Clymer Motorcycle Repair Series

HONDA
600 HURRICANE • 1987-1989

By
RON WRIGHT

RANDY STEPHENS
Editor

CLYMER PUBLICATIONS

The world's finest publisher of mechanical how-to manuals

INTERTEC PUBLISHING CORPORATION
P.O. Box 12901, Overland Park, Kansas 66212

FIRST EDITION
First Printing July, 1990

Printed in U.S.A.
ISBN: 0-89287-515-1
Library of Congress: 90-055389

MOTORCYCLE INDUSTRY COUNCIL

Technical illustrations by Steve Amos and Carl Rohkar. Technical assistance by Curt Jordan.

COVER: Photographed by Mark Clifford, Mark Clifford Photography, Los Angeles, California. Motorcycle courtesy of Rice Honda of La Puente, La Puente, California.

CONTENTS

QUICK REFERENCE DATA

GENERAL SPECIFICATIONS

Engine type	Water cooled, 4-stroke
Compression ratio	11.0:1
Bore and stroke	63 x 48 mm (2.48 × 1.89 in.)
Cylinder arrangement	Vertical inline 4
Cylinder numbering	Left to right, 1-2-3-4
Firing order	1-2-4-3
Air filtration	Paper filter
Engine weight (dry)	
49-state	63 kg (138.9 lb.)
California	62 kg (136.7 lb.)
Valve timing at 1 mm lift	
49-state	
Intake opens	7° BTDC
Intake closes	40° ABDC
Exhaust opens	40° BBDC
Exhaust closes	9° ATDC
California	
Intake opens	-5° BTDC
Intake closes	40° ABDC
Exhaust opens	40° BBDC
Exhaust closes	-5° ATDC
Lubrication system	Forced pressure and wet sump
Overall length	2,050 mm (80.7 in.)
Overall width	685 mm (27.0 in.)
Overall height	1,110 mm (43.7 in.)
Wheelbase	1,410 mm (55.5 in.)
Ground clearance	140 mm (5.5 in.)
Curb weight	199 kg (439 lb.)
Dry weight	180 kg (397 lb.)
Frame type	Diamond
Suspension travel	
Front	130 mm (5.1 in.)
Rear	110 mm (4.3 in.)
Caster	26°
Trail	104 mm (4.1 in.)
Fuel capacity	16.5 liters (4.4 U.S. gal., 3.6 Imp. gal.)
Fuel reserve capacity	3.0 liters (4.4 gal., 3.6 Imp. gal.)
Clutch type	Wet, multi-plate
Transmission	
Type	6-speeds, constant-mesh
Primary reduction ratio	1.775 (71/40)
Final reduction ratio	2.933 (44/15)
Transmission ratios	
1st	3.230 (32/13)
2nd	2.235 (38/17)
3rd	1.800 (36/20)
4th	1.500 (33/22)
5th	1.272 (28/22)
6th	1.130 (26/23)
Ignition system	Capacitor discharge ignition (CDI)
Starting system	Electric starter only
Battery	12-volt, 8-amp/hour
Drive chain number	RK50MFO-Z1; 110 links

TUNE-UP SPECIFICATIONS

Air filtration	Paper element
Engine firing order	1-2-4-3
Valve clearance	
Intake	0.14-0.18 mm (0.006-0.007 in.)
Exhaust	0.18-0.22 mm (0.007-0.009 in.)
Compression pressure	
(at sea level)	13.0 $\pm$2.0 kg/cm^2 (185 $\pm$28 psi)
Spark plug type	
Standard heat range	ND X24EPR-U9 or NGK DPR8EA-9
Cold weather	ND X22EPR-U9 or NGK DPR7EA-9
Extended high-speed riding	ND X27EPR-U9 or NGK DPR9EA-9
Spark plug gap	0.8-0.9 mm (0.031-0.040 in.)
Ignition timing	"F" mark at idle
Idle speed	
49-state	1200 $\pm$100 rpm
California	1300 $\pm$100 rpm

IGNITION SYSTEM SPECIFICATIONS

Ignition coil resistance	
Primary	2.5-3.1 ohms
Secondary	
With plug wire	21,000-25,000 ohms
Without plug wire	11,000-15,000 ohms
Pulse generator coil resistance	450-550 ohms

CHARGING SYSTEM SPECIFICATIONS

Battery	
Capacity	12V-8 amp hours
Voltage @ 68° F (20° C)	
Fully charged	13.0-13.2 volts
Requires charging	12.3 volts or less
Charging current	0.9 amps
Charging time	5 hours
Alternator	
Charging coil resistance*	0.1-1.0 ohms
Output	See text
Charging test rpm	1,000 $\pm$100 rpm

* Tests made at 68° F (20° C).

TIRE SPECIFICATIONS

Tire size	Air pressure (cold)*	Minimum tread depth
Front		
110/80-17	36 psi (2.50 kg/cm^2)	1.5 mm (1/16 in.)
Rear		
130/80-17	42 psi (2.90 kg/cm^2)	2.0 mm (3/32 in.)

* Up to maximum load limit of 200 lb. (89 kg) including total weight of motorcycle with accessories, rider(s) and luggage.

x

RECOMMENDED LUBRICANTS

Engine oil	SAE 10W-40 SE/SF
Battery refilling	Distilled water
Brake fluid	DOT 4
Drive chain	SAE 80 or SAE 80 gear oil or drive chain lubricant recommended for use with O-ring drive chains
Fork oil	Automatic transmission fluid (ATF)
Cables	Light weight oil or cable lubricant
Pivot points	Light weight oil
Grease points	Molybdenum disulfide grease

ENGINE OIL CAPACITY

Oil change only	3.0 L (3.17 qt.)
Oil and filter change	3.5 L (3.59 qt.)
Engine rebuild	4.0 L (4.23 qt.)

FRONT FORK OIL CAPACITY

Left-hand side	371 cc (12.5 oz.)
Right-hand side	361 cc (12.2 oz.)

FRONT FORK AIR PRESSURE*

Normal	0-6 psi (0-0.4 kg/cm^2)

* Do not exceed the maximum air pressure or internal parts of the fork will be damaged.

COOLING SYSTEM SPECIFICATIONS

Coolant capacity	
Total system	2.0 liters (2.11 qt.)
Radiator cap relief pressure	0.95-1.25 kg/cm^2 (14-18 psi)
Thermostat	
Begins to open	80-84° C
	(176-183° F)
Valve lift	Minimum of 8 mm @ 95° C
	(0.32 in. at 203° F)
Boiling point (50/50 mixture)	
Unpressurized	107.7° C (226° F)
Pressurized (cap on)	125.6° C (258° F)
Freezing point (hydrometer test)	
45:55 Water:antifreeze ratio	-32° C (-25° F)
50:50 Water:antifreeze ratio	-37° C (-34° F)
45:55 Water:antifreeze ratio	-44.5° C (-48° F)

REAR SHOCK ADJUSTMENT

Adjuster position	Road condition
1	Smooth roads and typical freeways
2	City roads and conditions
3	Winding roads

MAINTENANCE TORQUE SPECIFICATIONS

Item	N·m	ft.-lb.
Spark plug	14	10
Oil filter	10	7
Oil drain bolt	35	25
Tappet lock nut	23	17
Timing hole cap	3.5	2.5
Crankshaft hole cap	7	5
Rear axle nut	90	65
Sidestand		
Bolt	15	11
Locknut	35	25
Bracket bolt	40	29
Handlebar pinch bolt	22	16
Right-hand footpeg bracket bolts	27	20
Top fork cap	22	16

ELECTRICAL SYSTEM TIGHTENING TORQUES

	N·m	ft.-lb.
Ignition switch bolts	25	18
Flywheel bolt	85	61
Starter clutch bolt	85	61
Starter clutch setting socket bolt*	16	12
Pulse generator socket bolt*	5.3	3.8
Oil pressure switch	12	9

* Apply Loctite 242 (blue) to threads before installation.

REPLACEMENT BULBS

	Voltage/wattage
Headlight	12V 60/55W
Stop/taillight	12V 32/3cp
Front turn signal/position light	12V 32/3cp
Rear turn signal light	12V 32cp
License light	12V 3cp
Instrument lights	
1987-1988	12V 3W
1989	12V 1.7W
Indicator lights	
1987-1988	12V 3W
1989	12V 3.4W

HONDA

600 HURRICANE • 1987-1989

CHAPTER ONE

GENERAL INFORMATION

This detailed, comprehensive manual covers Honda CBR600F Hurricane models.

Troubleshooting, tune-up, maintenance and repair are not difficult, if you know what tools and equipment to use and what to do. Anyone with some mechanical ability can perform most of the procedures in this manual.

The manual is written simply and clearly enough for owners who have never worked on a motorcycle, but is complete enough for use by experienced mechanics.

Some of the procedures require the use of special tools. Using an inferior substitute tool for a special tool is not recommended as it can be dangerous to you and may damage the part.

Engine and frame serial numbers for all models are listed in **Table 1**.

Table 2 lists general specifications.

Metric and U.S. standards are used throughout this manual. Metric to U.S. conversion is given in **Table 3**.

MANUAL ORGANIZATION

This chapter provides general information and discusses equipment and tools useful both for preventive maintenance and troubleshooting.

Chapter Two provides methods and suggestions for quick and accurate diagnosis and repair of problems. Troubleshooting procedures discuss typical symptoms and logical methods to pinpoint the trouble.

Chapter Three explains all periodic lubrication and routine maintenance necessary to keep your Honda operating well. Chapter Three also includes recommended tune-up procedures, eliminating the need to constantly consult other chapters on the various assemblies.

Subsequent chapters describe specific assemblies and systems such as the engine, clutch, transmission, fuel, exhaust, cooling, suspension, steering, brakes and fairing. Each chapter provides disassembly, repair, and assembly procedures in simple step-by-step form. If a repair is impractical for a home mechanic, it is so indicated. It is usually faster and less expensive to take such repairs to a Honda dealer or competent repair shop. Specifications concerning a particular system are included at the end of the appropriate chapter.

NOTES, CAUTIONS AND WARNINGS

The terms *NOTE, CAUTION* and *WARNING* have specific meanings in this manual. A *NOTE* provides additional information to make a step or procedure easier or clearer. Disregarding a *NOTE* could cause inconvenience, but would not cause damage or personal injury.

A *CAUTION* emphasizes areas where equipment damage could occur. Disregarding a *CAUTION* could cause permanent mechanical damage; however, personal injury is unlikely.

A *WARNING* emphasizes areas where personal injury or even death could result from negligence. Mechanical damage may also occur. *WARNINGS* are to be taken *seriously*. In some cases, serious injury and death have resulted from disregarding similar warnings.

SAFETY FIRST

Professional mechanics can work for years and never sustain a serious injury. If you observe a few rules of common sense and safety, you can enjoy many safe hours servicing your own machine. If you ignore these rules you can hurt yourself or damage the equipment.

1. Never use gasoline as a cleaning solvent.
2. Never smoke or use a torch in the vicinity of flammable liquids, such as cleaning solvent, in open containers.
3. If welding or brazing is required on the machine, remove the fuel tank and rear shock to a safe distance, at least 50 feet away. Welding on a gas tank requires special safety precautions and must be performed by someone skilled in the process. Do not attempt to weld or braze a leaking gas tank.
4. Use the proper size wrenches to avoid damage to fasteners and injury to yourself.
5. When loosening a tight or stuck nut, be guided by what would happen if the wrench should slip. Be careful; protect yourself accordingly.
6. When replacing a fastener, make sure to use one with the same measurements and strength as the old one. Incorrect or mismatched fasteners can result in damage to the vehicle and possible personal injury. Beware of fastener kits that are filled with cheap and poorly made nuts, bolts, washers and cotter pins. Refer to *Fasteners* in this chapter for additional information.
7. Keep all hand and power tools in good condition. Wipe greasy and oily tools after using them. They are difficult to hold and can cause injury. Replace or repair worn or damaged tools.
8. Keep your work area clean and uncluttered.

9. Wear safety goggles during all operations involving drilling, grinding, the use of a cold chisel or anytime you feel unsure about the safety of your eyes. Safety goggles should also be worn anytime compressed air is used to clean or dry a part.
10. Keep an approved fire extinguisher nearby. Be sure it is rated for gasoline (Class B) and electrical (Class C) fires.
11. When drying bearings or other rotating parts with compressed air, never allow the air jet to rotate the bearing or part; the air jet is capable of rotating them at speeds far in excess of those for which they were designed. The bearing or rotating part is very likely to disintegrate and cause serious injury and damage.

SERVICE HINTS

Most of the service procedures covered are straightforward and can be performed by anyone reasonably handy with tools. It is suggested, however, that you consider your own capabilities carefully before attempting any operation involving major disassembly of the engine or transmission.

1. "Front," as used in this manual, refers to the front of the motorcycle; the front of any component is the end closest to the front of the motorcycle. The "left-" and "right-hand" sides refer to the position of the parts as viewed by a rider sitting on the seat facing forward. For example, the throttle control is on the right-hand side. These rules are simple, but confusion can cause a major inconvenience during service.

2. Whenever servicing the engine or transmission, or when removing a suspension component, the bike should be secured in a safe manner. If the bike is to be parked on its sidestand, check the stand

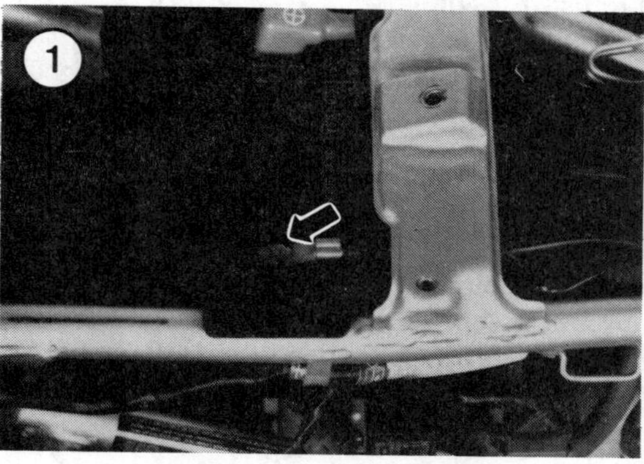

To make sure it is secure and not damaged. Block the front and rear wheels if they remain on the ground. A small hydraulic jack and a block of wood can be used to raise the chassis. If the transmission is not going to be worked on and the drive chain is connected to the rear wheel, shift the transmission into first gear.

NOTE
The CBR600 Hurricane is not equipped with a centerstand. Sold as an accessory item, a centerstand can be purchased from Honda dealers and installed on all non-California models. The Honda centerstand cannot be installed on California models. Because it will be necessary to raise your Hurricane's front and rear wheels during many of the service procedures described in this manual, some type of wheel stand will be required. If you do not want to install the factory stand or if you have a California model, see a Honda dealer or a motorcycle accessory store for wheel stands. Wheel stands are also sold through many aftermarket mail order dealers that specialize in high-performance four-stroke parts and accessories.

3. Disconnect the negative battery cable (**Figure 1**) when working on or near the electrical, clutch or starter systems and before disconnecting any wires. On most batteries, the negative terminal will be marked with a minus (−) sign and the positive terminal with a plus (+) sign. See **Figure 2**.

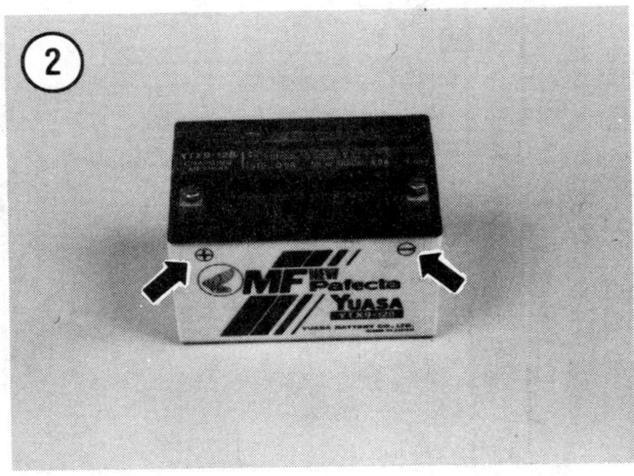

4. When disassembling a part or assembly, it is a good practice to tag the parts for location and mark all parts which mate together. Small parts, such as bolts, can be identified by placing them in plastic sandwich bags. Seal the bags and label them with masking tape and a marking pen. When reassembly will take place immediately, an accepted practice is to place nuts and bolts in a cupcake tin or egg carton in the order of disassembly.

5. Finished surfaces should be protected from physical damage or corrosion. Keep gasoline and brake fluid off painted, plated or plastic surfaces.

6. Use penetrating oil on frozen or tight bolts, then strike the bolt head a few times with a hammer and punch (use a screwdriver on screws). Avoid the use of heat where possible, as it can warp, melt or affect the temper of parts. Heat also ruins finishes, especially paint and plastics.

7. Keep flames and sparks away from a charging battery or flammable fluids and do not smoke near them. It is a good idea to have a fire extinguisher handy in the work area. Remember that many gas appliances in home garages (water heater, clothes drier, etc.) have pilot lights.

8. No parts removed or installed (other than bushings and bearings) in the procedures given in this manual should require unusual force during disassembly or assembly. If a part is difficult to remove or install, find out why before proceeding.

9. Cover all openings after removing parts or components to prevent dirt, small tools, etc. from falling in.

10. Read each procedure *completely* while looking at the actual parts before starting a job. Make sure you *thoroughly* understand what is to be done and then carefully follow the procedure, step by step.

11. Recommendations are occasionally made to refer service or maintenance to a Honda dealer or a specialist in a particular field. In these cases, the work will be done more quickly and economically than if you performed the job yourself.

12. In procedural steps, the term "replace" means to discard a defective part and replace it with a new or exchange unit. "Overhaul" means to remove, disassemble, inspect, measure, repair, reassemble and install major systems or parts.

13. Some operations require the use of a hydraulic press. It would be wiser to have these operations

performed by a shop equipped for such work, rather than to try to do the job yourself with makeshift equipment that may damage your machine.

14. Repairs go much faster and easier if your machine is clean before you begin work. There are many special cleaners on the market, like Bel-Ray Degreaser, for washing the engine and related parts. Follow the manufacturer's directions on the container for the best results. Clean all oily or greasy parts with cleaning solvent as you remove them.

> *WARNING*
> *Never use gasoline as a cleaning agent. It presents an extreme fire hazard. Be sure to work in a well-ventilated area when using cleaning solvent. Keep a fire extinguisher, rated for gasoline fires, handy in any case.*

15. Much of the labor charged for by dealers is for the time involved during removal, disassembly, assembly, and reinstallation of other parts in order to reach the defective part. It is frequently possible to perform the preliminary operations yourself and then take the defective unit to the dealer for repair at considerable savings.

16. If special tools are required, make arrangements to get them before you start. It is frustrating and time-consuming to get partly into a job and then be unable to complete it.

17. Make diagrams (or take a Polaroid picture) wherever similar-appearing parts are found. For instance, crankcase bolts are often not the same length. You may think you can remember where everything came from—but mistakes are costly. There is also the possibility that you may be sidetracked and not return to work for days or even weeks—in which the time carefully laid out parts may have become disturbed.

18. When assembling parts, be sure all shims and washers are replaced exactly as they came out.

> *NOTE*
> *The triangular mark cast into a housing or cover next to a bolt indicates that the bolt uses a special washer (usually copper). See **Figure 3**.*

19. Whenever a rotating part butts against a stationary part, look for a shim or washer. Use new gaskets if there is any doubt about the condition of the old ones.

20. If it is necessary to make a gasket, and you do not have a suitable old gasket to use as a guide, apply engine oil to the gasket surface of the part. Then place the part on the new gasket material and press the part slightly. The oil will leave a very accurate outline on the gasket material from which a gasket can be cut out.

21. Heavy grease can be used to hold small parts in place if they tend to fall out during assembly. However, keep grease and oil away from electrical and brake components.

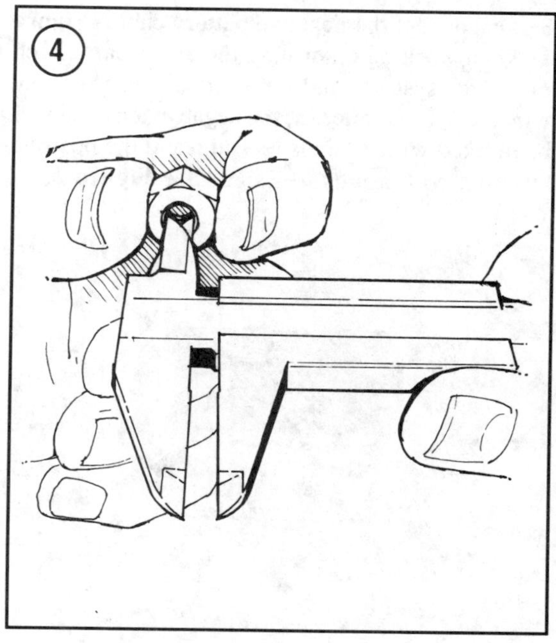

22. A carburetor is best cleaned by disassembling it and cleaning it. Motorcycle carburetors have much smaller air and fuel passages than automotive carburetors. For this reason, soaking the carburetor parts in an automotive type carburetor motorcycle carburetors is usually coated with a corrosion-protective clear coating. These caustic liquid cleaners will remove the protective coatings from the outside of the carburetor body. The dissolved coating could plug air or fuel passages within the carburetor and damage the exterior appearance of the carburetors. Also, if the cleaner was used previously there will be sediment held in suspension within the solution. This could plug a passage.

23. Take your time and do the job right. Do not forget that a newly rebuilt engine must be broken in just like as a new one.

TORQUE SPECIFICATIONS

Torque specifications throughout this manual are given in Newton-meters (N·m) and foot-pounds (ft.-lb.).

Table 4 lists general torque specifications for nuts and bolts that are not listed in the respective chapters. To use the table, first determine the size of the nut or bolt. **Figure 4** and **Figure 5** show how to measure fasteners with a vernier caliper.

FASTENERS

The materials and designs of the various fasteners used on your Honda are not arrived at by chance or accident. Fastener design determines the type of tool required to work the fastener. Fastener material is carefully selected to decrease the possibility of physical failure.

Nuts, bolts and screws are manufactured in a wide range of thread patterns. To join a nut and bolt, the diameter of the bolt and the diameter of the hole in the nut must be the same. It is just as important that the threads on both be properly matched.

The best way to tell if the threads on 2 fasteners are matched is to turn the nut on the bolt (or the bolt into the threaded hole in a piece of equipment) with fingers only. Be sure both pieces are clean. If much force is required, check the thread condition on each fastener. If the thread condition is good, but the fasteners jam, the threads are not compatible. A thread pitch gauge can also be used to determine pitch. Honda motorcycles are manufactured with ISO (International Organization for Standardization) metric fasteners. The threads are cut differently than those of American fasteners (**Figure 6**).

Most threads are cut so that the fastener must be turned clockwise to tighten it. These are called right-hand threads. Some fasteners have left-hand threads; they must be turned counterclockwise to be tightened. Left-hand threads are used in locations where normal rotation of the equipment would tend to loosen a right-hand threaded fastener.

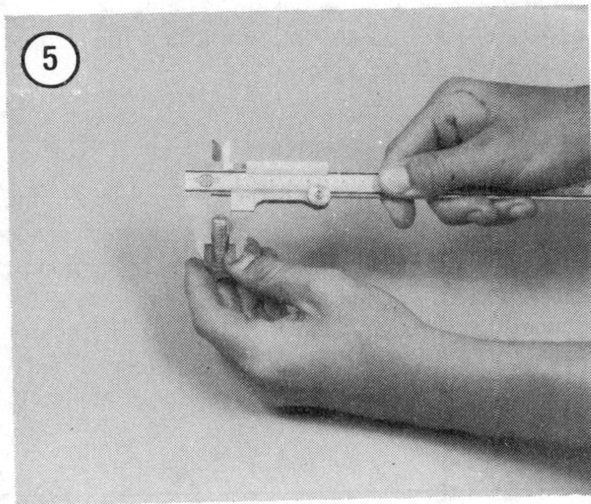

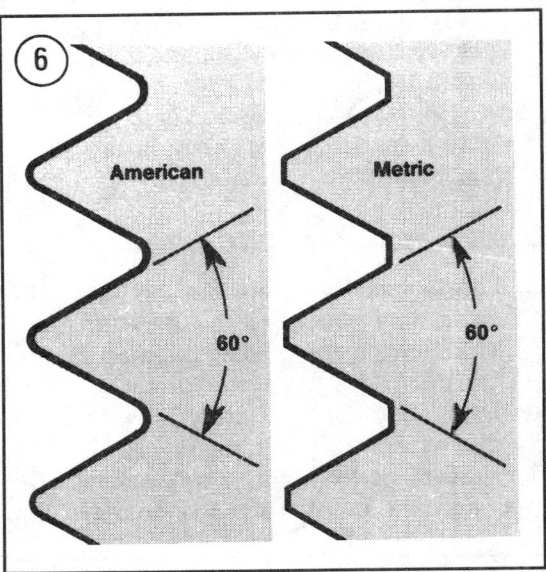

ISO Metric Screw Threads

ISO (International Organization for Standardization) metric threads come in 3 standard thread sizes: coarse, fine and constant pitch. The ISO coarse pitch is used for most all common fastener applications. The fine pitch thread is used on certain precision tools and instruments. The constant pitch thread is used mainly on machine parts and not for fasteners. The constant pitch thread, however, is used on all metric thread spark plugs. ISO metric threads are specified by the capital letter M followed by the diameter in millimeters and the pitch (or the distance between each thread) in millimeters separated by the sign ×. For example, a M8 × 1.25 bolt is one that has a diameter of 8 millimeters with a distance of 1.25 millimeters between each thread. The measurement across 2 flats on the head of the bolt indicates the proper wrench size to be used. **Figure 5** shows how to determine bolt diameter.

Machine Screws

There are many different types of machine screws. **Figure 7** shows a number of screw heads requiring different types of turning tools. Heads are also designed to protrude above the metal (round) or to be slightly recessed in the metal (flat). See **Figure 8**.

Nuts

Nuts are manufactured in a variety of types and sizes. Most are hexagonal (6-sided) and fit on bolts, screws and threaded studs with the same diameter and pitch.

Figure 9 shows several types of nuts. The common nut is generally used with a lockwasher. Self-locking nuts have a nylon insert which prevents the nut from loosening; no lockwasher is required. Wing nuts are designed for fast removal by hand. Wing nuts are used for convenience in non-critical locations.

To indicate the size of a nut, manufacturers specify the diameter of the opening and the thread pitch. This is similar to bolt specifications, but without the length dimension. The measurement across 2 flats on the nut indicates the proper wrench size to be used.

Prevailing Torque Fasteners

Several types of bolts, screws and nuts incorporate a system that develops an interference between the bolt, screw, nut or tapped hole threads. Interference is achieved in various ways: by distorting threads, coating threads with dry adhesive or nylon, distorting the top of an all-metal nut, using a nylon insert in the center or at the top of a nut, etc.

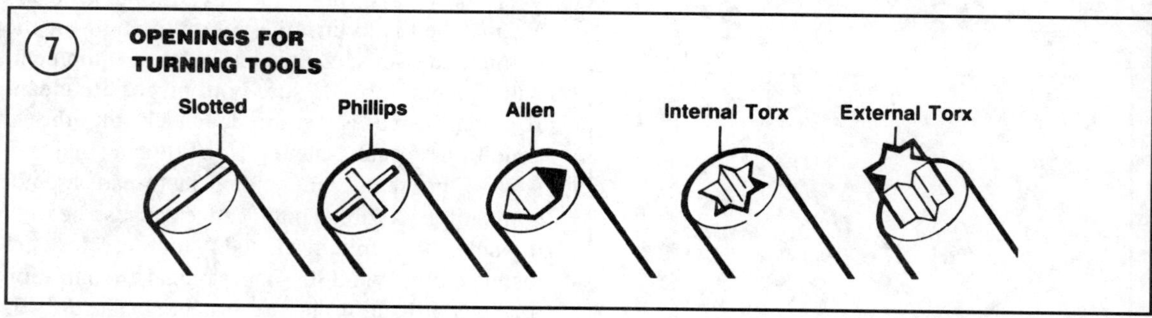

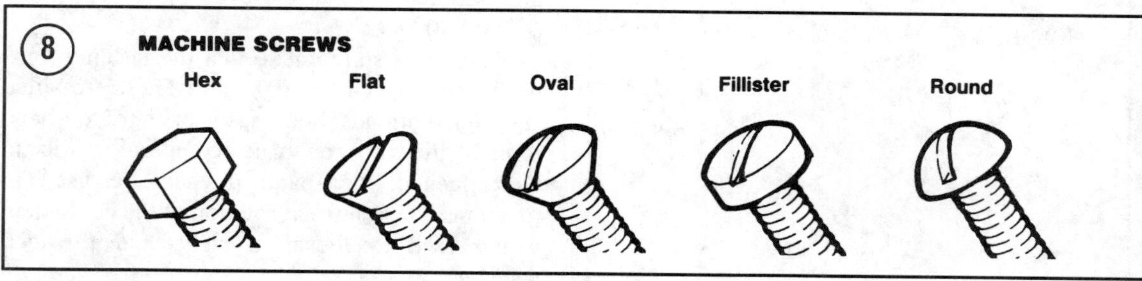

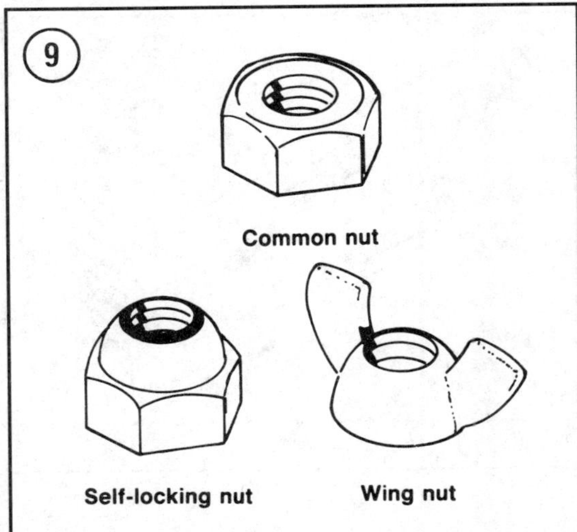

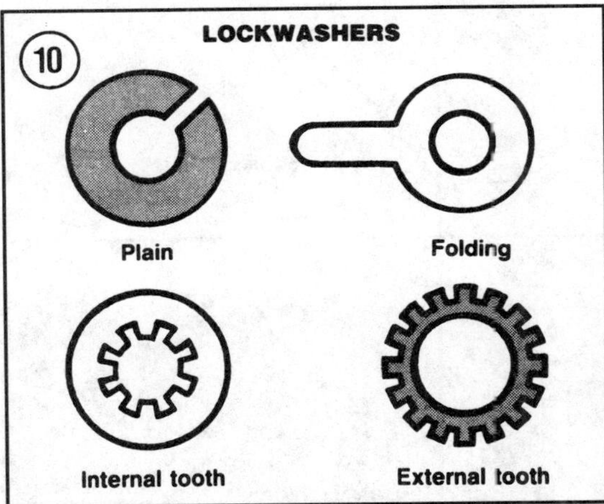

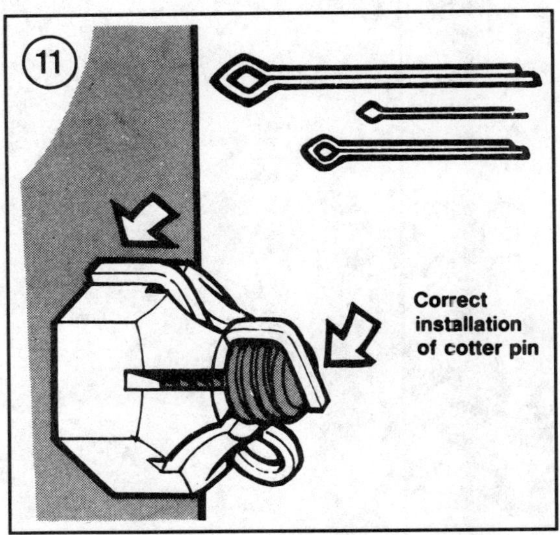

Prevailing torque fasteners offer greater holding strength and better vibration resistance. Some prevailing torque fasteners can be reused if in good condition. Others, like the nylon insert nut, form an initial locking condition when the nut is first installed; the nylon forms closely to the bolt thread pattern, thus reducing any tendency for the nut to loosen. When the nut is removed, the locking efficiency is greatly reduced. For greatest safety, it is recommended that you install new prevailing torque fasteners whenever they are removed.

Washers

There are 2 basic types of washers: flat washers and lockwashers. Flat washers are simple discs with a hole to fit a screw or bolt. Lockwashers are designed to prevent a fastener from working loose due to vibration, expansion and contraction. **Figure 10** shows several types of washers. Washers are also used in the following functions:

a. As spacers.
b. To prevent galling or damage of the equipment by the fastener.
c. To help distribute fastener load during torquing.
d. As seals.

Note that flat washers are often used between a lockwasher and a fastener to provide a smooth bearing surface. This allows the fastener to be turned easily with a tool.

Cotter Pins

Cotter pins (**Figure 11**) are used to secure special kinds of fasteners. The threaded stud must have a hole in it; the nut or nut lock piece has castellations around which the cotter pin ends wrap. Cotter pins should not be reused after removal as the ends could break off allowing the cotter pin to fall out.

Snap Rings

Snap rings can be internal or external design. They are used to retain items on shafts (external type) or within tubes (internal type). In some applications, snap rings of varying thicknesses are used to control the end play of parts assemblies. These are often called selective snap rings. Snap rings should be replaced during installation, as removal weakens and deforms them.

Two basic styles of snap rings are available: machined and stamped snap rings. Machined snap rings (**Figure 12**) can be installed in either direction (shaft or housing) because both faces are machined, thus creating two sharp edges. Stamped snap rings (**Figure 13**) are manufactured with one sharp edge and one rounded edge. When installing stamped snap rings in a thrust situation (transmission shafts, fork tubes, etc.), the sharp edge must face away from the part producing the thrust. When installing snap rings, observe the following:

a. Compress or expand snap rings only enough to install them.

b. After the snap ring is installed, make sure it is completely seated in its groove.

LUBRICANTS

Periodic lubrication assures long life for any type of equipment. The *type* of lubricant used is just as important as the lubrication service itself, although in an emergency the wrong type of lubricant is better than none at all. The following paragraphs describe the types of lubricants most often used on motorcycle equipment. Be sure to follow the manufacturer's recommendations for lubricant types.

Generally, all liquid lubricants are called "oil." They may be mineral-based (including petroleum bases) or natural-based (vegetable and animal bases), synthetic-based or emulsions (mixtures). "Grease" is an oil to which a thickening base has been added so that the end product is semi-solid. Grease is often classified by the type of thickener added; lithium soap is commonly used.

Engine Oil

Oil for motorcycle and automotive engines is graded by the American Petroleum Institute (API) and the Society of Automotive Engineers (SAE) in several categories. Oil containers display these ratings on the top or label.

API oil grade is indicated by letters; oils for gasoline engines are identified by an "S". The engines covered in this manual require SE or SF graded oil.

Viscosity is an indication of the oil's thickness. The SAE uses numbers to indicate viscosity; thin oils have low numbers while thick oils have high

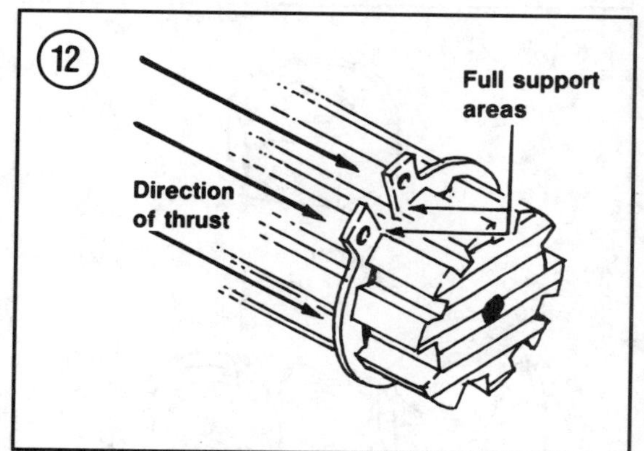

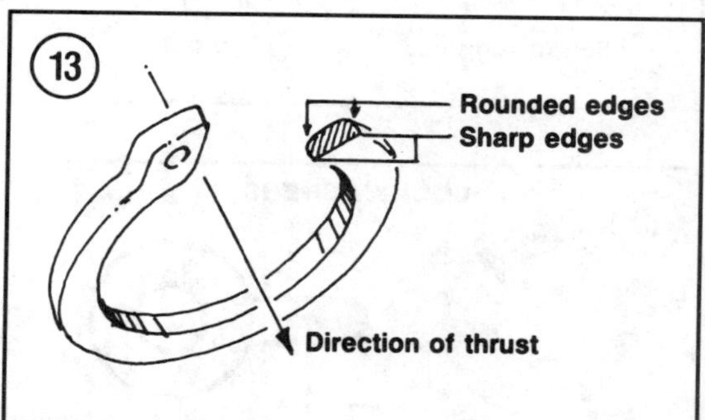

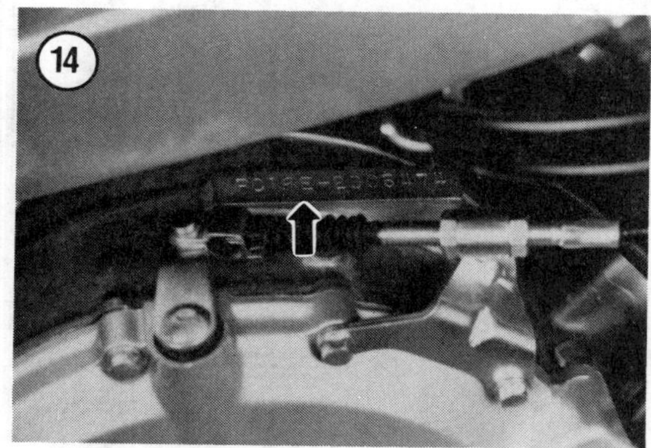

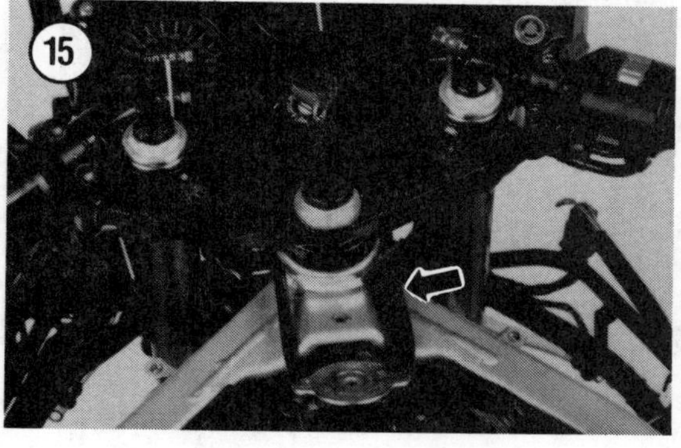

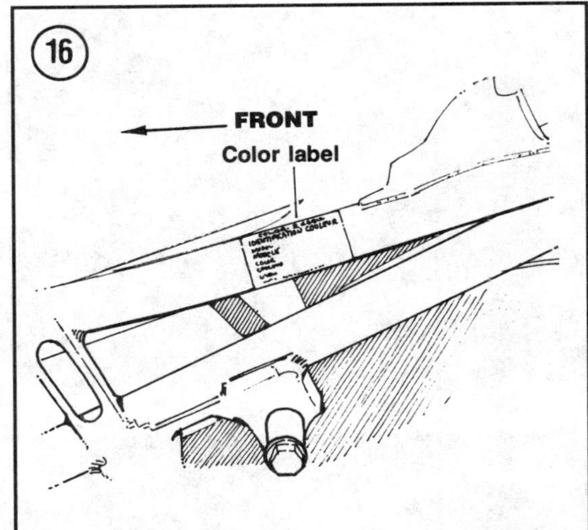

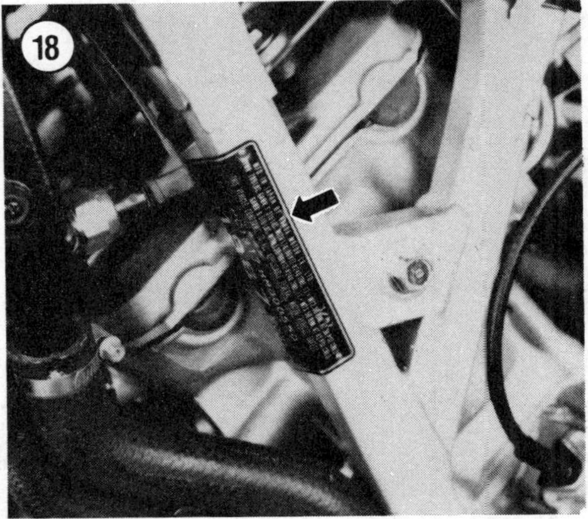

numbers. A "W" after the number indicates that the viscosity testing was done at low temperature to simulate cold-weather operation. Engine oils fall into the 5W-30 and 20W-50 range.

Multi-grade oils (for example 10W-40) maintain a consistent viscosity at low temperatures and at high temperatures. This allows the oil to perform efficiently across a wide range of engine operating conditions. The lower the number, the better the engine will start in cold climates. Higher numbers are usually recommended for engines running in hot weather conditions.

Grease

Greases are graded by the National Lubricating Grease Institute (NLGI). Greases are graded by number according to the consistency of the grease; these range from No. 000 to No. 6, with No. 6 being the most solid. A typical multipurpose grease is NLGI No. 2. For specific applications, equipment manufacturers may require grease with an additive such as molybdenum disulfide (MOS2).

SERIAL NUMBERS AND PARTS REPLACEMENT

Honda makes frequent changes during a model year, some minor, some relatively major. When you order parts from the dealer or other parts distributor, always order by engine and frame numbers. Write the numbers down and carry them with you. Compare new parts to old before purchasing them. If they are not alike, have the parts manager explain the difference to you. The engine number is stamped on the right-hand crankcase (**Figure 14**). The frame number is stamped is stamped on the right-hand side of the steering head (**Figure 15**). The color code label is fixed to the left-hand frame tube under the seat (**Figure 16**). When ordering any painted or color coded part, order by this number. The carburetor identification number is stamped on the rear of each carburetor body (**Figure 17**).

MANUFACTURER'S LABEL

The manufacturer's label is mounted on the left-hand frame tube (**Figure 18**).

EMISSION CONTROL INFORMATION LABELS (U.S.A. ONLY)

An emission control label is mounted on the right-hand frame tube as shown in **Figure 19**. This label lists tune-up specifications and fuel requirements.

NOTE
Your model may be equipped with an emission control information update label. This label is attached by a Honda dealer if the carburetor has been adjusted for high altitudes. If you purchased a used bike and it has an update label, you may want to ask a Honda dealer what adjustments were made and if they apply to the area where the bike is going to be ridden.

A vacuum hose routing diagram label is mounted on the air cleaner housing cover (**Figure 20**). This label shows vacuum and emission hose routing for your model.

BASIC HAND TOOLS

Many of the procedures in this manual can be carried out with simple hand tools and test equipment familiar to the average home mechanic. Keep your tools clean and in a tool box. Keep them organized with the sockets and related drives together, the open-end combination wrenches together, etc. After using a tool, wipe off dirt and grease with a clean cloth and return the tool to its correct place.

Top quality tools are essential; they are also more economical in the long run. If you are now starting to build your tool collection, stay away from the "advertised specials" featured at some parts houses, discount stores and chain drug stores. These are usually a poor grade tool that can be sold cheaply and that is exactly what they are—*cheap*. They are usually made of inferior material, and are thick, heavy and clumsy. Their rough finish makes them difficult to clean and they usually don't last very long. If it is ever your misfortune to use such tools, you will probably find out that the wrenches do not fit the heads of bolts and nuts correctly and damage the fastener.

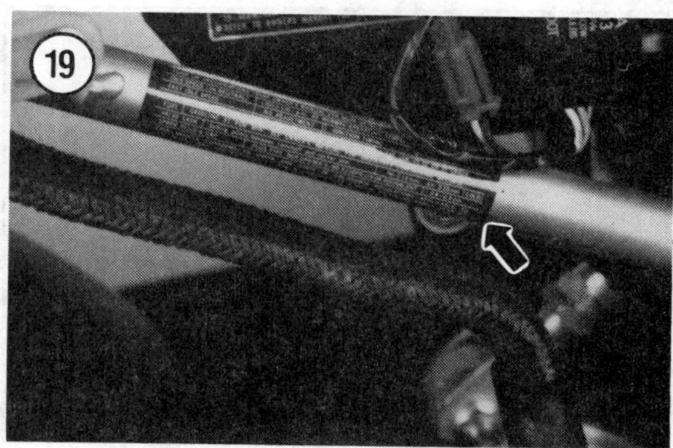

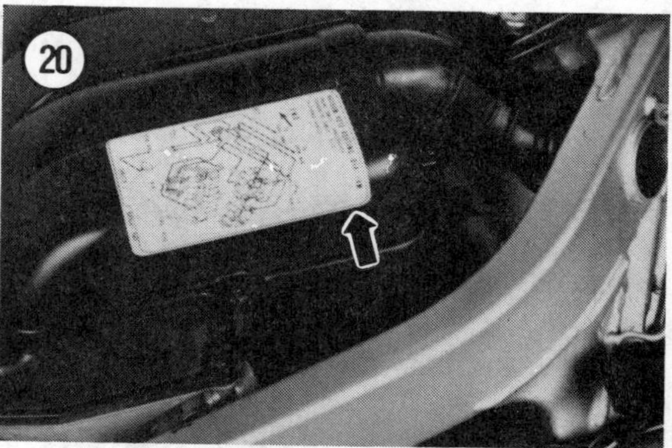

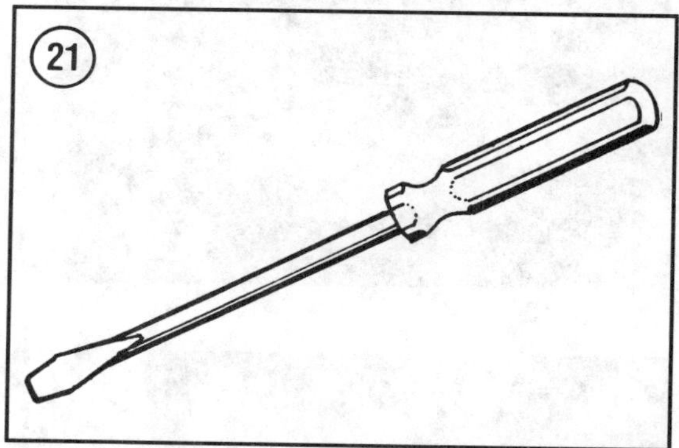

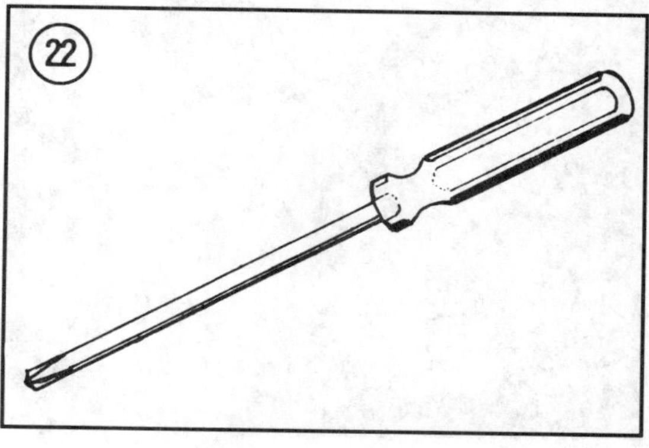

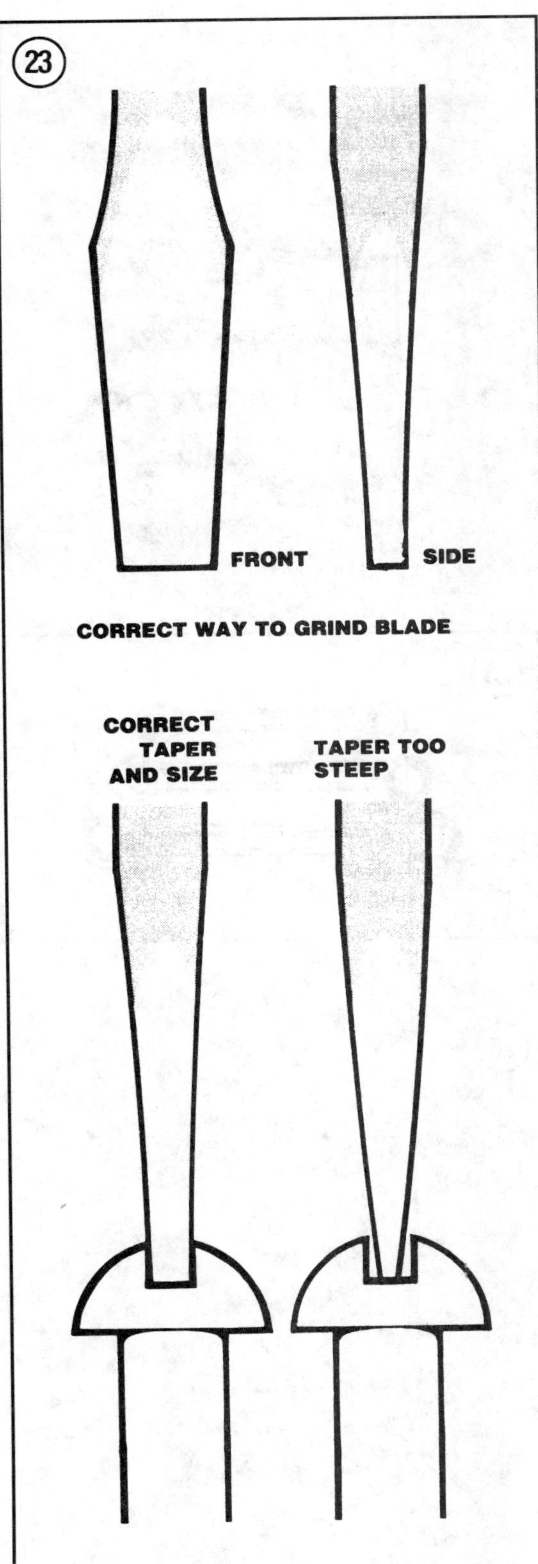

Quality tools are made of alloy steel and are heat treated for greater strength. They are lighter and better balanced than cheap ones. Their surface is smooth, making them a pleasure to work with and easy to clean. The initial cost of good quality tools may be more but they are cheaper in the long run. Don't try to buy everything in all sizes in the beginning; do it a little at a time until you have the necessary tools.

The following tools are required to perform virtually any repair job. Each tool is described and the recommended size given for starting a tool collection. Additional tools and some duplicates may be added as you become familiar with the vehicle. Honda motorcycles are built with metric standard fasteners—so if you are starting your collection now, buy metric sizes.

Screwdrivers

The screwdriver is a very basic tool, but if used improperly it will do more damage than good. The slot on a screw has a definite dimension and shape. A screwdriver must be selected to conform with that shape. Use a small screwdriver for small screws and a large one for large screws or the screw head will be damaged.

Two basic types of screwdriver are required: common (flat-bladed) screwdrivers (**Figure 21**) and Phillips screwdrivers (**Figure 22**).

Screwdrivers are available in sets which often include an assortment of common and Phillips blades. If you buy them individually, buy at least the following:

    a. Common screwdriver—5/16 × 6 in. blade.
    b. Common screwdriver—3/8 × 12 in. blade.
    c. Phillips screwdriver—size 2 tip, 6 in. blade.

Use screwdrivers only for driving screws. Never use a screwdriver for prying or chiseling metal. Do not try to remove a Phillips or Allen head screw with a common screwdriver (unless the screw has a combination head that will accept either type); you can damage the head so that the proper tool will be unable to remove it.

Keep screwdrivers in the proper condition and they will last longer and perform better. Always keep the tip of a common screwdriver in good condition. **Figure 23** shows how to grind the tip to the proper shape if it becomes damaged. Note the symmetrical sides of the tip.

Pliers

Pliers come in a wide range of types and sizes. Pliers are useful for cutting, bending and crimping. They should never be used to cut hardened objects or to turn bolts or nuts. **Figure 24** shows several pliers useful in motorcycle repairs.

Each type of pliers has a specialized function. Slip-joint pliers are general purpose pliers and are used mainly for holding things and for bending. Vise Grips are used as pliers or to hold objects very tightly like a vise. Needlenose pliers are used to hold or bend small objects. Channel lock pliers can be adjusted to hold various sizes of objects; the jaws remain parallel to grip around objects such as pipe or tubing. There are many more types of pliers.

Box and Open-end Wrenches

Box and open-end wrenches are available in sets or separately in a variety of sizes. The size number stamped near the end refers to the distance between 2 parallel flats on the hex head bolt or nut.

Box wrenches (**Figure 25**) are usually superior to open-end wrenches (**Figure 26**). Open-end wrenches grip the nut on only 2 flats. Unless a wrench fits well, it may slip and round off the points on the nut. The box wrench grips on all 6 flats. Both 6-point and 12-point openings on box wrenches are available. The 6-point gives superior holding power; the 12-point allows a shorter swing.

Combination wrenches which are open on one side and boxed on the other are also available. Both ends are the same size.

Adjustable Wrenches

An adjustable wrench can be adjusted to fit a variety of nuts or bolt heads (**Figure 27**). However, it can loosen and slip, causing damage to the nut and perhaps to your knuckles. Use an adjustable wrench only when other wrenches are not available.

Adjustable wrenches come in sizes ranging from 4-18 in. overall. A 6 or 8 in. wrench is recommended as an all-purpose wrench.

Socket Wrenches

This type is undoubtedly the fastest, safest and most convenient to use. Sockets which attach to

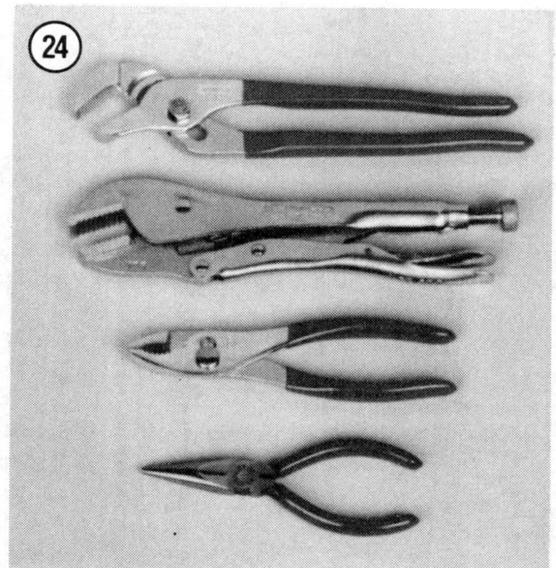

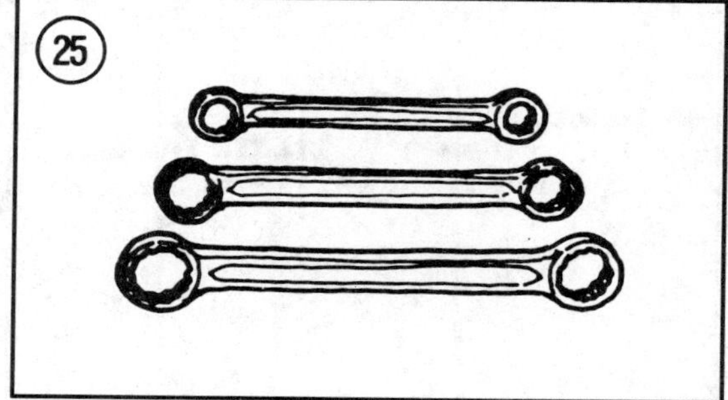

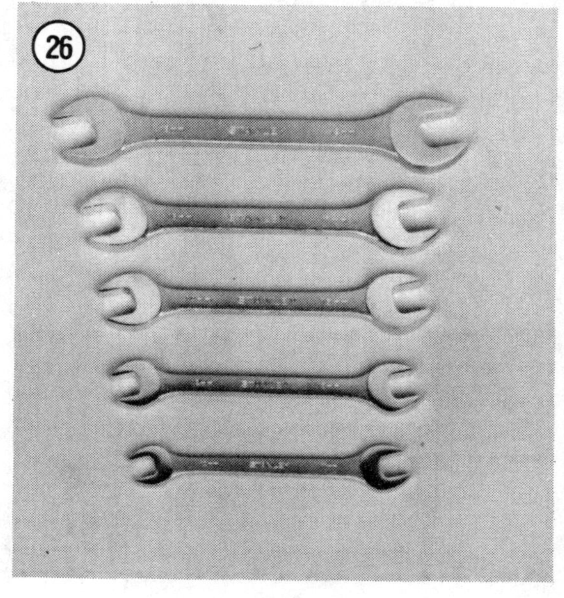

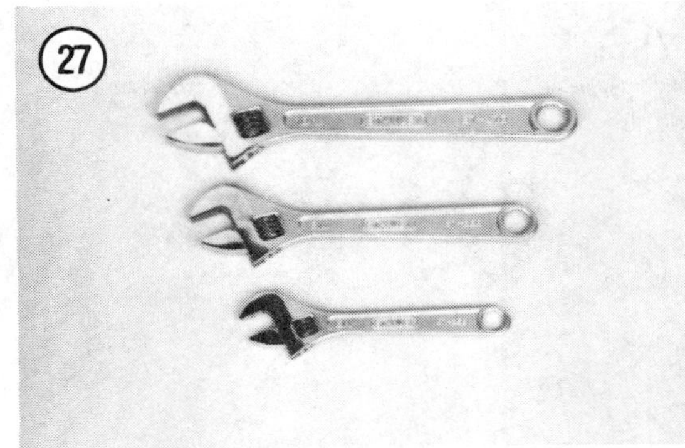

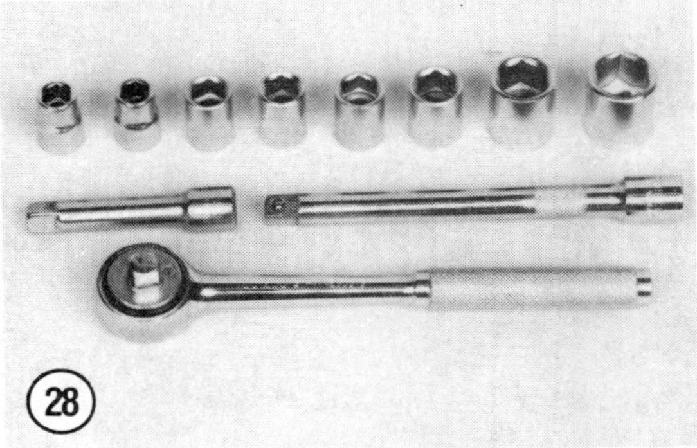

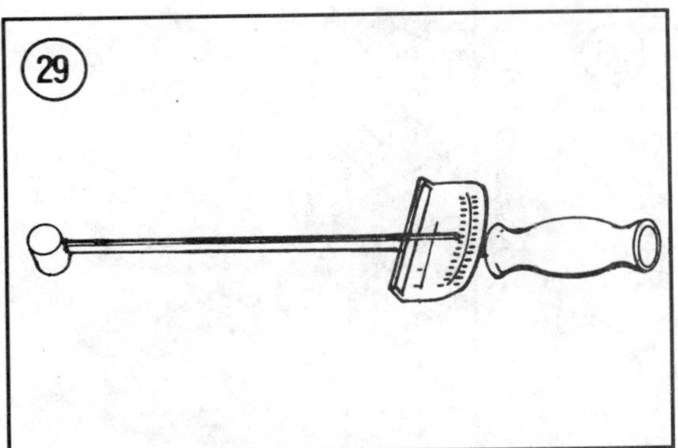

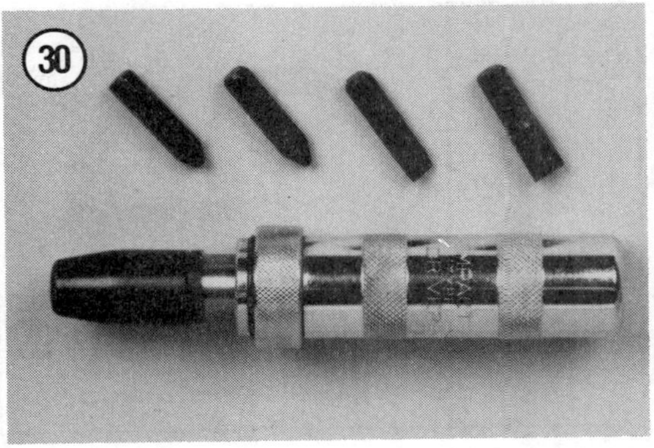

a ratchet handle (**Figure 28**) are available with 6-point or 12-point openings and 1/4, 3/8, 1/2 and 3/4 inch drives. The drive size indicates the size of the square hole which mates with the ratchet handle.

Torque Wrench

A torque wrench (**Figure 29**) is used with a socket to measure how tightly a nut or bolt is installed. They come in a wide price range and with either 3/8 or 1/2 in. square drive. The drive size indicates the size of the square drive which mates with the socket.

Impact Driver

This tool makes removal of tight fasteners easy and eliminates damage to bolts and screw slots. Impact drivers and interchangeable bits (**Figure 30**) are available at most large hardware and motorcycle dealers. Sockets can also be used with a hand impact driver. However, make sure the socket is designed for impact use (usually a dark color from heat treatment). Do not use regular hand type sockets, as they may shatter.

Hammers

The correct hammer is necessary for repairs. Use only a hammer with a face (or head) of rubber or plastic or the soft-faced type that is filled with buckshot. These are sometimes necessary in engine teardowns. *Never* use a metal-faced hammer, as severe damage will result in most cases. You can always produce the same amount of force with a soft-faced hammer.

Feeler Gauge

This tool has both flat and wire measuring gauges and is used to measure spark plug gap. See **Figure 31**. Wire gauges are used to measure spark plug gap; flat gauges are used for all other measurements.

Vernier Caliper

This tool is invaluable when reading inside, outside and depth measurements to close precision. The vernier caliper can be purchased from large dealers or mail order houses. See **Figure 32**.

Special Tools

A few special tools may be required for major service. These are described in the appropriate chapters and are available either from Honda dealers or other manufacturers as indicated.

TEST EQUIPMENT

Voltmeter, Ammeter and Ohmmeter

A good voltmeter is required for testing ignition and other electrical systems. Voltmeters are available with analog meter scales or digital readouts. An instrument covering 0-20 volts is satisfactory. It should also have a 0-2 volt scale for testing points or individual contacts where voltage drops are much smaller. Accuracy should be ±1/2 volt.

An ohmmeter measures electrical resistance. This instrument is useful in checking continuity (for open and short circuits) and testing lights. A self-powered 12-volt test light can often be used in its place.

The ammeter measures electrical current. These are useful for checking battery starting and charging currents.

Some manufacturers combine the 3 instruments into one unit called a multimeter or VOM. See **Figure 33**.

Compression Gauge

An engine with low compression cannot be properly tuned and will not develop full power. A compression gauge measures the amount of pressure present in the engine's combustion chambers during the compression stroke. This indicates general engine condition.

The Honda models described in this manual require the use of a screw-in compression gauge that threads into the spark plug holes (**Figure 34**).

Dial Indicator

A dial indicator (**Figure 35**) is a precision tool used to check dimension variations on machined parts such as transmission shafts and axles and to check crankshaft and axle shaft end play. Dial indicators are available with various dial types for different measuring requirements. When using a dial indicator, a stand or mounting fixture will be

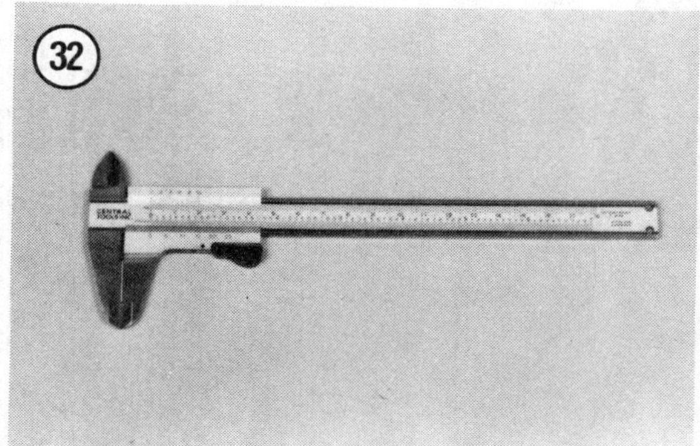

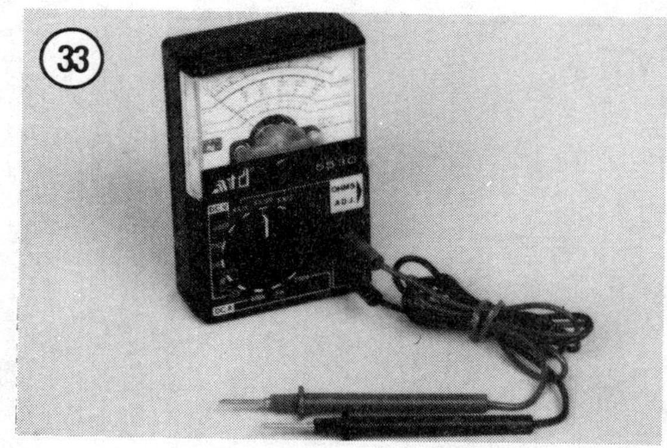

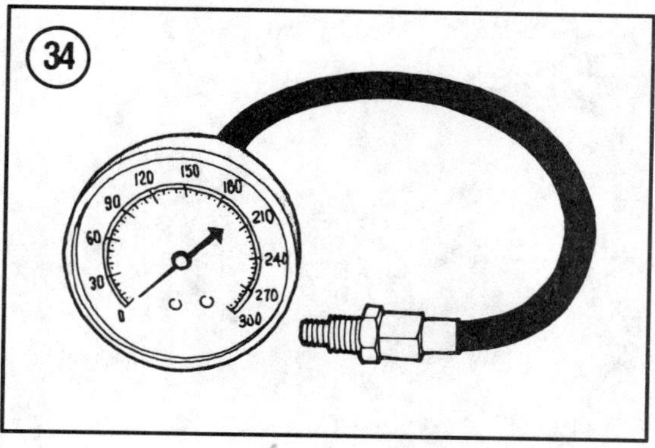

required to position and hold the dial indicator. **Figure 35** shows a dial indicator secured by a stand with a magnetic base. Mechanical clamp supports are also available.

Strobe Timing Light

This instrument is necessary for checking ignition timing. By flashing a light at the precise instant the spark plug fires, the position of the timing mark can be seen. The flashing light makes a moving mark appear to stand still opposite a stationary mark.

Suitable lights range from inexpensive neon bulb types to powerful xenon strobe lights. See **Figure 36**. A light with an inductive pickup is recommended to eliminate any possible damage to ignition wiring.

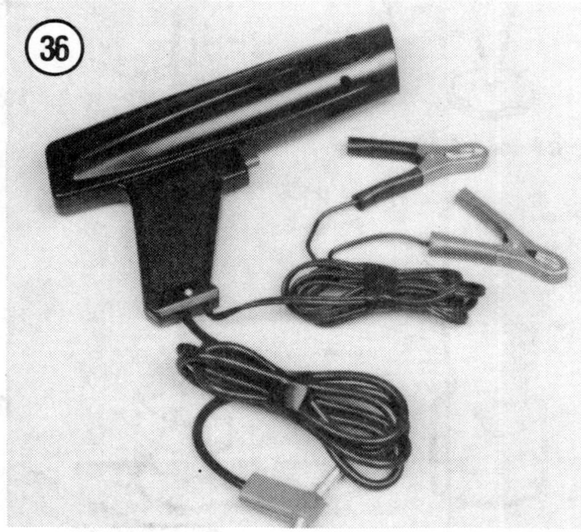

Portable Tachometer

A portable tachometer is necessary for tuning. See **Figure 37**. Ignition timing and carburetor adjustments must be performed at the specified idle speed. The best instrument for this purpose is one with a low range of 0-1,000 or 0-2,000 rpm and a high range of 0-4,000 rpm. Extended range (0-6,000 or 0-8,000 rpm) instruments lack accuracy at lower speeds. The instrument should be capable of detecting changes of 25 rpm on the low range.

Expendable Supplies

Certain expendable supplies are also required. These include grease, oil, gasket cement, shop rags and cleaning solvent. Ask your dealer for the special locking compounds, silicone lubricants and lube products which make vehicle maintenance simpler and easier. Cleaning solvent is available at some service stations.

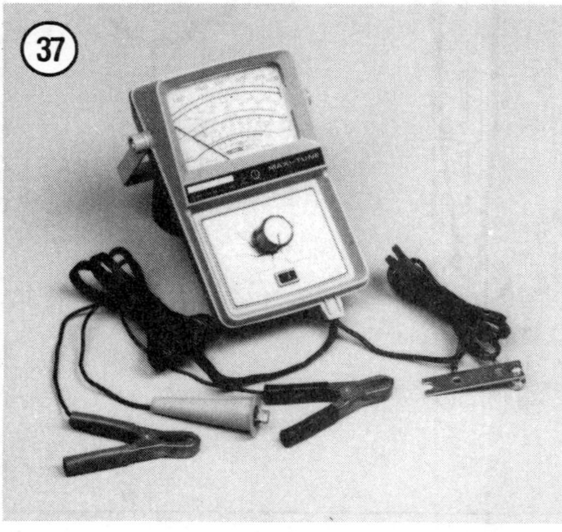

MECHANIC'S TIPS

Removing Frozen Nuts and Screws

When a fastener rusts and cannot be removed, several methods may be used to loosen it. First, apply penetrating oil such as Liquid Wrench or WD-40 (available at hardware or auto supply stores). Apply it liberally and let it penetrate for 10-15 minutes. Rap the fastener several times with a small hammer; do not hit it hard enough to cause damage. Reapply the penetrating oil if necessary.

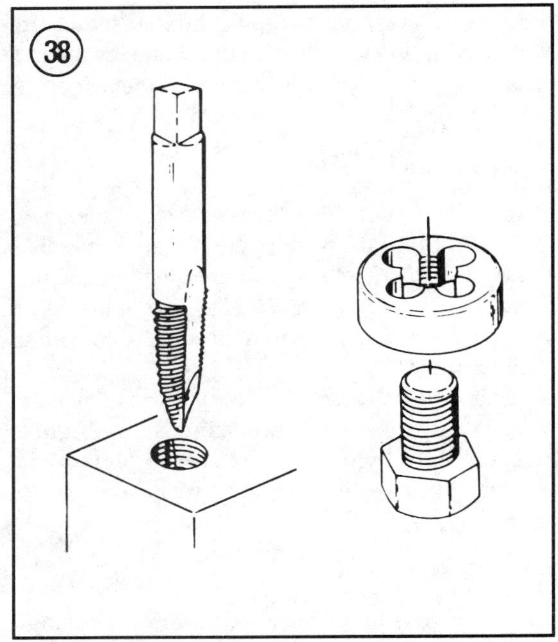

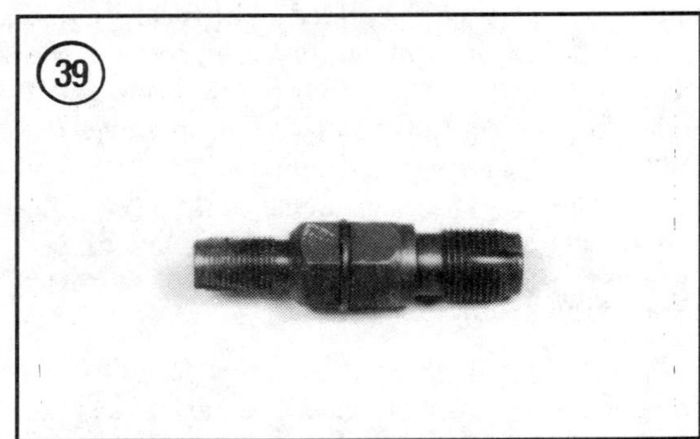

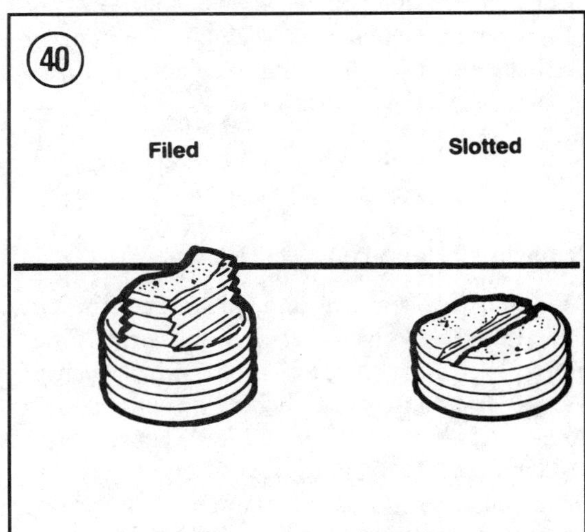

Filed
Slotted

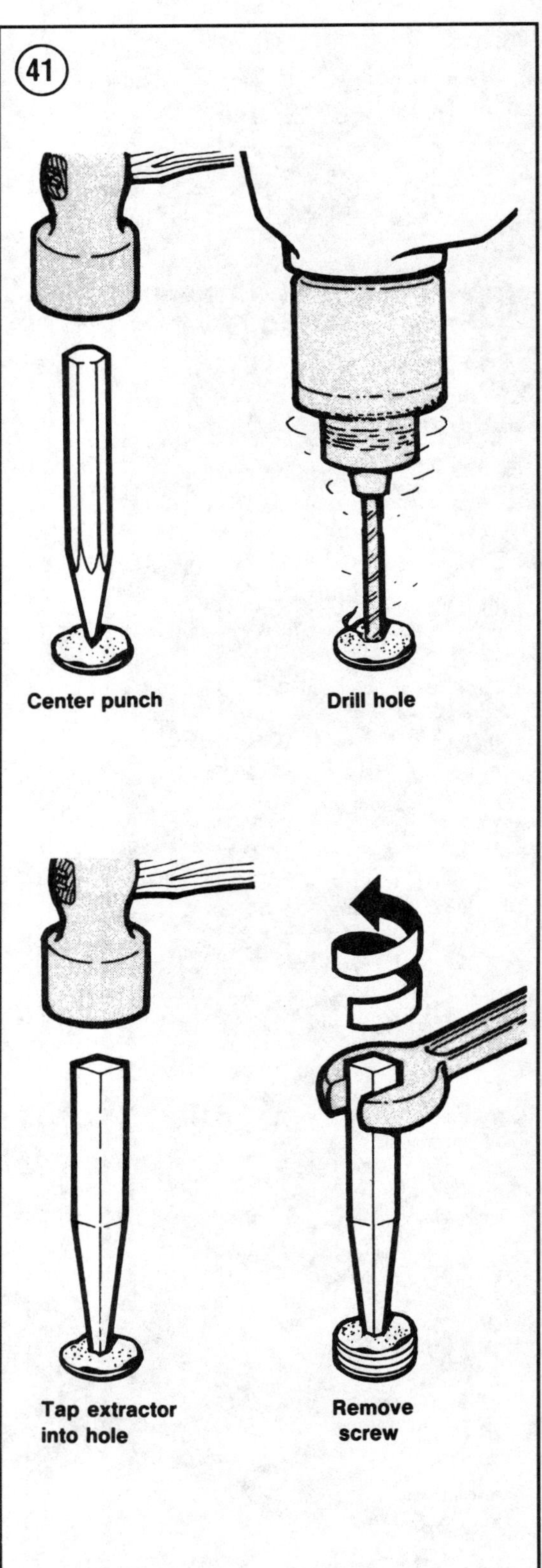

Center punch
Drill hole
Tap extractor
into hole
Remove
screw

For frozen screws, apply penetrating oil as described, then insert a screwdriver in the slot and rap the top of the screwdriver with a hammer. This loosens the rust so the screw can be removed in the normal way. If the screw head is too chewed up to use this method, grip the head with Vise Grip pliers and twist the screw out.

Avoid applying heat unless specifically instructed, as it may melt, warp or remove the temper from parts.

Remedying Stripped Threads

Occasionally, threads are stripped through carelessness or impact damage. Often the threads can be cleaned up by running a tap (for internal threads on nuts) or die (for external threads on bolts) through the threads. See **Figure 38**. To clean or repair spark plug threads, a spark plug tap can be used (**Figure 39**).

Removing Broken Screws or Bolts

When the head breaks off a screw or bolt, several methods are available for removing the remaining portion.

If a large portion projects out, try gripping it with Vise Grips. If the projecting portion is too small, file it to fit a wrench or cut a slot in it to fit a screwdriver. See **Figure 40**.

If the head breaks off flush, use a screw extractor. To do this, centerpunch the exact center of the remaining portion of the screw or bolt. Drill a small hole in the screw and tap the extractor into the hole. Back the screw out with a wrench on the extractor. See **Figure 41**.

Table 1 ENGINE AND FRAME SERIAL NUMBERS

Model number and year	Engine serial No. start to end	Frame serial No. start to end
1987 CBR600F		
49-state	PC19E-2000032-on	PC190*HM000014-on
California	PC19E-2000022-on	PC191*HM000002-on
1988 CBR600F		
49-state	PC19E-2100001-on	PC190*JM100001-on
California	PC19E-2100004-on	PC190*JM100001-on
1989 CBR600F		
49-state	PC19E-2200001-on	PC190*KM200001-on
California	PC19E-2202101-on	PC190*KM200001-on

Table 2 GENERAL SPECIFICATIONS

Engine type	Water cooled, 4-stroke
Compression ratio	11.0:1
Bore and stroke	63 x 48 mm (2.48 × 1.89 in.)
Cylinder arrangement	Vertical inline 4
Cylinder numbering	Left to right, 1-2-3-4
Firing order	1-2-4-3
Air filtration	Paper filter
Engine weight (dry)	
49-state	63 kg (138.9 lb.)
California	62 kg (136.7 lb.)
Valve timing at 1 mm lift	
49-state	
Intake opens	7° BTDC
Intake closes	40° ABDC
Exhaust opens	40° BBDC
Exhaust closes	9° ATDC

(continued)

Table 2 GENERAL SPECIFICATIONS (continued)

Valve timing at 1 mm lift (continued)	
California	
Intake opens	-5° BTDC
Intake closes	40° ABDC
Exhaust opens	40° BBDC
Exhaust closes	-5° ATDC
Lubrication system	Forced pressure and wet sump
Overall length	2,050 mm (80.7 in.)
Overall width	685 mm (27.0 in.)
Overall height	1,110 mm (43.7 in.)
Wheelbase	1,410 mm (55.5 in.)
Ground clearance	140 mm (5.5 in.)
Curb weight	199 kg (439 lb.)
Dry weight	180 kg (397 lb.)
Frame type	Diamond
Suspension travel	
Front	130 mm (5.1 in.)
Rear	110 mm (4.3 in.)
Caster	26°
Trail	104 mm (4.1 in.)
Fuel capacity	16.5 liters (4.4 U.S. gal., 3.6 Imp. gal.)
Fuel reserve capacity	3.0 liters (4.4 gal., 3.6 Imp. gal.)
Clutch type	Wet, multi-plate
Transmission	
Type	6-speeds, constant-mesh
Primary reduction ratio	1.775 (71/40)
Final reduction ratio	2.933 (44/15)
Transmission ratios	
1st	3.230 (32/13)
2nd	2.235 (38/17)
3rd	1.800 (36/20)
4th	1.500 (33/22)
5th	1.272 (28/22)
6th	1.130 (26/23)
Ignition system	Capacitor discharge ignition (CDI)
Starting system	Electric starter only
Battery	12-volt, 8-amp/hour
Drive chain number	RK50MF0-Z1; 110 links

Table 3 DECIMAL AND METRIC EQUIVALENTS

Fractions	Decimal in.	Metric mm	Fractions	Decimal in.	Metric mm
1/64	0.015625	0.39688	13/64	0.203125	5.15937
1/32	0.03125	0.79375	7/32	0.21875	5.55625
3/64	0.046875	1.19062	15/64	0.234375	5.95312
1/16	0.0625	1.58750	1/4	0.250	6.35000
5/64	0.078125	1.98437	17/64	0.265625	6.74687
3/32	0.09375	2.38125	9/32	0.28125	7.14375
7/64	0.109375	2.77812	19/64	0.296875	7.54062
1/8	0.125	3.1750	21/64	0.328125	8.33437
9/64	0.140625	3.57187	11/32	0.34375	8.73125
5/32	0.15625	3.96875	23/64	0.359375	9.121812
11/64	0.171875	4.36562	3/8	0.375	9.52500
3/16	0.1875	4.76250	25/64	0.390625	9.92187

(continued)

Table 3 DECIMAL AND METRIC EQUIVALENTS (continued)

Fractions	Decimal in.	Metric mm	Fractions	Decimal in.	Metric mm
13/32	0.40625	10.31875	45/64	0.703125	17.85937
27/64	0.421875	10.71562	23/32	0.71875	18.25625
7/16	0.4375	11.11250	47/64	0.734375	18.65312
29/64	0.453125	11.50937	3/4	0.750	19.05000
15/32	0.46875	11.90625	49/64	0.765625	19.44687
31/64	0.484375	12.30312	25/32	0.78125	19.84375
1/2	0.500	12.70000	51/64	0.796875	20.24062
33/64	0.515625	13.09687	53/64	0.828125	21.03437
17/32	0.53125	13.49375	27/32	0.84375	21.43125
35/64	0.546875	13.89062	55/64	0.859375	21.82812
9/16	0.5625	14.28750	7/8	0.875	22.22500
37/64	0.578125	14.68437	57/64	0.890625	22.62187
19/32	0.59375	15.08125	29/32	0.90625	23.01875
39/64	0.609375	15.47812	59/64	0.921875	23.41562
5/8	0.625	15.87500	15/16	0.9375	23.81250
41/64	0.640625	16.27187	61/64	0.953125	24.20937
21/32	0.65625	16.66875	31/32	0.96875	24.60625
43/64	0.671875	17.06562	63/64	0.984375	25.00312
11/16	0.6875	17.46250	1	1.00	25.40000

Table 4 GENERAL TORQUE SPECIFICATIONS*

Thread diameter	N·m	ft.-lb.
5 mm		
Bolt and nut	5	3.5
Screw	4	3
6 mm		
Bolt and nut	10	8
Screw	9	7
6 mm flange bolt and nut	12	9
6 mm bolt with 8 mm head	9	7
8 mm		
Bolt and nut	22	16
Flange bolt and nut	27	20
10 mm		
Bolt and nut	35	25
Flange bolt and nut	40	29
12 mm		
Bolt and nut	55	40

* The torque specifications in this table are listed by Honda to be used for tightening non-critical fasteners. Always refer to the tightening torque table listed at the end of the respective chapter(s) for torque specifications for critical applications. If a torque specification is not included in the tightening torque table, use the specifications in this table.

CHAPTER TWO

TROUBLESHOOTING

Every motorcycle engine requires an uninterrupted supply of fuel and air, proper ignition and adequate compression. If any of these are lacking, the engine will not run.

Diagnosing mechanical problems is relatively simple if you use orderly procedures and keep a few basic principles in mind.

The troubleshooting procedures in this chapter analyze typical symptoms and show logical methods of isolating causes. These are not the only methods. There may be several ways to solve a problem, but only a systematic approach can guarantee success.

Never assume anything. Do not overlook the obvious. If you are riding along and the bike suddenly quits, check the easiest, most accessible problem spots first. Is there gasoline in the tank? Has a spark plug wire pulled apart or broken?

If nothing obvious turns up in a quick check, look a little further. Learning to recognize and describe symptoms will make repairs easier for you or a mechanic at the shop. Describe problems accurately and fully. Saying that "it won't run" isn't the same thing as saying "it quit at high speed and won't start," or that "it sat in my garage for 3 months and then wouldn't start."

Gather as many symptoms as possible to aid in diagnosis. Note whether the engine lost power gradually or all at once. Remember that the more complicated a machine is, the easier it is to troubleshoot because symptoms point to specific problems.

After the symptoms are defined, areas which could cause problems are tested and analyzed. Guessing at the cause of a problem may provide the solution, but it can easily lead to frustration, wasted time and a series of expensive, unnecessary parts replacements.

You do not need fancy equipment or complicated test gear to determine whether repairs can be attempted at home. A few simple checks could save a large repair bill and lost time while the bike sits in a dealer's service department. On the other hand, be realistic and don't attempt repairs beyond your abilities. Service departments tend to charge heavily for putting together a disassembled engine that may have been abused. Some won't even take on such a job—so use common sense and don't get in over your head.

Charging system specifications are listed in **Table 1**. Ignition system specifications are listed in **Table 2**. **Table 1** and **Table 2** are found at the end of the chapter.

OPERATING REQUIREMENTS

An engine needs 3 basics to run properly: correct fuel/air mixture, compression and a spark at the correct time. If one or more are missing, the engine will not run. Four-stroke engine operating principles are described under *Engine Principles* in Chapter Four. The electrical system is the weakest link of the 3 basics. More problems result from electrical breakdowns than from any other source. Keep that in mind before you begin tampering with carburetor adjustments and the like.

If the machine has been sitting for any length of time and refuses to start, check and clean the spark plugs and then look to the gasoline delivery system. This includes the fuel tank, fuel pump, fuel shutoff valve and fuel line to the carburetors. Gasoline deposits may have formed and gummed up the carburetor jets and air passages. Gasoline tends to lose its potency after standing for long periods. Condensation may contaminate the fuel with water. Drain the old fuel (fuel tank, fuel lines and carburetors) and try starting with a fresh tankful.

TROUBLESHOOTING INSTRUMENTS

Chapter One lists the instruments needed and instruction on their use.

STARTING THE ENGINE

When experiencing engine starting troubles, it is easy to work out of sequence and forget basic engine starting procedures. The following is the factory recommended procedure for starting the Honda CRB600 engine.

> *NOTE*
> *Never operate the electric starter for more than 5 seconds at a time. Wait approximately 10 seconds between starting attempts.*

Starting Notes

1. The electric starter can operate when the transmission is in gear and the clutch disengaged. On 1989 models, the sidestand must be in the UP position.
2. Before starting the engine, shift the transmission into NEUTRAL, turn the fuel valve to ON and push the engine stop switch to RUN.
3. The engine is now ready to start. Refer to the starting procedure in this section that best pertains to your engine's temperature.
4. If the engine is idled at a fast speed for 5 minutes or more and/or the throttle is snapped on and off repeatedly at normal air temperatures, the exhaust pipes may discolor.
5. Excessive use of the choke may cause a rich mixture and result in piston and cylinder wall scuffing.

> *CAUTION*
> *Once the engine starts, the red oil pressure warning light should go off in a few seconds. If the light stays on longer than a few seconds, immediately stop the engine. Check the engine oil level as described in Chapter Three and correct if necessary. If the oil level is okay, the oil pressure may be too low or the switch may be shorted. Check the oiling system and correct the problem before starting the engine. Severe engine damage will occur if the engine is run with low oil pressure.*

Starting Procedure
(Cold Engine With Normal Air Temperature)

Normal air temperature is considered to be between 50-95° F (10-35° C).
1. Perform the procedures under *Starting Notes*.
2. Install the ignition key and turn the ignition switch to ON.
3. Pull the choke lever to the fully open position (**Figure 1**).
4. Operate the starter button and start the engine. Do not open the throttle.

> *NOTE*
> *When a cold engine is started with the throttle open and the choke open, a lean mixture will result and cause hard starting.*

5. With the engine running, operate the choke lever as required to keep the engine idle at 1,500-2,500 rpm.

6. After approximately 30 seconds, push the choke lever to the fully closed position (**Figure 1**). If the idling is rough, open the throttle to help warm the engine.

Starting Procedure
(Cold Engine With Low Air Temperature)

Low air temperature is considered to be 50° F (10° C) or lower.

1. Perform the procedures under *Starting Notes*.
2. Install the ignition key and turn the ignition switch to ON.
3. Pull the choke lever to the fully open position.
4. Operate the starter button and start the engine. Do not open the throttle when pressing the starter button.
5. Once the engine is running, open the throttle slightly to help warm the engine. Continue warming the engine until the choke can be turned to the fully closed position (**Figure 1**) and the engine responds to the throttle cleanly.

Starting Procedure
(Warm Engine and/or High Air Temperature)

High air temperature is considered to be 95° F (35° C) or higher.

1. Perform the procedures under *Starting Notes*.
2. Install the ignition key and turn the ignition switch to ON.
3. Operate the starter button, open the throttle slightly and start the engine.

Starting Procedure
(Flooded Engine)

If the engine does not start after a few attempts it may be flooded. A good indicator of a flooded engine is the smell of gasoline after attempting to start the engine. To start a flooded engine, perform the following.

1. Turn the engine stop switch off.
2. Push the choke lever to the closed position (**Figure 1**).
3. Open the throttle grip completely and push the starter button and crank the engine for 5 seconds.

4. After waiting 10 seconds, proceed with Step 5.
5. Perform the procedures under *Starting Notes*.
6. With the ignition key, turn the ignition switch to ON.
7. Operate the starter button, open the throttle slightly and start the engine.

EMERGENCY TROUBLESHOOTING

When the bike is difficult to start, or won't start at all, it doesn't help to wear down the battery using the electric starter. Check for obvious problems even before getting out your tools. Go down the following list step by step. Do each one; you may be embarrassed to find the engine stop switch off, but that is better than wearing down the battery. If the bike still will not start, refer to the appropriate troubleshooting procedures which follows in this chapter.

1. Is there fuel in the tank? Open the filler cap and rock the bike. Listen for fuel sloshing around.

> *WARNING*
> *Do not use an open flame to check in the tank. A serious explosion is certain to result.*

2. Is the fuel supply valve in the ON position? Turn the valve to the RES position to be sure you get the last remaining gas.

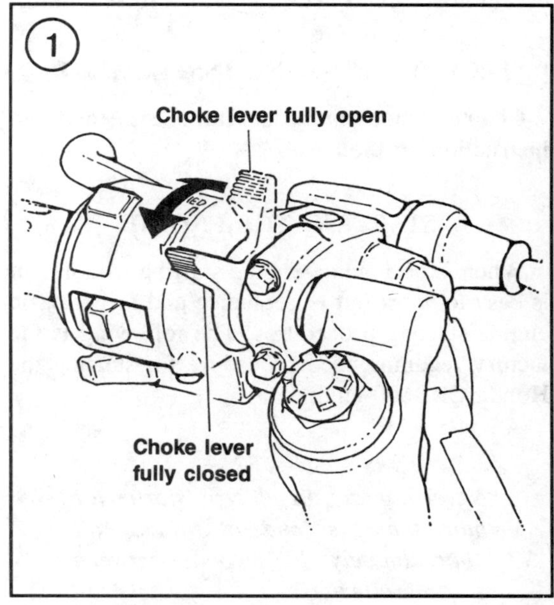

3. Make sure the engine stop switch (**Figure 2**) is not stuck in the OFF position or that the wire is not broken and shorting out. Test the switch as described under *Switches* in Chapter Eight.

4. Are the spark plug wires on tight? Remove the maintenance covers (Chapter Thirteen). Push all 4 spark plug caps on and slightly rotate them to clean the electrical connection between the plug and the connector.

5. Is the choke lever (**Figure 1**) in the right position? The choke lever should be *closed* for a warm engine and *open* for a cold engine.

6. On 1989 models, is the sidestand in the UP position?

ENGINE STARTING TROUBLESHOOTING

An engine that refuses to start or is difficult to start is very frustrating. More often than not, the problem is very minor and can be found with a simple and logical troubleshooting approach.

The following items will help isolate engine starting problems.

Engine Fails to Start

Perform the following spark test to determine if the ignition system is operating properly.

1. Remove one of the spark plugs as described in Chapter Three.

2. Connect the spark plug wire and connector to the spark plug and touch the spark plug base to a good ground like the engine cylinder head. Position the spark plug so you can see the electrodes.

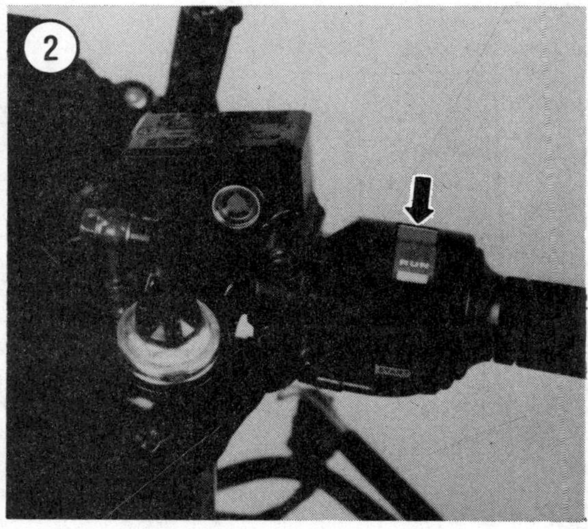

WARNING
During the next step, do not hold the spark plug, wire or connector with fingers or a serious electrical shock may result. If necessary, use a pair of insulated pliers to hold the spark plug or wire. The high voltage generated by the ignition system could produce serious or fatal shocks.

3. Crank the engine over with the starter. A fat blue spark should be evident across the spark plug electrodes.

NOTE
*If the starter does not operate or if the starter motor rotates but the engine does not turn over, refer to **Engine Will Not Crank** in this section.*

4. If the spark is good, check for one or more of the following possible malfunctions:
   a. Obstructed fuel line or fuel filter.
   b. Leaking head gasket.
   c. Low compression.

5. If the spark is not good, check for one or more of the following:
   a. Loose electrical connections.
   b. Dirty electrical connections.
   c. Loose or broken ignition coil ground wire.
   d. Broken or shorted high tension lead to the spark plug(s).
   e. Discharged battery.
   f. Disconnected or damaged battery connection.
   g. Pulse generator malfunction.
   h. Spark unit malfunction.
   i. Ignition or engine stop switch malfunction.
   j. Blown fuse.

Engine is Difficult to Start

Check for one or more of the following possible malfunctions:
   a. Fouled spark plug(s).
   b. Improperly adjusted choke.
   c. Intake manifold air leak.
   d. Contaminated fuel system.
   e. Improperly adjusted carburetors.
   f. Ignition system malfunction.
   g. Weak ignition coil(s).
   h. Poor compression.
   i. Engine and transmission oil too heavy.

Engine Will Not Crank

Check for one or more of the following possible malfunctions:
a. Blown fuse.
b. Discharged battery.
c. Defective starter motor.
d. Seized piston(s).
e. Seized crankshaft bearing(s).
f. Broken connecting rod(s).

ENGINE PERFORMANCE

In the following checklist, it is assumed that the engine runs, but is not operating at peak performance. This will serve as a starting point from which to isolate a performance malfunction.

NOTE
Where ignition timing is mentioned as a problem, remember that there is no method of adjusting the ignition timing on these Honda models. If ignition timing is incorrect, there is a faulty part(s) within the ignition system that must be replaced as described in Chapter Eight.

Engine Will Not Start or is Hard to Start

a. Fuel tank empty.
b. Fuel pump not operating properly.
c. Obstructed fuel line, fuel shutoff valve or fuel filter.
d. Sticking float valve in carburetor(s).
e. Carburetors incorrectly adjusted.
f. Improper starter valve (choke) operation.
g. Improper throttle operation.
h. Fouled or improperly gapped spark plug(s).
i. Ignition timing incorrect.
j. Broken or shorted ignition coil(s).
k. Weak or faulty spark unit(s) or pulse generator(s).
l. Improper valve timing.
m. Clogged air filter element.
n. Contaminated fuel.
o. Engine flooded with fuel.
p. Improper valve clearance.
q. Detective switches in the ignition and/or starter system(s).

Engine Will Not Idle

a. Carburetors incorrectly adjusted (too lean or too rich).
b. Fouled or improperly gapped spark plug(s).
c. Leaking head gasket(s) or vacuum leak.
d. Ignition timing incorrect.
e. Weak spark unit(s) or pulse generator(s).
f. Improper valve timing.
g. Obstructed fuel line or fuel shutoff valve.
h. Low engine compression.
i. Slow air cutoff valve faulty.
j. Starter valve (choke) stuck in the open position.
k. Incorrect pilot screw adjustment.
l. Clogged slow jet(s) in the carburetor(s).
m. Clogged air filter element.
n. Improper valve clearance.
o. Valve(s) and valve seat(s) require service.

Engine Misses at High Speed

a. Fouled or improperly gapped spark plugs.
b. Improper carburetor main jet selection.
c. Improper ignition timing.
d. Weak ignition coil(s).
e. Weak or faulty spark unit(s) or pulse generator(s).
f. Obstructed fuel line or fuel shutoff valve.
g. Obstructed fuel filter.
h. Clogged carburetor jets.
i. Dirty air cleaner.
j. Fuel pump not working properly.

Engine Overheating

a. Incorrect carburetor adjustment or jet selection.
b. Ignition timing retarded due to defective ignition component(s).
c. Improper spark plug heat range.
d. Cooling system malfunction.
e. Incorrect coolant level.
f. Oil level low.
g. Oil not circulating properly.
h. Valves leaking.
i. Heavy engine carbon deposits.
j. Dragging brake(s).
k. Clutch slipping.

Engine Overheating
(Cooling System Malfunction)

Note the previous procedure, then check the following items:
a. Clogged radiator.
b. Damaged thermostat.
c. Worn or damaged radiator cap.
d. Water pump worn or damaged.
e. Fan relay malfunction.
f. Thermostatic fan switch malfunction.
g. Damaged fan blade(s).

Smoky Exhaust and Engine Runs Roughly

a. Clogged air filter element.
b. Carburetor adjustment incorrect—mixture too rich.
c. Choke not operating correctly.
d. Water or other contaminants in fuel.
e. Clogged fuel line.
f. Spark plugs fouled.
g. Ignition coil defective.
h. Loose or defective ignition circuit wire(s).
i. Short circuit from damaged wire insulation.
j. Loose battery cable connection(s).
k. Valve timing incorrect.

Engine Loses Power at Normal Riding Speed

a. Carburetor incorrectly adjusted.
b. Engine overheating.
c. Improper ignition timing.
d. Incorrectly gapped spark plug(s).
e. Weak ignition coil(s).
f. Weak spark unit(s).
g. Weak pulse generator(s).
h. Obstructed muffler.
i. Dragging brake(s).
j. Improper valve clearance.

Engine Lacks Acceleration

a. Carburetor mixture too lean.
b. Clogged fuel line.
c. Improper ignition timing.
d. Dragging brake(s).
e. Slipping clutch.
f. Fuel pump not working properly.

Engine Backfires

a. Improper ignition timing.
b. Carburetor(s) improperly adjusted.
c. Lean fuel mixture.

Engine Misfires During Acceleration

a. Improper ignition timing.
b. Lean fuel mixture.

ENGINE NOISES

Often the first evidence of an internal engine problem is a strange noise. That knocking, clicking or tapping sound which you never heard before may be warning you of impending trouble.

While engine noises can indicate problems, they are difficult to interpret correctly; inexperienced mechanics can be seriously misled by them.

Professional mechanics often use a special stethoscope (which looks like a doctor's stethoscope) for isolating engine noises. You can do nearly as well with a "sounding stick" which can be an ordinary piece of doweling, or a section of small hose. By placing one end in contact with the area to which you want to listen and the other end to the front of your ear (not directly on your ear), you can hear sounds emanating from that area. The first time you do this, you may be confused at the strange sounds coming from even a normal engine. If you can, have an experienced friend or mechanic help you sort out the noises.

Consider the following when troubleshooting engine noises:

1. *Knocking or pinging during acceleration—* Caused by using a lower octane fuel than recommended. May also be caused by poor fuel. Pinging can also be caused by a spark plug of the wrong heat range or carbon buildup in the combustion chamber. Refer to *Correct Spark Plug Heat Range* and *Compression Test* in Chapter Three.

2. *Slapping or rattling noises at low speed or during acceleration—*May be caused by piston slap, i.e., excessive piston-cylinder wall clearance.

NOTE
Piston slap is easier to detect when the engine is cold and before the pistons have expanded. Once the engine has

warmed up, piston expansion reduces piston-to-cylinder clearance.

3. *Knocking or rapping while decelerating—* Usually caused by excessive rod bearing clearance.
4. *Persistent knocking and vibration occurring every crankshaft rotation—*Usually caused by worn rod or main bearing(s). Can also be caused by broken piston rings or damaged piston pins.
5. *Rapid on/off squeal—*Compression leak around cylinder head gasket or spark plug(s).
6. *Valve train noise—*Check for the following:
   a. Valves adjusted incorrectly.
   b. Loose valve adjuster.
   c. Valve sticking in guide.
   d. Low oil pressure.
   e. Damaged rocker arm or shaft. Rocker arm may be binding on shaft.

ENGINE LUBRICATION

An improperly operating engine lubrication system will quickly lead to engine seizure. The engine oil level should be checked weekly and topped up, as described in Chapter Three. Oil pump service is described in Chapter Four.

Oil Consumption High or Engine Smokes Excessively

   a. Worn valve guides.
   b. Worn or damaged piston rings.

Excessive Engine Oil Leaks

   a. Clogged air cleaner breather hose.
   b. Loose engine parts.
   c. Damaged gasket sealing surfaces.

Black Smoke

   a. Clogged air filter element.
   b. Incorrect carburetor fuel level (too high).
   c. Choke stuck open.
   d. Incorrect main jet(s) (too large).

White Smoke

   a. Worn valve guide.
   b. Worn valve oil seal.
   c. Worn piston ring oil ring.
   d. Excessive cylinder and/or piston wear.

Oil Pressure Too High

   a. Clogged oil filter.
   b. Clogged oil gallery or metering orifices.
   c. Pressure relief valve stuck closed.

Low Oil Pressure

   a. Damaged oil pump.
   b. Low oil level.
   c. Clogged oil screen.
   d. Clogged oil filter.
   e. Pressure relief valve stuck open.
   f. Internal oil leakage.

No Oil Pressure

   a. Damaged oil pump.
   b. Excessively low oil level.
   c. No oil.
   d. Internal oil leakage.
   e. Damaged oil pump drive chain.
   f. Damaged oil pump drive shaft.

Oil Pressure Warning Light Stays On

   a. Low oil pressure.
   b. No oil pressure.
   c. Damaged oil pressure switch.
   d. Short in warning light circuit.

Oil Level Too Low

   a. Oil not maintained at correct level.
   b. Worn piston rings.
   c. Worn cylinder(s).
   d. Worn valve guides.
   e. Worn valve stem seals.
   f. Piston rings incorrectly installed during engine rebuilding.
   g. External oil leakage.

Oil Contamination

   a. Blown head gasket allowing coolant leakage.
   b. Water contamination.
   c. Oil and filter not changed at specified intervals or when abnormal operating conditions demand more frequent changes.

CLUTCH

The four basic clutch troubles are:

a. Clutch slipping.
b. Clutch dragging.
c. Excessive clutch noise.
d. Rough clutch operation.

All clutch troubles, except adjustments, require partial clutch disassembly to identify and cure the problem. The troubleshooting chart in **Figure 3** lists clutch troubles and checks to make. Refer to Chapter Five for clutch service procedures.

GEARSHIFT LINKAGE

The gearshift linkage assembly connects the gearshift pedal (external shift mechanism) to the shift drum (internal shift mechanism). Basic gearshift linkage troubles are:

a. Difficult shifting.
b. Gearshift pedal does not return.
c. Transmission gears pop out of mesh.

The external shift mechanism can be examined after removing the clutch assembly. The internal shift mechanism can only be examined once the engine has been removed and the crankcase disassembled. The troubleshooting chart in **Figure 4** lists gearshift linkage troubles and checks to make.

TRANSMISSION

The basic transmission troubles are:

a. Excessive gear noise.
b. Difficult shifting.
c. Gears pop out of mesh.
d. Incorrect shift lever operation.

Transmission symptoms are sometimes hard to distinguish from clutch symptoms. The troubleshooting chart in **Figure 5** lists transmission troubles and checks to make. Refer to Chapter Six for transmission service procedures. Be sure that the clutch is not causing the trouble before working on the transmission.

ELECTRICAL TROUBLESHOOTING

This section describes the basics of electrical troubleshooting, how to use test equipment and the basic test procedures with the various pieces of test equipment.

Electrical troubleshooting can be very time consuming and frustrating without proper knowledge and a suitable plan. Refer to the wiring diagrams at the end of the book and to the individual system diagrams included with the charging system, ignition. system and starting system sections in this chapter. Wiring diagrams will help you determine how the circuit should work by tracing the current paths from the power source through the circuit components to ground. Also check any circuits that share the same fuse, ground or switch, etc. If the other circuits work properly, the shared wiring is okay and the cause must be in the wiring used only by the suspect circuit. If all related circuits are faulty at the same time the probable cause is a poor ground connection or a blown fuse(s).

As with all troubleshooting procedures, analyze typical symptoms in a systematic procedure. Never assume anything and don't overlook the obvious like a blown fuse or an electrical connector that has separated. Test the simplest and most obvious cause first and try to make tests at easily accessible points on the bike.

Preliminary Checks and Precautions

Before starting any electrical troubleshooting procedure perform the following:

a. Check the main fuse. Make sure it is not blown. Replace it if necessary.

b. Check the individual fuse(s) for each circuit. Make sure it is not blown; replace if necessary.

c. Inspect the battery. Make sure it is fully charged, the electrolyte level is correct and that the battery leads are clean and securely attached to the battery terminals. Refer to *Battery* in Chapter Three.

d. Disconnect each electrical connector in the suspect circuit and check that there are no bent metal pins on the male side of the electrical connector (**Figure 6**). A bent pin will not connect to its mating receptacle in the female end of the connector, causing an open circuit.

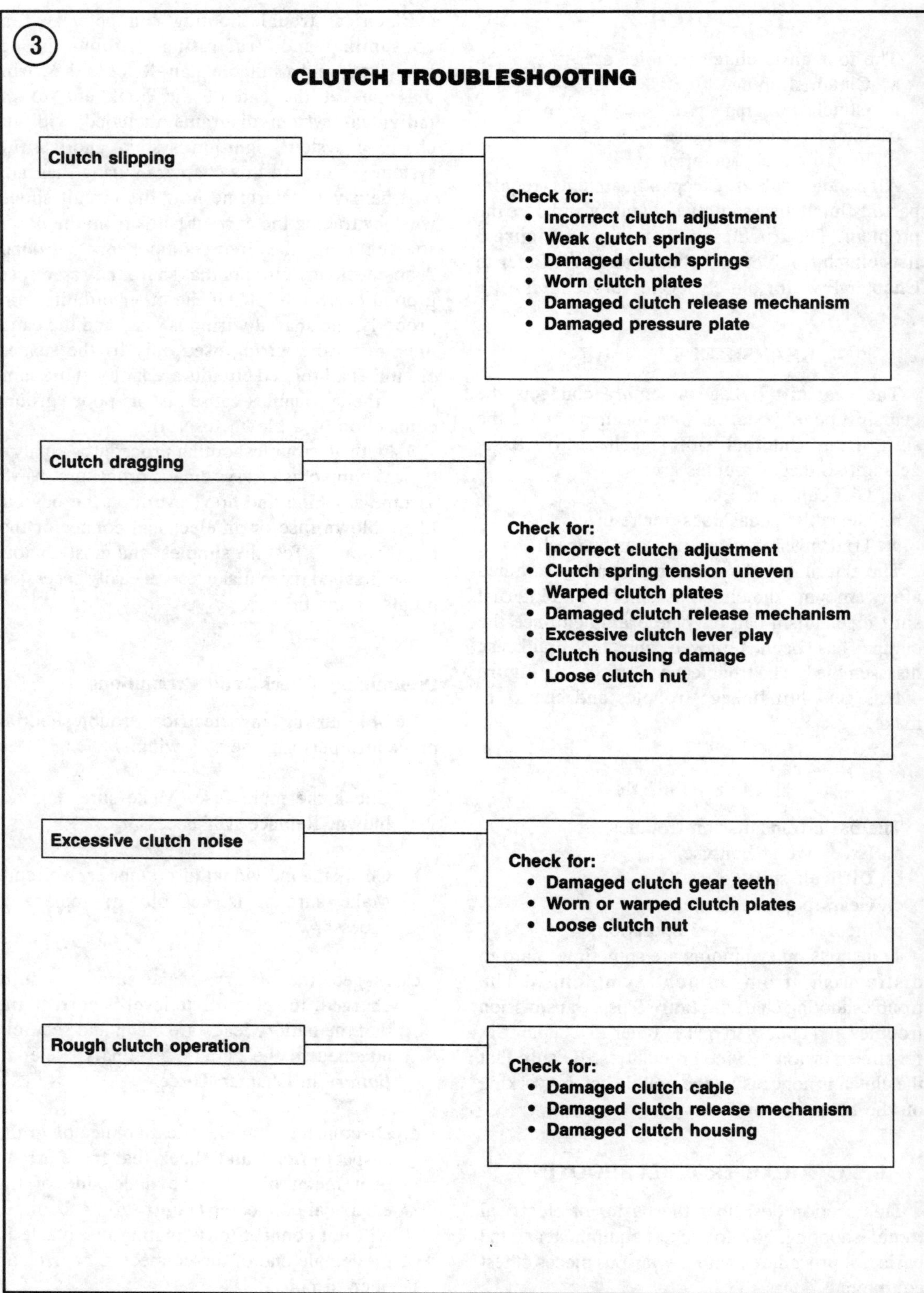
3

CLUTCH TROUBLESHOOTING

Clutch slipping

Check for:
• Incorrect clutch adjustment
• Weak clutch springs
• Damaged clutch springs
• Worn clutch plates
• Damaged clutch release mechanism
• Damaged pressure plate

Clutch dragging

Check for:
• Incorrect clutch adjustment
• Clutch spring tension uneven
• Warped clutch plates
• Damaged clutch release mechanism
• Excessive clutch lever play
• Clutch housing damage
• Loose clutch nut

Excessive clutch noise

Check for:
• Damaged clutch gear teeth
• Worn or warped clutch plates
• Loose clutch nut

Rough clutch operation

Check for:
• Damaged clutch cable
• Damaged clutch release mechanism
• Damaged clutch housing

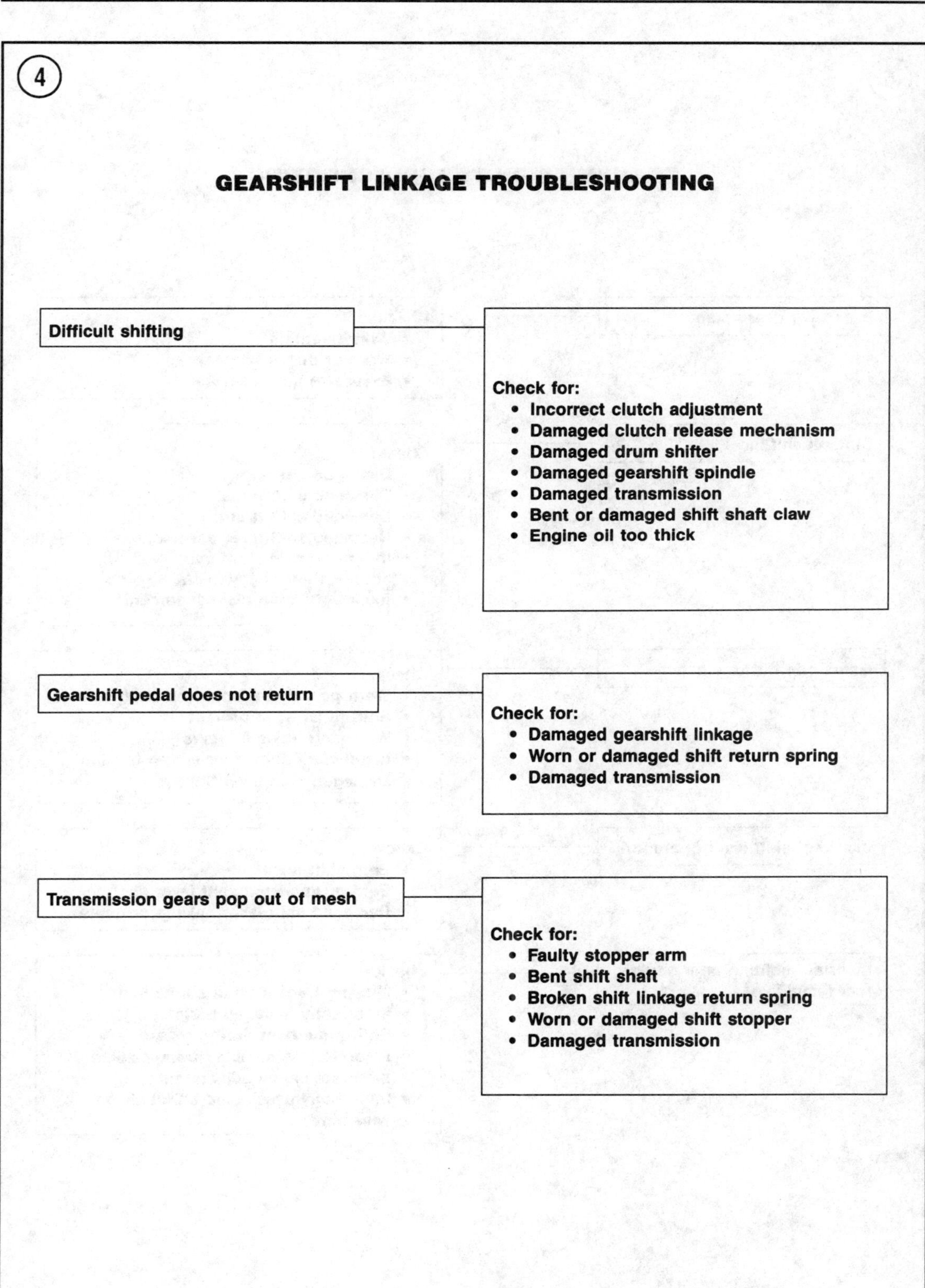

4

GEARSHIFT LINKAGE TROUBLESHOOTING

Difficult shifting

Check for:
• Incorrect clutch adjustment
• Damaged clutch release mechanism
• Damaged drum shifter
• Damaged gearshift spindle
• Damaged transmission
• Bent or damaged shift shaft claw
• Engine oil too thick

Gearshift pedal does not return

Check for:
• Damaged gearshift linkage
• Worn or damaged shift return spring
• Damaged transmission

Transmission gears pop out of mesh

Check for:
• Faulty stopper arm
• Bent shift shaft
• Broken shift linkage return spring
• Worn or damaged shift stopper
• Damaged transmission

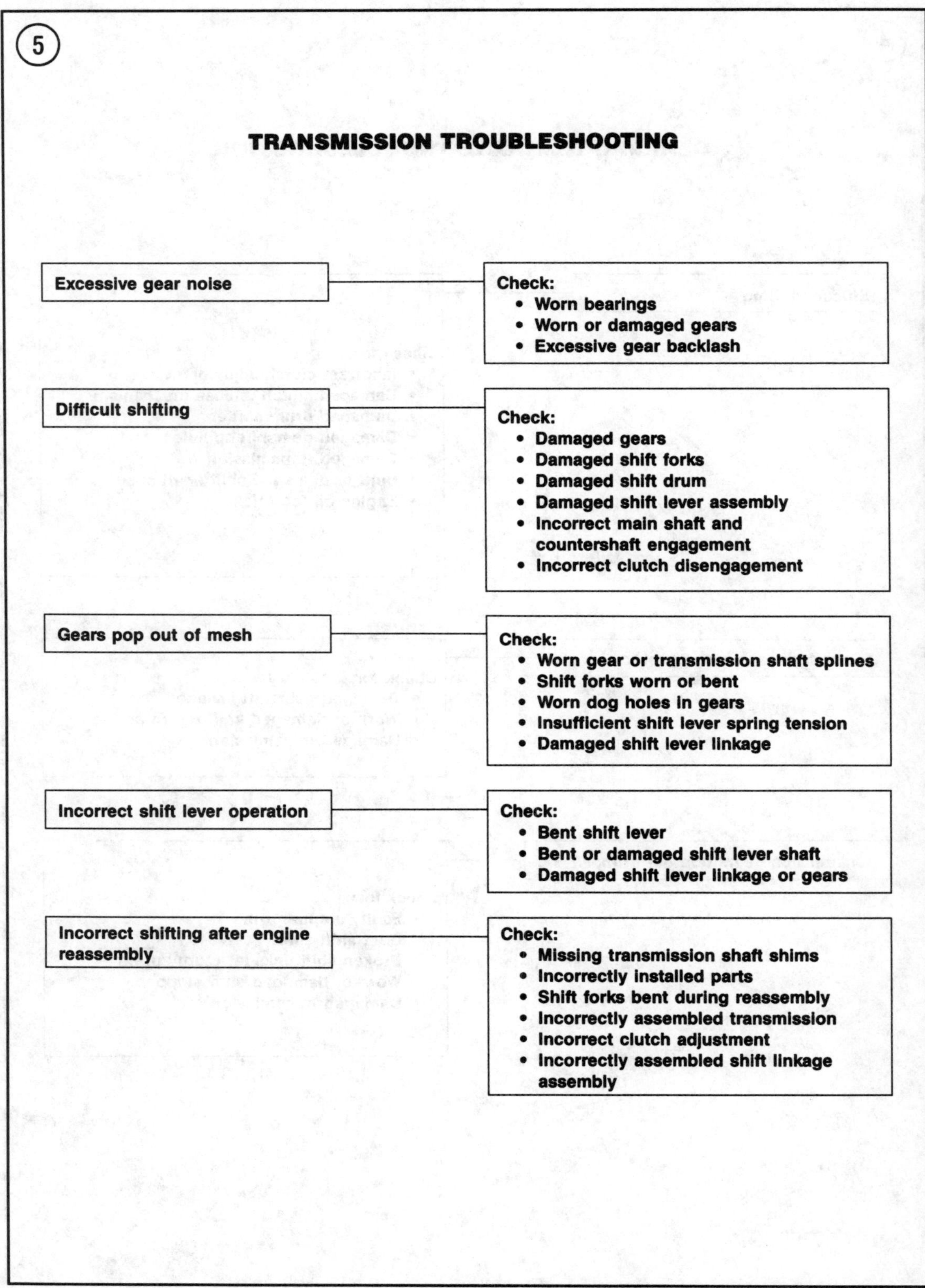
5

TRANSMISSION TROUBLESHOOTING

Excessive gear noise

Check:
• Worn bearings
• Worn or damaged gears
• Excessive gear backlash

Difficult shifting

Check:
• Damaged gears
• Damaged shift forks
• Damaged shift drum
• Damaged shift lever assembly
• Incorrect main shaft and countershaft engagement
• Incorrect clutch disengagement

Gears pop out of mesh

Check:
• Worn gear or transmission shaft splines
• Shift forks worn or bent
• Worn dog holes in gears
• Insufficient shift lever spring tension
• Damaged shift lever linkage

Incorrect shift lever operation

Check:
• Bent shift lever
• Bent or damaged shift lever shaft
• Damaged shift lever linkage or gears

Incorrect shifting after engine reassembly

Check:
• Missing transmission shaft shims
• Incorrectly installed parts
• Shift forks bent during reassembly
• Incorrectly assembled transmission
• Incorrect clutch adjustment
• Incorrectly assembled shift linkage assembly

e. Check each female end of the connector. Make sure that the metal connector on the end of each wire (**Figure 7**) is pushed all the way into the plastic connector. If not, carefully push them in with a narrow-blade screwdriver.

f. Check all electrical wires where they enter the individual metal connector in both the male and female plastic connector.

g. Make sure all electrical connectors within the connector are clean and free of corrosion. Clean, if necessary, and pack the connectors with a dielectric grease as described under *Electrical Connectors* in this chapter.

h. After all is checked out, push the connectors together and make sure they are fully engaged and locked together (**Figure 8**).

i. Never pull on the electrical wires when disconnecting an electrical connector—pull only on the connector plastic housing.

j. Never use a self-powered test light on circuits that contain solid-state devices. The solid-state devices may be damaged.

TEST EQUIPMENT

Test Light or Voltmeter

A test light can be constructed of a 12-volt light bulb with a pair of test leads carefully soldered to the bulb. To check for battery voltage (12 volts) in a circuit, attach one lead to ground and the other lead to various points along the circuit. Where battery voltage is present the light bulb will light.

A voltmeter is used in the same manner as the test light to find out if battery voltage is present in any given circuit. The voltmeter, unlike the test light, will also indicate how much voltage is present at each test point. When using a voltmeter, attach the red lead (+) to the component or wire to be checked and the black negative (−) lead to a good ground.

Self-powered Test Light and Ohmmeter

A self-powered test light can be constructed of a 12-volt light bulb, a pair of test leads and a 12-volt battery. When the test leads are touched together the light bulb will go on.

Use a self-powered test light as follows:

a. Touch the test leads together to make sure the light bulb goes on. If not, correct the problem before using it in a test procedure.

b. Disconnect the bike's battery or remove the fuse(s) that protects the circuit to be tested.

c. Select 2 points within the circuit where there should be continuity.

d. Attach one lead of the self-powered test light to each point.

e. If there is continuity, the self-powered test light bulb will come on.

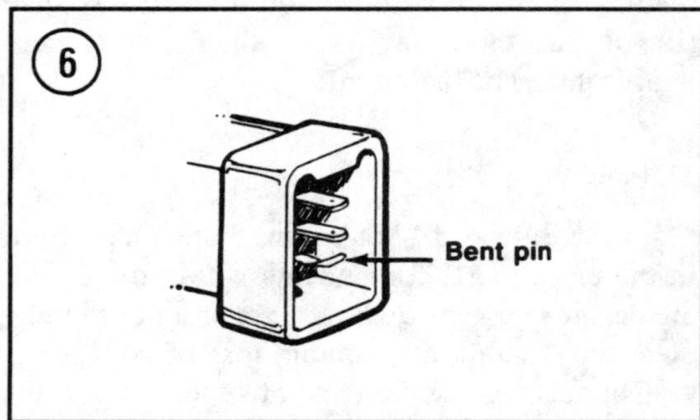

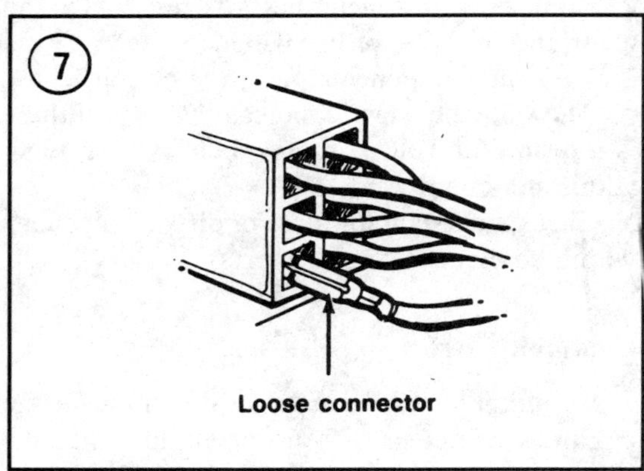

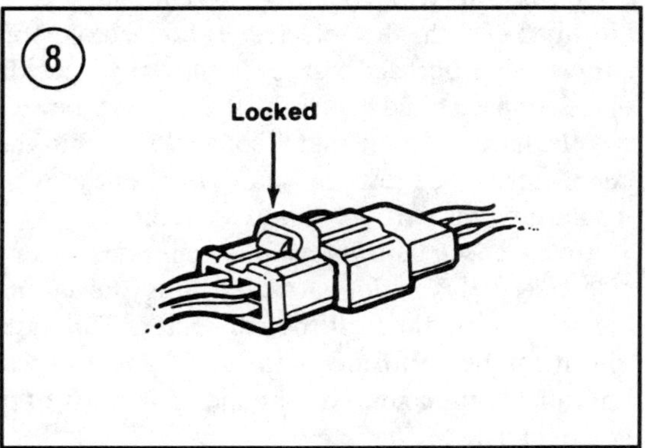

f. If there is no continuity, the self-powered test light bulb will *not* come on, which indicates an open circuit.

An ohmmeter can be used in place of the self-powered test light. The ohmmeter, unlike the test light, will also indicate how much resistance is present between each test point. Low resistance means good continuity in a complete circuit. Before using an ohmmeter, it must first be calibrated. This is done by touching the leads together and turning the ohms calibration knob until the meter reads "zero."

> *CAUTION*
> *An ohmmeter must never be connected to any circuit which has power applied to it. Always disconnect the battery negative lead before using the ohmmeter.*

Jumper Wire

When using a jumper wire always install an inline fuse/fuse holder (available at most auto supply stores or electronic supply stores) to the jumper wire. Never use a jumper wire across any load (a component that is connected and turned on). This would result in a direct short and will blow the fuse(s).

BASIC TEST PROCEDURES

Voltage Testing

Unless otherwise specified, all voltage tests are made with the electrical connector still *connected*. Insert the test leads into the backside of the connector and make sure the test lead touches the electrical wire or metal connector within the connector. If the test lead only touches the wire insulation you will get a false reading.

Always check both sides of the connector as one side may be loose or corroded thus preventing electrical flow through the connector. This type of test can be performed with a test light or a voltmeter. A voltmeter will give the best results.

> *NOTE*
> *If using a test light, it doesn't make any difference which test lead is attached to ground.*

1. Attach the negative test lead (if using a voltmeter) to a good ground (bare metal). If necessary, scrape away paint from the frame or engine (retouch later with paint). Make sure the part used for ground is not insulated with a rubber gasket or rubber grommet.
2. Attach the positive test lead (if using a voltmeter) to the point (electrical connector, etc.) you want to check.
3. Turn the ignition switch on. If using a test light, the test light will come on if voltage is present. If using a voltmeter, note the voltage reading. The reading should be within 1 volt of battery voltage (12 volts). If the voltage is less than 11 volts there is a problem in the circuit.

Voltage Drop Test

A voltage drop of 1 volt means there is a problem in the circuit. All components within the circuit are designed for low resistance in order to conduct electricity within a minimum loss of voltage.
1. Connect the voltmeter positive test lead to the end of the wire or switch closest to the battery.
2. Connect the voltmeter negative test lead to the other end of the wire or switch.
3. Turn the components on in the circuit.
4. The voltmeter should indicate 12 volts. If there is a drop of 1 volt or more, there is a problem within the circuit.
5. Check the circuit for loose or dirty connections within an electrical connector(s).

Continuity Test

A continuity test is made to determine if the circuit is complete with no opens in either the electrical wires or components within that circuit.

Unless otherwise specified, all continuity tests are made with the electrical connector still *connected*. Insert the test leads into the backside of the connector and make sure the test lead touches the electrical wire or metal connector within the connector. If the test lead only touches the wire insulation you will get a false reading.

Always check both sides of the connectors as one side may be loose or corroded thus preventing electrical flow through the connector. This type of test can be performed with a self-powered test light or a ohmmeter. An ohmmeter will give the best results.

If using an ohmmeter, calibrate the meter by touching the leads together and turning the ohms calibration knob until the meter reads "zero." This is necessary in order to get accurate results.

1. Disconnect the battery negative lead.

2. Attach one test lead (test light or ohmmeter) to one end of the part of the circuit to be tested.

3. Attach the other test lead to the other end of the part of the circuit to be tested.

4. The self-powered test light will come on if there is continuity. The ohmmeter will indicate either a low or no resistance (means good continuity in a complete circuit) or infinite resistance (means an open circuit).

**Testing For a Short
With a Self-powered Test Light
or Ohmmeter**

This test can be performed with either a self-powered test light or an ohmmeter.

1. Disconnect the battery negative lead.

2. Remove the blown fuse from the fuse panel.

3. Connect one test lead of the test light or ohmmeter to the load side (the side that connects to the circuit being tested) of the fuse terminal in the fuse panel.

4. Connect the other test lead to a good ground (bare metal). If necessary, scrape away paint from the frame or engine (retouch later with paint). Make sure the part used for a ground is not insulated with a rubber gasket or rubber grommet.

5. With the self-powered test light or ohmmeter attached to the fuse terminal and ground, wiggle the wiring harness relating to the suspect circuit at 6 in. intervals. Start next to the fuse panel and work your way away from the fuse panel. Watch the self-powered test light or ohmmeter as you progress along the harness.

6. If the test light blinks or the needle on the ohmmeter moves, there is a short to ground at that point in the harness.

**Testing For a Short
With a Test Light or Voltmeter**

This test can be performed with either a test light or voltmeter.

1. Remove the blown fuse from the fuse panel.

2. Connect the test light or voltmeter across the fuse terminals in the fuse panel. Turn the ignition switch on and check for battery voltage (12 volts).

3. With the test light or voltmeter attached to the fuse terminals, wiggle the wiring harness relating to the suspect circuit at 6 in. intervals. Start next to the fuse panel and work your way away from the fuse panel. Watch the test light or voltmeter as you progress along the harness.

4. If the test light blinks or the needle on the voltmeter moves, there is a short-to-ground at that point in the harness.

ELECTRICAL PROBLEMS

If bulbs burn out frequently, the cause may be excessive vibration, loose connections that permit sudden current surges, or the installation of the wrong type of bulb.

Most light and ignition problems are caused by loose or corroded ground connections. Check these before replacing a bulb or electrical component.

CHARGING SYSTEM

The charging system consists of the battery, alternator and a voltage regulator/rectifier. A 30-amp main fuse protects the circuit. See **Figure 9**.

Alternating current generated by the alternator is rectified to direct current. The voltage regulator maintains the voltage to the battery and additional electrical loads (lights, ignition, etc.) at a constant voltage regardless of variations in engine speed and load.

Charging system test specifications are listed in **Table 1**.

Troubleshooting

Before troubleshooting the charging system, check battery voltage as follows.

1. Remove the side covers and seat. See Chapter Thirteen.

2. Remove the bolts securing the battery case cover and remove the cover (**Figure 10**).

3. Connect a voltmeter between the battery negative and positive leads (**Figure 11**). Interpret results as follows:

    a. 13.0-13.2 volts: Fully charged.

    b. 12.3 volts or less: Undercharged.

4. If the battery is overcharged, replace the regulator/rectifier assembly as described in Chapter Eight. If the battery is undercharged, perform the troubleshooting procedures in **Figure 12** step-by-step. **Figure 12** will instruct you when to perform a test procedure in this chapter.

Battery Leakage Test

Perform this test before performing the output test.

1. Remove the side covers and seat. See Chapter Thirteen.

2. Remove the fuel tank as described in Chapter Seven.

3. Remove the bolts securing the battery case cover and remove the cover (**Figure 10**).

4. Turn the ignition switch off.

5. Disconnect the battery negative (−) lead (**Figure 13**). Tie the lead so that it doesn't contact any part of the frame or any component.

6. Connect a voltmeter between the battery negative lead and the negative terminal on the battery.

7. The voltmeter should read 8 volts.

8. Disconnect the 3-pin (A, **Figure 14**) and 4-pin (B, **Figure 14**) regulator/rectifier connectors at the holder at the rear of the air filter housing.

9. Check the voltage once again. The voltmeter should read 0 volts (with ignition switch off).

10. If the readings in Step 6 and Step 8 are incorrect, this indicates a voltage drain in the system that will drain the battery. Test the charging system as described in **Figure 12**.

11. Disconnect and remove the voltmeter.

12. Reinstall all parts.

Output Test

Whenever the charging system is suspected of trouble, make sure the battery is fully charged and in good condition before going any further. Clean and test the battery as described in Chapter Eight.

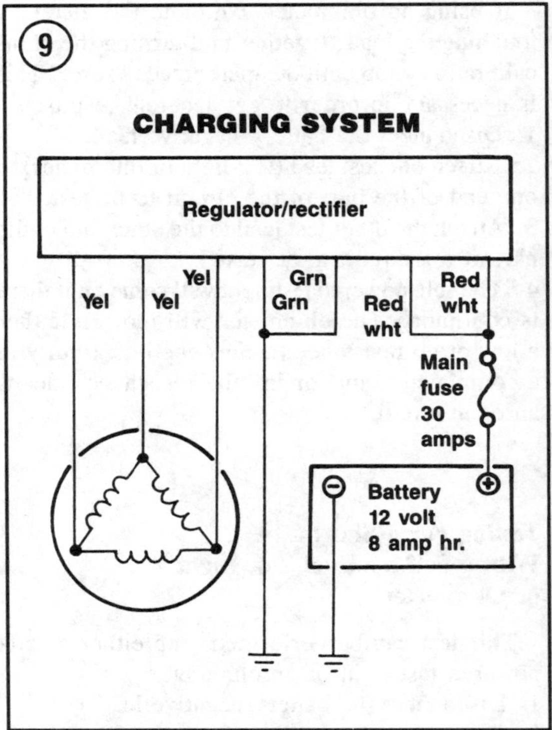

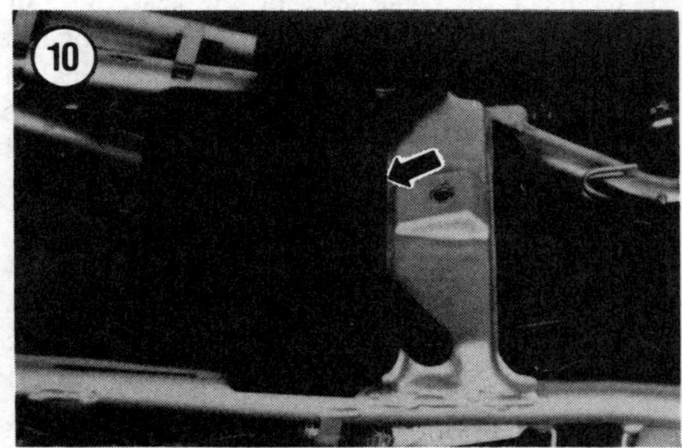

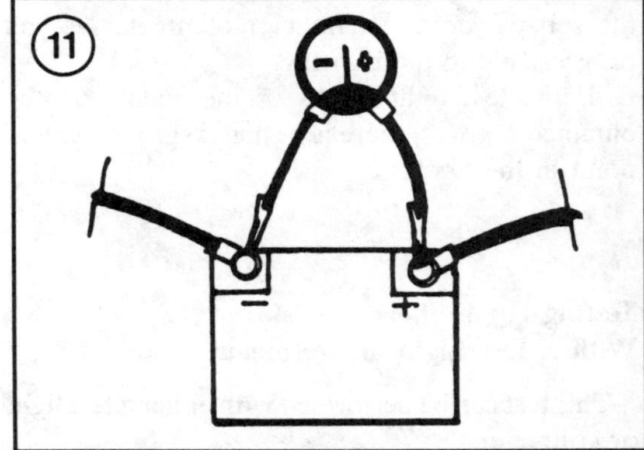

1. Remove the side covers and seat. See Chapter Thirteen.
2. Remove the bolts securing the battery case cover and remove the cover (**Figure 10**).
3. Start the engine and let it reach normal operating temperature; turn the engine off.
4. Leave the battery wires connected to the battery and connect a 0-15 volt DC voltmeter between the battery terminals. Connect the red voltmeter lead to the positive battery terminal and the black voltmeter lead to the negative battery terminal.

CAUTION
Make sure the positive voltmeter cable does not touch any component on the frame.

5. Start the engine and let it idle. Gradually increase engine speed to 5,000 rpm. At 5,000 rpm, the voltmeter should read 13.5-15.5 volts. If the output voltage is not within specifications, perform the following:
   a. Check the alternator-to-battery wire harness for loose or damaged connectors. Repair or replace any damaged component. If these connectors are okay, make the following checks.
   b. Check the alternator stator as described in this chapter.
   c. Check the voltage regulator/rectifier as described in this chapter.
6. Disconnect the voltmeter and reinstall all parts previously removed.

VOLTAGE REGULATOR/RECTIFIER

Testing

1. Remove the fuel tank as described in Chapter Seven.
2. Disconnect the 3-pin (A, **Figure 14**) and 4-pin (B, **Figure 14**) regulator/rectifier connectors at the holder at the rear of the air filter housing.
3. Clean the connectors with electrical contact cleaner.
4. Reconnect the 3-pin and 4-pin connectors.

NOTE
The following tests should be made when the stator is at an approximate temperature of 68° F (20° C).

5. *4-pin connector:* Connect the positive (+) voltmeter lead to the red/white wire and the negative (−) voltmeter lead to the green wire. The voltmeter should read battery voltage (13.0-13.2 volts).
6. *3-pin connector:* Disconnect the 3-pin connector (A, **Figure 14**). Connect the positive (+) ohmmeter lead to a yellow lead and the negative (−) ohmmeter lead to a different yellow lead. The ohmmeter should read 0.1-1.0 ohms.
7. If the voltage regulator/rectifier fails to pass any of these tests the unit is defective and must be replaced. See *Voltage Regulator/Rectifier Removal/Installation* in Chapter Eight.

ALTERNATOR

An alternator is a form of electrical generator in which a magnetized field called a rotor revolves within a set of stationary coils called a stator. As the rotor revolves, alternating current is induced in the stator. The current is then rectified to direct current and used to operate the electrical accessories on the motorcycle and to charge the battery. The rotor is permanently magnetized.

Rotor removal and installation procedures are covered in Chapter Four.

Rotor Testing

The rotor is permanently magnetized and cannot be tested except by replacement with a rotor known to be good. A rotor can lose magnetism from old age or a sharp blow. If defective, the rotor must be replaced; it cannot be remagnetized.

Stator Testing

1. Remove the fuel tank as described in Chapter Eight.
2. Disconnect the 3-pin (A, **Figure 14**) regulator/rectifier connector at the holder at the rear of the air filter housing.

NOTE
The following tests should be made when the stator is at an approximate minimum temperature of 68° F (20° C).

⑫

CHARGING SYSTEM TROUBLESHOOTING
Problem: Battery undercharged.

TEST 1: Check all connections. Make sure all are tight and free of corrosion. → **Perform TEST 2**

TEST 2: Perform the battery leakage test as described in this chapter. →

- **If the battery tested okay, perform TEST 3.**
- **If the battery tested incorrectly, there is an open or short circuit in the wiring.**

TEST 3: Test the Voltage Regulator/Rectifier as described in this chapter. →

- **If the voltage reading was 13.5-15.5 volts, the battery is in good condition. Perform TEST 4.**
- **If the voltage reading was incorrect, the battery is faulty. Replace the battery.**

(continued)

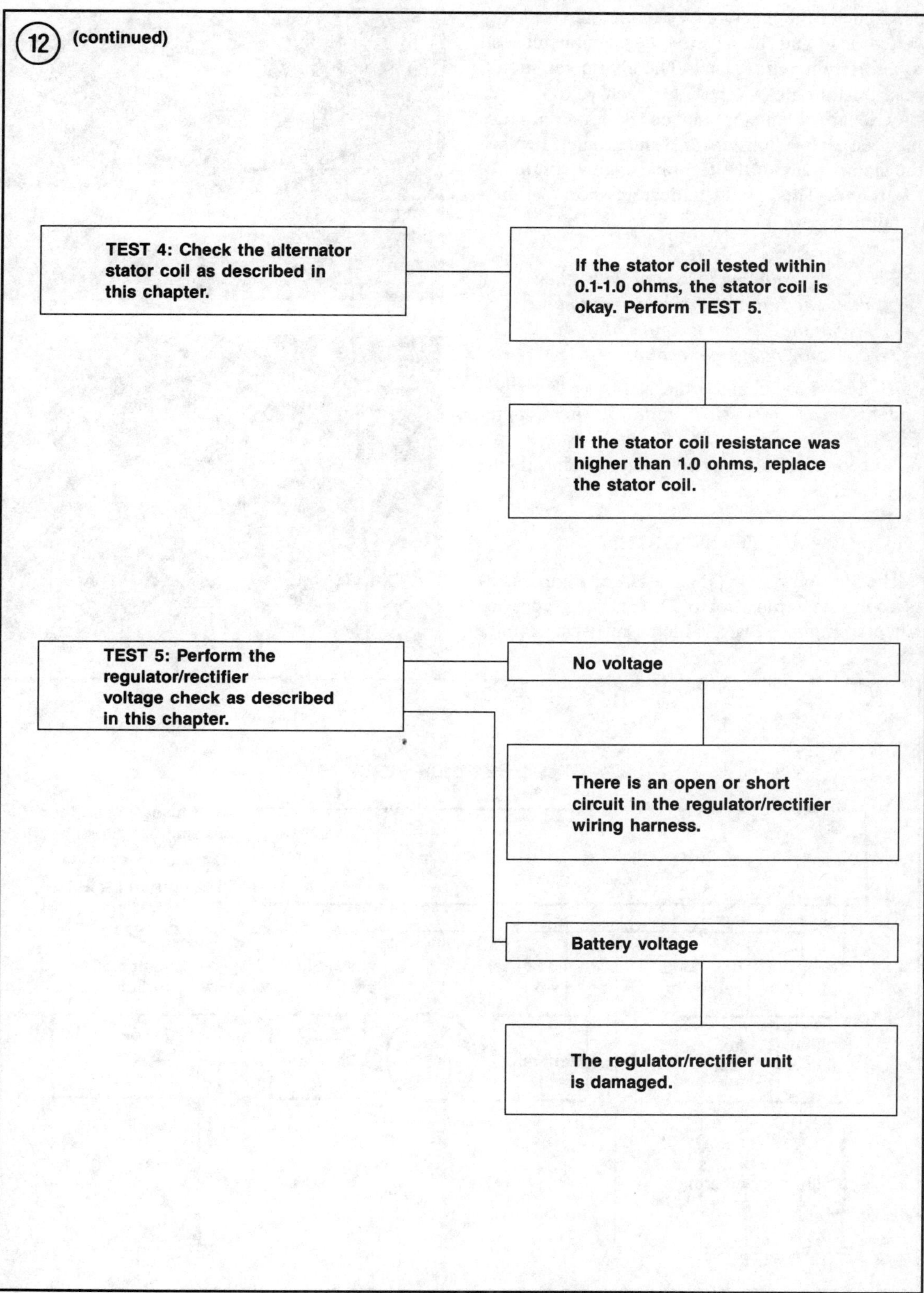
12 (continued)

TEST 4: Check the alternator stator coil as described in this chapter.

If the stator coil tested within 0.1-1.0 ohms, the stator coil is okay. Perform TEST 5.

If the stator coil resistance was higher than 1.0 ohms, replace the stator coil.

TEST 5: Perform the regulator/rectifier voltage check as described in this chapter.

No voltage

There is an open or short circuit in the regulator/rectifier wiring harness.

Battery voltage

The regulator/rectifier unit is damaged.

2

3. Connect the positive (+) ohmmeter lead to a yellow lead and the negative (−) ohmmeter lead to a different yellow lead. The ohmmeter should read 0.1-1.0 ohms. Repeat for each yellow wire.

4. Use an ohmmeter and check for continuity between each yellow terminal and ground. Replace the stator if any of the terminals show continuity to ground. This would indicate a short within a winding.

> *NOTE*
> *Before replacing the stator with a new one, check the electrical wires to and within the electrical connector for any opens or poor connections.*

5. If necessary, replace the stator as described under *Stator Removal/Installation* in Chapter Eight.

6. Reconnect the 3-pin connector. Reinstall the fuel tank.

IGNITION SYSTEM

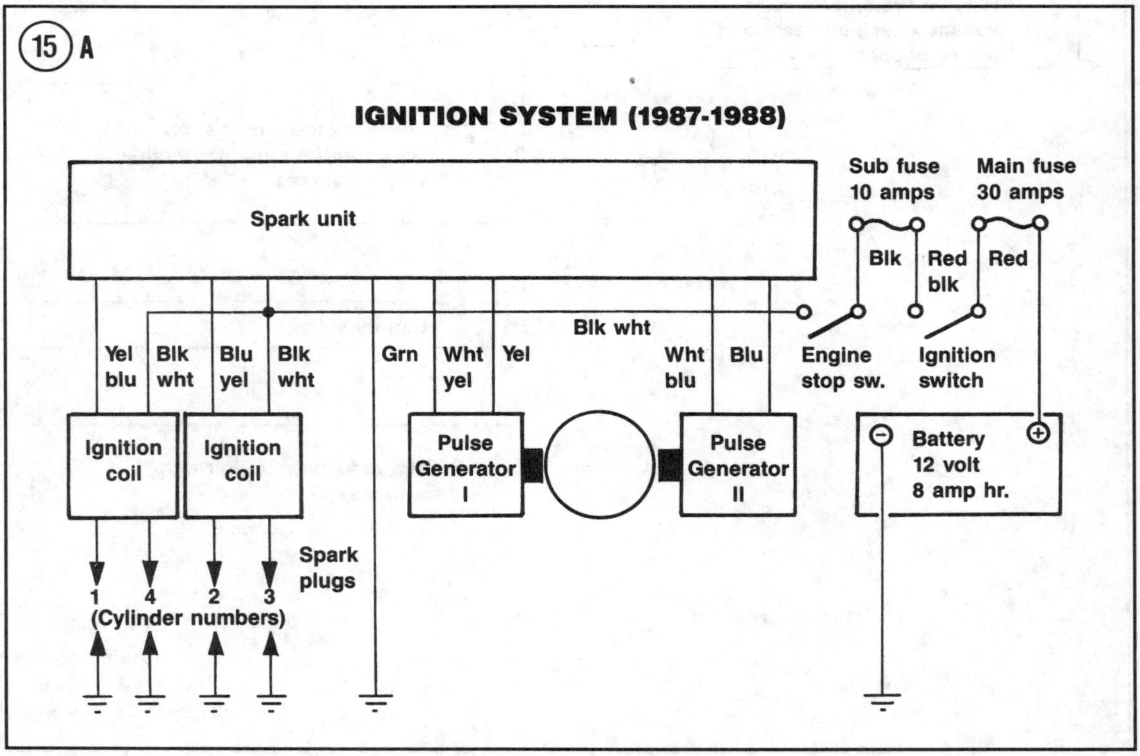

The ignition system (**Figure 15A** or **Figure 15B**) is a solid state transistorized breakerless type. See Chapter Eight. Most problems involving failure

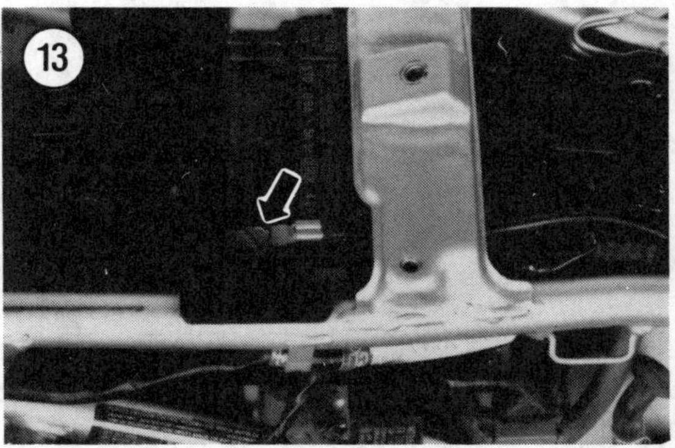

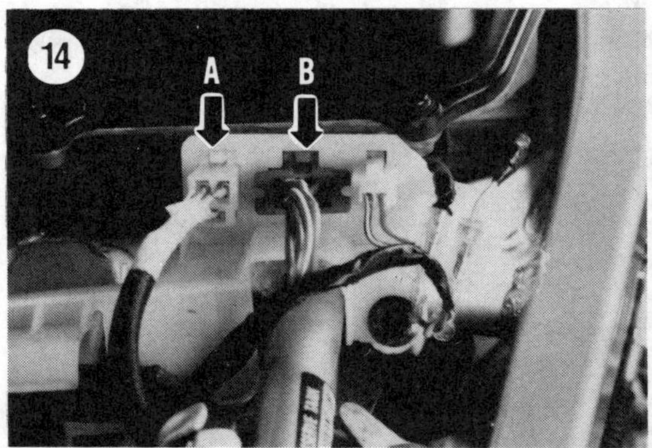

to start, poor driveablility or rough running are caused by trouble in the ignition system.

Note the following symptoms:

a. Engine misses.

b. Stumbles on acceleration (misfiring).

c. Loss of power at high speed (misfiring).

d. Hard starting (or failure to start).

e. Rough idle.

Most of the symptoms can also be caused by carburetors that are worn or improperly adjusted, but the odds are far better that the source of the problem will be found in the ignition system rather than the fuel system.

Troubleshooting

Basic ignition system troubles are:

a. No spark at all spark plugs.

b. No spark at spark plugs No. 1 and 4 or No. 2 and 3.

Test procedures for troubleshooting the ignition system are found in the diagnostic charts in **Figure 16** and **Figure 17**. A multimeter, as described in Chapter One, is required to perform the test procedures.

Before beginning actual troubleshooting, read the entire test procedure (**Figure 16** or **Figure 17**). When required, the diagnostic chart will refer you to a certain procedure for testing. **Figure 16** describes troubleshooting procedures when there is no spark at all spark plugs. **Figure 17** describes troubleshooting procedures when there is no spark at plugs No. 1 and 4 or No. 2 and 3.

Ignition Spark Test

Perform the following spark test to determine if the ignition system is operating properly.

NOTE
Because of the difficulty in removing and checking spark plugs on the CBR600, use an inductive pickup timing light (described in Chapter One) to check spark plug operation. With the engine turned off, connect the timing light to the number one spark plug wire. Connect the timing light red lead to the positive battery terminal and the black lead to the negative battery terminal. Start the engine and

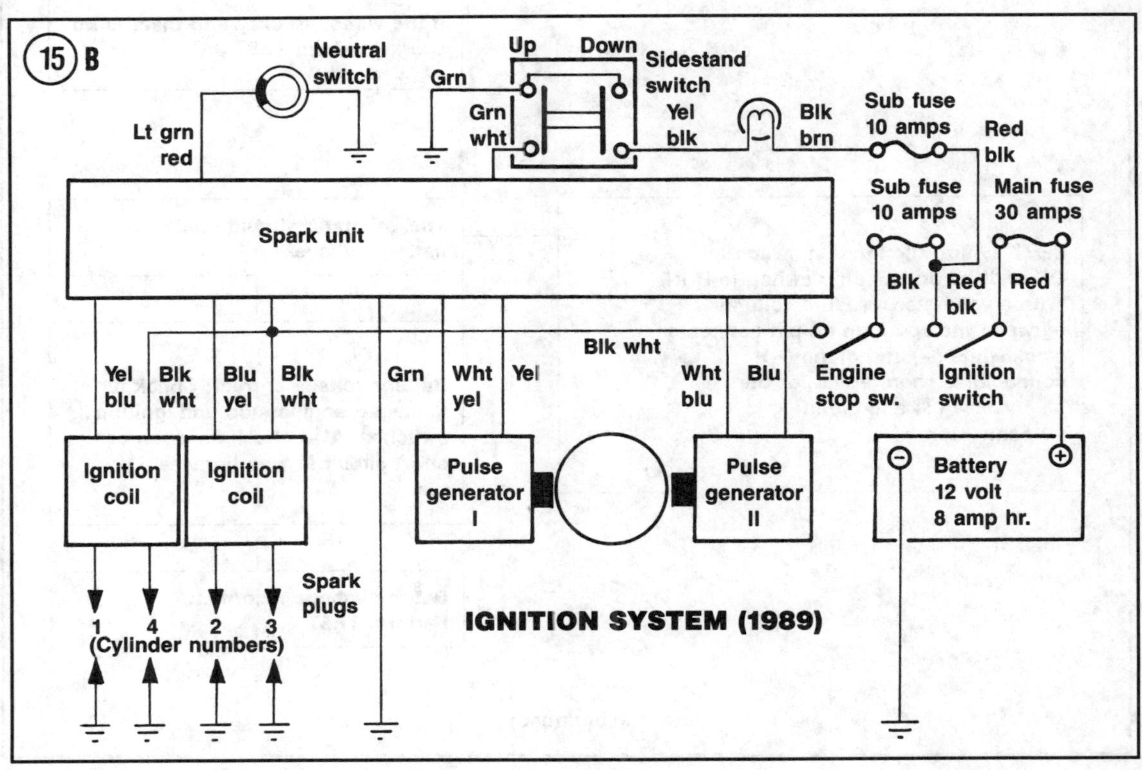

(16)

IGNITION SYTEM TROUBLESHOOTING
Problem: No spark at all spark plugs.

TEST 1: Disconnect one spark plug lead from the spark plug. Insert screwdriver into the spark plug cap and hold it about 5 mm (1/4 in.) from any ground. Turn the ignition switch ON and the engine stop switch to RUN. Crank the engine over and watch for a spark between the screwdriver shank and ground.

If there is a spark, inspect all spark plugs (Chapter Three) and the fuel delivery system (Chapter Six).

If there is no spark, perform TEST 2.

TEST 2: Check all connectors in the ignition system for damaged, loose contacts or contamination. Clean all connector contacts. Reconnect connectors and retest.

If there is spark, the engine should run. If not, inspect all spark plugs (Chapter Three) and the fuel delivery system (Chapter Six).

If the wires are okay and there is no spark, perform TEST 3.

TEST 3: Turn the ignition switch to ON and the engine stop switch to RUN. With a voltmeter measure voltage between the spark unit 6-pin connector black/white (+) and green (−) connectors. Then repeat for the blue/yellow (+) and green (−) connectors.

The voltmeter should read battery voltage.

Battery voltage correct: Check for damaged engine stop and ignition switches. Also check for open or short circuit in wire harness.

Battery voltage incorrect: Perform TEST 4.

(continued)

(16) **(continued)**

TEST 4: Turn the ignition switch OFF. Use an ohmmeter and check resistance between the spark unit 4-pin connector white/yellow and blue connectors.

The ohmmeter should read 450-550 ohms.

Reading correct: Perform TEST 5.

Reading incorrect: Replace the spark unit.*

TEST 5: Check pulse generator as described in this chapter.

Reading correct: There is probably a short or open circuit in the wire harness or the contact connectors are loose or damaged.

Reading incorrect: If pulse generator resistance reading is correct, replace the pulse generator(s).**

*Prior to replacing the spark unit, have the unit tested by a Honda dealer to verify the test results.

**Prior to replacing the pulse generator(s), have the generator(s) tested by a Honda dealer to verify the test results.

⑰

IGNITION SYSTEM TROUBLESHOOTING
PROBLEM: NO SPARK AT SPARK PLUGS NO. 1-4 OR NO. 2-3

TEST 1: Disconnect one spark plug lead from the spark plug. Insert screwdriver into the spark plug cap and hold it about 5 mm (1/4 in.) from any ground. Turn the ignition switch ON and the engine stop switch to RUN. Crank the engine over and watch for a spark between the screwdriver shank and ground.

→ If there is a spark, inspect all spark plugs (Chapter Three) and the fuel delivery system (Chapter Six).

→ If there is no spark, perform TEST 2.

TEST 2: Check all connectors in the ignition system for damaged, loose contacts or contamination. Clean all connector contacts. Reconnect connectors and retest.

→ If there is spark, the engine should run. If not, inspect all spark plugs (Chapter Three) and the fuel delivery system (Chapter Six).

→ If the wires are okay and there is no spark, perform TEST 3.

TEST 3: Check the ignition coil secondary coil resistance as described in this chapter.

→ Reading correct: Perform Test 4.

→ Reading incorrect: If the resistance is beyond the specified resistance range, check the spark plug wire resistance as described in this chapter. If the spark plug wire resistance is okay, replace the ignition coil.*

(continued)

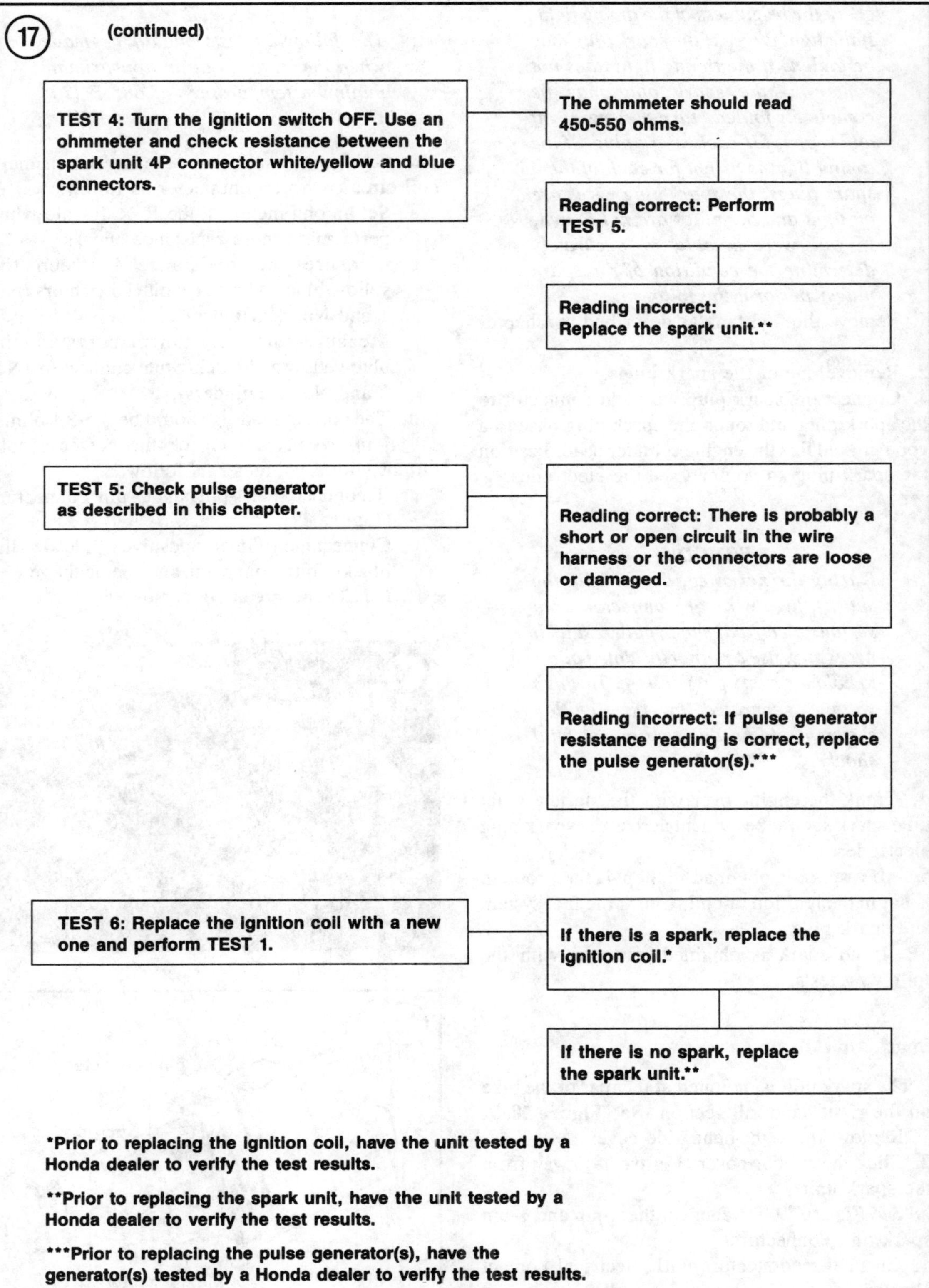

(17)   (continued)

TEST 4: Turn the ignition switch OFF. Use an ohmmeter and check resistance between the spark unit 4P connector white/yellow and blue connectors.

The ohmmeter should read 450-550 ohms.

Reading correct: Perform TEST 5.

Reading incorrect: Replace the spark unit.**

TEST 5: Check pulse generator as described in this chapter.

Reading correct: There is probably a short or open circuit in the wire harness or the connectors are loose or damaged.

Reading incorrect: If pulse generator resistance reading is correct, replace the pulse generator(s).***

TEST 6: Replace the ignition coil with a new one and perform TEST 1.

If there is a spark, replace the ignition coil.*

If there is no spark, replace the spark unit.**

*Prior to replacing the ignition coil, have the unit tested by a Honda dealer to verify the test results.

**Prior to replacing the spark unit, have the unit tested by a Honda dealer to verify the test results.

***Prior to replacing the pulse generator(s), have the generator(s) tested by a Honda dealer to verify the test results.

check the brightness of the timing light. If the light is weak, the spark plug may be fouled. If the timing light does not come on, the spark plug may be completely fouled. Turn the engine off and repeat for each spark plug. If the timing light is bright for each of the 4 spark plugs, the spark plug wires are on tight and the plugs are not fouled. If you were unable to accurately determine the condition of the spark plugs, perform the following.

1. Remove the fuel tank as described in Chapter Seven.

2. Remove one of the spark plugs.

3. Connect the spark plug wire and connector to the spark plug and touch the spark plug base to a good ground like the engine cylinder head. Position the spark plug so you can see the electrodes.

WARNING
During the next step, do not hold the spark plug, wire or connector or a serious electrical shock may result. If necessary, use a pair of insulated pliers to hold the spark plug or wire. The high voltage generated by the ignition system could produce serious or fatal shocks.

4. Crank the engine over with the starter. A fat blue spark should be evident across the spark plug electrodes.

5A. If a spark is obtained in Step 4, the problem is not in the ignition or coil. Check the fuel system and spark plugs.

5B. If no spark is obtained, proceed with the following tests.

Spark Unit Testing

The spark unit is mounted at the rear of the bike on the right-hand tail section. See **Figure 18**.

1. Remove the right-hand side cover.

2. Slide the rubber cover (**Figure 18**) away from the spark unit.

3. See **Figure 19**. Disconnect the 4-pin and 6-pin spark unit connectors.

4. Clean the connectors with electrical contact cleaner.

NOTE
The following tests should be made when the stator is at an approximate minimum temperature of 68° F (20° C).

5A. *6-pin connector:* Check the ignition primary coil circuit with an ohmmeter as follows:

   a. Set an ohmmeter on the R × 1 scale when performing these resistance checks.

   b. Measure the resistance between the yellow/blue and black/white connectors (No. 1 and No. 4 cylinders).

   c. Measure the resistance between the blue/yellow and black/white connectors (No. 2 and No. 3 cylinders).

   d. The correct reading should be 2.5-3.1 ohms.

5B. *6-pin connector:* Check the power supply circuit with a voltmeter as follows:

   a. Reconnect the 4-pin and 6-pin connectors (**Figure 19**).

   b. Connect the voltmeter positive (+) lead to the black/white connector and the negative (−) lead to the green connector.

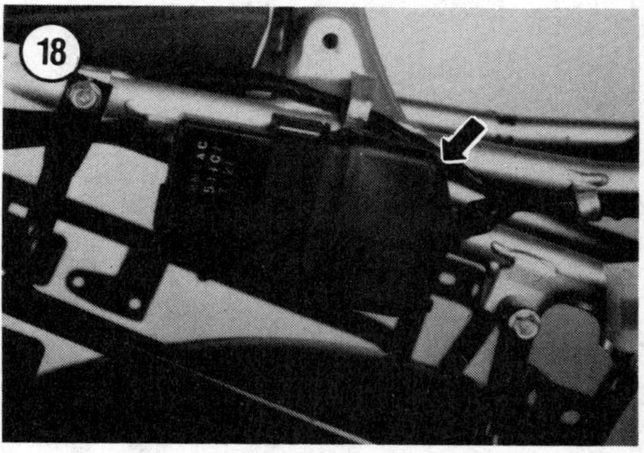

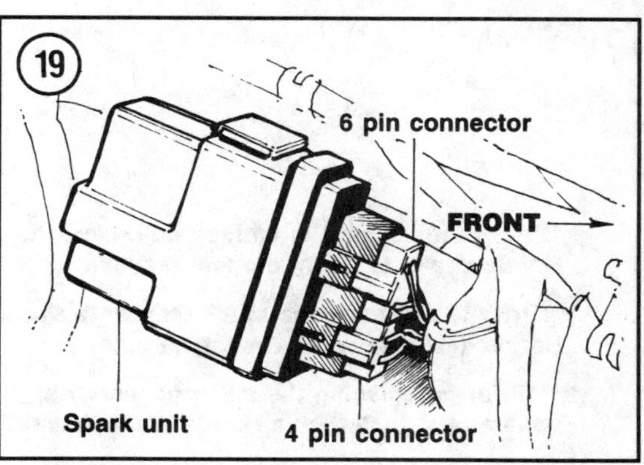

c. Turn the ignition switch on and the engine stop switch to RUN.

d. The voltmeter should read battery voltage (13.0-13.2 volts).

6A. *4-pin connector:* Check the pulse generator coil circuit with an ohmmeter as follows:

a. Set an ohmmeter on the R × 100 scale when performing these resistance checks.

b. Measure the resistance between the white/yellow connector and the yellow connector (No. 1 pulse generator).

c. Measure the resistance between the white/blue connector and the blue connector (No. 2 pulse generator).

d. The correct readings should be 450-550 ohms.

6B. *4-pin connector:* Check the pulse generator for an internal short with an ohmmeter as follows:

a. Connect one ohmmeter test lead to a good ground.

b. Connect the other test lead to each of the 4-pin connector terminals. If the needle on the ohmmeter moves, there is a short-to-ground.

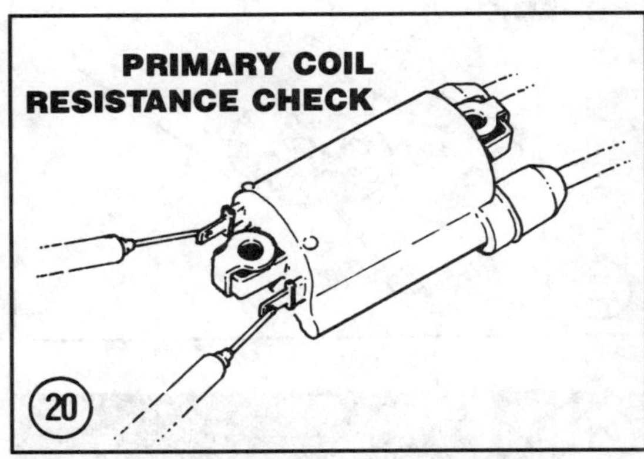

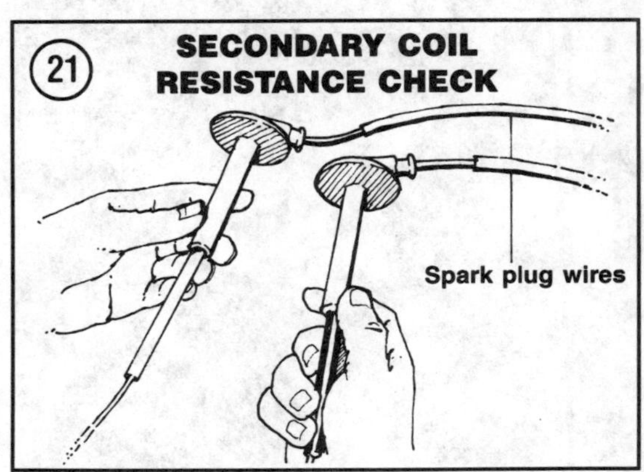

7. If the spark unit failed any one test, it must be replaced as described under *Spark Unit Removal/Installation* in Chapter Eight. It cannot be serviced.

Ignition Coil Testing

The following describes ignition coil static testing procedures. If the coils test okay and you're still experiencing ignition related troubles, remove the coils and have a Honda dealer perform a 3-point arc test. The arc test is the most accurate way to determine ignition coil condition. If ignition coil replacement is required, you should look into installing aftermarket coils available from aftermarket distributors and manufacturers.

1. Remove the ignition coils as described under *Ignition Coil Removal/Installation* in Chapter Eight.

2. Measure the coil primary resistance using an ohmmeter set at R × 1. Measure between the coil's primary terminals as shown in **Figure 20**. The correct primary resistance is listed in **Table 2**.

3. Measure the secondary resistance using an ohmmeter set at R × 100. Measure between the spark plug caps as shown in **Figure 21**. The correct secondary resistance is listed in **Table 2**. If the resistance reading is incorrect, remove the spark plug cable at the coil by unscrewing the cable fitting. Then measure the resistance between the secondary terminals on the coil as shown in **Figure 22**. See **Table 2** for specifications. Interpret results as follows:

a. If the secondary coil readings are incorrect with the spark plug wires attached and correct with the wires removed, replace the spark plug wires and retest.

b. If the secondary coil readings are incorrect both times, replace the ignition coil and retest with the old coil wires.

4. Replace the ignition coil(s) if it doesn't test within the specifications in Step 2 or Step 3. See *Ignition Coil Removal/Installation* in Chapter Eight.

Switches

Test the following switches as described under *Switches* in Chapter Eight:

a. Ignition switch.
b. Starter switch.
c. Engine stop switch.

Pulse Generator Testing

1. Remove the fuel tank as described in Chapter Eight.
2. Disconnect the 4-pin pulse generator electrical connector (**Figure 23**).
3. Set an ohmmeter on the R × 100 scale.
4. Connect the ohmmeter leads between the white/yellow and the yellow leads (No. 1 pulse generator) and then between the white/blue and the blue leads (No. 2 pulse generator).
5. The resistance for each coil is listed in **Table 2**. If the pulse generator coils do not meet these specifications, the ignition pulse generator assembly must be replaced as described under *Pulse Generator Removal/Installation* in Chapter Eight. It cannot be serviced.

STARTING SYSTEM

The starting system consists of the starter motor, starter gears, solenoid, starter button, ignition switch, clutch switch, neutral switch, sidestand switch (1989 models), main and auxiliary fuses and battery. See **Figure 24A** or **Figure 24B**.

When the starter button is pressed, it allows current flow through the solenoid coil. The coil contacts close, allowing electricity to flow from the battery to the starter motor.

> *CAUTION*
> *Do not operate the starter for more than 5 seconds at a time. Let it rest approximately 10 seconds, then use it again.*

Troubleshooting

The starter should turn when the starter button is depressed when the transmission is in neutral, the clutch disengaged and on 1989 models, with the sidestand in the UP position. If the starter does not operate properly, perform the following test procedures. Starter troubleshooting is grouped under the following:
a. Preliminary checks.
b. Starter motor does not turn.

c. Starter motor turns slowly.
d. Starter motor turns but the engine does not.
e. The starter motor and engine turns, but the engine does not start.

When testing the starter, first perform the preliminary checks. Then if the starter still does not operate properly, perform the necessary test procedure(s).

Preliminary checks

Before testing the starter, perform the following:
a. Check the main and the sub fuses as described under *Fuses* in Chapter Eight.
b. Check the starter cables for loose or damaged connections.
c. Check the battery cables for loose or damaged connections. Then check the battery state of charge as described under *Battery Testing* in Chapter Eight.

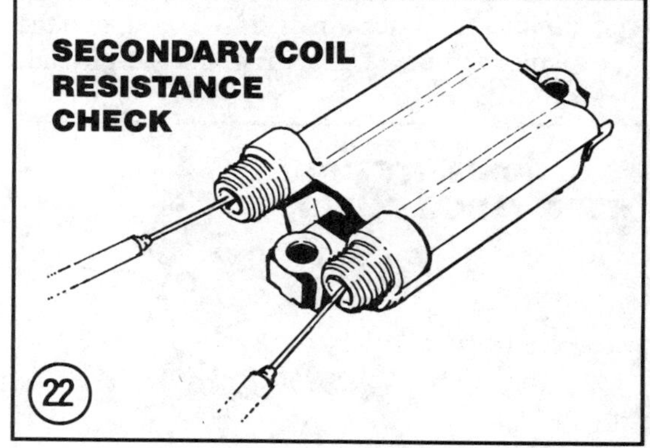

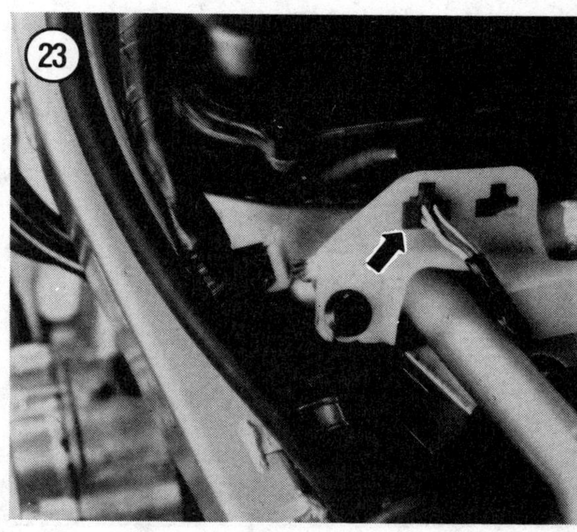

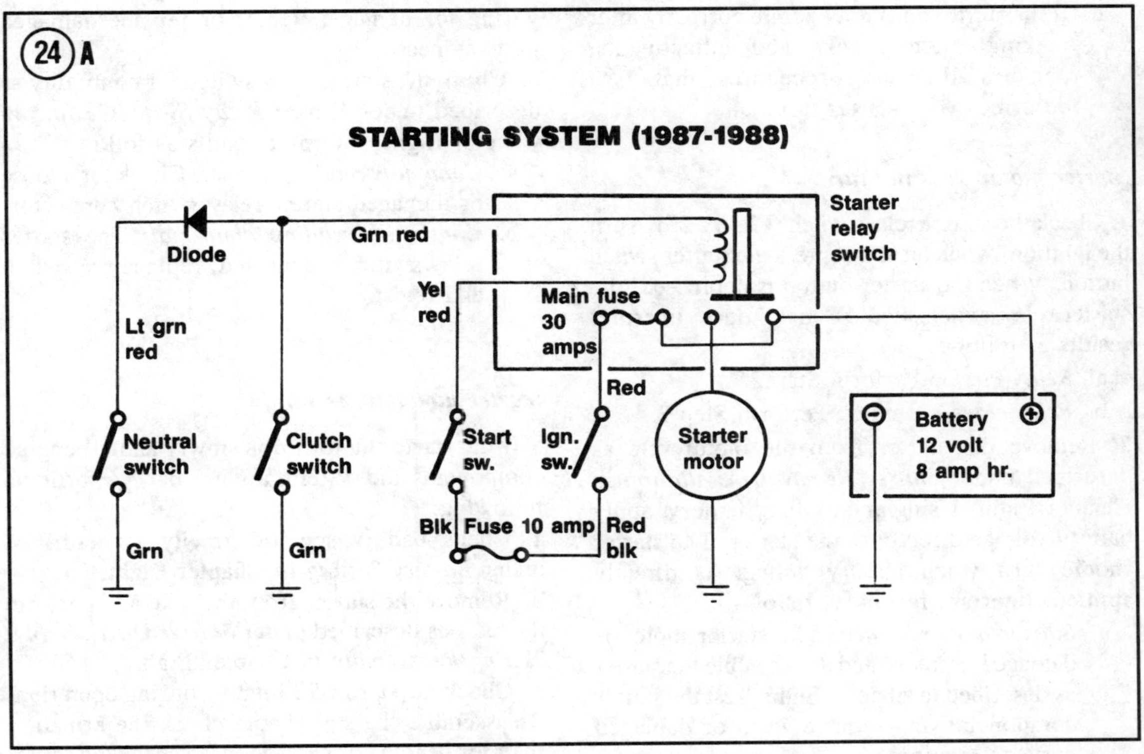
24 A
STARTING SYSTEM (1987-1988)
Starter relay switch
Grn red
Diode
Yel red
Main fuse 30 amps
Lt grn red
Red
Battery 12 volt 8 amp hr.
Neutral switch
Clutch switch
Start sw.
Ign. sw.
Starter motor
Blk
Fuse 10 amp
Red blk
Grn
Grn

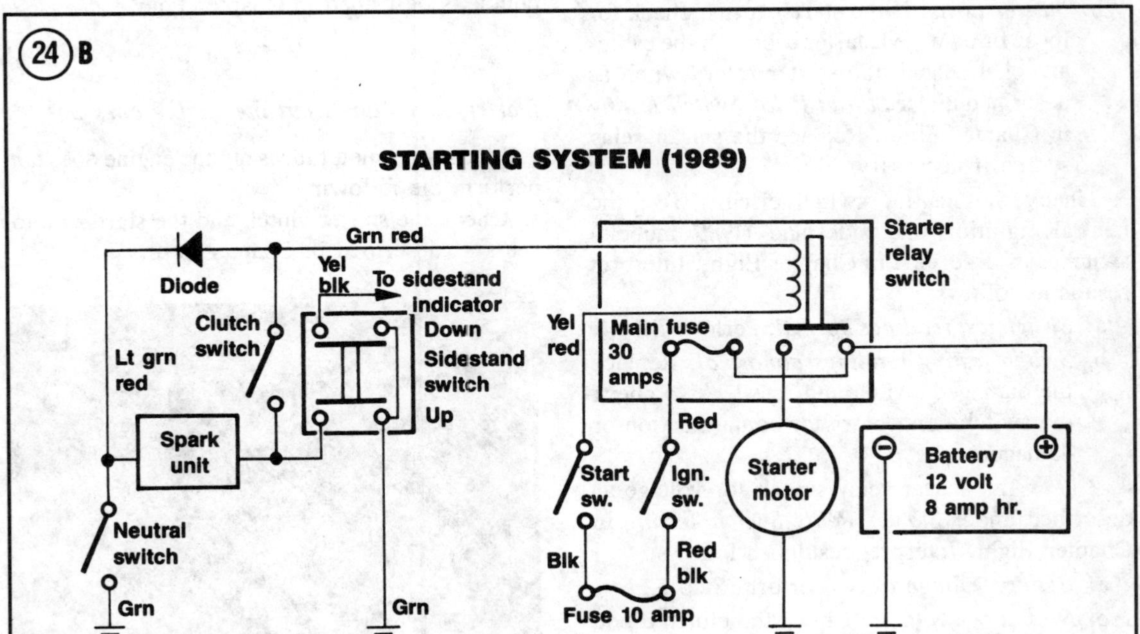
24 B
STARTING SYSTEM (1989)
Grn red
Starter relay switch
Diode
Yel blk
To sidestand indicator
Clutch switch
Down
Sidestand switch
Up
Lt grn red
Yel red
Main fuse 30 amps
Red
Spark unit
Start sw.
Ign. sw.
Starter motor
Battery 12 volt 8 amp hr.
Neutral switch
Red blk
Blk
Fuse 10 amp
Grn
Grn

d. If the starter does not operate correctly after making these checks and adjustments, perform the test procedures that best describes your starter trouble.

Starter motor does not turn

1. Check the starter relay switch (**Figure 25**). Turn the ignition switch on and depress the starter switch button. When the starter button is depressed, the starter relay switch should "click" once. Interpret results as follows:

   a. *Relay clicks:* Perform Step 2.

   b. *Relay does not click:* Perform Step 3.

2. Remove the starter from the motorcycle as described under *Starter Removal/Installation* in Chapter Eight. Using an auxiliary battery, apply battery voltage directly to the starter. The starter should turn when battery voltage is directly applied. Interpret results as follows:

   a. *Starter does not turn:* The starter motor is damaged. Remove and disassemble the starter as described in Chapter Eight. Test the starter components and replace worn or damaged parts as required.

   b. *Starter turns:* If the starter turns, check for loose or damaged starter cables. If the cables are okay, check the starter relay switch as described under *Starter Relay Switch Testing* in Chapter Eight. Replace the starter relay switch if necessary.

3. Check the neutral switch circuit. Test the neutral, ignition and sidestand (1989 models) switches as described in Chapter Eight. Interpret results as follows:

   a. *Switch test readings normal:* Perform Step 4.

   b. *Switch testing readings abnormal:* Replace the damaged switch and retest. Also check the switch connectors for contamination or damaged.

4. Check the starter relay switch for voltage as described under *Starter Relay Switch Testing* in Chapter Eight. Interpret results as follows:

   a. *Battery voltage okay:* Perform Step 5.

   b. *No battery voltage:* Check the clutch diode as described under *Clutch Diode Testing* in Chapter Eight. Also check the clutch diode wiring connector and wire harness for damage. If the clutch diode is okay, check the starter switch (Chapter Eight) and all related

wiring for damage. Repair or replace damaged parts as necessary.

5. Check the starter relay switch for continuity as described under *Starter Relay Switch Testing* in Chapter Eight. Interpret results as follows:

   a. *Continuity reading normal:* Check for a loose or damaged starter relay switch connector.

   b. *Continuity reading abnormal:* The starter relay switch is damaged; replace the switch and retest.

Starter motor turns slowly

If the starter motor turns slowly and all engine components and systems are normal, perform the following:

1. Check battery specific gravity as described under *Battery Testing* in Chapter Eight.

2. Remove the starter from the bike and perform the tests as described under *Starter Disassembly/ Testing/Reassembly* in Chapter Eight.

3. Check the starter for binding during operation. Disassemble the starter and check the armature shaft for bending or damage. Also check the starter clutch as described in Chapter Four.

Starter motor turns but the engine does not

If the starter motor turns but the engine does not, perform the following:

1. Check the starter clutch and the starter motor gears as described in Chapter Four.

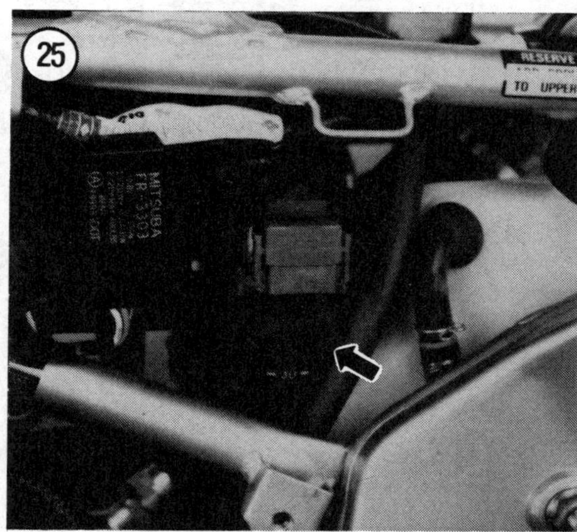

2. Check the starter motor and idle gear for wear or damaged. Remove the starter as described in Chapter Eight.

Starter motor and engine turns, but the engine does not start

1. Check engine compression as described under *Compression Test* in Chapter Three.
2. Check the spark plugs as described under *Spark Plugs* in Chapter Three.
3. Check the ignition system as described under *Ignition System Troubleshooting* in this chapter.

CARBURETOR TROUBLESHOOTING

Basic carburetor troubleshooting procedures are found in **Figure 26**.

FRONT SUSPENSION AND STEERING

Poor handling may be caused by improper tire pressure, a damaged or bent frame or steering components, worn wheel bearings or dragging brakes. Possible causes of suspension and steering malfunctions are listed below.

Irregular or Wobbly Steering

a. Loose wheel axle nuts.
b. Loose or worn steering head bearings.
c. Excessive wheel hub bearing play.
d. Damaged wheel.
e. Unbalanced wheel assembly.
f. Worn hub bearings.
g. Incorrect wheel alignment.
h. Bent or damaged steering stem or frame (at steering neck).
i. Tire incorrectly seated on rim.
j. Excessive front end loading from non-standard equipment.
k. Damaged fairing assembly.
l. Loose fairing mounts or brackets.

Stiff Steering

a. Low front tire air pressure.
b. Bend or damaged steering stem or frame (at steering neck).
c. Loose or worn steering head bearings.

Stiff or Heavy Fork Operation

a. Incorrect fork springs.
b. Incorrect fork oil viscosity.
c. Excessive amount of fork oil.
d. Incorrect fork air pressure.
e. Bent fork tubes.
f. Fluid passages clogged.

Poor Fork Operation

a. Worn or damage fork tubes.
b. Fork oil level low due to leaking fork seals.
c. Bent or damaged fork tubes.
d. Contaminated fork oil.
e. Worn fork springs.
f. Heavy front end loading from non-standard equipment.

Poor Rear Shock Absorber Operation

a. Damper unit leaking.
b. Incorrect rear shock adjustment.
c. Heavy rear end loading from non-standard equipment.
d. Incorrect loading.
e. Weak spring.
f. Worn shock linkage pivot bearings.
g. Bent swing arm.

BRAKE PROBLEMS

Sticking disc brakes may be caused by a stuck piston(s) in a caliper assembly, warped pad shim(s) or improper rear brake adjustment. See **Figure 27** for disc brake troubles and checks to make.

FUEL SYSTEM TROUBLESHOOTING

Rich fuel mixture

Check for:
- Clogged air filter element
- Incorrect fuel level (too high)
- Clogged carburetor air jet
- Defective float valve and seat
- Worn needle jet
- Worn jet needle
- Bystarter valve stuck open

Lean fuel mixture

Check for:
- Incorrect fuel level (too low)
- Defective float valve and seat
- Blocked fuel tank cap vent hole
- Clogged jets
- Intake air leak
- Restricted or damaged fuel line
- Clogged or damaged air vent tube
- Defective fuel pump
- Defective fuel pump relay
- Carburetor vacuum piston stuck closed

Engine cranks but will not start

Check for:
- Engine flooded
- Clogged air filter element
- No fuel in tank
- Incorrect choke operation or adjustment
- Incorrect throttle operation or adjustment
- Defective fuel pump
- Defective fuel pump relay

(continued)

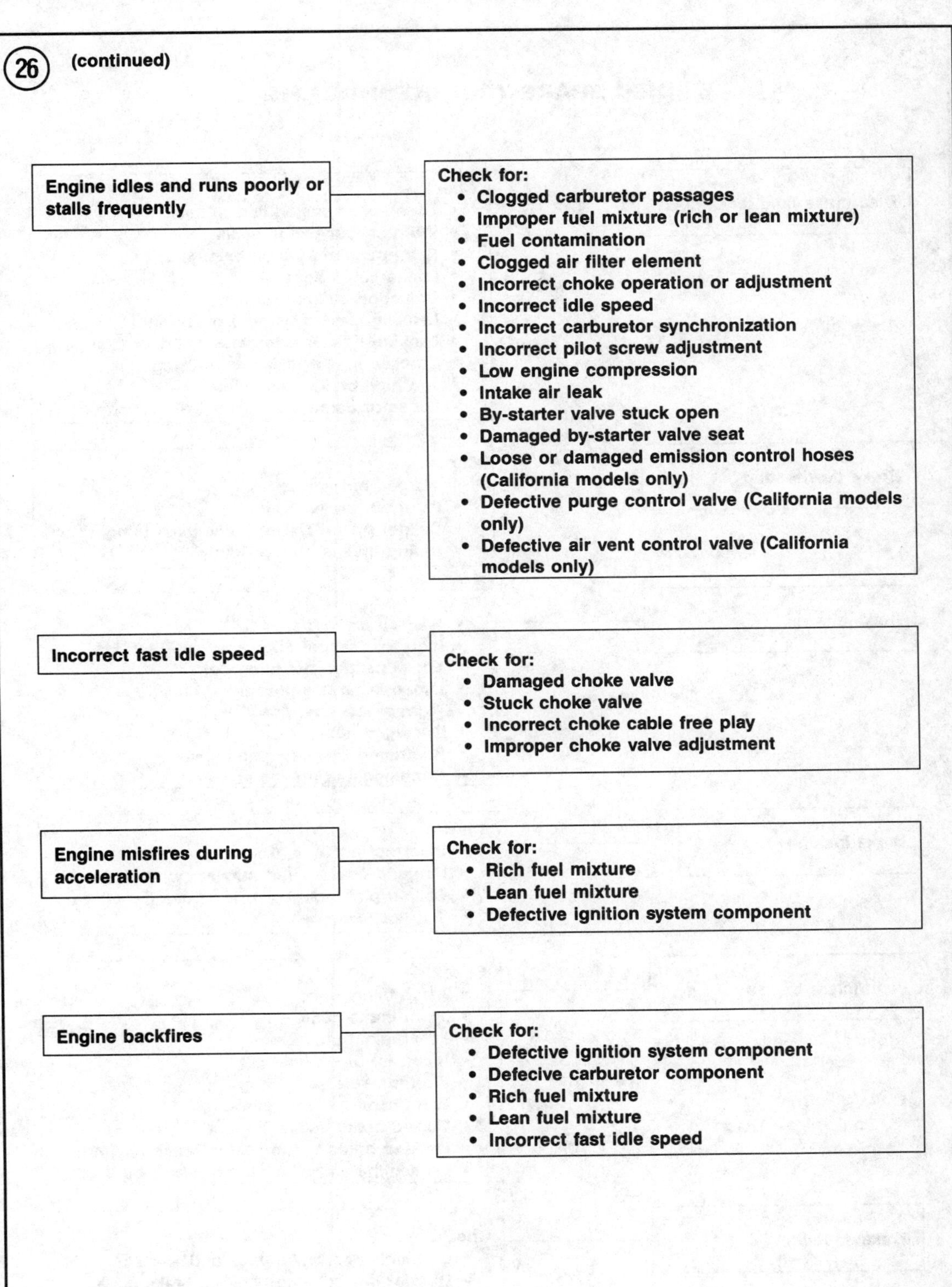

26 (continued)

Engine idles and runs poorly or stalls frequently

Check for:
• Clogged carburetor passages
• Improper fuel mixture (rich or lean mixture)
• Fuel contamination
• Clogged air filter element
• Incorrect choke operation or adjustment
• Incorrect idle speed
• Incorrect carburetor synchronization
• Incorrect pilot screw adjustment
• Low engine compression
• Intake air leak
• By-starter valve stuck open
• Damaged by-starter valve seat
• Loose or damaged emission control hoses (California models only)
• Defective purge control valve (California models only)
• Defective air vent control valve (California models only)

Incorrect fast idle speed

Check for:
• Damaged choke valve
• Stuck choke valve
• Incorrect choke cable free play
• Improper choke valve adjustment

Engine misfires during acceleration

Check for:
• Rich fuel mixture
• Lean fuel mixture
• Defective ignition system component

Engine backfires

Check for:
• Defective ignition system component
• Defecive carburetor component
• Rich fuel mixture
• Lean fuel mixture
• Incorrect fast idle speed

2

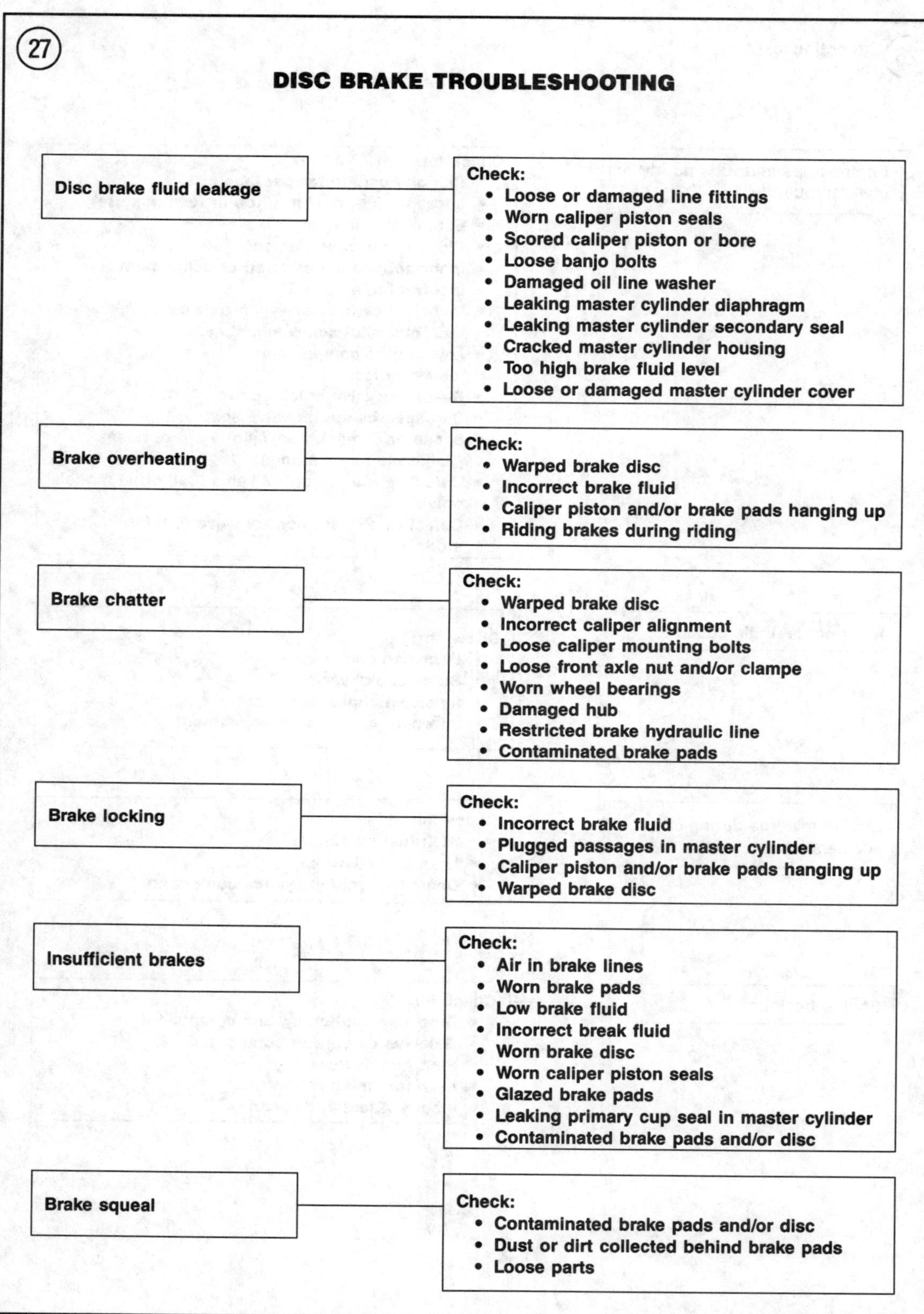
27

DISC BRAKE TROUBLESHOOTING

Disc brake fluid leakage

Check:
• Loose or damaged line fittings
• Worn caliper piston seals
• Scored caliper piston or bore
• Loose banjo bolts
• Damaged oil line washer
• Leaking master cylinder diaphragm
• Leaking master cylinder secondary seal
• Cracked master cylinder housing
• Too high brake fluid level
• Loose or damaged master cylinder cover

Brake overheating

Check:
• Warped brake disc
• Incorrect brake fluid
• Caliper piston and/or brake pads hanging up
• Riding brakes during riding

Brake chatter

Check:
• Warped brake disc
• Incorrect caliper alignment
• Loose caliper mounting bolts
• Loose front axle nut and/or clampe
• Worn wheel bearings
• Damaged hub
• Restricted brake hydraulic line
• Contaminated brake pads

Brake locking

Check:
• Incorrect brake fluid
• Plugged passages in master cylinder
• Caliper piston and/or brake pads hanging up
• Warped brake disc

Insufficient brakes

Check:
• Air in brake lines
• Worn brake pads
• Low brake fluid
• Incorrect break fluid
• Worn brake disc
• Worn caliper piston seals
• Glazed brake pads
• Leaking primary cup seal in master cylinder
• Contaminated brake pads and/or disc

Brake squeal

Check:
• Contaminated brake pads and/or disc
• Dust or dirt collected behind brake pads
• Loose parts

Table 1 CHARGING SYSTEM SPECIFICATIONS

Battery	
Capacity	12V-8 amp hours
Voltage @ 68° F (20° C)	
Fully charged	13.0-13.2 volts
Requires charging	12.3 volts or less
Charging current	0.9 amps
Charging time	5 hours
Alternator	
Charging coil resistance*	0.1-1.0 ohms
Output	See text
Charging test rpm	1,000 ±100 rpm

* Tests made at 68° F (20° C).

Table 2 IGNITION SYSTEM SPECIFICATIONS

Ignition coil resistance	
Primary	2.5-3.1 ohms
Secondary	
With plug wire	21,000-25,000 ohms
Without plug wire	11,000-15,000 ohms
Pulse generator coil resistance	450-550 ohms

CHAPTER THREE

PERIODIC LUBRICATION, MAINTENANCE AND TUNE-UP

Your bike can be cared for by two methods: preventive and corrective maintenance. Because a motorcycle is subjected to tremendous heat, stress and vibration—even in normal use—preventive maintenance prevents costly and unexpected corrective maintenance. When neglected, any bike becomes unreliable and actually dangerous to ride. When properly maintained, your Honda is one of the most reliable bikes available and will give many miles and years of dependable and safe riding. By maintaining a routine service schedule as described in this chapter, costly mechanical problems and unexpected breakdowns can be prevented.

The procedures presented in this chapter can be easily performed by anyone with average mechanical skills. **Table 1** is a suggested factory maintenance schedule. **Tables 1-10** are located at the end of this chapter.

ROUTINE CHECKS

The following simple checks should be carried out at each fuel stop.

Engine Oil Level

Refer to *Engine Oil Level Check* under *Periodic Lubrication* in this chapter.

Coolant Level

1. Remove the right-hand side cover (see Chapter Thirteen).
2. Start the engine and allow it to idle until it reaches normal operating temperature.
3. With the engine at idle, hold the bike upright and check the coolant level in the coolant reserve tank (**Figure 1**). The level should be between the UP and LOW marks.

> *CAUTION*
> *Do not add coolant to the radiator. If the coolant tank was completely empty, there may be a leak in the cooling system. Wait until the engine cools to room temperature and then remove the radiator cap and check the level in the radiator. If necessary, refer to Cooling System Inspection in this chapter.*

> *WARNING*
> *Do not remove the radiator cap when the engine is hot. The coolant is under pressure and scalding and severe burns could result.*

4. If necessary, add coolant as follows:
   a. Turn the engine off.

b. Remove the coolant reserve tank cap (**Figure 1**) and add a 50:50 mixture of distilled water and antifreeze into the reserve tank (not the radiator) to bring the level to the UP mark.

c. Reinstall the reserve tank cap.

5. After adding coolant, repeat this procedure to make sure the coolant level is correct.

6. Install the right-hand side cover.

General Inspection

1. Examine the engine for signs of oil or fuel leakage.

2. Check the tires for embedded stones. Pry them out with your ignition key.

3. Make sure all lights work.

NOTE
At least check the brake light. It can burn out anytime. Motorists can not stop as quickly as you and need all the warning you can give.

Tire Pressure

Tire pressure must be checked with the tires cold. Correct tire pressure depends on the load you are carrying. See **Table 2**. See *Tires and Wheels* in this chapter.

Battery

The CBR600 is equipped with a maintenance-free battery. These batteries have no filler caps and do not require the addition of water. Maintenance-free batteries do require periodic inspection and cleaning of the cables and battery housing. See *Battery* in this chapter. Battery testing is described in Chapter Eight.

Lights and Horn

With the engine running, check the following.

1. Pull the front brake lever on and check that the brake light comes on.

2. Push the rear brake pedal down and check that the brake light comes on soon after you have begun depressing the pedal.

3. Move the dimmer switch up and down between the high and low positions, and check to see that both headlight elements are working.

4. Push the turn signal switch to the left position and the right position and check that all 4 turn signal lights are working.

5. Push the horn button and note that the horn blows loudly.

6. If the horn or any light failed to work properly, refer to Chapter Eight.

MAINTENANCE INTERVALS

The services and intervals shown in **Table 1** are recommended by the factory. Strict adherence to these recommendations will ensure long life from your Honda. If the bike is run in an area of high humidity, the lubrication services must be done more frequently to prevent possible rust damage.

For convenience when maintaining your motorcycle, most of the services shown in **Table 1** are described in this chapter. Those procedures which require more than minor disassembly or adjustment are covered elsewhere in the appropriate chapter. The *Table of Contents* and *Index* can help you locate a particular service procedure.

TIRES AND WHEELS

Tire Pressure

Tire pressure should be checked weekly to provide maximum tire performance, ride comfort and stability. Incorrect tire inflation will cause rapid and uneven tire wear and create a severe safety hazard during all riding conditions. Underinflation results in excessive tire heat that causes tire wear and failure. Severe underinflation may cause the tire to slip on the rim and break its

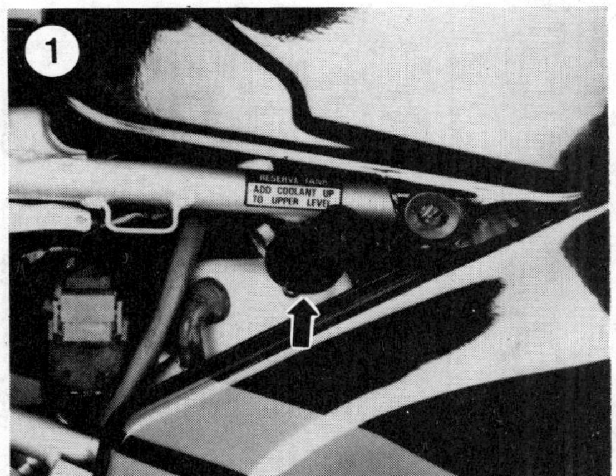

sealing bead. Uneven tread wear shortens tire life. Overinflation makes the tire more susceptible to damage from holes or objects in the road.

Tire pressure should be checked and adjusted to accommodate rider and luggage weight. A simple, accurate gauge (**Figure 2**) can be purchased for a few dollars and should be carried in your motorcycle tool kit. The appropriate tire pressures are shown in **Table 2**. Check tire pressure when the tires are *cold* because pressure builds in the tires when they are in motion.

> *NOTE*
> *After checking and adjusting the air pressure, make sure to reinstall the air valve cap (**Figure 3**). The cap prevents small pebbles and/or dirt from collecting in the valve stem; this could allow air leakage or result in incorrect tire pressure readings.*

Tire Inspection

The likelihood of tire failure increases with tread wear. It is estimated that most tire failures occur during the last 10% of usable tread wear. Check tire tread for excessive wear, deep cuts, embedded objects such as stones, nails, etc. Check also for high spots that indicate internal tire damage. Replace tires that show high spots or swelling. If you find a nail in a tire, mark its location with a light crayon before pulling it out. This will help locate the hole for repair. Refer to *Tubeless Tires* and *Tubeless Tire Changing* in Chapter Ten.

> *NOTE*
> *Tubeless tires have the ability to self-seal when punctured. If the foreign object was very small, air leakage may be very slow. Check the tires carefully and if necessary, wash the tires to obtain a better view of the tread.*

Measure tread wear at the center of the tire with a tread depth gauge (**Figure 4**) or small ruler. Because tires sometimes wear unevenly, measure wear at several points. **Table 2** lists minimum tread depth for stock tires.

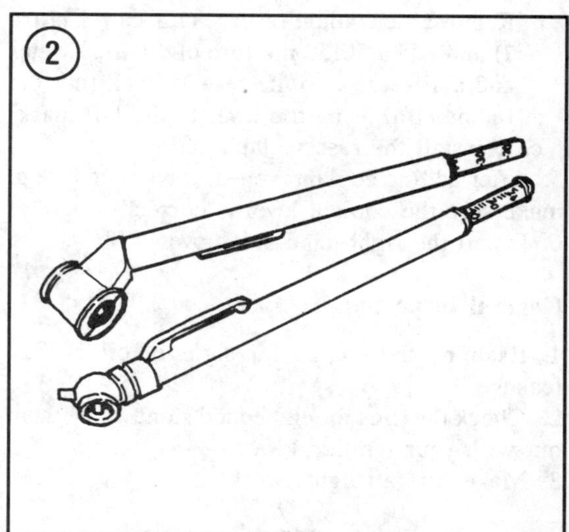

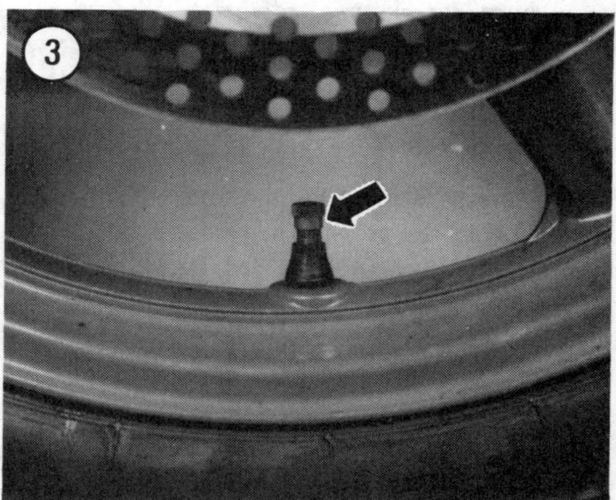

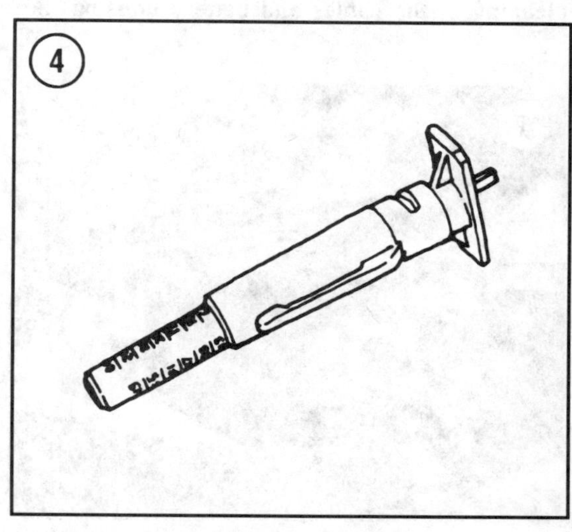

Rim Inspection

Frequently inspect the wheel rims. If a rim has been damaged it might have been knocked out of alignment. Improper wheel alignment can cause severe vibration and result in an unsafe riding condition. If the rim portion of an alloy wheel is damaged, the wheel must be replaced as it cannot be repaired.

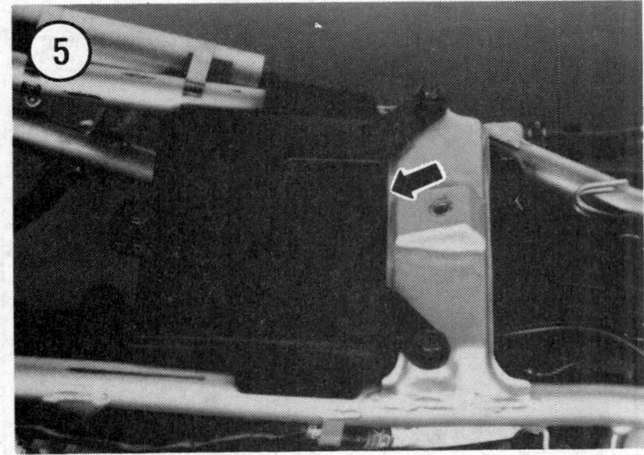

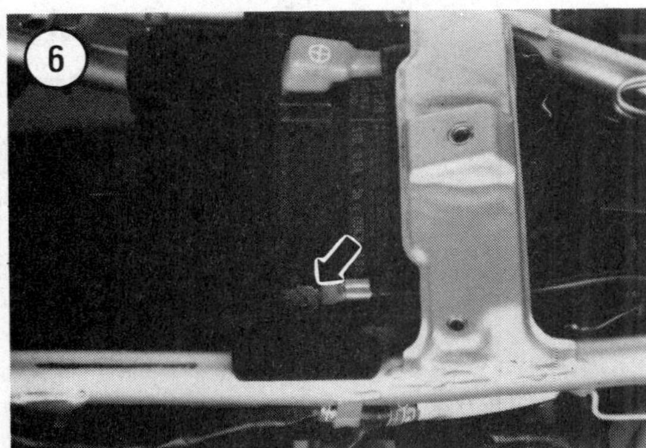

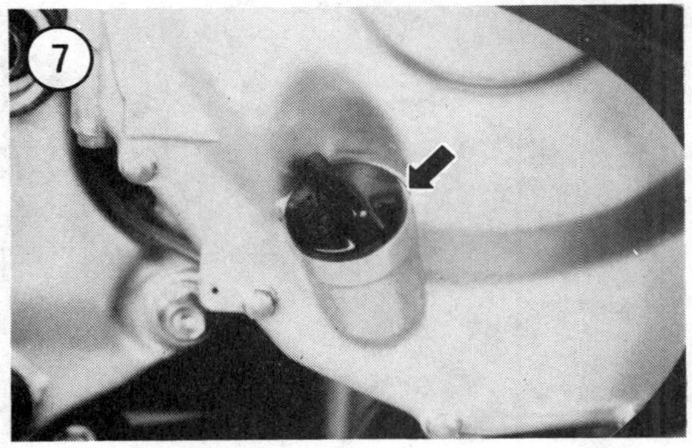

BATTERY

Inspection

All Hurricane models come equipped with a maintenance-free battery. Maintenance-free batteries have no filler caps and do not require the addition of water. This procedure describes a quick check of the maintenance-free battery. Complete battery cleaning, testing and replacement is described in Chapter Eight under *Battery*.

1. Remove the seat.
2. Remove the battery cover bolts and remove the cover (**Figure 5**).
3. Check the condition of the battery cables and the battery (**Figure 6**). If the cables are corroded or if the top of the battery shows signs of leakage or damage, refer to *Battery* in Chapter Eight.
4. Reinstall the battery cover and bolts.
5. Install the seat.

PERIODIC LUBRICATION

Oil

Oil is graded according to its viscosity, which is an indication of how thick it is. The Society of Automotive Engineers (SAE) system distinguishes oil viscosity by numbers. Thick oils have higher viscosity numbers than thin oils.

Grease

A good quality grease (preferably waterproof) should be used. Water does not wash grease off parts as easily as it washes oil off. In addition, grease maintains its lubricating qualities better than oil on long and strenuous rides.

In many cases in this book a special grease called molybdenum disulfide grease is specified. It is used on some parts during engine reassembly and on some suspension components. Whenever this type of grease is specified it should be used as it has special lubricating qualities. Be sure to use this type of grease, even though it may be more expensive than ordinary multipurpose grease.

Engine Oil Level Check

The engine oil level is checked with the dipstick located on the right-hand crankcase/clutch cover (**Figure 7**).

1. Place the bike on level ground. Have an assistant hold the bike upright.

2. Start the engine and let it idle for 2-3 minutes.

3. Stop the engine and allow the oil to settle for 2-3 minutes.

4. Unscrew the dipstick/filler cap (**Figure 8**) and wipe it clean. Reinsert the dipstick/filler cap onto the threads in the hole; do not screw it in.

5. Remove the dipstick/filler cap and check the oil level.

6. The level should be between the 2 level marks on the dipstick and not above the upper mark (**Figure 9**). If the level is below the lower mark, add the recommended oil (**Table 3**) to correct the level. Do not overfill.

7. Reinstall the dipstick/filler cap.

Engine Oil and Filter Change

The factory-recommended oil and filter change interval is specified in **Table 1**. This assumes that the motorcycle is operated in moderate climates. The time interval is more important than the mileage interval because combustion acids, formed by gasoline and water vapor, will contaminate the oil even if the motorcycle is not run for several months. If a motorcycle is operated under dusty conditions, the oil will get dirty more quickly and should be changed more frequently than recommended.

Use only a detergent oil with an API rating of SE or SF. The quality rating is stamped on top of the can or printed on the container (**Figure 10**). Try always to use the same brand of oil. Use of oil additives is not recommended. Honda recommends the use of SAE 10W-40 oil viscosity under normal conditions. Refer to **Figure 11** for the correct weight of oil to use under anticipated ambient temperatures (not engine oil temperature). Use of oil additives is not recommended as they may cause clutch slippage.

> *CAUTION*
> *Honda does not recommend the use of vegetable, non-detergent or castor based racing oils.*

To change the engine oil and filter you will need the following:

  a. Drain pan.

  b. Funnel.

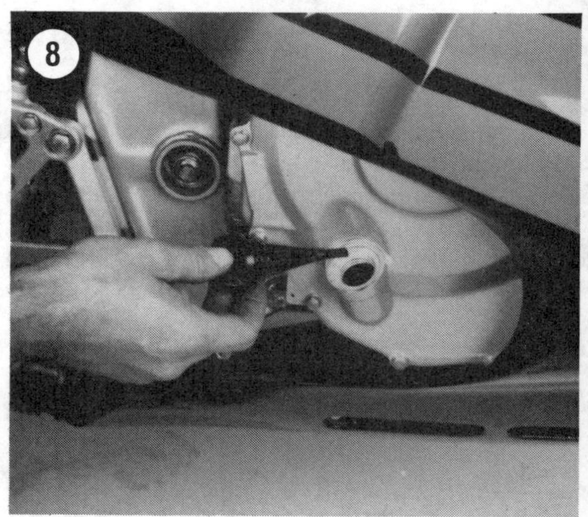

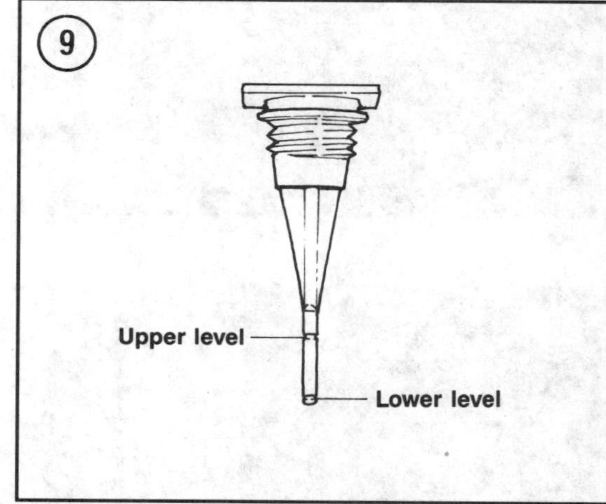

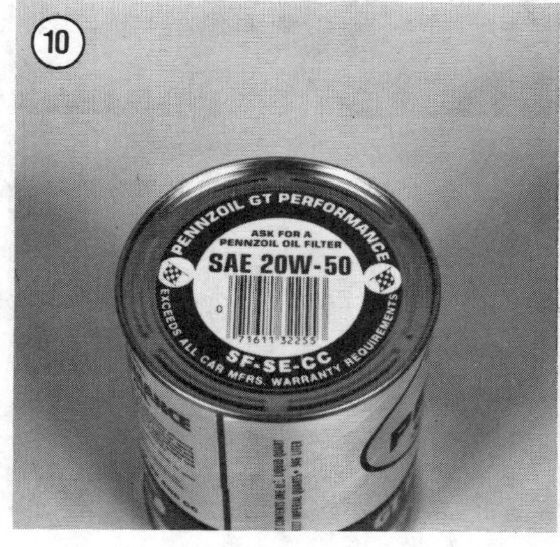

c. Can opener or pour spout (oil in cans).
d. Wrench or socket to remove drain plug.
e. New drain plug washer (if necessary).
f. 4 quarts of oil (**Table 4**).
g. Oil filter element.
h. Socket type oil filter wrench (**Figure 12**). See *NOTE* following.

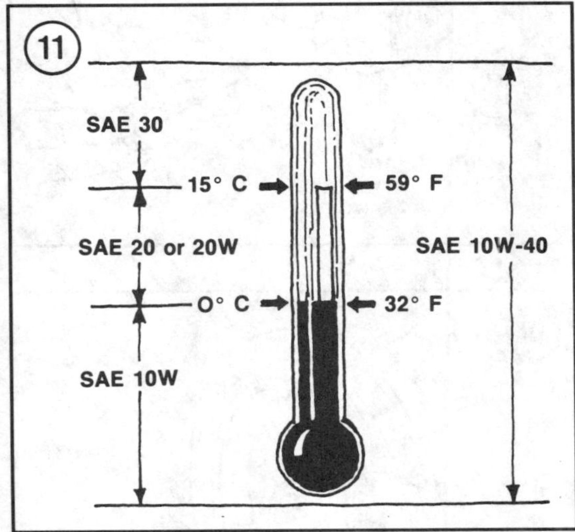

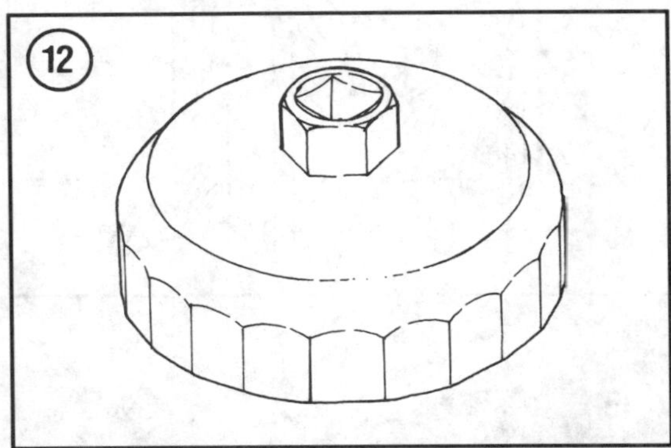

NOTE
The CBR600 uses a new style oil filter that is overall smaller in size than oil filters used on similar models. The new filter can be manufactured smaller because of a new paper folding system. If you have an old style filter wrench (socket type) it will not work on these filters. A new filter wrench can be ordered from a Honda dealer or motorcycle accessory store.

NOTE
A socket type oil filter wrench must be used when removing the oil filter because of the small working area between the oil filter, exhaust pipes and lower fairing assembly.

There are a number of ways to discard the used oil safely. The easiest way is to pour it from the drain pan into a gallon plastic bleach, juice or milk container for disposal.

NOTE
Some service stations and oil retailers will accept your used oil for recycling. Do not discard oil in your household trash or pour it onto the ground.

1. Support the bike so that it is positioned upright.

NOTE
It is not necessary to remove the lower fairing assembly when replacing the oil filter.

2. Start the engine and run it until it is at normal operating temperature, then turn it off.

NOTE
Warming the engine causes the oil to heat up, allowing it to flow freely and carry contamination and sludge with it.

WARNING
The oil will be hot! Work quickly and carefully when removing the plug to avoid burning your hand.

3. Place a drip pan under the crankcase and remove the drain plug (**Figure 13**) and washer.
4. Remove the dipstick/oil filler cap (**Figure 7**) and rest the cap in the filler hole; this will speed up the flow of oil.

5. Let the oil drain for at least 15-20 minutes, then move the drain pan under the oil filter.

6. Install a socket type oil filter wrench on the end of the oil filter. Insert the end of a 3/8 in. ratchet extension into the oil filter wrench (**Figure 14**). Turn the oil filter counterclockwise and loosen it until oil begins to run out the engine. Wait until the oil stops then loosen the filter all the way and remove it.

7. Hold the oil filter over the drain pan and pour out any remaining oil before discarding the filter. Place the oil filter in a plastic bag to contain any residual oil. Close off the end of the plastic bag to prevent oil from draining out.

> *CAUTION*
> *Before installing the new oil filter, clean off the crankcase mating surface with a lint-free cloth—do not allow any road dirt to enter the lubrication system.*

8. Apply a light coat of new engine oil to the rubber seal on the new oil filter (**Figure 15**) and screw on the oil filter. Tighten the filter to the torque specification in **Table 5**.

9. Replace the oil drain plug gasket if deformed.

10. Install the oil drain plug and gasket and tighten to the torque specification in **Table 5**.

11. Remove the dipstick/oil filler cap (**Figure 7**) and fill the crankcase with the correct weight (**Table 3**) and quantity of oil (**Table 4**).

12. Screw in the dipstick/oil filler cap securely.

13. Start the engine and allow to idle; the oil pressure warning light should go out within 1-3 seconds. If it stays on, shut off the engine immediately and locate the problem. Do not run the engine with the oil warning light on.

14. Let the engine idle and check for leaks.

15. Turn the engine off after 2-3 minutes and check the oil level; adjust as necessary.

Front Fork Oil Change

1. These models are not equipped with a centerstand. If an accessory front wheel bike stand is available, support the front of the bike so that the front tire is clear of the ground. If a front wheel stand is not available, remove the lower fairing assembly (Chapter Thirteen) and support the bike with a jack and wood blocks. Then pivot the front

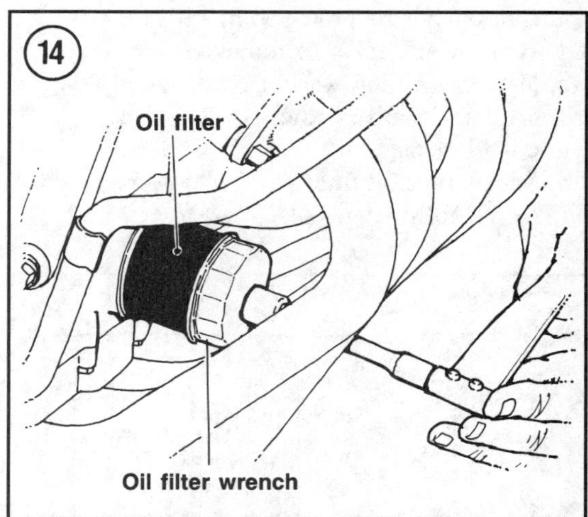

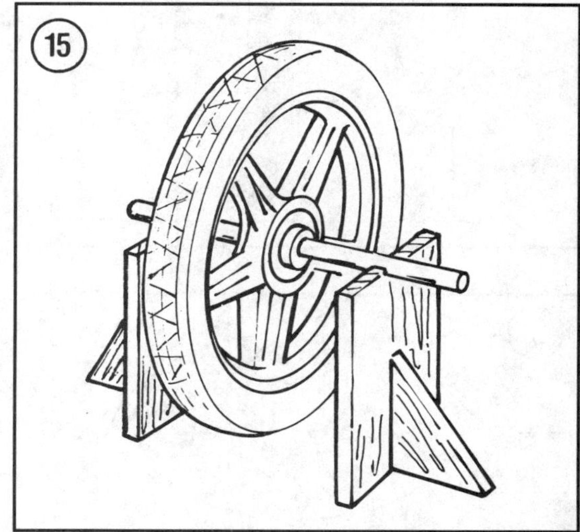

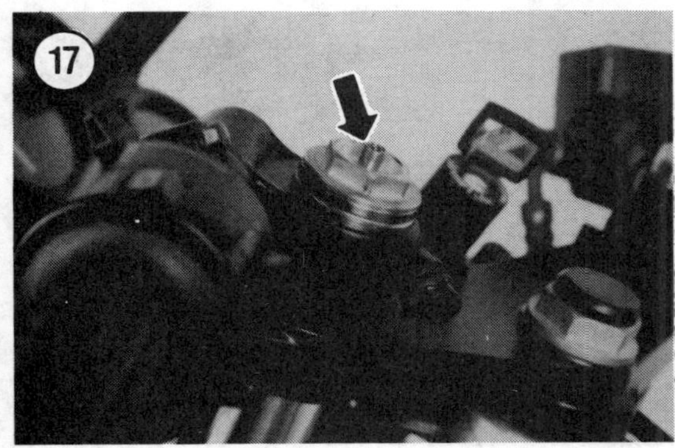

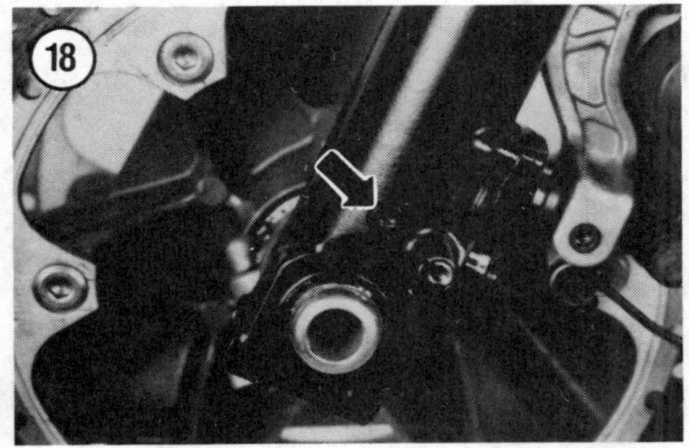

end up and support the back end. Block the rear wheel so that the bike cannot move in either direction.

> *NOTE*
> *Service one fork tube at a time.*

2. Turn the air valve cap (A, **Figure 16**) counterclockwise and remove it.
3. Depress the valve stem (**Figure 17**) with a screwdriver to release all air from the fork tube.

> *NOTE*
> *When removing the fork tube drain screw in Step 4, make sure to use a 5 mm Allen wrench to prevent rounding out the screw head.*

4. Place a drip pan beside the fork tube and remove the drain screw and washer (**Figure 18**) with an Allen wrench. Allow the oil to drain until it stops.
5. Remove the bike from the stand or blocks. With both of the bike's wheels on the ground, apply the front brake and push down on the front end and allow it to return. Repeat to remove as much oil as possible.

> *WARNING*
> *Do not allow the fork oil to come in contact with any of the brake components.*

6. Install the drain screw (**Figure 18**) and washer.
7. Repeat Steps 2-6 for the opposite fork.
8. Support the bike once again as described in Step 1.
9. Loosen, but do not remove, the handlebar pinch bolt (B, **Figure 16**).

> *NOTE*
> *A speeder wrench or a T-handle equipped with a long extension and a socket will allow you to control the top fork cap more easily when removing it.*

10. Unscrew the top fork cap (**Figure 19**) slowly as it is under pressure from the fork spring. Remove the top fork cap and the socket.
11. Lift the spacer (**Figure 20**) out of the fork tube.

12. Remove the spring seat (**Figure 21**).

13. Lift the fork spring (**Figure 22**) out of the fork tube. The fork spring will drip oil so wrap the bottom of the spring with a rag when removing it. Place the spring on clean newspapers to prevent dirt contamination.

NOTE
*The left- and right-hand fork tubes differ in fork oil quantity. See **Table 6**.*

NOTE
In order to measure the correct amount of fluid, use a baby bottle. These bottles have measurements in cubic centimeters (cc) and fluid ounces (oz.) imprinted on the side.

14. Fill the fork tube with the specified quantity of DEXRON automatic transmission fluid or 10W fork oil. Refer to **Table 6** for fork oil quantity.

15. Install the fork spring. Position the fork spring with the closer wound coils at the bottom end (**Figure 23**) and slowly guide the spring into the fork tube.

16. Install the spring seat (**Figure 21**) and spacer (**Figure 20**).

17. Inspect the O-ring on the top fork cap (**Figure 24**); replace if necessary.

18. Lubricate the top fork cap threads with clean fork oil.

19. Use the same tool setup used during disassembly. Insert the top fork cap into the socket. Align the cap with the fork tube and install the cap while pushing down on the spring. Start the top fork cap slowly; it is easy to cross thread the cap's aluminum threads. Tighten the top fork cap to the torque specification in **Table 5**.

20. Tighten the handlebar pinch bolt to the torque specification in **Table 5**.

21. Repeat Steps 8-20 for the opposite fork.

WARNING
When refilling the fork tube air pressure in Step 22, never use any type of compressed gas as an explosion may be lethal. Never heat the fork assembly with a torch or place it near an open flame or extreme heat as this will also result in an explosion.

22. Using a small hand-operated air pump, inflate the front forks to the pressure listed in **Table 7**.

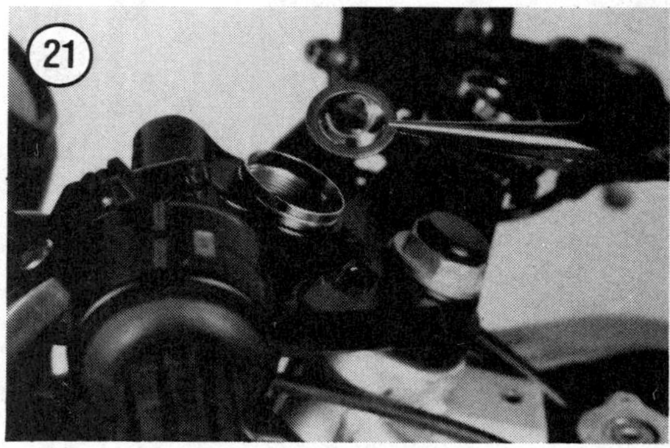

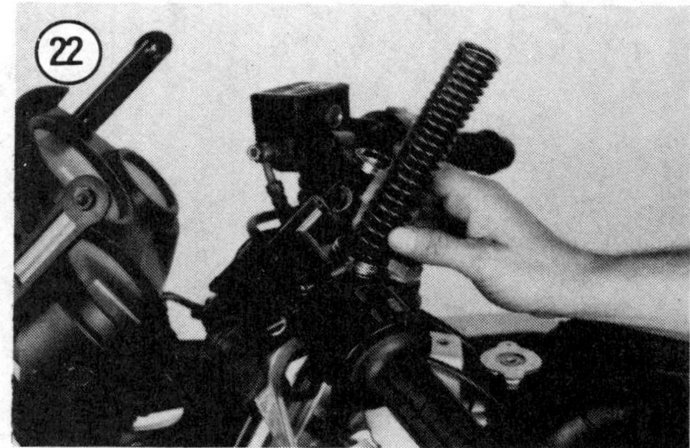

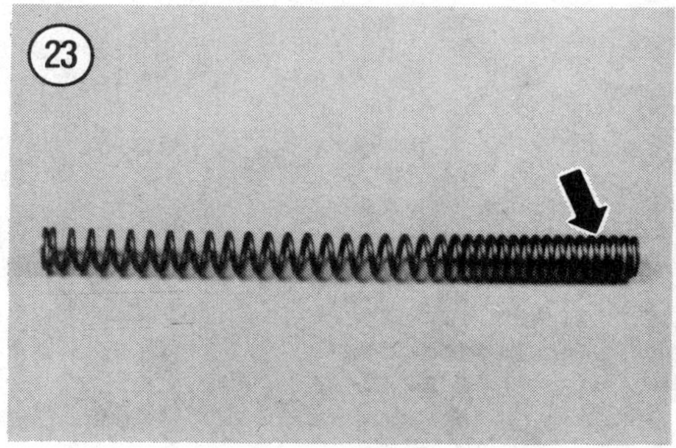

Do not use compressed air as the fork will fill quickly and the pressure may damage the oil seal.

23. Remove the bike from the stand or blocks. Install the lower fairing assembly, if removed, as described in Chapter Thirteen.

24. Road test the bike and check for oil and air leaks.

Control Cables

The control cables should be lubricated at the intervals specified in **Table 1**. At this time, they should also be inspected for fraying, and the cable sheath should be checked for chafing. The cables are relatively inexpensive and should be replaced when found to be faulty.

They can be lubricated with a cable lubricant and a cable lubricator available at most motorcycle dealers.

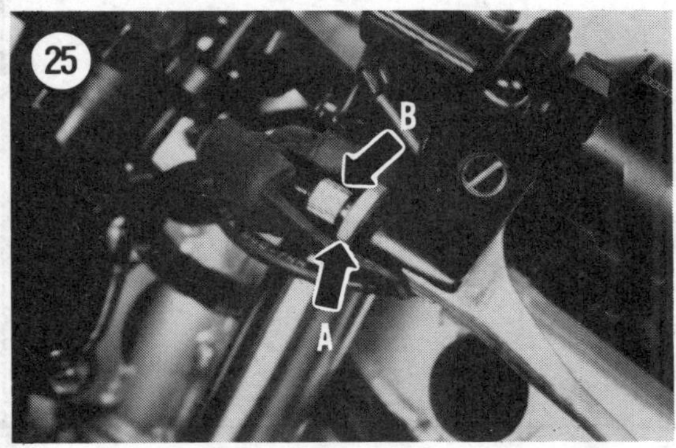

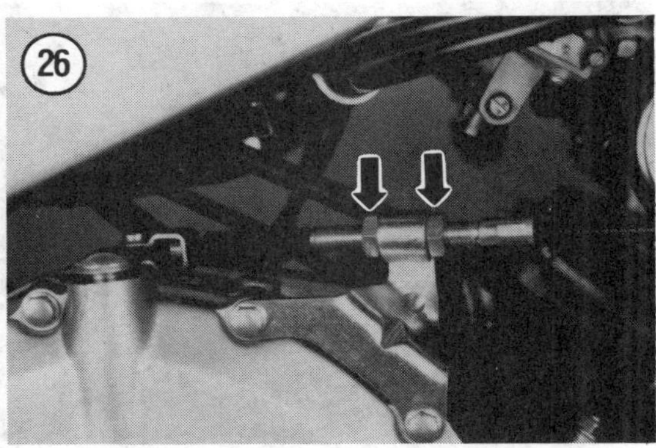

> *NOTE*
> *The main cause of cable breakage or cable stiffness is improper lubrication. Maintaining the cables as described in this section will assure long service life.*

1. Disconnect the clutch cable as follows:
   a. Slide the rubber boot away from the clutch cable handlebar adjuster.
   b. Loosen the clutch cable handlebar adjuster locknut (A, **Figure 25**). Turn the adjuster (B, **Figure 25**) all the way in to loosen the clutch cable.
   c. Align the slots in the locknut and adjuster so that they face to the front of the bike.
   d. Pull the clutch lever all the way in with your left hand and grab the clutch cable with your right hand.
   e. Then release the clutch lever slowly while at the same time pulling the cable out of the adjuster and through the aligned slots with your right hand. Pull the cable end out of the clutch lever.

> *NOTE*
> *If the clutch cable is still tight after loosening the clutch cable handlebar adjuster and you cannot disconnect the cable as just described, loosen the clutch cable mid-line adjuster locknuts at the engine (**Figure 26**). Remove the right-hand maintenance cover to gain access to the clutch cable mid-line adjuster (**Figure 27**).*

2. Disconnect the choke cable from the left-hand handlebar.

3. Disconnect the throttle cables as follows:
   a. Remove the screw securing the metal weight on the end of the handlebar and remove the weight.

b. Loosen the throttle cable adjuster locknuts at the handlebar and loosen the throttle cables.

c. Remove the screws securing the throttle cable/switch housing and partially separate the housings (**Figure 28**).

d. Disconnect the throttle cables from the twist grips and remove the cables.

4. Attach a cable lubricator (**Figure 29**) to the cable following the manufacturer's instructions.

> *NOTE*
> *Place a shop cloth at the end of the cable(s) to catch all excess lubricant that will flow out.*

5. Insert the nozzle of the lubricant can into the lubricator, press the button on the can and hold it down until the lubricant begins to flow out of the other end of the cable.

> *NOTE*
> *If lubricant does not flow out the end of the cable, check the entire cable for fraying, bending or other damage.*

6. Remove the lubricator, reconnect and adjust the cable(s) as described in this chapter.

Swing Arm Bearing Lubrication

The rear swing arm needle bearings should be cleaned in solvent and lubricated with a molybdenum disulfide grease at the intervals specified in **Table 1**. The swing arm must be removed to service the needle bearings. Refer to *Swing Arm Removal/Installation* in Chapter Eleven.

Shock Linkage Lubrication

The rear shock absorber tie-rod and connecting rod needle bearings should be cleaned in solvent and lubricated with molybdenum disulfide grease at the intervals specified in Table 1. The linkage must be removed to service the needle bearings. Refer to Chapter Eleven.

Speedometer Cable Lubrication

Lubricate the speedometer cable every year or whenever needle operation is erratic.

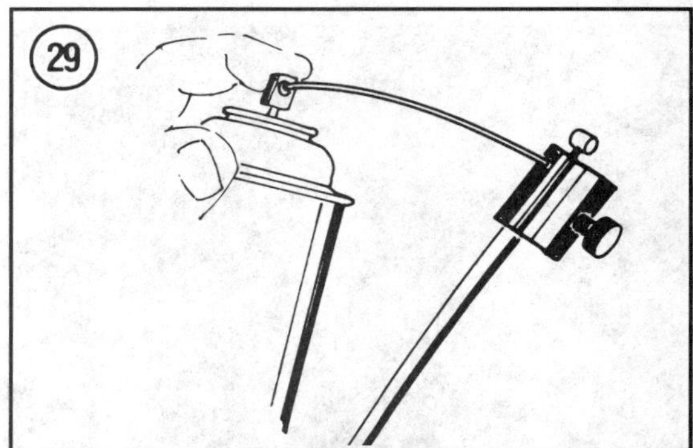

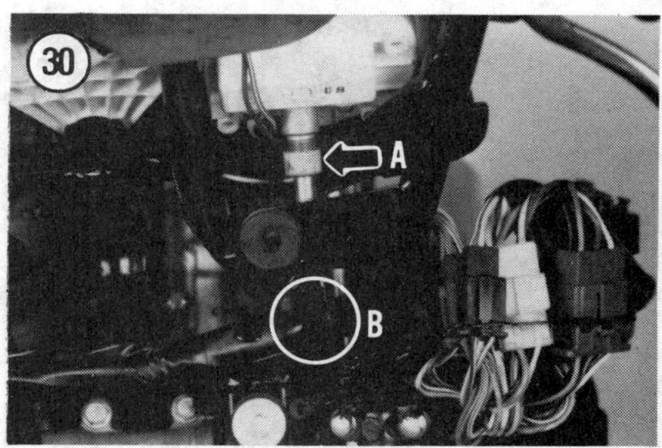

1. Remove the upper fairing as described in Chapter Thirteen.

2. Unscrew the end of the speedometer cable (A, **Figure 30**) at the instrument cluster.

3. At the front wheel, remove the speedometer cable Phillips screw and pull the cable (**Figure 31**) out of the speedometer gear housing.

4. Pull the cable from the sheath.

5. If the grease is contaminated, thoroughly clean off all old grease with solvent and dry thoroughly.

6. Thoroughly coat the cable with a good grade of multi-purpose grease and reinstall into the sheath.

7. Installation is the reverse of these steps. Note the following:

   a. Hook the upper end of the speedometer behind the cable guide as shown in B, **Figure 30**.

   b. Hook the lower end of the speedometer into the front wheel guide as shown in **Figure 32**.

   c. Before installing the upper fairing assembly, stand on the left-hand side of the bike and with the front wheel off the ground, turn the front wheel counterclockwise and make sure the needle in the speedometer moves.

Speedometer Gear Lubrication

Refer to *Speedometer Gear Inspection and Lubrication* in Chapter Ten.

Steering Stem Lubrication

Refer to *Steering Head and Stem* in Chapter Ten.

Drive Chain Lubrication

Honda recommends SAE 80 or 90 gear oil for chain lubrication; it is less likely to be thrown off the chain than lighter oils. Many commercial drive chain lubricants are also available that do an excellent job.

> *NOTE*
> *If the drive chain is very dirty, remove and clean it as described under **Drive Chain Cleaning** in Chapter Eleven before lubricating it as described in this procedure.*

> *CAUTION*
> *The factory drive chain is equipped with O-rings between the side plates (**Figure 33**) that seal grease between*

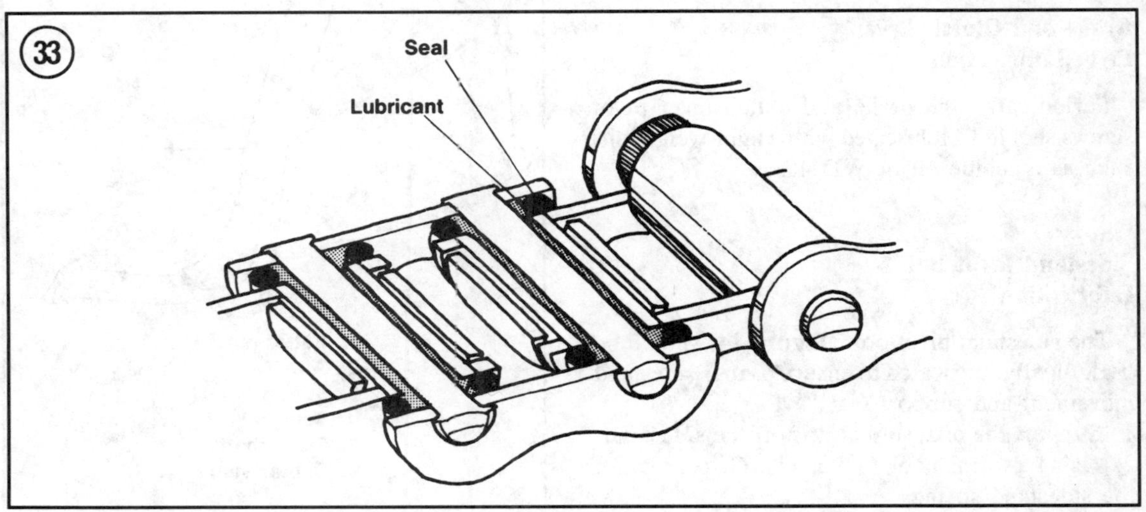

the pins and bushings. To prevent damaging these O-rings, use only kerosene for cleaning. Do not use gasoline or other solvents that will cause the O-rings to swell or deteriorate. Refer to cleaning procedures in Chapter Eleven.

1. Ride the bike a few miles to warm the drive chain. A warm chain increases lubricant penetration.
2. These models are not equipped with a centerstand. Support the bike with a rear wheel stand so that the rear wheel clears the ground.
3. Oil the bottom chain run with SAE 90 gear oil or a commercial chain lubricant *recommended* for use on O-ring equipped drive chains. Concentrate on getting the oil down between the side plates of the chain links (**Figure 33**).

> *CAUTION*
> *Not all commercial chain lubricants are recommended for use on O-ring equipped drive chains. Read the label on the can carefully before use or purchase to be sure it is formulated for O-ring chains.*

4. Rotate the chain and continue lubricating until the entire chain has been lubricated.
5. Wipe off any oil or chain lubricant that has run onto the swing arm or rear wheel.

Brake and Clutch Lever Pivot Lubrication

Periodically, the brake and clutch lever pivot screws should be lubricated with a light-weight oil, such as machine oil or WD-40.

Sidestand Pivot Bolt Lubrication

The sidestand pivot bolt (**Figure 34**) should be periodically lubricated to ensure proper sidestand movement and support.
1. Support the bike so that it is off the sidestand.
2. Using a spring hook tool or Vise Grips, remove the sidestand spring.

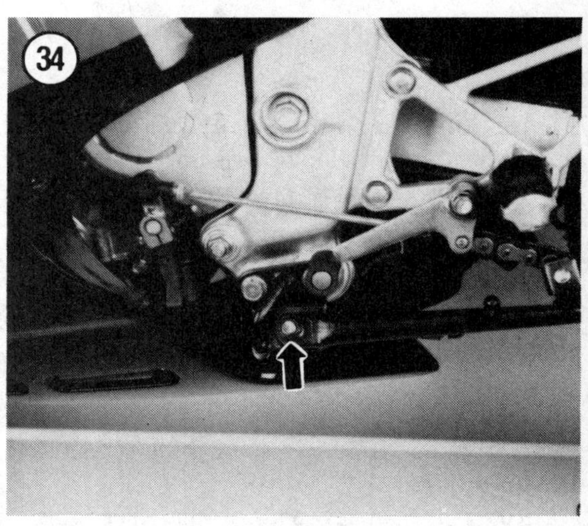

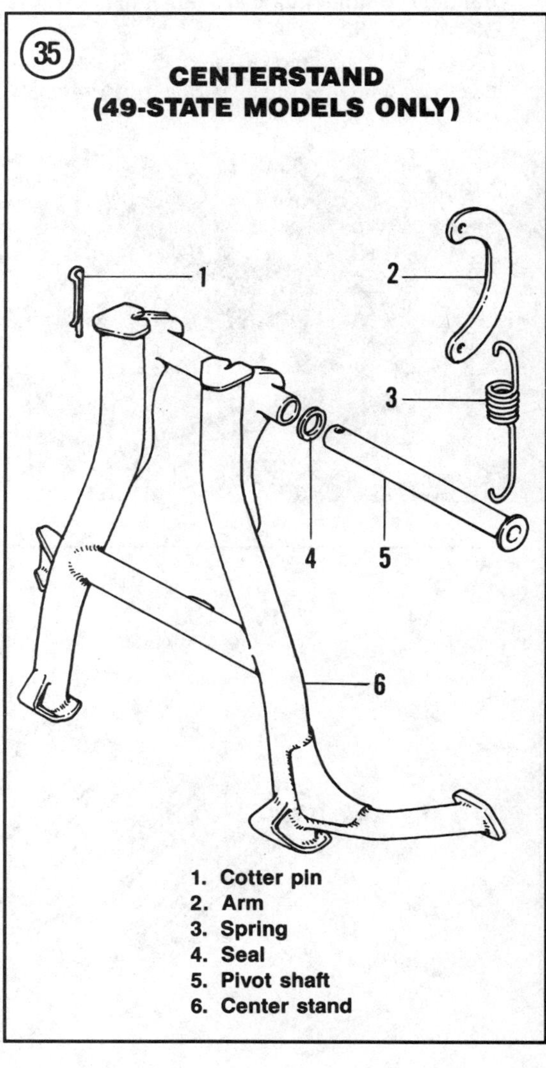

1. Cotter pin
2. Arm
3. Spring
4. Seal
5. Pivot shaft
6. Center stand

3. Remove the sidestand nut, washers and pivot bolt and slip the sidestand off its bracket.
4. Clean all parts thoroughly in solvent and dry thoroughly.
5. Inspect the sidestand pivot bolt for metal fatigue or other damage. Also inspect the sidestand pivot point for fatigue or damage that would allow the bike to fall when the sidestand is used.

CAUTION
Expensive fairing damage could result from sidestand failure.

6. Replace worn or damaged parts.
7. Apply a coat of molybdenum disulfide grease to the pivot.
8. Install the sidestand by reversing these steps. Note the following:

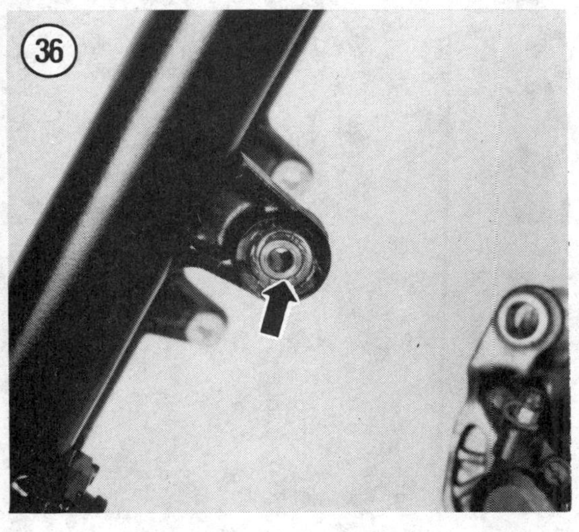

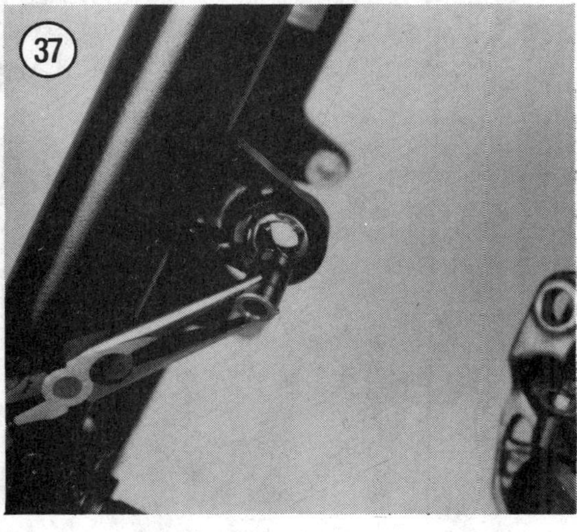

a. Tighten the sidestand mounting bolt to the torque specification in **Table 5**.
b. Install the sidestand washers and locknut. Tighten the locknut to the torque specification in **Table 5**.
c. Make sure the spring contacts the mounting bracket and sidestand completely.
9. Operate the sidestand to make sure it pivots smoothly. If the spring feels fatigued or at the maintenance intervals in **Table 1**, check spring tension as described under *Sidestand Inspection* in this chapter.

Center Stand Pivot Shaft Lubrication

Offered as an accessory item, Honda sells a center stand (**Figure 35**) that will fit all 49-state models; the center stand cannot be installed on California models. If you have installed the accessory center stand, it should be removed periodically and the pivot bolt lubricated with a coat of molybdenum disulfide grease. During installation, make sure the center stand return spring is mounted properly and that the center stand does not sag in its raised position. During installation, install a *new* cotter pin and bend the ends over completely to lock it.

Left-hand Front Caliper Mount Needle Bearing Lubrication

Periodically, the lefthand fork needle bearing (**Figure 36**) should be lubricated with grease. The lefthand front brake caliper must be able to pivot freely in its fork mount for the antidive unit to function properly.
1. Remove the left-hand front brake caliper as described in Chapter Twelve.
2. Remove the fork needle bearing pivot spacer (**Figure 37**).
3. Check the needle bearing for color change (dark blue), abrasion or needle damage. If the bearing is damaged, replace it as described in Chapter Ten.
4. Inspect the spacer for scoring, color change or abrasion. Replace if necessary.
5. If the needle bearing and pivot spacer are okay, clean the needle bearing with solvent or contact cleaner and allow to dry thoroughly. Apply grease

to the needle bearing rollers and install the pivot spacer (**Figure 37**). Thoroughly work the grease between the needles.

6. Install the left-hand front brake caliper as described in Chapter Twelve.

Front Brake Caliper
Pivot Bolt Lubrication

The brake caliper pivot bolts should be periodically cleaned and then lubricated with a silicone grease. See **Figure 38** and **Figure 39**. Brake caliper removal will be required to service the pivot bolts. Refer to *Front Brake Caliper Removal* in Chapter Twelve.

Brake Pedal
Pivot Shaft Lubrication

The brake pedal should be removed periodically and the pivot shaft lubricated with grease. Refer to *Rear Brake Pedal Removal/Installation* in Chapter Ten.

Wheel Bearings and Seals
Inspection/Lubrication

Worn wheel bearings cause excessive wheel play that result in vibration and other steering troubles. At the intervals specified in **Table 1**, the bearing should be inspected and lubricated with wheel bearing grease. Refer to *Front Hub* in Chapter Ten and *Rear Hub* in Chapter Eleven.

> *NOTE*
> *Sealed bearings (**Figure 40**) do not require periodic lubrication.*

Worn or improperly lubricated wheel bearing seals (**Figure 41**) allow bearing contamination. When the wheels are removed for bearing lubrication and inspection, apply a light coat of waterproof grease to the inside of the seal lip.

PERIODIC MAINTENANCE

Drive Chain Adjustment

To prevent drive chain tension related problems, adjust the chain at the intervals specified in **Table 1**. If the bike is operated at sustained high speeds or if it is repeatedly accelerated very hard, check the drive chain adjustment more often. Drive chain

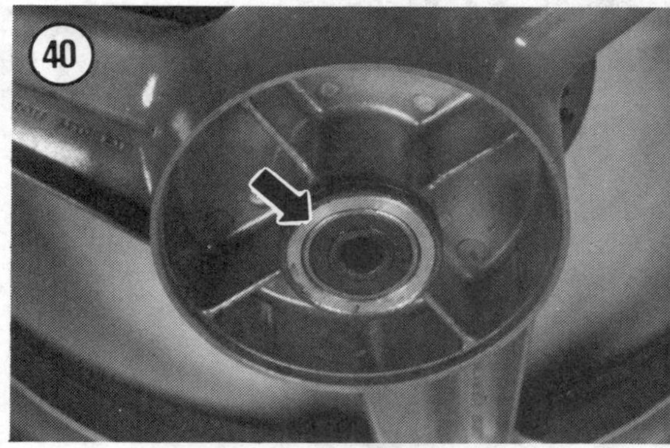

slack that exceeds 50 mm (1 5/8 in.) may damage the bottom of the frame.

NOTE
As drive chains stretch and wear in use, the chain will become tighter at one point. The chain must be checked and adjusted at this point.

1. With the engine off, shift the transmission into NEUTRAL.

NOTE
When performing Step 2, it is easier to check the chain for tight spots if the rear wheel can be raised off the ground. Use an accessory rear wheel stand or remove the lower fairing and raise the rear wheel off the ground with a small hydraulic jack.

2. Check the chain for its tightest point. Mark this spot with chalk and turn the wheel so that the mark is located on the chain's lower run, midway between both drive sprockets (Figure 42). Check and adjust the drive chain as follows.

NOTE
*If the drive chain is kinked or feels tight, it may require cleaning and lubrication. Refer to **Drive Chain Lubrication** in this chapter. If the chain is still tight, it may be damaged due to damaged rollers, loose pins or binding links. Refer to **Drive Sprocket and Drive Chain** in Chapter Eleven and remove the drive chain.*

3. Remove the bike from the accessory stand or hydraulic jack (if used). Park the bike on its sidestand.

4. With thumb and forefinger, lift up, then press down on the chain at that point, measuring the distance the chain moves vertically (**Figure 42**).

5. The drive chain should have approximately 15-25 mm (5/8-1 in.) of vertical travel at midpoint (**Figure 42**). If necessary, adjust the chain as follows.

6. Loosen the axle nut on the right-hand side (A, **Figure 43**).

7. Loosen the axle adjuster locknut (B, **Figure 43**) on both sides of the wheel.

8. Turn each adjuster nut (C, **Figure 43**) an equal number of turns to obtain the correct drive chain slack. Alignment is checked by observing the left- and right-hand adjuster marks; align the marks with the rear edge of the swing arm axle slots on

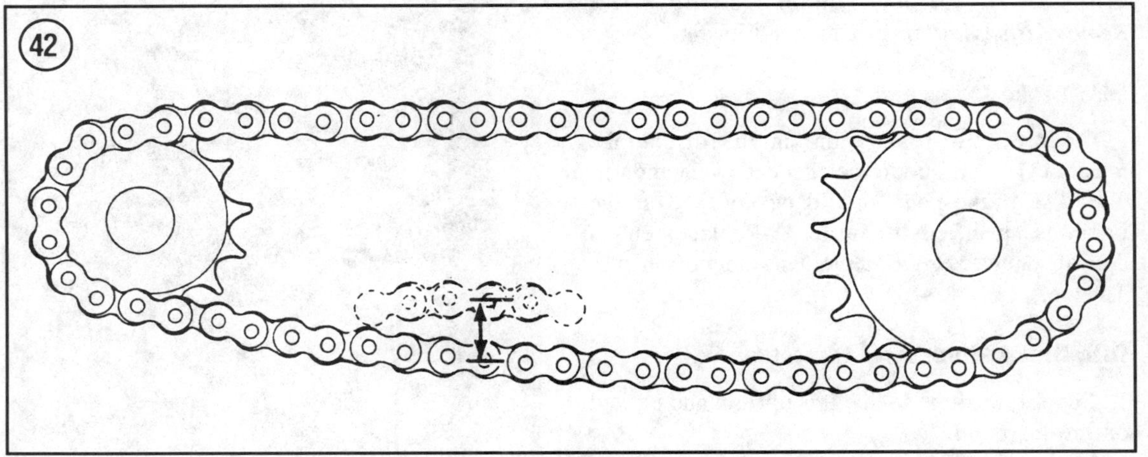

both sides. Adjust the chain until the correct amount of free play is obtained (Step 5). See **Figure 42**.

NOTE
*A drive chain wear label is mounted on the left-hand side of the swing arm. If the arrow mark on the adjuster aligns with the red zone on the label (**Figure 44**), and the chain slack is correct, the drive chain is excessively worn and must be replaced. See **Drive Sprocket and Drive Chain** in Chapter Eleven.*

9. To verify the swing arm adjuster marks, remove the chain guard and check rear wheel alignment by sighting along the chain as it runs over the rear sprocket. It should not appear to bend sideways. See **Figure 45**.
10. Tighten the rear axle nut to the torque specification in **Table 5**.
11. Tighten the adjusting nut (C, **Figure 43**) *lightly*. Then hold the adjusting nut with a 10 mm wrench and tighten the locknut (B, **Figure 43**). Repeat for the opposite side.
12. Recheck chain play.
13. Perform the *Rear Brake Pedal Free Play Adjustment* in this chapter.

Swing Arm Slider Inspection

A slider is installed on the left-hand side of the swing arm (**Figure 46**) to protect the swing arm from chain damage. The slider should be inspected frequently for advanced wear or damage that would allow the chain to cut into the swing arm. If necessary, replace the slider by removing the swing arm as described under *Swing Arm Removal/Installation* in Chapter Eleven.

Disc Brake Inspection

The hydraulic brake fluid in the disc brake master cylinders should be checked every month. The disc brake pads should be checked at the intervals specified in **Table 1**. Replacement is described under *Brake Pad Replacement* in Chapter Twelve.

Disc Brake Fluid Level Inspection

1. Support the bike so that it is upright and parked on level ground.

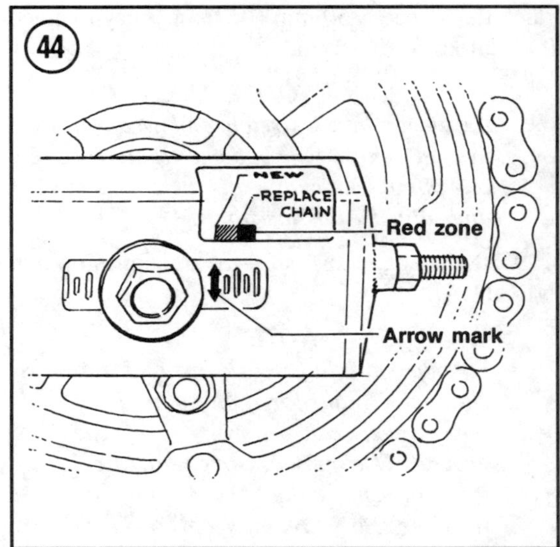

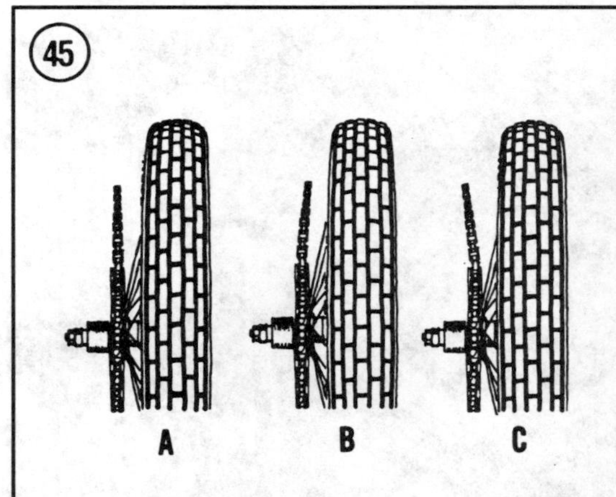

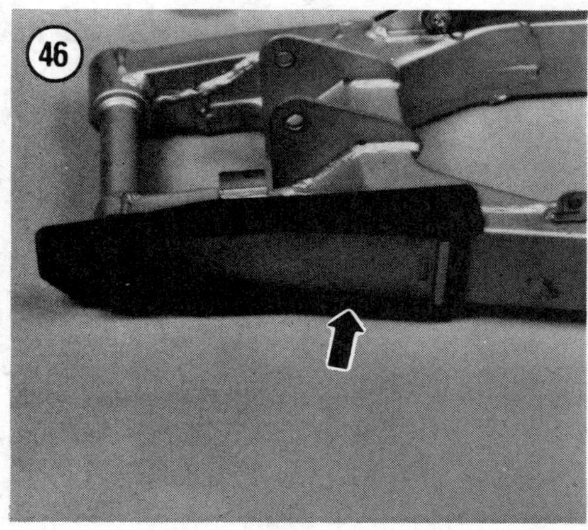

2. Turn the handlebars so that the front master cylinder is level.

3. The brake fluid must be kept above the lower level lines. See **Figure 47** (front) or **Figure 48** (rear).

Adding Brake Fluid

1. *Rear master cylinder:* Remove the seat and the right-hand side cover as described in Chapter Thirteen.

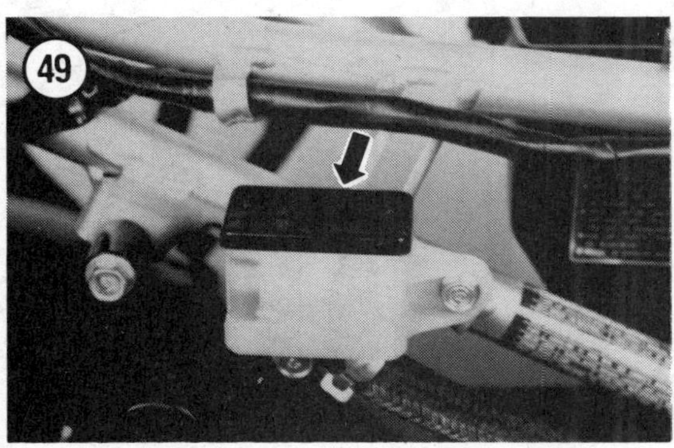

2. Clean the outside of the reservoir cap thoroughly with a dry rag and remove the reservoir cap. See **Figure 47** (front) or **Figure 49** (rear). Remove the diaphragm under the reservoir cap.

> *WARNING*
> *Use brake fluid clearly marked DOT 4 only and specified for disc brakes. Others may vaporize and cause brake failure.*

> *CAUTION*
> *Be careful not to spill brake fluid on painted or plated surfaces as it will destroy the surface. Wash immediately with soapy water and thoroughly rinse it off.*

3. The fluid level in the reservoir should be up to the upper level line. Add fresh DOT 4 brake fluid as required.

4. Reinstall all parts. Make sure the cap is tightly secured.

> *NOTE*
> *If the brake fluid was so low as to allow air in the hydraulic system, the brakes will have to be bled. Refer to **Bleeding the System** in Chapter Twelve.*

Disc Brake Lines and Seals

Check the brake lines between the master cylinder and the brake caliper. If there is any leakage, tighten the connections and bleed the brakes as described in Chapter Twelve. If this does not stop the leak or if a line is obviously damaged, cracked, or chafed, replace the line and seals and bleed the brake.

Disc Brake Pad Inspection

There is no recommended mileage interval for changing the friction pads on the disc brake. Pad wear depends greatly on riding habits and conditions. The pads should be checked for wear every 4,000 miles (6,400 km) by observing the pads through the slot in the caliper housing—**Figure 50** (front) or **Figure 51** (rear)—and replaced when the wear indicator (**Figure 52**) reaches the edge of the brake disc. To maintain an even brake pressure on the disc, always replace both pads in each caliper at the same time. Replace the brake pads as described in Chapter Twelve.

> *NOTE*
> *If it is difficult to observe the thickness and condition of the brake pads, remove them as described under **Brake Pad Replacement** in Chapter Twelve.*

Disc Brake Fluid Change

Every time you remove the reservoir cap a small amount of dirt and moisture enters the brake fluid. The same thing happens if a leak occurs or when any part of the hydraulic system is loosened or disconnected. Dirt can clog the system and cause unnecessary wear. Water in the fluid vaporizes at high temperatures, impairing the hydraulic action and reducing brake performance.

To change brake fluid, drain the master cylinders as described under *Front Master Cylinder Removal/Installation* or *Rear Master Cylinder Removal/Installation* in Chapter Twelve. Add new fluid to the master cylinder and bleed at the caliper until the fluid leaving the caliper is clean and free of contaminants and air bubbles. Refer to *Bleeding the System* in Chapter Twelve.

> *WARNING*
> *Use brake fluid clearly marked DOT 4 only. Others may vaporize and cause brake failure.*

Front Brake Lever Adjustment

Periodic adjustment of the front disc brake is not required because disc pad wear is automatically compensated. If there is excessive play in the front brake lever, check the front brake lever pivot hole and bolt for excessive wear. Replace worn parts. See *Front Master Cylinder* in Chapter Twelve. If the brake lever pivot bolt is okay, check for air in the brake line.

Rear Brake Pedal Height Adjustment

The rear brake pedal (A, **Figure 53**) height should be set to your personal preference.

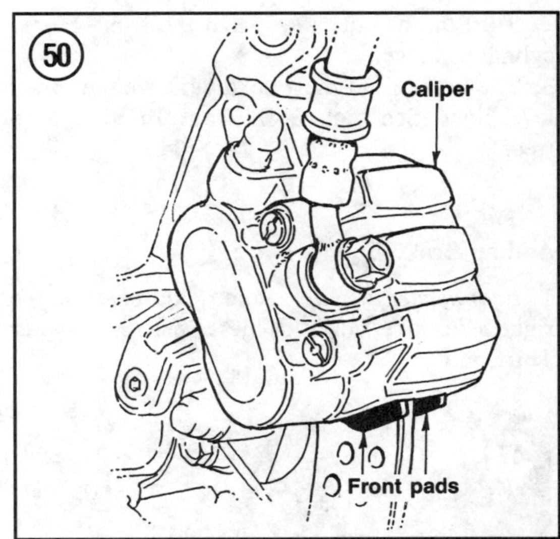

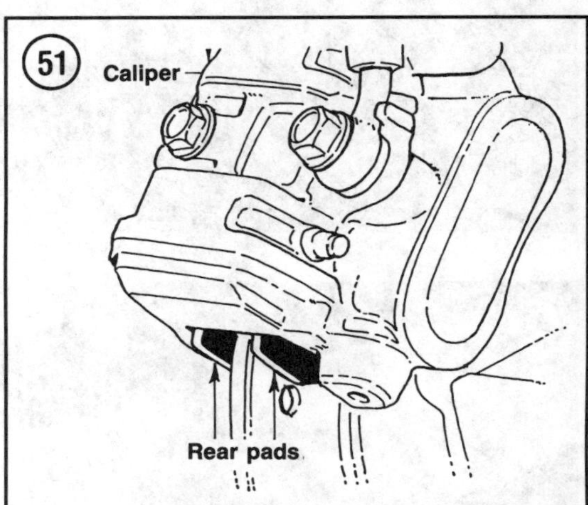

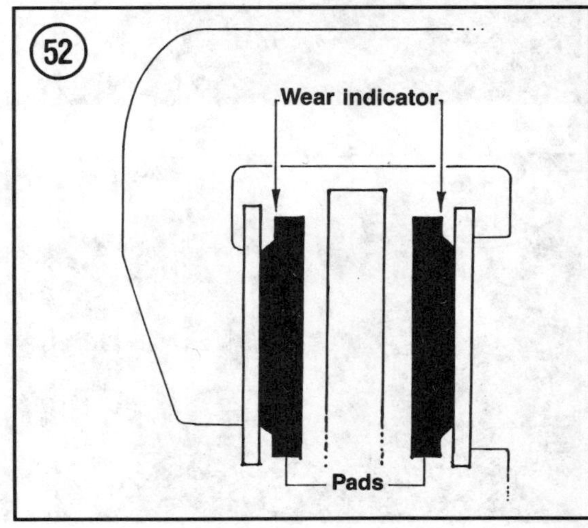

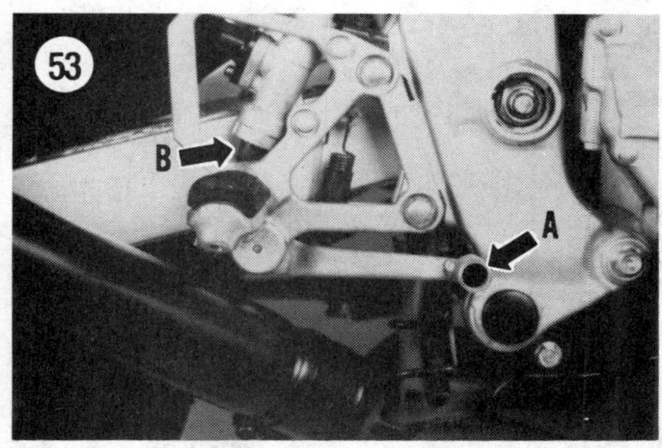

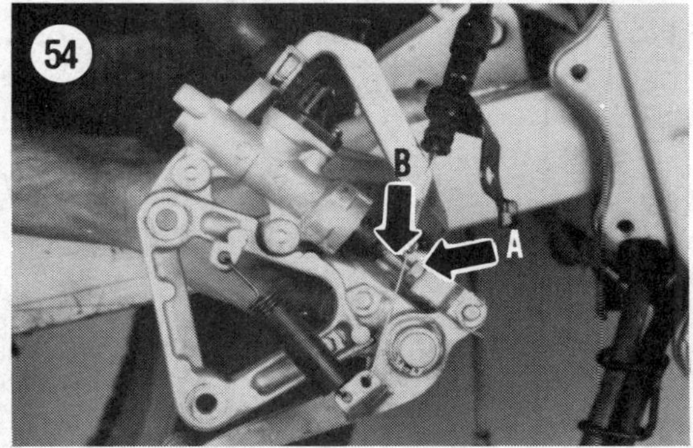

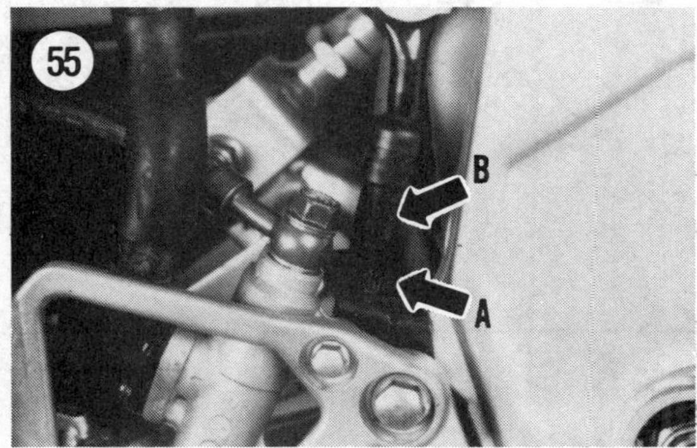

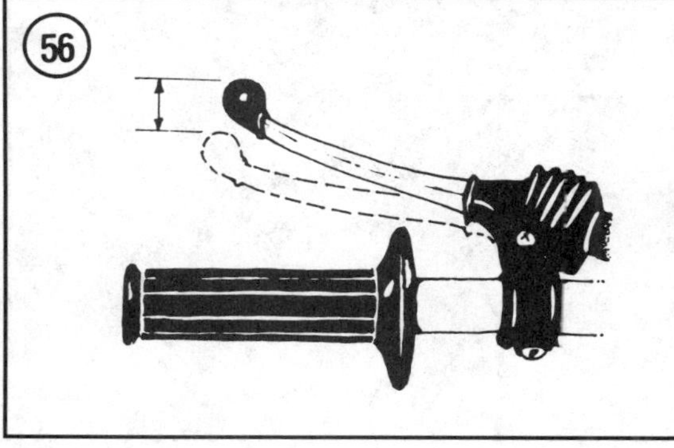

1. Park the motorcycle on the sidestand.
2. Check to be sure the brake pedal is in the "at rest" position.
3. Loosen the rear master cylinder pushrod locknuts (B, Figure 53). Then turn the pushrod in either direction to adjust rear brake pedal height.

> *NOTE*
> *Figure 54 shows the rear brake/master cylinder assembly with the mounting bracket removed for clarity. It is not necessary to remove the bracket for adjustment. See (A) locknuts and (B) pushrod in **Figure 54**.*

4. Recheck the brake pedal height and readjust if necessary.
5. Check the *Rear Brake Light Switch Adjustment* as described in the next procedure.

Rear Brake Light Switch Adjustment

1. Turn the ignition switch ON.
2. Depress the brake pedal. The brake light should come on after the brake pedal is depressed. If necessary, adjust as follows.
3. Turn the rear brake light switch adjuster (A, **Figure 55**) to move the switch body (B, **Figure 55**) up or down as required.
4. Recheck the rear brake light switch adjustment.

Clutch Lever Adjustment

1. Pull the clutch until resistance is felt and measure free play at the end of the clutch lever (**Figure 56**). The clutch cable should have 10-20 mm (3/8-3/4 in.) free play.
2. Minor adjustment can be made at the hand lever. Pull the rubber cover away from the clutch lever handlebar adjuster. Loosen the locknut (A, **Figure 57**) and turn the adjuster (B, **Figure 57**) as required to obtain the correct free play. Tighten the locknut and recheck the adjustment.

> *NOTE*
> *If sufficient free play cannot be obtained at the hand lever, additional adjustment can be made at the clutch cable mid-line adjuster.*

3. Remove the right-hand maintenance cover. See Chapter Thirteen.

4. Loosen the clutch cable mid-line adjuster locknuts (**Figure 58**).

5. At the hand lever, loosen the locknut (A, **Figure 57**) and turn the adjuster (B, **Figure 57**) to loosen the clutch cable.

6. At the mid-line adjuster, pull the clutch cable forward and tighten the adjuster locknuts (**Figure 58**) to lock the cable.

7. Now turn the handlebar adjuster as described in Step 2 and adjust the clutch cable. Tighten the adjuster locknut.

8. Make sure all locknuts are tight.

9. Start the engine and make sure the clutch operates correctly.

10. Install the right-hand maintenance cover (if removed).

Throttle Cable Adjustment

Always check the throttle cables before you make any carburetor adjustments. Too much free play causes delayed throttle response; too little free play will cause unstable idling.

Check the throttle cables from grip to carburetors. Make sure they are not kinked or chafed. Replace them if necessary.

Make sure that the throttle grip rotates smoothly from fully closed to fully open. Check at center, full left and full right position of steering.

Check free play at the throttle grip flange (**Figure 59**); Honda specifies 2-6 mm (3/32-1/4 in.) free play. If adjustment is required proceed as follows.

> *WARNING*
> *If idle speed increases when the handlebar is turned to right or left, check throttle cable routing. Correct this problem immediately. Do not ride the motorcycle in this unsafe condition.*

1. If minor adjustment is required, perform the following:
   a. Loosen the locknut and turn the throttle cable adjuster (**Figure 60**) at the throttle grip in or out to achieve proper free play rotation.
   b. Tighten the locknut and recheck the adjustment.
2. If major adjustment is necessary, perform the following:
   a. Remove the seat (Chapter Thirteen).
   b. Remove the fuel tank (Chapter Seven).

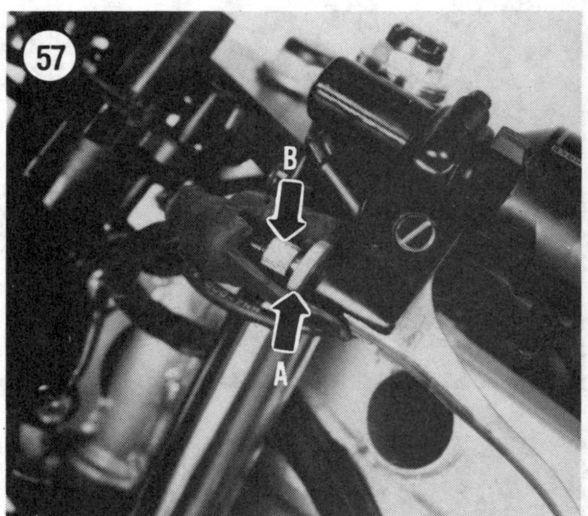

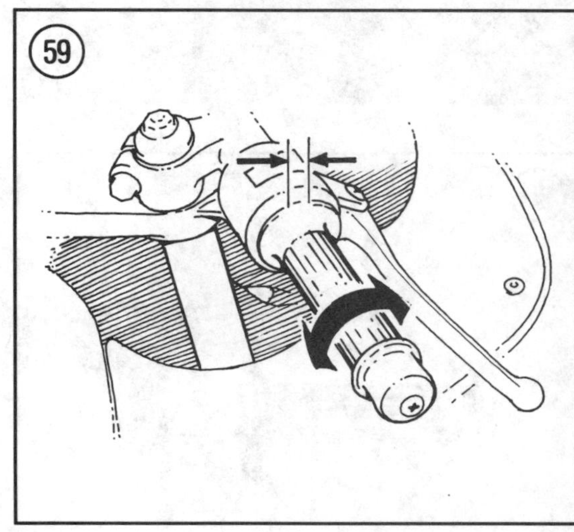

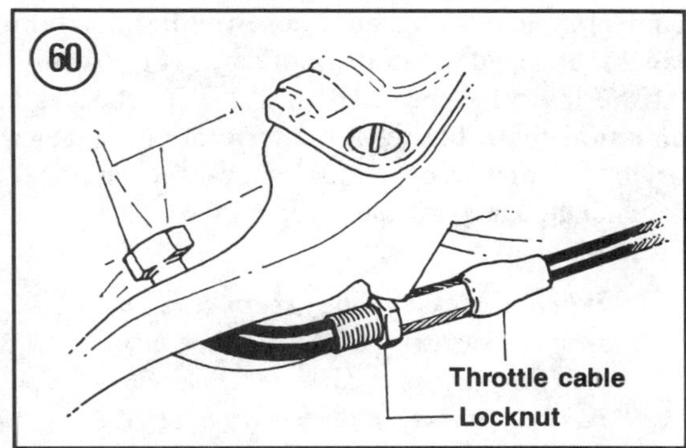

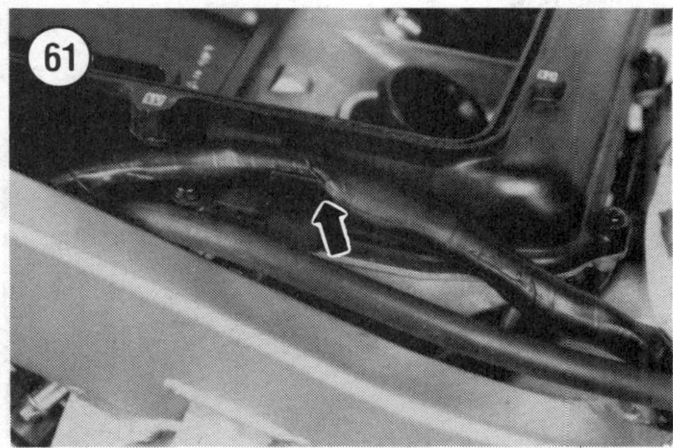

c. Remove the air filter as described in this chapter.

> *NOTE*
> *The intake sides of the carburetors are now exposed; stuff a clean, lint-free rag into each carburetor opening to prevent dropping small screws or other parts into the carburetors.*

d. Lift the wire harness (**Figure 61**) out of the harness guide on the lower air filter housing.

e. Remove the screws securing the lower air filter housing and lift the housing (**Figure 62**) off the engine.

f. Loosen the cable locknuts at the carburetors (**Figure 63**) and reposition the cable to achieve proper free play rotation at the throttle grip. Tighten the locknuts and recheck the free play. If necessary, readjust the cable at the throttle grip.

3. Tighten all locknuts.

4. Operate the throttle grip a few times. The throttle grip should now be adjusted correctly. If not, the throttle cables may be stretched and should be replaced.

5. Reinstall all parts previously removed. Make sure to route the wire harness through the guide in the lower air filter housing (**Figure 61**).

6. Sit on the seat and start the engine. Turn the handlebars from right to left to check for abnormal idle speed variances due to improper cable routing.

> *WARNING*
> *If idle speed increases when the handlebar is turned to right or left, check throttle cable routing. Correct this problem immediately. Do not ride the motorcycle in this unsafe condition.*

Choke Cable Adjustment

The choke lever should move smoothly when pushed between the fully open and fully closed positions (**Figure 64**). If necessary, lubricate the choke cable as described under *Control Cables* in this chapter. If the choke lever does not operate the choke properly, perform the following.

1. Remove the seat (Chapter Thirteen).

2. Remove the fuel tank (Chapter Seven).

3. Remove the air filter as described in this chapter.

NOTE
The intake sides of the carburetors are now exposed. Stuff a clean, lint-free rag into each carburetor opening to prevent dropping small screws or other parts into the carburetors.

4. Lift the wire harness (**Figure 61**) out of the harness guide on the lower air filter housing.

5. Remove the screws securing the lower air filter housing and lift the housing (**Figure 62**) off the engine.

6. Move the choke lever at the handlebar to the fully *open* position (**Figure 64**). Check the carburetor by-starter valve operation by attempting to move the choke lever (A, **Figure 65**) at the carburetor; the choke lever should be tight (no free play). If there is free play at the choke lever (A, **Figure 65**), perform the following:

  a. Loosen the choke cable clamp screw (B, **Figure 65**).

  b. Move the choke cable in the clamp as required so that the choke lever at the engine (A, **Figure 65**) is fully open with no free play. Tighten the clamp screw.

  c. Move the choke lever at the handlebar to the fully *closed* position (**Figure 64**). Now check that there is choke cable free play when checked between the choke lever on the carburetor (A, **Figure 65**) and the cable clamp (B, **Figure 65**). Readjust the choke cable if necessary.

7. Operate the choke lever a few times. If the choke lever still does not operate correctly, the choke cable may be damaged or stretched excessively; replace the choke cable.

8. Reinstall all parts previously removed. Make sure to route the wire harness through the guide in the lower air filter housing (**Figure 61**).

Fuel and Vacuum Line Inspection

Inspect all fuel and vacuum lines for cracks or deterioration; replace if necessary. Make sure the hose clamps are in place and holding securely.

Emission Control Hoses
(California Models)

Models sold in California are equipped with a secondary air supply and evaporative emission control system. A vacuum hose routing diagram label is attached to the air filter cover (**Figure 66**). At the intervals specified in **Table 1**, check all emission control hoses for deterioration, damage or loose connections. Also check the charcoal canister housing for damage.

NOTE
When checking the secondary air supply system, look at the hoses carefully for heat damage. If any hose has been damaged from heat, check the reed valve as described in Chapter Seven.

Replace any parts or hoses as required.

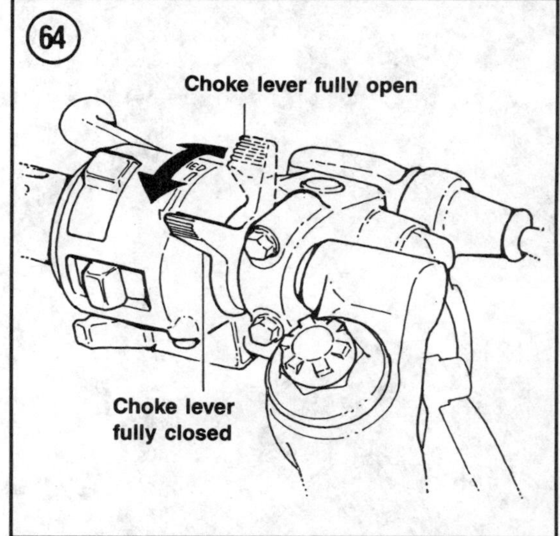

Fuel Filter

The fuel filter should be replaced at the intervals specified in **Table 1**.

> *WARNING*
> *A small amount of fuel may dribble from the hose(s) and fuel filter when performing this procedure. Because gasoline is extremely flammable and explosive, work in an area that is free of all flames or sparks. Do not allow anyone to smoke when performing this procedure.*

1. Remove the seat and disconnect the negative battery cable.
2. Remove the left-hand side cover.
3. Turn the fuel valve off.

4. Disconnect the front hose (inlet side) at the fuel filter (A, **Figure 67**). Then pull the filter's rubber stay (B, **Figure 67**) out of the frame. Slide the rubber stay off of the filter.
5. Check the filter for contamination, sludge buildup or other damage; replace the fuel filter if necessary.
6. Install a new fuel filter by performing the following:
   a. Disconnect the rear hose (outlet side) (C, **Figure 67**).
   b. Replace the hose clamps if fatigued or damaged.
   c. Slide the hose clamps onto the inlet and outlet hoses.
   d. Install a new filter so that the arrow on the filter faces toward the rear (outlet side) (C, **Figure 67**). Insert the hoses onto the filter so that the hoses go on all the way. Do not leave a gap between the hose and filter.
   e. Secure the inlet and outlet hoses with the hose clamps.
7. Reconnect the negative battery cable.
8. Turn the fuel valve on and start the engine. Check for leaks.

> *WARNING*
> *Repair any fuel leakage before riding the bike.*

9. Install the left-hand side cover.

Sidestand Inspection

The sidestand should be periodically inspected to prevent failure that could allow the bike to fall on its side or the sidestand to fall during riding.

> *CAUTION*
> *Your CBR600 is equipped with a full body fairing assembly. If the bike should fall off of the sidestand, very expensive body fairing damage will result.*

1. The sidestand is equipped with a rubber pad. When the rubber pad is worn to the wear line (arrow on pad), replace the pad (**Figure 68**) by removing the mounting bolt and sliding the pad off the sidestand. When installing a new pad, apply a small amount of Loctite 242 (blue) onto the mounting bolt; tighten the bolt securely.

2. Check the sidestand return spring as follows:
   a. Check spring for cracks or other damage.
   b. Have an assistant hold the bike upright. Then swing the sidestand up and down by hand. The sidestand should move smoothly with no binding. If the sidestand binds or moves roughly, check the stand and its mounting bracket for damage; replace worn or damaged parts as required. Tighten the sidestand bolts to the torque specifications in **Table 5**.
   c. Have an assistant hold the bike upright and swing the sidestand down. Then attach a spring scale to the sidestand (**Figure 69**) and measure the force required to pull the sidestand up. It should take approximately 2-3 kg (4.4-6.6 lb.) to pull the stand up. If the spring scale read less than the force specified, replace the return spring.

Exhaust System

Check for leakage at all fittings. Tighten all bolts and nuts; replace any gaskets as necessary. Refer to *Exhaust System* in Chapter Seven.

Air Filter Element Replacement

The air filter element should be replaced as indicated in **Table 1**.

> *NOTE*
> *The service intervals specified in **Table 1** should be followed with general use. However, the air filter element should be replaced more often if the bike is ridden in dusty areas.*

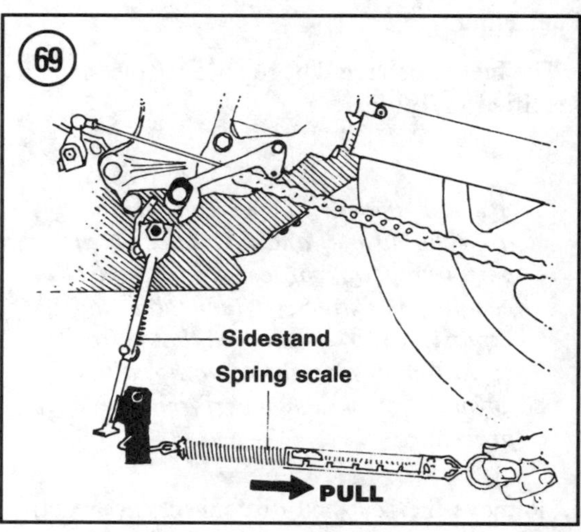

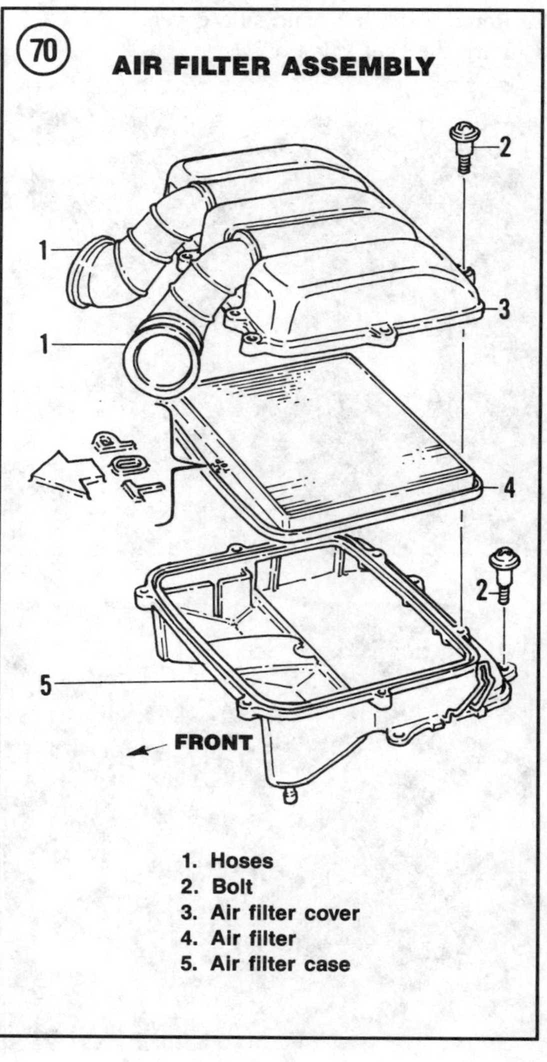

1. Hoses
2. Bolt
3. Air filter cover
4. Air filter
5. Air filter case

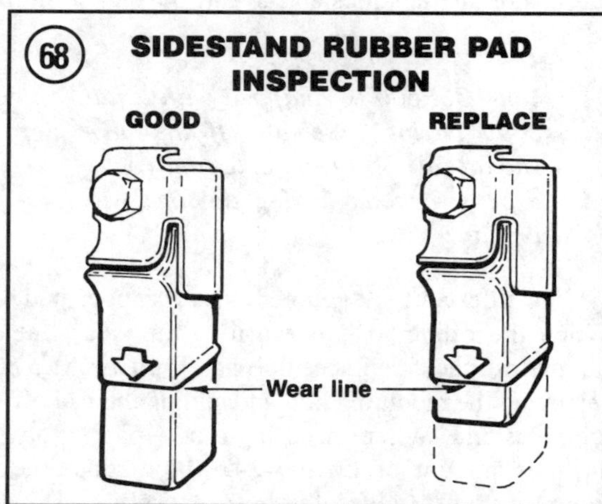

The air filter removes dust and abrasive particles from the air before the air enters the carburetors and engine. A clogged air filter element will decrease the efficiency and life of the engine. With a damaged air filter element, very fine particles could enter the engine and cause rapid wear of the piston rings, cylinder and bearings and might clog small passages in the carburetors. Never run the bike without the air filter element installed.

Refer to **Figure 70** for this procedure.

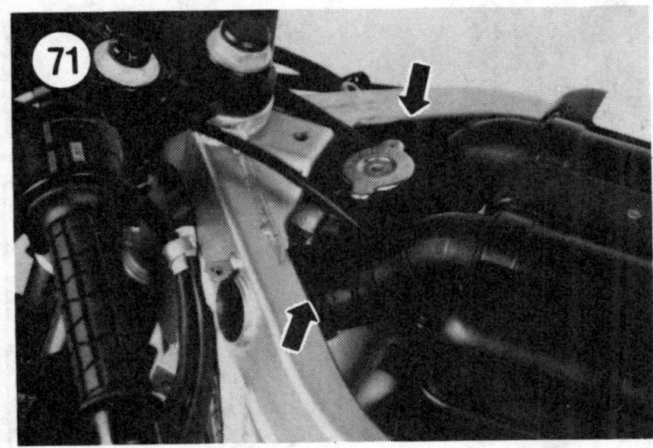

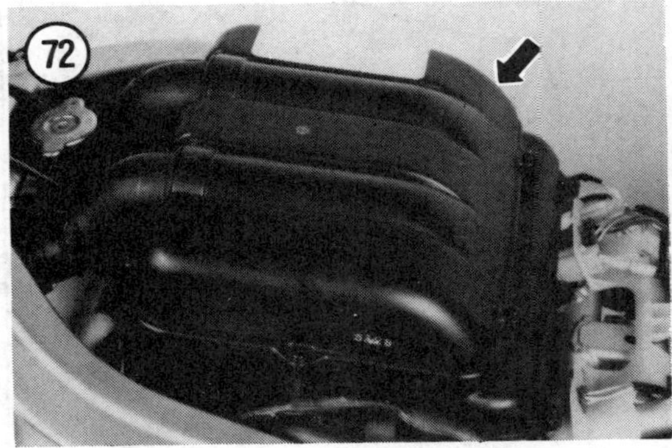

1. Remove the fuel tank as described in Chapter Seven.
2. Pull the air filter case hoses out of the frame hose joints (**Figure 71**).
3. Remove the air filter housing cover screws and lift the cover (**Figure 72**) off the housing.
4. Lift the air filter element (**Figure 73**) out of the housing.

NOTE
The intake sides of the carburetors are now exposed. If the air filter element is going to be off the housing for some time, stuff a clean, lintfree rag into each carburetor opening to prevent dropping small screws or other parts into the carburetors.

5. At the specified service intervals (**Table 1**) replace the air filter element. If the bike's mileage is between replacement intervals, check the element for damage or dirt buildup; replace the element if necessary.
6. Check the inside of the air filter housing for dust and other contamination.
7. Wipe out the interior of the air box with a damp cloth. Remove any foreign matter that may have passed through a broken element.
8. Install the air filter element so that the arrow on the element is at the top and facing to the front (**Figure 70**).
9. Install the air filter housing cover (**Figure 72**) and its screws; tighten the screws securely. Check the housing cover to make sure it is seated completely around the lower housing.
10. Connect the air filter case hoses to the frame hose joints (**Figure 71**).
11. Install the fuel tank (Chapter Seven).

Steering Play

The steering head should be checked for looseness at the intervals specified in **Table 1**. Refer to *Steering Play* in Chapter Ten.

Cooling System Inspection

At the intervals indicated in **Table 1**, the following items should be checked. If you do not have the test equipment, the tests can be done by a Honda dealer, radiator shop or service station.

1. Remove the fuel tank as described in Chapter Seven.

WARNING
Do not remove the radiator cap when the engine is hot.

2. Remove the radiator cap (**Figure 74**).
3. Have the radiator cap pressure tested (**Figure 75**). The specified radiator cap relief pressure is 0.95-1.25 kg/cm² (14-18 psi). The cap must be able to sustain this pressure for 6 seconds. Replace the radiator cap if it does not hold pressure or if the relief pressure is too high or too low.
4. Leave the radiator cap off and have the entire cooling system pressure tested (**Figure 76**). The entire cooling system should be pressurized up to, but not exceeding, 1.25 kg/cm² (18 psi). The system must be able to sustain this pressure for 6 seconds. Replace or repair any components that fail this test.

CAUTION
If test pressures exceed specifications the radiator may be damaged.

5. Test the specific gravity of the coolant with an antifreeze tester (**Figure 77**) to ensure adequate temperature and corrosion protection. Never let the mixture become less than 40% antifreeze or corrosion protection will be impaired. See **Table 8** for antifreeze protection and capacity specifications.
6. Check all cooling system hoses for damage or deterioration. Replace any hose that is questionable. Make sure all hose clamps are tight.
7. Carefully clean any road dirt, bugs, mud, etc. from the radiator core. Use a whisk broom, compressed air or low-pressure water. If the radiator has been hit by a small rock or other item, *carefully* straighten out the fins with a screwdriver.

Coolant Change

The cooling system should be completely drained and refilled at the interval indicated in **Table 1**.

CAUTION
Use only a high quality ethylene glycol antifreeze specifically labeled for use with aluminum engines. Do not use an alcohol-based antifreeze.

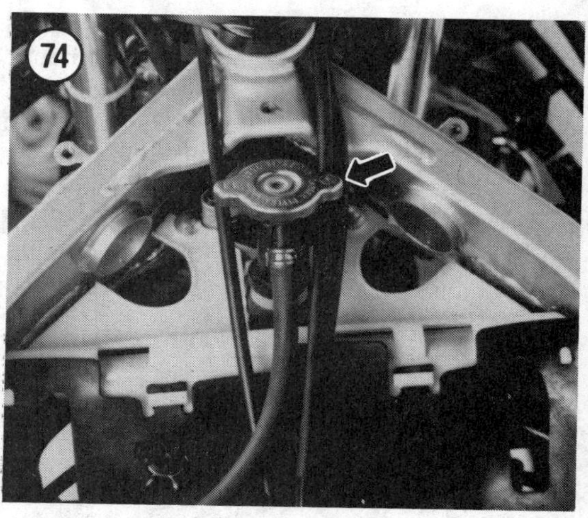

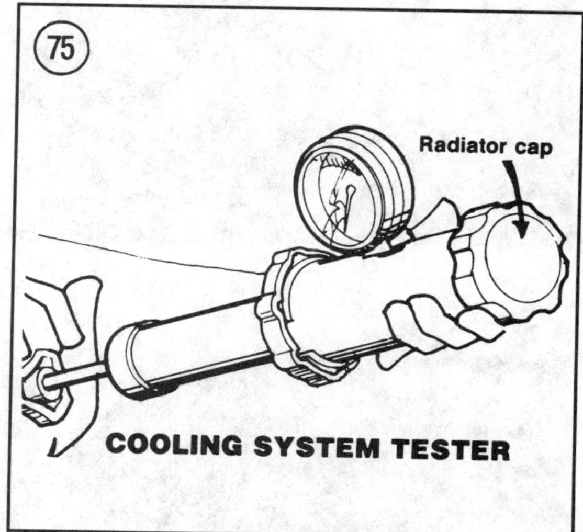

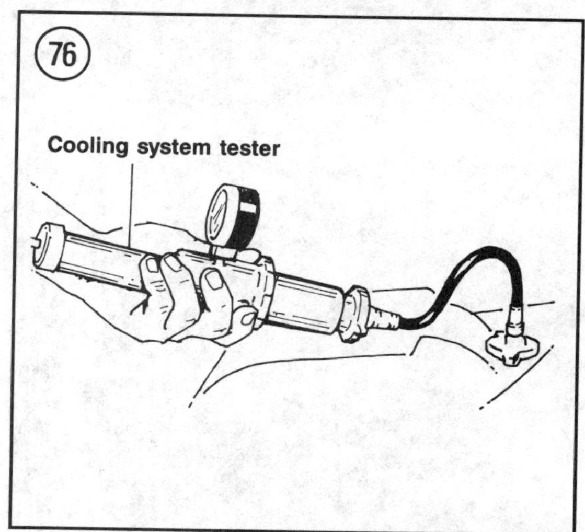

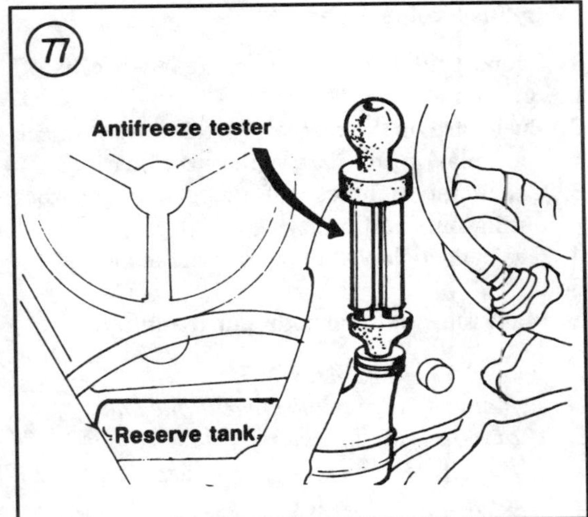

In areas where freezing temperatures occur, add a higher percentage of antifreeze to protect the system to temperatures far below those likely to occur. **Table 8** lists the recommended amount of antifreeze for protection. The following procedure must be performed when the engine is *cool*.

> *CAUTION*
> *Be careful not to spill antifreeze on painted surfaces as it will destroy the surface. Wash immediately with soapy water and rinse thoroughly with clean water.*

1. Support the bike so that it is level with both tires on the ground.
2. Remove the fuel tank as described in Chapter Seven.

> *WARNING*
> *Do not remove the radiator cap when the engine is hot.*

3. Remove the radiator cap (**Figure 74**).
4. Remove the lower fairings. See Chapter Thirteen.
5. Place a drain pan under the frame on the left-hand side of the bike under the water pump. Remove the drain screw (**Figure 78**) and sealing washer on the water pump.
6. Place a drain pan under the front of the engine. Remove the cylinder drain screws (**Figure 79**) and sealing washers.
7. Allow the coolant to completely drain into the drain pans.
8. If necessary, remove the coolant reservoir tank as described in Chapter Nine and drain the tank. Reinstall the tank.
9. Reinstall the drain screw and sealing washer on the water pump cover (**Figure 78**). Tighten the drain screw securely.
10. Reinstall the drain screws and sealing washers on the cylinder (**Figure 79**). Tighten the drain screws securely.

> *NOTE*
> *When filling the radiator in Step 11, have an assistant lean the bike from side to side. This step will release air bubbles in the coolant mixture. Continue until the radiator is full.*

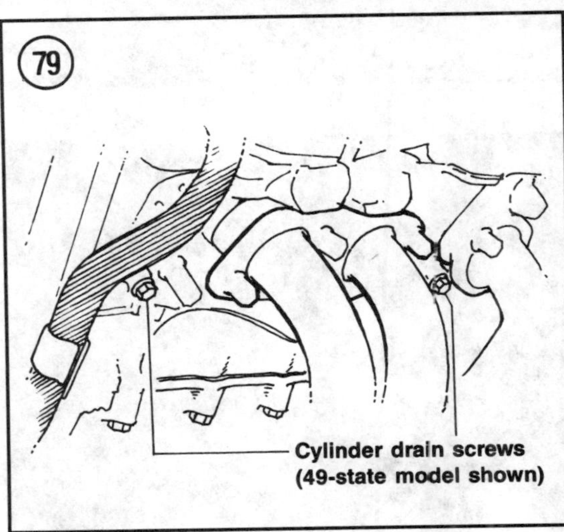

11. Pour coolant through the radiator filler neck (**Figure 80**) very slowly. Use the recommended mixture of antifreeze and distilled water. See **Table 8**. Fill to the radiator filler neck (just below the reservoir tank tube opening).

12. Fill the reserve tank (**Figure 81**) to the UPPER level mark.

13. After filling the radiator, bleed the cooling system as follows:

  a. Start the engine and bring the idle up to 4,000-5,000 rpm.

  b. Snap the throttle a few times. When the radiator coolant level drops, add coolant to bring the level to the filler neck.

  c. When the radiator coolant level has stabilized, perform Step 14.

14. Install the radiator cap (**Figure 74**). Turn the radiator cap clockwise to the first stop. Then, push the cap down and turn it clockwise until it stops.

15. Start the engine and let it run at idle speed until the engine reaches normal operating temperature. Make sure there are no air bubbles in the coolant and that the coolant level stabilizes at the correct level. Add coolant as necessary.

16. Add coolant to the reservoir tank (**Figure 81**) to correct the level.

17. Install the lower fairings (Chapter Thirteen).

18. Test ride the bike and readjust the coolant level in the reservoir tank if necessary.

Front Headlight Aim

At the intervals in **Table 1**, check the front headlight aim as described in Chapter Eight. Adjust the headlight beam as specified by local regulations.

Front Suspension Check

1. Apply the front brake and pump the fork up and down as vigorously as possible. Check for smooth operation and check for any oil leaks.

2. Make sure the upper and lower steering stem bolts are tight.

3. Check that the front axle pinch bolt is tight.

4. Check that the front axle nut is tight.

> *WARNING*
> *If any of the previously mentioned bolts and nuts are loose, refer to Chapter Ten for correct procedures and torque specifications.*

Rear Suspension Check

1. Support the bike so that the rear wheel is off the ground.

2. Push hard on the rear wheel sideways to check for side play in the rear swing arm bearings.

3. Check the tightness of the shock absorber mounting nuts and bolts.

4. Check the tightness of the rear brake torque arm bolts.

5. Make sure the rear axle nut is tight.

> *WARNING*
> *If any of the previously mentioned nuts or bolts are loose, refer to Chapter Eleven for correct procedures and torque specifications.*

Nuts, Bolts and Other Fasteners

Constant vibration can loosen many fasteners on a motorcycle. Check the tightness of all fasteners, especially those on:

  a. Engine mounting hardware.

  b. Engine crankcase covers.

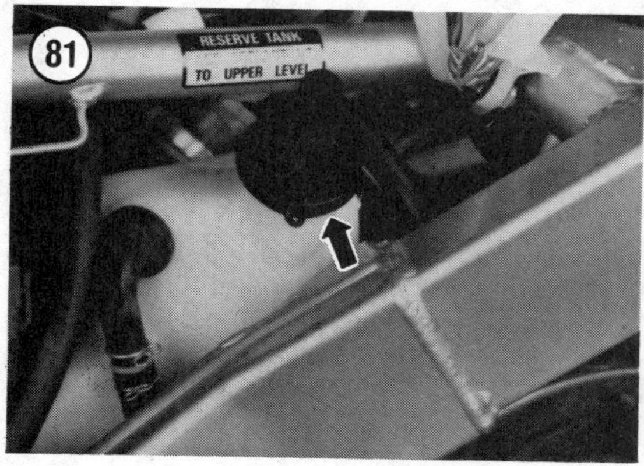

c. Handlebars and front forks.
d. Gearshift lever.
e. Sprocket bolts and nuts.
f. Brake pedal and lever.
g. Exhaust system.
h. Lighting equipment.

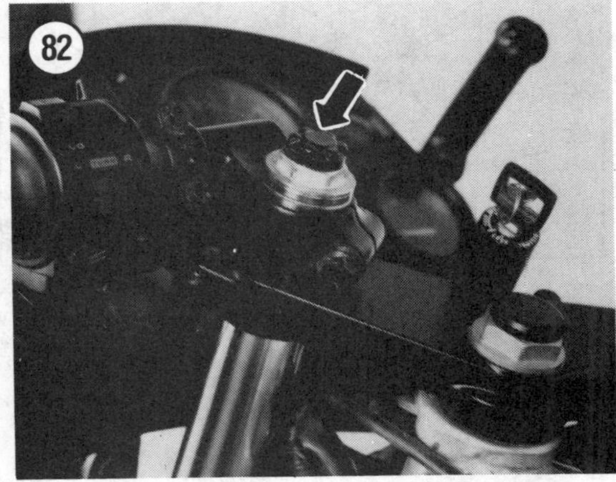

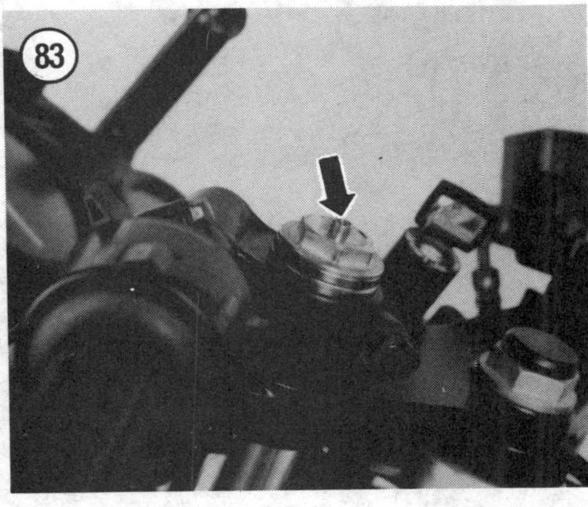

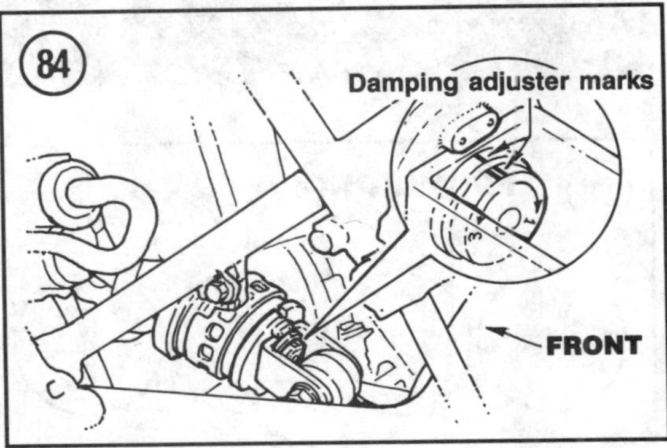

SUSPENSION ADJUSTMENT

Front Fork Air Adjustment

Both the fork springs and air pressure support the motorcycle and rider. Air pressure should be measured when the forks are cold.

The air pressure can be varied to suit the load and your ride preference. Don't use a high-pressure hose or bottle to pressurize the forks; a tire pump is a lot closer to the scale you need. Note the following when adjusting the front fork air pressure:

a. Increase air pressure for heavy loads.
b. If the suspension is too hard, reduce air pressure.
c. If the suspension is too soft, increase air pressure.

1. Support the bike with the front wheel off the ground.
2. Unscrew the air valve cap (**Figure 82**) from each fork tube.
3. Connect a pump to the air valve (**Figure 83**) and pump the forks to the desired air pressure within the limits listed in **Table 7**.

> *CAUTION*
> *Do not exceed the air pressure in **Table 7**.*

> *NOTE*
> *Each application of a pressure gauge bleeds off some air pressure in the process of applying and removing the gauge.*

4. Install the air valve caps.

Rear Shock Absorber Adjustment

The Honda rear shock absorber can be adjusted for damping and spring preload.

Damping adjustment

The damping can be adjusted to 3 different positions to best suit riding, load and speed conditions. **Table 9** lists adjuster positions in relation to various road and riding conditions.

The damping is changed by turning the adjuster (**Figure 84**) at the end of the shock absorber. Align the adjuster number with the mark on the shock (**Figure 84**) in one of the 3 positions listed in **Table 9**.

Spring preload

The spring preload adjuster has 7 different positions (Figure 85) to suit riding and load conditions. Adjustment positions 1-3 are for light load conditions; positions 4-7 increase spring preload for higher load conditions. The hook spanner tool enclosed in the tool kit (**Figure 86**) should be used to adjust the rear shock.

1. Remove the left-hand side cover.
2. Using the hook spanner, turn the spring preload adjuster (**Figure 85**) to the desired shock position.
3. Install the left-hand side cover and test ride the bike.

TUNE-UP

A complete tune-up restores performance and power that is lost due to normal wear and deterioration of engine parts. Because engine wear occurs over a combined period of time and mileage, the engine tune-up should be performed at the intervals specified in **Table 1**. More frequent tune-ups may be required if the bike is ridden primarily in stop-and-go traffic or used in competition.

The Vehicle Emission Control Information label is attached to the frame behind the right-hand side cover (**Figure 87**). The VECI label lists tune-up information for your model. **Table 10** lists tune-up specifications for all Honda CBR600 models.

> *NOTE*
> *Always refer to the tune-up specifications on your bike's Vehicle Emission Control Information label if available. If specifications on the label differ from those in* **Table 10**, *use the information listed on the label.*

Before starting a tune-up procedure, make sure to have all the necessary new parts on hand.

Because different systems in an engine interact, the procedures should be done in the following order:

a. Clean or replace the air filter element.
b. Adjust valve clearances.
c. Check engine compression.

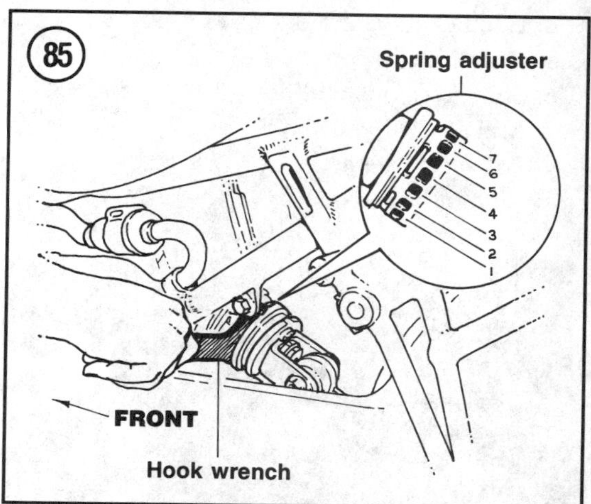

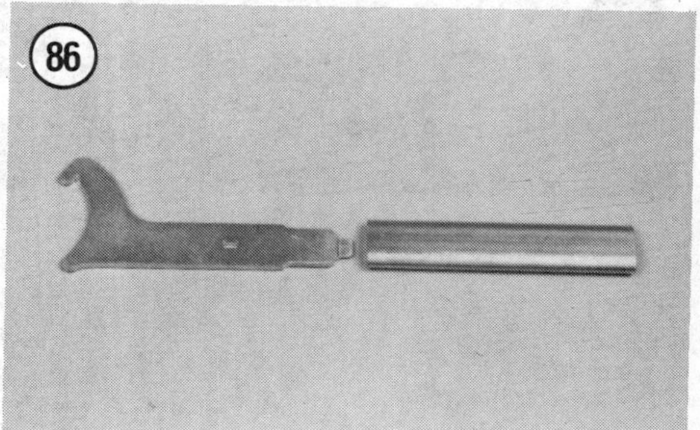

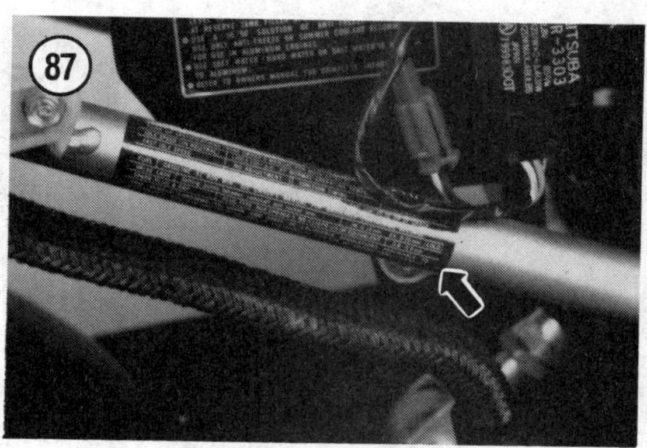

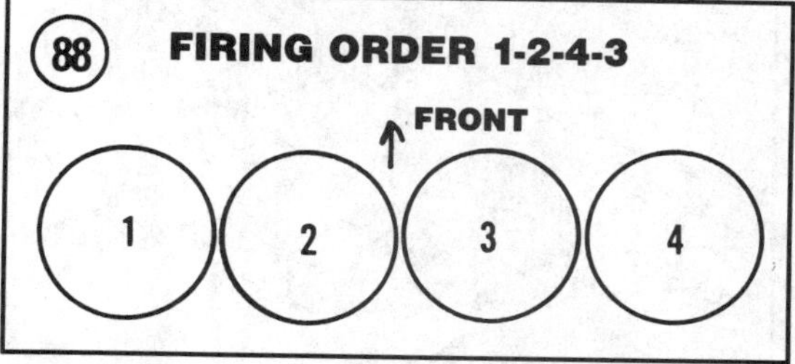

d. Check or replace the spark plugs.
e. Check the ignition timing.
f. Synchronize carburetors and set idle speed.

Tools

To perform a tune-up on your Honda, you will need the following tools:
a. Spark plug wrench.
b. Socket wrench and assorted sockets.
c. Flat feeler gauge.
d. Honda valve tappet locknut wrench (part No. 07GMA-ML70120) or equivalent.
e. Honda valve tappet adjusting driver (part No. 07GMA-ML70110) or equivalent.
f. Compression gauge.
g. Spark plug wire feeler gauge and gapper tool.

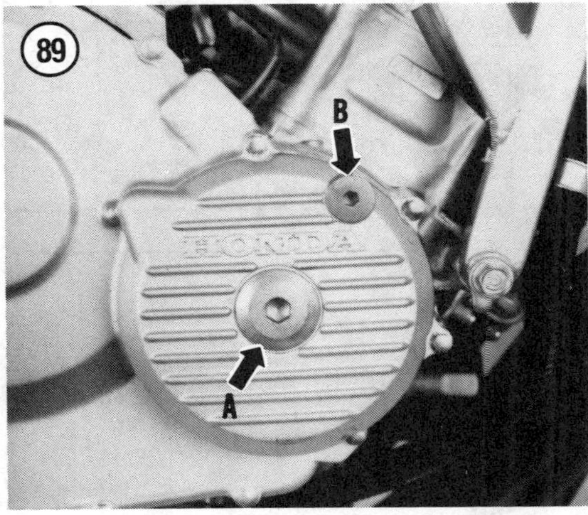

h. Ignition timing light.
i. Carburetor synchronization tool—to measure manifold vacuum.

Firing Order

The cylinder firing order for all Honda CBR600 engines is 1-2-4-3. Cylinder No. 1 is on the left-hand side (**Figure 88**).

Air Filter Element

The air filter element should be cleaned or replaced before doing other tune-up procedures. Refer to *Air Filter* in this chapter.

Valve Clearance

CAUTION
Valve clearance check and adjustment must be performed with the engine cool, at room temperature (below 35° C/95° F).

1. Remove the cylinder head cover. Refer to *Cylinder Head Cover Removal/Installation* in Chapter Four.
2. Remove the spark plugs as described in this chapter. This will make it easier to turn the engine by hand.

NOTE
After removing the spark plugs, stuff clean, lintfree shop rags into the spark plug tunnels to prevent dropping small screws or other objects into the cylinder.

3. Remove the crankshaft hole cap (A) and the timing hole cap (B) from the right-hand crankcase cover. See **Figure 89**.

NOTE
The cylinders are numbered 1-4, starting with the left cylinder and reading left to right (Figure 88).

4. Turn the crankshaft clockwise with the bolt on the end of the crankshaft (**Figure 90**) until the "T" mark on the flywheel is aligned with the timing mark on the right-hand crankcase cover (**Figure 91**).

5. Check the position of the camshaft sprocket timing marks; they should be aligned with the cylinder head upper surface as shown in **Figure 92**. Now check the position of the No. 4 cylinder camshaft lobes. They should face to the *outside* as shown in **Figure 92**. If the lobes are positioned correctly, proceed to Step 6. If the camshaft lobes face in, rotate the crankshaft 360° as described in Step 4 and align the "T" mark on the flywheel with the right-hand crankcase cover timing mark (**Figure 91**). The camshaft timing marks should be aligned with the cylinder head surface and the No. 4 camshaft lobes should face to the *outside* (**Figure 92**). Proceed to Step 6.

6. Insert a feeler gauge (**Figure 93**) between the following rocker arms and camshaft (**Figure 94**):
   a. No. 2 intake valves only.
   b. No. 3 exhaust valves only.
   c. No. 4 intake and exhaust valves.

The correct valve clearance is listed in **Table 10**. The clearance is measured correctly when there is a slight drag on the feeler gauge when it is inserted and withdrawn. If the clearance is within tolerance, go on to Step 8. If adjustment is required, continue with Step 7.

> *NOTE*
> *Valve adjustment requires the Honda tappet lock nut wrench (part No. 07GMA-ML70120) and the Honda tappet adjusting driver (part No. 07GMA-ML70110) or equivalent.*

7. See **Figure 95**. Adjust by loosening the adjuster locknut (**Figure 93**) and turning the adjuster as required to get the proper clearance. Hold the adjuster steady and tighten the locknut securely. Check that the locknut is tightened securely.

8. Turn the crankshaft clockwise 360° and align the "T" mark on the flywheel with the right-hand crankcase cover timing mark (**Figure 91**). The camshaft timing marks should be aligned with the cylinder head surface and the No. 4 camshaft lobes should face to the *inside*.

9. Insert a feeler gauge (**Figure 93**) between the following rocker arms and camshaft (**Figure 96**):
   a. No. 1 intake and exhaust valves.
   b. No. 2 exhaust valves only.
   c. No. 3 intake valves only.

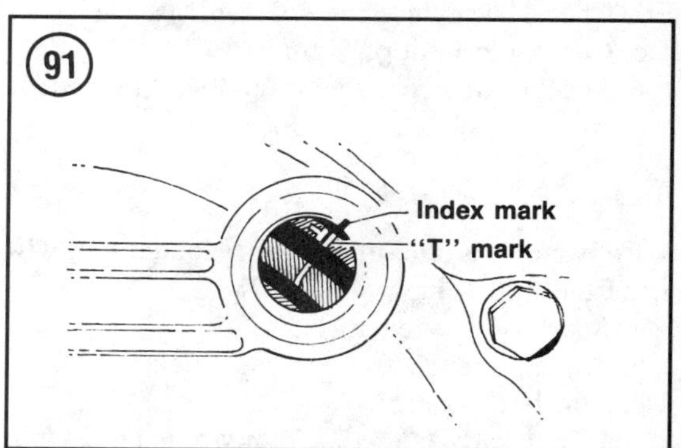

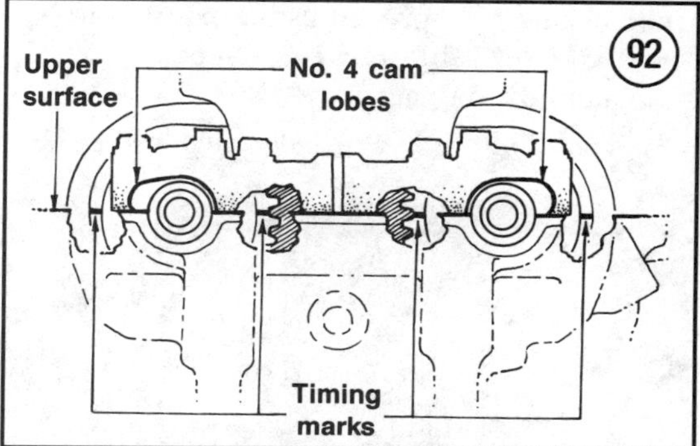

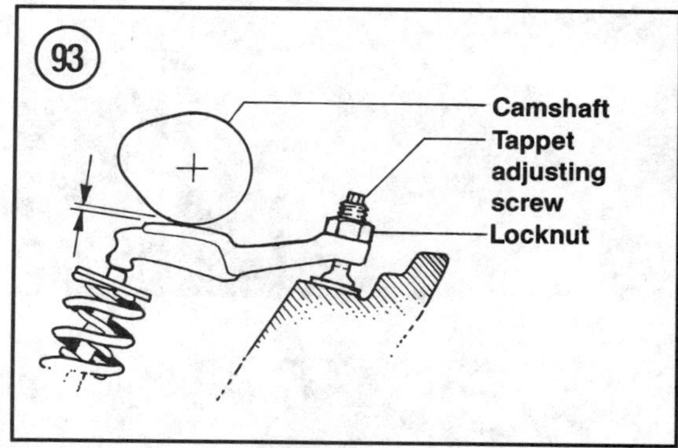

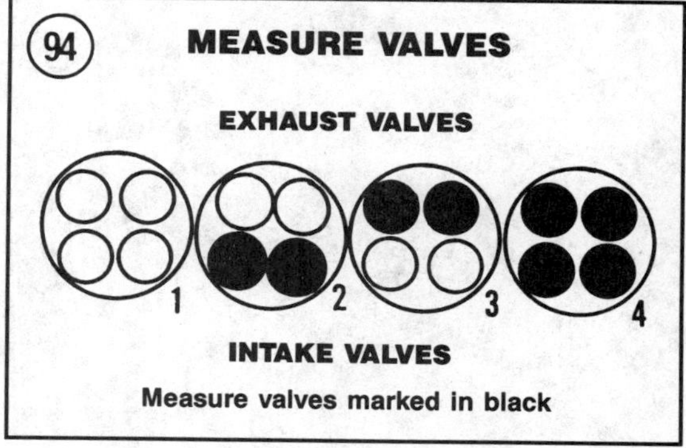

The correct valve clearance is listed in **Table 10**. The clearance is measured correctly when there is a slight drag on the feeler gauge when it is inserted and withdrawn. If the clearance is within tolerance, go on to Step 10. If adjustment is required, adjust as described in Step 7.

10. Reinstall the spark plugs.

11. Refer to **Figure 89**. Make sure an O-ring is installed on each cap. Install the crankshaft hole cap (A) and the timing hole cap (B) on the right-hand crankcase cover.

12. Install the cylinder head cover. Refer to *Cylinder Head Cover Removal/Installation* in Chapter Four.

Compression Test

At every tune-up, check cylinder compression. Record the results and compare them at the next check. A running record will show trends in deterioration so that corrective action can be taken before complete failure.

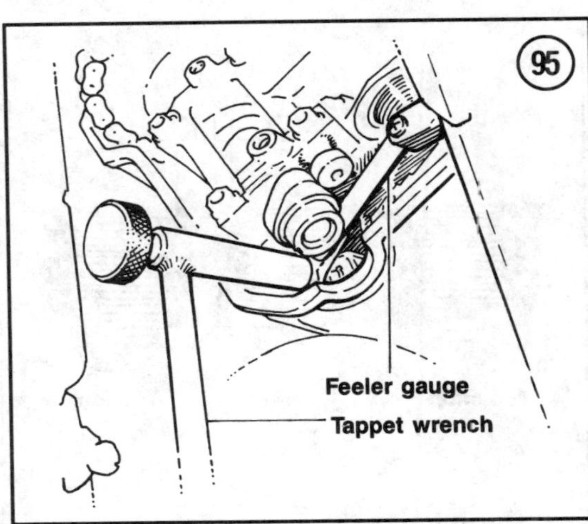

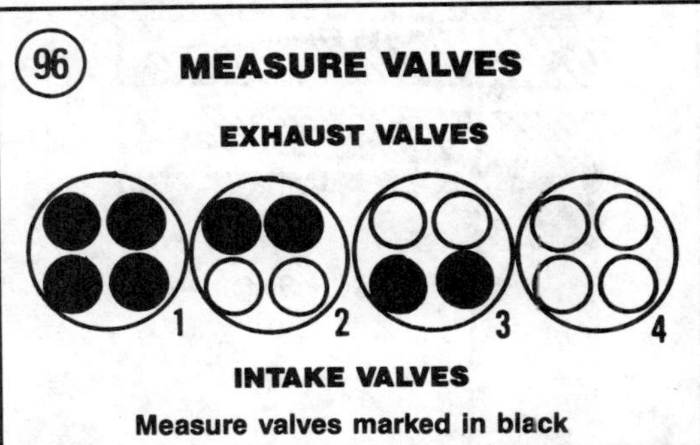

The results, when properly interpreted, can indicate general cylinder, piston ring and valve condition.

> *NOTE*
> *The valves must be properly adjusted to correctly interpret the results of this test.*

1. Warm the engine to normal operating temperature. Ensure that the choke valve is completely open and that the engine stop switch is in the OFF position.

2. Remove all spark plugs from cylinders as described in this chapter.

> *NOTE*
> *A screw-in type compression gauge with a flexible adapter is required for this procedure. See **Compression Gauge** in Chapter One. Before using the gauge, check that the rubber gasket on the end of the adapter is not cracked or damaged; the gasket seals the cylinder to ensure accurate compression readings.*

3. Connect the compression gauge to one cylinder following manufacturer's instructions. Lubricate the adapter threads with engine oil to prevent damaging the spark plug threads.

4. Open the throttle *completely* and, using the starter, crank the engine over until there is no further rise in pressure. Maximum pressure is usually reached within 4-7 seconds of engine cranking.

> *CAUTION*
> *Do not turn the engine over more than absolutely necessary. When spark plug leads are disconnected, the electronic ignition will produce the highest voltage possible and the coils may overheat and be damaged.*

5. Remove the gauge and record the reading.

6. Repeat Steps 3-5 for the remaining cylinders.

7. When interpreting the results, actual readings are not as important as the difference between the readings. Standard compression pressure is specified in **Table 10**. Greater differences indicate worn or broken rings, leaky or sticky valves, blown head gasket or a combination of these.

a. If compression reading does not differ between cylinders by more than 10 psi, the rings and valves are in good condition.

b. If a low reading (10% or more) is obtained on one of the cylinders, it indicates valve or ring trouble. To determine which, pour about a teaspoon of engine oil through the spark plug hole onto the top of the piston. Turn the engine over once to clear some of the excess oil, then take another compression test and record the reading. If the compression returns to normal, the valves are good but the rings are defective on that cylinder. If compression does not increase, the valves require servicing. A valve could be hanging open or burned, or a piece of carbon could be on a valve seat.

NOTE
If the compression is low, the engine cannot be tuned to maximum performance. The worn parts must be replaced and the engine rebuilt.

Correct Spark Plug Heat Range

Spark plugs are available in various heat ranges that are hotter or colder than the spark plugs originally installed at the factory.

Select plugs in a heat range designed for the loads and temperature conditions under which the engine will operate. Using incorrect heat ranges, however, can cause piston seizure, scored cylinder walls or damaged piston crowns.

In general, use a hotter plug for low speeds, low loads and low temperatures. Use a colder plug for high speeds, high engine loads and high temperatures.

NOTE
In areas where seasonal temperature variations are great, the factory recommends a "two-plug system"—a cold plug for hard summer riding and a hot plug for slower winter operation—which may prevent spark plug and engine problems.

The reach (length) of a plug (**Figure 97**) is also important. A longer than normal plug could interfere with the valves and pistons, causing permanent and severe damage. The standard heat range spark plugs are listed in **Table 10**.

Spark Plug Removal/Cleaning

A spark plug can be used to help determine the operating condition of its cylinder when properly read. As each spark plug is removed, label it with its cylinder number.

1. Remove the left- and right-hand side maintenance covers. See Chapter Thirteen.

2. The spark plug caps form a tight seal on the plugs. Grab the caps and twist from side to side to break their seal. Then pull the cap off of the spark plug. Do not remove the cap by pulling on the spark plug wire.

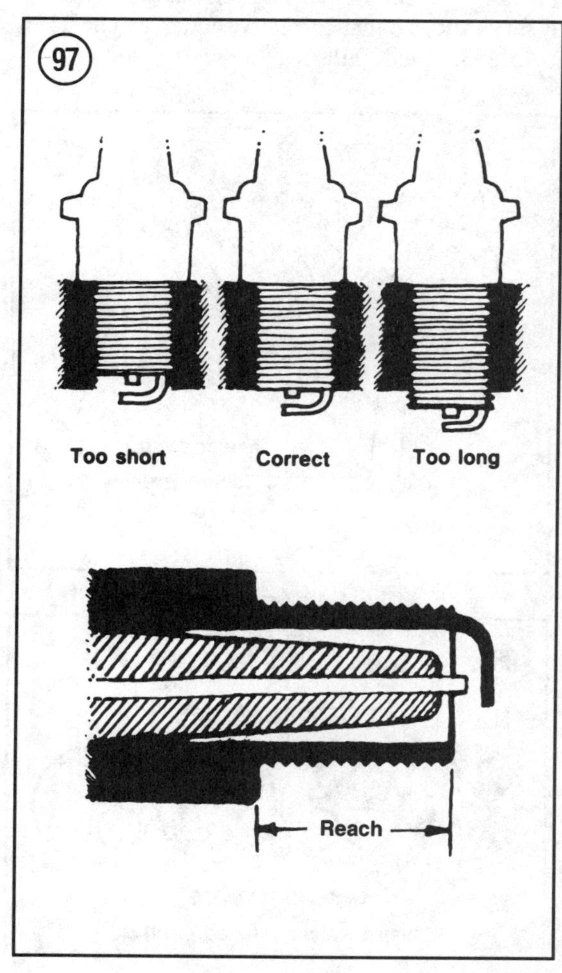

3. Using compressed air, clean the spark plug tunnel in the cylinder head of all dirt and debris.

CAUTION
The dirt collected in this area could fall into the cylinders when the plugs are removed and cause serious engine damage.

4. Remove the spark plugs with the plug socket and wrench furnished in the Honda tool kit.

NOTE
If plugs are difficult to remove, apply penetrating oil, like WD-40 or Liquid Wrench, around base of plugs and let it soak in for about 10-20 minutes.

5. Inspect the spark plugs carefully. Look for plugs with broken center porcelain, excessively eroded electrodes and excessive carbon or oil fouling. Replace such plugs. See **Figure 98**.

CAUTION
Spark plug cleaning with the use of a sand-blast type device is not recommended. While this type of cleaning is thorough, the plug must be perfectly free of all abrasive cleaning material when done. If not, it is possible for the cleaning material to fall into the engine during operation and cause damage.

Gapping and Installing the Plugs

New plugs should be carefully gapped to ensure a reliable, consistent spark. You must use a special spark plug gapping tool with a wire gauge.
1. Remove the new plugs from the box. Do *not* screw in the small pieces that are loose in each box (**Figure 99**); they are not used.
2. Insert a wire gauge between the center and the side electrode of each plug (**Figure 100**). The correct gap is found in **Table 10**. If the gap is correct, you will feel a slight drag as you pull the wire through. If there is no drag, or the gauge won't pass through, bend the side electrode *with the gapping tool* (**Figure 101**) to set the proper gap (**Table 10**).
3. Put a small drop of anti-seize on the threads of each spark plug.
4. Make sure a washer is installed on each spark plug.
5. Screw each spark plug in by hand until it seats. Very little effort is required. If force is necessary, you have the plug cross-threaded; unscrew it and try again.

CAUTION
Do not overtighten. Besides making the plug difficult to remove, the excessive torque will squash the gasket and destroy its sealing ability.

6. Tighten the spark plugs to the torque specification in **Table 5**. If you don't have a torque wrench, an additional 1/4 to 1/2 turn is sufficient after the gasket has made contact with the head. If you are reinstalling old, regapped plugs and are reusing the old gasket, tighten only an additional 1/4 turn.
7. Install each spark plug wire. Make sure it goes to the correct spark plug.
8. Install the maintenance covers (Chapter Thirteen). Insert the spark plug socket and wrench back into the tool kit.

Reading Spark Plugs

Much information about engine and spark plug performance can be determined by careful examination of the spark plugs. This information is only valid after performing the following steps.
1. Ride bike a short distance at full throttle in any gear.
2. Turn off kill switch before closing throttle, and simultaneously, pull in clutch and coast to a stop. Do *not* downshift transmission in stopping.
3. Remove spark plugs and examine them. Compare them to **Figure 98**.

SPARK PLUG CONDITION

NORMAL

- Identified by light tan or gray deposits on the firing tip.
- Can be cleaned.

GAP BRIDGED

- Identified by deposit buildup closing gap between electrodes.
- Caused by oil or carbon fouling. If deposits are not excessive, the plug can be cleaned.

OIL FOULED

- Identified by wet black deposits on the insulator shell bore and electrodes.
- Caused by excessive oil entering combustion chamber through worn rings and pistons, excessive clearance between valve guides and stems, or worn or loose bearings. Can be cleaned. If engine is not repaired, use a hotter plug.

CARBON FOULED

- Identified by black, dry fluffy carbon deposits on insulator tips, exposed shell surfaces and electrodes.
- Caused by too cold a plug, weak ignition, dirty air cleaner, too rich a fuel mixture, or excessive idling. Can be cleaned.

LEAD FOULED

- Identified by dark gray, black, yellow, or tan deposits or a fused glazed coating on the insulator tip.
- Caused by highly leaded gasoline. Can be cleaned.

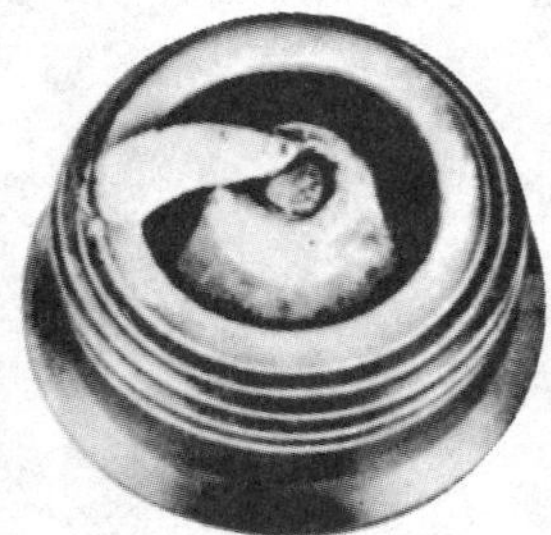

WORN

- Identified by severely eroded or worn electrodes.
- Caused by normal wear. Should be replaced.

FUSED SPOT DEPOSIT

- Identified by melted or spotty deposits resembling bubbles or blisters.
- Caused by sudden acceleration. Can be cleaned.

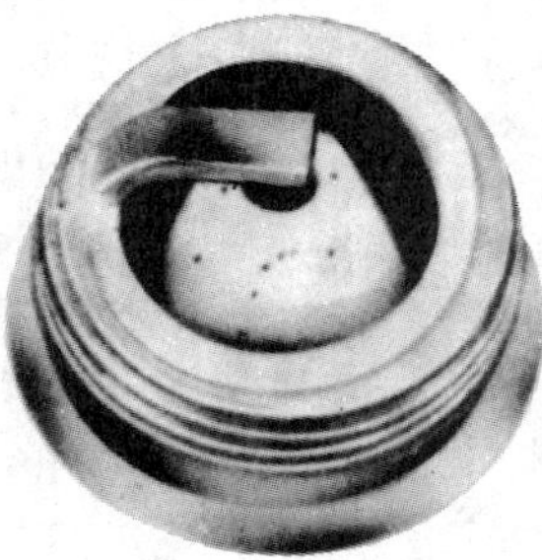

OVERHEATING

- Identified by a white or light gray insulator with small black or gray brown spots and with bluish-burnt appearance of electrodes.
- Caused by engine overheating, wrong type of fuel, loose spark plugs, too hot a plug, or incorrect ignition timing. Replace the plug.

PREIGNITION

- Identified by melted electrodes and possibly blistered insulator. Metallic deposits on insulator indicate engine damage.
- Caused by wrong type of fuel, incorrect ignition timing or advance, too hot a plug, burned valves, or engine overheating. Replace the plug.

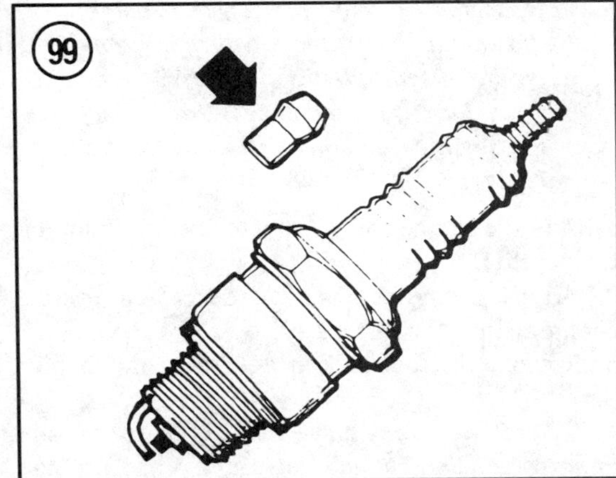

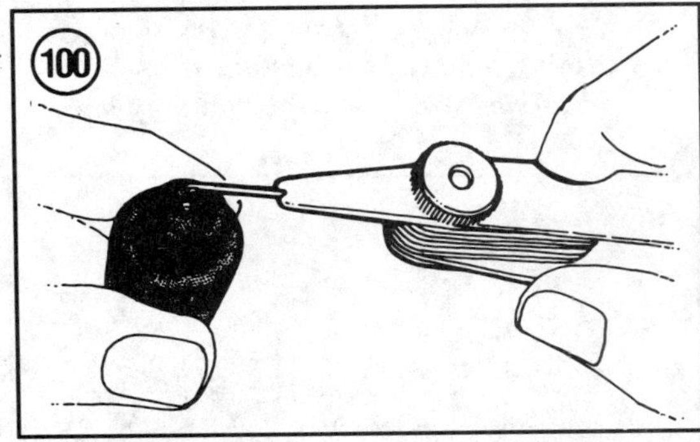

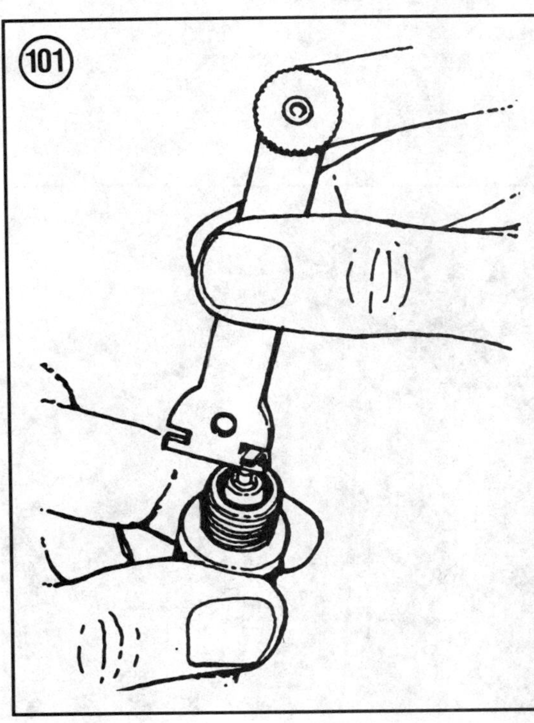

If the insulator tip is white or burned, the plug is too hot and should be replaced with a colder one.

A too-cold plug will have sooty deposits ranging in color from dark brown to black. Replace with a hotter plug and check for too-rich carburetion or evidence of oil blowby at the piston rings.

If any one plug is found unsatisfactory, replace all 4.

IGNITION TIMING

The models covered in this manual are equipped with a capacitor discharge ignition (CDI) system. This system uses no breaker points and is non-adjustable. The timing should be checked to make sure all ignition components are operating correctly.

Incorrect ignition timing can cause a drastic loss of engine performance and efficiency. It may also cause overheating.

Before starting on this procedure, check all electrical connections related to the ignition system. Make sure all connections are tight and free of corrosion and that all ground connections are tight. Refer to *Ignition System* in Chapter Eight.

1. Start the engine and let it reach normal operating temperature. Shut the engine off.
2. Remove the timing hole cap (B, **Figure 89**) from the right-hand crankcase cover.
3. Connect a portable tachometer following the manufacturer's instructions. The bike's tachometer is not accurate enough in the low rpm range for this adjustment.
4. Connect a timing light to the No. 1 spark plug following the manufacturer's instructions.
5. Start the engine and let it idle at the idle speed listed in **Table 10**.
6. Aim the timing light at the timing hole in the right-hand crankcase and pull the trigger. If the "F" mark aligns with the index mark on the crankcase (**Figure 102**), the timing is correct. Now increase engine rpm and note the "F" timing mark; it should begin to rotate counterclockwise.
7. Turn the engine off and connect the timing light to the No. 2 spark plug and repeat Step 6.
8. If the timing is incorrect, refer to *Ignition System Troubleshooting* in Chapter Two. There is no method of adjusting ignition timing.
9. Shut off the engine and disconnect the timing light and portable tachometer.
10. Install the timing hole cap with its O-ring.

CARBURETOR

Idle Speed

Proper idle speed setting is necessary to prevent stalling and to provide adequate engine compression braking, but you can't set it perfectly with the bike's tachometer—it's not accurate at the low rpm range. A portable tachometer is required for this procedure.

1. Remove the left-hand maintenance cover as described in Chapter Thirteen.
2. Attach a portable tachometer, following the manufacturer's instructions.
3. Start the engine and warm it to normal operating temperature.
4. Sit on the seat while the engine is idling. Turn the front wheel from side to side without touching the throttle grip. If the engine speed increases when the wheel is turned, the throttle cable(s) may be damaged or incorrectly adjusted. Perform the *Throttle Cable Adjustment* as described in this chapter.
5. Turn the throttle stop screw (A, **Figure 103**) to set the idle speed as specified in **Table 10**.
6. Rev the engine a couple of times to see if it settles down to the set speed. Readjust, if necessary.
7. Remove all test equipment and install the maintenance cover.

Carburetor Synchronization

When the carburetors are properly synchronized the engine will warm up faster and there will be an improvement in throttle response, performance and mileage.

Before synchronizing the carburetors, the air filter element must be clean and valve clearances must be properly adjusted. The ignition timing must also be checked to make sure that all components are operating correctly.

This procedure requires special tools. You will need a mercury manometer (carb-synch tool). This is a tool that measures the manifold vacuum for all 4 cylinders simultaneously. A carb-synch tool can be purchased from a Honda dealer or mail order firm.

> *CAUTION*
> *When purchasing this tool, check that it is equipped with restrictors. These restrictors keep the mercury from being drawn into the engine when engine rpm is increased during the adjustment procedure. If the mercury is drawn into the engine the tool will have to be replaced.*

1. Start the engine and warm it to normal operating temperature.
2. Adjust the idle speed as described in this chapter. Shut the engine off.
3. Remove the fuel tank as described in Chapter Seven.
4. Install an auxiliary fuel tank onto the motorcycle and attach its fuel hose to the carburetor.

> *NOTE*
> *Carburetor synchronization cannot be performed with the stock fuel tank in*

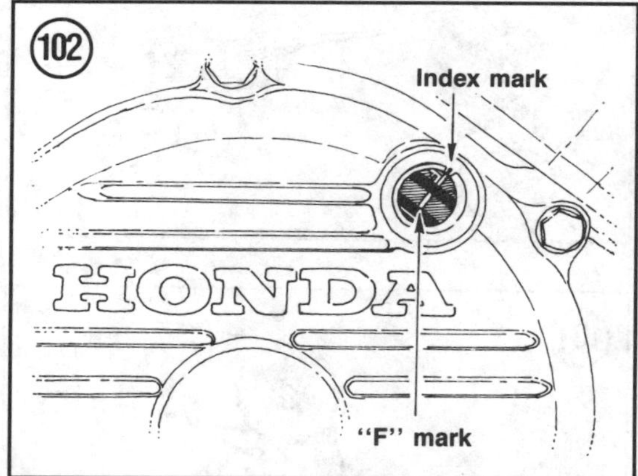

place because of the lack of room required to install the gauges and make adjustments. An auxiliary fuel tank is required to supply fuel to the carburetors during this procedure.

NOTE
Fuel tanks from small displacement motorcycles and ATV's make excellent auxiliary fuel tanks. Make sure the tank is mounted securely and positioned so

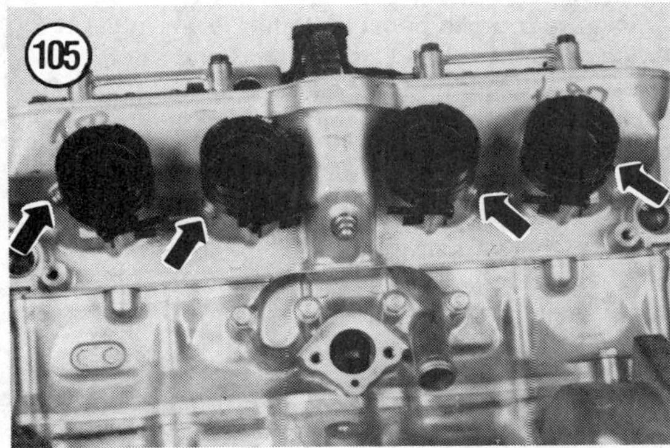

that the connecting fuel hose is not kinked or obstructed.

WARNING
When supplying fuel by temporary means, make sure the fuel tank is secure and that all fuel lines are tight—no leaks.

NOTE
The vacuum plugs being removed in Step 5 consist of a Phillips screw and flat washer.

5A. *49-state models:* Remove the 4 Phillips head vacuum plugs from the cylinder head ports. See B, **Figure 103**.

5B. *California models:* Remove the Phillips head vacuum plugs from the cylinder head ports and disconnect the vacuum hose(s) from the boost joint(s). Refer to **Figure 104** and **Figure 105**.

NOTE
***Figure 105** shows the vacuum plugs and boost joint(s) on a California model with the engine removed for clarity.*

6. Connect the vacuum lines from the carb-synch tool, following the manufacturer's instructions. Be sure to route the vacuum lines to the correct cylinder. Most carb-synch tools have the cylinder number indicated on them next to each tube containing mercury.

NOTE
The No. 2 carburetor has no synchronization screw; the other 3 carburetors must be synchronized to it.

7. Start the engine and let it idle at the speed listed in **Table 10**.

8. If the difference in gauge readings is 40 mm Hg (1.6 in. Hg) or less among all 4 cylinders, the carburetors are considered synchronized. If not, proceed as follows.

NOTE
***Figure 106** is shown with the carburetor assembly removed for clarity. Do not remove the carburetor assembly to perform this procedure.*

9. Remove the air filter case cover (**Figure 107**). Do not remove the air filter element.

10. Turn the adjusting screws and adjust the No. 1, 3 and 4 carburetors to have the same gauge readings as the No. 2 carburetor.

NOTE
To gain the utmost in performance and efficiency from the engine, adjust the carburetors so that the gauge readings are as close to each other as possible.

11. Reset the idle speed and stop the engine.
12. Disconnect the carb-synch tool vacuum lines.
13. Install the vacuum plugs or reconnect the hose(s). Make sure the plugs and hose(s) are tight to prevent a vacuum leak.
14. Install the fuel tank.

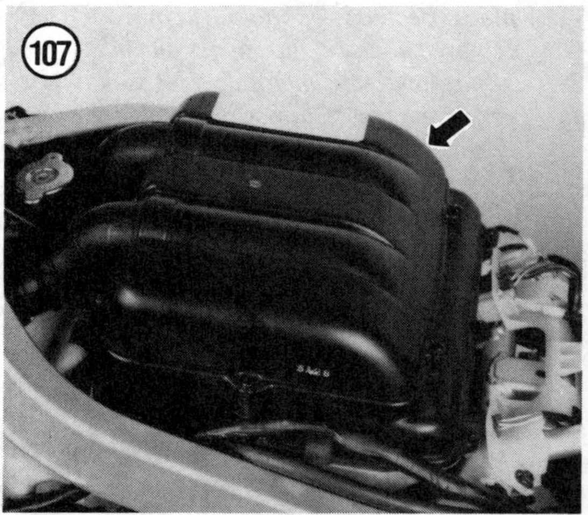

Table 1 SERVICE INTERVALS*

Initial 600 miles (1,000 km)**	Check valve clearance Replace engine oil and filter Check and adjust carburetor idle speed Synchronize carburetors Check clutch cable adjustments Check brake system Check steering head play Check all nuts, bolts and fasteners for tightnes
Every 600 miles (1,000 km) or 6 months	Check drive chain adjustment Check engine oil level Lubricate rear brake pedal and shift lever Lubricate sidestand and centerstand pivot points Inspect front steering for looseness Check wheel bearings for smooth operation Check wheel runout
Every 4,000 miles (6,400 km) or 6 months	Replace spark plugs Check and adjust carburetor idle speed Check hydraulic fluid level in brake master cylinder Inspect brake pads for wear Check clutch cable adjustment
Every 8,000 miles (12,000 km) or 1 year	Check the fuel line for deterioration or leakage Replace the fuel filter Check the throttle grip for operation and play; adjust if necessary Check the throttle cables for fraying or damage Lubricate the throttle cables if necessary Check the choke cable for fraying or damage Check the choke cable free play; adjust if necessary Swing arm bearing lubrication Shock linkage lubrication

(continued)

Table 1 SERVICE INTERVALS* (continued)

Every 8,000 miles (12,000 km) or 1 year (continued)	Check and adjust valve clearance Change the engine oil and filter Check carburetor synchronization; adjust if necessary Inspect the cooling system hoses for deterioration or leakage Check all cooling system hose clamps for damage Check the radiator for clogging or damage Inspect the coolant level Inspect the secondary air supply system*** Inspect brake pads for wear Check brake pedal height; adjust if necessary Check the rear brake light switch adjustment Check the headlight adjustment Check the sidestand bolt for tightness Check the sidestand rubber pad for wear or deterioration; replace if necessary Check the front forks for seal leakage Check the front fork for damage Check the front fork air pressure Check the rear shock absorber for leakage, looseness or damage Check the tires for tread wear or damage Check the rims for damage Inspect steering head bearings
Every 12,000 miles (19,000 km) or 18 months	Replace air cleaner element Inspect the evaporative emission control system*** Check centerstand spring tension
Every 2 years	Coolant change

*This maintenance schedule should be considered as a guide to general maintenance and lubrication intervals. Harder than normal use and exposure to mud, water, sand, high humidity, etc. will naturally dictate more frequent attention to most maintenance items.

** Also perform maintenance after engine rebuild.

*** California models only.

Table 2 TIRE SPECIFICATIONS

Tire size	Air pressure (cold)*	Minimum tread depth
Front 110/80-17	36 psi (2.50 kg/cm²)	1.5 mm (1/16 in.)
Rear 130/80-17	42 psi (2.90 kg/cm²)	2.0 mm (3/32 in.)

* Up to maximum load limit of 200 lb. (89 kg) including total weight of motorcycle with accessories, rider(s) and luggage.

Table 3 RECOMMENDED LUBRICANTS

Engine oil	SAE 10W-40 SE/SF
Battery refilling	Distilled water
Brake fluid	DOT 4
Drive chain	SAE 80 or SAE 80 gear oil or drive chain lubricant recommended for use with O-ring drive chains
Fork oil	Automatic transmission fluid (ATF)
Cables	Light weight oil or cable lubricant
Pivot points	Light weight oil
Grease points	Molybdenum disulfide grease

Table 4 ENGINE OIL CAPACITY

Oil change only	3.0 L (3.17 qt.)
Oil and filter change	3.5 L (3.59 qt.)
Engine rebuild	4.0 L (4.23 qt.)

Table 5 MAINTENANCE TORQUE SPECIFICATIONS

Item	N·m	ft.-lb.
Spark plug	14	10
Oil filter	10	7
Oil drain bolt	35	25
Tappet lock nut	23	17
Timing hole cap	3.5	2.5
Crankshaft hole cap	7	5
Rear axle nut	90	65
Sidestand		
Bolt	15	11
Locknut	35	25
Bracket bolt	40	29
Handlebar pinch bolt	22	16
Right-hand footpeg bracket bolts	27	20
Top fork cap	22	16

Table 6 FRONT FORK OIL CAPACITY

Left-hand side	371 cc (12.5 oz.)
Right-hand side	361 cc (12.2 oz.)

Table 7 FRONT FORK AIR PRESSURE*

Normal	0-6 psi (0-0.4 kg/cm^2)

* Do not exceed the maximum air pressure or internal parts of the fork will be damaged.

Table 8 ANTIFREEZE PROTECTION AND CAPACITY

Temperature	Antifreeze-to-water ratio
Above -25° F (-32° C)	45:55
Above -34° F (-37° C)	50:50
Above -48° F (-44.5° C)	55:45
Coolant capacity Total system	2.0 liters (2.11 qt.)

Table 9 REAR SHOCK ADJUSTMENT

Adjuster position	Road condition
1	Smooth roads and typical freeways
2	City roads and conditions
3	Winding roads

Table 10 TUNE-UP SPECIFICATIONS

Air filtration	Paper element
Engine firing order	1-2-4-3
Valve clearance	
Intake	0.14-0.18 mm (0.006-0.007 in.)
Exhaust	0.18-0.22 mm (0.007-0.009 in.)
Compression pressure	
(at sea level)	13.0 $\pm$2.0 kg/cm^2 (185 $\pm$28 psi)
Spark plug type	
Standard heat range	ND X24EPR-U9 or NGK DPR8EA-9
Cold weather	ND X22EPR-U9 or NGK DPR7EA-9
Extended high-speed riding	ND X27EPR-U9 or NGK DPR9EA-9
Spark plug gap	0.8-0.9 mm (0.031-0.040 in.)
Ignition timing	"F" mark at idle
Idle speed	
49-state	1200 $\pm$100 rpm
California	1300 $\pm$100 rpm

CHAPTER FOUR

ENGINE

The engine is a liquid-cooled double overhead cam 16-valve inline four. Valves are operated by two chain-driven overhead camshafts.

This chapter provides complete service and overhaul procedures, including information for disassembly, removal, inspection, service and reassembly of the engine.

Before starting any work, read the service hints in Chapter One. You will do a better job with this information fresh in your mind.

Table 1 lists general engine specifications and **Table 2** lists engine service specifications. **Tables 1-7** are at the end of the chapter.

ENGINE PRINCIPLES

Figure 1 explains how the engine works. This will be helpful when troubleshooting or repairing your engine.

SERVICING ENGINE IN FRAME

Many components can be serviced while the engine is mounted in the frame:

a. Cylinder head.
b. Cylinders and pistons.
c. Gearshift mechanism.
d. Clutch.
e. Oil pump.
f. Carburetors.
g. Starter motor.
h. Alternator and electrical systems.

NOTE
The camshafts, cylinder head and cylinder block can be removed with the engine in the frame, but it's much easier to remove them after the engine has been removed.

ENGINE

Removal/Installation

One of the most important aspects of engine overhaul is removal and installation. Improper preparation before and failing to identify and store parts during removal will cause a headache when it comes time to reinstall and assemble the engine. Before removing the first bolt and to prevent frustration during installation, get a number of boxes, plastic bags and containers and store the parts as they are removed. Have on hand a roll of masking tape and a permanent, waterproof marking pen to label each part or assembly as

① 4-STROKE OPERATING PRINCIPLES

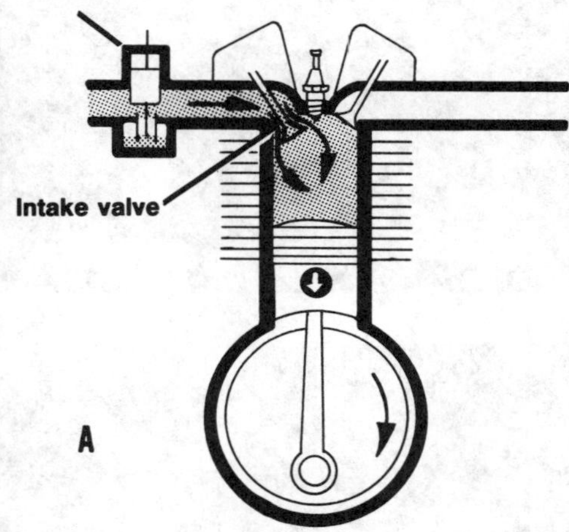

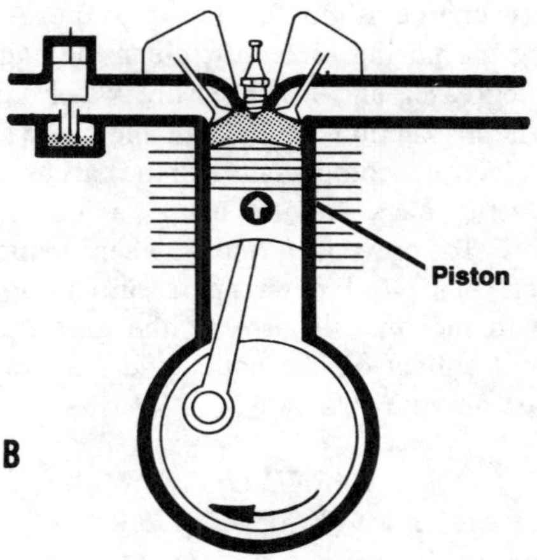

As the piston travels downward, the exhaust valve is closed and the intake valve opens, allowing the new air-fuel mixture from the carburetor to be drawn into the cylinder. When the piston reaches the bottom of its travel (BDC), the intake valve closes and remains closed for the next 1 1/2 revolutions of the crankshaft.

While the crankshaft continues to rotate, the piston moves upward, compressing the air-fuel mixture.

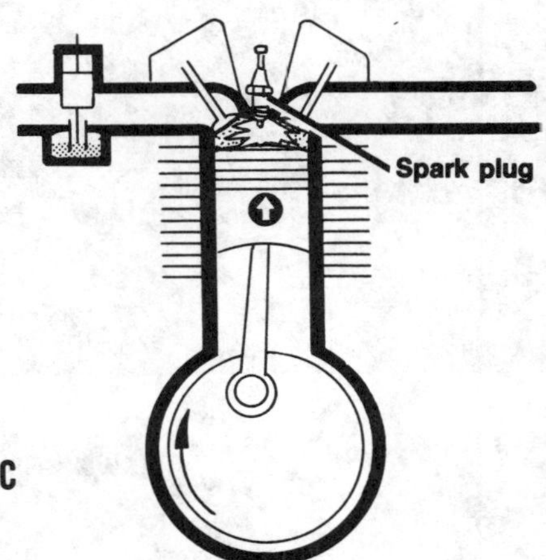

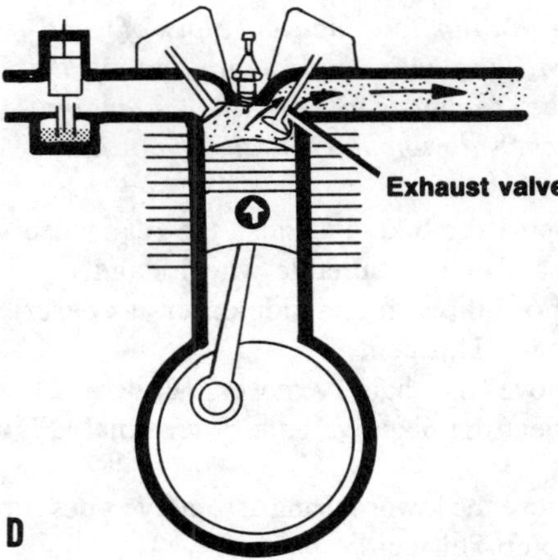

As the piston almost reaches the top of its travel, the spark plug fires, igniting the compressed air-fuel mixture. The piston continues to top dead center (TDC) and is pushed downward by the expanding gases.

When the piston almost reaches BDC, the exhaust valve opens and remains open until the piston is near TDC. The upward travel of the piston forces the exhaust gases out of the cylinder. After the piston has reached TDC, the exhaust valve closes and the cycle starts all over again.

required. If your bike was purchased second hand, and it appears that some of the wiring may have been changed or replaced, label each electrical connection before disconnecting it.

A dirty engine is no fun to work on. After removing the fairing assembly, clean the engine with a degreaser and low-pressure water hose. Follow the instructions on the can and make sure to cover electrical components and the carburetors with plastic bags before using a chemical degreaser. To prevent a mess when using a degreaser, place old newspapers or cardboard underneath the bike. That way, the grease and grime will collect on the paper and not on the ground or on your driveway.

WARNING
The engine weighs 63 kg (138.9 lb.). Due to its weight and bulk, it is essential that a minimum of 2, preferably 3, people be used during engine removal and installation.

CAUTION
The engine can be detached and reattached with basic hand tools as described in Chapter One. However, a hydraulic floor jack and block of wood will be required to remove and install the engine. Do not attempt engine removal without a hydraulic floor jack.

1. Support the bike and raise the rear wheel off the ground with a suitable wheel stand.
2. Remove the seat and side covers as described in Chapter Thirteen.
3. Remove the battery cover (**Figure 2**) and disconnect the negative battery terminal (**Figure 3**).
4. Remove the lower fairing assembly as described in Chapter Thirteen.
5. Remove the fuel tank as described in Chapter Seven.
6. Drain the engine oil as described in Chapter Three.
7. Drain the cooling system as described in Chapter Three.
8. Remove the air filter case and the carburetor assembly as described in Chapter Seven.
9. Remove the drive sprocket cover as described in Chapter Six.

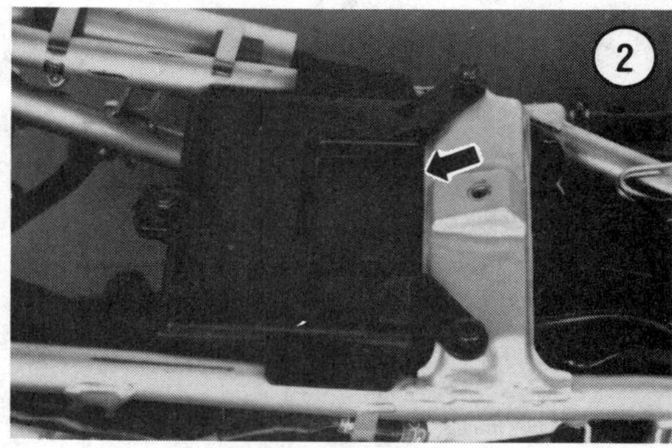

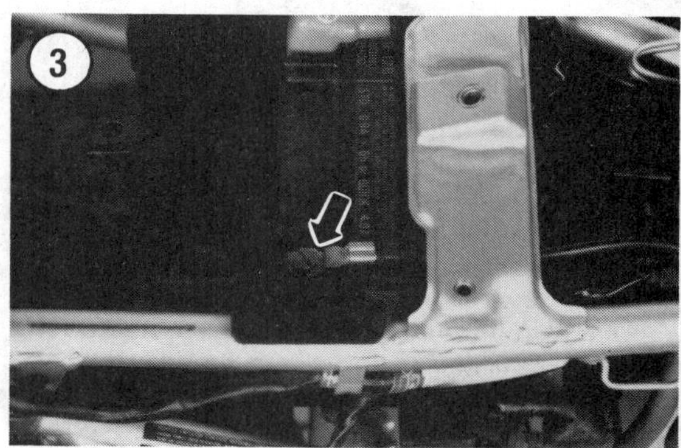

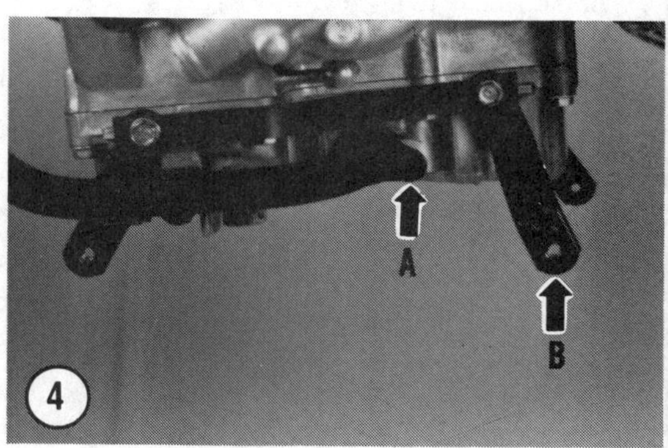

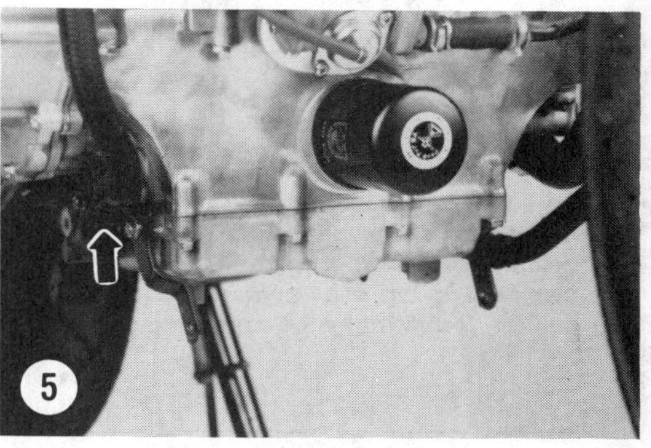

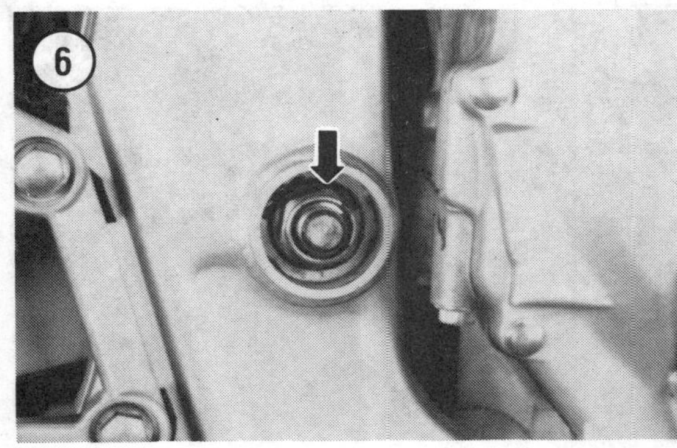

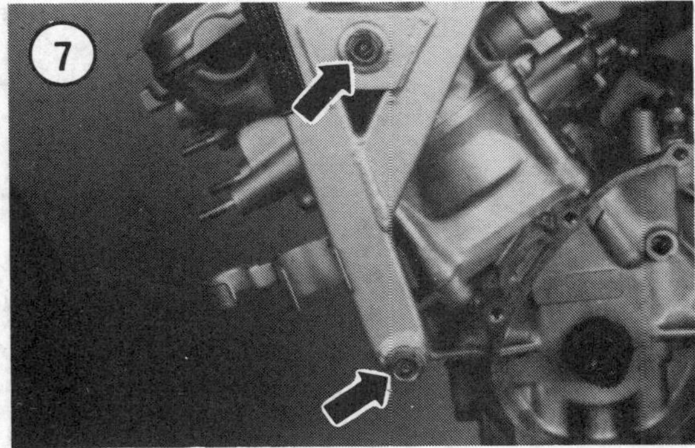

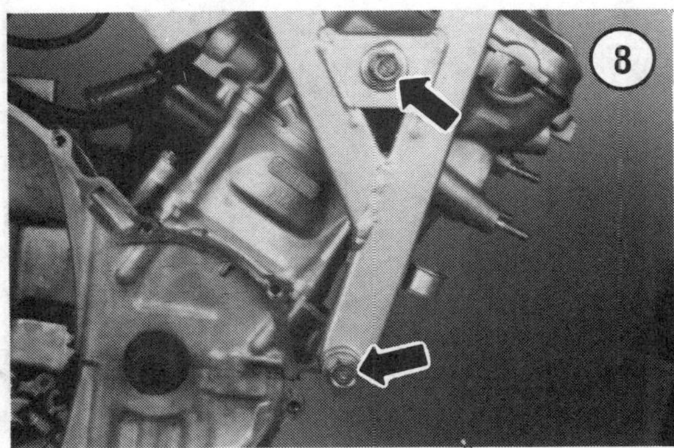

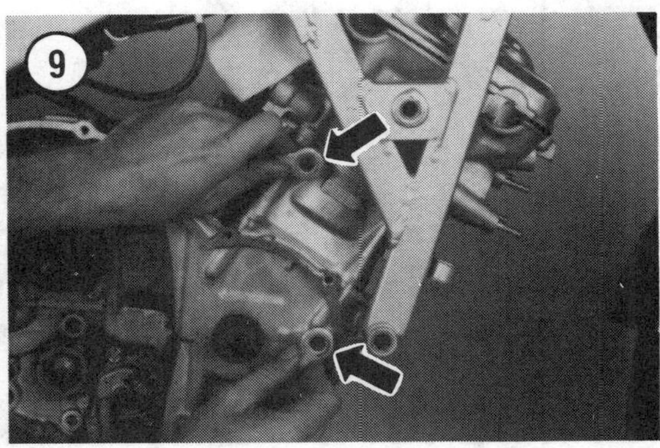

10. Remove the drive sprocket as described in Chapter Six.

11. Remove the exhaust system as described in Chapter Seven.

12. Disconnect the left- (A, **Figure 4**) and right-hand (**Figure 5**) oil pipes at the oil pan.

13. Remove the exhaust system mounting bracket (B, **Figure 4**).

14. Remove the radiator as described in Chapter Nine.

15. Remove the clutch as described in Chapter Five.

16. Remove the starter motor as described in Chapter Eight.

17. Remove the alternator as described in this chapter.

18. Disconnect the engine ground strap and all electrical connectors going to the engine.

19. Loosen, but do not remove, all engine mounting bolts and nuts.

20. Place a hydraulic floor jack, with a piece of wood to protect the oil pan, under the engine. Apply a *small amount* of jack pressure up on the engine.

21. Loosen the swing arm pivot shaft nut (**Figure 6**).

NOTE
The engine is a tight fit in the frame. Loosening the swing arm pivot shaft nut will ease engine removal and installation.

22. On the left-hand side, remove the upper front engine mount bolts (**Figure 7**).

23. On the right-hand side, remove the upper front engine mount bolts (**Figure 8**). Remove the large washers between the engine and frame (**Figure 9**).

24. On the right-hand side, remove the upper rear engine mount nut (A, **Figure 10**). Remove the engine mount bolt from the left-hand side (**Figure 11**).

25. On the left-hand side, remove the lower rear engine mount nut (A, **Figure 12**).

WARNING
The engine assembly is very heavy. This final step requires a minimum of 2, preferably 3, people to safely remove the engine from the frame.

26. Jack the engine up a little to remove tension from the lower engine mount bolt.

27. On the right-hand side, remove the lower rear engine mount bolt (B, **Figure 10**) halfway. Remove the spacer (B, **Figure 12**) from the left-hand side.

28. With an assistant steadying the engine on the jack, completely remove the lower engine mount bolt from the right-hand side.

29. Carefully and slowly pivot the engine on the floor jack (**Figure 13**) out of the frame in order to gain access to all sides. Move it out far enough so that everyone can get a good handhold on the engine.

30. Slide the jack and the engine out from underneath the bike.

31. Place the engine in an engine stand or take it to a workbench for further disassembly.

32. Before servicing the engine, store all of the engine mounts, spacers and nuts back in the frame. Label and store parts as required.

33. While the engine is removed for service, check all of the frame engine mounts for cracks or other damage. If any cracks are detected, take the chassis assembly to a Honda dealer for further examination.

34. Install by reversing the removal steps. Note the following.

35. Tighten the engine mounting bolts and nuts to the torque specification listed in **Table 3**.

36. Fill the crankcase with the recommended type and quantity of engine oil. Refer to *Engine Oil and Filter Change* in Chapter Three.

37. Refill the cooling system. See *Coolant Change* in Chapter Three.

38. Adjust the following items as described in Chapter Three:
   a. Clutch.
   b. Drive chain.
   c. Rear brake.

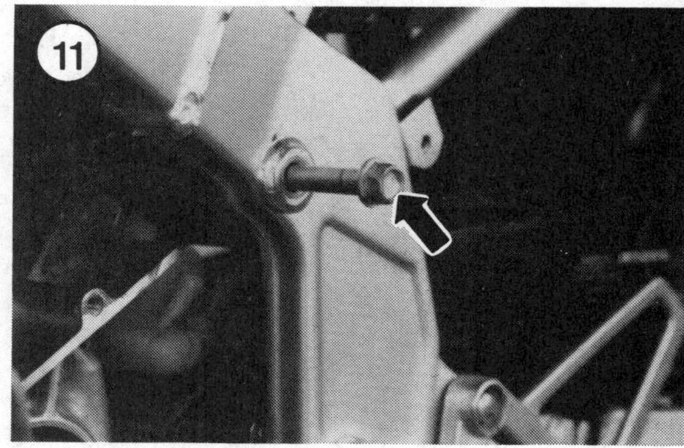

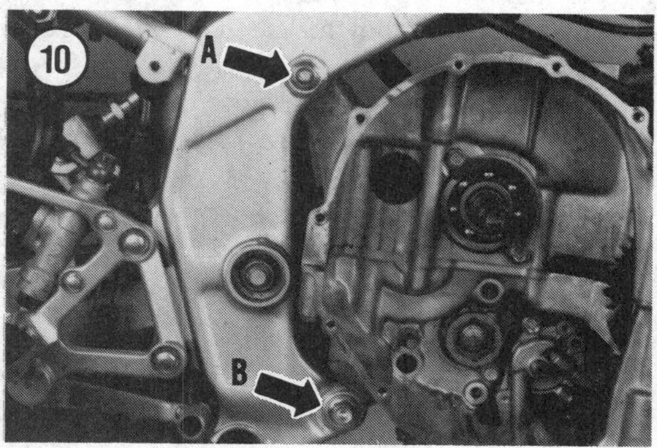

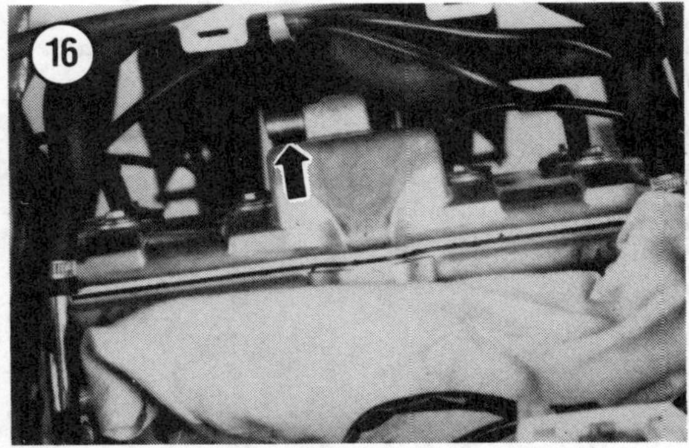

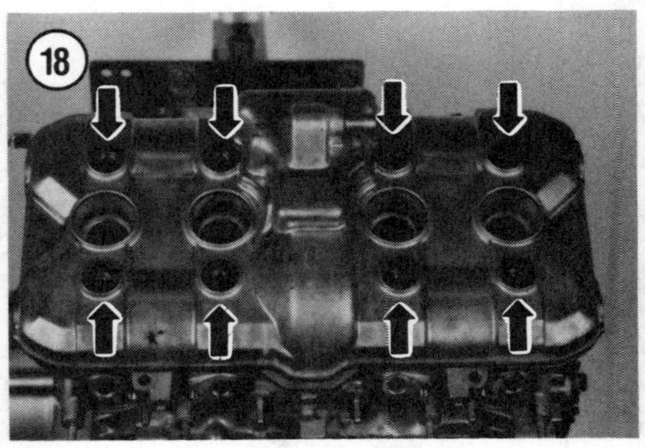

   d. Throttle cables.

   e. Choke cable.

39. Start the engine and check for leaks.

CYLINDER HEAD COVER

Removal/Installation

1. Support the bike and raise the rear wheel off the ground with a suitable wheel stand.

2. Remove the lower fairings as described in Chapter Thirteen.

3. Loosen the radiator upper mounting bolt (A, **Figure 14**).

4. Remove the radiator grille (B, **Figure 14**).

5. Remove the radiator lower mounting bolts (A, **Figure 15**) underneath the radiator.

6. Swing the radiator (B, **Figure 15**) upwards and secure it with a piece of heavy wire or a Bunjee cord.

> *NOTE*
> *If the radiator is still in the way, it may be necessary to remove it. Refer to Chapter Nine.*

7. Label and disconnect the spark plug caps at the spark plugs. Position the caps up and away from the cylinder head cover.

8. Disconnect the breather tube (**Figure 16**) at the cylinder head cover.

> *NOTE*
> *Some of the photographs in the following steps are shown with the engine removed for clarity.*

9. Remove the cylinder head cover mounting bolts (**Figure 17**) and washers (**Figure 18**).

10. Lift the cylinder head cover (**Figure 19**) and gasket off of the cylinder head and remove from underneath the radiator.

11. Installation is the reverse of these steps, noting the following.

12. Replace the cylinder head cover gasket if necessary. Note the following:

   a. Remove all residue from the head cover and cylinder head mating surfaces.

   b. Apply a non-hardening gasket sealer to the cylinder head cover gasket groove.

   c. Install the gasket (A, **Figure 20**) onto the cylinder head cover so that the arrows on the sides of the gasket face to the front.

   d. Apply a non-hardening gasket sealer to the 4 cylinder head cavity gasket surfaces (B, **Figure 20**).

13. If the breather plate (**Figure 21**) was removed, install it using a new gasket. Apply Loctite 242 (blue) onto the breather plate bolts and tighten securely.

14. Install the cylinder head cover so that the arrow (**Figure 22**) on the cover faces to the front of the bike.

15. Install the cylinder head cover washers (**Figure 23**) so that the UP mark on the washers faces up.

16. Install the cylinder head cover bolts in a crisscross pattern (**Figure 24**) to the torque specification in **Table 3**. Make sure to tighten bolts 1 and 2 in order to help position the cylinder head cover gasket.

CAMSHAFTS

This section describes removal, inspection and installation procedures for the camshaft components.

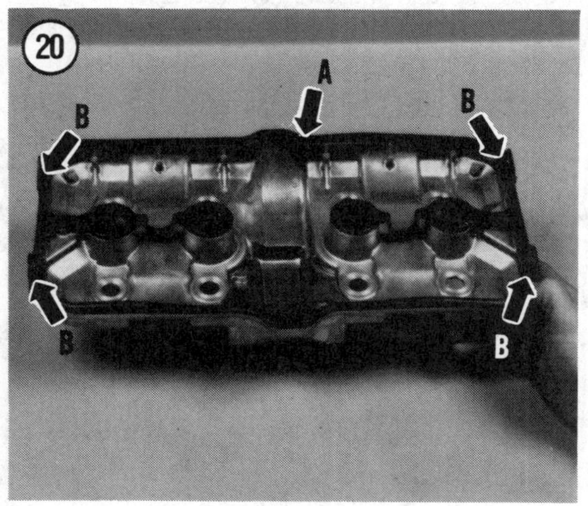

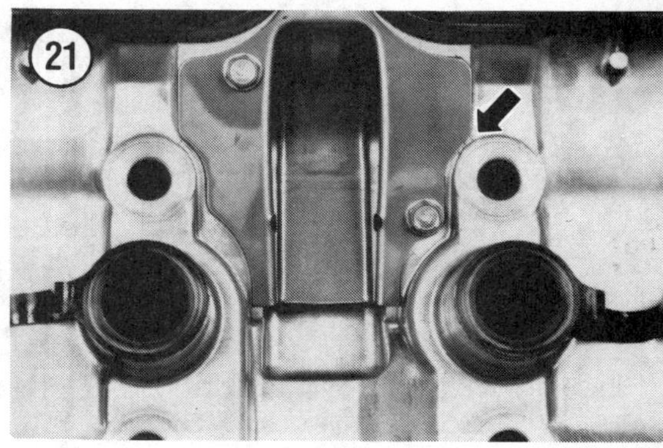

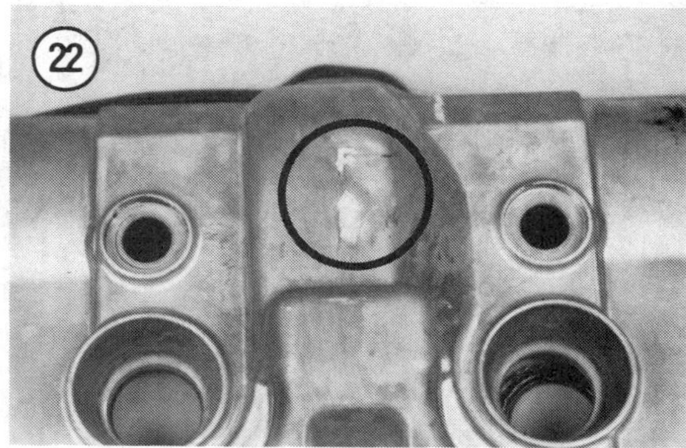

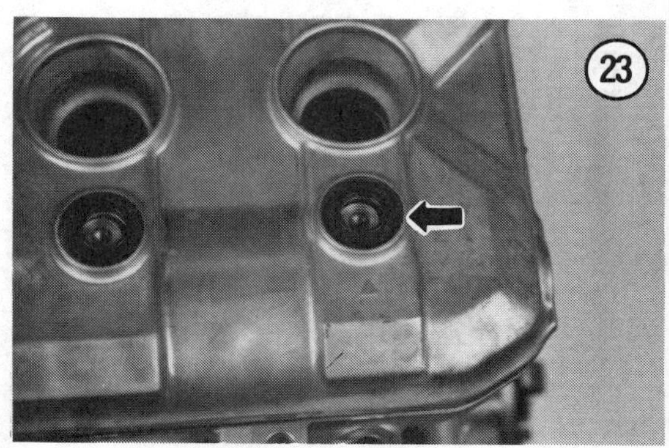

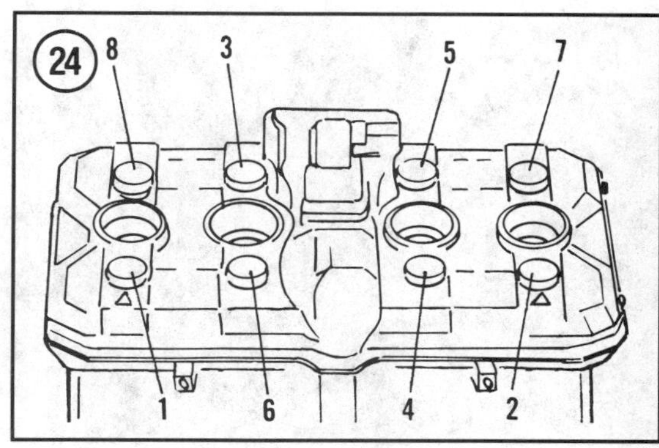

NOTE
The cams can be removed with the engine in the frame but it is much easier with the engine removed. This procedure is shown with the engine removed.

Removal

1. Remove the engine as described in this chapter.
2. Remove the cylinder head cover as described in this chapter.
3. Remove the spark plugs as described in Chapter Three. This will make it easier to turn the engine by hand.
4. Remove the camshaft chain tensioner bolts and remove the tensioner assembly (**Figure 25**).
5. Remove the camshaft chain top guide bolts and remove the chain top guide (**Figure 26**).
6. If removed, temporarily install the alternator rotor and the right-hand crankcase/clutch cover.
7. Remove the timing hole cap and the crankshaft hole cap (**Figure 27**).
8. Using the bolt on the alternator rotor (**Figure 28**), rotate the engine *clockwise* to expose 2 of the camshaft sprocket bolts (**Figure 29**). Remove the bolts.
9. Rotate the engine *clockwise* and remove the remaining cam sprocket bolts.
10. Carefully slide the camshaft sprockets (**Figure 30**) off the shoulder on each camshaft. See **Figure 31**.

NOTE
*During the next step, loosen the bolts
in 2-3 stages on all 4 camshaft holders.
This will gradually release the pressure
on the camshaft as the lobes on one
cylinder will be under pressure.*

NOTE
*The camshaft holders have a cast
identification mark as indicated in
Figure 32. The marks are:*
  a. EXR: Exhaust right-hand side.
  b. EXL: Exhaust left-hand side.
  c. INR: Intake right-hand side.
  d. INL: Intake left-hand side.

NOTE
*Each camshaft holder is equipped with
2 dowel pins (**Figure 33**).*

11. Remove the bolts securing the camshaft holders
(**Figure 34**).
12. Secure the camshaft chain with wire.
13. Remove both camshafts with their sprockets
(**Figure 35**). Remove the camshafts slowly to
prevent damaging any camshaft lobe or bearing
surface.

CAUTION
*The crankshaft can be turned with the
camshafts removed. However, pull the
camshaft chain tight to prevent it from
binding at the crankshaft sprocket.*

Camshaft Inspection

1. Check camshaft lobes (A, **Figure 36**) for wear.
The lobes should not be scored and the edges
should be square. Slight damage may be removed

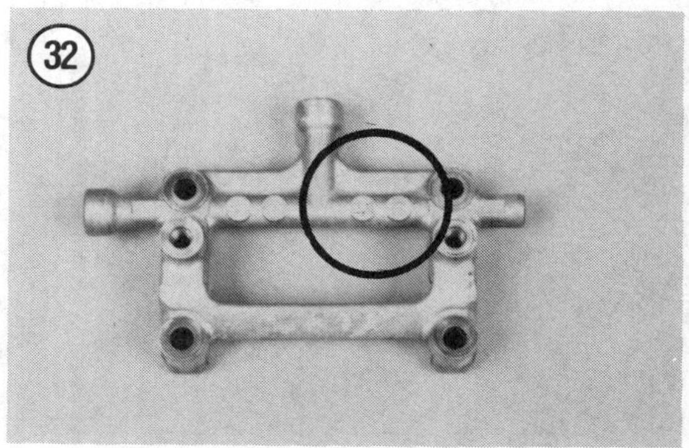

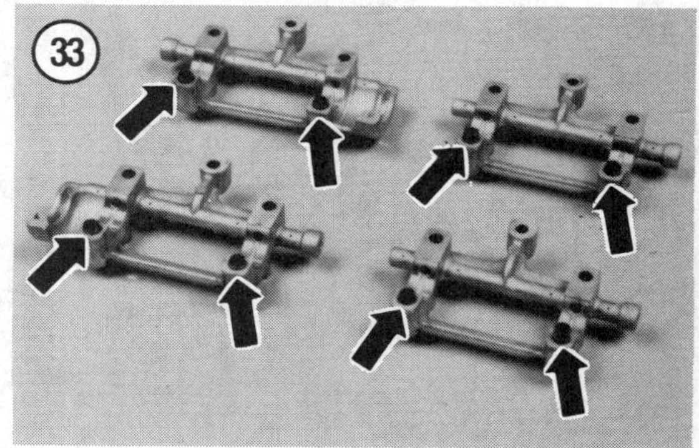

Figure 35

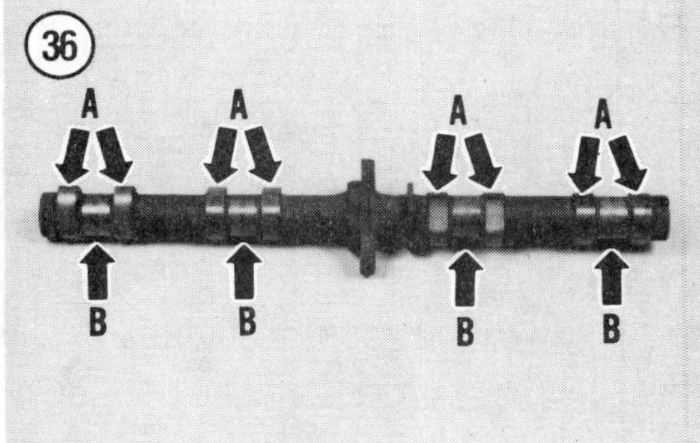

Figure 36

with a silicon carbide oilstone. Use No. 100-120 grit initially, then polish with a No. 280-320 grit.

2. Even though the camshaft lobe surface appears to be satisfactory, with no visible signs of wear, they must be measured with a micrometer as shown in **Figure 37**. Replace the camshaft(s) if worn to or beyond the service limits (measurements less than those given in **Table 2**).

3. Check the camshaft bearing journals (B, **Figure 36**) for wear and scoring.

4. Even though the camshaft bearing journal surface appears satisfactory, with no visible signs of wear, the camshaft bearing journals must be measured with a micrometer (**Figure 38**). Replace the camshaft(s) if worn to or beyond the service limits (measurements less than those given in **Table 2**).

5. Place the camshaft on a set of V-blocks and check its runout with a dial indicator (**Figure 39**). Replace the camshaft if runout exceeds specifications in **Table 2**. Repeat for the opposite camshaft.

6. Inspect the camshaft sprockets (**Figure 40**) for wear; replace if necessary.

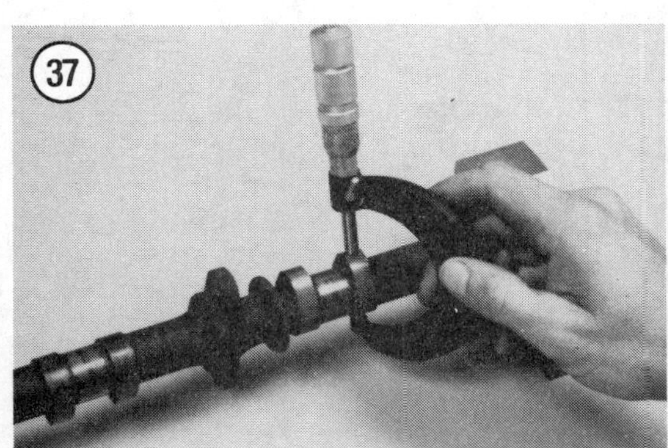

Figure 37

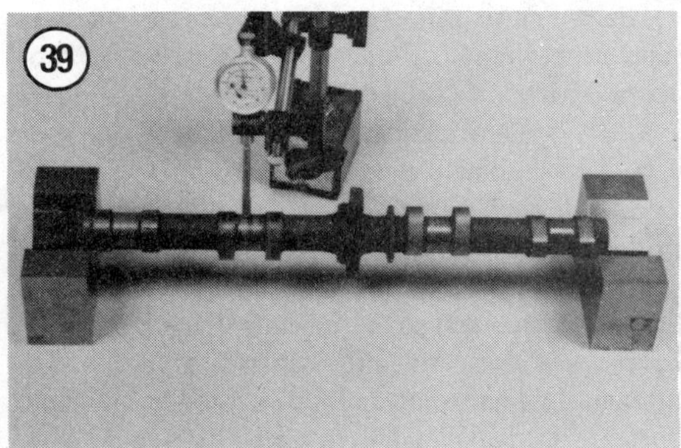

Figure 39

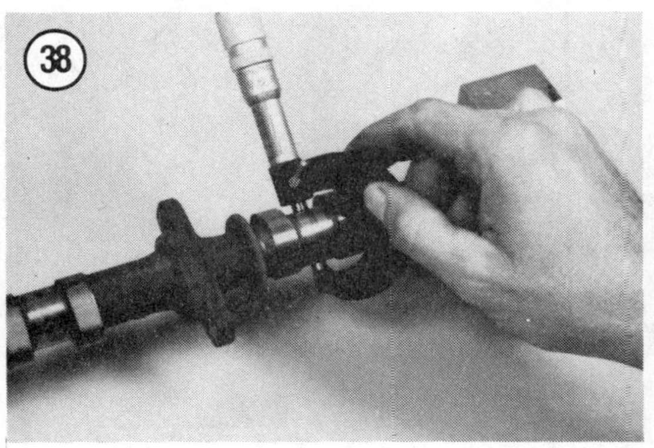

Figure 38

Figure 40

NOTE
If the camshaft sprockets are worn,
also check the camshaft chain, chain
guides and chain tensioner.

7. Check the camshaft bearing journals in the cylinder head (**Figure 41**) and camshaft holders (A, **Figure 42**) for wear and scoring. They should not be scored or excessively worn. If necessary, replace the cylinder head and camshaft holders as a matched pair.

8. Check the camshaft holder oil orifices (B, **Figure 42**) for clogging. Clean the camshaft holder in solvent and check that the oil orifices are clean. Blow out the holes with compressed air if necessary.

9. Check the camshaft chain guide (**Figure 43**) for wear or damage; replace if necessary.

Camshaft Bearing Clearance Measurement

This procedure requires the use of a Plastigage set. The camshaft must be installed into the head. Prior to installation, wipe all oil residue from each camshaft bearing journal and bearing surface in the cylinder head and all camshaft caps.

1. Each camshaft is identified for correct placement in the cylinder head (**Figure 44**). They are identified as follows:
   a. IN—intake camshaft.
   b. EX—exhaust camshaft.

2. Install each camshaft into its correct location in the head. Position the camshaft lobes so they are not depressing any rocker arms (or back off the valve adjusters) so the valves will not be pressed open when the camshaft is installed.

3. Install all camshaft holder locating dowels into position in the camshaft holder (**Figure 33**).

4. Wipe all oil from camshaft bearing journals before using the Plastigage material.

5. Place a strip of Plastigage material on top of each camshaft bearing journal (**Figure 45**), parallel to the cam.

6. Each camshaft holder is identified for correct placement in the cylinder head. Identification marks are shown in **Figure 32**. They are identified as follows:
   a. EXR: Exhaust right-hand side.
   b. EXL: Exhaust left-hand side.
   c. INR: Intake right-hand side.
   d. INL: Intake left-hand side.

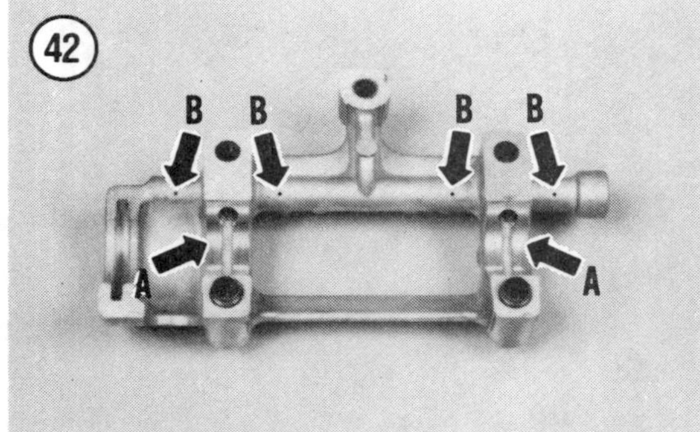

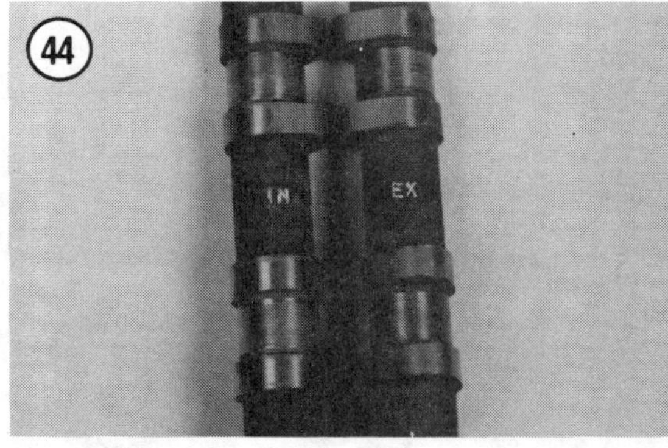

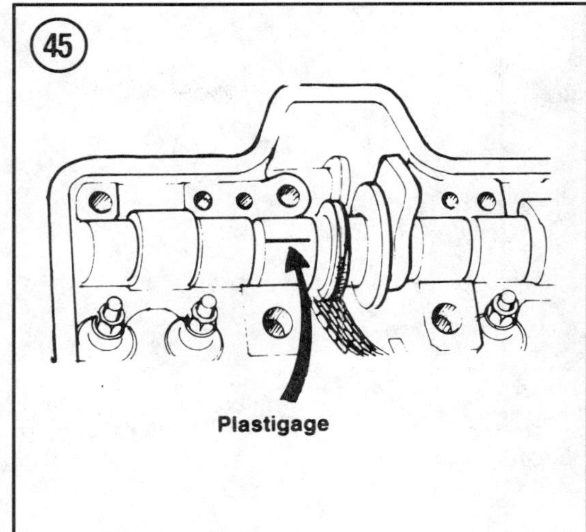

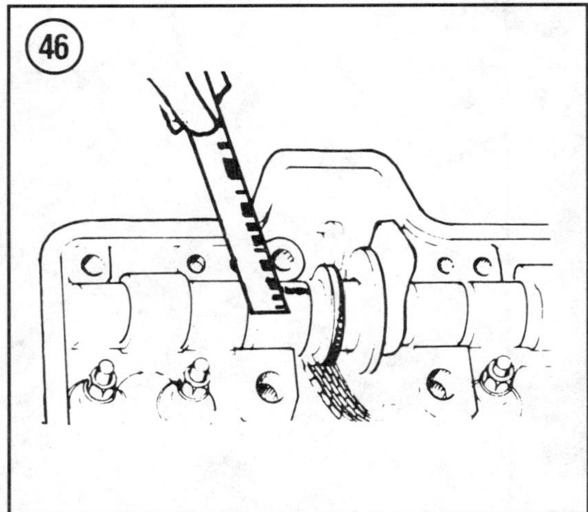

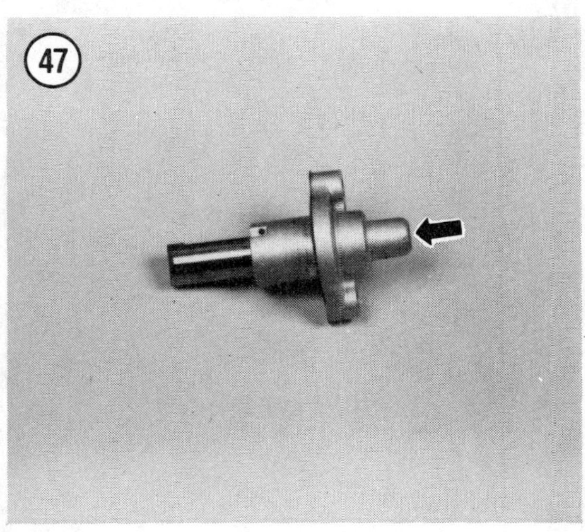

7. Place the camshaft holders into their correct position.

8. Install all camshaft holder bolts and the bolts that hold the cam chain guide in place. Install finger-tight at first, then tighten in a crisscross pattern to the final torque specification listed in **Table 3**.

> *CAUTION*
> *Do not rotate the camshaft with the Plastigage material in place.*

9. Gradually remove the camshaft holder bolts in a crisscross pattern. Remove the camshaft holders carefully.

10 Measure the width of the flattened Plastigage according to manufacturer's instructions (**Figure 46**).

11. If the clearance exceeds the wear limits in **Table 2**, measure the camshaft bearing journals (**Figure 38**) with a micrometer and compare to the limits in **Table 2**. If the camshaft bearing journal is less than dimension specified, replace the camshaft. If the camshaft is within specifications, the cylinder head and camshaft holders must be replaced as a matched set.

> *CAUTION*
> *Remove all particles of Plastigage from all camshaft bearing journals and the camshaft holder. Be sure to clean the camshaft holder groove. This material must not be left in the engine as it can plug up an oil control orifice and cause severe engine damage.*

Camshaft Chain Tensioner Inspection

The camshaft chain tensioner cannot be rebuilt or serviced. Check the tensioner for operation by moving the tensioner pushrod (**Figure 47**) in and out by hand. The pushrod should operate smoothly. Replace the camshaft chain tensioner assembly if necessary.

Camshaft Installation

1. If camshaft bearing clearance was checked, make sure all Plastigage material has been removed from the camshaft and bearing cap surfaces.

CAUTION
When rotating the crankshaft in Step 2, lift the cam chain tightly and make sure it is meshed with the crankshaft sprocket. Pull on the exhaust side (front) to prevent it from binding on the crankshaft sprocket and crankcase.

2. Use a socket on the alternator rotor nut (**Figure 48**) and rotate the engine *clockwise* until the top dead center (TDC) "T" mark aligns with the fixed pointer on the right-hand crankcase cover. See **Figure 49**.

3. Coat all camshaft lobes and bearing journals with molybdenum disulfide grease or assembly oil.

4. Coat the bearing surfaces in the cylinder head and camshaft bearing caps.

5. Each camshaft is identified for correct placement in the cylinder head (**Figure 44**). They are identified as follows:
   a. IN—intake camshaft.
   b. EX—exhaust camshaft.

NOTE
*Position the camshaft sprockets with their identification marks (**Figure 50**) facing the right-hand side (toward the clutch). This is necessary for camshaft timing.*

6. See **Figure 50**. Install a camshaft into each sprocket from the left-hand side. Then install the camshafts into the cylinder head. Do not install the sprockets onto the camshaft shoulders at this time.

7. Position the camshafts so that the No. 4 cylinder lobes face out, away from the center of the cylinder head, as shown in **Figure 50**.

8. Install the dowel pins into each camshaft holder (**Figure 51**).

9. Each camshaft holder is identified for correct placement in the cylinder head. Identification marks are shown in **Figure 52**. They are identified as follows:
   a. EXR—Exhaust right-hand side.
   b. EXL—Exhaust left-hand side.
   c. INR—Intake right-hand side.
   d. INL—Intake left-hand side.

10. Place the camshaft holders into their correct position.

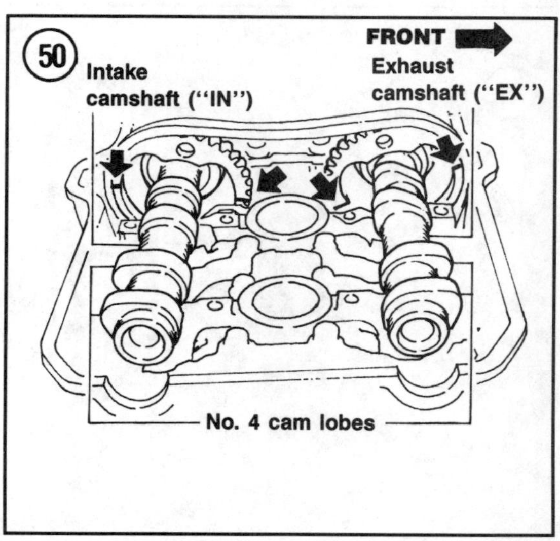

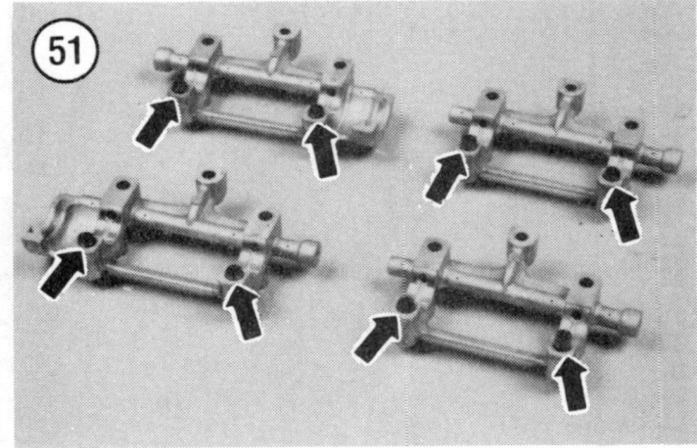

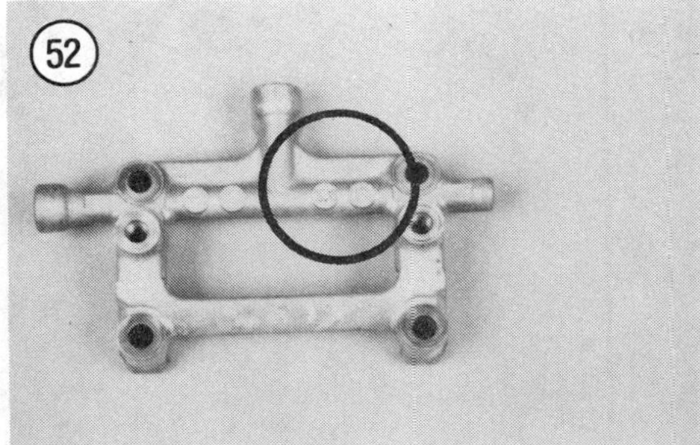

11. Install finger-tight at first, then tighten in a cirsscross pattern to the final torque specification listed in **Table 3.**

12. Turn the camshaft sprockets so that the alignment mark on each sprocket is aligned with the cylinder head gasket surface.

13. Pull the camshaft chain up and engage it with the cam sprockets (**Figure 53**).

14. Pull the camshaft chain and both sprockets up onto the shoulder on each camshaft. See **Figure 54.**

15. Apply Loctite 242 (blue) onto all 4 sprocket bolts and install one bolt into each camshaft sprocket (**Figure 55**). Tighten the bolts to only a firm finger-tight at this time. They will be tightened later.

> *CAUTION*
> *If there is any binding while turning the crankshaft, stop. Recheck the camshaft timing marks. Improper timing can cause valve and piston damage.*

16. Use a socket on the alternator rotor nut (**Figure 48**) and rotate the engine *clockwise* 360° (1 turn). Install the remaining 2 sprocket bolts. Tighten the bolts to only a firm finger-tight at this time. They will be tightened later along with the other 2 bolts.

17. Use a socket on the alternator rotor nut (**Figure 48**) and rotate the engine *clockwise* until the top dead center (TDC) "T" mark aligns with the fixed pointer on the right-hand crankcase cover. See **Figure 49**.

18. Check the alignment of the index marks on both camshaft sprockets (**Figure 50**). If the alignment is incorrect, correct by removing the

camshaft sprocket bolts and repositioning the sprockets. If the alignment is correct, proceed to Step 19.

19. Tighten the camshaft sprocket bolts installed in Step 15 in 2-3 steps to the torque specification in **Table 3**.

20. Rotate the engine *clockwise* 360° (1 turn) and tighten the camshaft sprocket bolts installed in Step 16 in 2-3 steps to the torque specification in **Table 3**.

> *CAUTION*
> *Very expensive damage could result from improper camshaft and chain alignment. Make this final check to be sure alignment is correct. If alignment is incorrect, it must be corrected at this time.*

21. Install the camshaft chain top guide (**Figure 56**) and its bolts. Tighten the bolts to the torque specification in **Table 3**.

22. Replace the chain tensioner gasket (**Figure 57**). Then install the chain tensioner (**Figure 58**) and tighten the bolts securely.

23. Adjust the valves as described under *Valve Adjustment* in Chapter Three.

24. Install the cylinder head cover as described in this chapter.

ROCKER ARM ASSEMBLIES

The rocker arms are identical (same Honda part No.) but they will develop different wear patterns during use. It is recommended that all parts be marked during removal so that they can be assembled in their original positions.

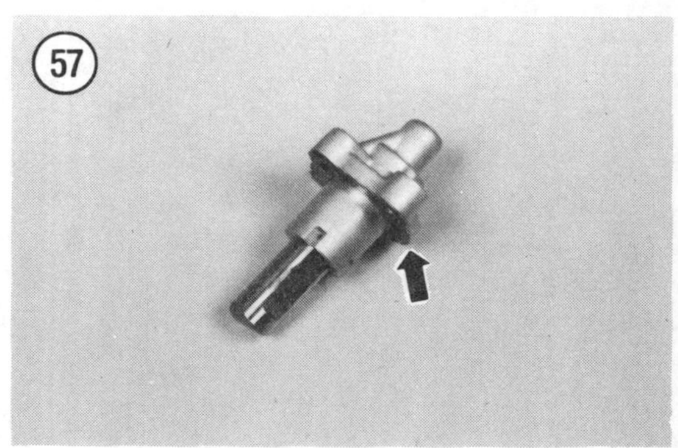

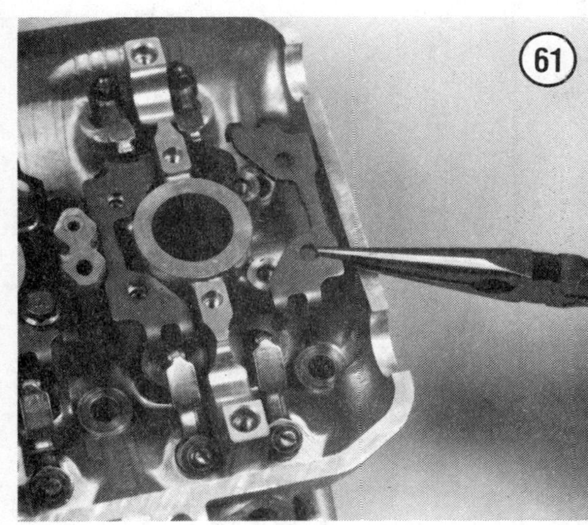

Figure 61

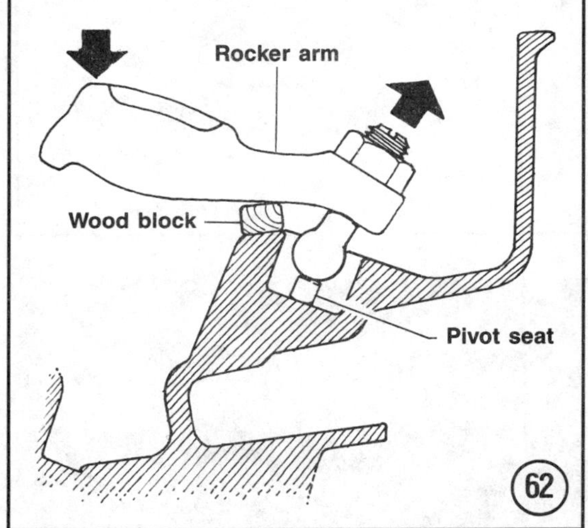

Figure 62

Figure 63

Removal

NOTE
This procedure is shown with the cylinder head removed for clarity.

1. Remove the camshafts as described in this chapter.
2. Remove the rocker arm holder bolts (**Figure 59**).
3. Lift the rocker arm spring (**Figure 60**) out of the cylinder head.
4. Lift the rocker arm holder (**Figure 61**) out of the cylinder head.
5. Place a small block of wood underneath the rocker arm as shown in **Figure 62**. Then carefully tap the end of the rocker arm (with a plastic mallet) and remove the rocker arm (**Figure 63**).
6. Repeat Steps 2-5 for the remaining rocker arms.

Inspection

1. Wash all parts in cleaning solvent and dry thoroughly.
2. Check each rocker arm spring (A, **Figure 64**) for fatigue, cracks or other damage; replace if necessary.
3. Examine each rocker arm holder (B, **Figure 64**) for cracks or other damage; replace if necessary.
4. Inspect the rocker arm pad where it rides on the valve stems (A, **Figure 65**). Then check the pivot bolt (B, **Figure 65**) where it rides in the pivot seat. If any part is scratched severely or unevenly worn, the damaged part must be replaced. To disassemble a rocker arm, perform the following:

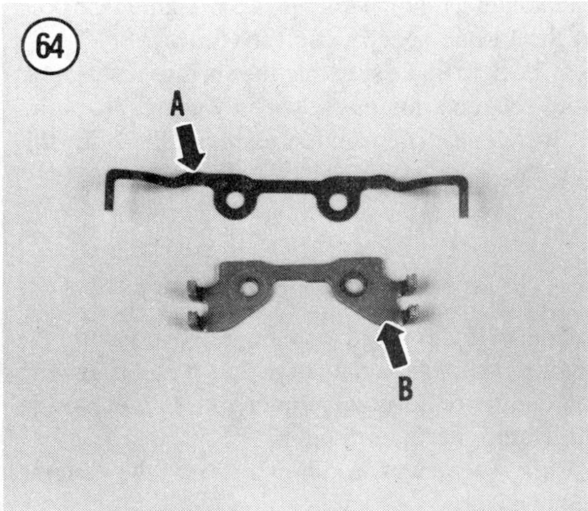

Figure 64

a. Loosen the locknut (C, **Figure 65**) and unscrew the pivot bolt.
b. Check the pivot bolt and rocker arm threads for damage.
c. Coat the pivot bolt threads with engine oil and screw it into the rocker arm. Turn the pivot bolt so that the distance indicated in **Figure 66** is maintained.

5. Check the pivot seats (**Figure 67**) in the cylinder head for looseness, excessive wear or other damage. If any one pivot seat is damaged or excessively worn, the cylinder head must be replaced.

Installation

1. Coat all parts with new engine oil.
2. Install the rocker arm assembly as follows:

a. Align the pivot bolt with the pivot seat in the cylinder head (**Figure 62** and **Figure 63**).
b. Place a socket over the rocker arm and tap the rocker arm so that the pivot bolt seats into the pivot seat (**Figure 68**). **Figure 69** shows the rocker arm/pivot bolt assembly properly installed.

3. Place the rocker arm holder over the 2 rocker arms as shown in **Figure 70**.
4. Place the rocker arm spring over the rocker arm holder (**Figure 60**).
5. Install the 2 rocker arm bolts through the spring and holder as shown in **Figure 71**. Tighten the bolts to the torque specification in **Table 3**.
6. Check to make sure that the springs rest against both rocker arms as shown in **Figure 71**.
7. Install the camshafts as described in this chapter.

CYLINDER HEAD

The cylinder head can be removed with the engine mounted in the frame but it is easier with the engine removed. If the engine is mounted in the frame, perform Step 1.

This sequence is shown with the engine removed.

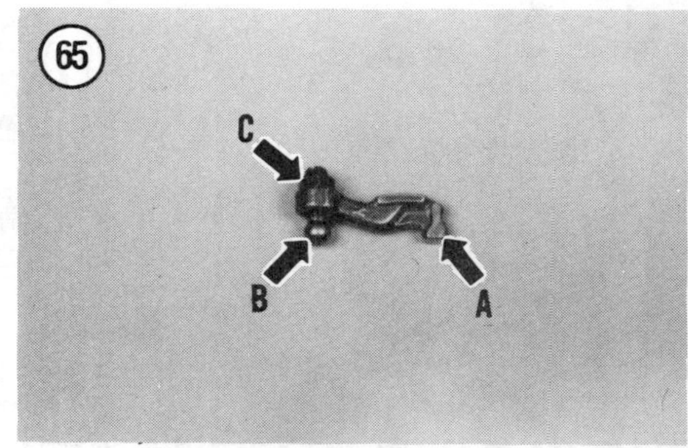

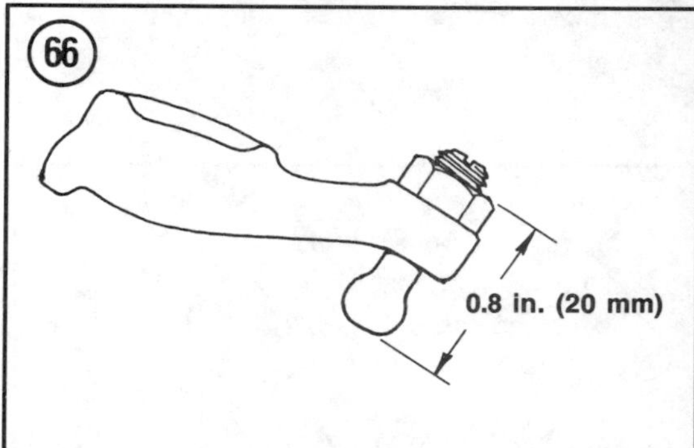

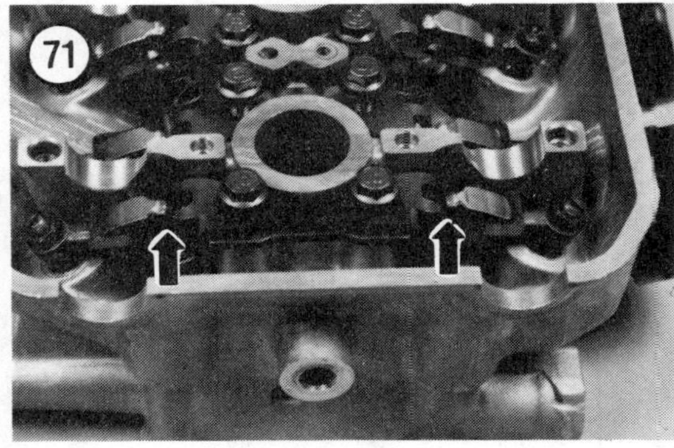

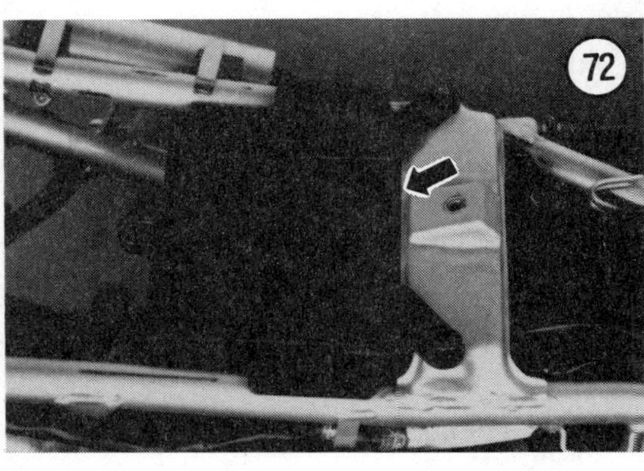

Removal

1. If the engine is mounted in the frame, perform the following:
   a. Remove the seat and both side covers. See Chapter Thirteen.
   b. Remove the battery cover (**Figure 72**) and disconnect the negative battery terminal (**Figure 73**).
   c. Remove the fuel tank as described in Chapter Seven.
   d. Remove the carburetors as described in Chapter Seven.
   e. Remove the exhaust pipe as described in Chapter Seven.
   f. Remove the cylinder head cover as described in this chapter.
   g. Remove the camshafts as described in this chapter.
   h. Remove the front/upper engine bolt from the left- and right-hand sides. See **Figure 74**.

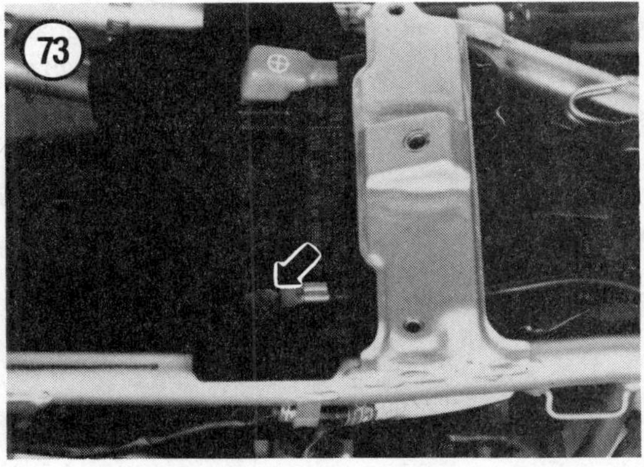

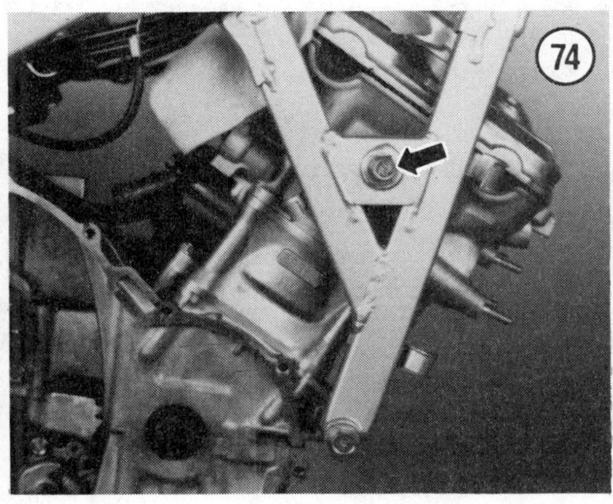

Remove the washer (**Figure 75**) from the right-hand side.

    i. Drain cooling system as described in Chapter Three.

    j. Remove the left- and right-hand water pipes (**Figure 76**) from the cylinder head. Don't lose the O-rings on the fittings.

2. Remove the camshafts as described in this chapter.

3. Remove the acorn nut (**Figure 77**) and washer at the rear of the cylinder head. Lift the rear camshaft chain tensioner (**Figure 78**) out of the engine.

4. Loosen the cylinder head nuts in a crisscross pattern (**Figure 79**) and remove the nuts and washers.

5. Loosen the cylinder head by tapping around the perimeter with a rubber or plastic mallet.

6. Remove the cylinder head (**Figure 80**) by pulling straight up and off the cylinder. Pull the camshaft chain and wire through the opening in the cylinder head and retie the wire to the exterior of the engine.

7. Place a clean shop rag into the cam chain tunnel in the cylinder to prevent the entry of foreign matter.

NOTE
After removing the cylinder head, check the top and bottom mating surfaces for any indications of coolant, oil or combustion leakage. Also check the head gasket for signs of leakage. A blown head gasket could indicate possible cylinder head warpage or other damage.

8. Remove the cylinder head gasket.

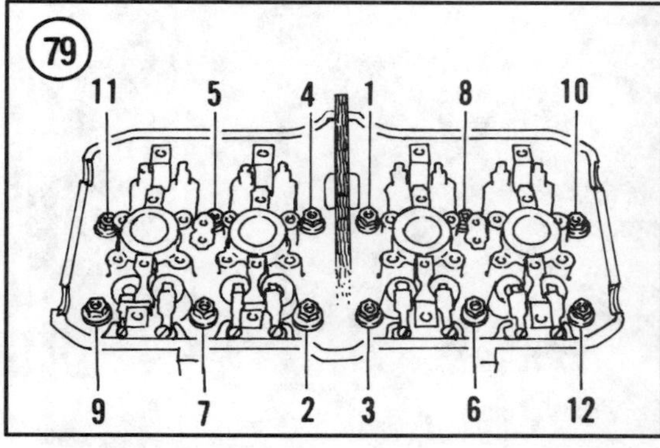

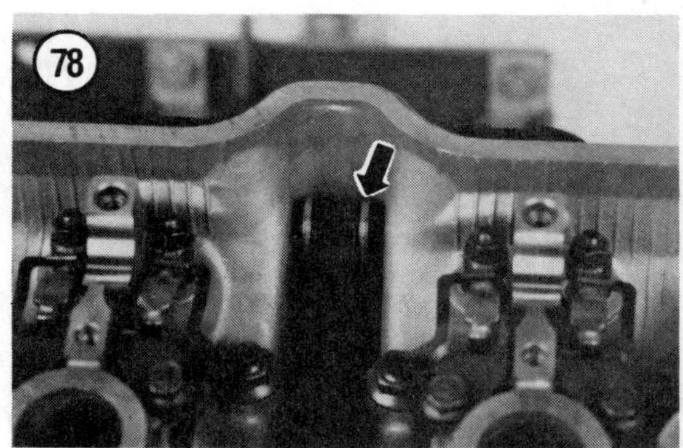

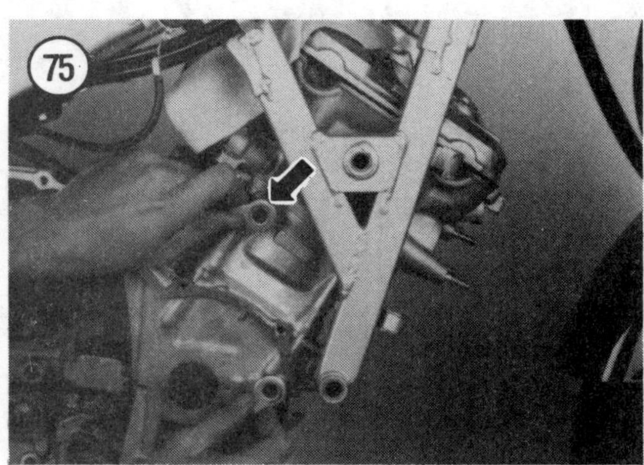

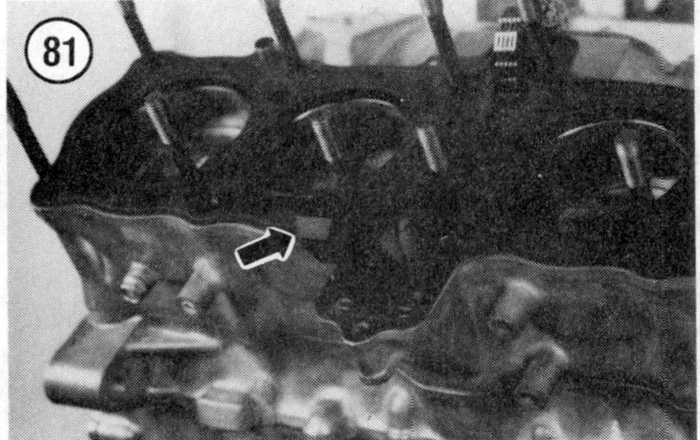

9. Lift the front camshaft chain guide (**Figure 81**) out of the engine.

10. If loose, remove the 2 dowel pins (**Figure 82**). If the dowel pins are secure there is no need to remove them.

Cylinder Head Inspection

1. Remove all traces of gasket residue from head (**Figure 83**) and cylinder mating surfaces. Do not scratch the gasket surface.

> *CAUTION*
> *If the combustion chambers are cleaned while the valves are removed, you stand a good chance of damaging the valve seat surfaces. A damaged or even slightly scratched valve seat will cause poor valve seating.*

2. Without removing the valves, remove all carbon deposits from the combustion chambers (**Figure 84**) with a wire brush or wooden scraper. Take care not to damage the head, valves or spark plug hole threads.

3. Examine the spark plug threads in the cylinder head for damage. If damage is minor or if the threads are dirty or clogged with carbon, use a spark plug thread tap to clean the threads following the manufacturer's instructions. If thread damage is severe, the thread can be restored by installing a steel thread insert. Thread insert kits can be purchased at automotive supply stores or you can have the inserts installed by a Honda dealer or machine shop.

> *NOTE*
> *When using a tap to clean spark plug threads, coat the tap with an aluminum tap cutting fluid or kerosene.*

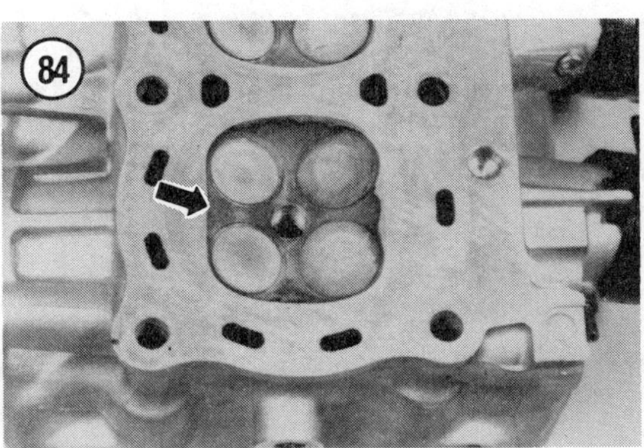

NOTE

Aluminum spark plug threads are commonly damaged due to galling, cross-threading and overtightening. It is easy to cross-thread spark plugs on the Hurricane because the plug holes are set deeply and hard to get to. To prevent galling, apply an anti-seize compound on the plug threads before installation and do not overtighten.

4. After all carbon is removed from the combustion chambers, and valve ports and the spark plug thread holes are repaired, clean the entire head in solvent.

CAUTION

If the cylinder head was bead-blasted, make sure to clean the head thoroughly with solvent and then with hot water and soap afterwards. Residual grit seats in small crevices and other areas and can be hard to remove. Chase each exposed thread with a tap to remove grit between the threads or you may damage a thread later. Residual grit left in the engine will wind up in the oil and cause premature piston, ring and bearing wear.

5. Examine the piston crowns. The crowns should show no signs of wear or damage. If the crown appears pecked or spongy-looking, also check the spark plug, valves and combustion chamber for aluminum deposits. If these deposits are found, the cylinder(s) are suffering from excessive heat caused by a lean fuel mixture or preignition.

CAUTION

Do not clean the piston crowns with the cylinder assembled on the crankcase. Carbon scraped from the tops of the pistons will inevitably fall between the cylinder wall and piston and onto the piston rings. Because carbon grit is very abrasive, premature cylinder, piston and ring wear will occur. If the piston crowns are heavily carboned, remove the pistons as described in this chapter and clean them off of the engine. Excessive carbon build-up on

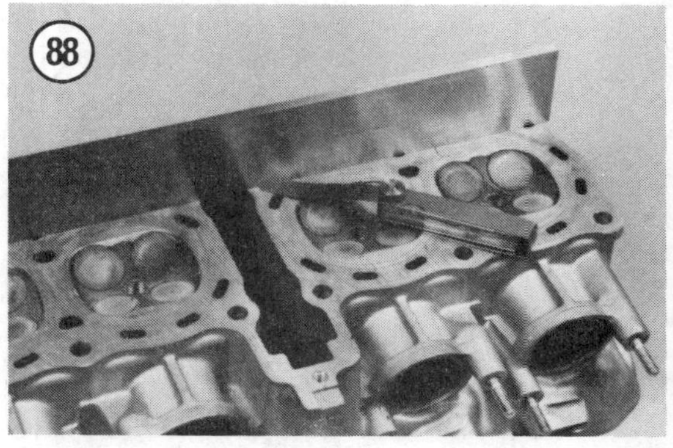

the piston crowns reduces piston cooling, raises engine compression and causes overheating.

6. Inspect the carburetor intake boots (**Figure 85**) for cracks or other damage that would allow unfiltered air to enter the engine. Also check the

(89)

(90)

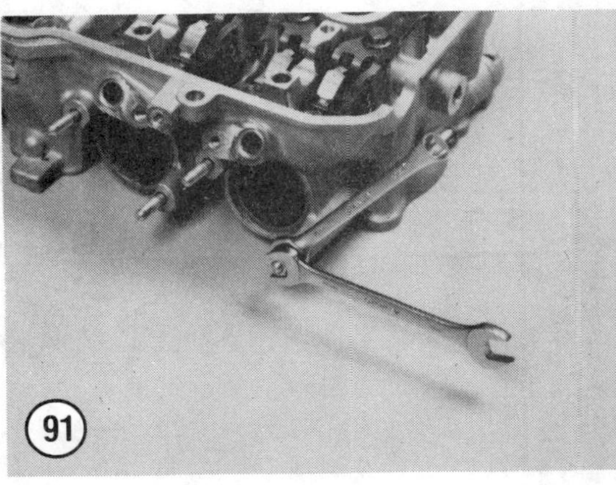

(91)

hose clamps for breakage or fatigue. When installing the intake boots, make sure to reinstall them with the CARB mark facing toward the carburetor and the UP mark facing up (**Figure 86**).

7. Check for cracks in the combustion chambers and exhaust ports (**Figure 87**). A cracked head must be replaced.

8. After the head has been thoroughly cleaned, place a straightedge across the gasket surface at several points (**Figure 88**). Measure warp by inserting a feeler gauge between the straightedge and cylinder head at each location. Maximum allowable warpage is listed in **Table 2**. Warpage or nicks in the cylinder head surface could cause an air leak and result in overheating. If warpage exceeds this limit, the cylinder head must be resurfaced or replaced.

9. Check the exhaust pipe studs (**Figure 89**) for looseness or thread damage. Slight thread damage can be repaired with a thread file or die. If thread damage is severe, replace the damaged stud(s) as follows:

a. Screw two 6 mm nuts onto the end of a stud as shown in **Figure 90**.
b. With 2 wrenches, tighten the nuts against each other (**Figure 91**).
c. Unscrew the stud with a wrench on the lower nut.
d. Clean the tapped hole with solvent and check for thread damage or carbon buildup. If necessary, clean the threads with a 6 × 1.00 metric tap.
e. Remove the nuts from the old stud and install them on the end of a new stud.
f. Tighten the nuts against each other.
g. Apply Loctite 271 (red) to the threads of the new stud.
h. Screw the stud into the cylinder head with a wrench on the upper nut. Tighten the stud securely.
i. Remove the nuts from the new stud.

10. Check the valves and valve guides as described under *Valves and Valve Components* in this chapter.

11. If the special Allen bolts (**Figure 92**) in the cylinder head were loosened or removed, apply Loctite 242 (blue) to the bolt threads and tighten the bolts securely.

Camshaft Chain Tensioner Guide Inspection

Inspect the front (**Figure 93**) and rear (**Figure 94**) camshaft chain tensioner guides for excessive wear or damage. If the guides are excessively worn, the chain tensioner may be damaged. Replace worn or damaged parts.

Installation

1. Clean the cylinder head (**Figure 83**) and cylinder mating surfaces of all gasket residue.

> *NOTE*
> *The cylinder head gasket is stamped with the word UP on one side (**Figure 95**). This side must face up. In addition, the side of the head gasket with the greater number of holes (**Figure 96**) faces to the front (exhaust) side of the engine.*

2. Refer to **Figure 97**. Install the 2 dowel pins (A), if removed, and a new head gasket (B).

3. Set the front cam chain guide so that it rests up on the cylinder as shown in **Figure 98**. Do not push it all the way in at this time.

4. Feed the camshaft chain and wire through the opening in the cylinder head.

> *NOTE*
> *As the cylinder head is installed in Step 5, push the front camshaft chain guide into cam chain tunnel and engage the guide at the top and bottom slots.*

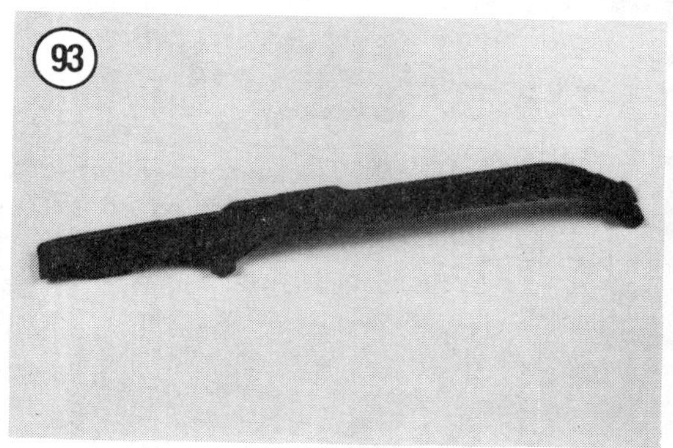

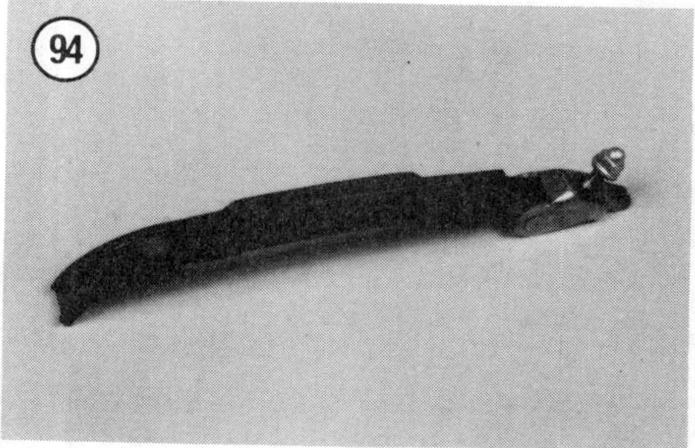

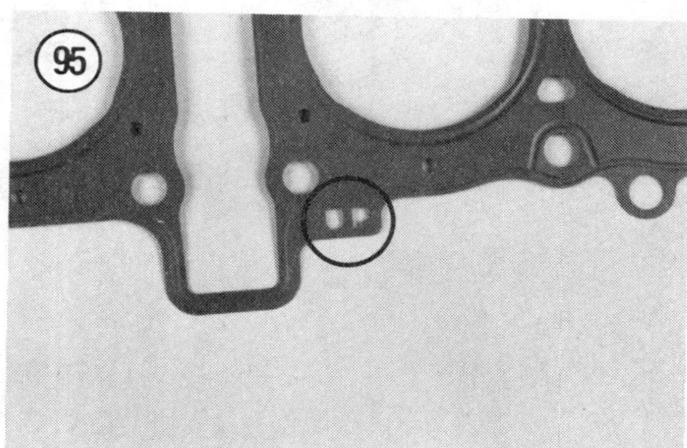

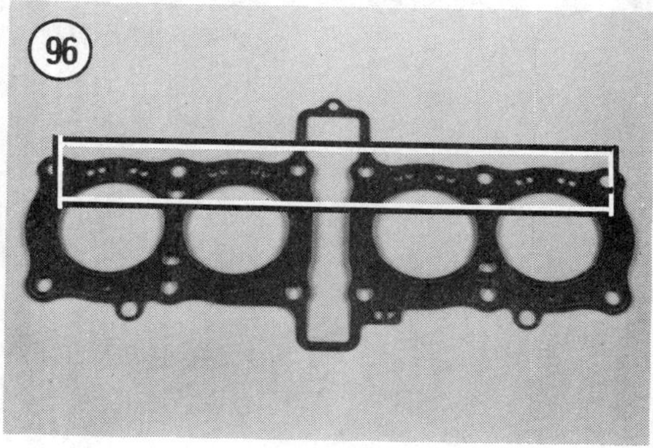

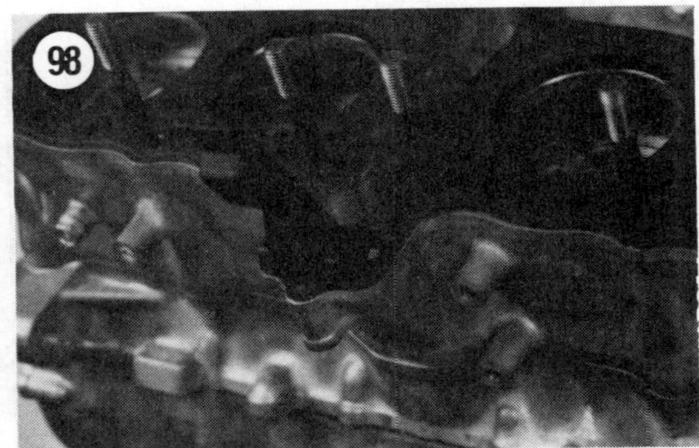

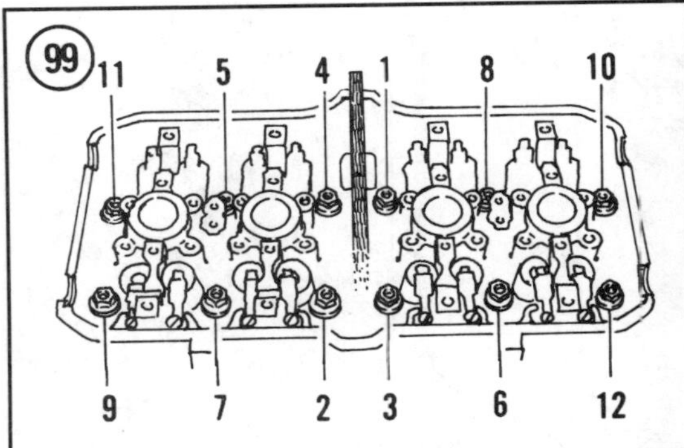

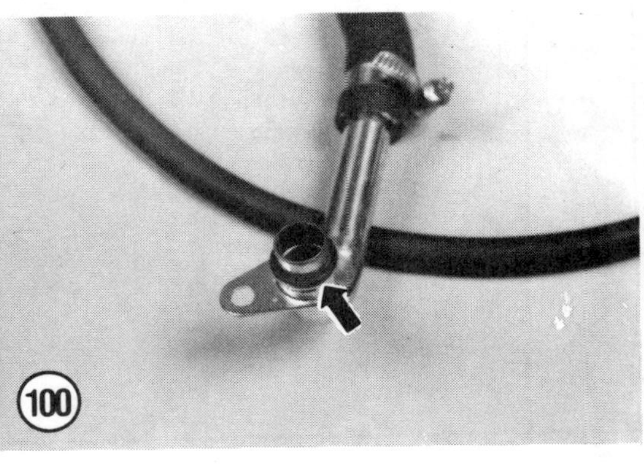

5. Install the cylinder head assembly (**Figure 80**). Check the installation of the front cam chain guide with a flashlight to make sure it is properly seated.

6. Secure the cam chain wire to the exterior of the engine.

7. Install the nuts and washers securing the cylinder head. Tighten the nuts in 2-3 stages in a crisscross pattern (**Figure 99**) to the torque specification listed in **Table 3**.

8. Install the rear camshaft chain tensioner into the cylinder head and push the mounting bolt through the hole in the cylinder head. Install the acorn nut and washer and tighten the nut securely.

9. Install the camshafts as described in this chapter.

10. If the engine was not removed, perform the following:

   a. Install a new O-ring onto each water pipe (**Figure 100**).

   b. Insert the left- and right-hand water pipes into the cylinder head (**Figure 101**). Tighten the mounting bolts securely.

   c. Install the left- and right-hand front/upper mounting bolts (**Figure 102**). Install the

washer (**Figure 103**) on the right-hand side. Tighten the bolts to the torque specification in **Table 3**.

d. Reverse Step 1 of *Removal* to complete installation.

VALVES AND VALVE COMPONENTS

Correct valve service requires a number of special tools. The following procedures describe how to check for valve component wear and to determine what type of service is required. In most cases, valve troubles are caused by poor valve seating, worn valve guides and burned valves. A valve spring compressor (Figure 104) is required to remove and install the valves.

Refer to **Figure 105** for this procedure.

1. Remove the cylinder head as described in this chapter.

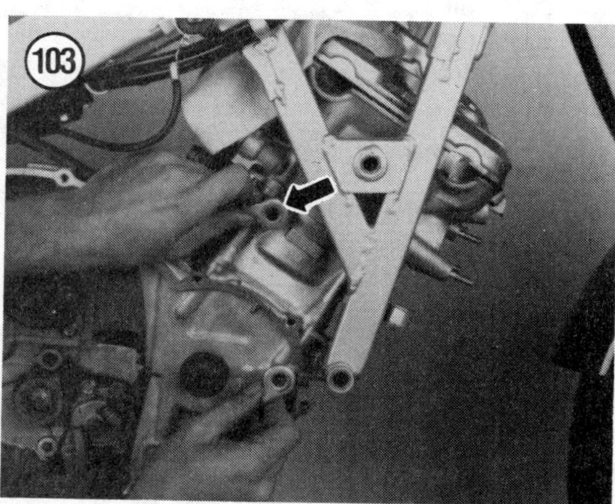

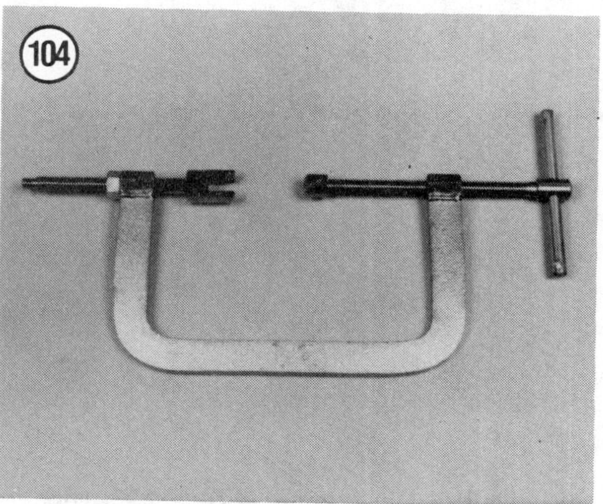

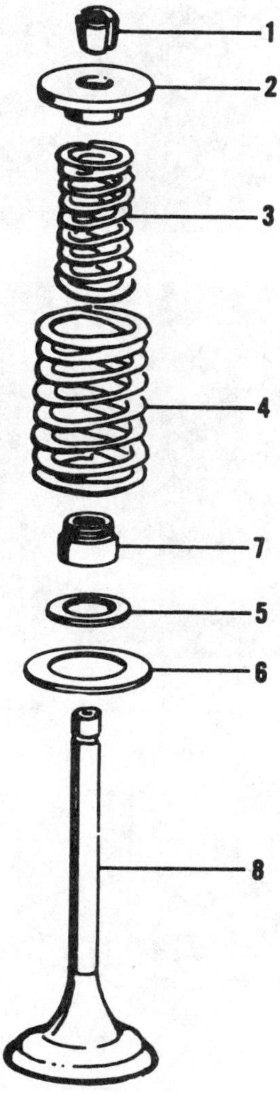

1. Keepers
2. Upper retainer
3. Inner spring
4. Outer spring
5. Inner spring seat
6. Outer spring seat
7. Oil seal
8. Valve

2. Remove the rocker arms as described in this chapter.

3. Install a valve spring compressor squarely over the valve retainer with other end of tool placed against valve head (**Figure 106**).

4. Tighten valve spring compressor until the valve keepers separate. Lift valve keepers out through the valve spring compressor (**Figure 107**) with needle nose pliers.

5. Gradually loosen the valve spring compressor and remove it from the head. Remove the upper retainer (**Figure 108**).

6. Remove the outer (**Figure 109**) and inner valve springs (**Figure 110**).

CAUTION
*Remove any burrs from the valve stem grooves before removing the valve (**Figure 111**). Otherwise the valve guides will be damaged.*

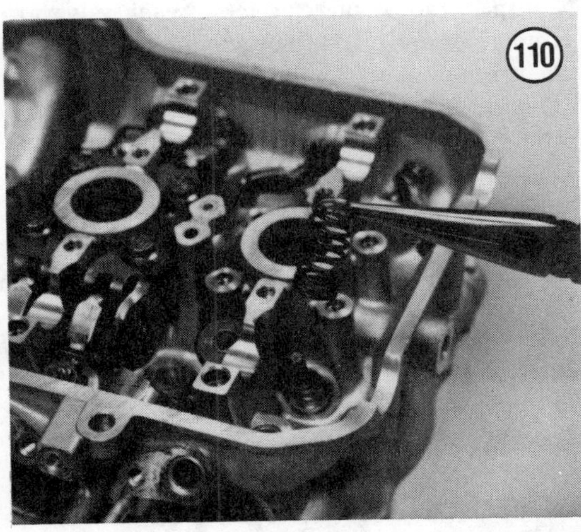

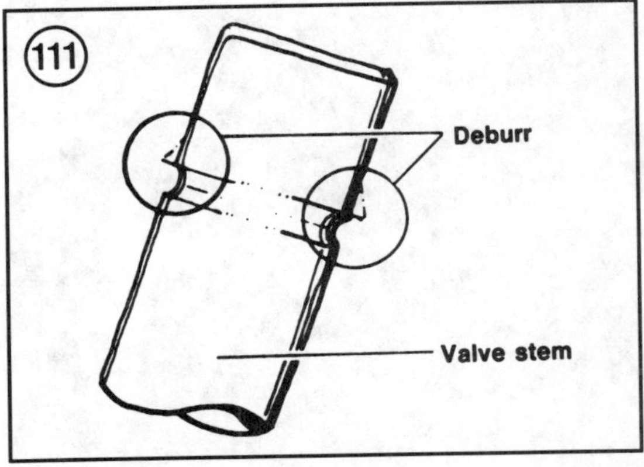

7. Turn the cylinder head over and remove the valve (**Figure 112**).

8. Pull the oil seal (**Figure 113**) off of the valve guide.

9. Remove the inner spring seat (**Figure 114**).

10. Remove the outer spring seat (**Figure 115**).

> *CAUTION*
> *All component parts of each valve assembly (**Figure 116**) must be kept together. Do not mix with similar components from other valves or excessive wear may result.*

11. Repeat Steps 3-10 and remove remaining valve(s).

Inspection

1. Clean valves in solvent. Do not gouge or damage the valve seating surface.

2. Inspect the contact surface of each valve for burning (**Figure 117**). Minor roughness and pitting can be removed by lapping the valve as described in this chapter. Excessive unevenness to the contact surface is an indication that the valve is not serviceable.

3. Inspect the valve stems for wear and roughness. Then measure the valve stem outside diameter for wear using a micrometer (**Figure 118**). Compare with specifications in Table 2.

4. Remove all carbon and varnish from the valve guides with a stiff spiral wire brush before checking wear.

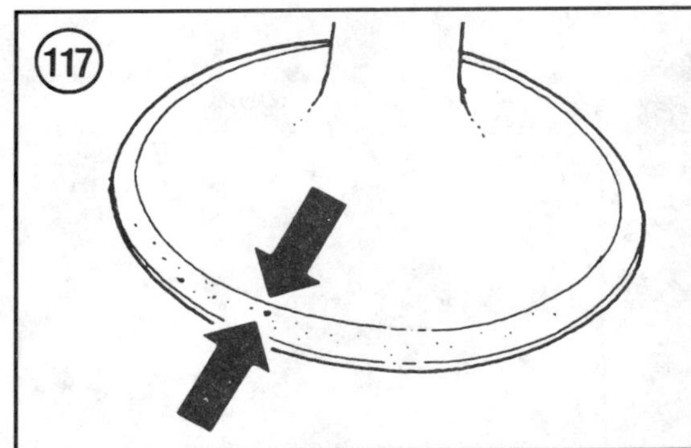

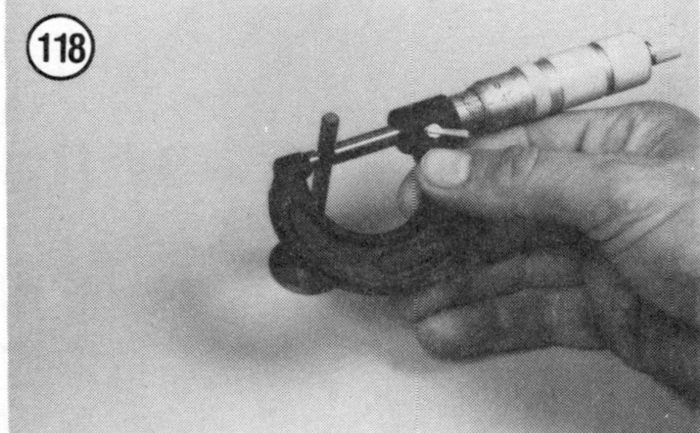

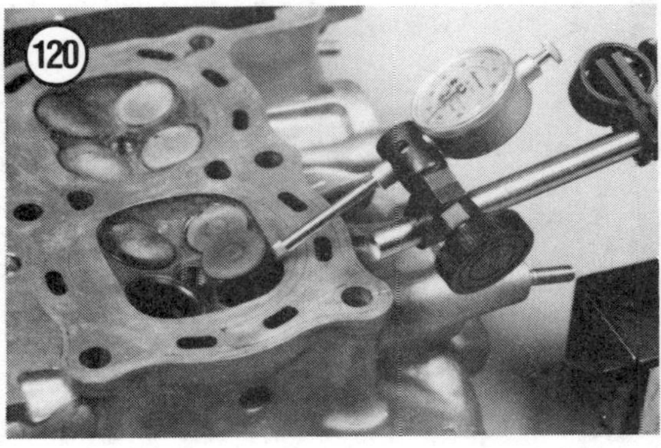

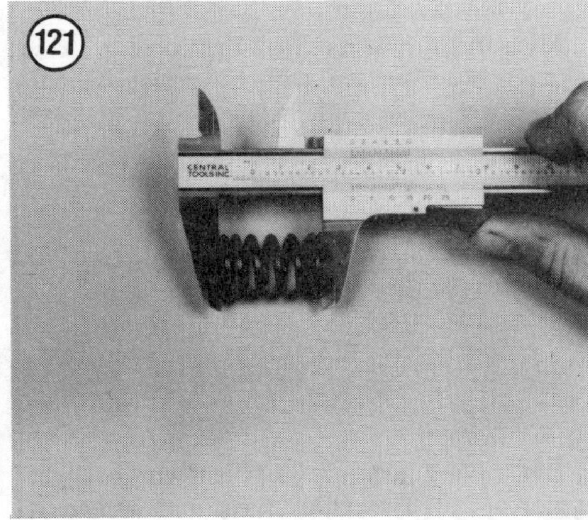

NOTE
If you do not have the required measuring devices, proceed to Step 7.

5. Measure each valve guide at top, center and bottom inside diameter with a small hole gauge. Compare measurements with specifications in **Table 2**.

6. Subtract the measurement made in Step 3 from the measurement made in Step 5. The difference is the valve guide-to-valve stem clearance. See specifications in **Table 2** for correct clearance. Replace any guide or valve that is not within tolerance. Valve guide replacement is described in this chapter.

7. If a small hole gauge is not available, insert each valve in its guide. Hold the valve just slightly off its seat and rock it sideways at 90° from each other (**Figure 119**) or use a dial indicator with its plunger against the upper valve stem (**Figure 120**). If the valve rocks more than slightly, the guide is probably worn and should be replaced. As a final check, take the cylinder head to a dealer or machine shop and have the valve guides measured.

8. Measure the valve spring length with a vernier caliper (**Figure 121**). All should be of length specified in **Table 2** without bends or other distortion. Replace defective springs as a set.

9. Check the valve spring retainer and valve keepers. If they are in good condition, they may be reused.

10. Inspect valve seats (**Figure 122**). If worn or burned, they may be reconditioned as described in this chapter. Valve seats and valves in near-perfect condition can be reconditioned by lapping with fine carborundum paste. Lapping, however, is always inferior to precision grinding. Check as follows:

   a. Clean the valve seat and valve mating areas with contact cleaner.

   b. Coat the valve seat with machinist's blue.

   c. Install the valve into its guide and rotate it against its seat with a valve lapping tool. See *Valve Lapping* in this chapter.

   d. Lift the valve out of the guide and measure the seat width with vernier calipers (**Figure 123**).

   e. The seat width for intake and exhaust valves should measure within the specifications listed in **Table 2** around the perimeter of the seat. If the seat width exceeds the service limit (**Table 2**), regrind the seats as described in this chapter.

   f. Remove all machinist's blue residue from the seats and valves.

Valve Guide Replacement

The valve guides must be removed and installed with special tools that are available from a Honda dealer. The required special tools are as follows:

   a. Valve guide driver, Honda part No. 07942-MA60000.

   b. 5.010 mm valve guide reamer, Honda part No. 07984-MA60001 or 07984-MA-6000A or 07984-MA6000B.

1. Measure the height of the valve guide from the cylinder head surface with a vernier caliper. Record each valve guide height.

> *CAUTION*
> *Do not heat the cylinder head with a torch (propane or acetylene)—never bring a flame into contact with the cylinder head. The direct heat may cause warpage of the cylinder head.*

2. The valve guides are installed with a slight interference fit. The cylinder head must be heated

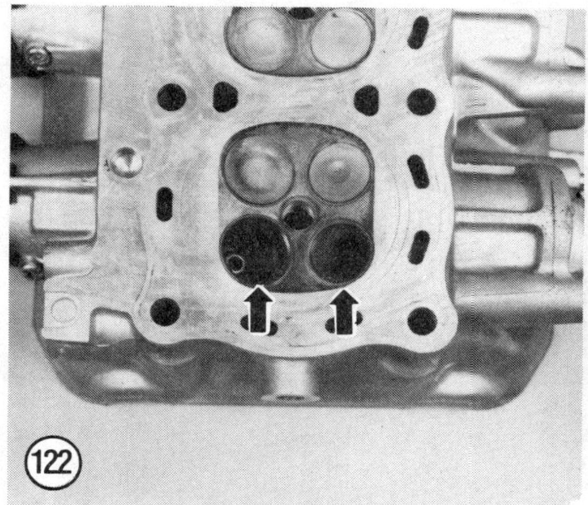

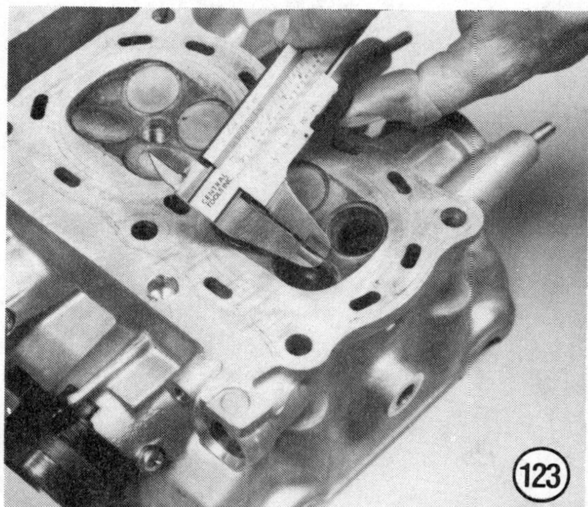

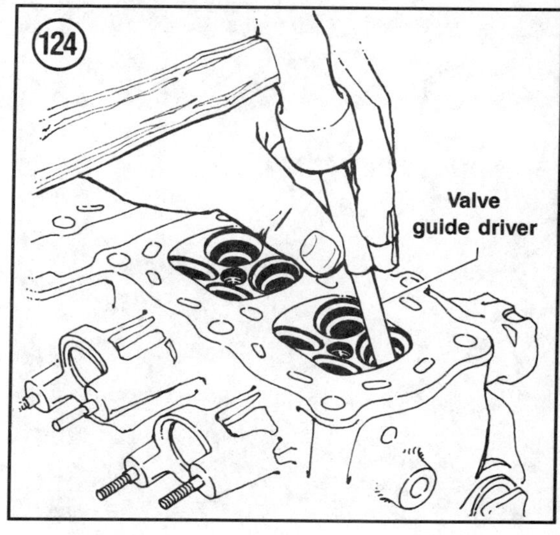

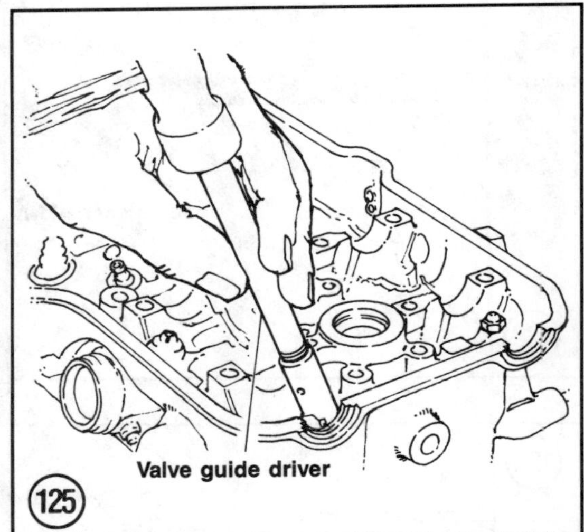

Valve guide driver

125

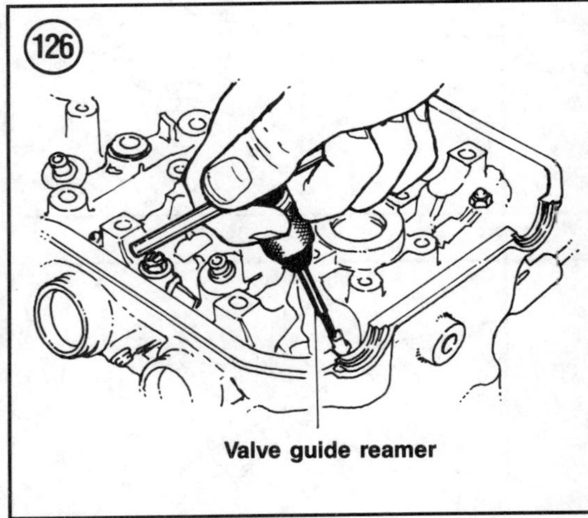

126

Valve guide reamer

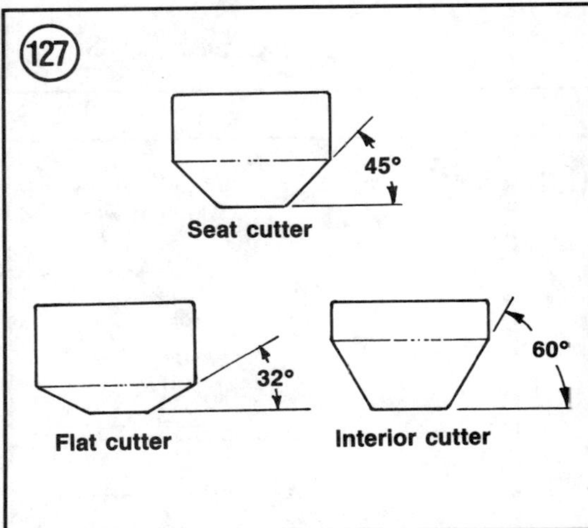

127

to a temperature of approximately 212-300° F (100-150° C) in an oven or on a hot plate.

WARNING
Heavy gloves must be worn when performing this procedure—the cylinder head will be very hot.

3. Remove the cylinder head from the oven or hot plate and place onto wood blocks with the combustion chamber facing *up*.

4. Drive the old valve guide out from the combustion chamber side of the cylinder head (**Figure 124**) with the valve guide driver.

5. Reheat the cylinder head to approximately 212-300° F (100-150° C).

6. Remove the cylinder head from the oven or hot plate and place it on wood blocks with the combustion chamber facing *down*.

7. Using the valve guide driver, install the new valve guide (**Figure 125**) so that distance from the cylinder head to the top of the valve guide is the same as that recorded in Step 1.

8. Repeat for each valve guide as necessary.

9. After the cylinder head has cooled to room temperature, ream the new valve guides as follows:

   a. Coat the valve guide and valve guide reamer with cutting oil.

   b. See **Figure 126**. Ream the valve guide by rotating the reamer *clockwise* only. Do not turn the reamer counterclockwise.

   c. Measure the valve guide inside diameter with a small hole gauge. The measurement should be within the service specifications listed in **Table 2**.

10. The valve seats must be refaced with a 45° cutter after replacing the valve guides. Reface the valve seats as described under *Valve Seat Reconditioning* in this chapter.

11. Clean the cylinder head thoroughly in solvent. Lightly oil the valve guides to prevent rust.

Valve Seat Reconditioning

The valve seats must be cut with special tools that are available from a Honda dealer or motorcycle accessory dealer. The following tools will be required:

   a. Valve seat cutters (see Honda dealer for part numbers) shown in **Figure 127** are required for this procedure.

b. Vernier caliper.
c. Machinist's blue.
d. Valve lapping tool.

NOTE
Follow the manufacturer's instructions with using valve seat facing equipment.

1. Inspect valve seats (**Figure 122**). If worn or burned, they may be reconditioned. Seats and valves in near-perfect condition can be reconditioned by lapping with fine carborundum paste. Lapping, however, is always inferior to precision grinding. Check as follows:

a. Clean the valve seat and valve mating areas with aerosol electrical contact cleaner.
b. Coat the valve seat with machinist's blue.
c. Install the valve into its guide and rotate it against its seat with a valve lapping tool. See *Valve Lapping* in this chapter.
d. Lift the valve out of the guide and measure the seat width with vernier calipers (**Figure 123**). See **Figure 128**.
e. The seat width for intake and exhaust valves should measure within the specifications listed in **Table 2** all the way around the seat. If the seat width exceeds the service limit (**Table 2**), regrind the seats as follows.

CAUTION
When grinding valve seats, work slowly to prevent grinding the seats too much. Overgrinding the valve seats will sink the valves too far into the cylinder head. Sinking the valves too far may reduce valve clearance and make it impossible to adjust valve clearance. If overgrinding occurs, the cylinder head must be replaced.

2. Install a 45° cutter onto the valve tool and lightly cut the seat to remove roughness (**Figure 129**).

3. Measure the valve seat with a vernier caliper (**Figure 128**). Record the measurement to use as a reference point when performing the following.

CAUTION
The 32° cutter removes material quickly. Work carefully and check your progress often.

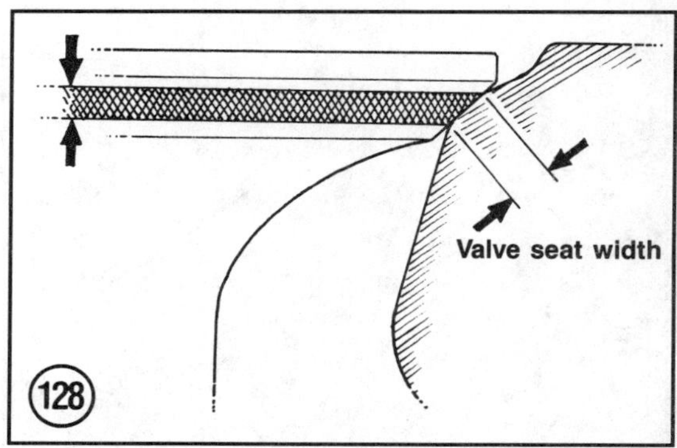

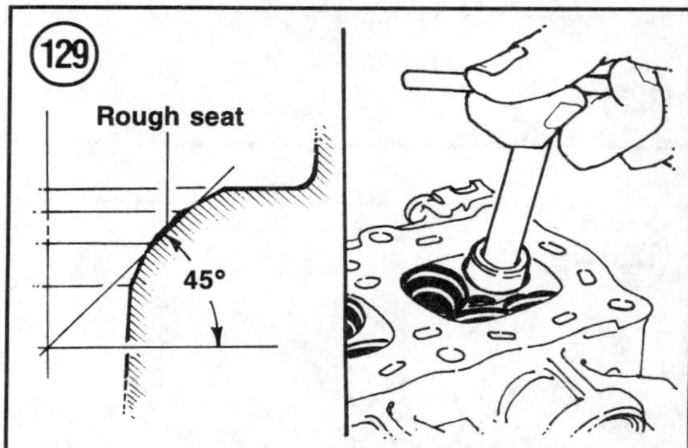

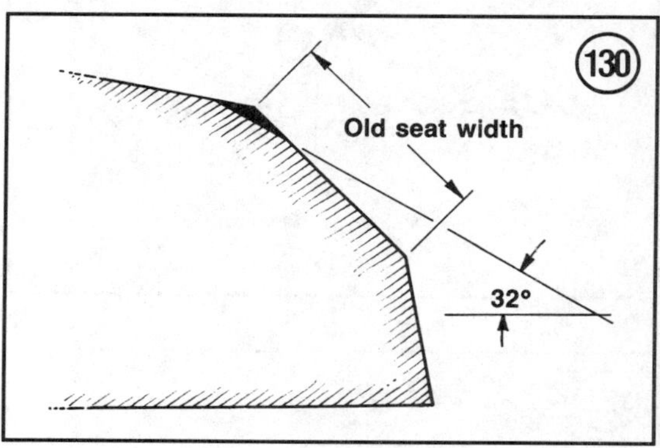

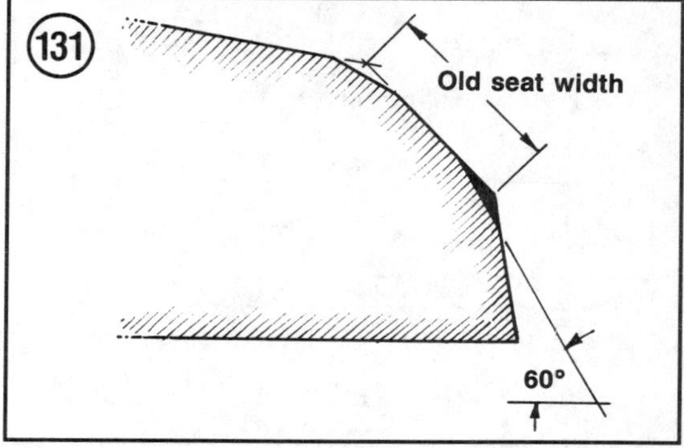

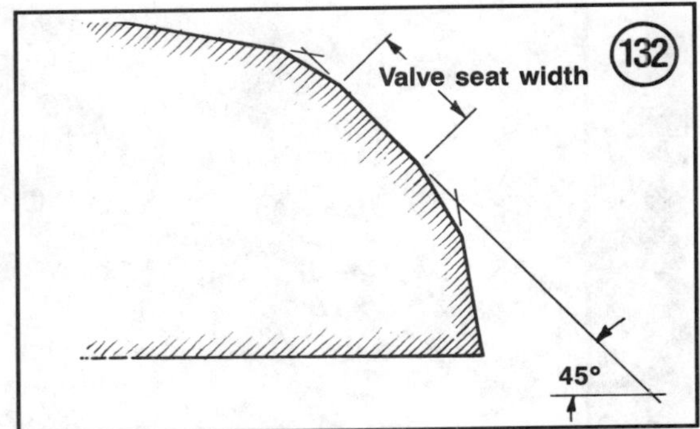

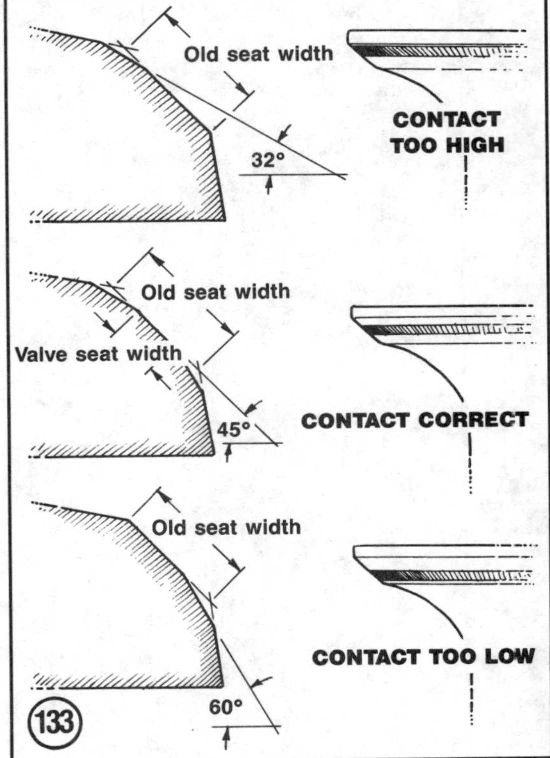

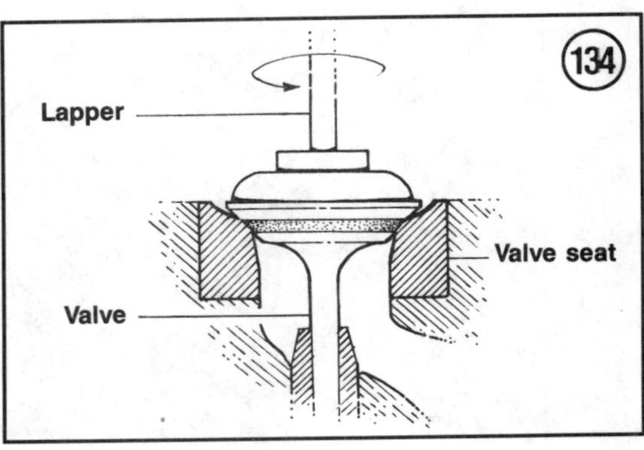

4. Install a 32° cutter onto the valve tool and lightly cut the seat to remove 1/4 of the existing valve seat (**Figure 130**).

5. Install a 60° cutter onto the valve tool and lightly cut the seat to remove the lower 1/4 of the existing valve seat (**Figure 131**).

6. Measure the valve seat with a vernier caliper (**Figure 128**). Then fit a 45° cutter onto the valve tool and cut the valve seat to the specified seat width listed in **Table 2**. See **Figure 132**.

7. When the valve seat width is correct, check valve seating as follows.

8. Clean the valve seat and valve mating areas with aerosol electrical contact cleaner.

9. Coat the valve seat with machinist's blue.

10. Insert the valve into the guide and seat it against the valve seat.

11. Remove the valve and check the contact area on the valve (**Figure 133**). Interpret results as follows:

   a. The valve contact area should be approximately in the center of the valve seat area.

   b. If the contact area is too high on the valve, lower the seat with a 32° flat cutter.

   c. If the contact area is too low on the valve, raise the seat with a 60° interior cutter.

   d. Refinish the seat using a 45° cutter.

12. When the contact area is correct, lap the valve as described in this chapter.

Valve Lapping

Valve lapping is a simple operation which can restore the valve seal without machining if the amount of wear or distortion is not too great.

This procedure should only be performed after determining that valve seat width and outside diameter are within specifications.

1. Smear a light coating of fine grade valve lapping compound on seating surface of valve.

2. Insert the valve into the head.

3. See **Figure 134**. Wet the suction cup of the lapping stick and stick it onto the head of the valve. Lap the valve to the seat by spinning the lapping stick in both directions. Every 5 to 10 seconds, rotate the valve 180° in the valve seat. Continue this action until the mating surfaces on the valve and seat are smooth and equal in size.

4. Closely examine valve seat in cylinder head (**Figure 122**). It should be smooth and even with a smooth, polished seating "ring."

5. Thoroughly clean the valves and cylinder head in solvent to remove all grinding compound. Any compound left on the valves or the cylinder head will end up in the engine oil and cause excessive wear and damage.

6. After the lapping has been completed and the valve assemblies have been reinstalled into the head the valve seal should be tested. Check the seal of each valve by pouring solvent into each of the intake and exhaust ports. There should be no leakage past the seat. If leakage occurs, combustion chamber will appear wet. If fluid leaks past any of the seats, disassemble that valve assembly and repeat the lapping procedure until there is no leakage.

Installation

1. Coat a valve stem with molybdenum disulfide paste and install into its correct valve guide.

2. Install the outer (**Figure 135**) and inner (**Figure 136**) valve spring seats.

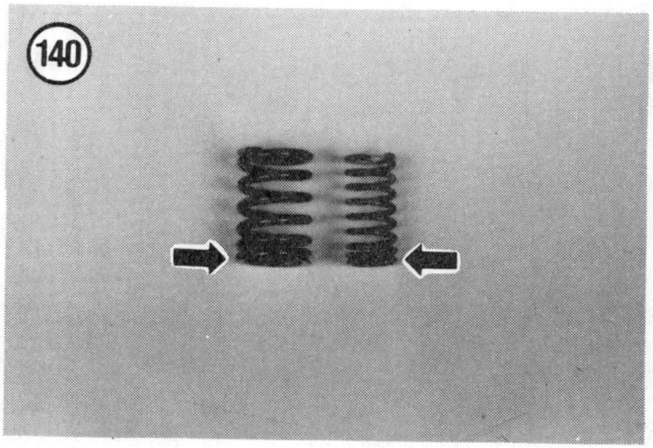

NOTE
Oil seals should be replaced whenever
a valve is removed or replaced.

3. Carefully slide a new oil seal (**Figure 137**) over the valve and seat it onto the end of the valve guide. See **Figure 138**.

4. Insert the valve into the cylinder head (**Figure 139**).

NOTE
Install valve springs with the narrow pitch end (end with coils closest together) facing the cylinder head. See Figure 140.

5. Install the inner (**Figure 141**) and outer (**Figure 142**) valve springs.

6. Install the valve spring retainer (**Figure 143**).

7. Push down on the upper valve seat with the valve spring compressor and install valve keepers (**Figure 144**). After releasing tension from compressor, examine valve keepers and make sure they are seated correctly (**Figure 145**).

8. Repeat Steps 1-7 for remaining valve(s).

CYLINDER BLOCK

The alloy cylinder block has pressed-in cylinder sleeves, which can be bored to 0.25 mm (0.010 in.) oversize and again to 0.5 mm (0.020 in.) oversize.

The cylinder block can be removed with the engine mounted in the frame but it is easier with the engine removed.

This procedure is shown with the engine removed.

Removal

1. Remove the cylinder head as described under *Cylinder Head Removal/Installation* in this chapter.

2. If the engine is mounted in the frame, loosen the hose clamp (**Figure 146**) at the cylinder block water pipe and disconnect the water hose.

3. Remove the cylinder block rear mounting bolt (**Figure 147**).

4. Loosen the cylinder block by tapping around the perimeter with a rubber or plastic mallet.

5. Pull the cylinder block (**Figure 148**) straight up and off the pistons and cylinder studs.

6. Pull the camshaft chain and wire through the opening in the cylinder block and retie the wire to the exterior of the engine to prevent it from falling into the lower crankcase.

7. If necessary, remove the pistons as described under *Piston Removal/Installation* in this chapter.

8. Remove the 2 oil jets (**Figure 149**). See **Figure 150**.

9. Remove the 2 dowel pins (**Figure 151**) and base gasket.

10. Stuff clean, lint-free shop rags into the crankcase opening to prevent objects from falling into the crankcase.

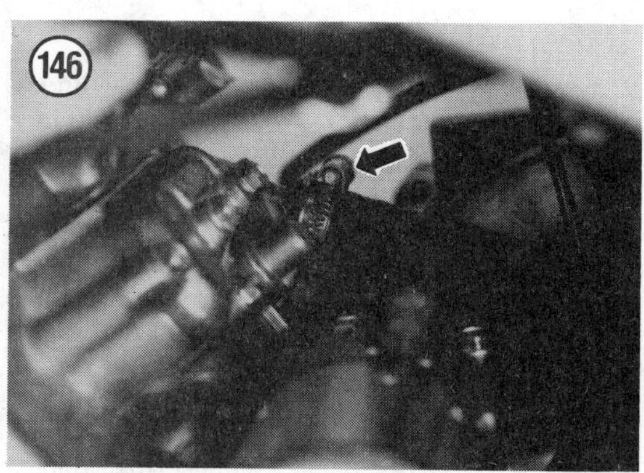

(152)

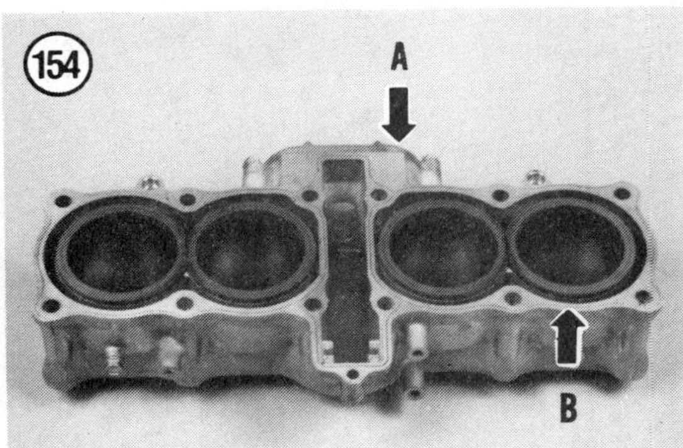

(153)

11. If necessary, remove the water joint cover bolts (**Figure 152**) and remove the cover and O-ring. See **Figure 153**.

Inspection

1. Wash the cylinder block in solvent to remove any oil and carbon particles. The cylinder bores must be cleaned thoroughly before attempting any measurement as incorrect readings may be obtained.

2. Remove all gasket residue from the top (A, **Figure 154**) and bottom (A, **Figure 155**) gasket surfaces.

3. Clean the cylinder block water ports (B, **Figure 154**) of all coolant sludge buildup.

4. Check the cylinder O-rings (B, **Figure 155**) for wear or deterioration; replace if necessary.

5. Measure cylinder block warpage with a feeler gauge and a straightedge as shown in **Figure 156**. Replace the cylinder block if the warpage exceeds the service limit in **Table 2**.

6. Measure the cylinder bores with a cylinder gauge or inside micrometer at the points shown in **Figure 157**.

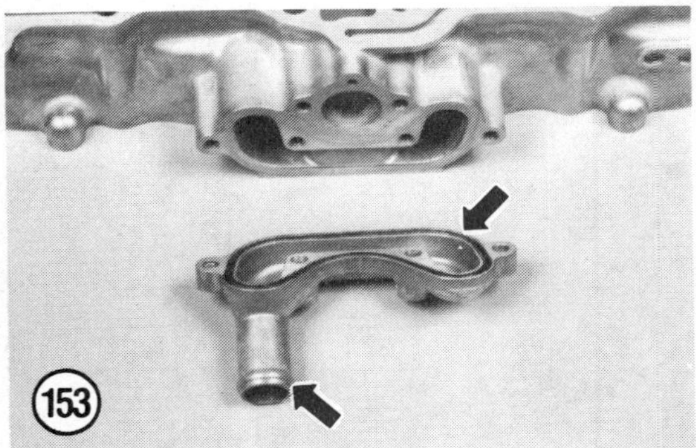

(154)

(156)

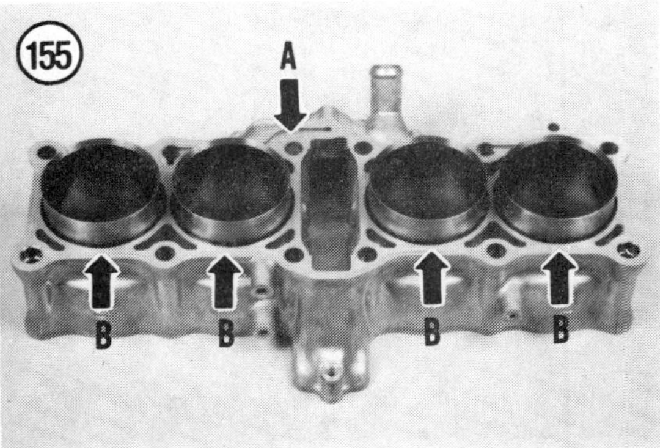

(155)

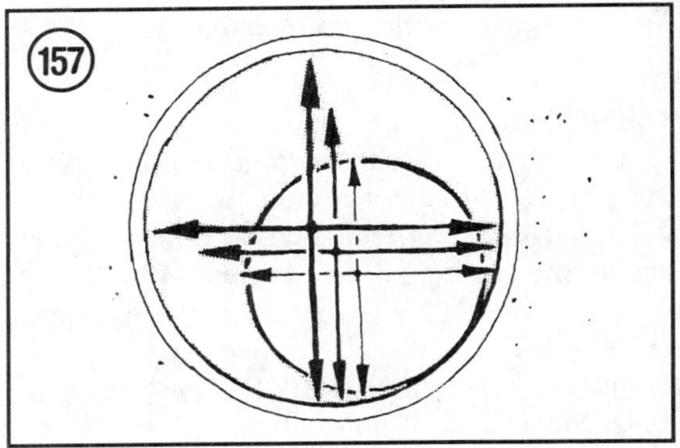

(157)

7. Measure in 2 axes—in line with the piston pin and at 90° to the pin. If the taper or out-of-round is greater than specifications (**Table 2**), the cylinders must be rebored to the next oversize and new pistons and rings installed. Rebore all 4 cylinders even though only one may be worn.

NOTE
*The new pistons should be obtained first before the cylinders are bored so that the pistons can be measured; each cylinder must be bored to match one piston only. Piston-to-cylinder clearance is specified in **Table 2**.*

8. If the cylinder(s) is not worn past the service limits, check the bore carefully for scratches or gouges. The bore still may require boring and reconditioning.

9. If the cylinders require reboring, remove all dowel pins from the cylinder block before leaving it with the dealer or machine shop for service.

10. After the cylinders have been serviced, wash each cylinder bore in hot soapy water. This is the only way to clean the cylinders of the fine grit material left from the bore or honing job. After washing the cylinder walls, run a clean white cloth through each wall; it should show no traces of grit or other debris. If the rag is dirty, the cylinder wall is not clean and must be rewashed. After the cylinder block is cleaned, lubricate the cylinder walls with clean engine oil to prevent the cylinder liners from rusting.

CAUTION
A combination of soap and water is the only solution that will completely clean cylinder walls. Solvent and kerosene cannot wash fine grit out of cylinder crevices. Grit left in the cylinder will act as a grinding compound and cause premature wear to the new rings.

Installation

1. Check that the top and bottom cylinder surfaces are clean of all gasket residue.

2. Install the 2 oil jets (**Figure 150**) with their *small* holes facing up. See **Figure 149**.

3. Install the 2 dowel pins onto the crankcase (**Figure 151**).

4. Install a new cylinder block base gasket (**Figure 158**). Make sure all holes align.

5. If removed, install the water joint cover as follows:
   a. Replace the water joint cover O-ring (**Figure 153**) if necessary.
   b. Align the cover with the cylinder block and install the 4 bolts and 2 copper washers. The 2 copper washers (A, **Figure 159**) are installed with the 2 center bolts (B, **Figure 159**).
   c. Tighten the bolts securely.

6. Install the pistons, if removed, as described in this chapter.

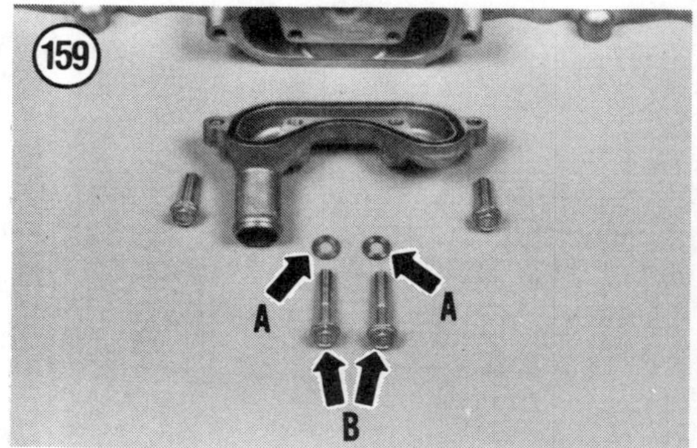

7. Install a piston holding fixture under the 2 pistons protruding out of the crankcase.

8. Lubricate the cylinder wall and pistons liberally with engine oil prior to installation.

9. Carefully align the cylinder block with the pistons.

NOTE
Once the cylinder block is installed, run the camshaft chain and wire up through the opening in the cylinder block.

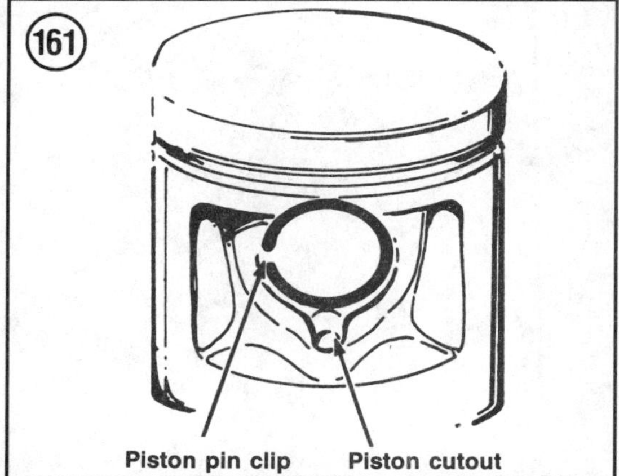

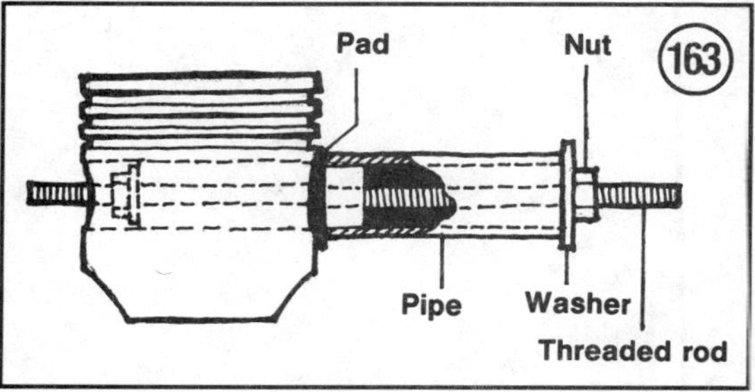

10. Compress each ring as it enters the cylinder with your fingers or by using aircraft type hose clamps of appropriate diameter.

CAUTION
Don't tighten the clamp any more than necessary to compress the rings. If the rings can't slip through easily, the clamp may gouge the rings.

11. Remove the piston holding fixtures and push the cylinder block (**Figure 148**) all the way down.

12. Install the cylinder block bolt (**Figure 147**) and tighten it securely.

13. If the engine is mounted in the frame, attach the water hose to the water pipe joint (**Figure 146**). Tighten the hose clamp.

14. Install the cylinder head as described in this chapter.

PISTONS AND PISTON RINGS

Piston
Removal/Installation

1. Remove the cylinder block as described in this chapter.

2. Stuff the crankcase with clean, lint-free shop rags to prevent objects from falling into the crankcase.

3. Lightly mark each piston crown (**Figure 160**) with an identification number (1-4), starting with the No. 1 piston (left-hand side).

4. Remove the piston rings as described in this chapter.

5. Before removing the piston, hold the rod tightly and rock the piston. Any rocking motion (do not confuse with the normal sliding motion) indicates wear on the piston pin, rod bushing, pin bore, or more likely, a combination of all three. Mark the piston and pin so that they will be reassembled into the same set.

6. Remove the circlips from the piston pin bores (**Figure 161**).

NOTE
Discard the piston circlips. New circlips must be installed during reassembly.

7. Push the piston pin out of the piston by hand (**Figure 162**). If the pin is tight, use a homemade tool (**Figure 163**) to remove it. Do not drive the

piston pin out as this action may damage the piston pin, connecting rod or piston.

8. Lift the piston off the connecting rod.

9. Repeat Steps 4-8 for the other pistons.

10. Inspect the piston as described in this chapter.

NOTE
New piston circlips must be installed.

11. Coat the connecting rod bushing, piston pin and piston with assembly oil.

12. Place the piston over the connecting rod. If you are installing old parts, make sure the piston is installed on the correct rod as marked during removal. If the cylinders were bored, install the new pistons as marked by the machinist. The IN mark on each piston crown (**Figure 164**) must face to the intake valve side of the engine (rear). Install the pistons in the following order:

   a. No. 2.
   b. No. 1.
   c. No. 3.
   d. No. 4.

13. Insert the piston pin through one side of the piston until it starts to enter the connecting rod. Then it may be necessary to move the piston around until the pin enters the connecting rod. Do not force installation or damage may occur. If the pin does not slide easily, use the home made tool (**Figure 163**) but eliminate the piece of pipe. Push the pin in until it is centered in the piston.

14. Install the new piston circlips in the circlip grooves. Make sure they are correctly seated and with the gap away from the cutout in the piston (**Figure 161**).

15. Install piston rings as described in this chapter.

16. Repeat Steps 13-15 for the opposite pistons.

Piston Inspection

1. Carefully clean the carbon from the piston crown (**Figure 164**) with a soft scraper or wire wheel. Large carbon accumulations reduce piston cooling and cause detonation and piston damage. Do not remove or damage the carbon ridge around the circumference of the piston above the top ring. If the pistons, rings and cylinders are found to be dimensionally correct and can be reused, removal of the carbon ring from the top of the piston or the carbon ridges from the cylinders will promote excessive oil consumption.

CAUTION
Do not wire brush the sides of the piston as the brush will leave scratches on the ring grooves and piston skirt.

NOTE
*Be sure to renumber the piston crown (**Figure 165**) after performing Step 1. Used pistons must be reinstalled in the same cylinder bore.*

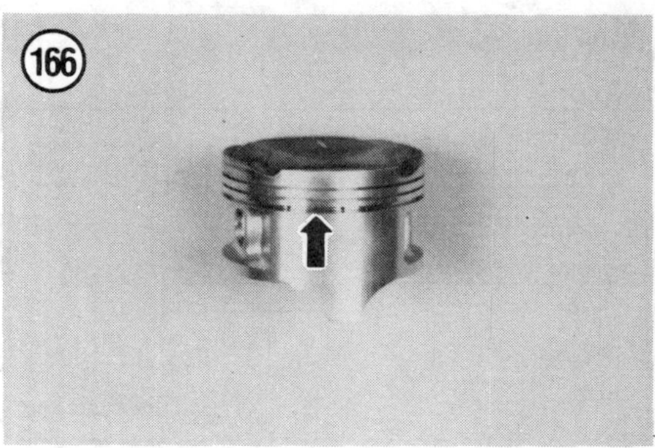

2. After cleaning the piston, examine the crown. The crown should show no signs of wear or damage. If the crown appears pecked or spongy-looking, also check the spark plug, valves and combustion chamber for aluminum deposits. If these deposits are found, the cylinder(s) are suffering from excessive heat caused by a lean fuel mixture or preignition.

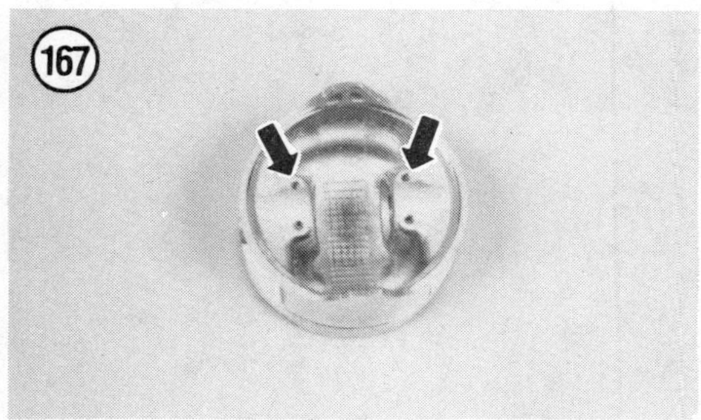

3. Examine each ring groove for burrs, dented edges and wide wear. Pay particular attention to the top compression ring groove, as it usually wears more than the others. Because the oil rings are constantly bathed in oiled, these rings and grooves wear little compared to compression rings and their grooves. If there is evidence of oil ring groove wear or if the oil ring assembly is tight and difficult to remove, the piston skirt may have collapsed due to excessive heat and is permanently deformed. Replace the pistons.

4. Check the oil control holes in the piston for carbon or oil sludge buildup. Clean the holes with a small diameter drill bit. See **Figure 166** and **Figure 167**.

5. Check the piston skirts for cracks or other damage. If a piston(s) shows signs of partial seizure (bits of aluminum build-up on the piston skirts), the pistons should be replaced and the cylinders bored (if necessary) to reduce the possibility of engine noise and further piston seizure.

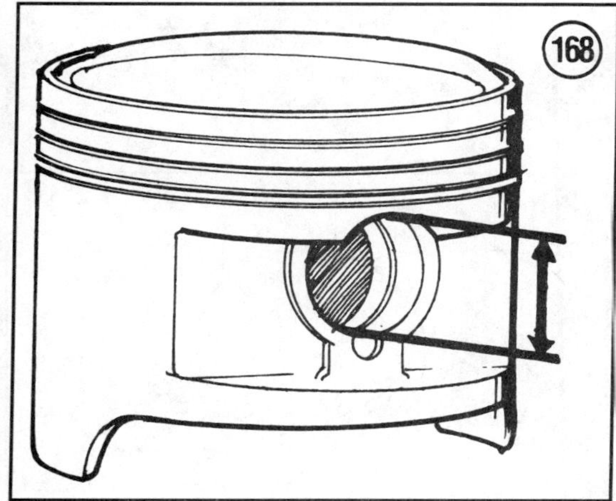

NOTE
If the piston skirts are worn or scuffed unevenly from side to side, the connecting rod may be bent or twisted.

6. Inspect the wrist pin for chrome flaking or cracks. Replace wrist pin if necessary.

7. Measure the piston pin bore (**Figure 168**) with a snap gauge and measure the outside diameter of the piston pin with a micrometer (**Figure 169**). Compare against dimensions given in **Table 2**. Replace the piston and piston pin as a set if either is worn.

8. Install a new piston pin circlip in each piston circlip groove and check the groove for wear or circlip looseness by pulling the circlip from side to side. If the circlip has any side play, the groove is worn and the pistons must be replaced.

9. Measure piston-to-cylinder clearance as described under *Piston Clearance* in this chapter.

10. If damage or wear indicate piston replacement, select new pistons as described under *Piston Clearance* in this chapter.

Piston Clearance

1. Make sure the piston and cylinder walls are clean and dry.

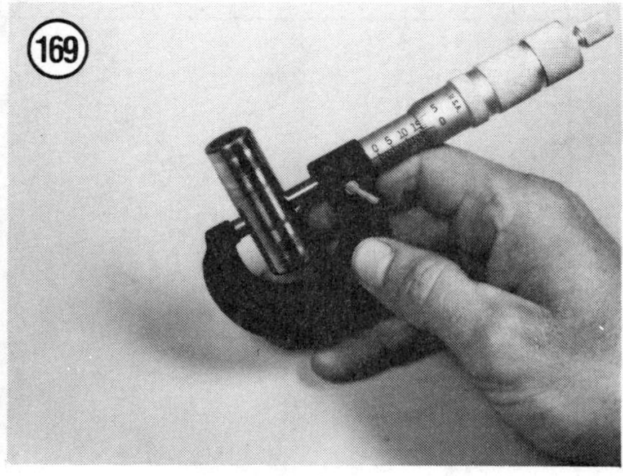

2. Measure the inside diameter of the cylinder at a point 13 mm (1/2 in.) from the upper edge with a bore gauge.

3. Measure the outside diameter of the piston at a point 10 mm (13/32 in.) from the lower edge of the piston 90° to piston pin axis (**Figure 170**).

4. Subtract the piston diameter from the cylinder bore diameter; the difference is piston-to-cylinder clearance. Compare to specification in **Table 2**. If clearance is excessive, the pistons should be replaced and the cylinders rebored. Purchase the new pistons first; measure its diameter and add the specified clearance to determine the proper cylinder bore diameters.

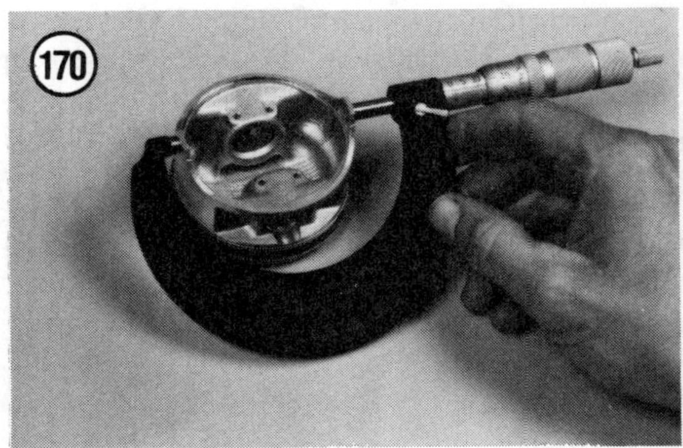

> *NOTE*
> *If one cylinder requires boring, the other cylinders must be bored also.*

**Piston Ring
Removal/Installation**

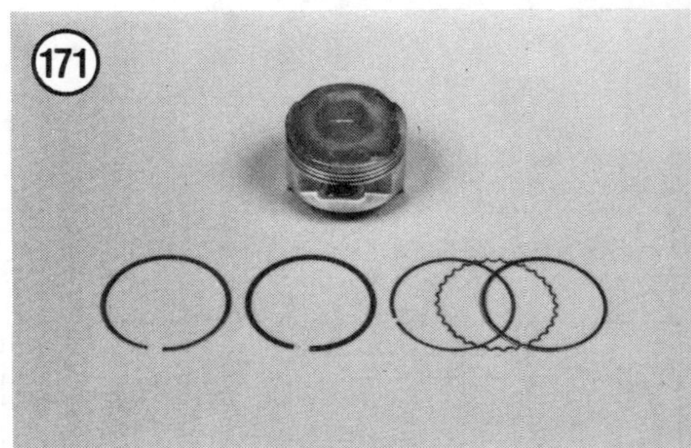

> *WARNING*
> *The edges of all piston rings are very sharp. Be careful when handling them to avoid cut fingers.*

> *NOTE*
> *Store the rings in order of removal and with their piston (**Figure 171**).*

1. Remove the old rings with a ring expander tool or by spreading the ring ends with your thumbs and lifting the rings up evenly (**Figure 172**).

2. Measure the side clearance of each ring in its groove with a flat feeler gauge (**Figure 173**) and compare with the specifications in **Table 2**. If the clearance is greater than specified, the rings must be replaced. If the clearance is still excessive with the new rings, the piston must be replaced.

3. Using a broken piston ring, remove all carbon from the piston ring grooves.

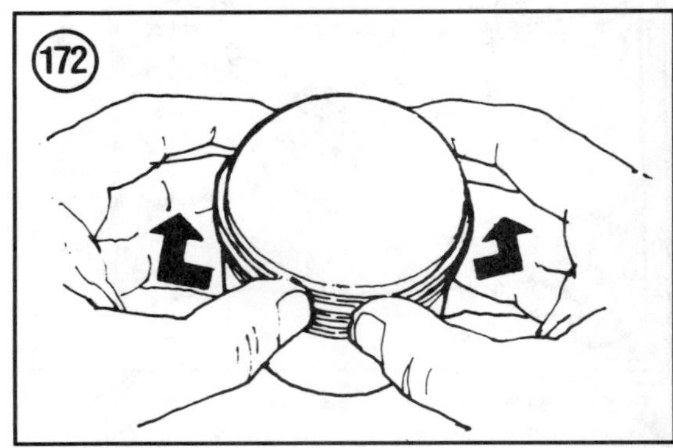

4. Inspect grooves carefully for burrs, nicks or broken or cracked lands. Replace piston if necessary.

5. Check end gap of each ring. To check ring, insert the ring into the bottom of the cylinder bore and square it with the cylinder wall by tapping it with the piston (**Figure 174**). The ring should be pushed in about 15 mm (5/8 in.). Insert a feeler gauge as shown in **Figure 175**. Compare gap with

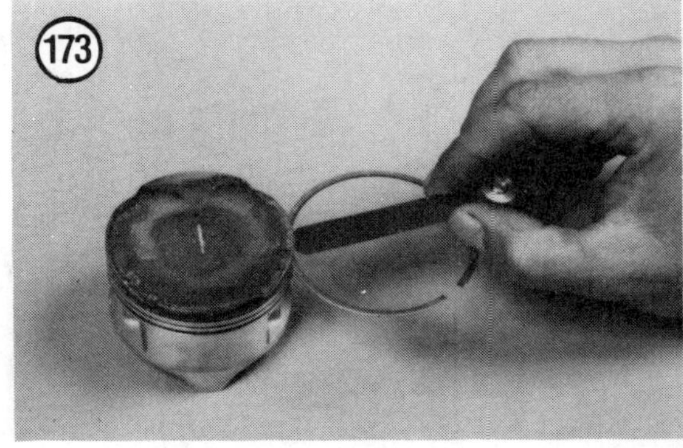

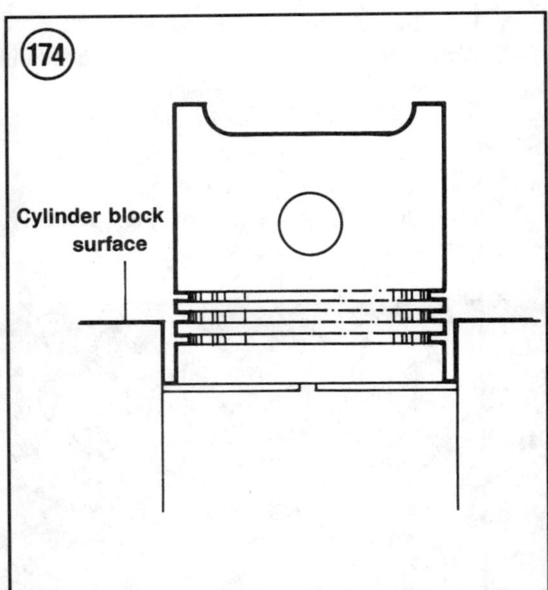

Table 2. Replace ring if gap is too large. If the gap on the new ring is smaller than specified, hold a small file in a vise, grip the ends of the ring with your fingers and enlarge the gap.

6. Roll each ring around its piston groove as shown in **Figure 176** to check for binding. Minor binding may be cleaned up with a fine-cut file.

> *NOTE*
> *Install the piston rings in the order shown in **Figure 177**.*

> *NOTE*
> *Install all rings with the manufacturer's markings facing up (**Figure 177**).*

7. Install the piston rings—first the bottom, then the middle, then the top ring—by carefully spreading the ends with your thumbs and slipping the rings over the top of the piston. Remember that

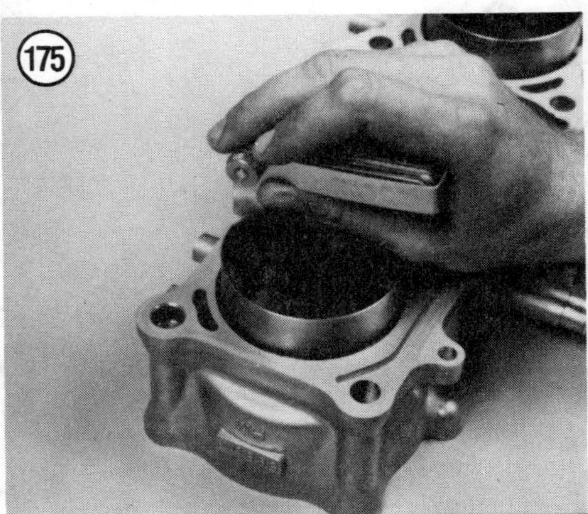

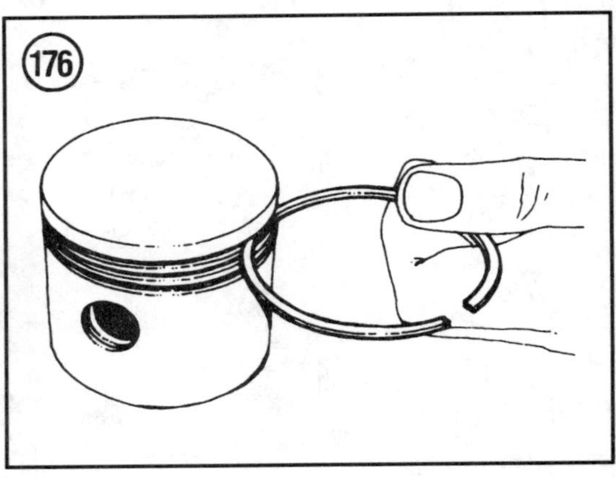

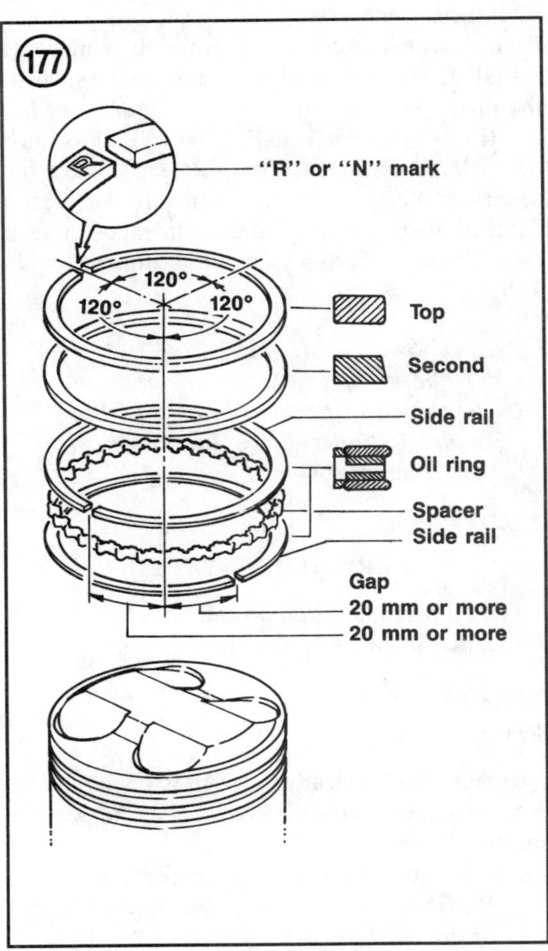

the piston rings must be installed with the marks on them facing up toward the top of the piston or there is the possibility of oil pumping past the rings.

   a. Install the oil ring assembly into the bottom ring groove. The assembly is comprised of 2 steel rails and 1 expander. The expander is installed in the middle of the steel rails.

   b. The top and second piston rings are different. The second ring is slightly tapered and must be installed as shown in **Figure 177**. The top ring is symmetrical and must be installed as shown in **Figure 177**.

8. Make sure the rings are seated completely in their grooves all the way around the piston and that the end gaps are distributed around the piston as shown in **Figure 177**. It is important that the ring gaps are not aligned with each other when installed to prevent compression pressures from escaping past them.

9. If installing oversize compression rings, check the number to make sure the correct rings are being installed. The ring numbers should be the same as the piston oversize number.

10. If new rings are installed, the cylinders must be deglazed or honed. This will help to seat the new rings. Refer honing service to a Honda dealer. After honing, measure the end clearance of each ring (**Figure 175**) and compare to dimensions in **Table 2**.

> *NOTE*
> *If the cylinders were deglazed or honed, clean the cylinders as described under **Cylinder Block Inspection** in this chapter.*

LUBRICATION SYSTEM

The oil pan and oil pump can be removed with the engine mounted in the frame.

Service Notes

Because the lubrication system is a vital key to engine reliability, note the following during service and inspection:

   a. Was the engine oil level correct?

   b. Was the engine oil contaminated with sludge or coolant?

   c. Was the oil pump properly mounted?

   d. Were external oil lines damaged or their fittings loose?

   e. Were banjo bolts loose or clogged?

   f. Was the oil filter element clogged?

   g. Was the oil pump screen clogged?

   h. Was the relief valve working properly, clogged or damaged?

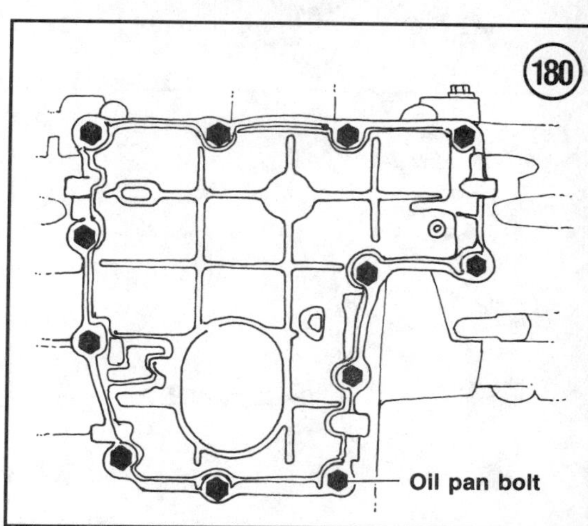

i. Were all O-rings properly installed or were they damaged?

j. Was the oil cooler damaged or improperly installed?

k. Were the oil passages partially restricted or clogged?

Oil Pan
Removal/Installation

The oil pan can be removed with the engine mounted in the frame.

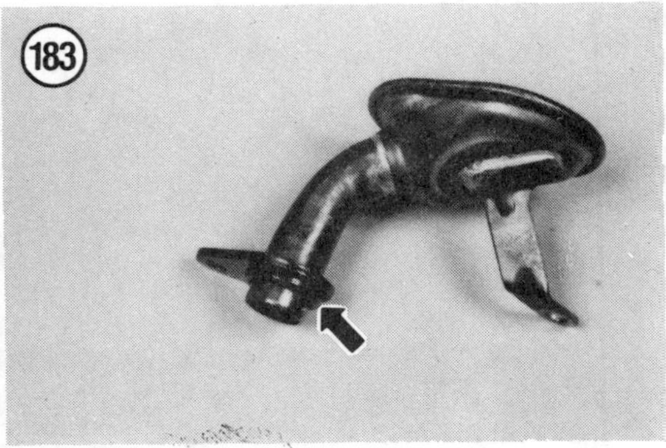

1. Remove the lower fairings as described in Chapter Thirteen.

2. Remove the mufflers as described under *Exhaust System Removal/Installation* in Chapter Seven.

3. Drain the engine oil and remove the oil filter as described under *Engine Oil and Filter Change* in Chapter Three.

4. Disconnect the left- (A, **Figure 178**) and right-hand (**Figure 179**) oil pipes at the oil pan.

5. Remove the exhaust system mounting bracket (B, **Figure 178**).

NOTE
Place an oil drain pan underneath the engine when performing Step 6.

6. Loosen the oil pan mounting bolts (**Figure 180**) all the way around the pan and allow residual oil to drain into the drain pan.

7. Completely remove the oil pan mounting bolts and lower the pan (**Figure 181**) from the crankcase and remove it.

8. Remove the O-rings and dowel pins (A, **Figure 182**). Discard the O-rings as they should be replaced.

9. Before cleaning the oil pan, check the inside for signs of excessive aluminum or metal debris that may indicate engine, clutch or transmission damage.

10. Installation is the reverse of these steps, noting the following:

    a. Apply clean engine oil to new O-rings.

    b. Install the new O-rings and dowel pins (A, **Figure 182**).

    c. Remove all gasket residue from the oil pan and crankcase. Then install a new pan gasket. Make sure the pan gasket bolt holes align properly.

    d. Install a new oil filter and refill the engine oil as described in Chapter Three.

Oil Strainer
Removal/Installation

1. Remove the oil pan as described in this chapter.

2. Remove the oil strainer bolts and remove the oil strainer assembly (B, **Figure 182**).

3. Check the O-ring (**Figure 183**) for wear or deterioration; replace if necessary.

4. Check the oil strainer screen (**Figure 184**) for clogging or damage. If the screen is clogged, clean in solvent and dry thoroughly. If the screen cannot be cleaned or if it is damaged, replace the oil strainer assembly.

5. Installation is the reverse of these steps, noting the following:

    a. Apply clean engine oil to the O-ring.

    b. Make sure the O-ring (**Figure 183**) is installed on the oil strainer before installation.

    c. Tighten the oil strainer bolts securely.

Oil Pressure Relief Valve Removal/Inspection/Installation

1. Remove the oil pan as described in this chapter.

2. Pull the oil pressure relief valve (**Figure 185**) out of the crankcase.

3. Check the relief valve operation by pushing the piston (A, **Figure 186**) with your finger. The piston should move smoothly. If the piston movement is tight, inspect the valve as described in Step 4.

4. Referring to **Figure 187**, perform the following:

    a. Remove the relief valve circlip (B, **Figure 186**).

    b. Remove the washer (**Figure 188**).

    c. Remove the spring (**Figure 189**).

    d. Remove the piston (**Figure 190**).

    e. Inspect the piston and piston bore (**Figure 191**) for scoring, excessive wear or cracks.

    f. Inspect the spring for fatigue or damage.

    g. Replace the oil pressure relief valve assembly if any one part is damaged or worn. The relief valve cannot be rebuilt.

5. Reverse Step 4 to assemble the relief valve. Make sure the circlip seats in the housing groove completely.

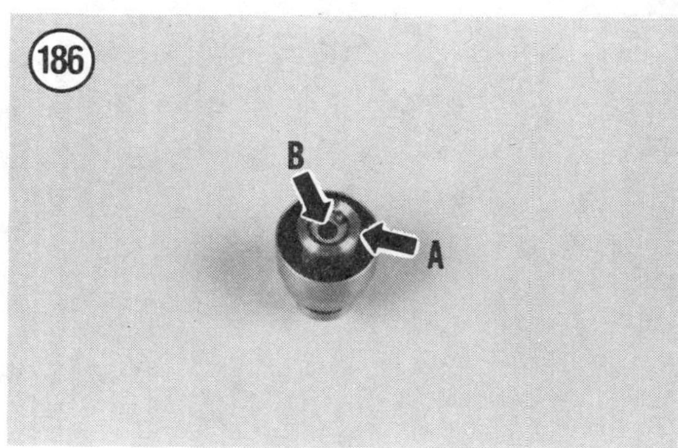

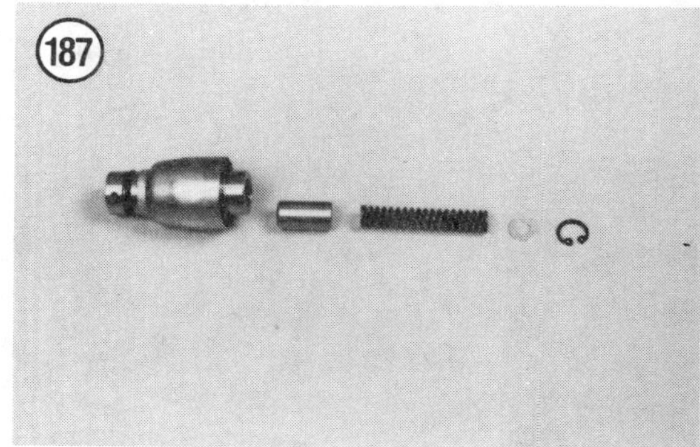

6. Inspect the O-ring (**Figure 192**) for wear or damage; replace if necessary.

7. Install by reversing Step 1 and Step 2.

Oil Pump
Removal/Installation

The oil pump can be removed with the engine installed in the frame.

1. Remove the clutch as described in Chapter Five.

2. Remove the oil pan as described in this chapter.

3. Remove the oil strainer as described in this chapter.

4. Remove the pressure relief valve as described in this chapter.

5. See **Figure 193**. Remove the oil pump mounting bolts (A) and remove the oil pump (B).

6. Installation is the reverse of these steps. Note the following:

    a. Align the oil pump shaft with the water pump shaft (**Figure 194**) and install the oil pump.

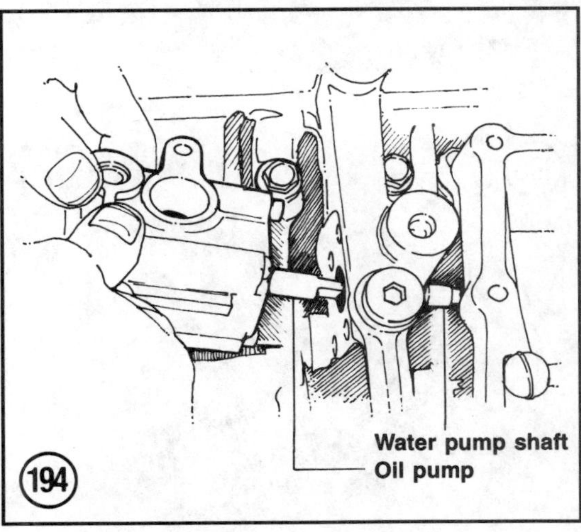

b. Install the oil pump mounting bolts (B, **Figure 193**) and tighten to the torque specification in **Table 3**.

c. Refill the engine oil as described in Chapter Three.

Oil Pump
Disassembly/Inspection/Assembly

1. Remove the oil pump as described in this chapter.

2. Remove the oil pump assembly screws (**Figure 195**).

3. Disassemble the feed portion of the oil pump as follows:

   a. Remove the feed pump cover (**Figure 196**).
   b. Remove the 2 dowel pins (**Figure 197**).
   c. Remove the feed pump outer (**Figure 198**) and inner (**Figure 199**) rotors.
   d. Remove the pin (**Figure 200**) from the hole in the pump shaft.
   e. Remove the washer (**Figure 201**) from the shaft.

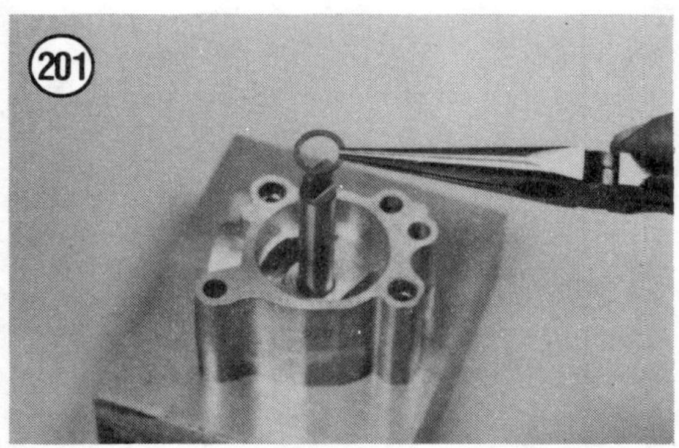

4. Disassemble the oil cooler portion of the pump as follows:

  a. Remove the cooler pump cover (**Figure 202**).
  b. Remove the dowel pin (**Figure 203**).
  c. Remove the outer rotor (**Figure 204**).
  d. Push the pump shaft out slightly and remove the inner rotor (**Figure 205**).
  e. Remove the pin (**Figure 206**) from the hole in the pump shaft.

5. Remove the pump shaft (**Figure 207**) from the pump housing.

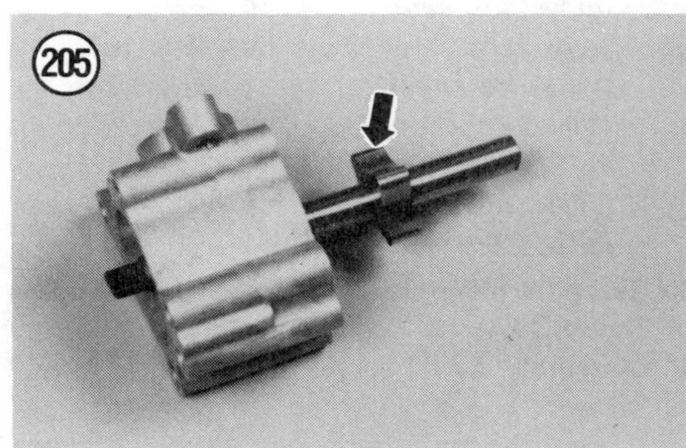

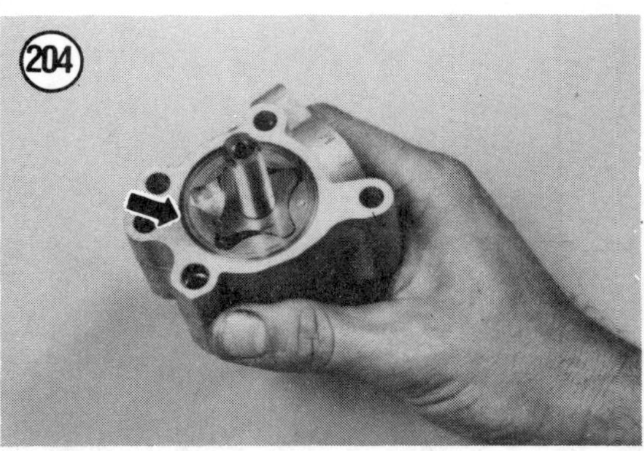

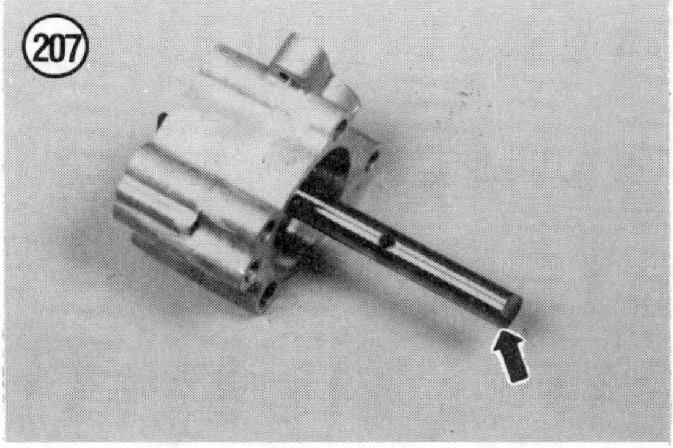

6. Inspect the rotors (**Figure 208**) for wear, cracks or other damage.

7. Inspect the housing rotor bores (**Figure 209**) for excessive wear or damage.

8. Inspect the feed pump and cooler pump covers (**Figure 210**) for wear or damage.

9. Check the oil pump shaft (**Figure 211**). Check the shaft for flatness by rolling it on a piece of glass. Then check the pin holes in the shaft for wear or damage.

NOTE
Proceed with Step 10 only when the above inspection and measurement steps have been completed and all parts are known to be good. If any component is worn or damaged, the oil pump assembly must be replaced; the pump cannot be rebuilt as individual parts are not available.

10. Insert the pump shaft into the housing as shown in **Figure 207**.

11. Assemble the oil cooler portion of the pump as follows:

   a. Insert the pin into the hole in the oil pump shaft as shown in **Figure 206**.

   b. Slide the inner rotor onto the pump shaft (**Figure 205**) and engage the notch in the back of the rotor with the pin. Then insert the rotor and shaft all the way into the pump housing.

   c. Install the outer rotor (**Figure 204**) so that the mark on the rotor (**Figure 212**) faces *up*.

12. Assemble the feed portion of the pump as follows:

   a. Install the washer over the pump shaft (**Figure 201**).

   b. Insert the pin into the hole in the oil pump shaft (**Figure 200**).

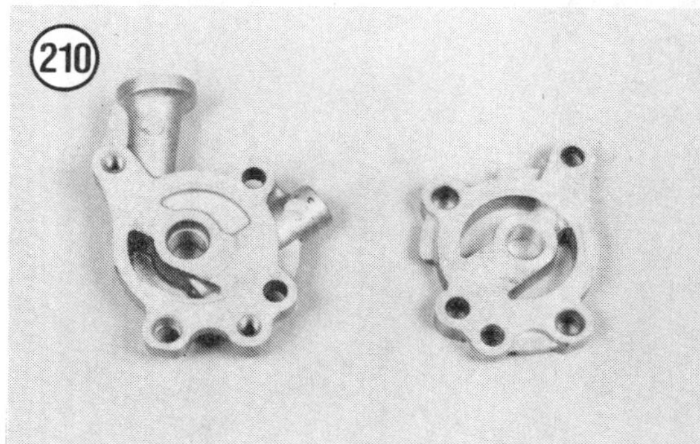

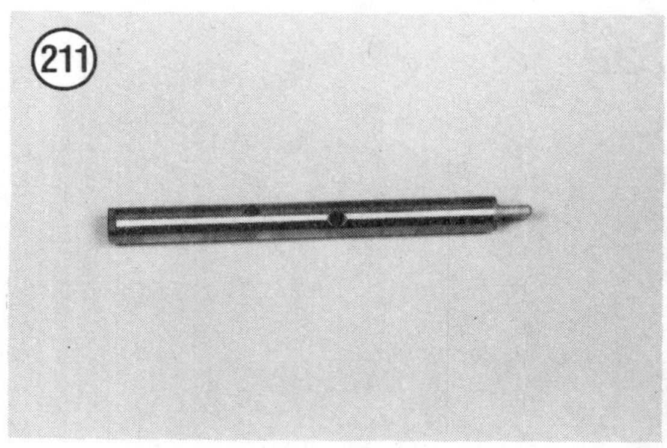

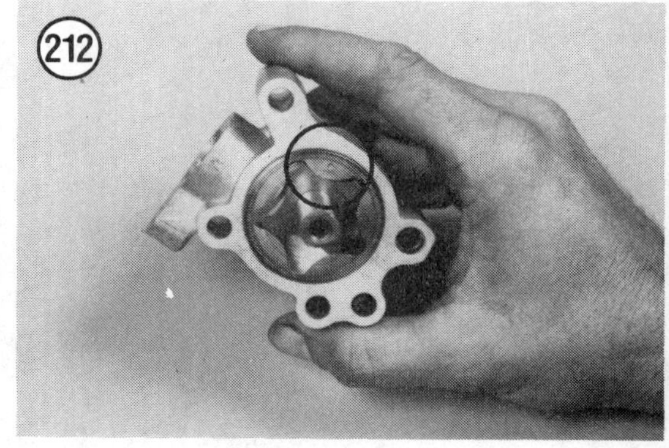

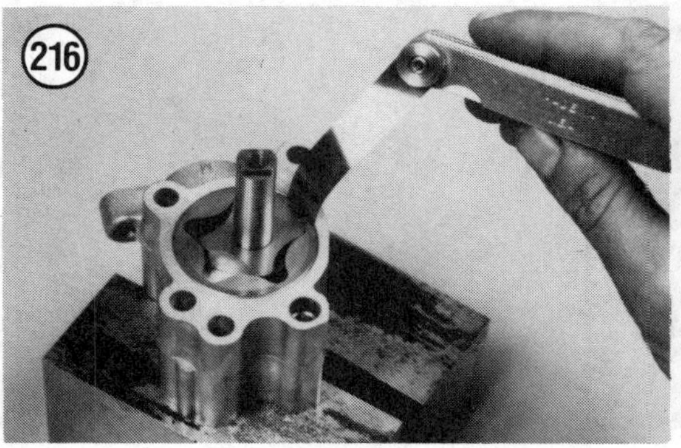

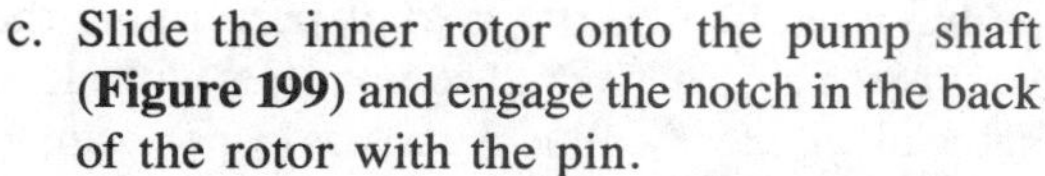

4

c. Slide the inner rotor onto the pump shaft (**Figure 199**) and engage the notch in the back of the rotor with the pin.

d. Install the outer rotor (**Figure 198**) so that the locator mark on the rotor faces *up*.

13. Inspect the rotors as follows:

a. Check the clearance between the inner tip and the outer rotor with a flat feeler gauge. If the clearance is greater than the service limit in **Table 2**, the oil pump must be replaced. See **Figure 213** (feed pump) or **Figure 214** (oil cooler pump).

b. Check the clearance between the outer rotor and the housing with a flat feeler gauge. If the clearance is greater than the service limit in **Table 2**, the oil pump must be replaced. See **Figure 215** (feed pump) or **Figure 216** (oil cooler pump).

c. Check the rotor end clearance with a straightedge and flat feeler gauge. If the clearance is greater than the service limit in **Table 2**, the oil pump must be replaced. See **Figure 217** (feed pump) or **Figure 218** (oil cooler pump).

14. Disassemble the rotors after performing the tests in Step 13. Then oil all components with clean engine oil and reassemble the rotors by performing Step 11 and Step 12. When the rotors are assembled, proceed to Step 15.

15. On the oil cooler pump side, install the dowel pin (**Figure 203**) and install the side cover (**Figure 202**).

16. On the feed pump side, install the 2 dowel pins (**Figure 197**) and install the side cover (**Figure 196**). Install the 2 oil pump housing screws (**Figure 195**) and tighten securely. Turn the pump shaft and make sure it turns smoothly. If the pump shaft is tight, something is wrong. Disassemble the pump, correct the problem and reassemble.

> *NOTE*
> *If the condition of the oil pump is doubtful, run the **Oil Pump Pressure Test** as described in this chapter.*

Oil Pump Relief Valve Removal/Inspection/Assembly

The oil pump relief valve is installed in the oil cooler pump side cover.

1. Remove the cotter pin (**Figure 219**). Then remove the following parts in order (**Figure 220**):
   a. Seat.
   b. Spring.
   c. Relief valve.
2. Check the relief valve and the housing bore for scratches or damage.
3. Check the spring for fatigue or wear.
4. Clean the parts in solvent and dry thoroughly before reassembly.
5. Reassemble the relief valve by reversing Step 1. Secure with a *new* cotter pin (**Figure 219**). Bend the ends over completely.

Oil Pump Pressure Test

If the oil pump output is doubtful, perform the following test. An oil pressure gauge and adapter is required for this procedure.

> *NOTE*
> *An oil pressure gauge and adapter can be purchased in an automotive or motorcycle supply store or from a Honda dealer. The Honda parts are*

No. 07506-3000000 (Oil Pressure Gauge) and No. 07510-MA70000 (Oil Pressure Gauge Attachment).

1. Warm the engine up to normal operating temperature (176° F/80° C). Shut off the engine.
2. Support the bike on the sidestand.
3. Check the engine oil level. It must be to the upper line on the dipstick (**Figure 221**); add oil if

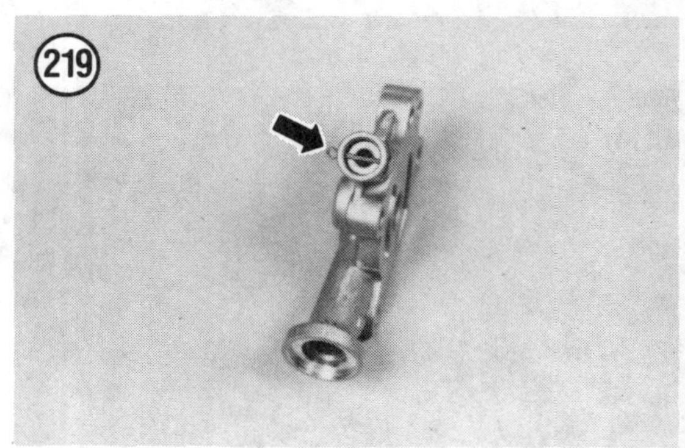

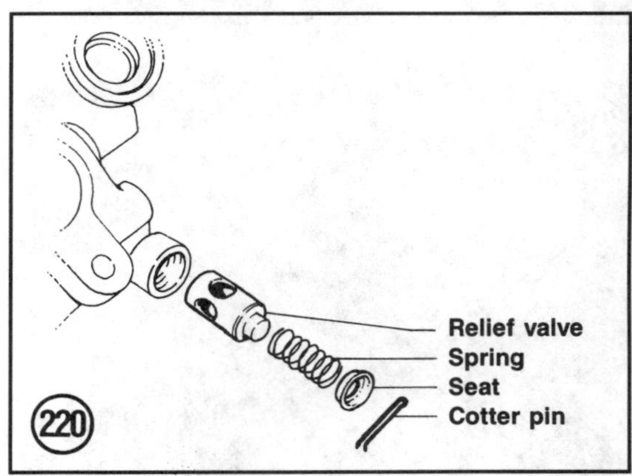

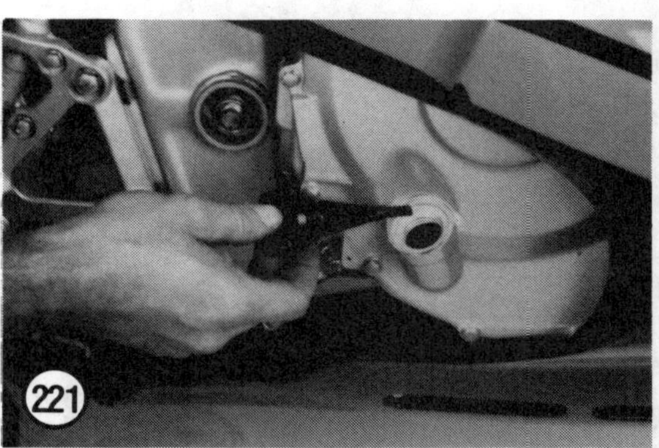

necessary. Do not run this test with the oil level low or the test readings will be false.

4. Disconnect the electrical wire from the oil pressure switch.

NOTE
Figure 222 shows the oil pressure switch with the engine removed for clarity.

5. Remove the oil pressure switch (**Figure 222**).
6. Screw a portable oil pressure gauge into the switch hole in the crankcase.
7. Start the engine and run it at 5,000 rpm. The standard pressure is 5.0-6.0 kg/cm² (71-85 psi) at 5,000 rpm and with the engine temperature at 176° F (80° C). If the pressure is less than specified the oil pump must be replaced as it cannot be serviced.
8. Remove the portable oil pressure gauge.
9. Apply liquid sealant (Gasgacinch or equivalent) to the oil pressure switch before installation. Tighten the switch to the torque specification in **Table 3**.

10. Clean the electrical terminal on the top of the switch. Install the electrical wire to the top of the switch. This connection must be free of oil to make good electrical contact.

OIL COOLER

Removal/Installation

1. Remove the upper fairing assembly. See Chapter Thirteen.
2. Disconnect the oil hoses (A, **Figure 223**) from the oil cooler.

NOTE
Support the hoses disconnected in Step 2 so that oil doesn't run out. In addition, cover the end of the hoses with small plastic resealable bags to prevent dirt and other debris from entering.

3. Remove the oil cooler mounting bolts (B, **Figure 223**).
4. Remove the oil cooler assembly.
5. To install the cooler, reverse the removal steps. Note the following:
   a. Replace the oil hose O-rings if worn or damaged.
   b. Oil the O-rings before assembly.
   c. After installing the oil cooler assembly and reconnecting the hoses, check the hose fittings for leaks.

ALTERNATOR ROTOR

The alternator is a form of electrical generator in which a magnetized field, called a rotor, revolves within a set of stationary coils called a stator. As the rotor revolves, alternating current is induced in the stator. The current is then rectified to direct current and used to operate the electrical accessories on the motorcycle and to charge the battery. The rotor is permanently magnetized.

Stator electrical testing is covered in Chapter Two.

Removal/Installation

1. Park and support the bike securely.
2. Remove the clutch cover as described in Chapter Five.

3. Remove the side covers and the seat. See Chapter Thirteen.

4. Remove the battery cover and disconnect the negative battery lead (**Figure 224**).

5. Use a strap wrench (**Figure 225**) to secure the rotor. Then remove the bolt and washer (**Figure 226**) securing the alternator rotor.

6. Screw in the rotor puller until it stops. Use the Honda rotor puller (part No. 07733-0020001) or equivalent.

CAUTION
Don't try to remove the rotor without a special puller; any attempt to do so will ultimately lead to some form of damage to the engine and/or rotor. Many aftermarket pullers are available from motorcycle dealers or mail order houses. If you can't buy or borrow one, have a dealer remove the rotor.

7. Turn the rotor puller with a wrench until the rotor is free.

NOTE
If the rotor is difficult to remove, strike the puller with a hammer a few times. This will usually break it loose.

CAUTION
If normal rotor removal attempts fail, do not force the puller as the threads may be stripped out of the rotor causing expensive damage. Take the bike to a dealer and have the rotor removed.

8. Remove the rotor from the crankshaft.

9. Remove the rotor puller from the rotor (**Figure 227**).

10. Install by reversing these removal steps. Note the following.

CAUTION
Carefully inspect the inside of the rotor (Figure 228) for small bolts, washers

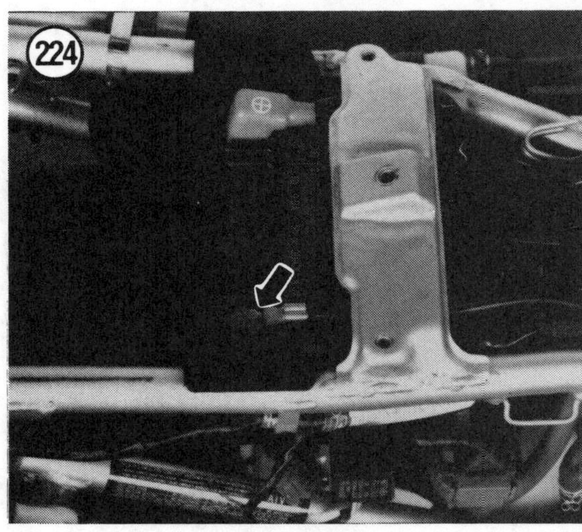

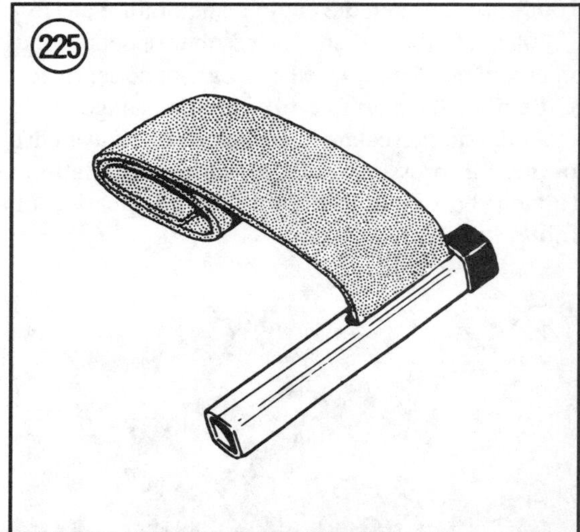

or other metal "trash" that may have been picked up by the magnets. These small metal bits can cause severe damage to the alternator stator assembly.

11. Make sure the Woodruff key is installed on the crankshaft (**Figure 229**) before installing the rotor.

12. Align the keyway in the rotor with the Woodruff key and install the rotor (**Figure 230**) onto the crankshaft.

13. Install the rotor bolt and washer (**Figure 226**) and tighten it to the torque specification in **Table 3**.

STARTER CLUTCH ASSEMBLY, STARTER GEARS AND PRIMARY DRIVE GEAR

The starter clutch assembly and gears can be removed with the engine in the frame. The starter motor can be left in place, if desired.

Refer to **Figure 231** when performing procedures in this section.

Removal

1. Remove the side covers and seat as described in Chapter Thirteen.

2. Remove the battery cover and disconnect the negative battery lead (**Figure 224**).

3. Remove the fuel tank as described in Chapter Seven.

4. Remove the left-hand side lower fairing as described in Chapter Thirteen.

5. Drain the engine oil as described in Chapter Three.

6. Disconnect the pulse generator 4-pin mini connector (**Figure 232**).

7. Remove the bolts securing the left-hand crankcase cover (**Figure 233**) and remove the cover and gasket. Remove the dowel pin (**Figure 234**).

8. Remove the starter clutch bolt (**Figure 235**).

9. Remove the pulse rotor (**Figure 236**).

10. Remove the starter clutch assembly (**Figure 237**).

11. Remove the starter drive gear (**Figure 238**) and shaft (**Figure 239**).

12. Remove the starter clutch washer (**Figure 240**) from the crankshaft.

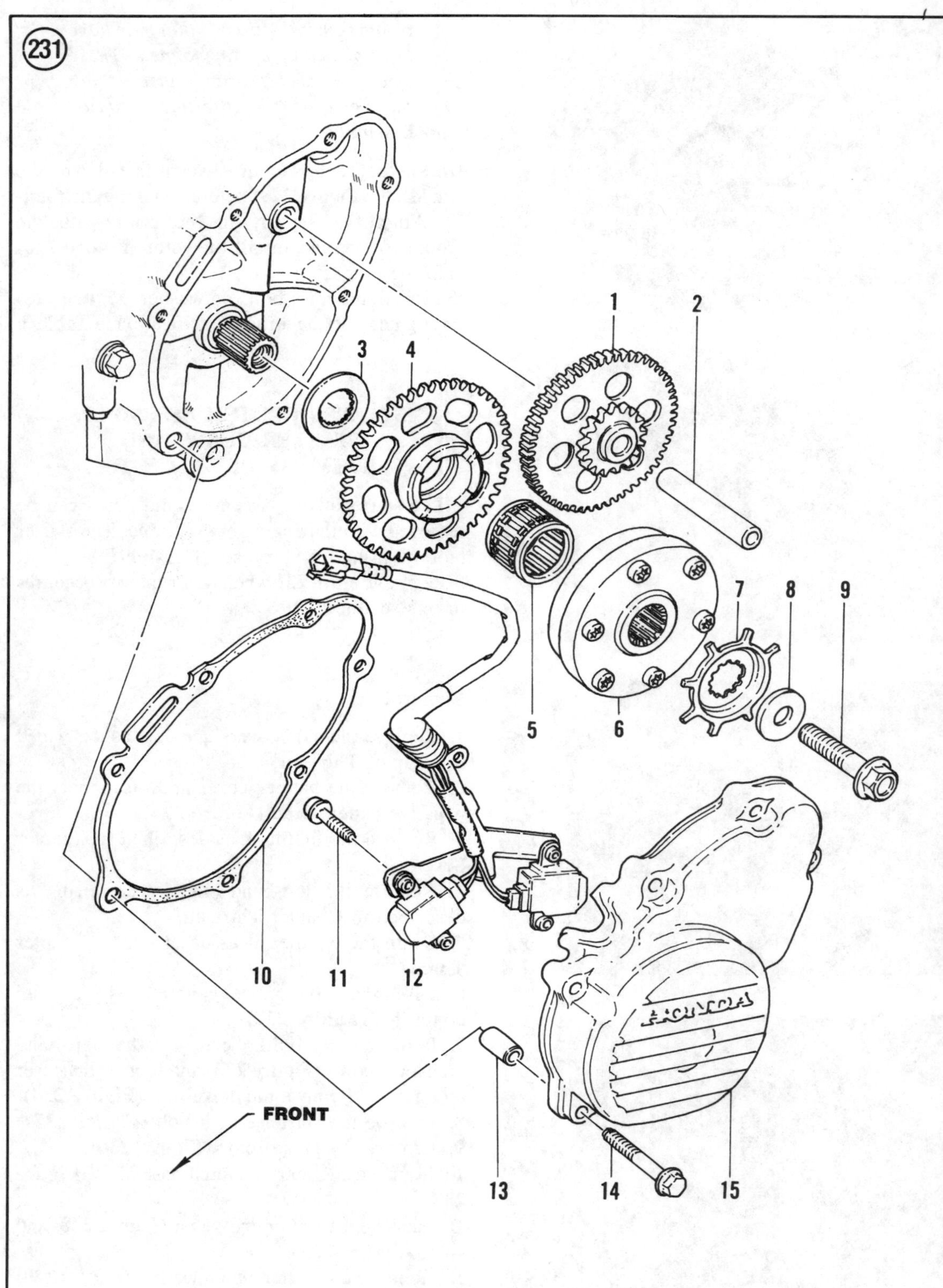
231
1
2
3
4
5
6
7
8
9
10
11
12
13
14
15
FRONT
HONDA

STARTER CLUTCH ASSEMBLY

1. Starter drive gear
2. Shaft
3. Washer
4. Starter driven gear
5. Needle bearing
6. Starter clutch
7. Pulse rotor
8. Washer
9. Bolt
10. Gasket
11. Bolt
12. Pulse generator assembly
13. Dowel pin
14. Bolt
15. Left-hand side cover

Disassembly/Inspection/Reassembly

1. Hold the starter clutch assembly as shown in **Figure 241**. Then attempt to turn the starter driven gear counterclockwise, then clockwise. The gear should only turn *counterclockwise*.

2. Pull the starter driven gear (**Figure 242**) out of the starter clutch assembly.

3. Remove the needle bearing (**Figure 243**) from the starter clutch.

4. Inspect the teeth on the starter driven gear (**Figure 244**) and on the idle gear (A, **Figure 245**). Check for chipped or missing teeth. Look for uneven or excessive wear on the gear faces; replace if necessary.

5. Check the idle gear pivot shaft (B, **Figure 245**) for uneven wear or damage. Check the pivot shaft journal in the left-hand crankcase (**Figure 246**) for cracks or damage.

6. Check the needle bearing (**Figure 243**) for wear or damage. It must rotate freely; replace if necessary.

7. Check the rollers (**Figure 247**) in the starter clutch for uneven wear or excessive wear; replace as a set if any are bad.

8. To replace the rollers, perform the following:
   a. Remove the Torx bolts (**Figure 248**) securing the starter clutch assembly.
   b. Remove the cover, rollers and clutch outer.
   c. During installation, install the one-way clutch onto the starter clutch outer so that its flange side faces toward the inside (**Figure 249**).
   d. Install the cover (**Figure 249**).

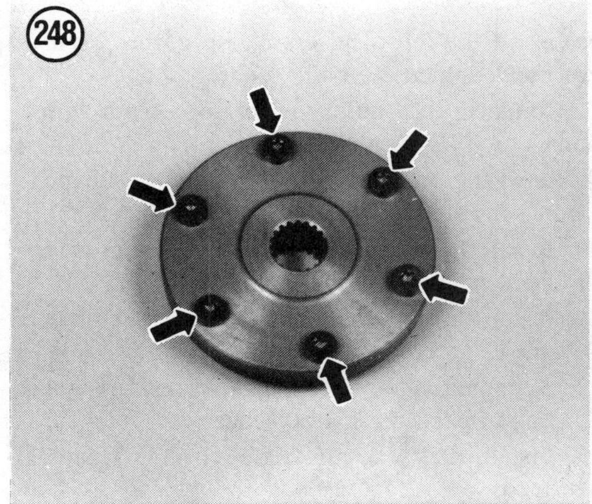

e. Apply Loctite 242 (blue) to the threads before installing the cover bolts and tighten to the torque specifications listed in **Table 3**.

9. Measure the starter gear contact surface outside diameter (**Figure 250**) where it rides against the rollers. Compare to the dimension listed in **Table 2**.

10. Assemble the starter clutch as follows:

a. Insert the needle bearing (**Figure 243**) into the starter clutch.

b. Install the driven gear (**Figure 242**) into the starter clutch by turning it counterclockwise. See **Figure 241**.

Installation

1. Install the washer (**Figure 240**) onto the crankshaft.

2. Install the starter drive shaft (**Figure 239**) and gear (**Figure 238**).

3. Install the starter clutch assembly (**Figure 237**) onto the crankshaft. Engage the driven gear with the drive gear.

4. Install the pulse rotor (**Figure 236**). Align the punch mark on the rotor with the extra wide crankshaft spline.

5. Install the starter clutch bolt and tighten to the torque specification in **Table 3**.

6. Install a new gasket and the dowel pin (**Figure 234**).

> *NOTE*
> *Make sure the rubber grommet in the left-hand side cover (**Figure 251**) is pushed in all the way.*

7. Install the left-hand crankcase cover (**Figure 233**) and tighten the bolts securely.

8. Connect the pulse generator 4-pin mini connector (**Figure 232**).

9. Refill the engine oil as described in Chapter Three.

10. Install the left-hand lower fairing as described in Chapter Thirteen.

11. Install the fuel tank as described in Chapter Seven.

12. Reconnect the battery negative lead (**Figure 224**) and install the battery cover.

13. Install the seat and side covers (Chapter Thirteen).

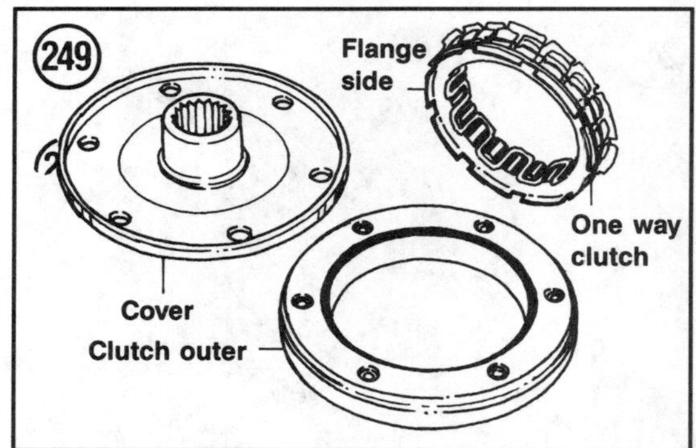

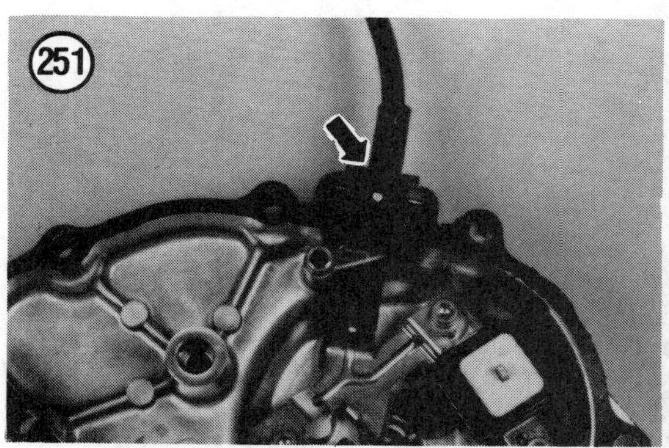

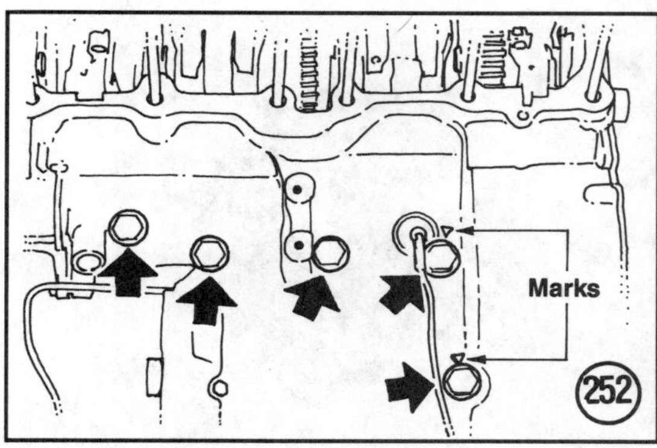

CRANKCASE

The crankcases are made of die-cast aluminum and matched as a set. The mating of the crankcases is a precision fit with no gasket at the joint, only a thin layer of gasket sealer. If a screwdriver or any other tool is used to pry the cases apart, the cases will leak and require expensive replacement.

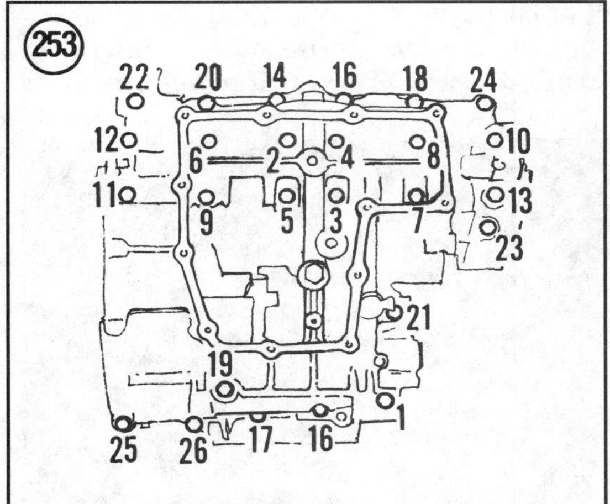

Service to the lower end requires that the crankcase assembly be removed from the motorcycle frame and disassembled (split).

Disassembly

1. Remove the engine as described in this chapter. Remove all exterior assemblies from the crankcase as described in this chapter and other related chapters.
2. Remove the upper crankcase bolts (**Figure 252**).
3. Turn the engine so that the bottom end faces up.
4. Loosen the lower crankcase bolts by reversing the bolt tightening sequence in **Figure 253**.

NOTE
Before attempting to separate the crankcase halves, make sure all bolts have been removed. In addition, the case halves are dowel-pinned together. To break the case seal, one of the case halves must be pulled straight up and not from side to side.

CAUTION
Do not pry the crankcase between any gasket surface. The crankcases are machined as a set and the damage of one will require replacement of both.

5. Remove the *lower* case half from the upper. This is because the crankshaft and transmission shafts will stay in the upper case half. Have an assistant hold the upper case half securely and lift up on the lower case half. If the lower case half is stubborn, lightly tap the crankcase at a point where one case half overhangs the other. Only tap the case halves with a plastic faced mallet. Once the mating crankcase seal is broken loose, the lower case half should lift off the upper case half easily.

NOTE
After separating the crankcase halves, the transmission and crankshaft assemblies will stay in the upper crankcase half.

6. Remove the dowel pins if they are loose. See **Figure 254** and **Figure 255**. If the dowel pins are secure it is not necessary to remove them.

7. Remove the oil jet orifices. See **Figure 256** and **Figure 257**.

8. Remove the transmission, shift forks and shift drum assemblies as described in Chapter Six.

9. Remove the crankshaft and the crankshaft bearing inserts as described in this chapter.

Inspection

1. Clean the crankcases in solvent. Clean the case half mating surfaces with a gasket scraper or a single-edge razor blade. Work slowly and do not damage mating surfaces.

> *CAUTION*
> *Never use a wire wheel chucked in an electric drill to clean gasket surfaces. The aluminum can become damaged from the wheel and cause an oil leak.*

2. Thoroughly clean the inside and outside of both crankcase halves with cleaning solvent. Dry with compressed air. After the case halves have been cleaned in solvent, clean a final time using soap and hot water and dry with compressed air.

> *CAUTION*
> *Make sure there is no solvent residue left in the cases as it will contaminate the engine oil.*

3. Make sure all oil passages are clean; blow them out with compressed air.

4. Check the crankcases for cracks or other damage. Inspect the mating surfaces of both halves. They must be free of gouges, burrs or any damage that could cause an oil leak.

5. Inspect the crankshaft bearing inserts as described in this chapter.

6. Inspect the shift shaft oil seal (**Figure 258**). If the seal is leaking, carefully pry it out of the crankcase (**Figure 259**). Install a new seal by driving it into the crankcase with a suitable size socket (**Figure 260**).

7. Inspect the mainshaft needle bearing journal (A, **Figure 261**). If the journal is worn or damaged, remove the bolt and bracket (B, **Figure 261**) and remove the journal with an internal bearing puller. Replace the mainshaft needle bearing as described in Chapter Six.

8. If the oil was contaminated or if the engine is being rebuilt because of engine damage, remove

the 3 special oil gallery bolts and flush the cases completely of all oil. See **Figure 262** and **Figure 263**. When installing the bolts, tighten to the torque specifications in **Table 3**.

Assembly

1. Prior to assembly, coat all parts with assembly oil or engine oil.

2. Install the crankshaft bearing inserts as described under *Crankshaft Removal/Installation*

in this chapter. If reusing old bearings, make sure that they are installed in the same location. Refer to marks made during crankshaft removal. Make sure each bearing is locked in place.

3. Install the shift drum, shift forks and transmission assemblies as described in Chapter Six.

4. *Transmission shift test:* This is an optional procedure to make sure the transmission has been assembled properly.

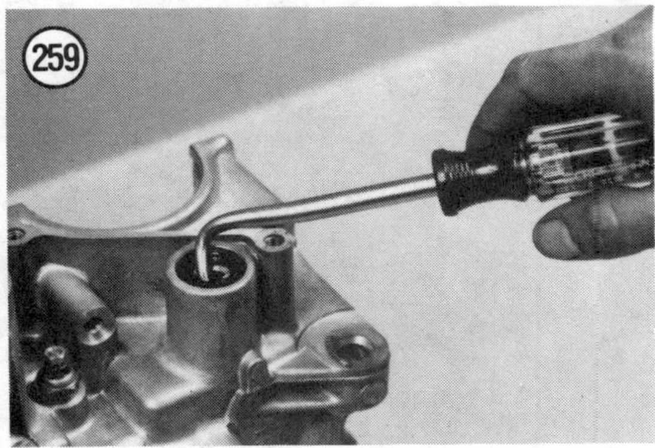

a. Carefully place the lower case half in position, aligning the shift forks (**Figure 264**) in their proper gear grooves (**Figure 265**).

b. Seat the upper case half onto the lower and tap lightly with a plastic or rubber mallet—do *not* use a metal hammer or it will damage the cases.

c. Carefully rotate the shift drum while turning the countershaft. Check that all gears engage smoothly and that each gear position can be identified. You will have to spin the countershaft quickly. Refer to Chapter Six if the transmission does not work correctly.

d. Remove the lower case half.

5. Install the crankshaft as described under *Crankshaft Removal/Installation* in this chapter.

6. Make sure the case half sealing surfaces are perfectly clean and dry.

7. If removed, install the 3 dowel pins. See **Figure 254** and **Figure 255**.

8. Install the oil jet orifices as follows:

a. Make sure the oil jet orifices are not clogged.

> *CAUTION*
> *An oil jet is installed in each of the crankcase halves. However, because the oil jet installed in the lower crankcase may fall out when the lower crankcase is installed, the lower crankcase oil jet can be installed upside down in the upper crankcase.*

b. Install the upper crankcase oil jet (**Figure 257**) into the upper crankcase with the larger hole facing *up*. See **Figure 266**.

c. Install the lower crankcase oil jet (**Figure 256**) into the upper crankcase with the small hole facing *up*. See **Figure 267**.

> *NOTE*
> *Use Gasgacinch Gasket Sealer, Three Bond or equivalent.*

9. Apply a light coat of gasket sealer to the lower crankcase half sealing surface. Cover only flat surfaces, not curved bearing surfaces. **Figure 268** shows the lower crankcase. Make the coating as thin as possible. Do not apply sealant close to the edge of the bearing inserts as it would restrict oil flow and cause damage.

10. Carefully place the lower case half in position, aligning the shift forks (**Figure 264**) in their proper gear grooves (**Figure 265**).

11. Lower the crankcase completely.

CAUTION
Do not install any crankcase bolts until the sealing surface around the entire crankcase perimeter has seated completely.

12. Before installing the bolts, slowly spin the transmission shafts and shift the transmission through all 6 gears. This is done to check that the shift forks are properly engaged.

13. Apply oil to the threads of all crankcase bolts and install them finger-tight. Copper washers are installed on bolts No. 1-13 and No. 21. See **Figure 269** for bolt numbering.

14. Tighten the lower crankcase bolts in 2-3 stages in the sequence shown in **Figure 269**. Refer to **Table 3** for tightening torques.

15. Turn the crankcase over and install the upper crankcase bolts. Install copper washers on the bolts with the special raised mark on the crankcase adjacent to the bolt hole. See **Figure 270**.

16. Spin the crankshaft and transmission shafts after tightening the crankcase bolts. If any part does not turn smoothly, disassemble the crankcase assembly and correct the problem.

17. Install all engine assemblies that were removed.

18. Install the engine in the frame as described in this chapter.

CRANKSHAFT

Removal/Installation

1. Split the crankcase as described under *Crankcase Disassembly* in this chapter.

2. Lift the crankshaft and camshaft chain out of the crankcase (**Figure 271**).

3. Slip the camshaft chain (**Figure 272**) off of the crankshaft.

NOTE
Remember that the left-hand side refers to the engine as it sits in the bike's frame, not as it sits on the workbench.

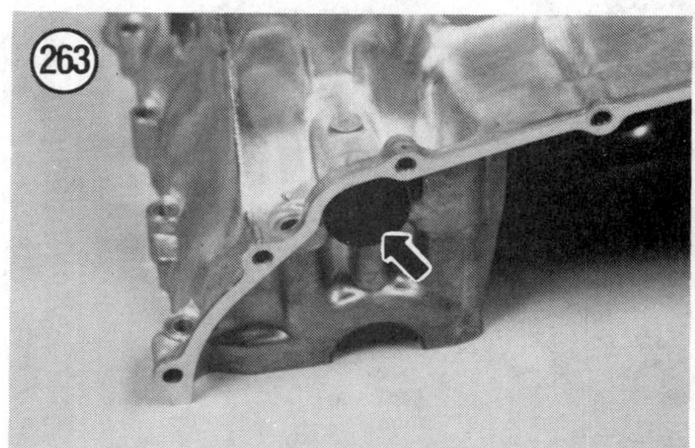

4. Remove the crankshaft bearing inserts (**Figure 273**) from the upper and lower crankcase halves. Mark the backsides of the bearings with a 1, 2, 3, 4, 5 or 6 and U (upper) or L (lower) starting from the left-hand side, so they can be reinstalled into the same positions.

5. Installation is the reverse of these steps. Note the following:

   a. Install the camshaft chain over the crankshaft (**Figure 272**).

   b. Install the bearing inserts into the upper and lower crankcase (**Figure 273**). Make sure the bearing tabs align with the crankcase grooves (**Figure 274**).

   c. Install the crankshaft so that it sits into the crankcase as shown in **Figure 271**.

Crankshaft Inspection

1. Clean the crankshaft thoroughly with solvent. Clean oil holes with rifle cleaning brushes; flush

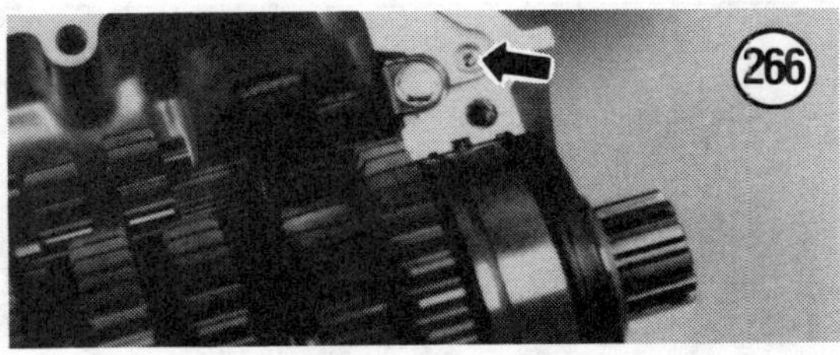

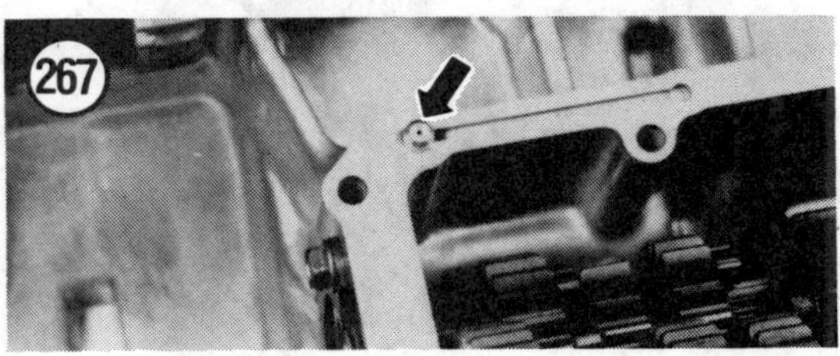

thoroughly and dry with compressed air. Lightly oil all oil journal surfaces immediately to prevent rust.

2. Inspect each bearing journal (**Figure 275**) for scratches, ridges, scoring, nicks, etc.

3. If the surface on all bearing journals is satisfactory, measure the journals with a micrometer (**Figure 276**) and check for out-of-roundness and taper.

4. See **Figure 277**. Inspect the camshaft sprocket (A) and primary gear (B). If they are worn or damaged, the crankshaft will have to be replaced.

5. Inspect the camshaft chain for damaged pins or links. Replace if necessary.

Crankshaft Main Bearing Clearance Measurement

1. Check the inside and outside surfaces of the bearing inserts for wear, bluish tint (burned), flaking, abrasion and scoring. If the bearings are good, they may be reused. If any insert is questionable, replace the entire set.

2. Clean the crankshaft and main bearing insert surfaces.

3. Measure the main bearing clearance by performing the following steps.

4. Set the upper crankcase upside down on the workbench on wood blocks to protect the crankcase studs.

5. Install the existing main bearing inserts into the upper and lower crankcase into their original positions. See **Figure 274**.

6. Install the crankshaft (**Figure 271**) into the upper crankcase.

7. Cut a piece of Plastigage (**Figure 278**) the width of the bearing. Place a piece of Plastigage over each main bearing journal parallel to the crankshaft.

> *CAUTION*
> *Do not rotate the crankshaft while the Plastigage is in place.*

8. Install the lower crankcase over the upper crankcase. Install and tighten the lower crankcase 8 mm bolts (**Figure 279**) to 24 N·m (17 ft.-lb.).

9. Remove the 8 mm bolts in the reverse order of installation.

10. Carefully remove the lower crankcase and measure the width of the flattened Plastigage according to the manufacturer's instructions (**Figure 280**). Measure at both ends of the strip.

A difference of 0.025 mm (0.001 in.) or more indicates a tapered crankpin. Confirm with a micrometer. Remove the Plastigage strips from all bearing journals.

11. New bearing clearance should be 0.023-0.047 mm (0.0009-0.0019 in.) with a service limit of 0.05 mm (0.002 in.).

12. If the bearing clearance is geater than specified, use the following steps for new bearing selection.

13. The upper crankcase is marked with a series of 6 letters, (A, B, or C) that represent each main bearing crankpin journal (No. 1-6) reading from left to right (**Figure 281**.) The left-hand crankshaft counterbalancer is stamped with a series of 6 code numbers (1 or 2) that represent each crankshaft main journal outside diameter (**Figure 282**).

NOTE
The letter on the left-hand end relates to the bearing insert in the left-hand side and so on, working across from left to right. Remember, the left-hand side relates to the engine as it sits in the bike's frame, not as it sits on your workbench. **Figure 283** *shows bearing insert numbering for the upper crankcase.*

14. Select new main bearing by cross referencing the crankpin code number (**Figure 281**) with the main journal code letter (**Figure 282**) in **Table 4**. Where the 2 columns intersect, the new bearing insert color is indicated. **Table 5** gives the bearing insert color and thickness.

15. Turn the crankcase over and install the upper crankcase bolts. Install copper washers on the bolts with the special raised mark on the crankcase adjacent to the bolt hole. See **Figure 270**.

16. Spin the crankshaft and transmission shafts after tightening the crankcase bolts. If any part does not turn smoothly, disassemble the crankcase assembly and correct the problem.

17. Install all engine assemblies that were removed.

18. Install the engine in the frame as described in this chapter.

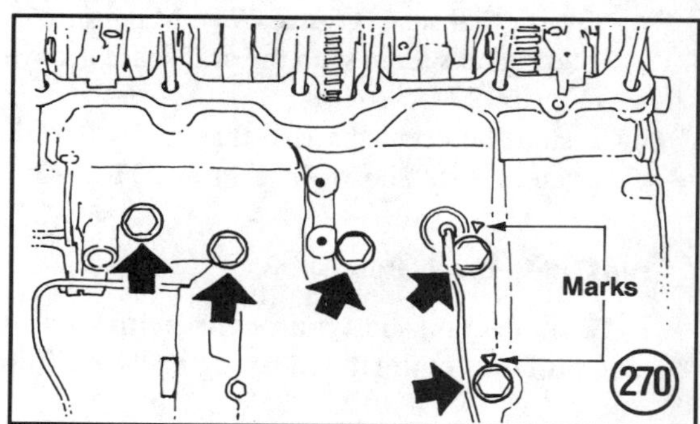

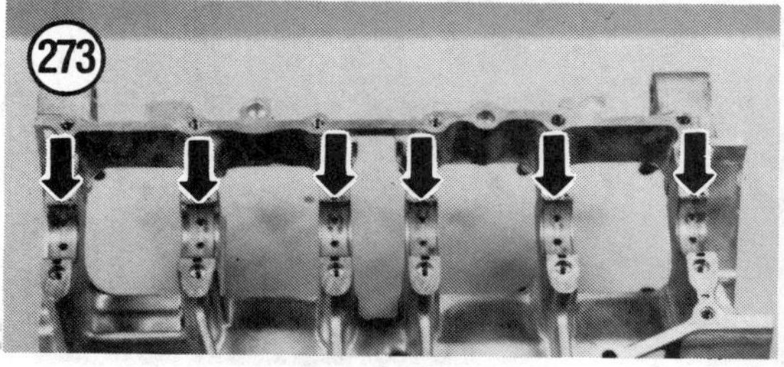

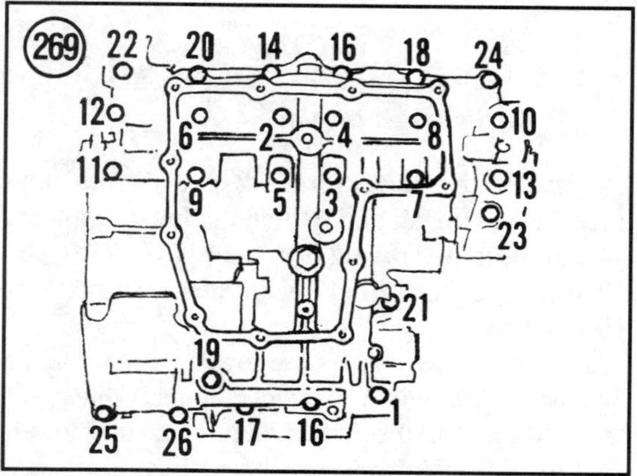

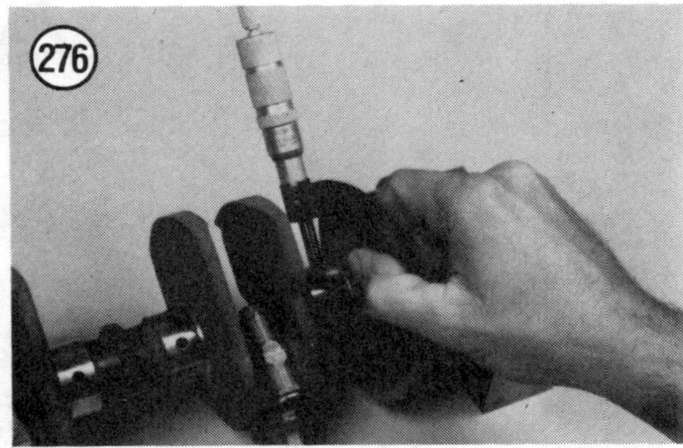

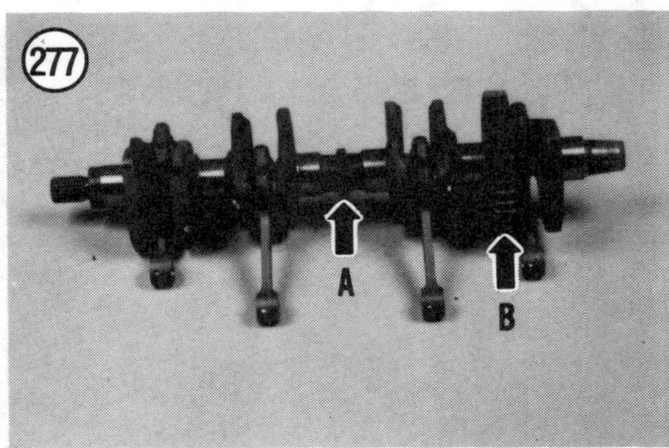

CONNECTING RODS

Removal/Installation

1. Remove the engine as described in this chapter.
2. Split the crankcase and remove the crankshaft (**Figure 284**) as described in this chapter.
3. Measure the crankshaft big end side clearance. Insert a feeler gauge between a connecting rod big end and either crankshaft machined web (**Figure 285**). Record the clearance for each connecting rod and compare to the specification in **Table 2**. If the clearance is excessive, replace the connecting rod(s) and recheck clearance. If clearance is still excessive, replace the crankshaft.

> *NOTE*
> *Prior to disassembly, mark the rods and caps with a "1", "2", "3" and "4" starting from the left-hand side. Remember, the left-hand side relates to the engine as it sits in the bike's frame, not as it sits on your workbench.*

4. Remove the connecting rod cap nuts (**Figure 286**) and separate the rods from the crankshaft (**Figure 287**). Keep each cap with its original rod.

> *NOTE*
> *Keep each bearing insert in its original place in the crankcase, rod or rod cap. If you are going to assemble the engine with the original inserts, they must be installed exactly as removed in order to prevent rapid wear.*

5. Install by reversing these removal steps. Note the following procedures.
6. Install the bearing inserts into each connecting rod and cap. Make sure they are locked in place correctly. See **Figure 288**.
7. Apply assembly lube to the bearing inserts.
8. If new bearing inserts are going to be installed, check the bearing clearance as described in this chapter.
9. If replacing connecting rods, make sure to match weight mark on side of rod (**Figure 289**).
10. Before installing connecting rods, align the bearing caps with the rod by matching the code letters (**Figure 290**) on side of cap and rod.

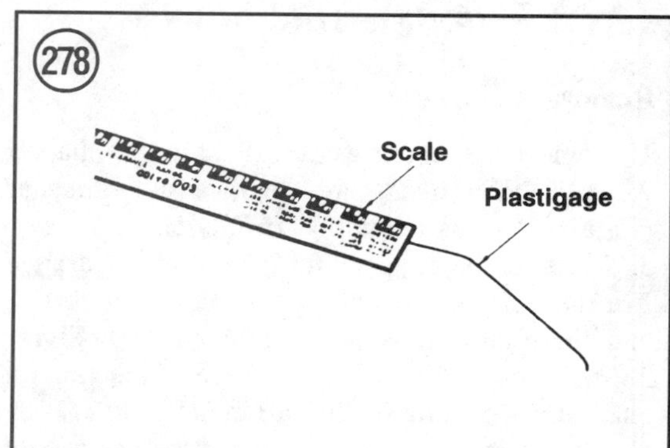

278

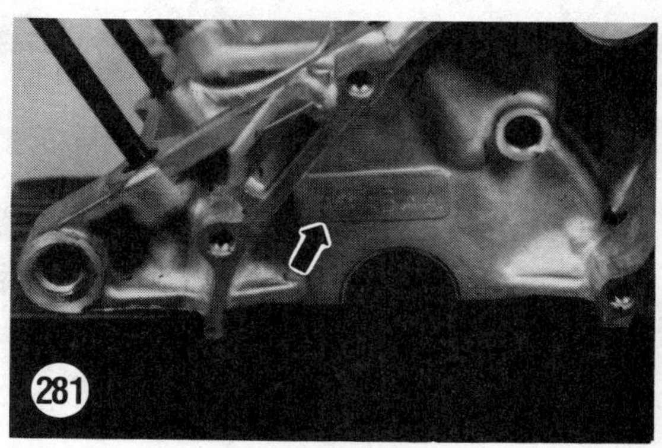

281

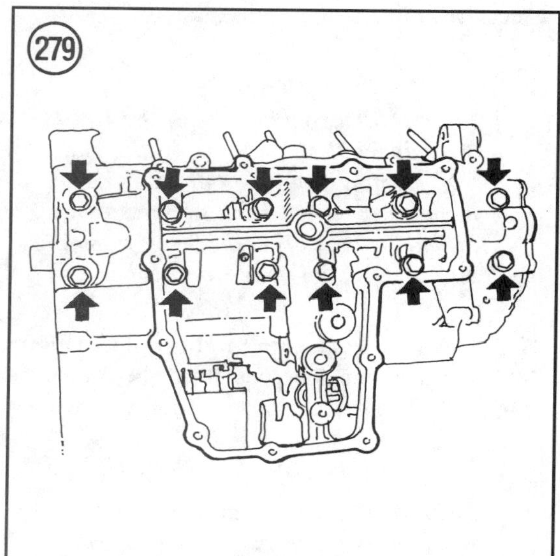

279

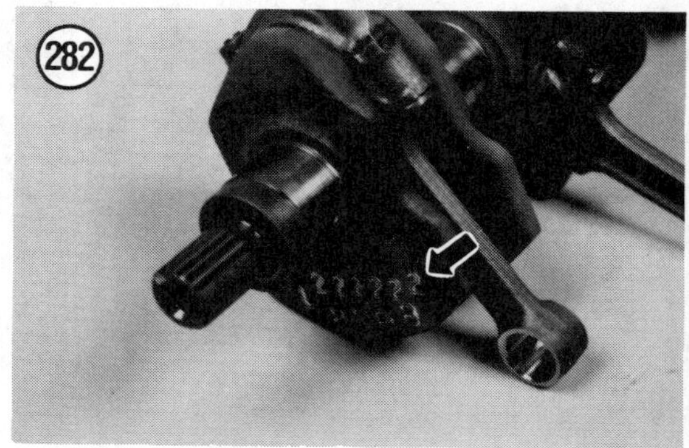

282

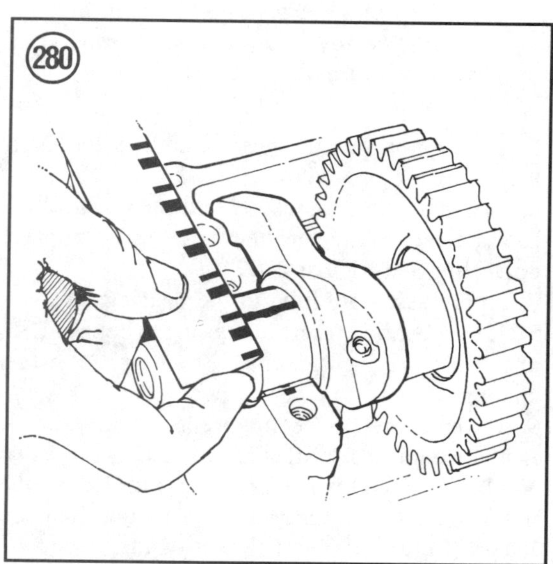

280

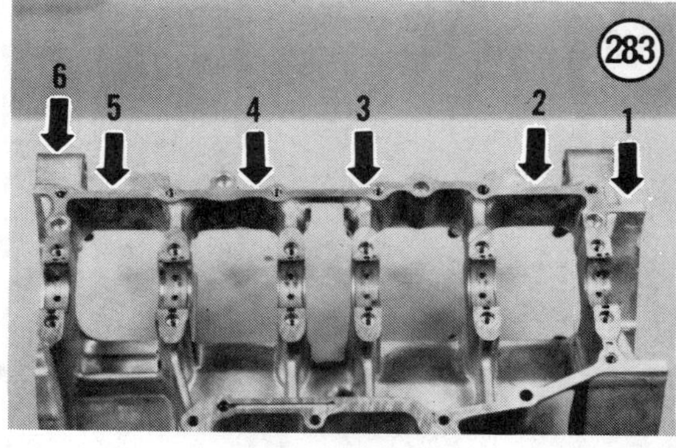

283

284

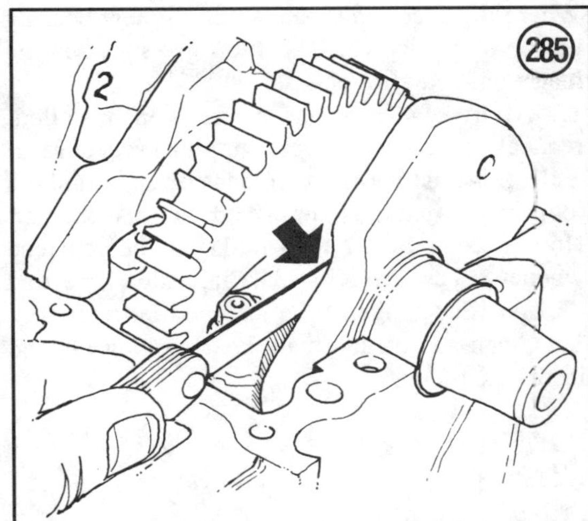

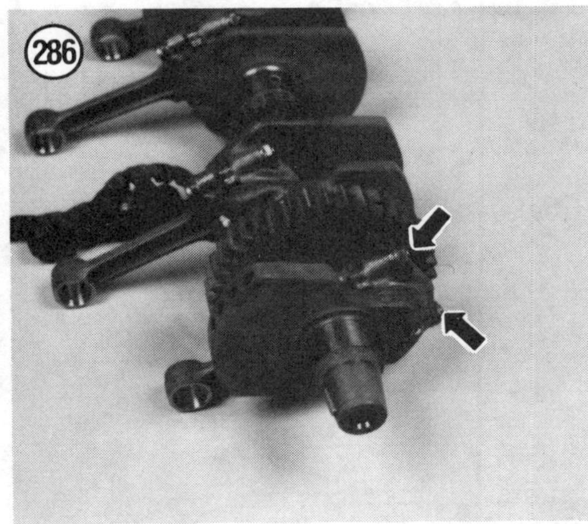

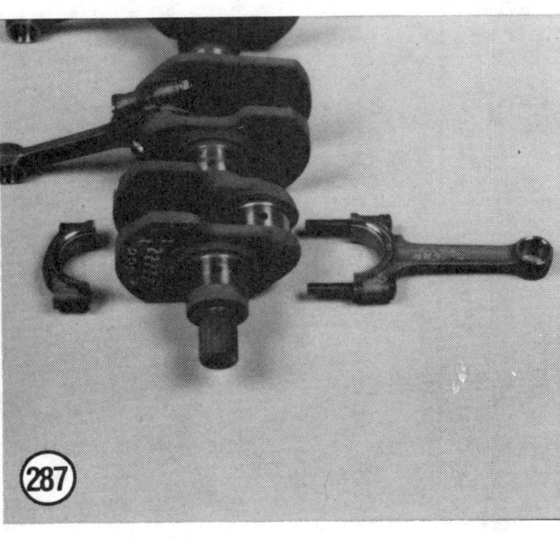

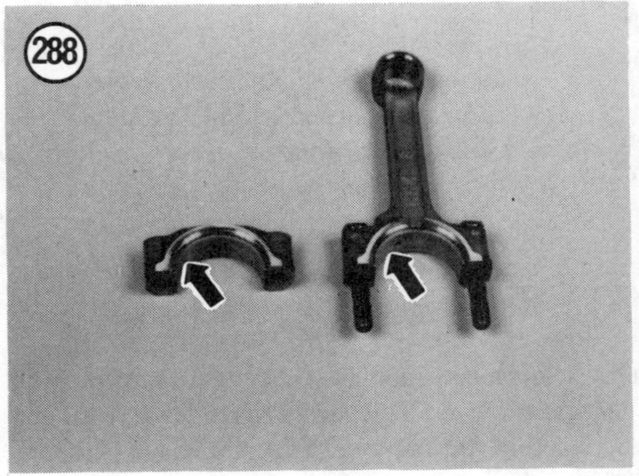

11. Install the connecting rods onto the crankshaft so that the marked side of rod (**Figure 290**) faces to the clutch side (right-hand side) of engine.

12. Apply engine oil onto the connecting rod bolt and nuts. Then tighten the nuts (**Figure 286**) in 2-3 steps to the torque specification in **Table 3**.

Connecting Rod Inspection

1. Check each rod for obvious damage such as cracks and burns.

2. Check the piston pin bushing for wear or scoring.

3. Take the rods to a machine shop and have them checked for twisting and bending.

4. Examine the bearing inserts (**Figure 288**) for wear, scoring or burning. They are reusable if in good condition. Make a note of the bearing color (if any) marked on the side of the insert if the bearing is to be discarded; a previous owner may have used undersize bearings.

5. Remove the connecting rod bearing bolts and check them for cracks or twisting. Replace any bolts as required.

6. Measure the crankpin journal and check for taper and out-of-round (**Figure 291**).

7. Check bearing clearance as described in this chapter.

**Connecting Rod Bearing
and Clearance Measurement**

*CAUTION
If the old bearings are to be reused, be
sure that they are installed in their
exact original locations.*

1. Wipe bearing inserts and crankpins clean. Install bearing inserts in rod and cap.

2. Place a piece of Plastigage (**Figure 278**) on one crankpin parallel to the crankshaft.

3. Install rod and cap. Tighten nuts to torque specification in **Table 3**.

> *CAUTION*
> *Do not rotate crankshaft while Plastigage is in place.*

4. Remove rod cap.

5. Measure width of flattened Plastigage according to the manufacturer's instructions (**Figure 292**). Measure at both ends of the strip. A difference of 0.025 mm (0.001 in.) or more indicates a tapered crankpin; the crankshaft must be replaced. Confirm with a micrometer measurement (**Figure 291**) of the journal OD.

6. If the crankpin taper is within tolerance, measure the bearing clearance with the same strip of Plastigage. Correct bearing clearance is specified in **Table 2**. Remove the Plastigage strips.

7. If the bearing clearance is greater than specified, use the following steps for new bearing selection.

8. New bearing clearance should be 0.028-0.052 mm (0.0011-0.0020 in.) with a service limit of 0.06 mm (0.0.0020 in.). Remove the Plastigage strips from all crankpin journals.

9. If the bearing clearance is greater than specified, use the following steps for new bearing selection.

10. The connecting rod and cap are marked with numbers "1" or "2" (**Figure 293**). The upper crankcase is marked with a series of 4 letters (A or B) that represent each crankpin journal (No. 1-4) reading from left to right (**Figure 294**).

> *NOTE*
> *The letter on the left-hand end relates to the bearing insert in the left-hand side and so on, working across from left to right. Remember, the left-hand side relates to the engine as it sits in the bike's frame, not as it sits on your workbench.*

11. Select a new main bearing by cross referencing the crankpin code letter (**Figure 294**) with the connecting rod number (**Figure 293**) in **Table 6**.

Where the 2 columns intersect, the new bearing insert color is indicated. **Table 7** gives the bearing insert color and thickness.

12. After new bearings have been installed, recheck clearance by repeating this procedure. If a clearance is incorrect, remeasure the crankpin journal diameter as described in this chapter. Honda recommends the crankshaft be replaced whenever a crankpin journal dimension is beyond the specified range of the stamped letter code.

13. Clean and oil the main bearing journals and insert faces.

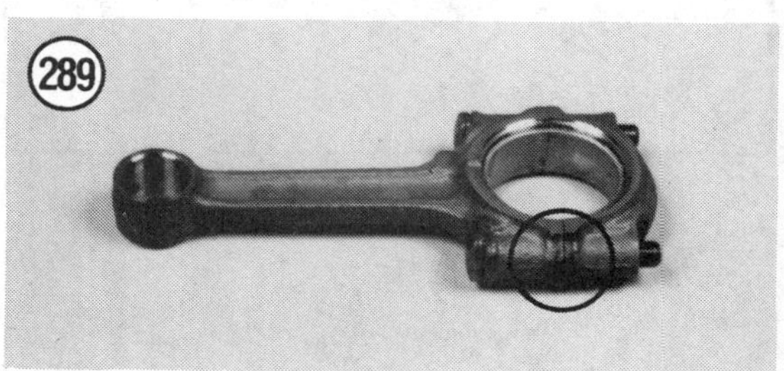

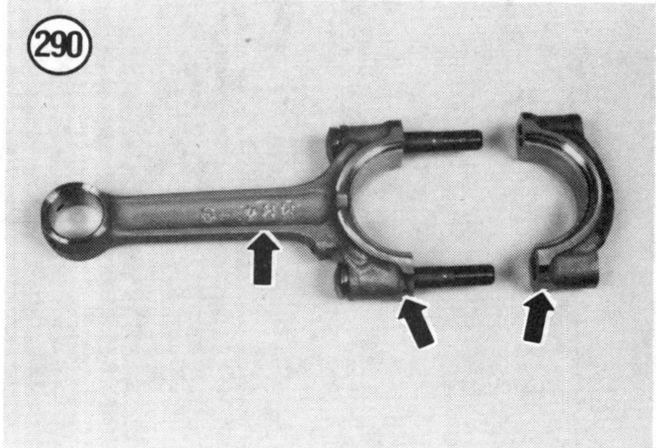

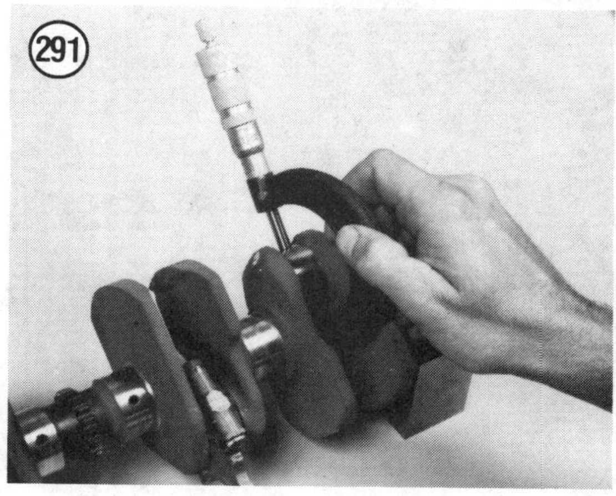

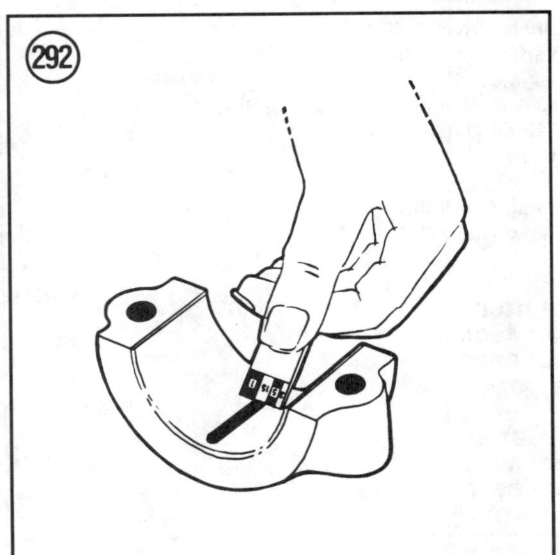

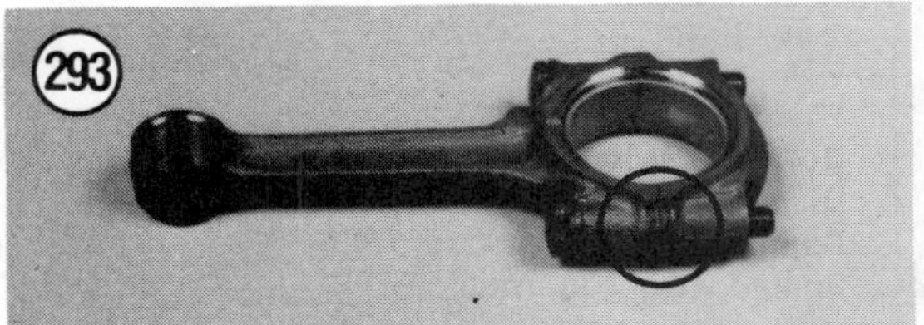

Tables are on the following pages.

Table 1 GENERAL ENGINE SPECIFICATIONS

Valve train	Chain driven DOHC
Cylinder alignment	Vertical inline four
Firing order	1-2-4-3
Bore and stroke	63.0 × 48.0 mm (2.48 × 1.98 in.)
Displacement	598 cc (3.65 cu. in.)
Compression ratio	11.0:1
Engine weight (dry)	
49-state	63 kg (138.9 lb.)
California	62 kg (136.7 lb.)
Valve timing at 1 mm lift	
49-state	
Intake opens	7° BTDC
Intake closes	40° ABDC
Exhaust opens	40° BBDC
Exhaust closes	9° ATDC
California	
Intake opens	-5° BTDC
Intake closes	40° ABDC
Exhaust opens	40° BBDC
Exhaust closes	-5° ATDC

Table 2 ENGINE SERVICE SPECIFICATIONS

	Specification mm (in.)	Wear limit mm (in.)
Cylinder head warpage	0.10	(0.004)
Camshaft		
Lobe height		
49-state		
Intake	31.582-31.882	31.53
	(1.2434-1.2552)	(1.241)
Exhaust	31.550-31.850	31.50
	(1.2421-1.2539)	(1.240)
California		
Intake	30.949-31.249	30.90
	(1.2185-1.2303)	(1.217)
Exhaust	30.980-31.280	30.93
	(1.2197-1.2315)	(1.218)
Runout	—	0.05
	—	(0.002)
Journal outside diameter	22.939-22.980	22.935
	(0.9031-0.9047)	(0.9030)
Journal oil clearance		
No. 1 and 4	0.020-0.062	0.10
	(0.0008-0.0024)	(0.004)
No. 2 and 3	0.020-0.082	0.12
	(0.0008-0.0032)	(0.005)
Valves		
Stem outside diameter		
Intake	4.975-4.990	4.97
	(0.1959-0.1965)	(0.196)
Exhaust	4.955-4.970	4.94
	(0.1951-0.1957)	(0.194)
Valve guide inside diameter	5.000-5.012	5.04
	(0.1969-0.1973)	(0.1980)

(continued)

Table 2 ENGINE SERVICE SPECIFICATIONS (continued)

	Specification mm (in.)	Wear limit mm (in.)
Valves (continued)		
Valve stem-to-guide clearance		
Intake	—	0.07
	—	(0.003)
Exhaust	—	0.09
	—	(0.004)
Valve seat width	0.9-1.1	1.5
	(0.035-0.043)	(0.06)
Valve springs		
Free length		
Inner	33.4	32.1
	(1.31)	(1.26)
Outer	34.2	32.7
	(1.35)	(1.29)
Cylinder block		
Bore diameter	63.000-63.010	63.10
	(2.4803-2.4807)	(2.484)
Taper	—	0.10
	—	(0.004)
Out of round	—	0.10
	—	(0.004)
Warpage at top	—	0.10
	—	(0.004)
Piston		
Piston-to-cylinder clearance	0.010-0.050	0.10
	(0.004-0.0020)	(0.004)
Outside diameter	62.960-62.990	62.90
	(2.4787-2.4799)	(2.476)
Piston pin bore	16.002-16.008	16.05
	(0.6300-0.6302)	(0.632)
Piston pin outside diameter	15.995-16.000	15.98
	(0.6297-0.6299)	(0.629)
Piston-to-pin clearance	0.002-0.014	0.04
	(0.0001-0.0006)	(0.002)
Piston rings		
End gap		
Top	0.20-0.35	0.50
	(0.008-0.014)	(0.020)
Second	0.3-0.5	0.008
	(0.01-0.20)	(0.003)
Oil	0.2-0.8	1.1
	(0.01-0.03)	(0.04)
Ring to groove clearance		
Top	0.025-0.060	0.08
	(0.0010-0.0023)	(0.003)
Second	0.015-0.050	0.08
Oil pump rotors		
Rotor tip clearance	0.15	0.20
	(0.006)	(0.008)
Pump end clearance	0.02-0.07	0.10
	(0.001-0.003)	(0.004)
Pump body clearance	0.15-0.22	0.35
	(0.006-0.009)	(0.014)
	(0.0006-0.0020)	(0.003)

(continued)

Table 2 ENGINE SERVICE SPECIFICATIONS (continued)

	Specification mm (in.)	Wear limit mm (in.)
Connecting rods		
Small end inside diameter	16.016-16.034 (0.6305-0.6313)	16.07 (0.633)
Small end side clearance	0.016-0.040 (0.0006-0.0016)	0.06 (0.002)
Crankshaft		
Connecting rod big end side clearance	0.05-0.20 (0.002-0.008)	0.3 (0.01)
Runout	—	0.05 (0.002)
Crankpin oil clearance	0.028-0.052 (0.0011-0.0020)	0.06 (0.0023)
Main journal oil clearance	0.023-0.047 (0.0009-0.0019)	0.05 (0.002)
Starter driven gear OD	74.57 (1.794)	— —

Table 3 ENGINE TIGHTENING TORQUES

	N·m	ft.-lb.
Oil drain bolt	35	25
Oil pump bolt	12	9
Oil pump driven sprocket*	15	11
Spark plug	14	10
Timing hole cap	3.5	2.5
Crankshaft hole cap	7	5
Shift drum center pin*	23	17
Alternator rotor bolt	85	61
Cylinder head nuts	37	27
Rocker arm holder bolts	12	9
Camshaft holder bolts	12	9
Cam sprocket bolts*	21	15
Cam chain guide bolt	12	9
Cylinder head cover bolts	10	7
Cylinder head cover breather plate*	12	9
Lower crankcase special oil gallery bolts		
Sealing bolt (20 mm)	30	22
Special bolt (14 mm)	25	18
Crankcase bolts		
6 mm	12	9
8 mm	24	17
10 mm	40	29
Connecting rod cap nut/bolt	24	17
Starter clutch		
Cover socket bolts (6 mm)*	16	12
Starter clutch bolt (10 mm)	85	61
Pulse generator socket bolt*	5.3	3.8
Neutral switch	12	9
Oil pressure switch	12	9
Engine mounting bolts and nuts	50	36
Drive sprocket bolt	55	40
Gearshift pedal bolt	27	20

* Apply Loctite 242 (blue) to threads before assembly.

Table 4 MAIN JOURNAL BEARING SELECTION

Crankcase ID code letter and dimension	Main journal OC number code and dimension		
	Letter A 36.000-36.008 mm (1.4173-1.4176 in.)	Letter B 36.008-36.016 mm (1.4176-1.4179 in.)	Letter C 36.016 86.024 mm (1.4179 1.4183 in.)
Number 1 32.992-33.000 mm (1.2989-1.2992 in.)	Pink (D)	Yellow (C)	Green (B)
Number 2 32.984-32.992 mm (1.2986-1.2989 in.)	Yellow (C)	Green (B)	Brown (A)

Table 5 MAIN JOURNAL BEARING INSERT THICKNESS

Color	mm	In.
Brown (A)	1.492-1.496	0.0587-0.0589
Green (B)	1.488-1.492	0.0586-0.0587
Yellow (C)	1.484-1.488	0.0584-0.0586
Pink (D)	1.480-1.484	0.0583-0.0584

Table 6 CONNECTING ROD BEARING SELECTION

Connecting rod ID code number and dimension	Crankpin journal DO size code letter and dimension	
	Number 1 36.000-36.008 (1.4173-1.4176)	Number 2 36.008-36.016 (1.4176-1.4179)
Letter A 32.992-33.000 mm (1.2989-1.2992 in.)	Yellow (C)	Green (B)
Letter B 32.984-32.992 mm (1.2986-1.2989)	Green (B)	Brown (A)

Table 7 CONNECTING ROD BEARING INSERT THICKNESS

Color	mm	In.
Brown (A)	1.494-1.498	0.0588-0.0590
Green (B)	1.490-1.494	0.0587-0.0588
Yellow (C)	1.486-1.490	0.0585-0.0587

CLUTCH

The clutch is a wet, multi-plate type which operates immersed in the engine oil. It is mounted on the right-hand end of the transmission mainshaft.

Clutch specifications are listed in **Table 1**. **Table 1** and **Table 2** are found at the end of the chapter.

CLUTCH COVER

Removal/Installation

1. Support the bike securely.
2. Drain the engine oil as described in Chapter Three.
3. Remove the lower right-hand fairing as described in Chapter Thirteen.
4. Remove the fuel tank as described in Chapter Seven.
5. Disconnect the alternator 3-pin connector (**Figure 1**).
6. At the left-hand handlebar, loosen the clutch cable adjuster locknut (A, **Figure 2**) and turn the adjuster (B, **Figure 2**) to loosen the clutch cable.
7. Remove the bolts securing the clutch cable adjuster bracket (A, **Figure 3**) and disconnect the clutch cable (B, **Figure 3**) from the release mechanism lever.

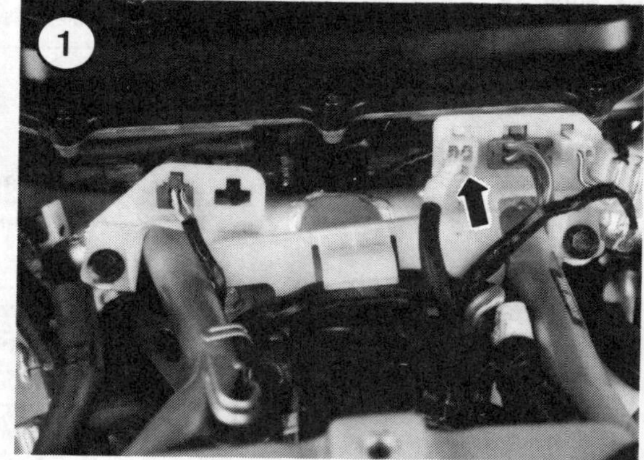

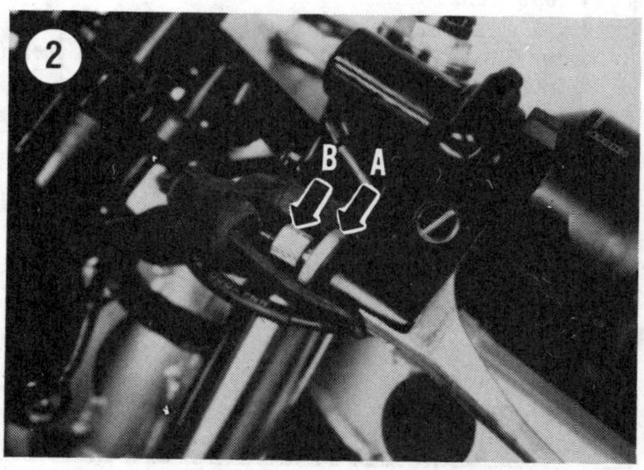

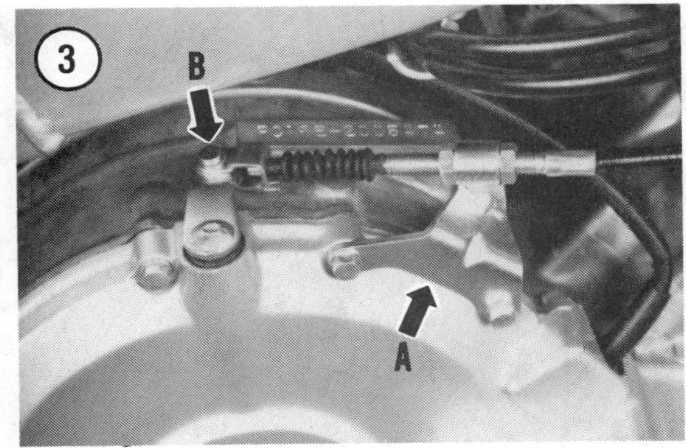

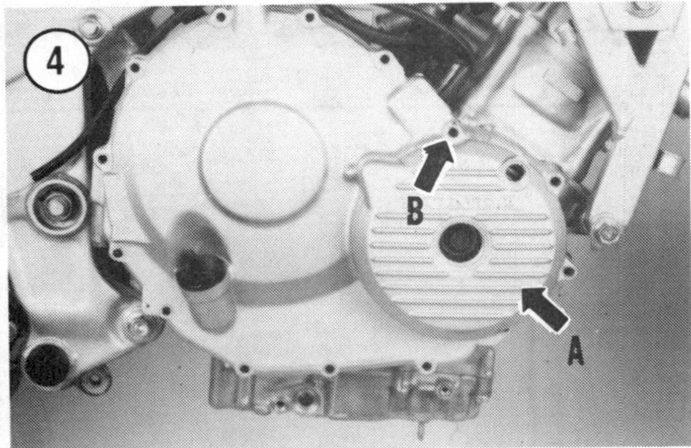

8. Remove the right-hand crankcase cover bolts and remove the cover (A, **Figure 4**). The bolt marked B in **Figure 4** had thread locking agent applied to it during assembly and may be difficult to loosen. Use an impact driver and socket to loosen this bolt.

9. Remove the crankcase cover gasket and the 2 dowel pins (**Figure 5**). If the dowel pins are secure it is not necessary to remove them.

10. Installation is the reverse of these steps. Note the following:

   a. Make sure the clutch lifter piece (A, **Figure 6**) is installed in the center of the crankcase cover.

   b. Install a new crankcase cover gasket.

   c. Make sure both dowel pins (**Figure 5**) are installed.

   d. Apply Loctite 242 (blue) to the bolt installed in B, **Figure 4**.

   e. Refill the engine oil as described in Chapter Three.

   f. Adjust the clutch as described in Chapter Three.

CLUTCH RELEASE MECHANISM

Removal/Installation

1. Remove the clutch cover as described in this chapter.

2. Remove the clutch lifter piece (A, **Figure 6**).

3. Remove the spring pin (B, **Figure 6**) and pull the shaft (**Figure 7**) out of the crankcase cover.

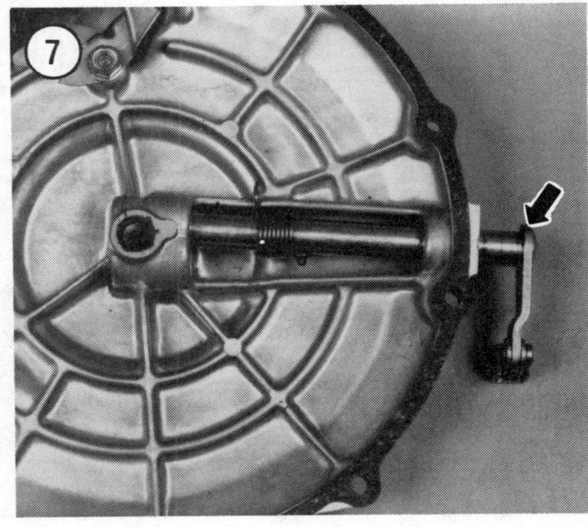

4. Check the oil seal at the top of the cover (**Figure 8**) for wear or damage. Replace the seal, if necessary, by prying it out of the cover with a small screwdriver. Install the new seal by carefully tapping it squarely into the cover with a suitable size socket and hammer.

5. Check the shaft for wear or damage; replace if necessary.

6. Installation is the reverse of these steps.

CLUTCH

Refer to **Figure 9** when performing procedures in this section.

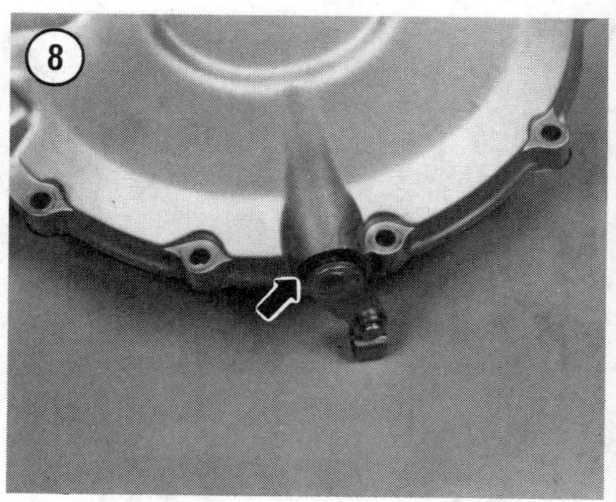

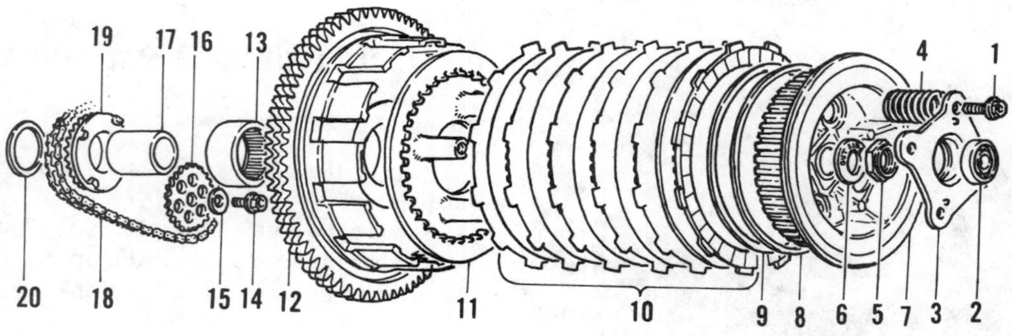

1. Bolt	11. Pressure plate
2. Bearing	12. Clutch outer
3. Lifter plate	13. Bearing
4. Spring	14. Bolt
5. Nut	15. Washer
6. Washer	16. Driven sprocket
7. Clutch center	17. Spacer
8. Spring seat	18. Chain
9. Judder spring	19. Drive sprocket
10. Clutch plates	20. Spacer

A new clutch locknut and the Honda universal clutch center holder (Part No. 2619906) (**Figure 10**) or equivalent are required for clutch removal and installation.

NOTE
Honda issued a product update program to replace the clutch in all 1987 CBR600F models. The new parts are designed to improve clutch engagement smoothness. If you have a 1987 CBR600F, a punch mark placed in front of the engine serial number (on the right-hand crankcase) indicates that the new clutch set was installed. All 1988 and later CBR600F models have this new clutch assembly.

Removal

1. Remove the right-hand crankcase cover as described in this chapter.
2. Slide the bearing (**Figure 11**) out of the lifter plate.
3. Loosen and remove the 4 lifter plate bolts (A, **Figure 12**).
4. Remove the lifter plate (B, **Figure 12**).
5. Remove the clutch springs (**Figure 13**).
6. Install the Honda clutch center holder (or equivalent) to prevent the pressure plate from rotating while removing the clutch locknut. Remove the clutch locknut (**Figure 14**). Remove the holder after removing the locknut.

7. Remove the lockwasher (**Figure 15**).

8. Remove the clutch center, clutch plates and pressure plate as a complete unit. See **Figure 16**.

NOTE
There are 3 different clutch friction plates used. Label each plate as they are removed in Step 9. See Figure 17.

9. Disassemble the clutch plate assembly as follows:

a. Remove the pressure plate (**Figure 18**).

b. Remove the first friction disc (**Figure 19**).

c. Remove all but the last 2 friction discs and clutch plates.

d. Remove friction disc B (**Figure 20**).

e. Remove the clutch plate (**Figure 21**).

f. Remove friction disc A (**Figure 22**).

g. Remove the judder spring (**Figure 23**).

h. Remove the spring seat (**Figure 24**).

10. Remove the clutch outer (**Figure 25**).

CLUTCH PLATE ASSEMBLY

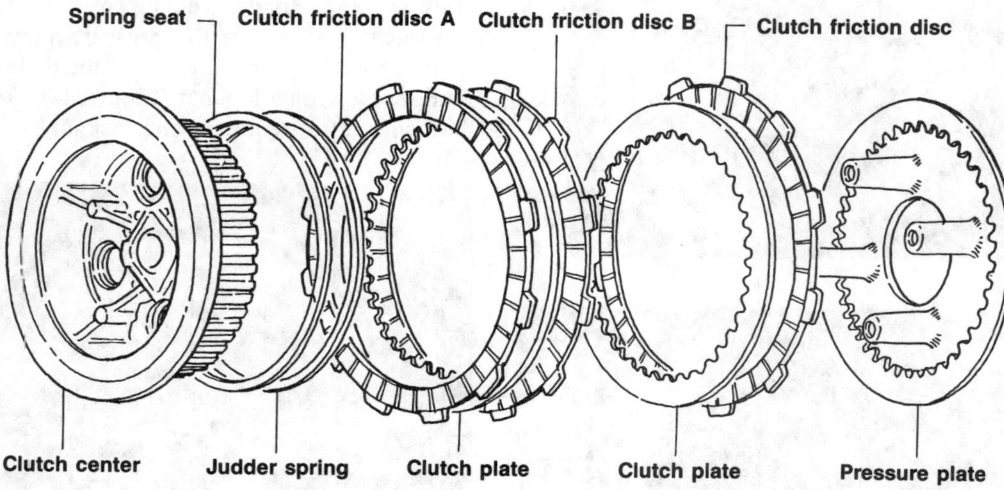

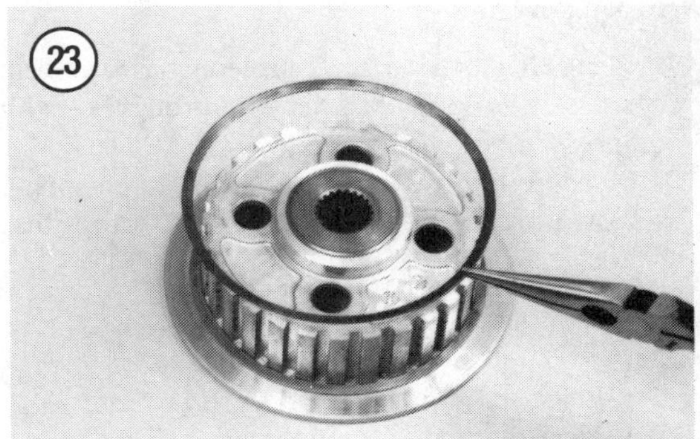

11. Remove the needle bearing (**Figure 26**).
12. Remove the oil pump sprockets as follows:
   a. Remove the oil pump driven sprocket bolt (**Figure 27**).
   b. Slide the oil pump sprockets and chain (**Figure 28**) off and remove them. See **Figure 29**.
   c. Remove the clutch outer guide (**Figure 30**).
   d. Remove the oil pump drive sprocket collar (**Figure 31**).

Inspection

1. Clean all clutch parts in petroleum based solvent such as kerosene and dry thoroughly with compressed air.
2. Measure the free length of each clutch spring as shown in **Figure 32**. Replace any springs that are too short (**Table 1**).

> *NOTE*
> *Refer to **Figure 17** for friction plate identification when performing Step 3.*

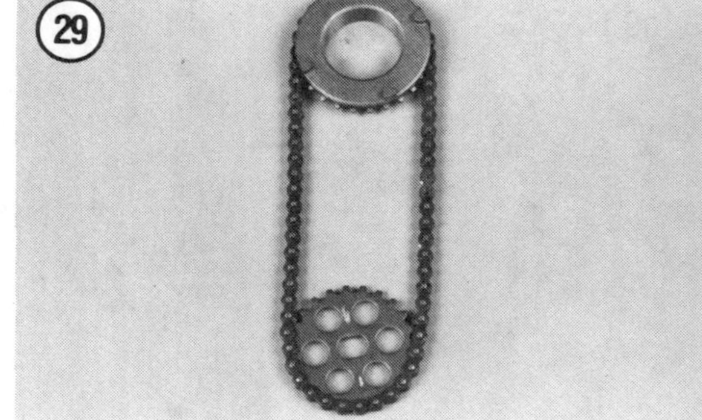

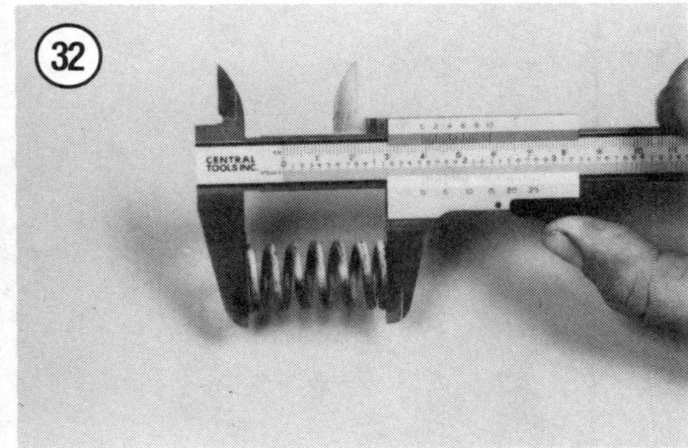

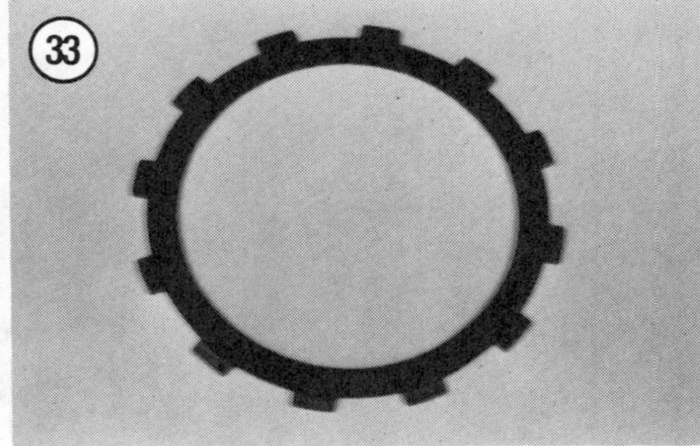

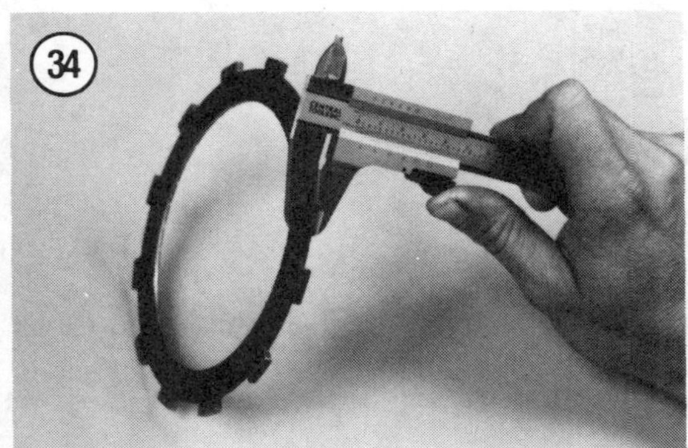

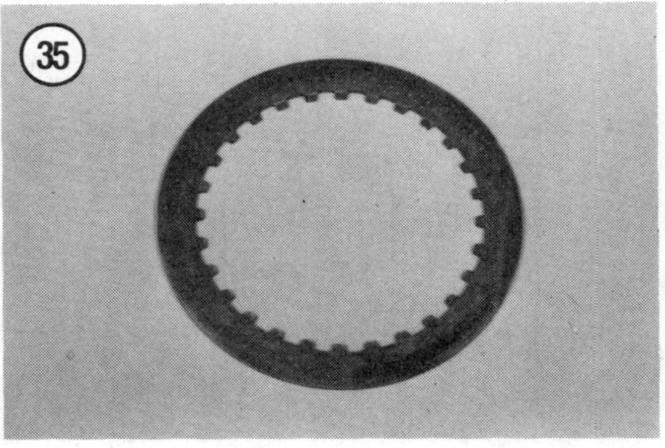

3. The friction plate (**Figure 33**) material is made of cork that is bonded onto an aluminum plate for warp resistance and durability. Measure the thickness of each friction plate at several places around the disc as shown in **Figure 34** with a vernier caliper. See **Table 1** for specifications. Replace worn or damaged friction plates. For best performance, replace all plates as a set. Do not replace only 1 or 2 plates.

4. The stock clutch assembly consists of 5 steel clutch plates (**Figure 35**). Place each clutch metal plate on a surface plate or a thick piece of glass and check for warpage with a feeler gauge as shown in **Figure 36**. If any plate is warped more than specified (**Table 1**), replace the entire set of plates for best performance. Do not replace only 1 or 2 plates.

5. The clutch metal plate inner teeth (**Figure 35**) mesh with the clutch center splines (A, **Figure 37**). Check the splines for cracks or galling. They must be smooth for chatter-free clutch operation. If the clutch center splines are worn, replace it. Check the clutch metal plate teeth for wear or damage; replace if necessary.

6. Inspect the shaft splines (B, **Figure 37**) in the clutch center assembly. If damage is only a slight amount, remove any small burrs with a fine cut file. If damage is severe, replace the clutch center.

7. Inspect the clutch boss bolt studs for thread damage or cracks at the base of the studs. Thread damage may be repaired with an M6 × 1 metric tap. Use kerosene on the tap threads. If a bolt stud is cracked, the clutch boss must be replaced.

8. Inspect the pressure plate (**Figure 38**) for signs of damage or warpage. Check the spring towers for cracks or damage. Check the pressure plate

teeth where they engage the clutch center for cracks or damage. Replace the pressure plate if necessary.

9. Check the clutch release bearing (**Figure 39**). Rotate the bearing race by hand and check for excessive play or roughness. Replace the bearing if necessary.

10. The friction plates (**Figure 33**) have tabs that slide in the clutch outer grooves (A, **Figure 40**). Inspect the tabs for cracks or galling in the grooves. They must be smooth for chatter-free clutch operation. Light damage can be repaired with an oilstone. Replace the clutch outer if damage is severe.

11. Check the clutch outer bearing bore (B, **Figure 40**) for cracks, deep scoring, excessive wear or heat discoloration. If the bearing bore is damaged, also check the needle bearing (**Figure 41**) for damage. Replace worn or damaged parts.

12. Check the clutch outer driven gear (**Figure 42**) for tooth wear, damage or cracks. Replace the clutch outer if necessary.

> *NOTE*
> *If the clutch outer driven gear teeth are damaged, the drive gear on the crankshaft may also be damaged. Refer to **Crankshaft** in Chapter Four and inspect it.*

13. See **Figure 43**. Inspect the spring seat (A) and the judder spring (B) for distortion, damage or wear; replace if necessary.

14. See **Figure 44**. Perform the following:
   a. Measure the oil pump drive sprocket inside diameter (A) with a vernier caliper.
   b. Measure the clutch outer guide inside diameter (B) with a vernier caliper.
   c. Measure the clutch outer guide length (C) with a vernier caliper.

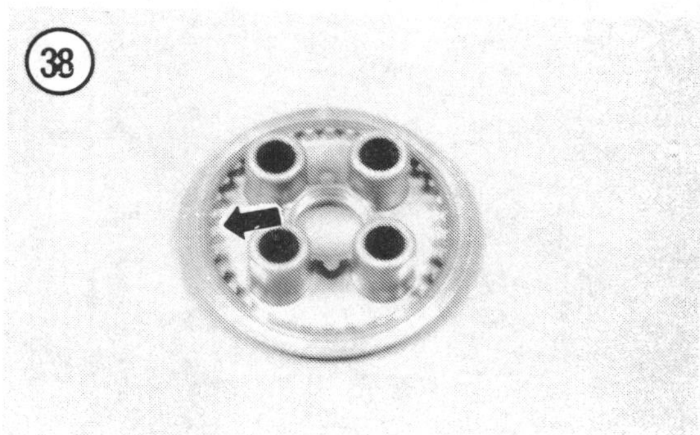

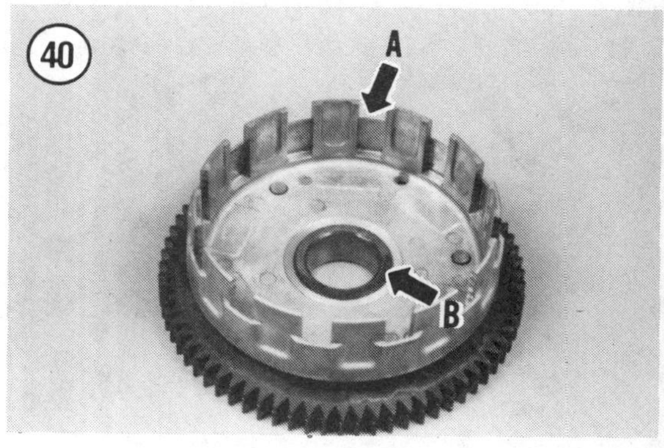

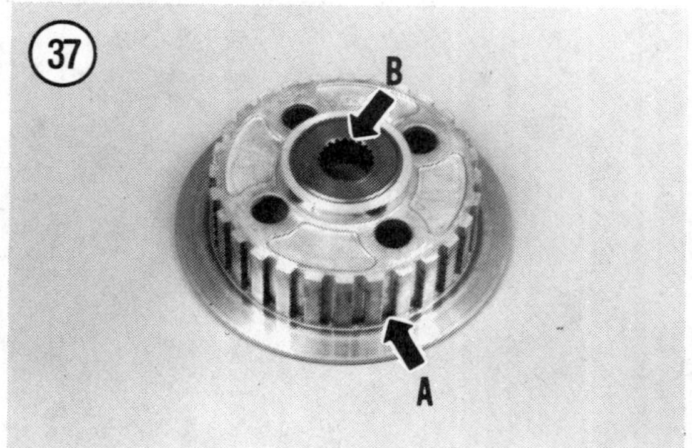

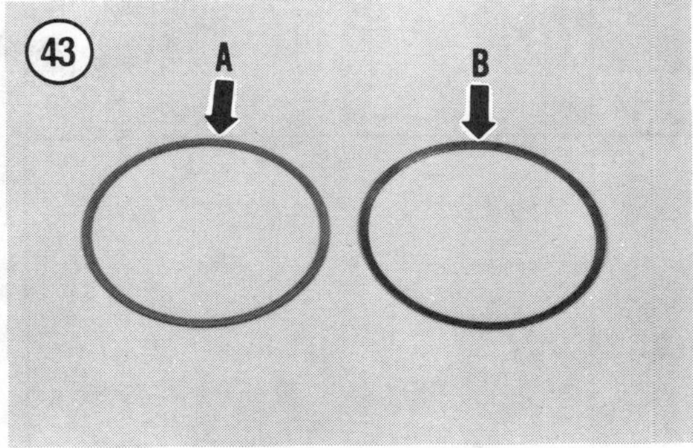

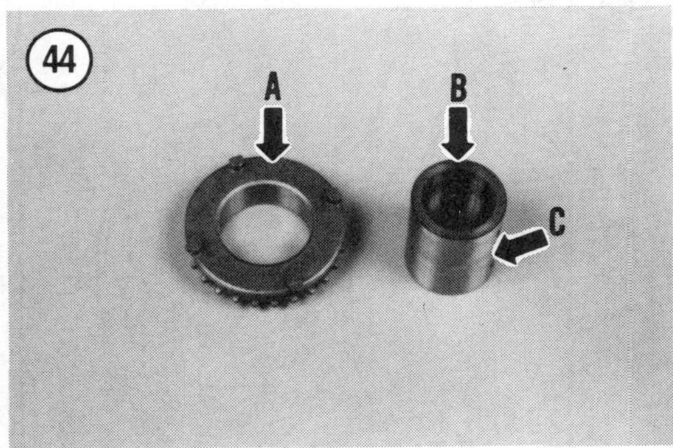

d. Replace worn or damaged parts. Refer to **Table 1** for service specifications.

15. Measure the transmission mainshaft outside diameter where the clutch outer guide rides (**Figure 30**). Compare to the specification in **Table 1**. If the mainshaft outside diameter is worn too small, replace the mainshaft as described in Chapter Six.

16. Check the oil pump driven sprocket and chain for wear or damage; replace if necessary.

Assembly/Installation

1. Oil all parts with clean engine oil before assembly.

2. If the clutch outer was removed, perform the following:

   a. Install the oil pump drive sprocket collar (**Figure 31**) onto the mainshaft.

   b. Install the clutch outer guide (**Figure 30**) onto the mainshaft.

   c. Assemble the oil pump sprocket assembly (**Figure 29**). Then install the assembly as shown in **Figure 28**. Make sure the mark on the driven sprocket (lower sprocket) faces out.

   d. Apply Loctite 242 (blue) onto the oil pump driven sprocket bolt (**Figure 45**). Install the bolt and tighten to the torque specification in **Table 2**.

   e. Oil the needle bearing pins and slide the needle bearing onto the clutch outer guide (**Figure 46**).

   f. Rotate the oil pump drive sprocket so the pins are lined up at the 12, 3, 6 and 9 o'clock positions (**Figure 47**).

   g. Align the index holes (**Figure 47**) in the backside of the clutch outer with the sprocket pins and install the clutch outer housing part way onto the transmission mainshaft.

   h. Align the crankshaft drive gear with the serrated teeth on the clutch outer as shown

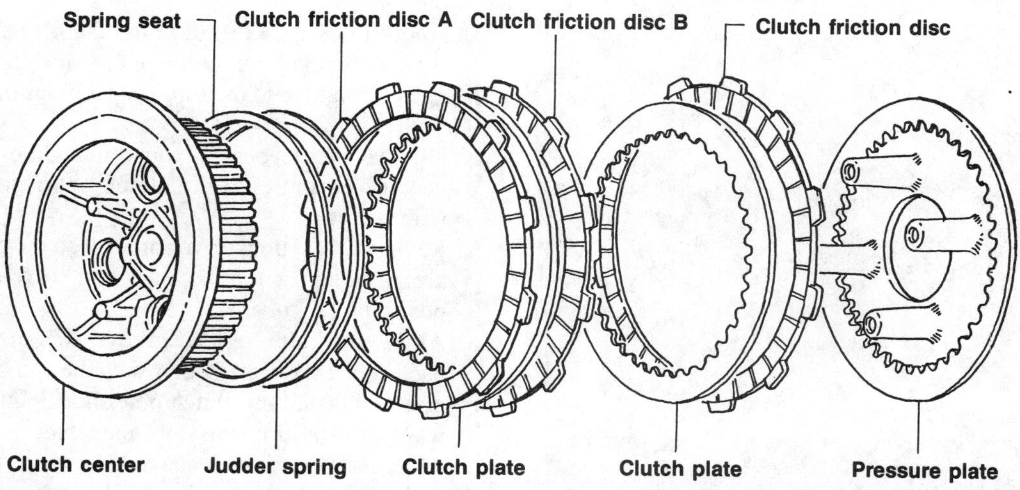

CLUTCH PLATE ASSEMBLY
Spring seat
Clutch friction disc A
Clutch friction disc B
Clutch friction disc
Clutch center
Judder spring
Clutch plate
Clutch plate
Pressure plate

in **Figure 48**. A screwdriver can be used to help engage the drive gear with the clutch outer gear serrated teeth. Then push the clutch outer on all the way and make sure that the pins and holes are indexed properly.

i. Slowly rotate the oil pump driven gear (with a socket placed onto the sprocket bolt) and drive chain until the pins and index holes align properly.

CAUTION
The oil pump sprocket and the clutch outer must index properly or the housing will not go on all the way. The clutch will not function properly nor will the oil pump rotate; severe engine damage will result.

3. Assemble the clutch plate assembly as follows (**Figure 49**):

a. Place the clutch center on the workbench so that it faces as shown in **Figure 50**.
b. Install the spring seat (**Figure 51**) over the clutch center.
c. Install the judder spring (**Figure 52**) with the convex side toward the outside.

NOTE
The spring seat Figure 51 is the flat spring; the judder spring Figure 52 is dished.

d. Install friction disc A (**Figure 53**).
e. Install a steel clutch plate (**Figure 54**).

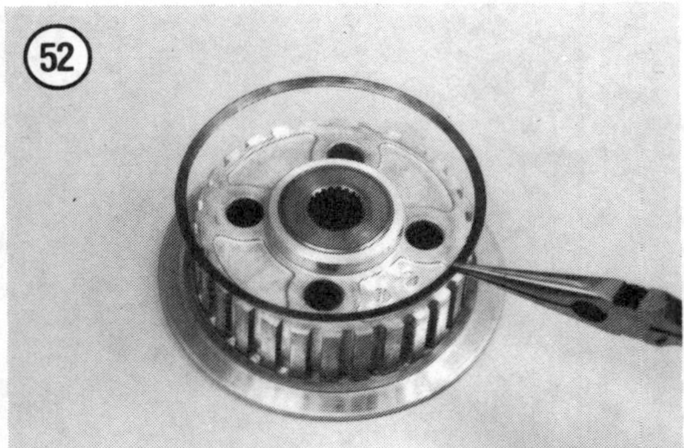

f. Install friction disc B (**Figure 55**).

g. Install a steel clutch plate and then a friction disc until all plates are installed. The last friction plate should be the first plate that was removed during disassembly.

h. Align the friction plate tabs (**Figure 56**).

i. Install the pressure plate (**Figure 57**) over the clutch center assembly.

4. Align the splines in the pressure plate with the transmission mainshaft and install the clutch plate assembly (**Figure 58**).

5. Install the lockwasher so that the side marked OUTSIDE faces out (**Figure 59**).

6. Install a *new* locknut.

7. Using the same tools as during disassembly, hold the clutch and tighten the locknut to the torque specification in **Table 2**.

8. Using a punch as shown in **Figure 60**, tap a portion of the locknut so that it engages the notch in the end of the transmission mainshaft.

9. Install the 4 clutch springs (**Figure 61**).

10. See **Figure 62**. Install the lifter plate (B) and the 4 lifter plate bolts (A). Tighten the bolts securely in a crisscross pattern.

11. Install the lifter plate bearing (**Figure 63**).

12. Install the clutch cover as described in this chapter.

Tables are on the following page.

Table 1 CLUTCH SPECIFICATIONS

	Specification mm (in.)	Wear limit mm (in.)
Spring free length	42.5 (1.67)	41.0 (1.61)
Friction plate thickness		
Disc A	3.22-3.38 (0.127-0.133)	2.90 (0.114)
Disc B	3.42-3.58 (0.135-0.141)	3.20 (0.126)
Clutch plate warpage	— —	0.30 (0.012)
Clutch outer guide		
Inside diameter	21.993-22.007 (0.8659-0.8664)	22.05 (0.868)
Length	39.9-40.0 (1.571-1.575)	39.8 (1.57)
Mainshaft outside diameter at outer guide	21.980-21.993 (0.8654-0.8659)	21.94 (0.864)
Oil pump drive sprocket inside diameter	30.025-30.075 (1.1821-1.1841)	30.11 (1.185)

Table 2 CLUTCH TIGHTENING TORQUES

	N·m	ft.-lb.
Clutch locknut	85	61
Shift drum center bolt*	23	17
Oil pump driven sprocket bolt*	15	11
Gearshift pedal bolt	27	20

* Apply Loctite 242 (blue) to threads before installation.

CHAPTER SIX

TRANSMISSION

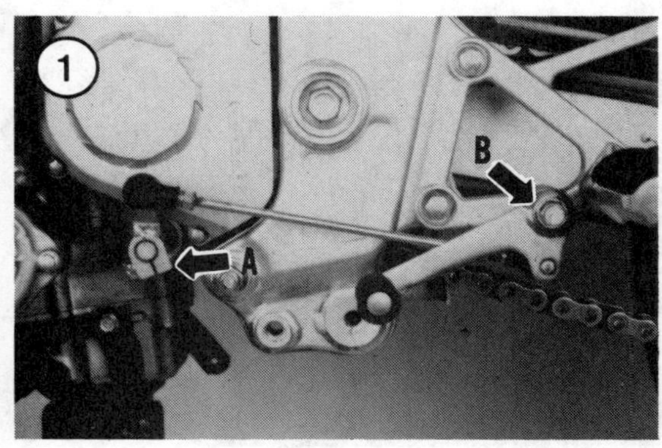

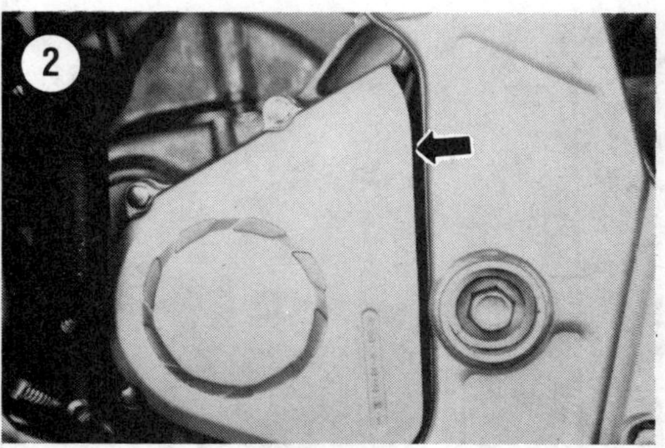

This chapter covers all the parts that transmit power from the clutch to the drive chain. These parts consist of the engine sprocket, transmission gears, shift drum and forks and shift linkage. Transmission specifications are listed in **Table 1**. **Tables 1-3** are at the end of the chapter.

SPROCKET COVER

Removal/Installation

1. Support the bike and raise the rear wheel off the ground with a suitable wheel stand or place it on wood blocks.
2. Remove the lower fairing assembly. See Chapter Thirteen.
3. Remove the shift linkage (**Figure 1**); remove the pinch screw (A) and the pivot screw (B) securing the shift linkage and pull the shift linkage off. If the pivot boss is tight on the shaft, spread open the slot with a screwdriver.
4. Remove the screws securing the engine sprocket cover and remove the cover (**Figure 2**). Remove

the case protector (A, **Figure 3**) and the washer gasket (B, **Figure 3**) from behind the cover.

5. Installation is the reverse of these steps. Note the following:

   a. Make sure to install the washer gasket (B, **Figure 3**) and the case protector (A, **Figure 3**) behind the sprocket cover.

   b. Tighten the sprocket cover screws securely.

NEUTRAL SWITCH

Removal/Installation

The neutral light is activated by a switch mounted behind the sprocket cover (**Figure 4**). The switch is turned on when the transmission and the shift drum end plate are in the NEUTRAL position.

1. Remove the sprocket cover as described in this chapter.

2. Disconnect the electrical connector at the neutral switch.

3. Unscrew the neutral switch and remove it.

4. Reverse to install.

5. Tighten the neutral switch securely.

ENGINE SPROCKET

The engine sprocket is on the left-hand end of the transmission countershaft, behind the sprocket cover. The drive chain is endless—it has no master link. To remove the drive chain, remove the engine sprocket from the countershaft and remove the rear wheel and the swing arm; see *Drive Sprocket and Drive Chain Removal/Installation* in Chapter Eleven.

Removal/Installation

1. Remove the engine sprocket cover as described in this chapter.

2. Have an assistant apply the rear brake to keep the drive chain taut and keep the drive sprocket from turning. Then, loosen and remove the drive sprocket bolt (**Figure 5**).

3. Loosen the rear axle adjuster locknuts (A, **Figure 6**) and loosen the axle nut (B, **Figure 6**). Loosen the rear axle adjusters to loosen the drive chain. Push the rear wheel forward to allow maximum drive chain slack.

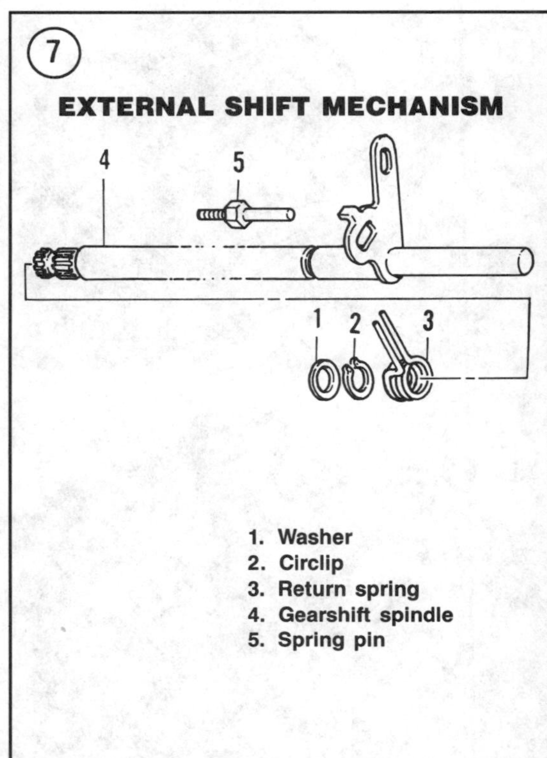

4. With slack in the drive chain, pull the drive sprocket and chain off of the transmission countershaft. See **Figure 5**. Remove the drive sprocket from the drive chain.

5. Install by reversing the removal steps. Note the following:

   a. Tighten the drive sprocket bolt to the torque specification in **Table 2**.

   b. Adjust the drive chain as described under *Drive Chain Adjustment* in Chapter Three.

   c. Rotate the wheel several times to make sure it rotates smoothly. Apply the brake several times to make sure it operates correctly.

   d. Adjust the rear brake as described under *Rear Brake Pedal Height Adjustment* and *Rear Brake Light Switch Adjustment* in Chapter Three.

EXTERNAL SHIFT MECHANISM

Refer to **Figure 7**. The external shift mechanism can be serviced with the engine in the frame.

Removal/Installation

1. Remove the lower fairing as described in Chapter Thirteen.

2. Remove the clutch as described in Chapter Five.

3. Remove the shift linkage (**Figure 1**); remove the pinch screw (A) and the pivot screw (B) securing the shift linkage and pull the shift linkage off. If the pivot boss is tight on the shaft, spread open the slot with a screwdriver.

4. Pull the shift lever (**Figure 8**) out of the crankcase. Note the washer (A, **Figure 9**) on the shift shaft.

5. Remove the shift collar (**Figure 10**) from the drum shifter.

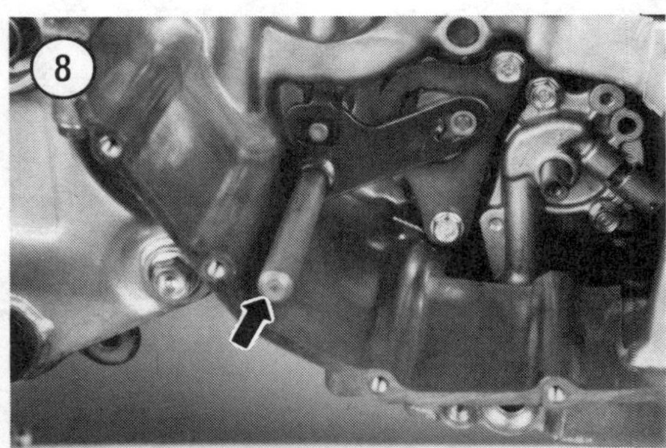

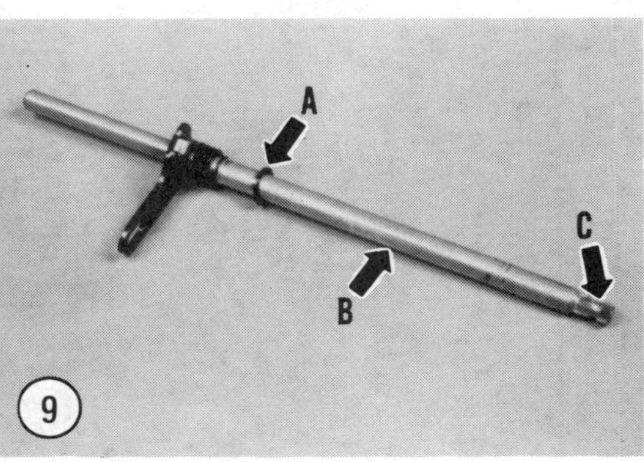

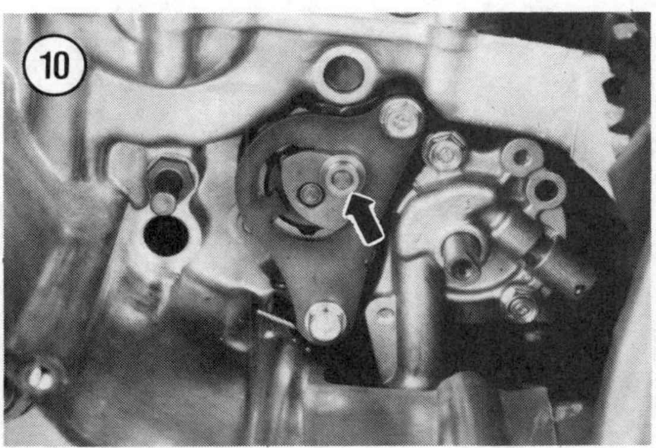

6. Remove the 2 guide plate bolts (**Figure 11**).

> *NOTE*
> *When removing the drum shifter in Step
> 7, hold onto the assembly carefully as
> the ratchet pawls, plungers and springs
> may fall out.*

7. See **Figure 12**. Remove the guide plate (A) and drum shifter (B) as an assembly.
8. Remove the stopper arm assembly as follows:
   a. Remove the stopper arm washer and dowel pin (**Figure 13**).
   b. Remove the stopper arm and spring as an assembly (**Figure 14**).
9. Remove the drum center as follows:
   a. See **Figure 15**. Remove the dowel pin (A) and bolt (B) and remove the drum center plate (C).
   b. Loosen and remove the center bolt (A, **Figure 16**).
   c. Slide the drum center (B, **Figure 16**) off of the shift drum assembly. Remove the pin from the end of the shift drum.

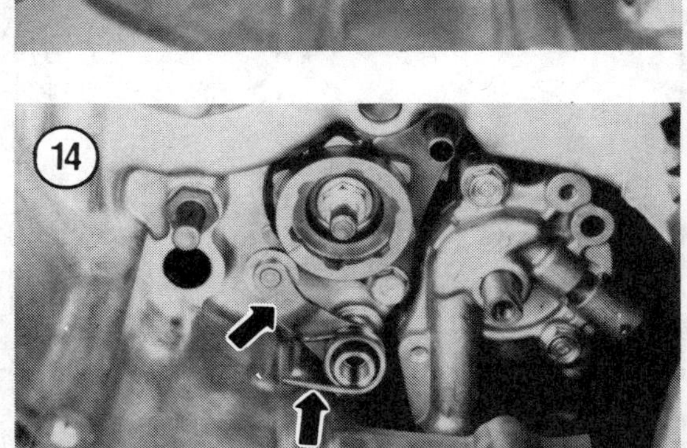

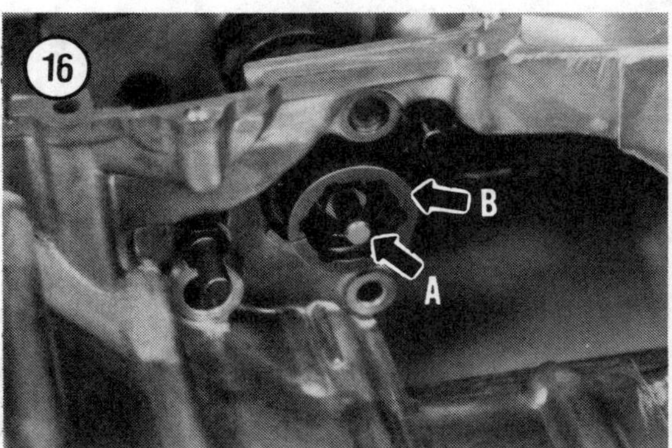

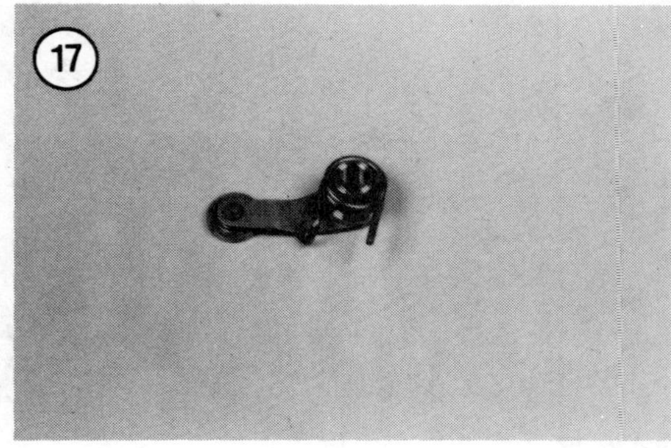

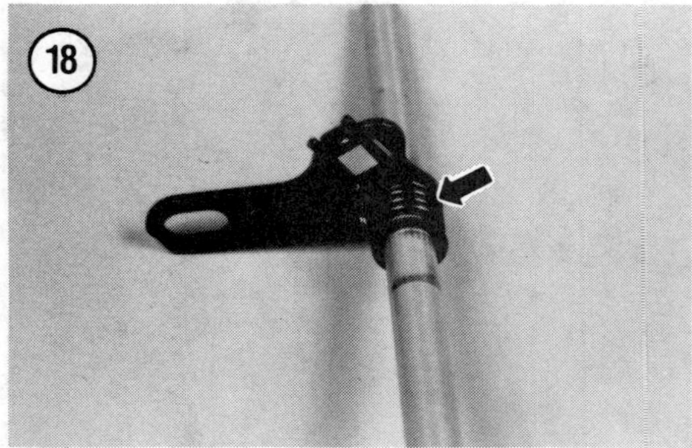

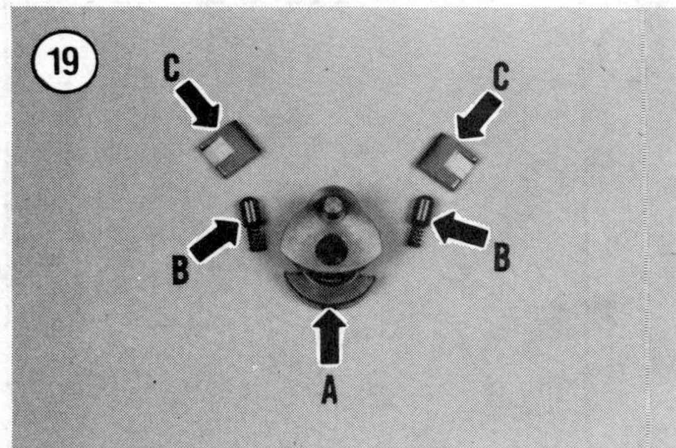

Inspection

1. If the transmission is hard to shift, check for a bent or damaged shift shaft (B, **Figure 9**) or a damaged drum shifter (B, **Figure 16**).

2. If the transmission jumps out of gear, check the stopper arm (**Figure 17**) for a damaged roller or spring pivot.

3. If the shift shaft will not return, check for a worn or broken shift return spring (**Figure 18**) and/or damaged shift lever linkage.

4. Inspect the drum shifter assembly (A, **Figure 19**). Check the plunger and springs (B) for wear or damage. Check the ratchet pawls (C) for scoring, excessive wear or damage. Replace worn or damaged parts.

5. Check the splines on the end of the shift shaft (C, **Figure 9**) for damage; replace the shift shaft if necessary.

6. Replace any other broken, bent, binding or worn shift mechanism parts.

7. Check the drum center (**Figure 20**) cam and detent areas for excessive wear or cracks. Replace the drum center if necessary.

Installation

> *NOTE*
> *Figure 21 shows the shift drum removed for clarity.*

1. Install the drum center as follows:
   a. Insert the pin (A, **Figure 21**) into the shift drum. Then align the notch in the back of the drum center (B, **Figure 21**) with the pin and install the drum center. See B, **Figure 16**.

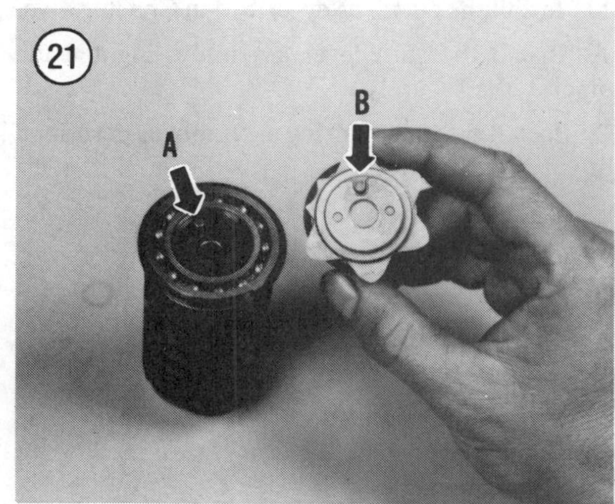

b. Apply Loctite 242 (blue) onto the shift drum center bolt and install the bolt (A, **Figure 16**). Tighten the shift drum center bolt to the torque specification in **Table 2**.

c. Install the drum center plate (C, **Figure 15**).

d. Install the dowel pin (A, **Figure 15**) and bolt (B, **Figure 15**). Tighten the bolt securely.

2. Install the stopper arm assembly as follows:

a. Install the collar (A, **Figure 22**) onto the stopper arm (B, **Figure 22**).

b. Install the spring onto the stopper arm as shown in **Figure 17**.

c. Install the dowel pin and washer (**Figure 23**).

d. Install the stopper arm assembly as shown in **Figure 13**.

3. See **Figure 24**. Install the plungers onto the springs. Then install the plunger/springs and pawls and assemble the drum shifter assembly. See **Figure 25** and **Figure 26**.

4. Install the drum shifter and guide plate as shown in **Figure 12**.

5. Apply Loctite 242 (blue) onto the guide plate bolts and install the bolts (**Figure 11**). Tighten the bolts securely.

6. Install the washer (A, **Figure 9**) onto the shift shaft.

7. Make sure the return spring is centered on the return spring pin as shown in **Figure 18**.

8. Install the collar (**Figure 10**) onto the drum shifter pin.

9. See **Figure 27**. Insert the shift shaft (A) into the crankcase so that the spring aligns with pin (B) and the shift shaft arm aligns with the collar (C).

10. Install the clutch as described in Chapter Five.

11. Install the shift lever assembly. Tighten the pinch bolts securely.

12. Install the lower fairing assembly as described in Chapter Thirteen.

TRANSMISSION GEARS

Removal

Refer to **Figure 28** for this procedure.

1. Remove the engine and split the crankcase as described under *Crankcase Disassembly* in Chapter Four.

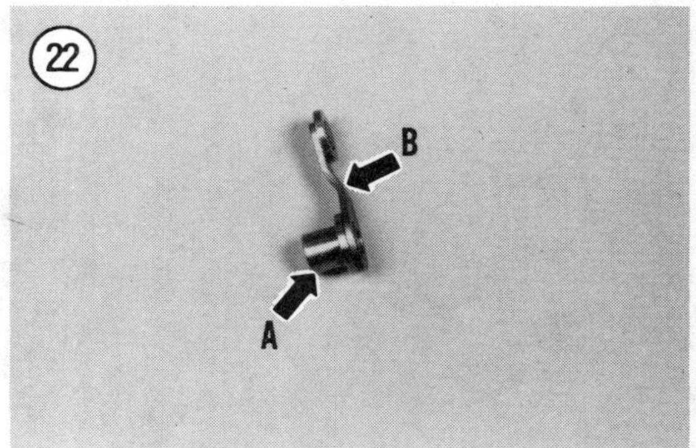

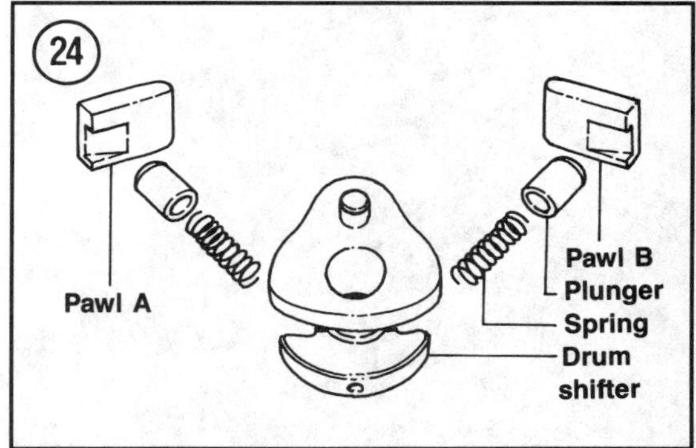

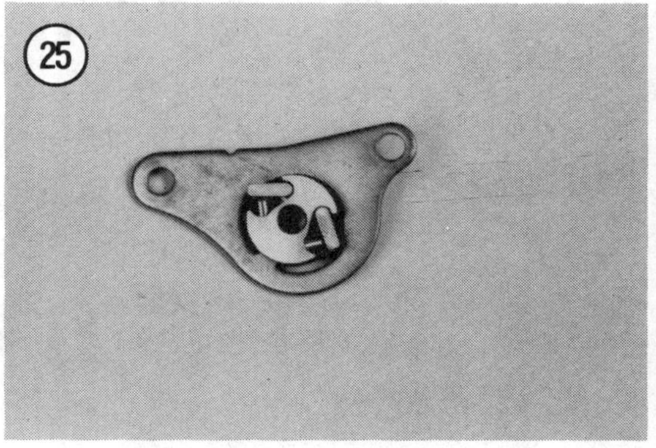

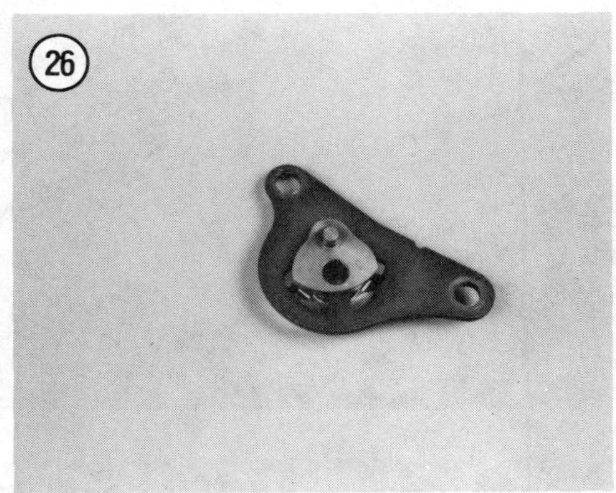

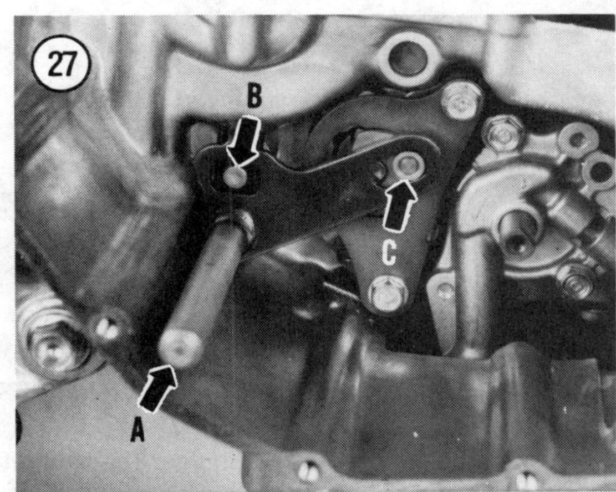

TRANSMISSION

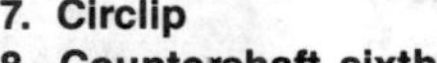
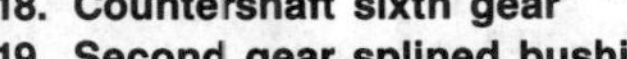

1. Circlip
2. Ball bearing
3. Plain washer
4. Countershaft first gear
5. Needle bearing
6. Plain washer
7. Countershaft fifth gear
8. Circlip
9. Splined washer
10. Countershaft third gear
11. Third gear bushing
12. Lockwasher (with tab)*
13. Stopper washer (with notches)*
14. Countershaft fourth gear
15. Fourth gear splined bushing
16. Splined washer
17. Circlip
18. Countershaft sixth gear
19. Second gear splined bushing
20. Countershaft second gear
21. Spline washer protector
22. Circlip
23. Countershaft
24. Ball bearing
25. Mainshaft/first gear
26. Plain washer
27. Mainshaft fifth gear
28. Fifth gear splined bushing
29. Splined washer
30. Circlip
31. Mainshaft third/fourth gear combination
32. Circlip
33. Splined washer
34. Mainshaft sixth gear
35. Sixth gear splined bushing
36. Stopper washer (with notches)
37. Lockwasher (with tabs)
38. Mainshaft second gear
39. Plain washer
40. Needle bearing

***These parts may appear slightly different on some models.**

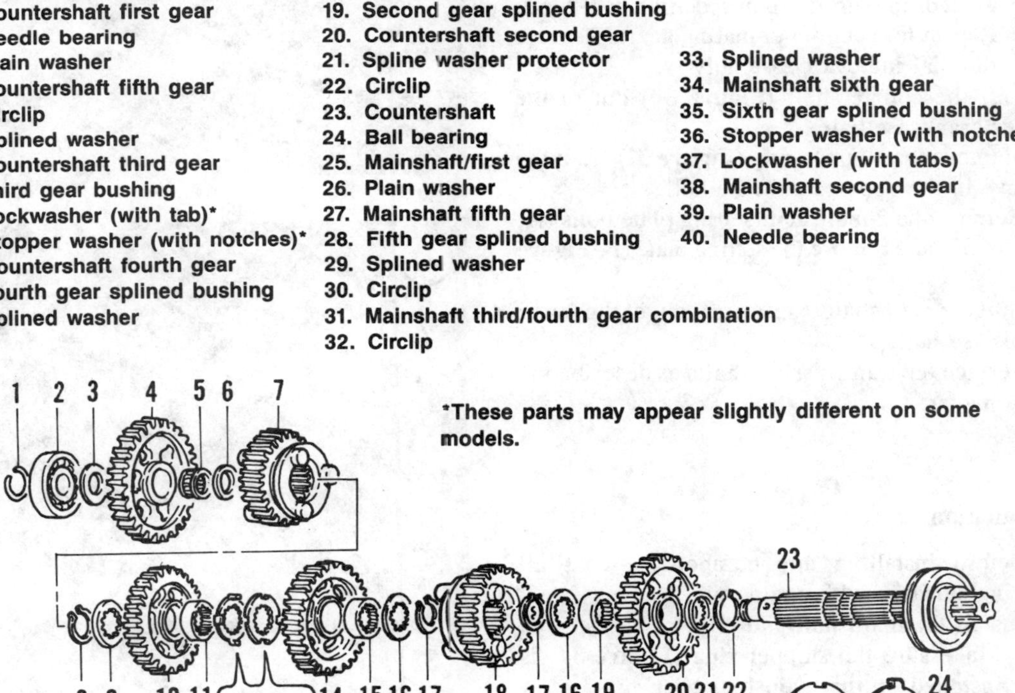

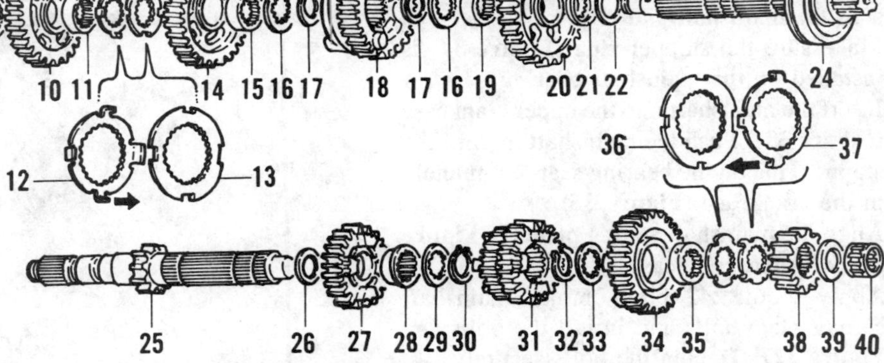

NOTE
It is not necessary to remove crankshaft, primary chain or starter clutch when removing the transmission shafts.

2. Before removing the transmission shafts, check gear backlash as follows:
   a. Mount a dial indicator onto a magnetic stand or some other support and place the plunger against one gear. See **Figure 29**.
   b. Rotate the gear with the plunger (back and forth) while holding the mating gear and note the dial indicator reading.
   c. The difference between the highest and lowest readings recorded in sub-step c is gear backlash. Replace both gears if the backlash exceeds the service limit specified in **Table 1**.
   d. Repeat for each set of mating gears. Remove the dial indicator assembly.

3. Lift the countershaft (**Figure 30**) out of the upper crankcase half.

4. Remove the stopper ring (**Figure 31**) from the groove in the upper crankcase half.

5. Remove the 2 mainshaft setting plate bolts (A, **Figure 32**) and remove the setting plate (B, **Figure 32**).

6. Pull the mainshaft (**Figure 33**) out of the lower crankcase half.

7. Service the transmission shafts as described in this chapter.

Installation

1. Before installing any component, coat all bearing surfaces with engine oil.

2. Install the mainshaft as follows:
   a. Make sure the stopper ring (**Figure 34**) is installed on the mainshaft bearing.
   b. Insert the mainshaft into the upper crankcase (**Figure 33**). Push the mainshaft in until the stopper ring on the bearing seats completely in the crankcase (**Figure 35**).
   c. Align the mainshaft setting plate (B, **Figure 32**) with the crankcase.
   d. Apply Loctite 242 (blue) onto the mainshaft setting plate bolts and install the bolts (A, **Figure 32**). Tighten the bolts securely.

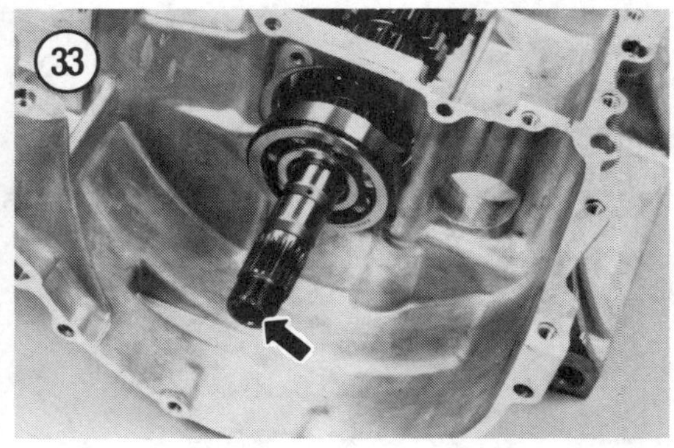

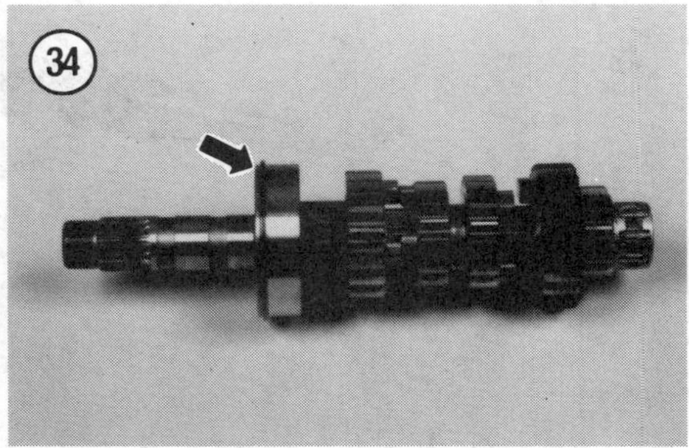

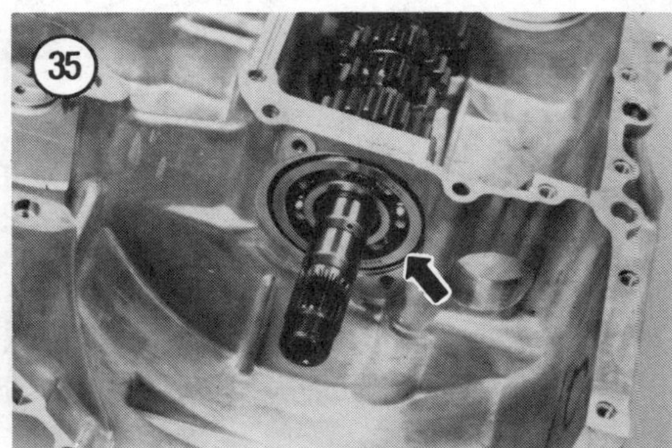

e. Spin the mainshaft assembly (**Figure 36**). It should spin smoothly and without any play or noise. If it does not, correct the problem.

3. Install the countershaft as follows:

a. Install the stopper ring into the inner crankcase half groove. See **Figure 31**.

b. Install the countershaft into the crankcase (**Figure 30**). When installing the countershaft, make sure the inner bearing groove (A, **Figure 37**) aligns with the stopper ring (**Figure 31**) and that the locating pin on the bearing seats in the notch in the crankcase (B, **Figure 37**).

> *CAUTION*
> *If the countershaft bearing is not installed correctly, there will be no clearance between the crankcase and the outer bearing race.*

4. Assemble the crankcase and install the engine as described in Chapter Four.

**Transmission
Service Notes**

1. A divided container, such as an egg carton, can be used to help maintain correct alignment and positioning of the parts as they are removed from the transmission shaft.

2. The circlips are a tight fit on the transmission shafts. It is recommended to replace all circlips during reassembly.

3. Circlips will turn and fold over making removal and installation difficult. To ease replacement, open the circlips with a pair of circlip pliers while

at the same time holding the back of the circlip with a pair of pliers and remove them. See **Figure 38**. Repeat for installation.

Mainshaft
Disassembly/Assembly

Refer to **Figure 28**.
1. Remove the needle bearing (**Figure 39**).
2. Remove the plain washer (**Figure 40**).
3. Slide off mainshaft second gear (**Figure 41**).
4. Remove the lockwasher (**Figure 42**).

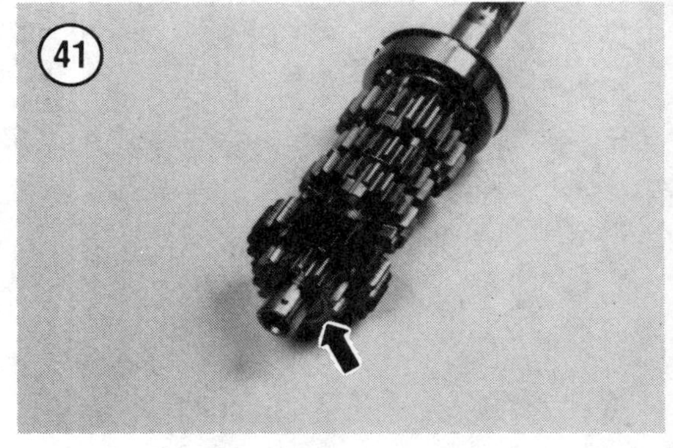

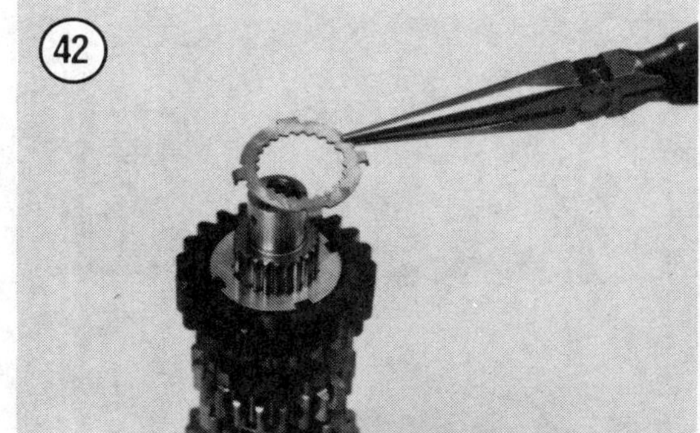

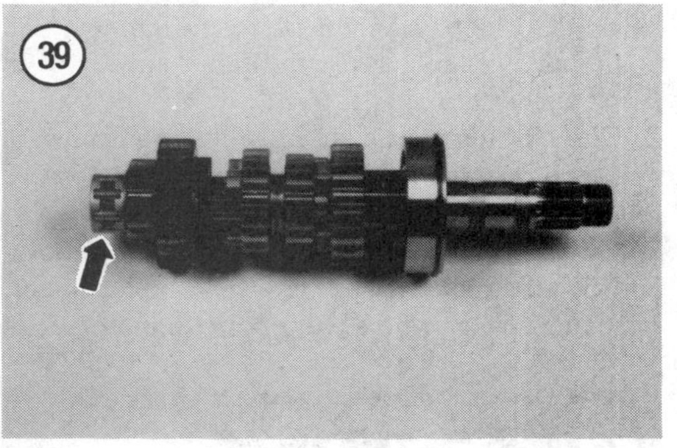

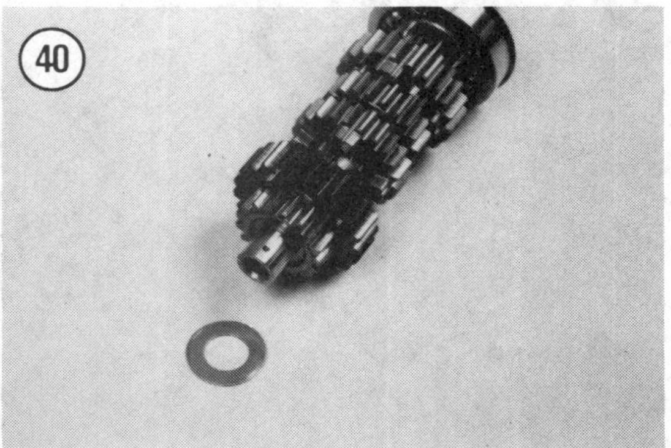

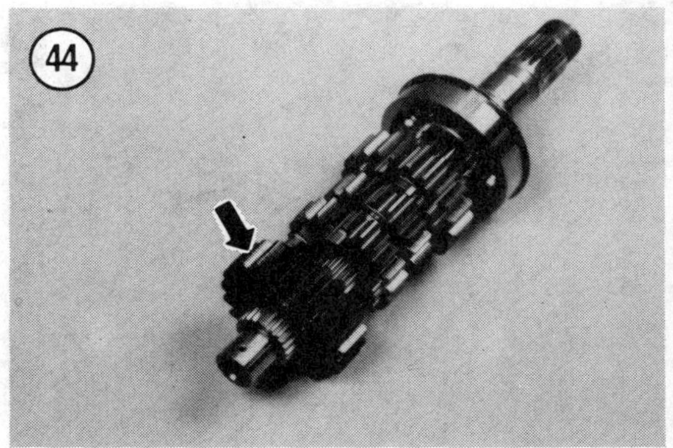

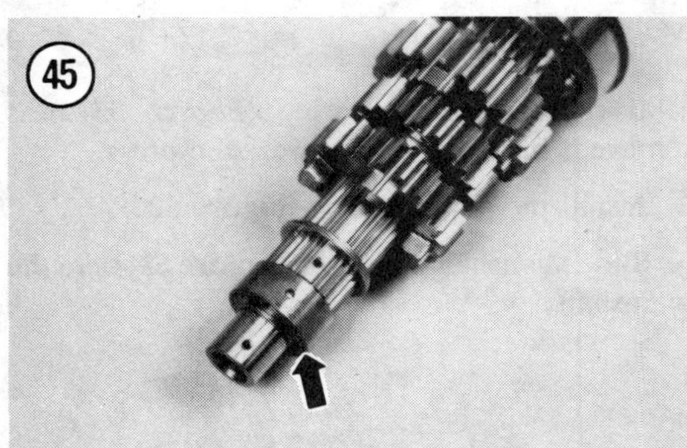

5. Remove the stopper washer (**Figure 43**).

6. Slide off mainshaft sixth gear (**Figure 44**).

7. Remove the sixth gear bushing (**Figure 45**) and the splined washer (**Figure 46**).

8. Remove the circlip (**Figure 47**).

9. Slide off mainshaft third/fourth gear combination (**Figure 48**).

10. Remove the circlip (**Figure 49**).

11. Remove the splined washer and the bushing (**Figure 50**).

12. Slide off mainshaft fifth gear (**Figure 51**).

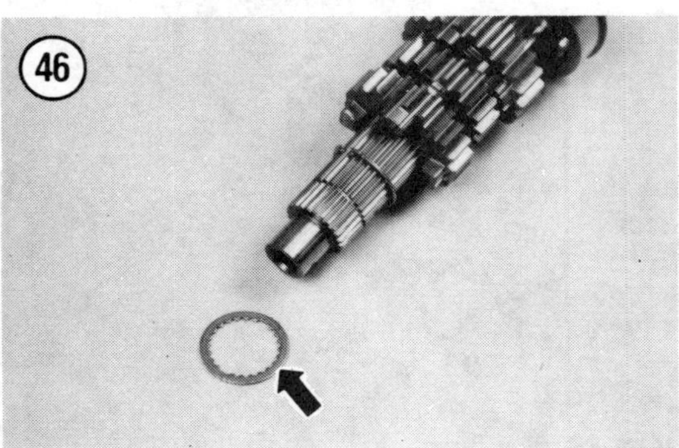

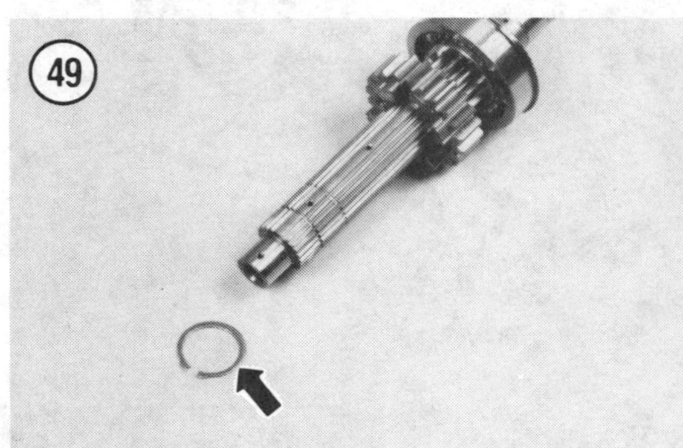

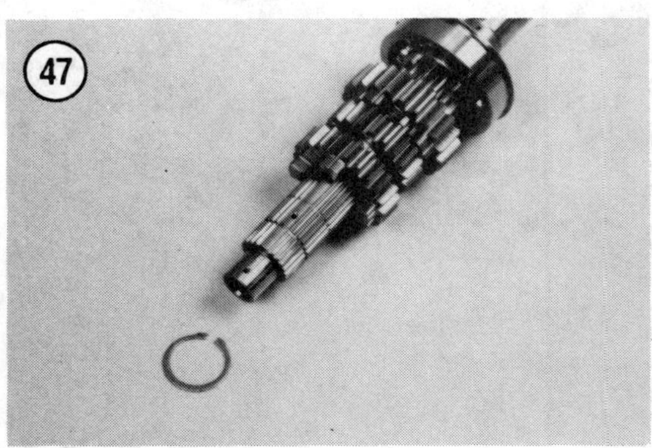

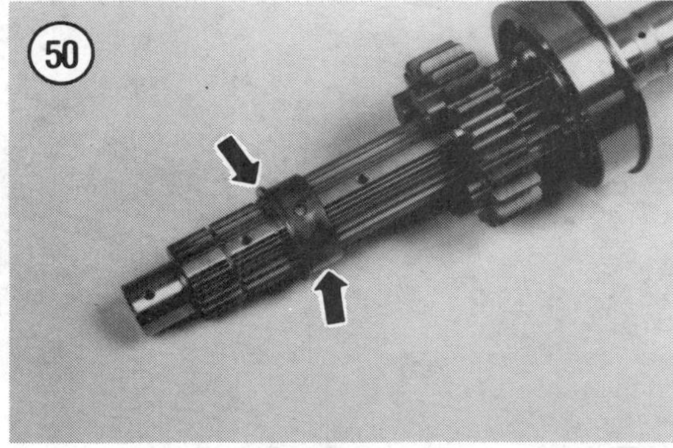

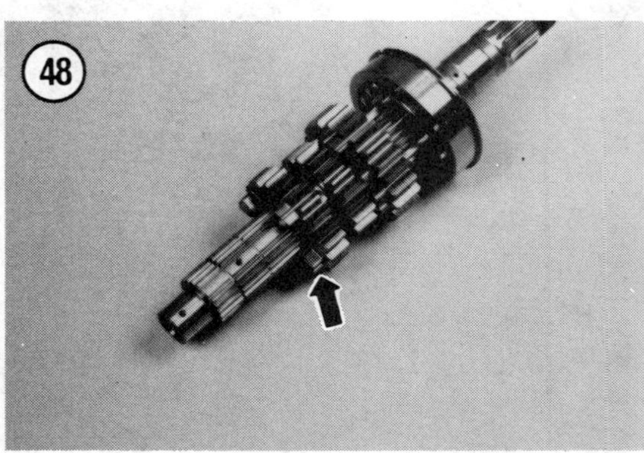

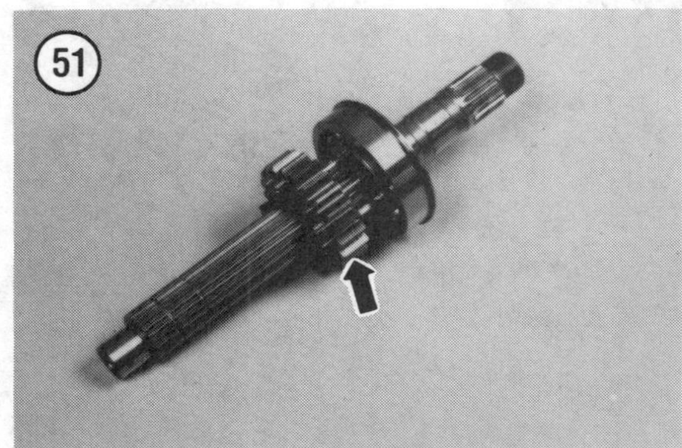

13. Remove the plain washer (**Figure 52**).

14. If necessary, remove the mainshaft bearing (**Figure 53**) with a bearing puller. Install a new bearing with a hydraulic press.

15. Inspect the mainshaft assembly as described in this chapter.

Mainshaft Assembly

1. If the mainshaft bearing (**Figure 53**) was removed, install it with a hydraulic press.

2. Install the plain washer (**Figure 52**).

3. Slide mainshaft fifth gear (**Figure 51**) onto the mainshaft.

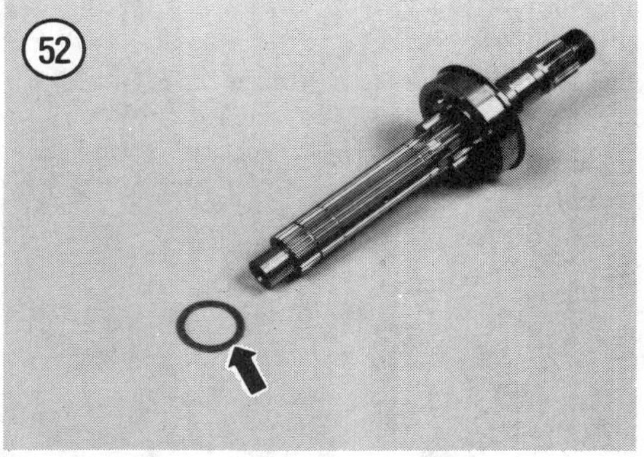

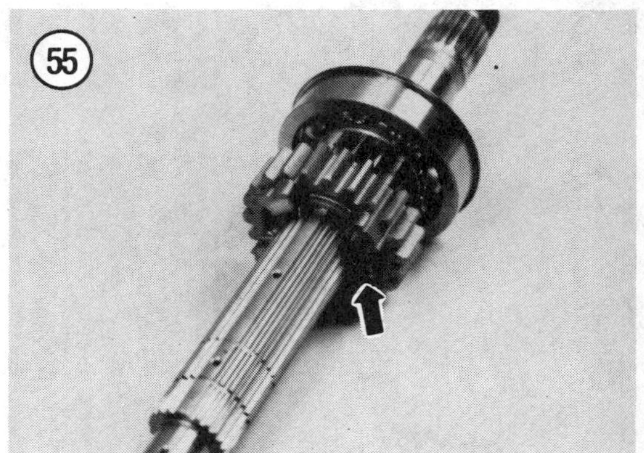

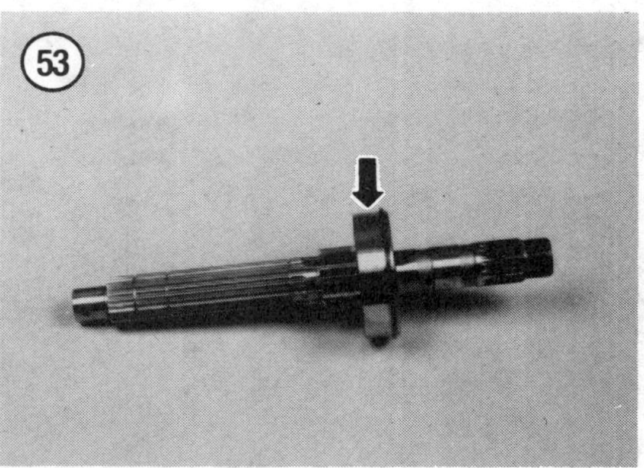

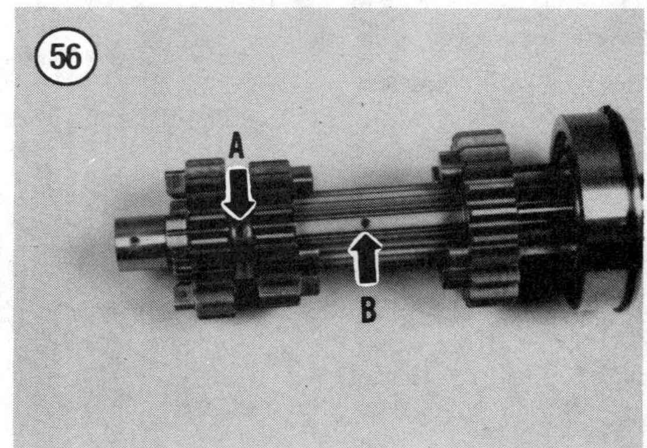

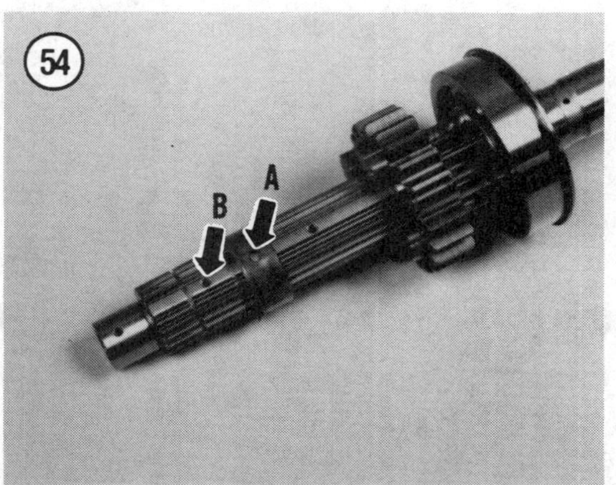

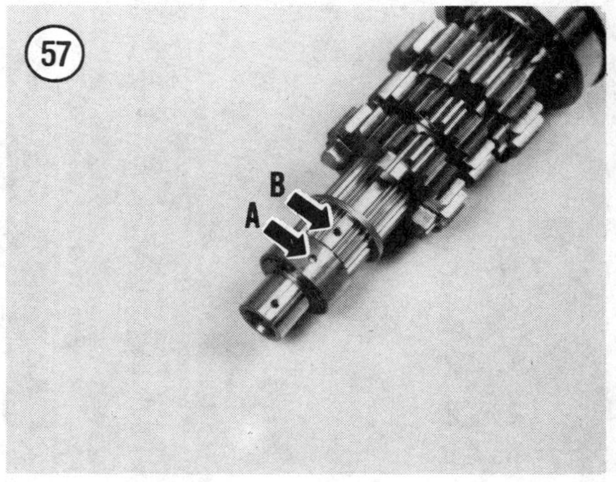

4. See **Figure 54**. Install the mainshaft fifth gear bushing. Align the hole in the bushing (A) with the oil hole in the mainshaft (B) and install the bushing. Fit the bushing into fifth gear.

5. Install the splined washer (**Figure 55**).

6. Install the circlip (**Figure 49**).

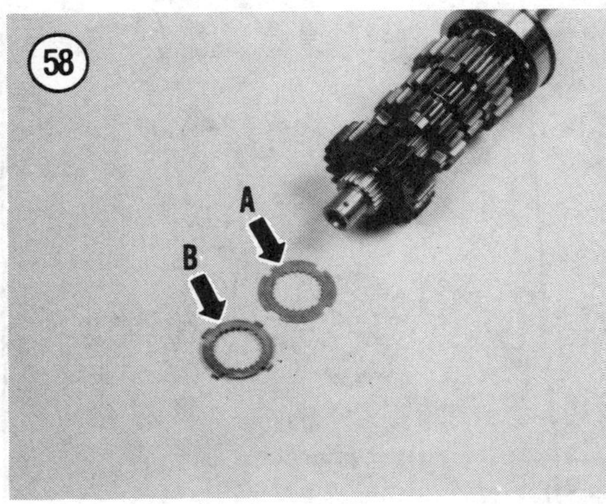

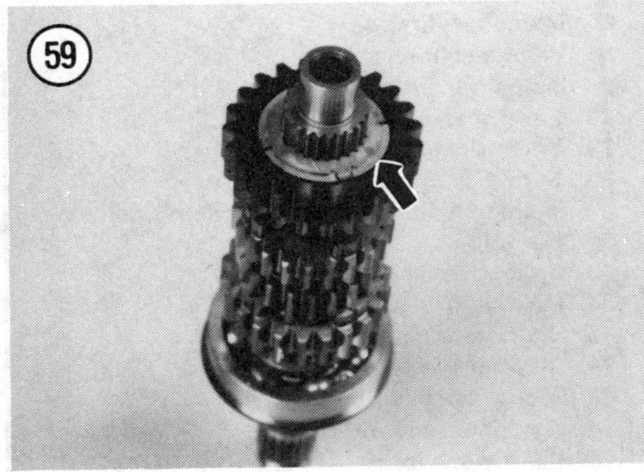

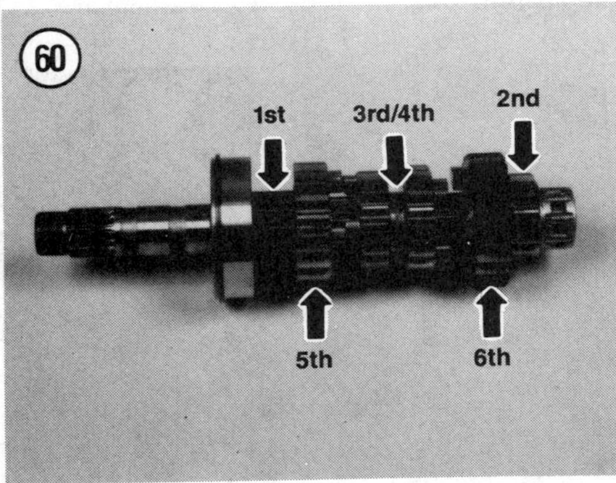

7. Position the mainshaft third/fourth gear with the smaller diameter gear (third gear) going on first. Align the hole in the mainshaft third/fourth gear (A, **Figure 56**) with the oil hole (B, **Figure 56**) in the mainshaft and install the gear assembly. See **Figure 48**.

8. Install the circlip (**Figure 47**) and splined washer (**Figure 46**).

9. See **Figure 57**. Install the mainshaft sixth gear bushing. Align the hole in the bushing (A) with the oil hole in the mainshaft (B) and install the bushing.

10. Slide mainshaft sixth gear (**Figure 44**) onto the mainshaft.

11. See **Figure 58**. Install the stopper washer (A) and the lockwasher (B) as follows:

   a. Install the stopper washer (**Figure 43**).

   b. Install the lockwasher so that washer tabs (**Figure 42**) fit into the stopper washer notches. See **Figure 59**.

12. Slide mainshaft second gear (**Figure 41**) onto the mainshaft.

13. Install the plain washer (**Figure 40**).

14. Install the needle bearing (**Figure 39**).

15. Refer to **Figure 60** for correct placement of the gears. Make sure each gear engages properly to the adjoining gear where applicable.

Countershaft Disassembly

Refer to **Figure 61** for this procedure.

1. Pry the circlip (**Figure 62**) out of the countershaft. See **Figure 63**.

2. Slide the roller bearing (**Figure 64**) off of the countershaft.

3. Remove the plain washer (**Figure 65**).

4. Slide off countershaft first gear (**Figure 66**).

5. Remove the needle bearing and plain washer (**Figure 67**).

6. Slide off countershaft fifth gear (**Figure 68**).

7. Remove the circlip and splined washer (**Figure 69**).

8. Slide off countershaft third gear (**Figure 70**).

9. Remove the third gear bushing (**Figure 71**).

10. See **Figure 72**. Remove the lockwasher (A) and stopper washer (B).

11. Slide off countershaft fourth gear (**Figure 73**).

12. See **Figure 74**. Remove the fourth gear splined bushing (A) and the splined washer (B).

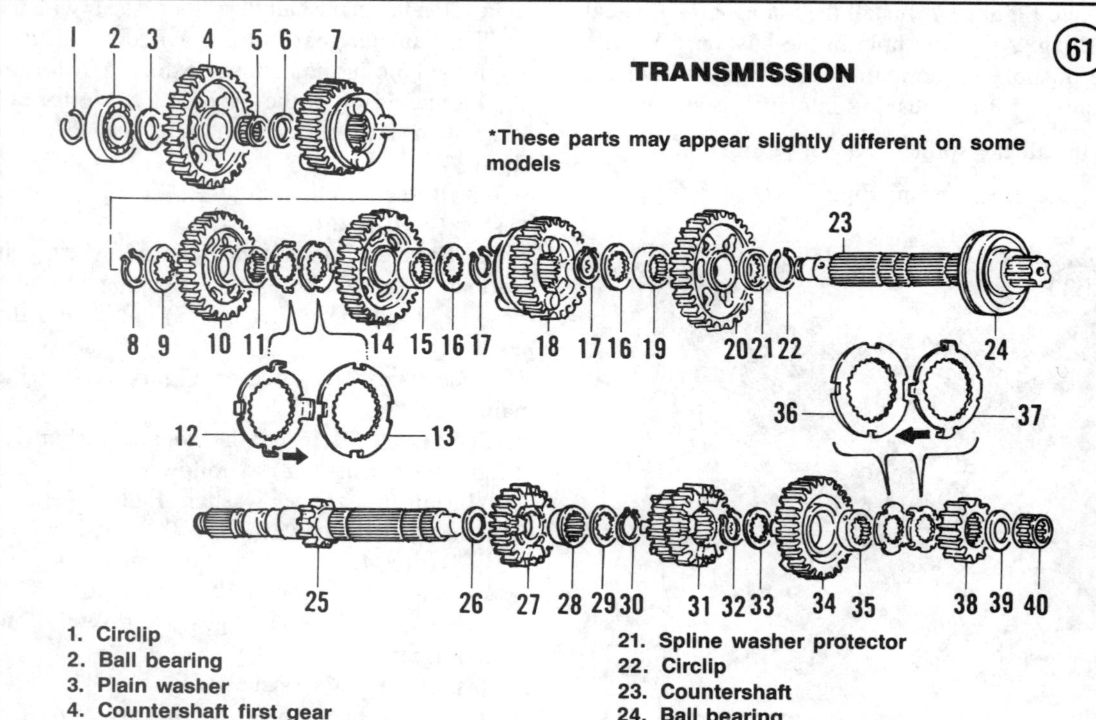

1. Circlip
2. Ball bearing
3. Plain washer
4. Countershaft first gear
5. Needle bearing
6. Plain washer
7. Countershaft fifth gear
8. Circlip
9. Splined washer
10. Countershaft third gear
11. Third gear bushing
12. Lockwasher (with tab)*
13. Stopper washer (with notches)*
14. Countershaft fourth gear
15. Fourth gear splined bushing
16. Splined washer
17. Circlip
18. Countershaft sixth gear
19. Second gear splined bushing
20. Countershaft second gear
21. Spline washer protector
22. Circlip
23. Countershaft
24. Ball bearing
25. Mainshaft/first gear
26. Plain washer
27. Mainshaft fifth gear
28. Fifth gear splined bushing
29. Splined washer
30. Circlip
31. Mainshaft third/fourth gear combination
32. Circlip
33. Splined washer
34. Mainshaft sixth gear
35. Sixth gear splined bushing
36. Stopper washer (with notches)
37. Lockwasher (with tabs)
38. Mainshaft second gear
39. Plain washer
40. Needle bearing

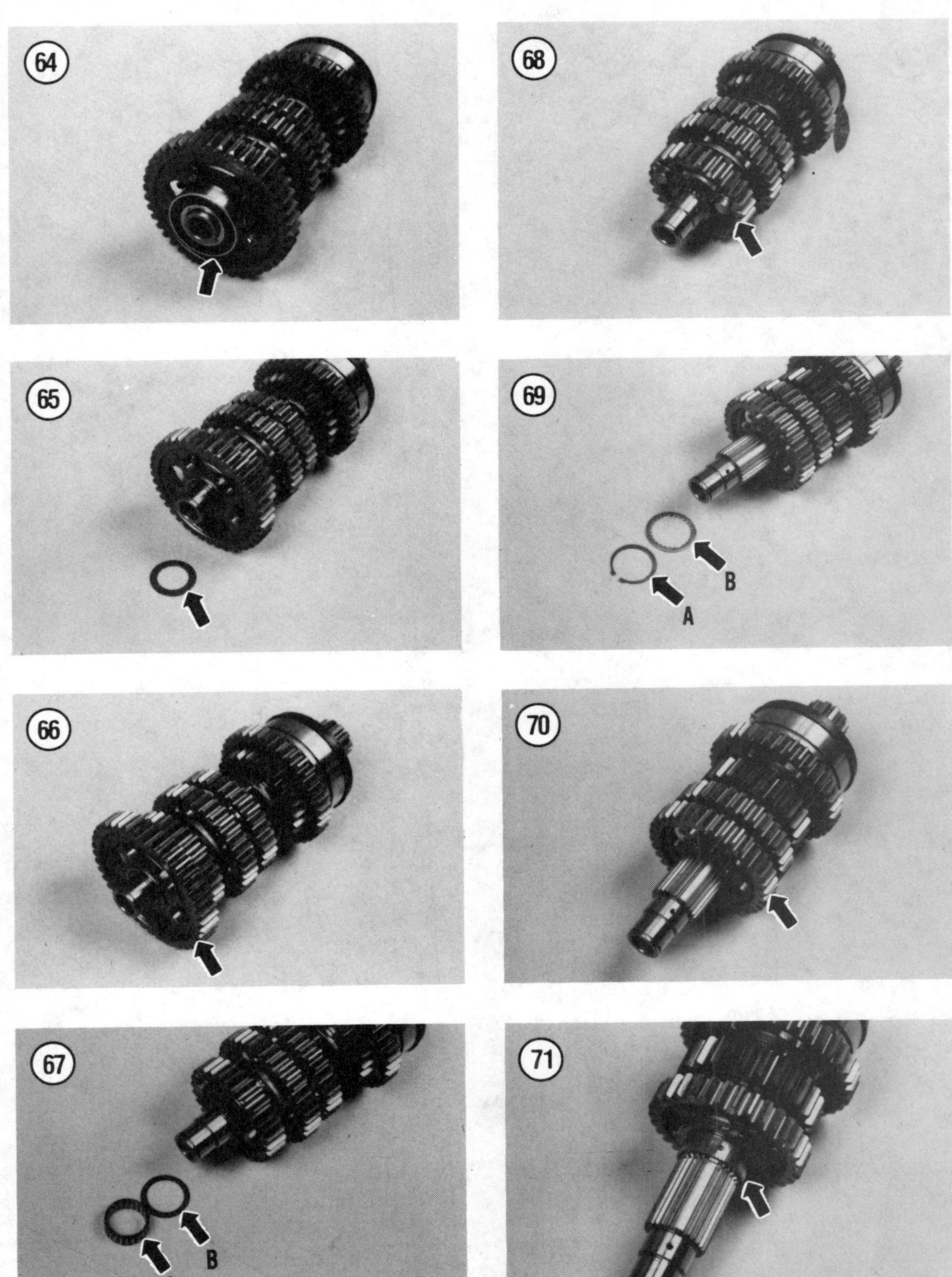
64
68
65
69
B
A
66
70
67
B
A
71
6

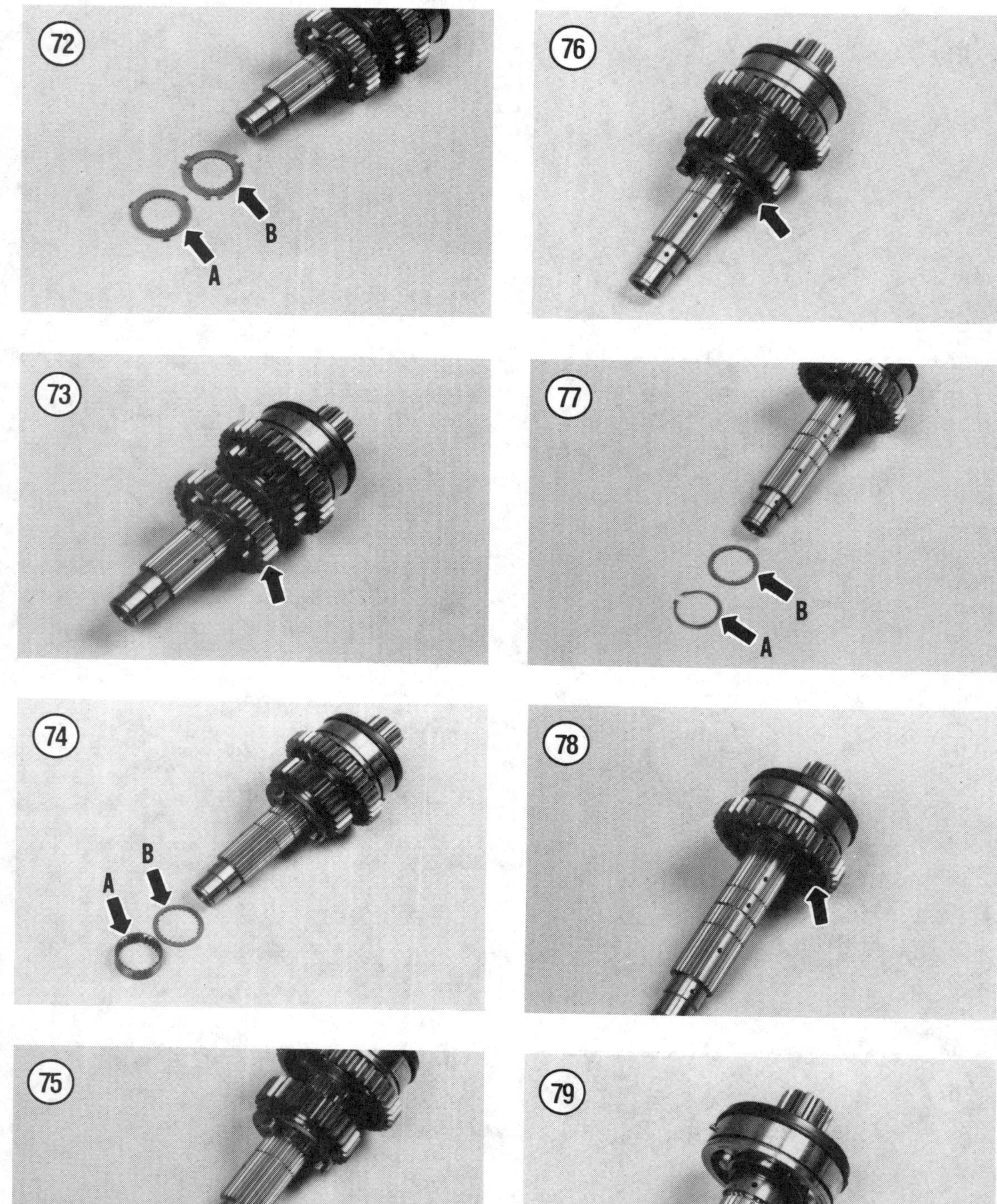
72
B
A
73
74
A B
75
76
77
B
A
78
79

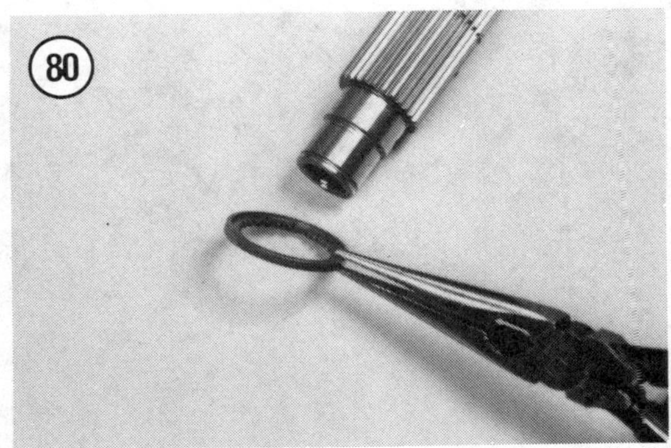

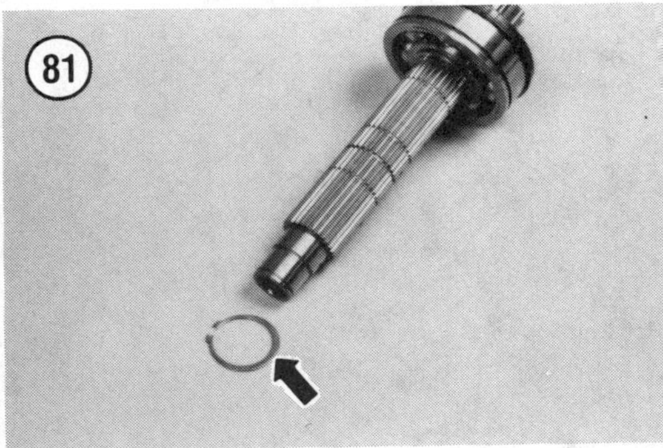

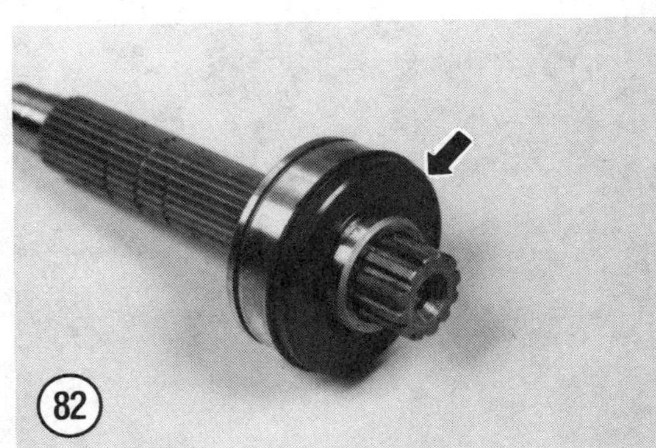

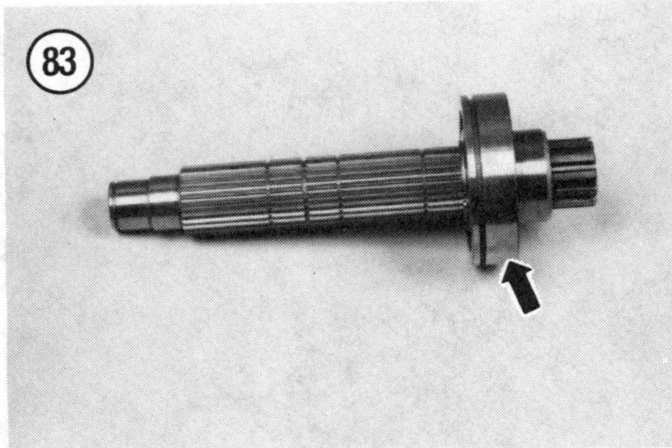

13. Remove the circlip (**Figure 75**).
14. Slide off countershaft sixth gear (**Figure 76**).
15. See **Figure 77**. Remove the circlip (A) and splined washer (B).
16. Slide off countershaft second gear (**Figure 78**).
17. Remove the second gear splined bushing (**Figure 79**).
18. Remove the splined washer protector (**Figure 80**).
19. Remove the circlip (**Figure 81**).
20. Remove the oil seal (**Figure 82**).
21. If necessary, remove the bearing (**Figure 83**) with a bearing puller.

Countershaft Assembly

Refer to **Figure 61** for this procedure.
1. If removed, install the countershaft bearing (**Figure 83**) with a hydraulic press.
2. Install a new oil seal onto the countershaft. See **Figure 82**.
3. Install the circlip (**Figure 81**). Make sure the circlip seats against the bearing as shown in **Figure 84**.
4. Install the splined washer protector with the recessed side going on first (**Figure 80**). Make sure the splined washer protector covers the circlip as shown in **Figure 85**.
5. See **Figure 86**. Align the hole in the splined bushing (A) with the oil hole in the countershaft (B) and install the bushing.
6. Install countershaft second gear (**Figure 78**).
7. See **Figure 77**. Install the splined washer (B) and circlip (A).

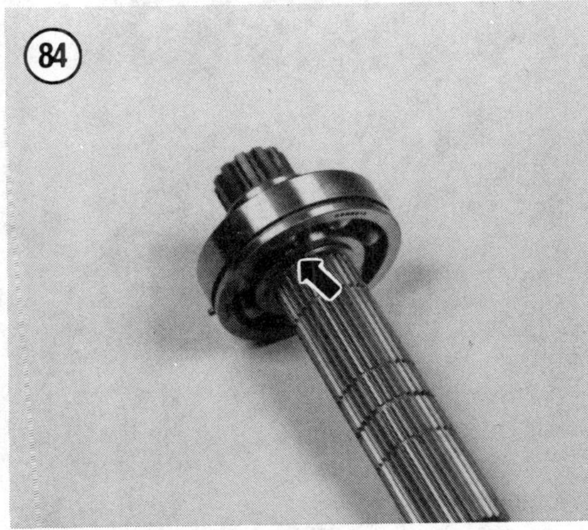

8. Install countershaft sixth gear (**Figure 76**).

9. Install the circlip (**Figure 75**). See **Figure 87**.

10. See **Figure 74**. Install the splined washer (B) and the fourth gear splined bushing (A).

11. Install countershaft fourth gear (**Figure 73**).

12. See **Figure 72**. Install the stopper washer (B) and the lockwasher (A) as follows:

   a. Install the stopper washer.

   b. Install the lockwasher so that washer tabs fit into the stopper washer notches. See **Figure 88**.

13. See **Figure 89**. Align the hole in the third gear splined bushing (A) with the oil hole in the countershaft (B) and install the bushing.

14. Install countershaft third gear (**Figure 70**).

15. See **Figure 69**. Install the splined washer (B) and the circlip (A).

16. Install countershaft fifth gear (**Figure 68**).

17. See **Figure 67**. Install the plain washer (B) and the needle bearing (A).

18. Install countershaft first gear (**Figure 66**).

19. Install the plain washer (**Figure 65**).

20. Install the ball bearing (**Figure 64**).

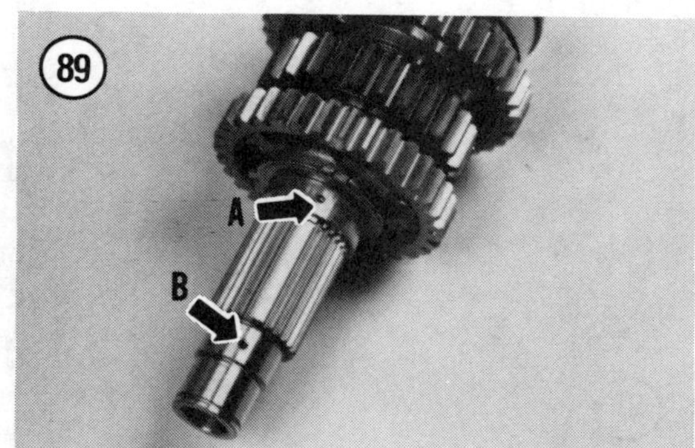

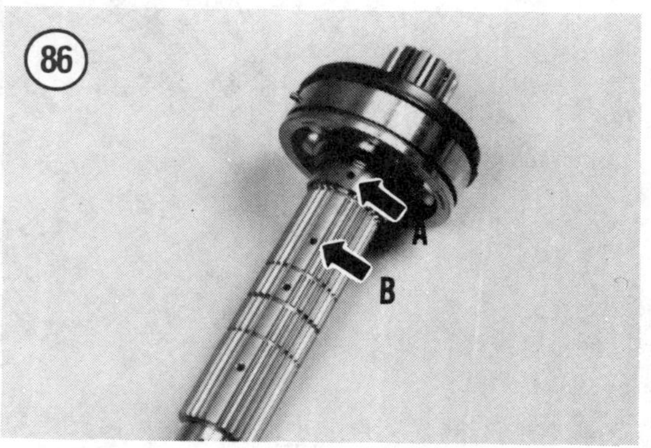

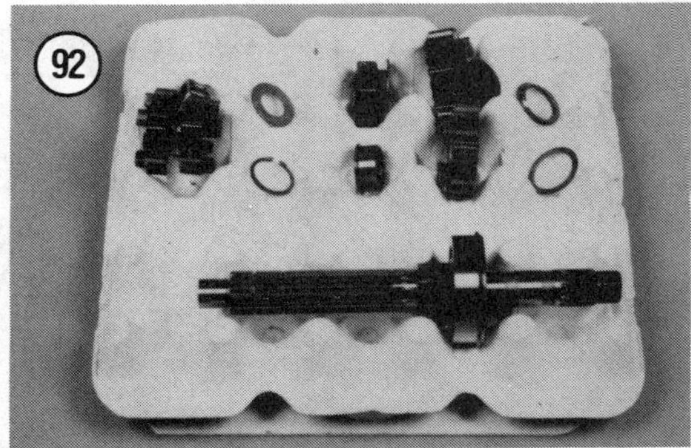

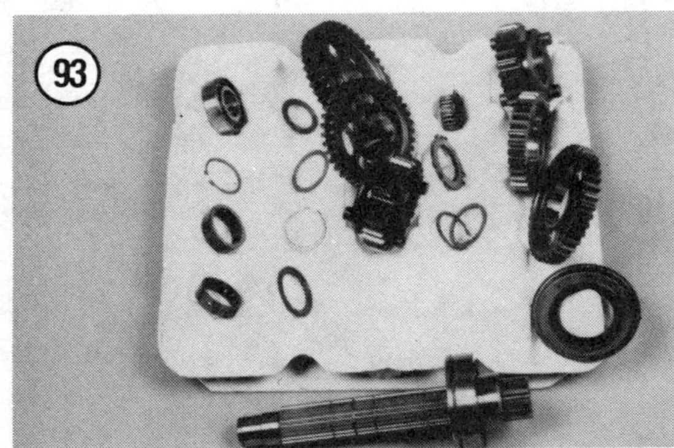

21. Install the circlip (**Figure 90**). Make sure the circlip is properly seated in the countershaft groove.

22. Refer to **Figure 91** for correct placement of the gears. Make sure each gear engages properly to the adjoining gear where applicable.

Inspection

NOTE
*After cleaning parts, make sure to place them in their exact order of disassembly. See **Figure 92** (mainshaft) and **Figure 93** (countershaft).*

1. Clean all parts in cleaning solvent and dry thoroughly.

2. Inspect the gears visually for cracks, chips, broken teeth and burnt teeth. Check the gear dogs (A, **Figure 94**) to make sure they are not rounded off. If dogs are rounded off, check the shift forks as described later in this chapter. More than likely, one or more of the shift forks is bent.

NOTE
*Defective gears should be replaced, and it is a good idea to replace the mating gear (**Figure 95**) even though it may not show as much wear or damage. Remember that accelerated wear to new parts is normally caused by contact with worn parts.*

3. Inspect all rotating gear bearing surfaces (B, **Figure 94**) for wear, discoloration and galling. Inspect the mating shaft bearing surface also. If there is any metal flaking or visible damage, replace both parts.

4. Determine the clearance between the mainshaft fifth and sixth gears and the countershaft second, third and fourth gears and their respective gear bushings as follows:

    a. Measure the inside diameter (A, **Figure 96**) of the gears. Compare with the dimensions listed in **Table 1**.

    b. Measure the outside diameter (B, **Figure 96**) of the gear bushings. Compare with the dimensions listed in **Table 1**.

    c. Subtract the bushing outside diameter from the gear inside diameter to determine gear-to-bushing clearance. Compare with the dimensions listed in **Table 1**.

    d. Replace worn gears and bushings as a set as required.

5. Inspect the mainshaft and countershaft splines (A, **Figure 97**) for wear or discoloration. Check the mating gear internal splines also (**Figure 98**). If no visible damage is apparent, install each sliding gear on its respective shaft and work the gear back and forth to make sure gear operates smoothly.

NOTE
A hydraulic press will be required to replace the countershaft and mainshaft bearings described in Step 6.

6. Inspect the countershaft and mainshaft bearings. See B, **Figure 97**. Make sure they rotate freely with no binding. Replace the bearing by pressing or pulling it off of the shaft. Reverse to install.

7. Inspect the mainshaft needle bearing (**Figure 99**). Check the bearing needle for galling or damage. Check the bearing cage for cracks or other damage. Replace the bearing if necessary. If the needle bearing is replaced, also replace the needle

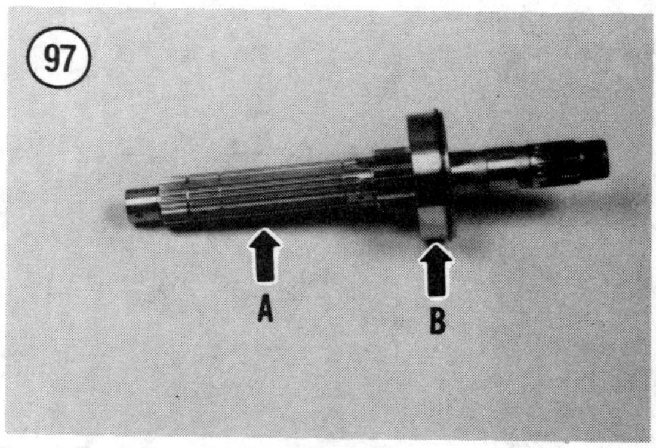

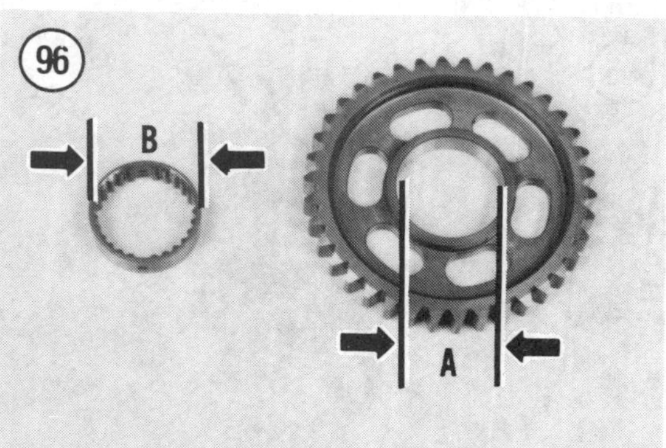

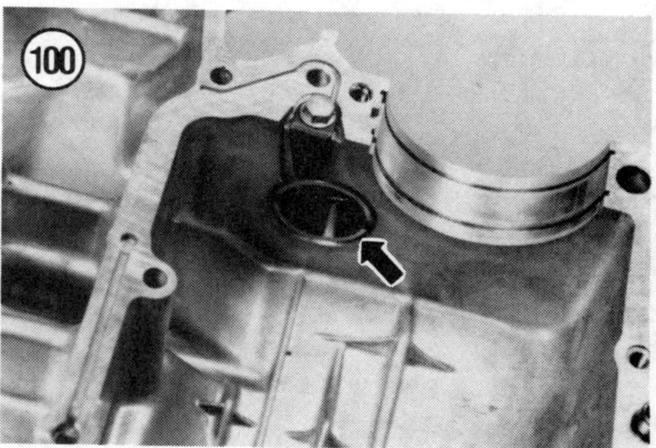

bearing race (**Figure 100**) in the upper crankcase half. A special bearing tool (available from a Honda dealer) will be required to replace the bearing race.

8. Inspect the remaining needle bearings as described in Step 7.

9. Replace any washers that show wear.

10. Discard the circlips as they are to be replaced during assembly.

INTERNAL SHIFT MECHANISM

Refer to **Figure 101**.

1. Remove the external shift mechanism as described in this chapter.

2. Split the crankcase as described under *Crankcase Disassembly* in Chapter Four.

3. Remove the transmission assemblies as described in this chapter.

4. Pry the lockwasher tab away from the bolt securing the center shift fork shaft (**Figure 101**).

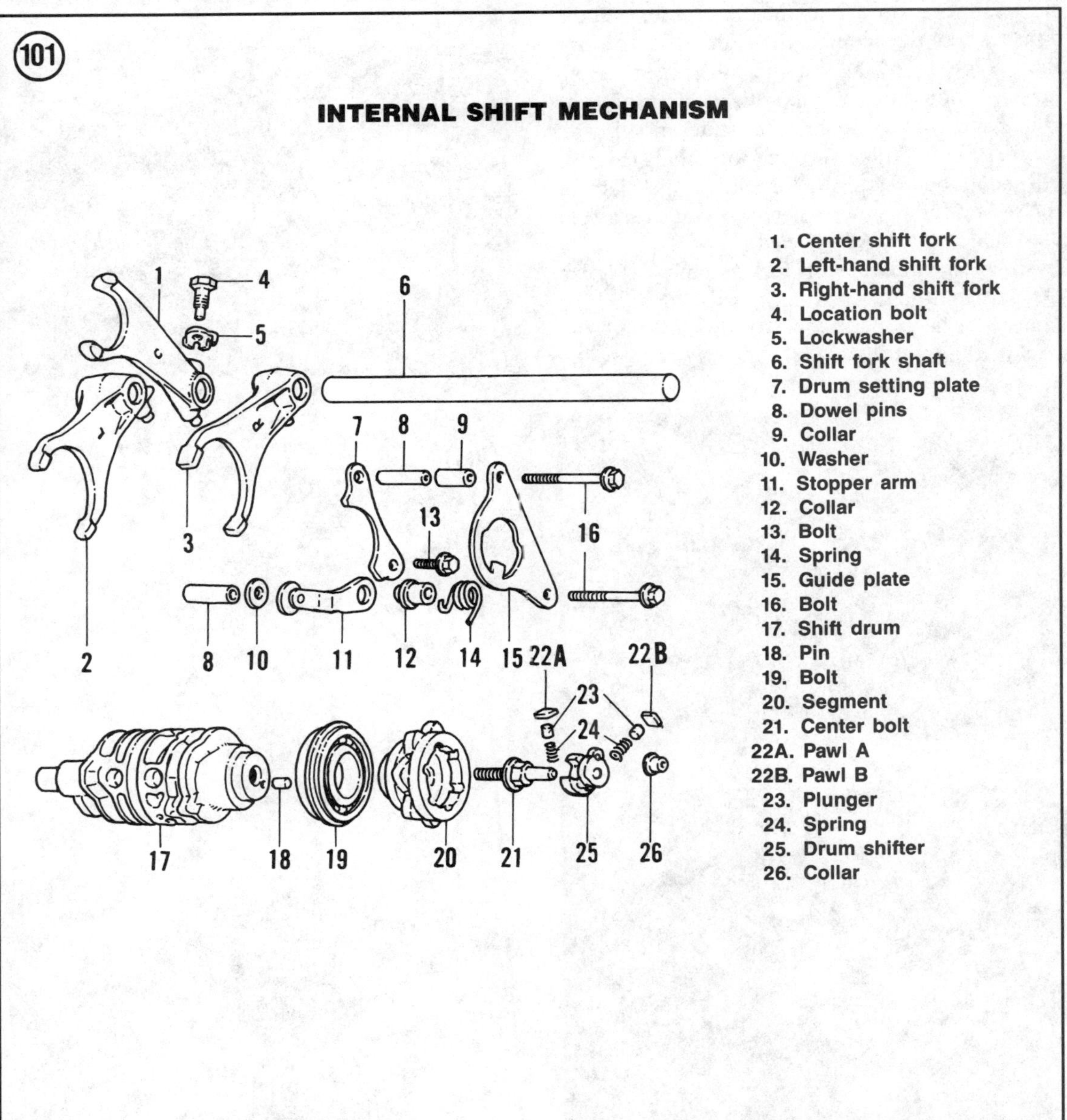

5. Withdraw the shift fork shaft and remove the 3 shift forks (**Figure 102**).

6. Remove the shift drum holding plate bolt (**Figure 103**) and remove the holding plate (**Figure 104**). Withdraw and remove the shift drum (**Figure 105**).

Inspection

Refer to **Table 3** for internal shift mechanism specifications.

1. Inspect each shift fork (**Figure 106**) for signs of wear or cracking. Examine the shift forks at the points where they contact the slider gear (**Figure 106**). **Figure 107** shows the slider gear. Both surfaces should be smooth with no signs of wear or damage. Make sure the forks slide smoothly on the fork shaft. Make sure the fork shaft (**Figure 108**) is not bent. Roll the fork shaft on a piece of glass. Any clicking noise detected indicates a bent shaft and it must be replaced.

2. Check the middle shift fork assembly (**Figure 109**). Check the threads in the shift fork (A) for damage. Check the bolt (B) threads and the machined end of the bolt for damage. Check the

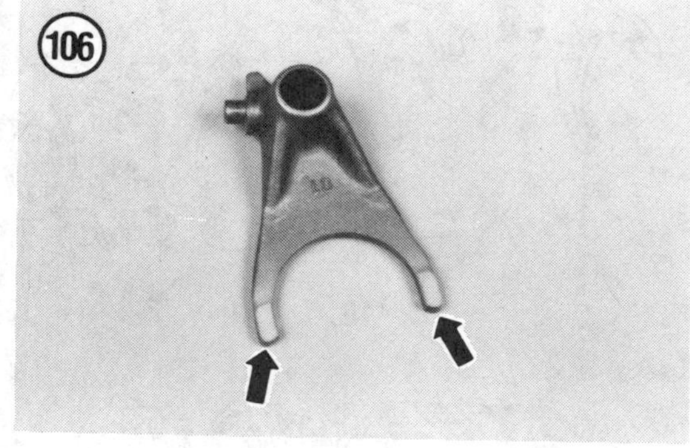

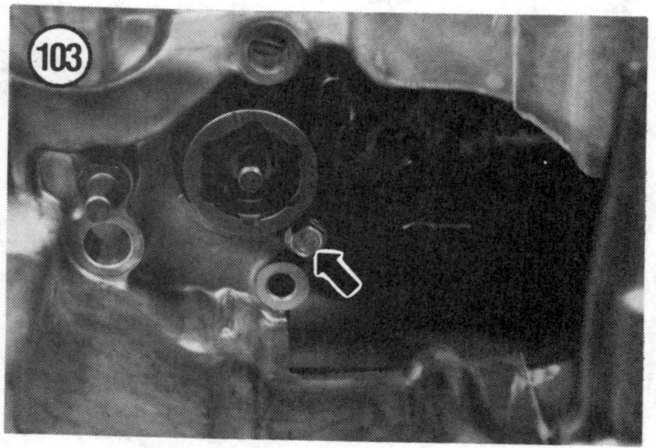

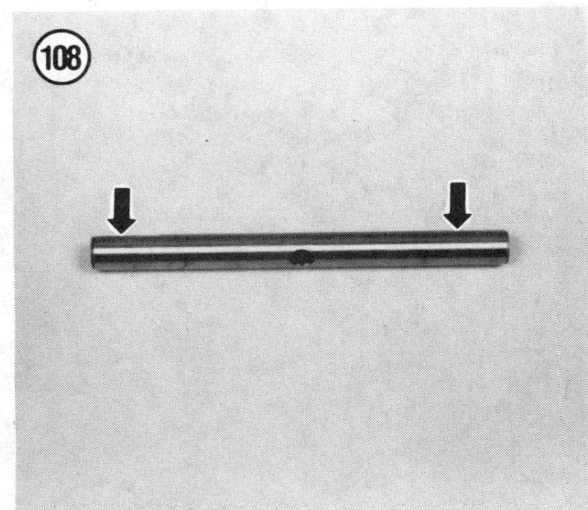

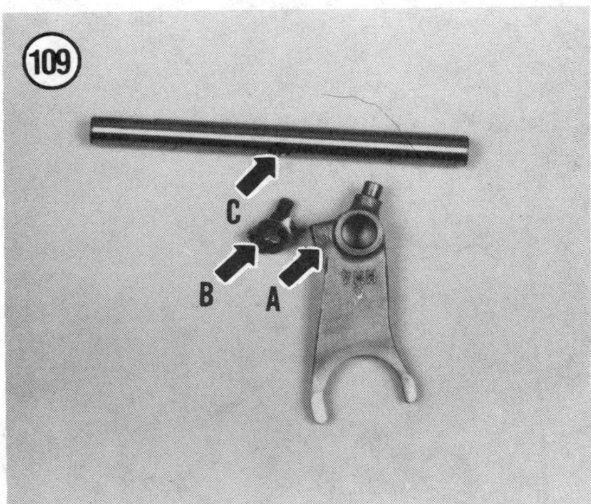

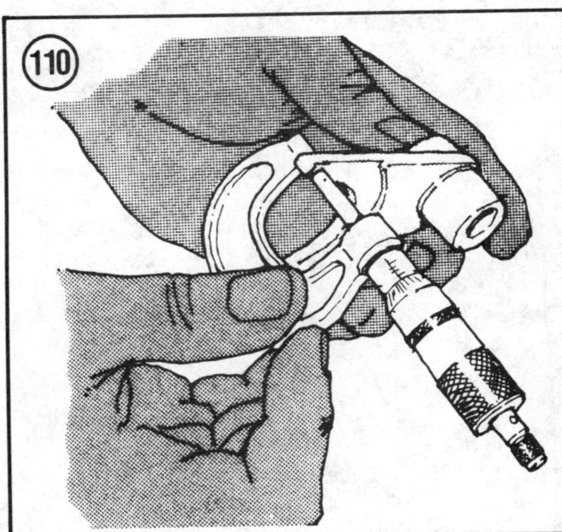

pin hole in the shift fork (C) for cracks or damage. Replace worn or damaged parts.

3. Measure the shift fork shaft at the left- and right-hand sides (**Figure 108**). Replace if worn to the wear limit or less as listed in **Table 3**.

4. Measure the tips of each shift fork (**Figure 110**) and compare to the specifications in **Table 3**. Replace a shift fork if the tip thickness is worn to the wear limit or less.

5. Measure the inside diameter of the shift forks with a small hole gauge (**Figure 111**). Replace any that are worn beyond the wear limit in **Table 1**.

6. Check the grooves in the shift drum (A, **Figure 112**) for wear or roughness. If any of the groove profiles have excessive wear or damage, replace the shift drum.

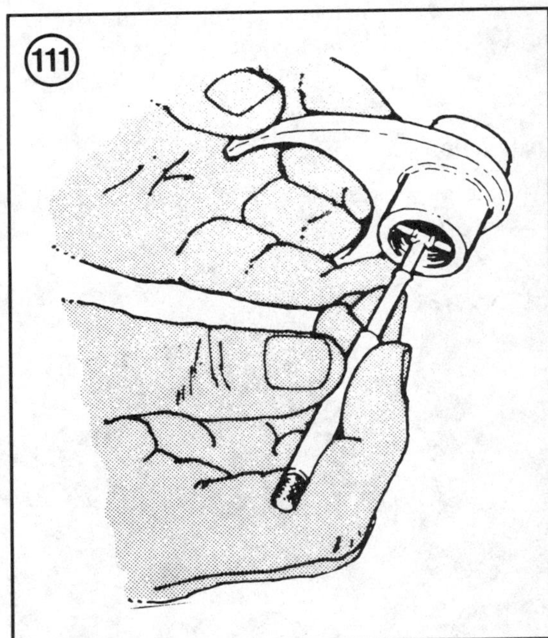

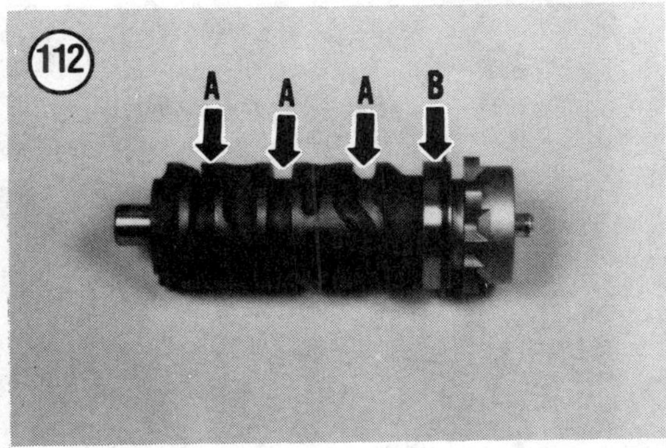

7. Check the shift drum bearing (B, **Figure 112**). Make sure the bearing rotates smoothly with no signs of wear or damage. If the bearing is faulty, replace the bearing as follows:

  a. Secure the shift drum in a vise with soft jaws and remove the center bolt (**Figure 113**).
  b. Lift the drum center (**Figure 114**) off of the shift drum.
  c. Lift the bearing (**Figure 115**) off of the shift drum.
  d. Remove the pin (**Figure 116**).
  e. Reverse to install the bearing. Note the following.
  f. Align the pin (A, **Figure 117**) with the notch (B, **Figure 117**) in the back of the drum center and install the drum center.
  g. Apply Loctite 242 (blue) onto the center bolt. Tighten the center bolt to the torque specification in **Table 2**.

Installation

1. Coat all bearing and sliding surfaces with assembly oil.

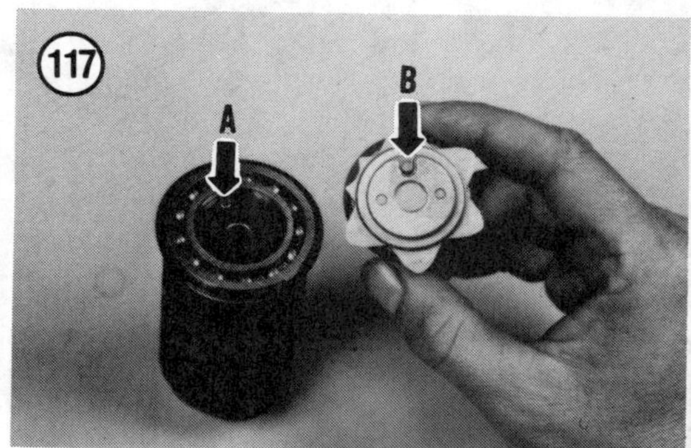

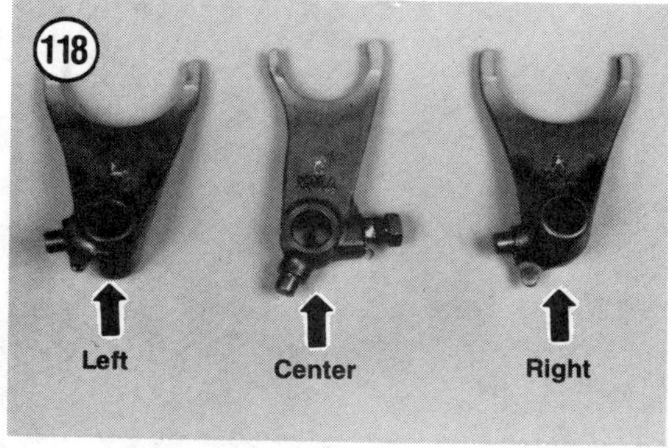

2. Install the shift drum into the lower crankcase half from the right-hand side (**Figure 105**).
3. Install the shift drum plate (**Figure 104**). Apply Loctite 242 (blue) onto the shift drum plate bolt and install the bolt (**Figure 103**). Tighten the bolt securely.

NOTE
*The shift forks are marked with an "R" (right-hand side), "C" (center) or "L" (left-hand side). See **Figure 118**. This relates to the engine as it sits in the bike's frame. These marks must face toward the clutch (right-hand side of the crankcase) when the shift forks are installed.*

4. Insert the shift fork shaft part way into the crankcase (**Figure 119**).
5. See **Figure 120**. Position the "R" (right-hand) shift fork into the crankcase and push the shift fork shaft through it.
6. See **Figure 121**. Position the "C" (center) shift fork and push the shift fork shaft through it.
7. See **Figure 122**. Position the "L" (left-hand) shift fork into the crankcase and push the shift fork shaft through it and into the crankcase.
8. Turn the shift fork shaft and align the pin hole in the shaft with the hole in the center shift fork. Install the bolt (**Figure 123**) and lockwasher. Tighten the bolt to the torque specification in **Table 2**. Bend the lockwasher tab over the bolt to lock it.
9. Install the transmission assemblies as described in this chapter.
10. Assemble the crankcase halves as described in Chapter Four.

Table 1 TRANSMISSION SPECIFICATIONS

	Specification mm (in.)	Wear limit mm (in.)
Backlash		
1st-5th gears	0.044-0.133 (0.0017-0.0052)	0.30 (0.012)
6th gear	0.068-0.136 (0.0027-0.0054)	0.18 (0.007)
Transmission gears ID		
Mainshaft		
5th and 6th gears	28.000-28.021 (1.1024-1.1032)	28.04 (1.104)
Countershaft		
2nd, 3rd, 4th gears	31.000-31.025 (1.2205-1.2215)	31.04 (1.222)
Transmission gear bushing OD		
Mainshaft		
5th and 6th gears	27.959-27.980 (1.1007-1.1016)	27.92 (1.099)
Countershaft		
2nd, 3rd, 4th gears	30.950-30.975 (1.2185-1.2195)	30.93 (1.218)
Gear to bushing clearance		
Mainshaft		
5th, 6th gears	0.020-0.062 (0.0008-0.0024)	0.10 (0.0039)
Countershaft		
2nd, 3rd, 4th gears	0.025-0.070 (0.0010-0.0028)	0.11 (0.0043)

Table 2 TRANSMISSION TIGHTENING TORQUES

	N·m	ft.-lb.
Center shift fork bolt	18	13
Shift drum center bolt	23	17
Drive sprocket bolt	55	40

Table 3 INTERNAL SHIFT MECHANISM SPECIFICATIONS

	Specification mm (in.)	Wear limit mm (in.)
Shift fork shaft OD	11.969-11.980 (0.4712-0.4717)	11.90 (0.469)
Shift fork finger tip thickness		
Left and right forks	5.43-5.50 (0.214-0.217)	5.10 (0.200)
Center fork	5.93-6.00 (0.233-0.236)	5.60 (0.220)
Shift fork ID	12.000-12.021 (0.4724-0.4733)	12.04 (0.474)

CHAPTER SEVEN

FUEL, EMISSION CONTROL AND EXHAUST SYSTEMS

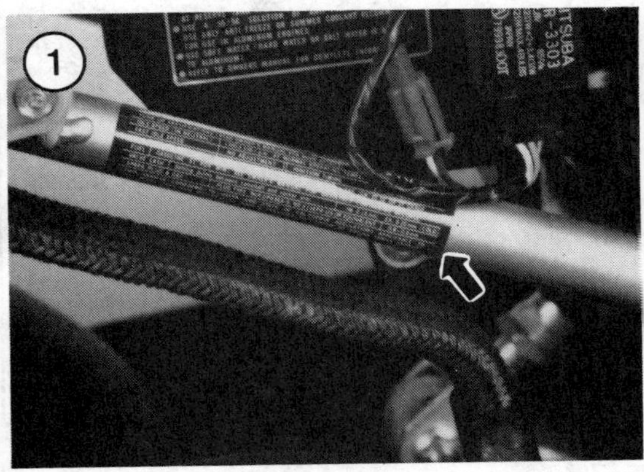

The fuel system consists of the fuel tank, shutoff valve, fuel pump and filter, 4 Keihin constant velocity carburetors and the air filter.

The exhaust system consists of a 4-exhaust pipe header assembly and a muffler.

Models sold in California are equipped with a secondary air supply system and an evaporative emission control system. On all U.S. models, an emission control information label is mounted on the right-hand frame tube (**Figure 1**). On California models, a vacuum hose routing diagram label is mounted on the air cleaner housing cover (**Figure 2**).

This chapter includes service procedures for all parts of the fuel, exhaust and emission control systems. Carburetor specifications are listed in **Table 1**. **Table 1** and **Table 2** are at the end of this chapter.

The carburetors on all U.S. models are engineered to meet stringent EPA (Environmental Protection Agency) regulations. The carburetors are flow tested and preset at the factory for maximum performance and efficiency within EPA regulations. Altering preset carburetor jet needle and pilot screw adjustments is forbidden by law. Failure to comply with EPA regulations may result in heavy fines.

Air filter service is covered in Chapter Three.

CARBURETOR OPERATION

An understanding of the function of each of the carburetor components and their relation to one another is a valuable aid for pinpointing a source of carburetor trouble.

The carburetor's purpose is to supply and atomize fuel and mix it in correct proportions with air that is drawn in through the air intake. At the primary throttle opening (idle), a small amount of fuel is siphoned through the pilot jet by the incoming air. As the throttle is opened further, the air stream begins to siphon fuel through the main jet and needle jet. The tapered needle increases the effective flow capacity of the needle jet as it is lifted, in that it occupies progressively less of the area of the jet.

At full throttle the carburetor venturi is fully open and the needle is lifted far enough to permit the main jet to flow at full capacity.

The choke circuit is a "bystarter" system in which the choke lever opens a valve rather than closing a butterfly in the venturi area as on many carburetors. In the open position, the slow jet discharges a stream of fuel into the carburetor venturi, to enrich the mixture when the engine is cold.

CARBURETOR SERVICE

Carburetor service (removal and cleaning) should be performed when poor engine performance or hesitation is observed. If, after servicing the carburetors and making the adjustments described in this chapter, the motorcycle does not perform correctly (and assuming that other factors affecting performance are correct, such as ignition timing and condition, etc.), the motorcycle should be checked by a dealer or a qualified performance tuning specialist.

Carburetor troubleshooting is covered in Chapter Two.

Carburetor Assembly
Removal/Installation

1. Support the bike securely.

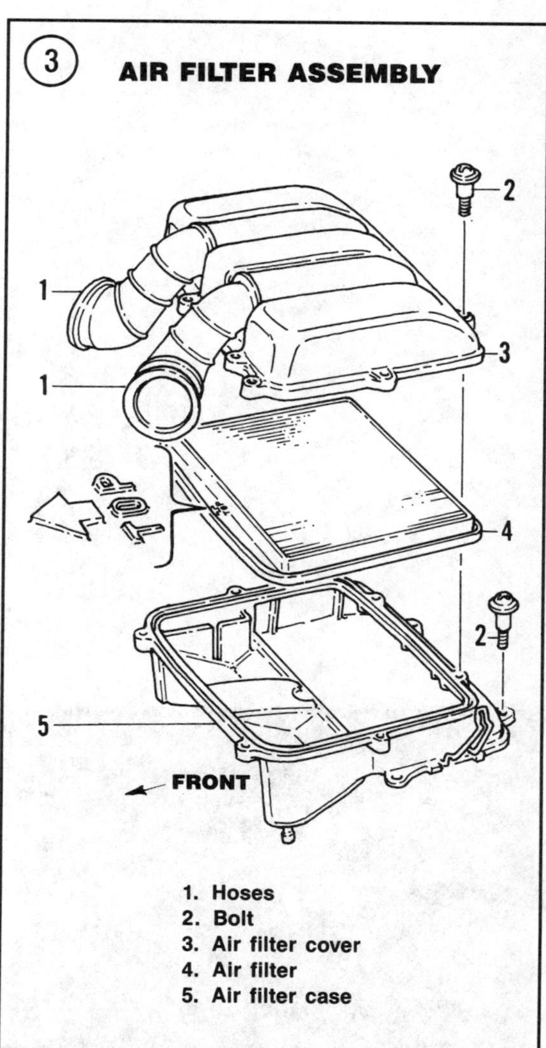

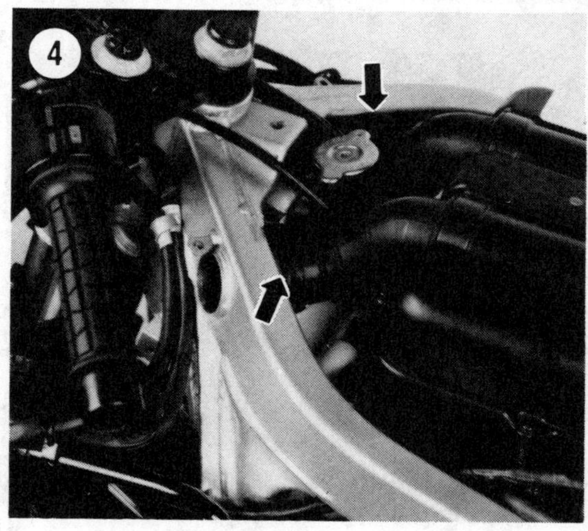

2. Remove the fuel tank as described in this chapter.

3. Remove the air filter housing (**Figure 3**) as follows:

  a. Pull the air filter case hoses out of the frame hose joints (**Figure 4**).

  b. Remove the air filter housing cover screws and lift the cover (**Figure 5**) off the housing.

  c. Lift the air filter element (**Figure 6**) out of the housing.

  d. Lift the wire harness (**Figure 7**) out of the guide on the left-hand side of the filter housing. Move the harness out of the way.

  e. Remove the housing screws and remove the housing (**Figure 8**).

NOTE

The intake sides of the carburetors are now exposed. If it is going to be some time before you remove the carburetors, stuff a clean, lint-free rag into each carburetor opening to prevent small screws or other parts from dropping into the carburetors.

4. Remove the screw (**Figure 9**) and disconnect the choke cable at the choke lever.

5. Loosen the intake manifold hose clamps. Then lift the carburetor assembly up (**Figure 10**) and remove it from the intake manifolds.

6. Disconnect the fuel line from the carburetor assembly.

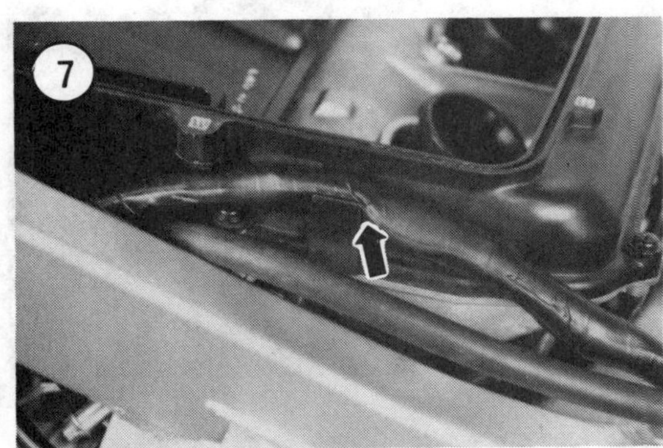

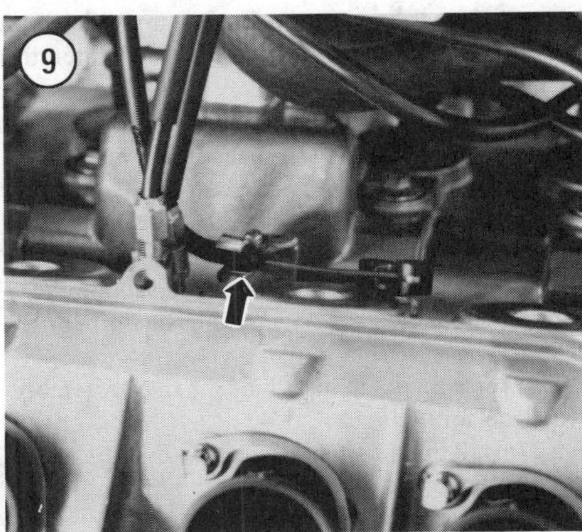

7. Loosen the throttle cable locknuts and remove
the cables from the cable holder (**Figure 11**). Then
disconnect the throttle cables from the throttle
drum (**Figure 12**).

8. Disconnect the drain tubes from the
carburetors. Leave the drain tubes routed through
the frame.

9. Cover the intake manifolds with a clean, lint-
free shop cloth (**Figure 13**).

10. Install by reversing these removal steps, noting
the following.

11. If the intake manifolds (**Figure 14**) were
removed, install them with the CARB mark facing
toward the carburetor and the UP mark on each
tube facing up.

12. Connect the ends of the throttle cables to the
correct position on the throttle drum as noted
during removal (**Figure 12**). Then attach the
throttle cables to the cable holder (**Figure 11**).
Tighten the locknuts.

13. Connect the fuel line to the carburetor
assembly.

14. Before installing the carburetor assembly, coat
the inside surface of all 4 rubber intake manifold
tubes with a light coat of engine oil. This will make
it easier to install the carburetor throats into the
intake tubes.

15. Be sure the throttle cables and choke cable are
correctly positioned in the frame—not twisted or
kinked and without any sharp bends. Tighten the
locknuts securely.

16. Remove the shop rags from the intake manifold
opening and install the carburetor assembly.
Tighten the hose clamps securely.

17. Attach the choke cable to the lever and secure
it with the screw (**Figure 9**).

18. *California models:* Refer to the vacuum hose
routing label and reconnect the vacuum hoses
(**Figure 2**).

19. Reverse Step 3 to install the air filter assembly.
Note the following:

   a. Install the air filter element so that the arrow
     on the element is at the top and facing to the
     front (**Figure 3**).

   b. Install the air filter housing cover (**Figure 5**)
     and its screws; tighten the screws securely.
     Check the housing cover to make sure it is
     seated completely around the lower housing.

   c. Connect the air filter case hoses to the frame
     hose joints (**Figure 4**).

d. Make sure to route the wire harness through the guide on the left-hand side of the air filter housing (**Figure 7**).

20. Adjust the throttle grip free play as described in Chapter Three.

21. Adjust the throttle cables as described in Chapter Three.

22. Adjust the carburetor idle speed as described in Chapter Three.

23. Adjust the choke cable as described in Chapter Three.

24. Install the fuel tank as described in this chapter.

Disassembly/Cleaning/Inspection

Refer to **Figure 15** for this procedure.

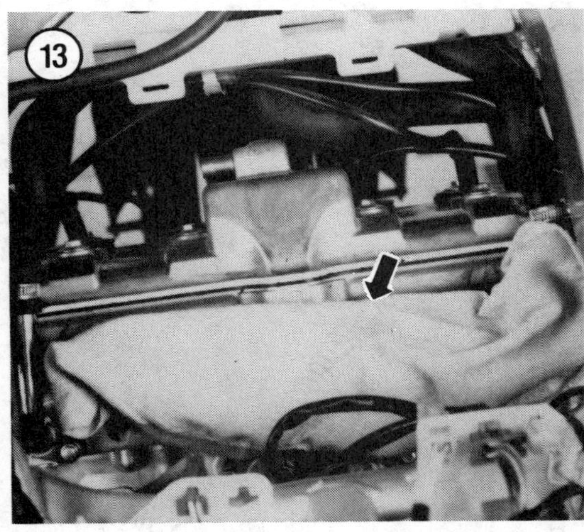

It is recommended that only one carburetor be disassembled and cleaned at a time. This will prevent an accidental interchange of parts.

1. Pry the lockwasher tabs away from the bolts securing the rear bracket (**Figure 16**) to the carburetor assembly. Then remove the bracket bolts and remove the bracket. Remove the 8 dowel pins from the bracket (**Figure 17**) or carburetor. The dowel pins may stay in either part.

2. Remove the bystarter arm shaft as follows:
   a. Remove the bystarter arm screws (A, **Figure 18**).
   b. Then slide the bystarter arm shaft (B, **Figure 18**) out of the carburetor assembly.
   c. Disconnect the bystarter arms from the choke knob on the carburetors and remove the arms. Remove the spring.

> *CAUTION*
> *An impact driver with a Phillips bit is required to loosen the front bracket screws in Step 3. Attempting to loosen the screws with a Phillips screwdriver may ruin the screw heads.*

3. Remove the front bracket Phillips screws and remove the front bracket (**Figure 19**).

4. Remove the throttle stop holder from the No. 1 and No. 2 carburetors (**Figure 20**).

5. Label each carburetor with a No. 1, 2, 3 and 4. The No. 1 carburetor is located on the left-hand side. The left-hand side refers to carburetor and engine as it sits in the bike's frame. Referring to **Figure 15**, separate the carburetors.

> *CAUTION*
> *When disassembling the carburetors in the following steps, it is critical not to mix the parts from one carburetor with another. Use separate storage containers for each carburetor during disassembly.*

6. Remove the bystarter valve as follows:
   a. Unscrew the nut (**Figure 21**) and remove it and the end cap.

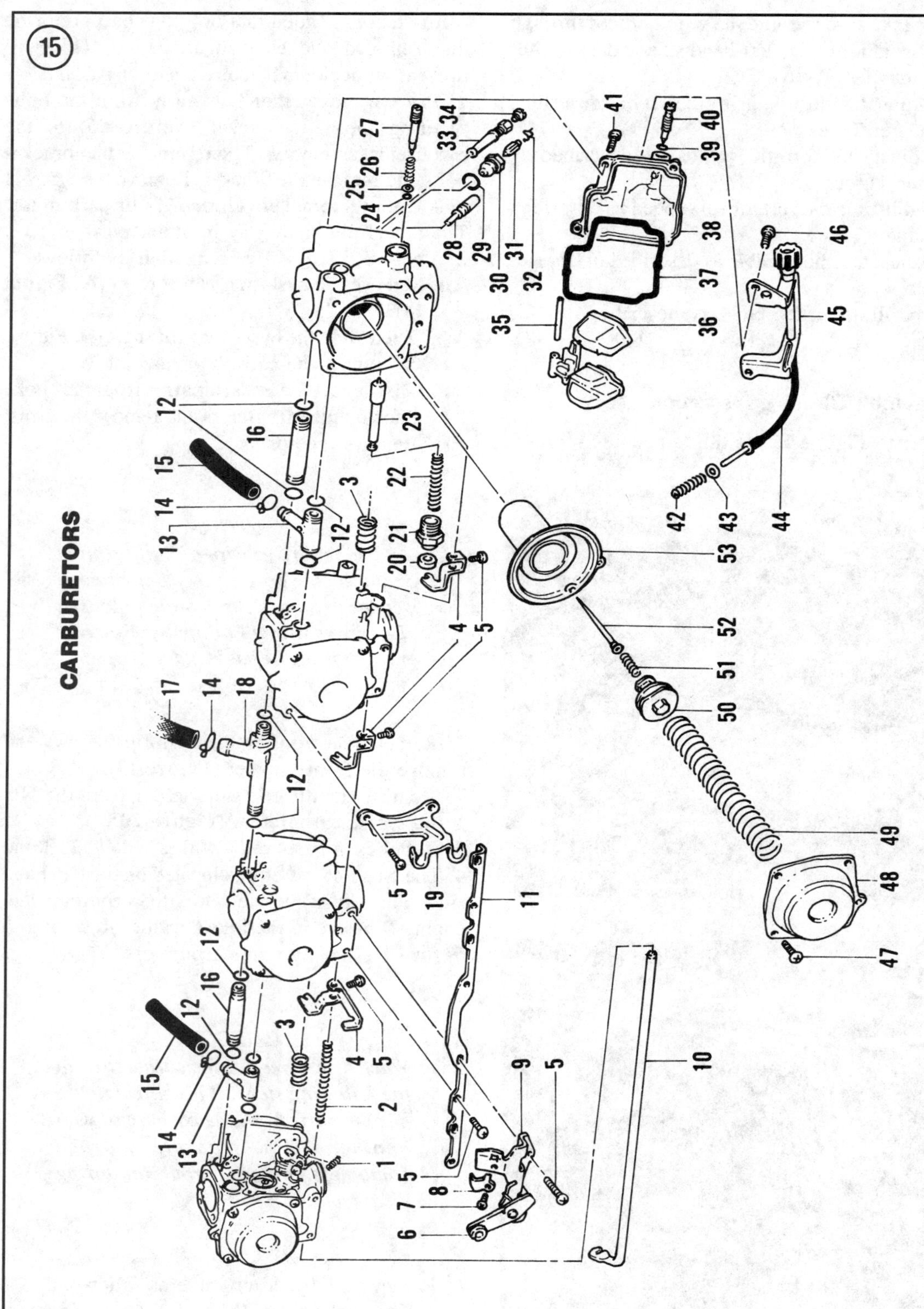
CARBURETORS

1. Synchronization spring
2. Spring
3. Thrust spring
4. Choke shaft arms
5. Screw
6. Choke lever
7. Screw
8. Bracket
9. Bracket
10. Choke shaft
11. Front bracket
12. O-rings
13. Air joint
14. Clip
15. Hose
16. Fuel joint
17. Fuel hose
18. Fuel joint
19. Cable guide
20. Cover
21. Nut
22. Spring
23. Choke valve
24. O-ring
25. Seat
26. Spring
27. Pilot screw
28. Pilot jet
29. Washer
30. Valve seat
31. Float valve
32. Clip
33. Needle jet holder
34. Main jet
35. Float pivot pin
36. Float
37. O-ring
38. Float bowl
39. O-ring
40. Drain bolt
41. Screw
42. Spring
43. Washer
44. Cable
45. Throttle adjust screw and bracket
46. Screw
47. Screw
48. Diaphragm cover
49. Spring
50. Jet needle holder
51. Spring
52. Jet needle
53. Vacuum piston

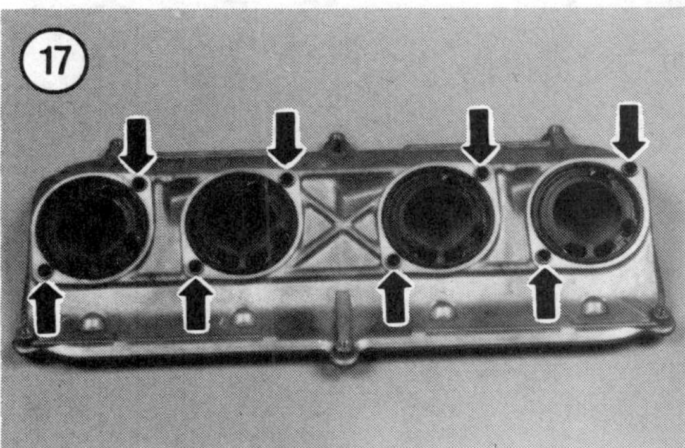

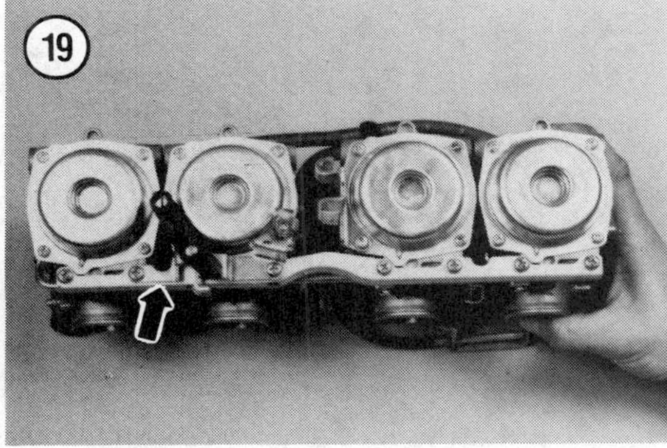

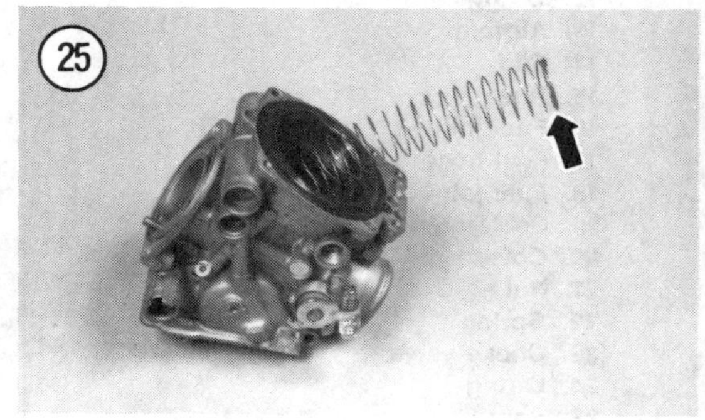

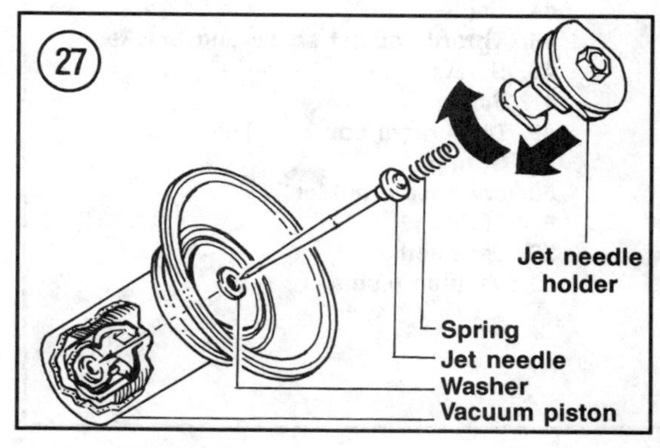
Jet needle
holder
Spring
Jet needle
Washer
Vacuum piston

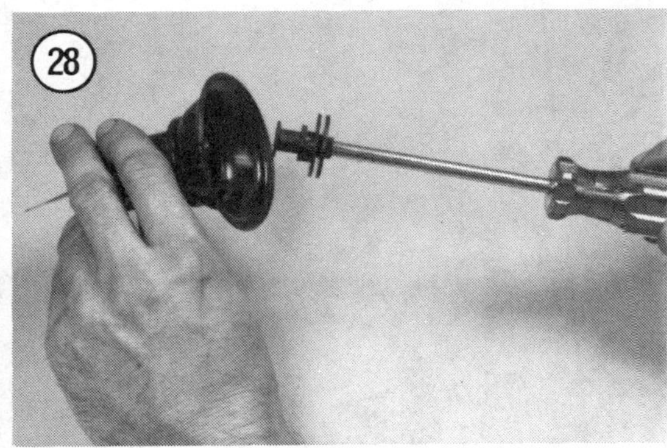

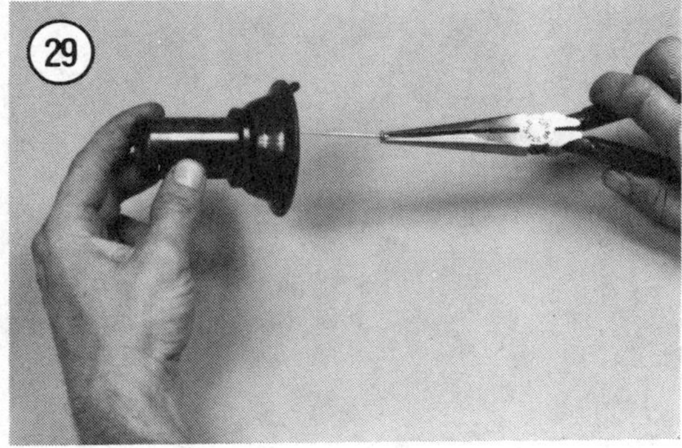

b. Remove the spring (**Figure 22**).

c. Remove the bystarter valve (**Figure 23**).

7. Remove the Phillips screws securing the vacuum chamber cover and remove it (**Figure 24**).

8. Remove the spring (**Figure 25**).

9. Carefully lift the vacuum piston (**Figure 26**) out of the carburetor.

10. Remove the jet needle as follows (**Figure 27**):

a. Put an 8 mm socket or screwdriver down into the vacuum cylinder cavity.

b. Place the socket or screwdriver on the jet needle holder and turn the holder 90° counterclockwise to unlock it from the tangs within the vacuum cylinder. Remove the jet needle holder (**Figure 28**).

c. Remove the spring (**Figure 27**).

d. Remove the jet needle (**Figure 29**) and washer.

11. Remove the screws securing the float bowl to the main body and remove the float bowl (**Figure 30**).

12. Unscrew and remove the main jet (**Figure 31**).

13. Unscrew and remove the needle jet (**Figure 32**).

14. Unscrew and remove the pilot jet (**Figure 33**).

15. Push out the float pin (A, **Figure 34**).

16. Lift the float and needle valve (B, **Figure 34**) out of the main body. See **Figure 35**.

17. Unscrew and remove the needle valve seat and washer (**Figure 36**).

18. *California models:* Remove the air cut off valve as follows:

   a. Remove the Phillips screws and remove the air cut off cover (**Figure 37**).

   b. Remove the spring (**Figure 38**).

   c. Remove the diaphragm (A, **Figure 39**).

   d. Remove the O-ring (B, **Figure 39**).

> *NOTE*
> *The pilot screws are covered by a metal plug (C, Figure 39) that has to be drilled out in order to remove the screw. If removal is necessary, refer to the separate procedure in this chapter.*

> *NOTE*
> *Further disassembly is neither necessary nor recommended. If throttle shafts or butterflies are damaged, the carburetor housing must be replaced.*

Cleaning/Inspection

1. Remove the float bowl O-ring (**Figure 40**). Replace if deteriorated, damaged or if there are signs of fuel leakage.

2. Clean the carburetor assembly and all parts in solvent.

> *NOTE*
> *If the carburetors are severely gummed with old gas or other contaminants, clean all carburetor parts, except rubber or plastic parts in a good solvent. Motorcycle carburetors have much smaller air and fuel passages than automotive carburetors. For this reason, soaking the carburetor parts in an automotive type carburetor cleaner is not recommended. The exterior of nearly all motorcycle carburetors is usually coated with a corrosion-protective clear coating. These caustic liquid cleaners will remove the protective coatings from the outside of the carburetor body. The*

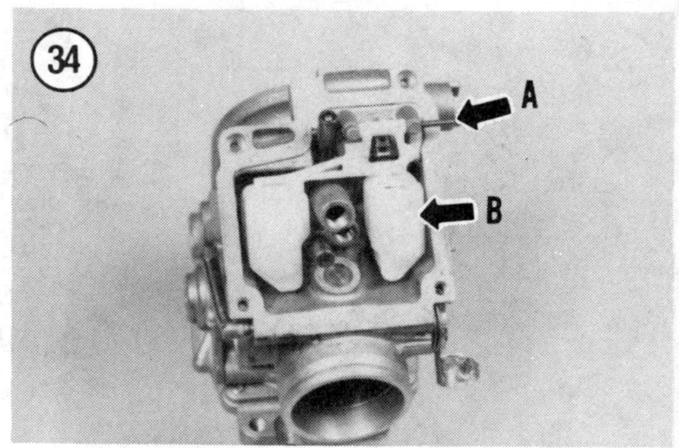

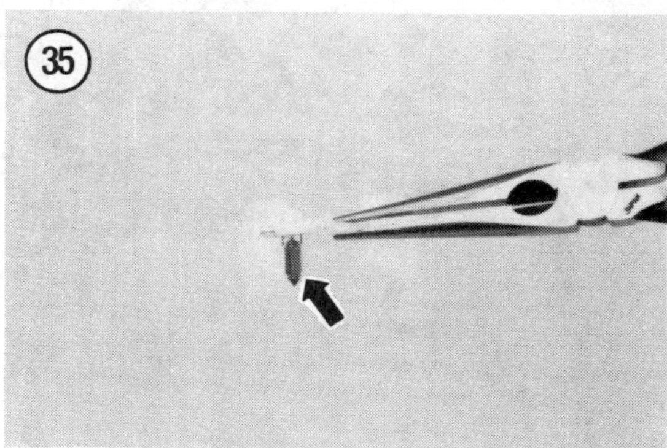

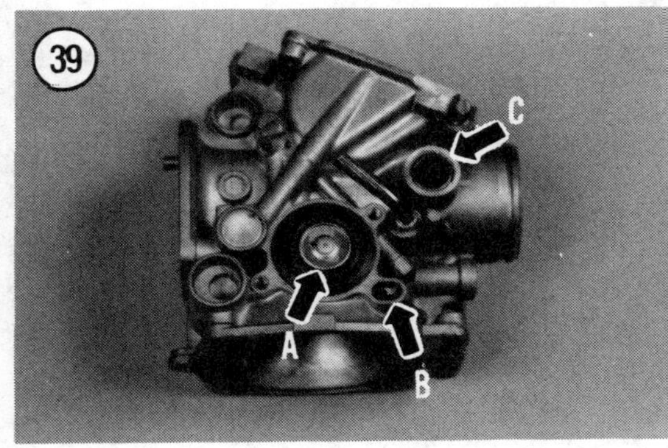

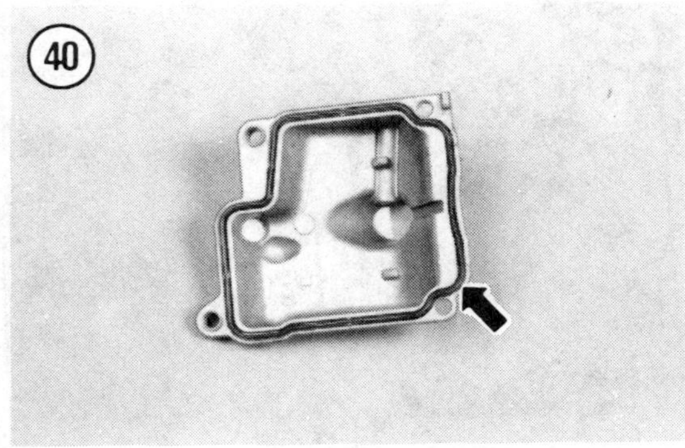

dissolved coating could plug passages within the carburetor and damage the exterior appearance of the carburetors. Also, if the cleaner was used previously there will be sediment held in suspension within the solution. This could also plug a passage. Many good aerosol carburetor cleaners (e.g. Zep Choke and Carburetor Cleaner) can help remove any residue not removed with the solvent. Thoroughly rinse off all parts with clean water and dry with compressed air. If you do not have access to compressed air, place the cleaned parts on a piece of newspaper and allow to dry.

3. Remove the parts from the cleaner and blow dry with compressed air. Blow out the jets with compressed air. Do *not* use a piece of wire to clean them as minor gouges in a jet can alter flow rate and upset the air/fuel mixture.

> *NOTE*
> *A small can of compressed air sold at photography stores can be used to clean the jets.*

4. Inspect the end of the float valve needle (**Figure 41**) and seat for wear or damage. Replace both parts if any one part is worn or damaged.

5. Inspect the filter on the float valve seat. If damaged, the float valve assembly must be replaced.

6. If removed, inspect the pilot screw for wear or damage that may have occurred during removal. Replace all 4 pilot screws even if only 1 requires replacement. This is necessary for correct pilot screw adjustment as described in this chapter.

7. See **Figure 42**. Check the bystarter valve (A) for scoring, nicks or other damage. Check the spring (B) and nut (C) for damage.

8. *California models:* Check the air cut off valve diaphragm for small holes, tearing or other damage; replace if necessary.

9. Check the vacuum piston diaphragm for small holes, tearing or other damage; replace if necessary.

Assembly

Refer to **Figure 15** for this procedure.

1. If removed, screw the pilot screw in to the exact same position (same number of turns) as recorded during disassembly.

> *NOTE*
> *If new pilot screws were installed, turn them out the number of turns indicated in **Table 1** from the **lightly seated** position.*

2. *California models:* Install the air cut off valve as follows:
   a. Install the diaphragm (A, **Figure 39**).
   b. Install the O-ring (B, **Figure 39**).
   c. Install the spring (**Figure 38**).
   d. Install the cover and screws (**Figure 37**). Tighten the screws securely.

3. Install a washer onto the needle valve seat and screw the needle valve seat into the carburetor (**Figure 36**). Tighten the seat securely.

4. Attach the needle valve onto the float assembly (**Figure 35**). Then align the needle valve with the needle valve seat and install the float assembly (B, **Figure 34**).

5. Align the float pivot hole and install the float pin (A, **Figure 34**). Push the float pin all the way in.

6. Inspect the float height and adjust, if necessary, as described in this chapter.

7. Install the pilot jet (**Figure 33**).

8. Install the needle jet holder (**Figure 32**).

9. Install the main jet (**Figure 31**).

10. Install the float bowl O-ring (**Figure 40**).

11. Install the float bowl and its mounting screws (**Figure 30**). Tighten the screws securely in a crisscross pattern.

12. Install the jet needle (**Figure 27**) as follows:
   a. Slide the washer onto the end of the jet needle.
   b. Insert the jet needle into the vacuum piston (**Figure 29**).
   c. Insert the spring into the end of the jet needle holder.
   d. Secure the end of the jet needle holder with an 8 mm socket or screwdriver (**Figure 43**) and insert the holder into the vacuum piston (**Figure 44**). Turn the jet needle holder 90° clockwise and lock the holder in place within the vacuum piston.

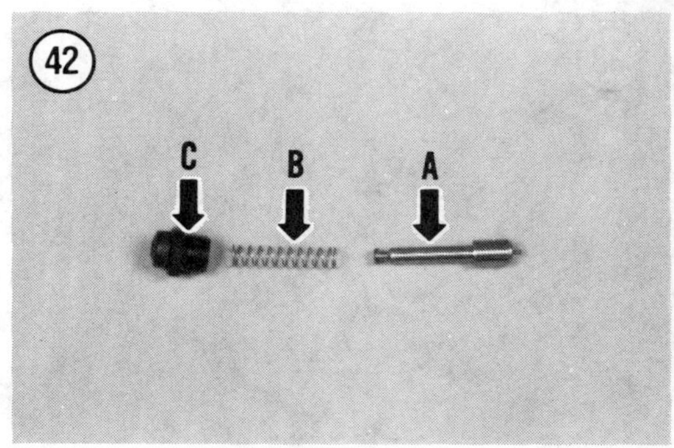

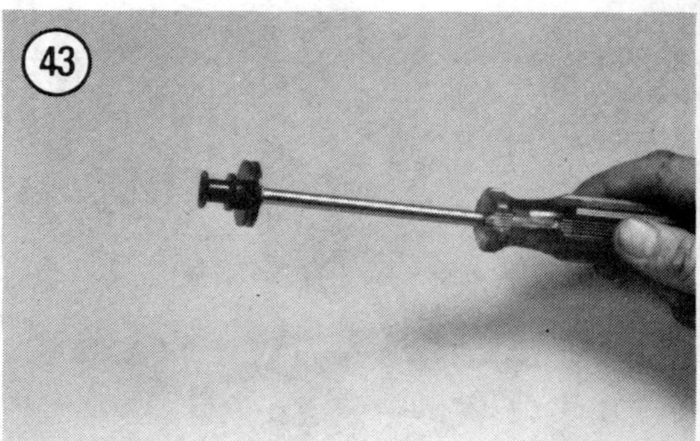

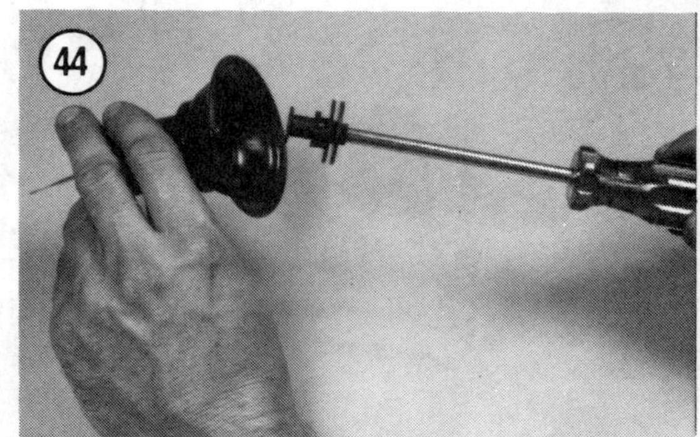

13. Install the vacuum piston into the carburetor body. Align the tab on the diaphragm with the hole (**Figure 45**) in the carburetor body.

14. Install the vacuum cylinder compression spring into the vacuum cylinder and index it onto the boss on the top cover (**Figure 25**).

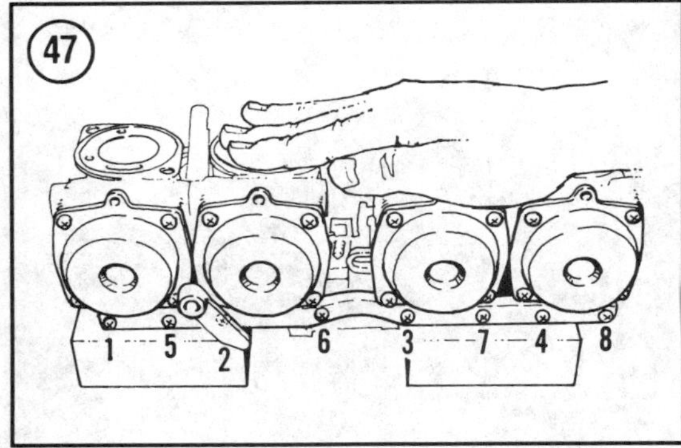

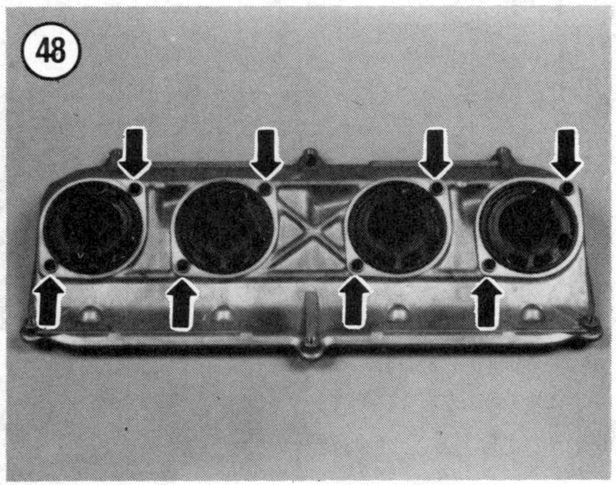

NOTE
Push the vacuum piston up slightly (from inside the carburetor) to raise the diaphragm slightly. Do not raise the piston too far or the diaphragm will unseat. Raising the vacuum piston prevents the vacuum chamber cover from pinching the diaphragm during installation.

15. Align the hole in the vacuum cylinder with the raised boss on the top cover. Install the top cover and tighten the screws securely.

16. Install the bystarter valve as follows:
   a. Insert the bystarter valve (**Figure 23**) into the carburetor housing.
   b. Install the spring over the end of the valve (**Figure 22**).
   c. Install the nut and end cap (**Figure 21**). Tighten the nut securely.

17. Referring to **Figure 15**, assemble the No. 1 and No. 2 carburetors as follows:
   a. Lay the carburetors on the workbench with the front side facing up.
   b. Install 2 new O-rings onto the fuel joint.
   c. Install 2 new O-rings onto the air joint.
   d. Assemble the carburetors with the fuel joint, air joint, thrust spring (**Figure 46**) and synchronization spring.

18. Repeat Step 17 for the No. 3 and No. 4 carburetors.

19. Install the throttle stop screw assembly onto the No. 1 and No. 2 carburetors (**Figure 20**).

20. Install 2 new O-rings onto the fuel joint connecting the No. 2 and No. 3 carburetors. Assemble the No. 2 and No. 3 carburetors.

21. Align the front bracket with the carburetors and install it with the mounting screws. Install the screws finger-tight at this time.

22. Place the carburetors on on a flat surface with the front side facing down. This is to make sure the rear side is completely horizontal. Then tighten the front bracket screws in 2 to 3 steps in the sequence shown in **Figure 47**. Tighten the screws securely.

23. Install the rear bracket as follows:
   a. Install the rear bracket dowel pins (**Figure 48**).

b. Install new lockwashers around the intake manifolds on the rear bracket (**Figure 49**).

c. Install the rear bracket Phillips screws and tighten in 2 to 3 steps in the sequence shown in **Figure 50**.

d. Bend the lockwasher tabs over the screws to lock them in place.

24. Referring to **Figure 15**, install the spring, bystarter arms and the bystarter arm shaft. Tighten the screws securely.

25. Operate the bystarter arm shaft lever (**Figure 51**) and check the bystarter arm shaft for sluggish or tight movement.

26. Referring to **Figure 52**, visually synchronize the carburetor throttle valves as follows:

a. Turn the throttle stop screw (A) and align the No. 2 carburetor throttle valve with the bypass hole in the carburetor bore (**Figure 53**). See B, **Figure 52**.

b. Align the No. 1, No. 3 and No. 4 throttle valves (C) with their respective bypass holes by turning the synchronization screws (D).

27. After installing the carburetor assembly onto the motorcycle, check and adjust carburetor synchronization as described in Chapter Three.

CARBURETOR ADJUSTMENTS

Pilot Screw Adjustment

The pilot screws are preset at the factory and do not require adjustment unless the carburetors are overhauled or the pilot screws replaced. A limiter cap has been installed over each pilot jet (**Figure 54**) to prevent routine adjustment.

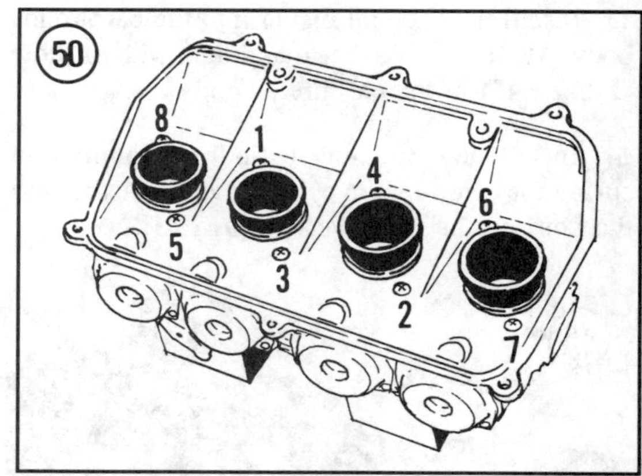

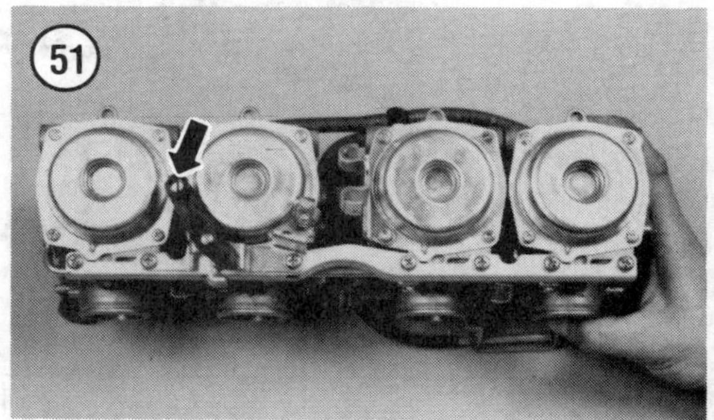

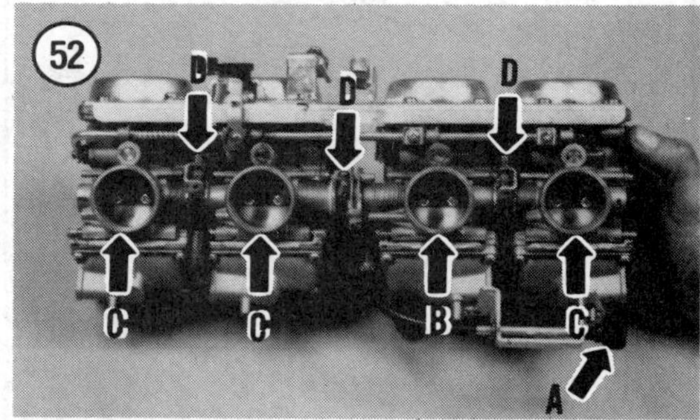

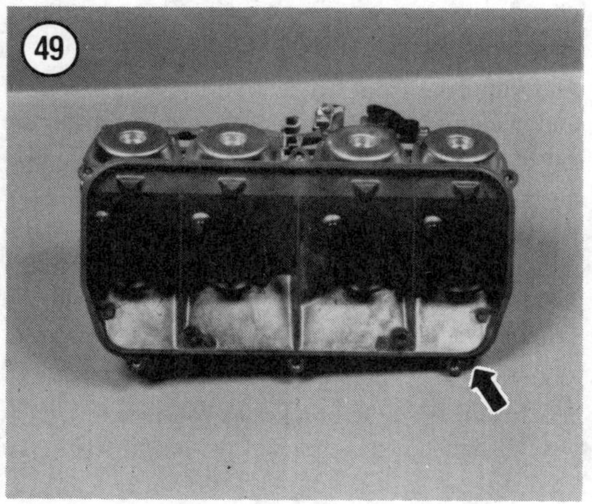

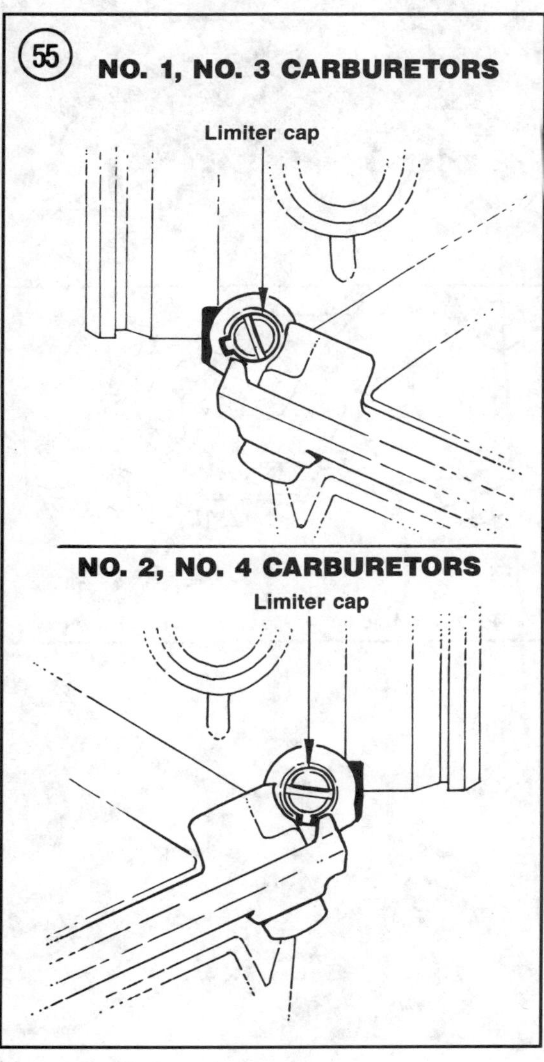

A tachometer able to detect changes as small as 50 rpm is required for this procedure.

1. Remove the fuel tank as described in this chapter.

2. Remove the fairing assembly as required to gain access to the carburetors.

3. Pull the limiter cap off of each pilot screw. See **Figure 55**.

> *CAUTION*
> *Before removing the pilot screw, record the number of turns necessary until the screw seats **lightly**. Record the number of turns for each individual carburetor as this setting can be used when reinstalling the pilot screws.*

> *CAUTION*
> *Tightening the pilot screw against its seat will damage the pilot screw.*

4. Remove the pilot screw (**Figure 56**), spring and O-ring (if necessary).

5. Install the O-ring onto the pilot screw. Then install the pilot screw and spring. Tighten the pilot screw until it seats lightly, then back it out the number of turns recorded during removal.

6. Install an auxiliary fuel tank to supply fuel to the carburetors. Make sure the fuel tank is properly secured and that the fuel hoses are secured tightly and positioned away from any component that could damage them.

7. Warm the engine up to normal operating temperature. Turn the engine off.

8. Connect a tachometer to the engine following the manufacturer's instructions.

9. Start the engine. Adjust the idle speed by turning the throttle stop screw (**Figure 57**). Adjust to the idle speed listed in **Table 1**.

10. Turn all pilot screws 1/2 turn counterclockwise from their initial setting. Interpret results as follows:

   a. If the idle speed increased by 50 rpm or more, turn all of the pilot screws counterclockwise in 1/2 turn increments until the idle speed does not increase. Then reset the idle speed with the throttle stop screw as described in Step 9. Proceed to Step 11.

   b. If the idle speed did not increase by more than 50 rpm, proceed to Step 11.

11. Turn the No. 2 carburetor pilot screw clockwise until the engine drops 50 rpm.

12. Turn the No. 2 carburetor pilot screw counterclockwise 1 turn. Reset the idle speed with the throttle stop screw as described in Step 9.

13. Repeat Step 11 and Step 12 to adjust the No. 1, 3 and 4 carburetor pilot screws.

14. Install the pilot screw limiter caps as follows:

   a. Apply Loctite 601 to the inside of a limiter cap.

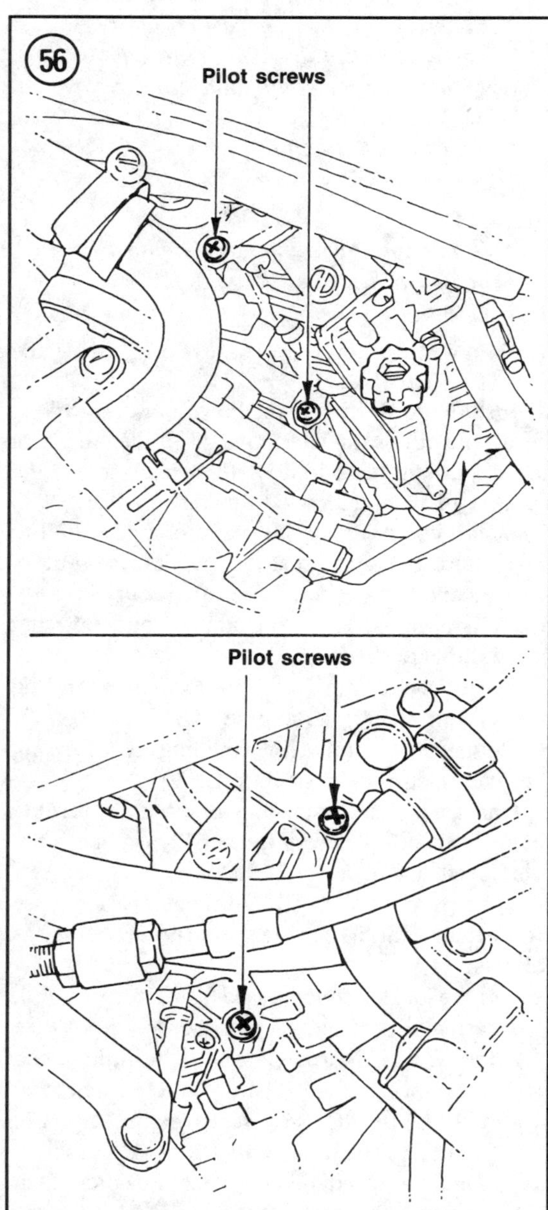

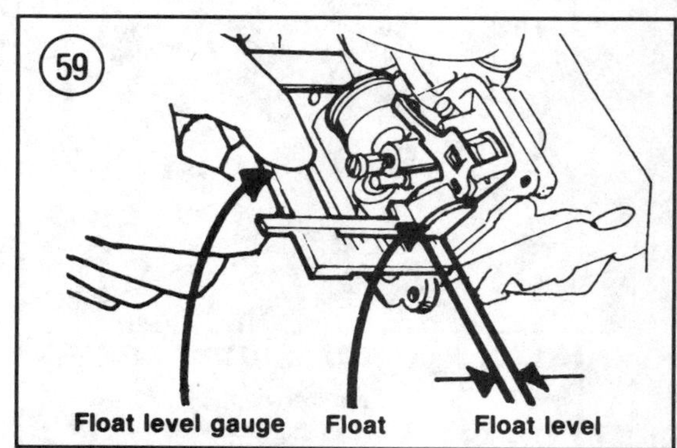

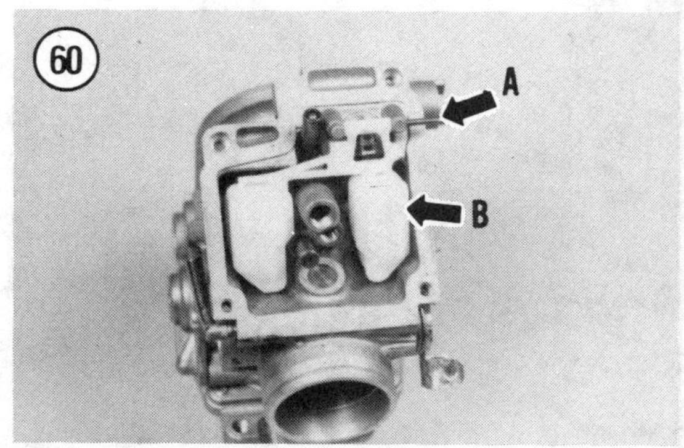

NOTE
Make sure you do not turn the pilot screw when installing the limiter cap.

b. Align the limiter cap with the pilot screw and install it so that the pilot screw can only be turned *clockwise*. This will prevent the pilot screws from being turned counterclockwise which enriches the air/fuel mixture.

c. Repeat for each pilot screw.

15. Remove the tachometer and reinstall the fuel tank and fairing.

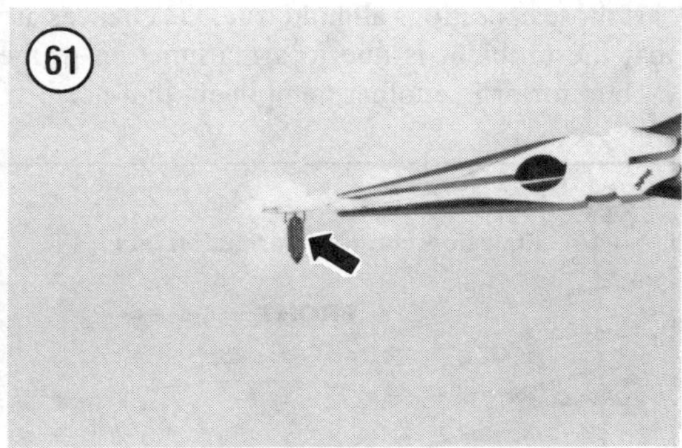

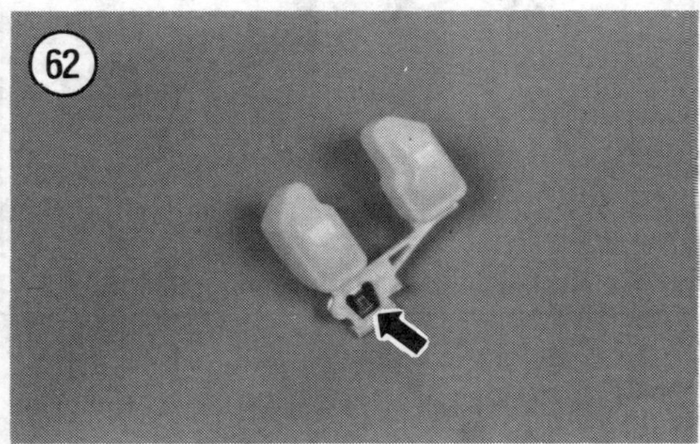

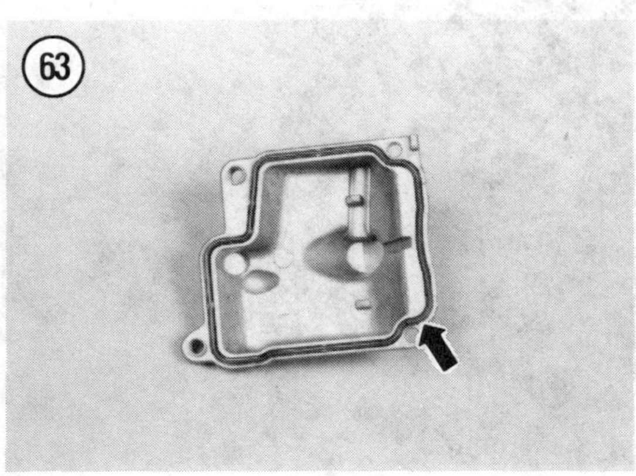

Float Adjustment

The carburetor assembly has to be removed and partially disassembled for this adjustment.

1. Remove the carburetor assembly as described in this chapter.

2. Remove the screws securing the float bowls (**Figure 58**) to the main bodies and remove them.

3. Hold the carburetor assembly with the carburetor inclined 15-45° from vertical so that the float arm is just touching the float needle. Use a float level gauge (Honda part No. 07401-001000 or equivalent) and measure the distance from the carburetor body to the float arm (**Figure 59**). The correct height is listed in **Table 1**.

4. If the float height adjustment is incorrect, perform the following:

a. Push out the float pin (A, **Figure 60**).

b. Lift the float and needle valve (B, **Figure 60**) out of the main body.

c. Remove the needle valve from the float tang (**Figure 61**).

d. Adjust by carefully bending the metal tang on the float arm (**Figure 62**).

e. Attach the needle valve onto the float assembly (**Figure 61**). Then align the needle valve with the needle valve seat and install the float assembly (B, **Figure 60**).

f. Align the float pivot hole and install the float pin (A, **Figure 60**). Push the float pin all the way in.

NOTE
If the float level is too high, the result will be a rich air/fuel mixture. If it is too low, the mixture will be too lean.

NOTE
The floats on all carburetors must be adjusted at the same height to maintain the same fuel/air mixture.

5. Check that the O-ring is installed in the float bowl groove (**Figure 63**); replace the O-ring if worn, damaged or if there are signs of fuel leakage.

6. Reinstall the carburetor assembly.

Needle Jet Adjustment

The needle jet is *non-adjustable* on all models.

High Elevation Adjustment

If the bike is going to be ridden for any sustained period of time at high elevation (2,000 m/6,500 ft.), the carburetors must be readjusted to improve performance and decrease exhaust emissions.

> *NOTE*
> *If this adjustment has been performed by a Honda dealer, there will be an emission control information update label placed to the right of the emission control information label. See **Figure 64**.*

1. Locate the pilot screws (**Figure 56**) and remove the limiter cap from each screw (**Figure 55**).
2. Start the engine and let it reach normal operating temperature. Stop-and-go riding for approximately 10 minutes is sufficient. Turn off the engine.
3. Connect a portable tachometer following the manufacturer's instructions. The bike's tachometer is not accurate enough at low rpm.
4. Turn each pilot screw *clockwise* 1/2 turn, as viewed from the left-hand side of the bike.
5. Restart the engine and turn the throttle stop screw (**Figure 57**) to set the idle speed to the specification listed in **Table 1**.
6. Turn the engine off and disconnect the portable tachometer.
7. Install the pilot screw limiter caps as follows:
   a. Apply Loctite 601 to the inside of a limiter cap.

> *NOTE*
> *Make sure you do not turn the pilot screw when installing the limiter cap.*

   b. Align the limiter cap with the pilot screw and install it so that the pilot screw can only be turned clockwise. This will prevent the pilot screws from being turned counterclockwise which enriches the air/fuel mixture.
   c. Repeat for each pilot screw.
8. When the bike is returned to lower elevations (near sea level), the pilot screws must be returned to their original position (1/2 turn counterclockwise) and the idle speed readjusted to the rpm listed in **Table 1**.

Rejetting the Carburetors

Do not try to solve a poor running engine problem by rejetting the carburetors if all of the following conditions hold true:
   a. The engine has held a good tune in the past with the standard jetting.
   b. The engine has not been modified.
   c. The motorcycle is being operated in the same geographical region under the same general climatic conditions as in the past.
   d. The motorcycle was and is being ridden at average highway speeds.

If those conditions all hold true, the chances are that the problem is due to a malfunction in the carburetor or in another component that needs to

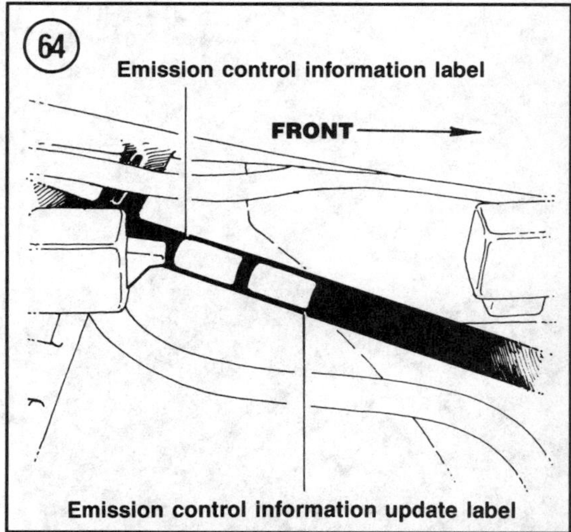

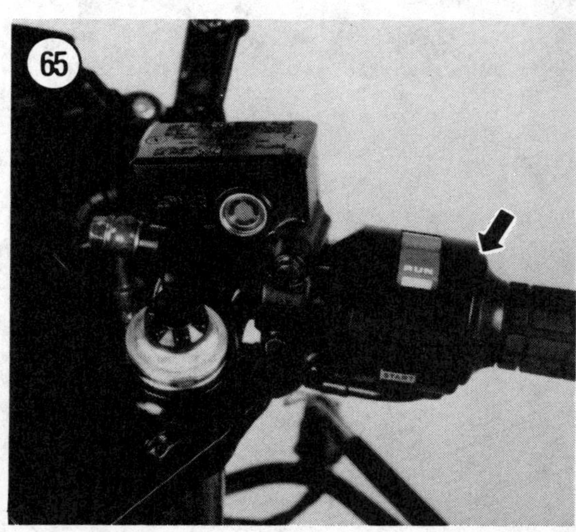

be adjusted or repaired. Changing carburetor jet size probably won't solve the problem. Rejetting the carburetors may be necessary if any of the following conditions hold true:

  a. A non-standard type of air filter element is being used.

  b. A non-standard exhaust system is installed on the motorcycle.

  c. Any of the top end components in the engine (pistons, cams, valves, compression ratio, etc.) have been modified.

  d. The motorcycle is in use at considerably higher or lower elevations or in a considerably hotter or colder climate than in the past.

  e. The motorcycle is being operated at considerably higher speeds than before and changing to colder spark plugs does not solve the problem.

  f. Someone has previously changed the carburetor jetting. Stock jet sizes are listed in **Table 1**.

  g. The motorcycle has never held a satisfactory engine tune.

If it is necessary to rejet the carburetors, check with a dealer or motorcycle performance tuner for recommendations as to the size of jets to install for your specific situation.

If you do change the jets do so only one size at a time. After rejetting, test ride the bike and perform a spark plug test; refer to *Reading Spark Plugs* in Chapter Three.

THROTTLE CABLE REPLACEMENT

The throttle cables should always be replaced as a set.

1. Park the bike and support it securely.
2. Remove the seat.
3. Remove the lower fairings and side covers as described in Chapter Thirteen.
4. Remove the fuel tank as described in this chapter.
5. Remove the air filter housing assembly as described under *Carburetor Removal/Installation* in this chapter.
6. Disconnect the front brake light switch electrical connectors.
7. Remove the screws securing the right-hand switch/throttle housing halves together (**Figure 65**).

NOTE
Use masking tape and label the old cables before removal. That way, you can use the old cables as a guide when installing the new cables as the 2 cables are different.

8. Remove the housing from the handlebar and disengage the throttle cables from the throttle grip.

NOTE
The carburetor assembly is shown in the following steps partially removed for clarity.

9. At the carburetor assembly, loosen the locknuts (**Figure 66**) securing the throttle cables to the cable bracket.
10. Disconnect the throttle cables (**Figure 67**) from the throttle wheel.

NOTE
The string attached in the next step will be used to pull the new throttle cables back through the frame so they will be routed in exactly the same position as the old ones.

11. Tie a piece of heavy string or cord (approximately 7 ft./2 m long) to the carburetor end of the throttle cables. Wrap this end with masking or duct tape. Do not use an excessive amount of tape as it must be pulled through the frame loop during removal. Tie the other 2end of the string to the frame.

12. At the throttle grip end of the cables, carefully pull the cables (and attached string) out through the frame. Make sure the attached string follows the same path as the cable through the frame.

13. Remove the tape and untie the string from the old cables.

14. Lubricate the new cables as described in Chapter Three.

15. Tie the string to the new throttle cables and wrap it with tape.

16. Carefully pull the string back through the frame, routing the new cables through the same path as the old cables.

17. Remove the tape and untie the string from the cables and the frame.

CAUTION
The throttle cables are the push/pull type and must not be interchanged. Attach the cables following the identification labels you made on the old cables.

18. Attach the cables to the correct position on the throttle drum as noted during removal (**Figure 67**) and connect the cables to the bracket (**Figure 66**).

19. Attach the throttle cables to the throttle grip.

20. Install the throttle/switch housing and tighten the screws securely.

21. Attach the front brake light switch connectors.

22. Operate the throttle grip and make sure the carburetor throttle linkage is operating correctly, with no binding. If operating incorrectly or if there is binding carefully check that the cables are attached correctly and there are no tight bends in the cables.

23. Install the carburetor assembly, fuel tank and seat.

24. Adjust the throttle cables as described in Chapter Three.

25. Install all parts previously removed. Make sure to route the throttle and choke cables through the cable guide at the front of the fuel tank.

26. Test ride the bike slowly at first and make sure the throttle is operating correctly.

CHOKE CABLE REPLACEMENT

1. Park the bike and support it securely.
2. Remove the seat.
3. Remove the lower fairings and side covers as described in Chapter Thirteen.
4. Remove the fuel tank as described in this chapter.
5. Remove the air filter housing assembly as described under *Carburetor Removal/Installation* in this chapter.
6. Disconnect the clutch switch wires at the clutch lever.
7. Remove the screws securing the left-hand switch assembly and separate the assembly.
8. Remove the choke cable from the switch and choke lever assembly (**Figure 68**) on the handlebar.
9. Remove the Phillips screw (A, **Figure 69**) and remove the arm clamp from the choke cable. Disconnect the end of the choke cable (B, **Figure 69**) from the lever.

NOTE
The piece of string attached in the next step will be used to pull the new choke cable back through the frame so it will be routed in the same position as the old cable.

10. Tie a piece of heavy string or cord (approximately 7 ft./2 m long) to the carburetor end of each choke cable. Wrap the end with masking or duct tape. Do not use an excessive amount of tape as it must be pulled through the frame loop during removal.
11. Unhook the choke cable from any clips on the frame.
12. At the choke lever end of the cable, carefully pull the cable assembly (and attached string) out through the frame. Make sure the attached string follows the same path as that of the choke cable.
13. Remove the tape and untie the string from the old cable assembly.
14. Lubricate the new cable assembly as described in Chapter Three.
15. Tie the string to the new choke cable assembly and wrap it with tape.

16. Carefully pull the string back through the frame, routing the new cable through the same path as the old cable.
17. Remove the tape and untie the string from the cable and the frame.
18. Attach the choke cable onto the choke lever assembly (B, **Figure 69**). Install the cable clamp with the Phillips screw (A, **Figure 69**).
19. Install the switch/choke assembly on the handlebar and tighten the screws securely.
20. Attach the clutch switch wires to the clutch lever.
21. Operate the choke lever and make sure the carburetor choke linkage is operating correctly, with no binding. If operation is incorrect or there is binding carefully check that the cable is attached correctly and there are no tight bends in the cable.
22. Adjust the choke cable as described under *Choke Cable Adjustment* in Chapter Three.
23. Install all parts previously removed. Make sure to route the choke and throttle cables through the cable guide at the front of the fuel tank.

FUEL TANK

Removal/Installation

WARNING
Do not store gasoline in an open container, since it is an extreme fire hazard. Store the gasoline in a sealed metal container, away from heat, sparks or flames.

Refer to **Figure 70** for this procedure.
1. Park and support the bike securely.
2. Remove the seat and both side covers.
3. Turn the fuel shutoff valve off.
4. Disconnect the fuel line that goes from the fuel tank to the fuel filter.
5. If it is necessary to drain the fuel tank, perform the following:
   a. Attach a piece of fuel line to the fitting on the fuel shutoff valve and place the loose end in a clean sealable metal container.
   b. Turn the fuel shutoff valve on.

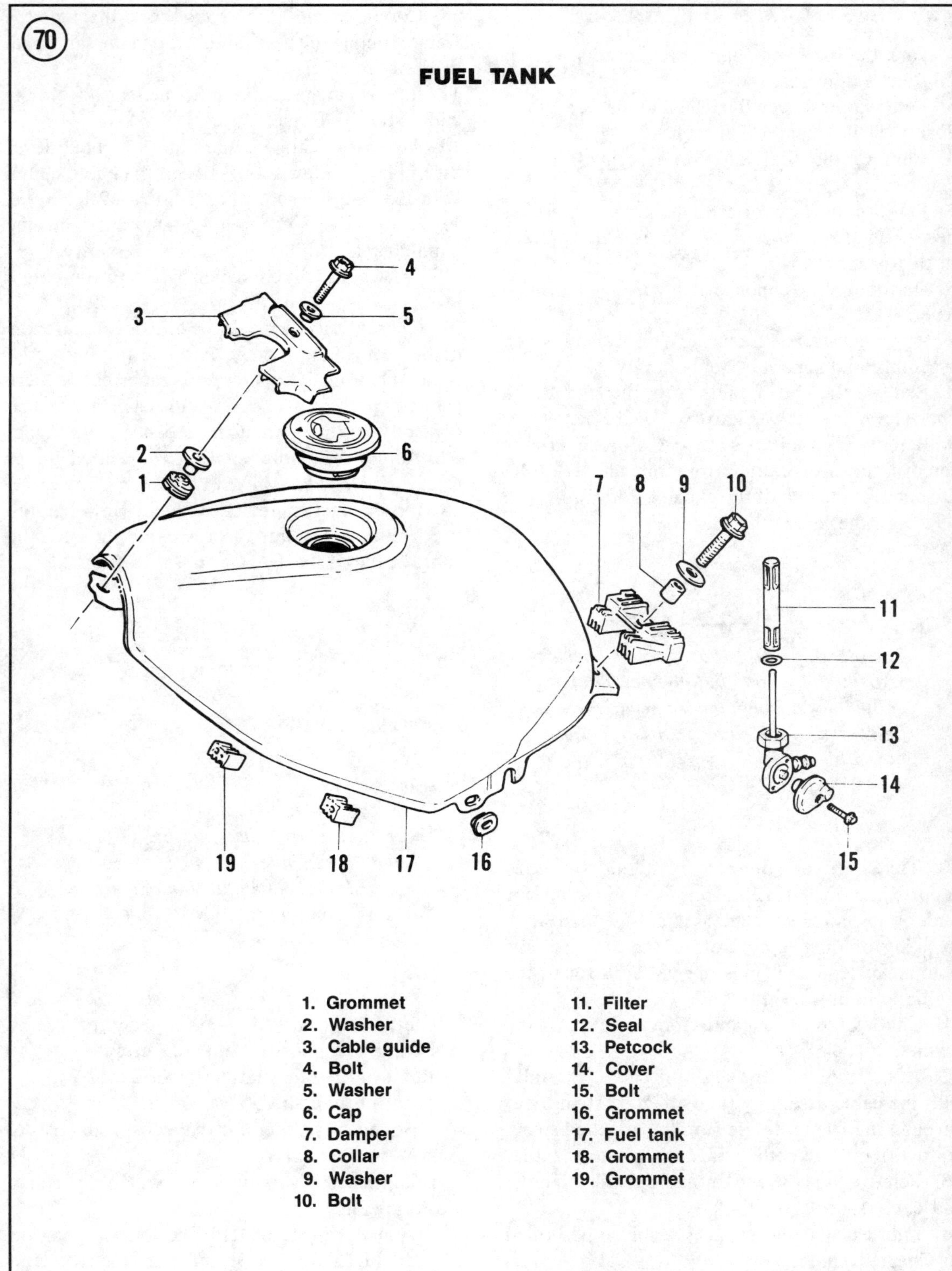

1. Grommet
2. Washer
3. Cable guide
4. Bolt
5. Washer
6. Cap
7. Damper
8. Collar
9. Washer
10. Bolt
11. Filter
12. Seal
13. Petcock
14. Cover
15. Bolt
16. Grommet
17. Fuel tank
18. Grommet
19. Grommet

c. Drain the fuel tank. If the fuel is kept clean it can be reused.
d. Open the fuel filler cap. This will speed up the flow of fuel.
e. Close the filler cap.

6. Remove the fuel tank mounting bolts (**Figure 70**).

7. *California models:* Lift up the tank and disconnect the fuel tank-to-canister vent hose (**Figure 71**).

8. Lift the fuel tank up and remove it.

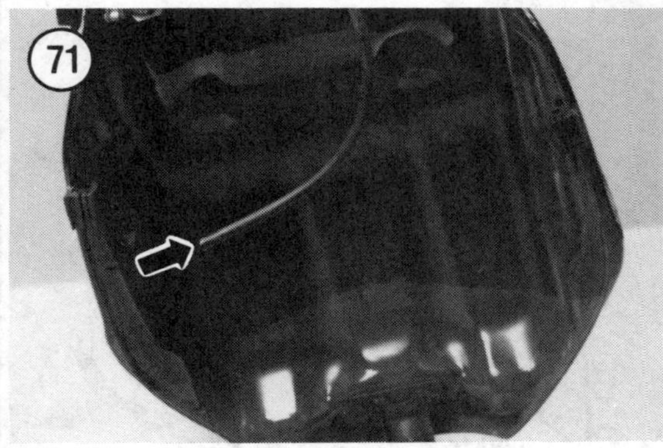

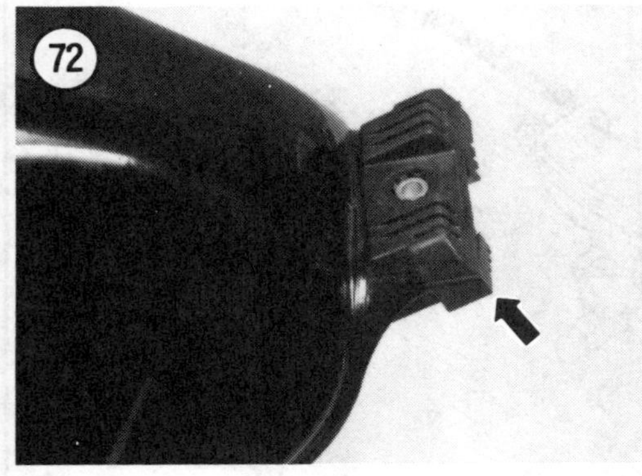

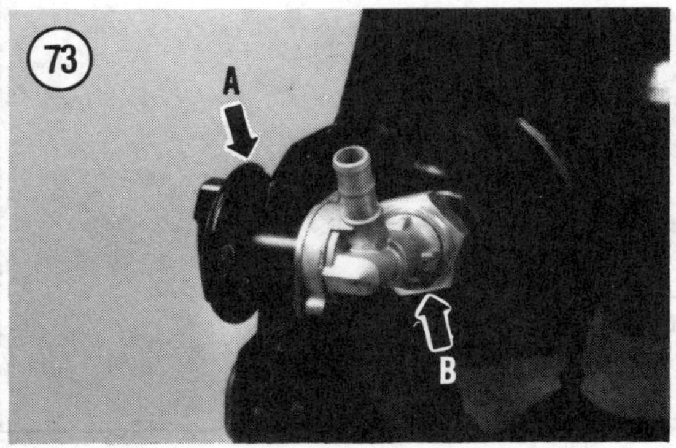

9. Install by reversing these removal steps, noting the following.

10. Make sure the fuel tank rubber dampers are in position before installing the fuel tank mounting bolts. **Figure 72** shows the rear damper.

11. Install the cable guide at the front of the fuel tank (**Figure 70**) and secure it with the bushing and bolt.

12. Tighten the front fuel tank mounting bolt to the torque specification in **Table 2**.

13. Tighten the rear fuel tank mounting bolt to the torque specification in **Table 2**.

14. Route the choke and throttle cables through the cable guide.

15. If the fuel tank was drained, refill it with the drained fuel.

FUEL SHUTOFF VALVE

Removal/Installation

Refer to **Figure 70** when performing this procedure.

1. Remove and drain the fuel tank as described under *Fuel Tank Removal/Installation* in this chapter.

> *WARNING*
> *Do not store gasoline in an open container, since it is an extreme fire hazard. Store the gasoline in a sealed metal container, away from heat, sparks or flames.*

2. Remove the screw securing the lever to the fuel shutoff valve and remove the lever. See A, **Figure 73**.

3. Loosen the fuel shutoff valve nut (B, **Figure 73**) and remove the fuel shutoff valve from the fuel tank.

4. Clean the filter of all grit and debris. Replace the fuel shutoff valve filter and O-ring if worn or damaged.

5. Install by reversing these removal steps. Tighten the nut securely and carefully check for fuel leaks.

FUEL FILTER

An external fuel filter is installed between the fuel tank and fuel pump. The stock fuel filter

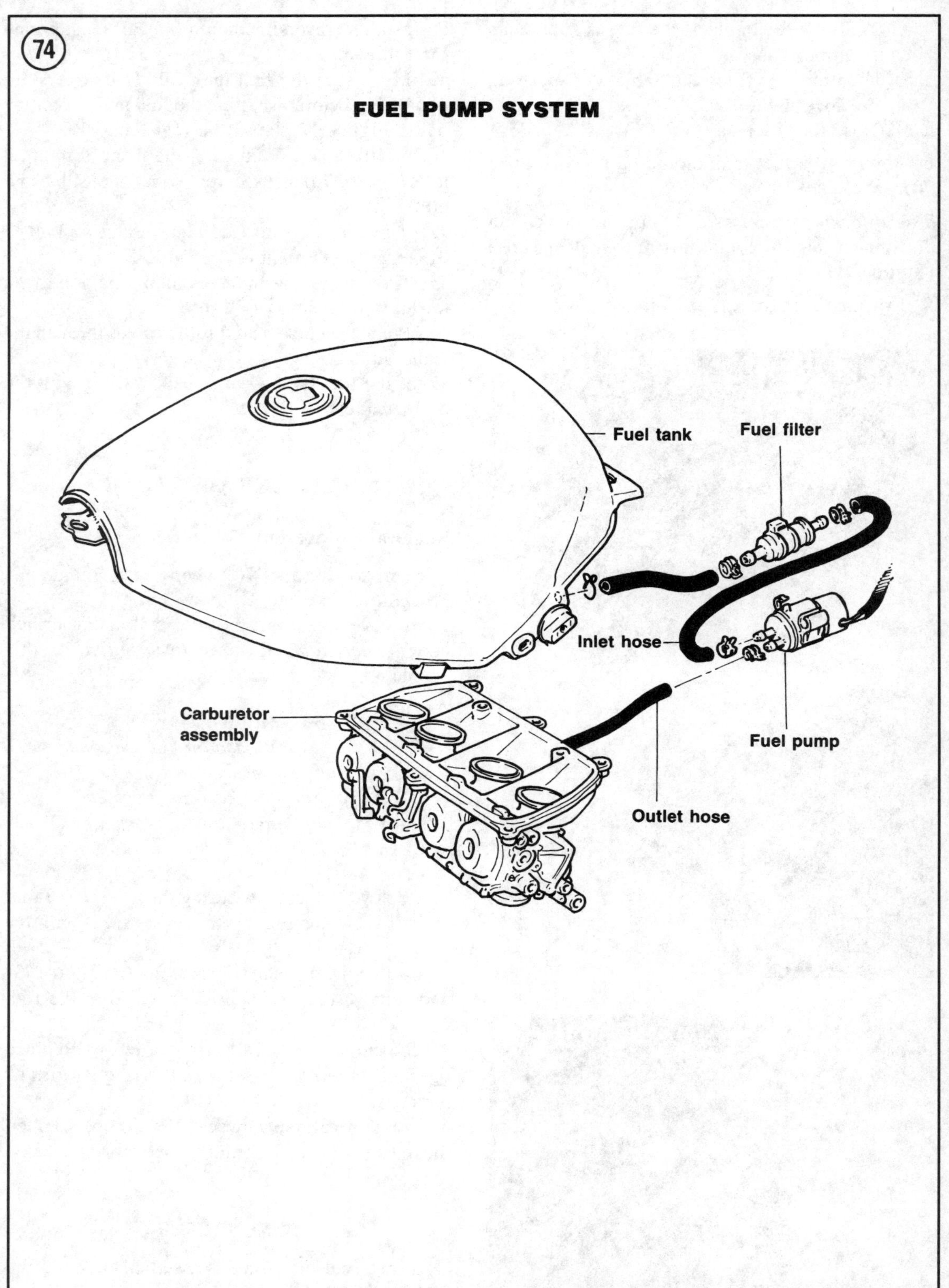
74
FUEL PUMP SYSTEM
Fuel tank
Fuel filter
Inlet hose
Fuel pump
Carburetor
assembly
Outlet hose

cannot be cleaned. If dirty, a new filter must be installed. It should be replaced at the interval specified in Chapter Three or when it becomes contaminated. Refer to *Fuel Filter Replacement* in Chapter Three.

FUEL PUMP

Fuel pump performance testing is covered in Chapter Eight.

Removal/Installation

Refer to **Figure 74** for this procedure.
1. Turn the fuel shutoff valve off.
2. Remove the seat and the left-hand side cover.
3. Disconnect the negative battery terminal.
4. Disconnect the fuel pump 2-pin electrical connector.
5. Label the inlet and outlet fuel hoses (**Figure 74**) at the fuel pump.
6. Disconnect the hoses from the fuel pump. In addition, pull the inlet hose out of the fuel pump rubber mount.
7. Remove the fuel pump (**Figure 75**) and its rubber mount from the frame.
8. Plug the ends of the fuel lines with golf tees to prevent fuel leakage.
9. Install by reversing these removal steps.
10. After installation is complete, thoroughly check for fuel leaks.

Fuel Pump Breather Tube Recall Notification

The Honda factory has determined that a problem exists with the fuel pump breather tube

on all 1989 CBR600 models and has issued a recall of these models. This problem was covered in Honda Service Bulletin CBR600F #3, August 1989. The models affected are as follows:
  a. 49-state models: VIN serial number JH2PC190*KM200001—JH2PC190*KM20 4-860.
  b. California models: VIN serial number JH2PC191*KM200001—JH2PC191*KM201 4-34.

The problem relates to the length and the routing of the fuel pump breather tube. Under certain conditions, it may be possible for the fuel/air mixture from the carburetor air vent to enter into this breather tube. This fuel/air mixture may become combustible and it may be ignited by the electrical arcing of the contacts within the electric fuel pump. This arcing could lead to a fire at the end of the breather tube that could spread to other components in the immediate area. If this happens a very serious fire may occur which could result in a total loss of the bike.

Replacement with a longer breather tube and the correct routing of this tube by a Honda dealer *will safely solve* this problem.

All Honda dealers were notified of this problem and all unsold 1989 bikes in dealers' stock were modified prior to the release of these bikes to customers. All owners that had taken delivery of affected bikes prior to the problem being discovered, were notified by U.S. mail and informed to bring their bike in to a Honda dealer and have this problem repaired at no charge.

If you are unsure if this problem has been corrected, take the bike to a Honda dealer and have them inspect it. If the problem has not been corrected, have them take care of the problem as soon as possible at no charge to you regardless of mileage or date of purchase.

CRANKCASE BREATHER SYSTEM

To comply with air pollution standards, the Honda CBR600 is equipped with a crankcase breather system (**Figure 76**). The system draws blowby gases from the crankcase and recirculates them into the air/fuel mixture and thus into the engine to be burned.

EVAPORATIVE EMISSION CONTROL SYSTEM (CALIFORNIA MODELS ONLY)

To comply with the California Air Resources Board, an evaporative emission control system (**Figure 77**) is installed on all models sold in California.

Fuel vapor from the fuel tank is routed into a charcoal canister (**Figure 77**). This vapor is stored when the engine is not running. When the engine is running these stored vapors are drawn through a purge control valve and into the carburetors to be burned. Make sure all hose clamps are tight. Check all hoses for deterioration and replace as necessary.

Refer to the vacuum hose routing label (**Figure 78**) mounted on the air filter cover for correct hose routing for your model.

Purge Control (PC) Valve

If the engine becomes difficult to start after it is warm or hot, test the purge control (PC) valve as follows.

The Honda vacuum pump (part No. ST-AH-260-MC7) or equivalent and the Honda pressure pump (part No. ST-AH-255-MC7) or equivalent are required to perform these tests.

Vacuum test

The Honda vacuum pump (part No. ST-AH-260-MC7) or equivalent will be required to perform this test.

1. Remove the fuel tank as described in this chapter. This will allow you access to the vacuum hose routing label (**Figure 78**) mounted on the air filter cover.

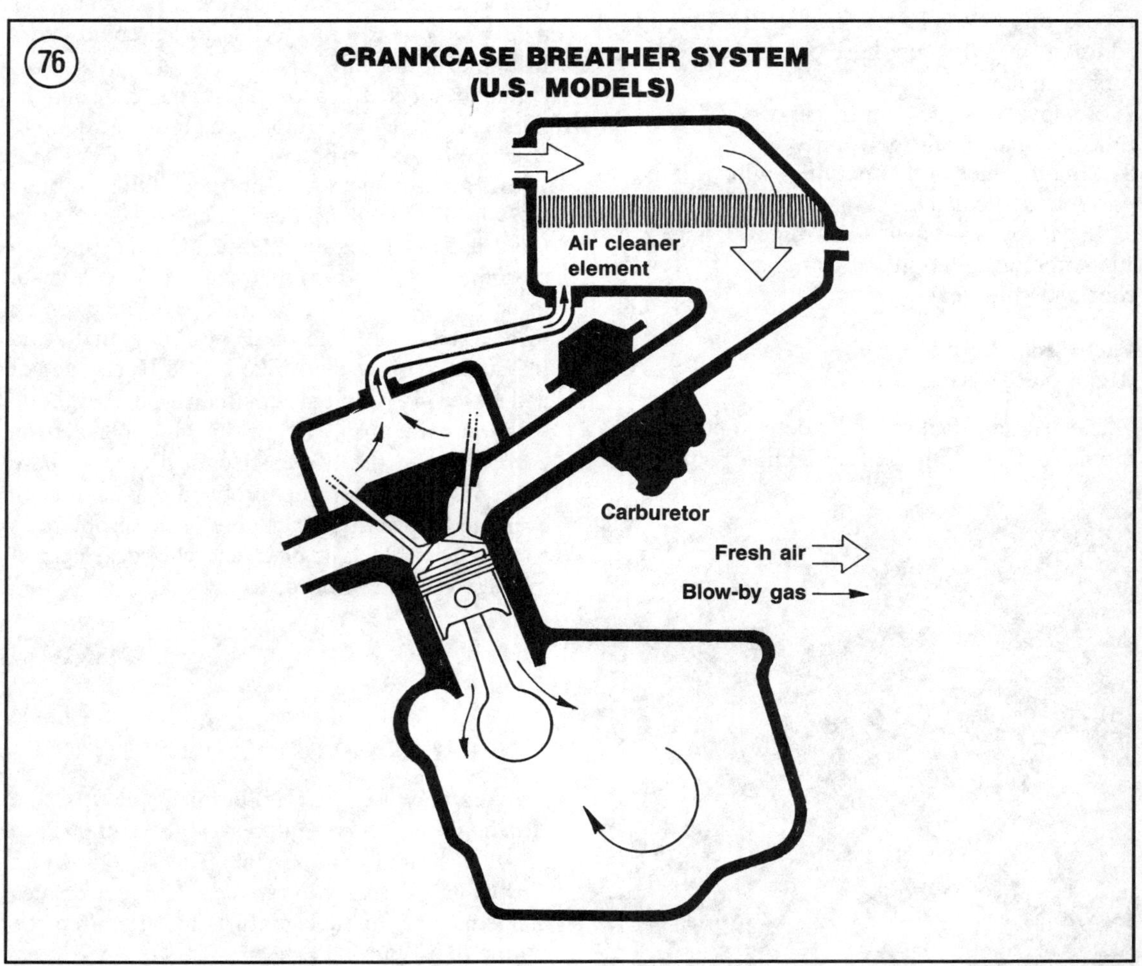

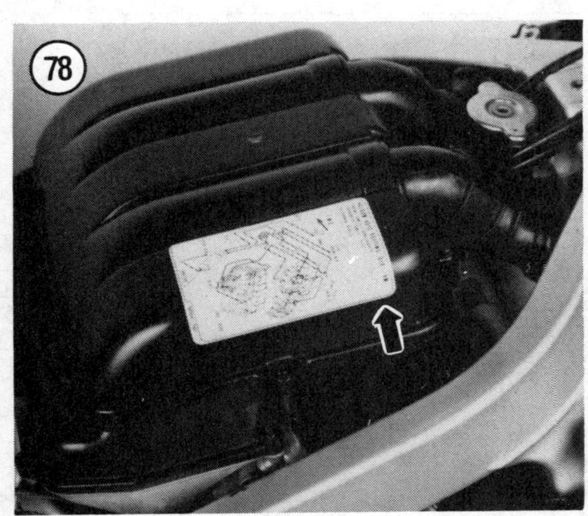

2. Disconnect the hoses from the purge control (PC) valve and remove it.

3. Referring to **Figure 79**, connect a vacuum pump to the PC valve. Apply a vacuum of 40 mm (1.6 in.) Hg to the valve. Interpret results as follows:

   a. Vacuum held: The PC valve is okay.

   b. Vacuum not held: The PC valve is damaged.

4. Disconnect the vacuum pump and perform Step 5.

5. Referring to **Figure 80**, connect the vacuum pump to the No. 3 carburetor outlet. Apply a vacuum of 40 mm (1.6 in.) Hg to the PC valve. Interpret results as follows:

   a. Vacuum held: The PC valve is okay.

   b. Vacuum not held: The PC valve is damaged.

EVAPORATIVE EMISSION CONTROL SYSTEM (CALIFORNIA MODELS ONLY)

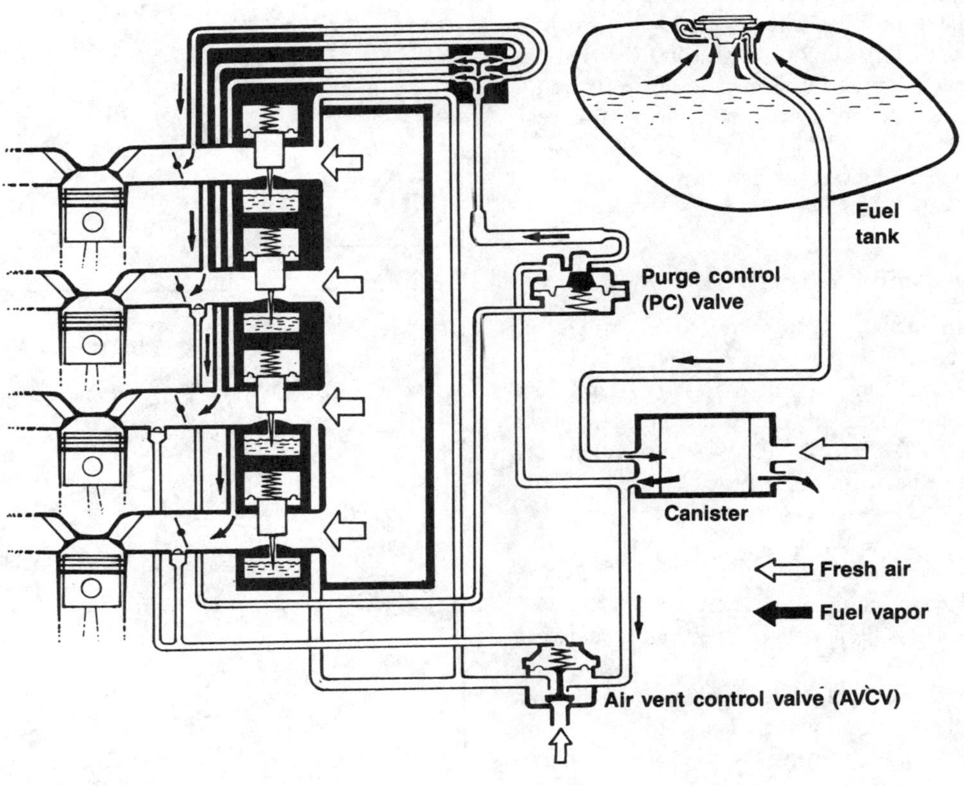

6. Replace the purge control valve if it failed either test procedure in Step 3 or Step 5.

7. If the purge control valve tested okay in Step 3 and Step 5, perform the flow test in the following procedure.

Flow test

The Honda vacuum pump (part No. ST-AH-260-MC7) or equivalent and the Honda pressure pump (part No. ST-AH-255-MC7) or equivalent are required to perform the flow test.

1. Remove the fuel tank as described in this chapter. This will allow you access to the vacuum hose routing label (**Figure 78**) mounted on the air filter cover.

2. Disconnect the hoses from the purge control (PC) valve and remove it.

3. Referring to **Figure 81**, connect a vacuum pump and pressure pump to the PC valve.

4. With the vacuum pump, apply a vacuum of 40 mm (1.6 in.) Hg to the PC valve. At the same time, operate the pressure pump and pump air through the canister hose. If the PC valve is working properly, air will flow through the PC valve and exit through the carburetor hose port. If the PC valve does not work properly during this test, replace it.

5. Disconnect the vacuum and pressure pumps and reverse Step 1 and Step 2.

Air Vent Control Valve (AVCV)

If the engine becomes difficult to restart, test the air vent control valve (AVCV) as follows:

The Honda vacuum pump (part No. ST-AH-260-MC7) or equivalent and the Honda pressure pump (part No. ST-AH-255-MC7) or equivalent are required to perform these tests.

Vacuum test

The Honda vacuum pump (part No. ST-AH-260-MC7) or equivalent will be required to perform this test.

1. Remove the fuel tank as described in this chapter. This will allow you access to the vacuum hose routing label (**Figure 78**) mounted on the air cleaner cover.

2. Disconnect the hoses from the air vent control valve (AVCV) and remove it.

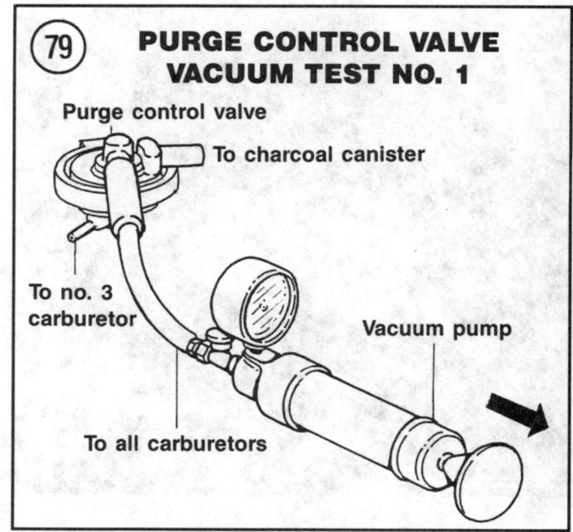

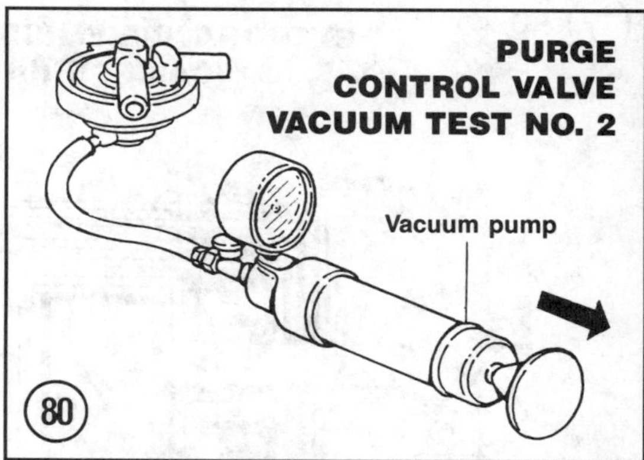

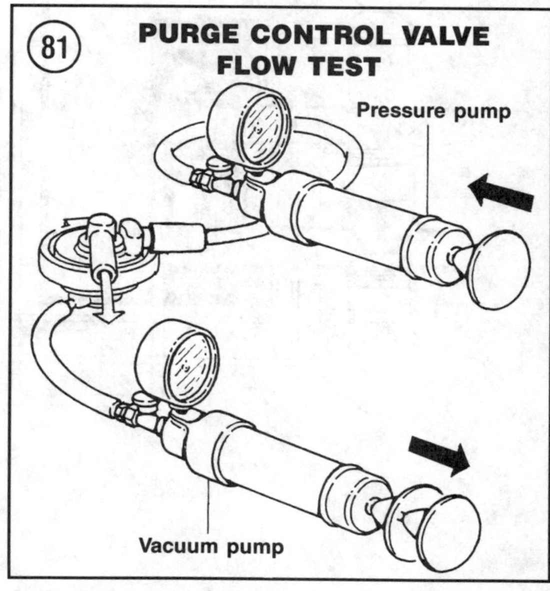

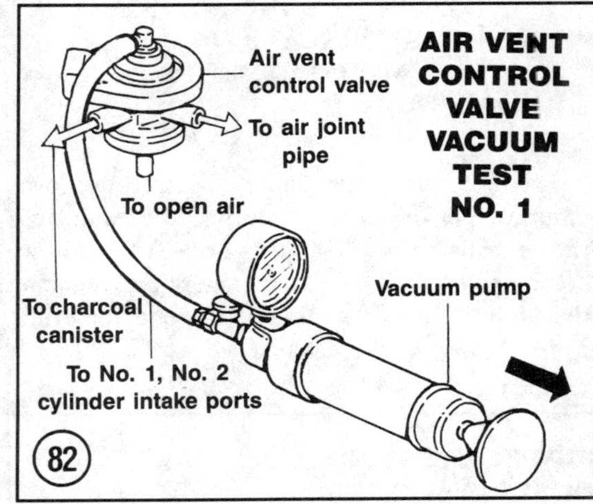

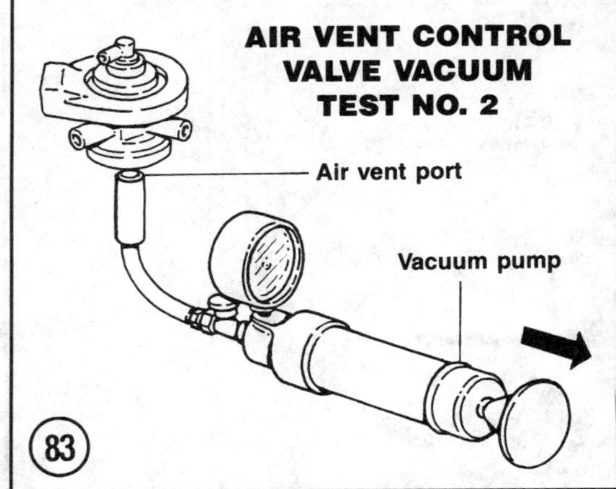

3. Referring to **Figure 82**, connect a vacuum pump to the AVCV. Apply a vacuum of 40 mm (1.6 in.) Hg to the valve. Interpret results as follows:

   a. Vacuum held: The AVCV is okay.

   b. Vacuum not held: The AVCV is damaged.

4. Disconnect the vacuum pump and perform Step 5.

5. Referring to **Figure 83**, connect the vacuum pump to the AVCV air vent port. Apply a vacuum of 40 mm (1.6 in.) Hg to the AVCV. Interpret results as follows:

   a. Vacuum held: The AVCV is okay.

   b. Vacuum not held: The AVCV is damaged.

6. Replace the air vent control valve if it failed either test procedure in Step 3 or Step 5.

7. If the air vent control valve tested okay in Step 3 and Step 5, perform Step 8.

8. Referring to **Figure 84**, connect a vacuum pump and pressure pump to the AVCV. With the vacuum pump, apply a vacuum of 40 mm (1.6 in.) Hg to the AVCV. At the same time, operate the pressure pump and pump air through the air joint pipe port. If the AVCV is working properly, air will flow through the AVCV and exit through the air vent port. If the AVCV does not work properly during this test, replace it.

9. If the air vent control valve tested okay in Step 8, perform Step 10.

10. Referring to **Figure 85**, connect a vacuum pump and pressure pump to the AVCV. Using a

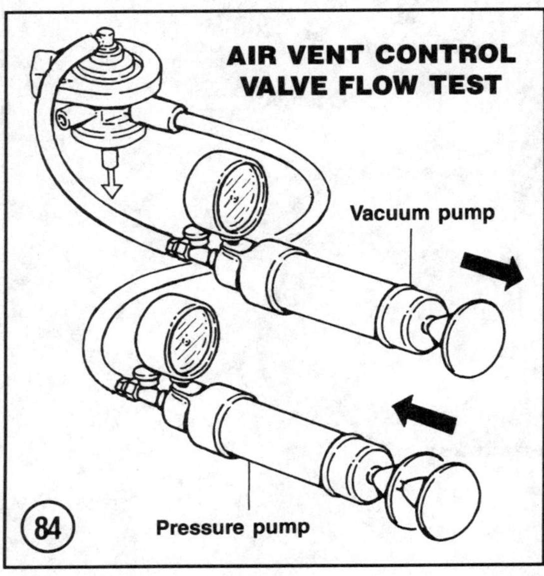

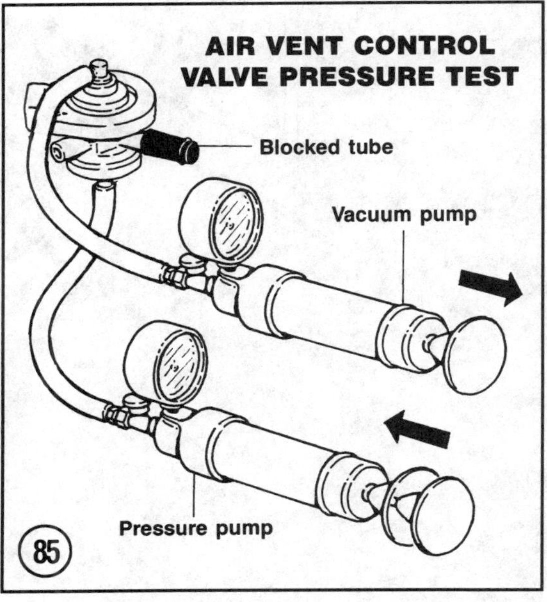

stopper, plug the carburetor air joint pipe. With the vacuum pump, apply a vacuum of 40 mm (1.6 in.) Hg to the AVCV. At the same time, operate the pressure pump and pump air through the air vent port. If the AVCV is working properly, air will flow through the AVCV and hold securely. If air exits one of the open ports, the AVCV is damaged and must be replaced. Remove the stopper from the carburetor air joint pipe.

11. Disconnect the vacuum and pressure pumps and reverse Step 1 and Step 2.

SECONDARY AIR SUPPLY SYSTEM (CALIFORNIA MODELS ONLY)

The secondary air supply system improves emission performance by routing filtered air into the exhaust port (**Figure 86**). This allows combustion to continue for a longer time, reducing the amount of carbon monoxide and unburned hydrocarbons in the exhaust.

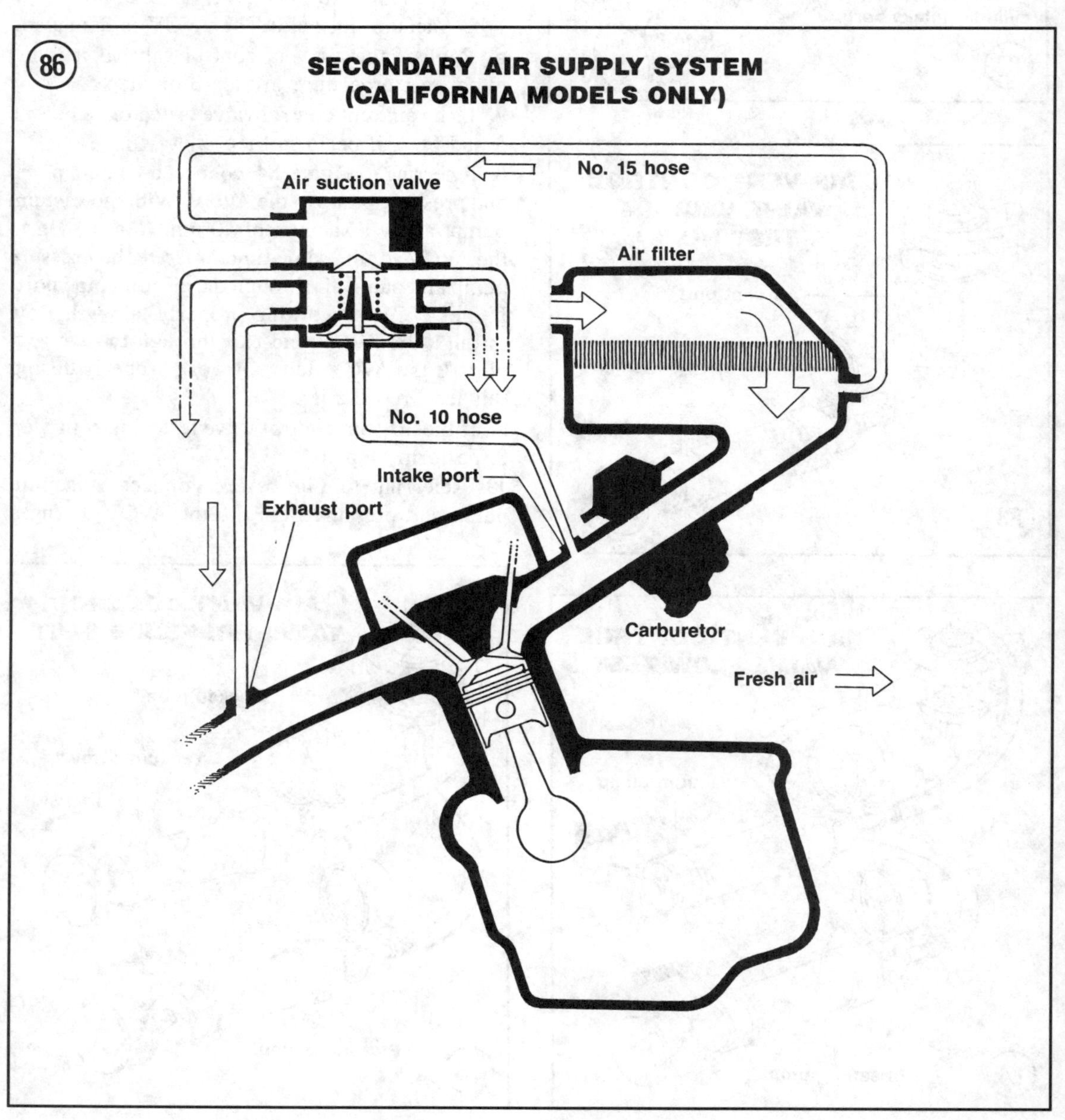

Testing

The Honda vacuum pump (part No. ST-AH-260-MC7) or equivalent will be required to perform this test.

1. Remove the fuel tank as described in this chapter. This will allow you access to the vacuum hose routing label (**Figure 78**) mounted on the air cleaner cover.

2. Disconnect the air suction valve No. 15 hose at the air filter case (**Figure 87**).

3. Disconnect the No. 10 intake pipe vacuum tube at the No. 1 carburetor (**Figure 87**). Plug the vacuum tube port.

4. Connect a vacuum pump to the No. 10 vacuum hose (**Figure 87**).

5. Start the engine and open the throttle slightly. Check that air is being sucked into the No. 15 hose (**Figure 87**). If there is no suction, check the No. 10 and No. 15 hoses for clogging or damage.

6. With the engine at idle, apply a vacuum of 40 mm (1.6 in.) Hg to the No. 10 hose. Now check the No. 15 hose; it should *not* be sucking air. Also check the vacuum pump gauge; it should show no signs of vacuum loss.

7. If air is being sucked into the No. 15 hose and/or there is a vacuum leak, replace the air suction valve.

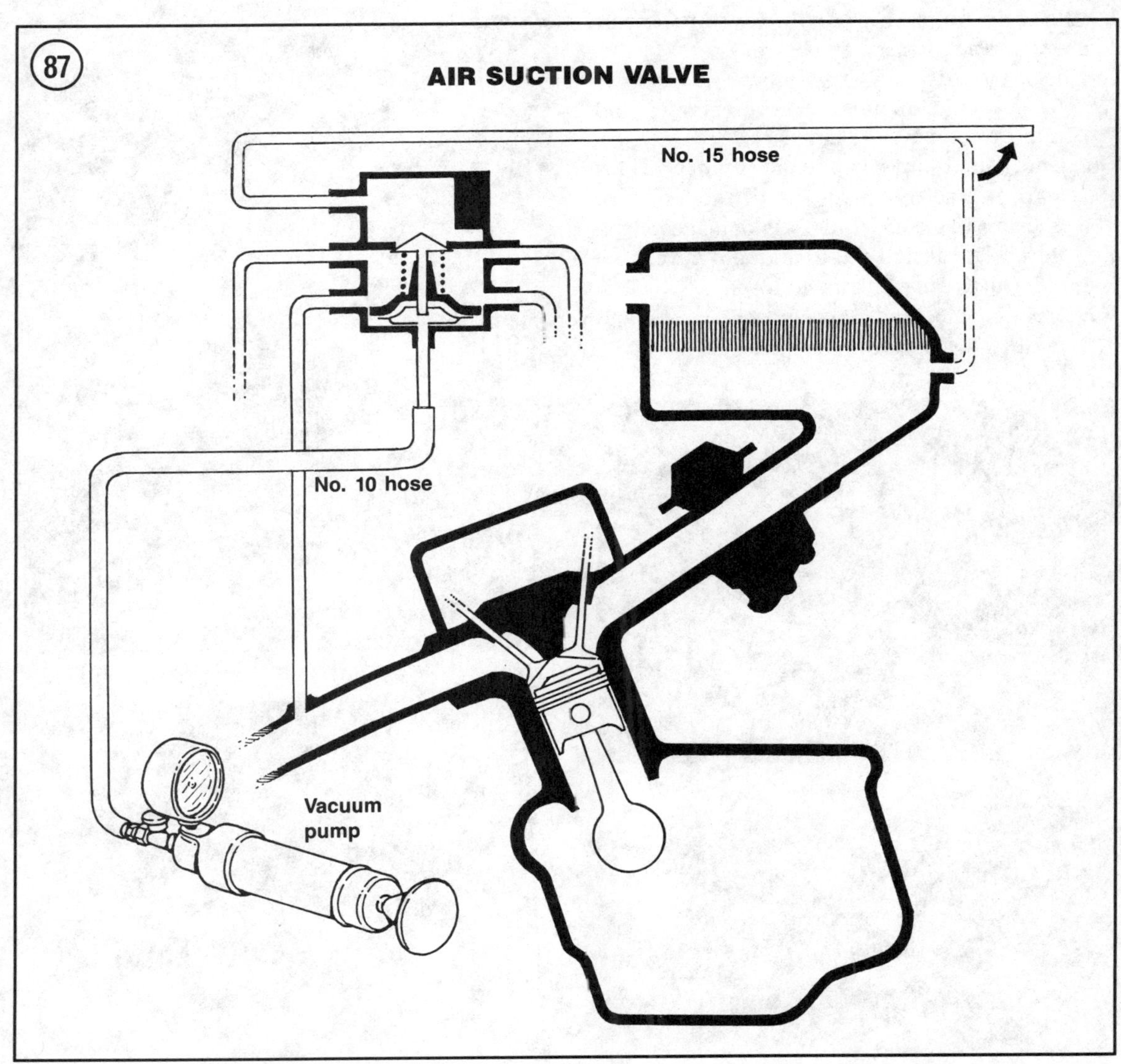

Air Suction Valve
Removal/Installation

1. Remove the exhaust pipes as described in this chapter.

2. Disconnect the vacuum hose (A, **Figure 88**) at the air suction valve diaphragm outlet port.

3. Remove the mounting bolts (B, **Figure 88**) and remove the pipe from the cylinder head.

4. Remove the mounting bolts and remove the air suction valve assembly (C, **Figure 88**).

5. Installation is the reverse of these steps. Replace the 4 O-rings (**Figure 89**) on the pipes if worn or damaged.

Inspection

1. Check the hoses (**Figure 90**) for soft spots or damage; replace hoses as necessary.

2. Check the diaphragm as follows:
   a. Remove the diaphragm cover screws and remove the cover (**Figure 91**).
   b. Check the rubber diaphragm (**Figure 92**) for tears or cracks; replace the air suction valve housing if the diaphragm is damaged.
   c. Reverse to install the diaphragm cover.

3. Inspect the reed valve as follows:
   a. Remove the reed valve cover screws and remove the cover.

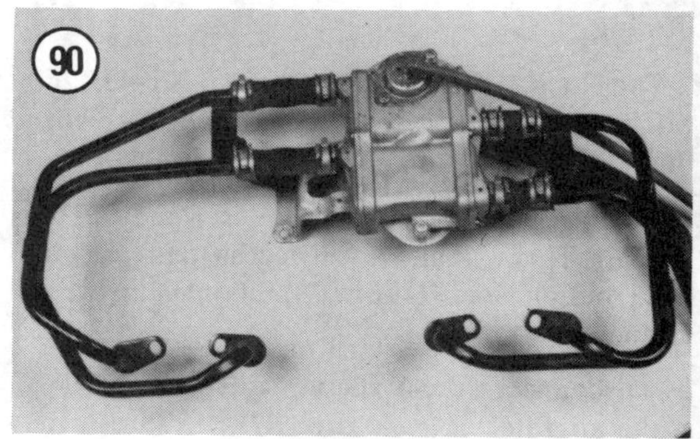

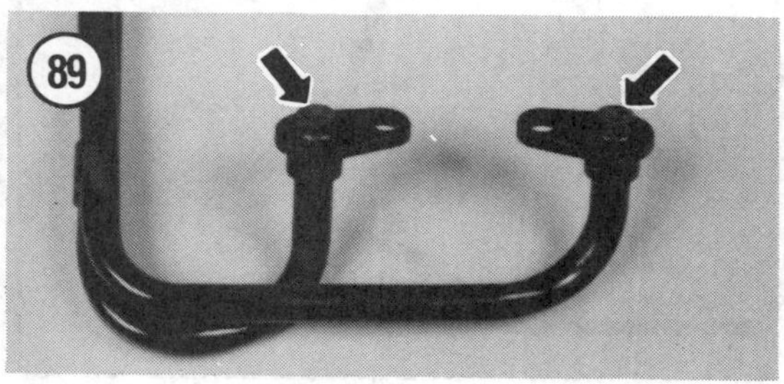

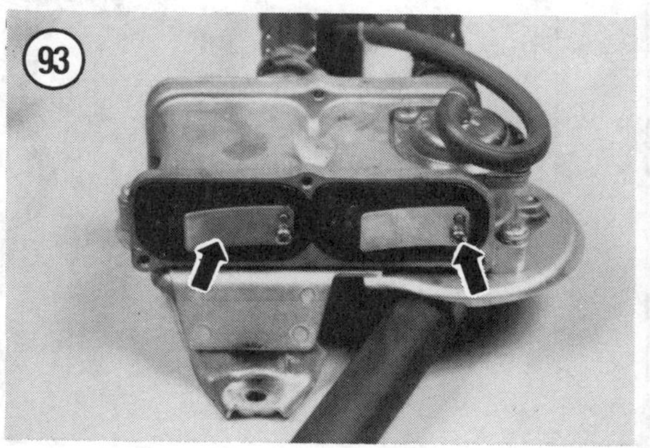

b. Lift the reed valves (**Figure 93**) out of the housing.

c. Inspect the reed valves (**Figure 94**) for fatigue or cracks. Check to see there is no clearance between the reed valve and seat. If there is clearance, check for debris that may be holding the valve open. Also check the reed valve rubber seat for cracks or damage. If any wear or damage is found, replace the air suction valve assembly; do not attempt replacement of the reed only.

d. Install the reed valves by reversing these steps.

EXHAUST SYSTEM

The stock Honda exhaust system consists of a header assembly and a single muffler (**Figure 95**).

Removal/Installation

1. Support the bike securely.
2. Remove the side covers as described in Chapter Thirteen.
3. Remove the lower fairings as described in Chapter Thirteen.

1. Bolt	8. Bolt
2. Washer	9. Bolt
3. Collar	10. Washer
4. Nut	11. Header pipe
5. Silencer	12. Gasket
6. Clamp	13. Collar
7. Gasket	14. Nut

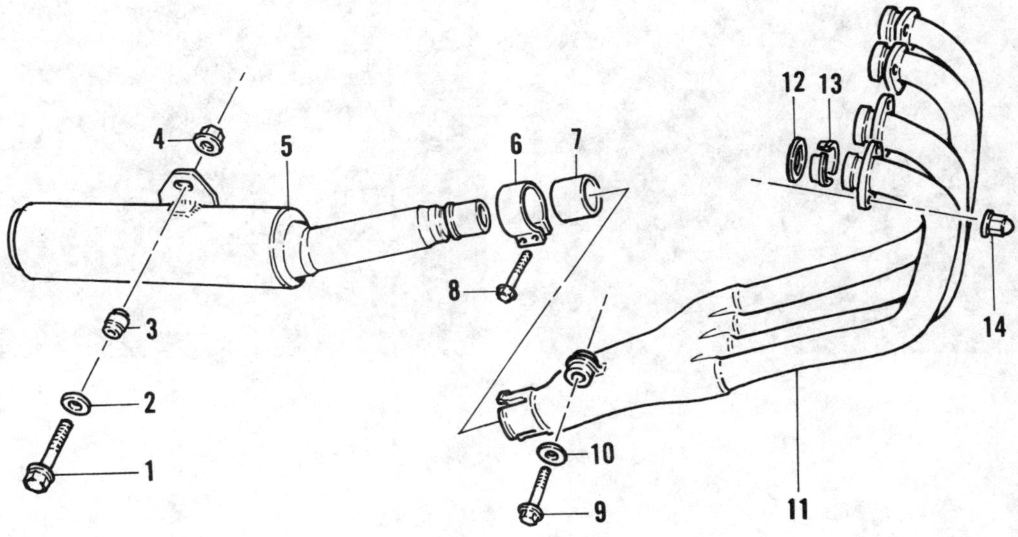

4. Loosen the muffler clamp band bolts (**Figure 96**). Then remove the rear muffler mounting bolt and nut and remove the muffler.

5. Loosen the header lower mounting bolt (**Figure 97**).

6. Loosen and remove the exhaust manifold acorn nuts (**Figure 98**) at the cylinder head.

7. Remove the header lower mounting bolt (**Figure 97**) and remove the header assembly.

8. Check the exhaust port gaskets (**Figure 99**). Replace if worn or damaged, or if there are signs of exhaust leakage.

9. Install the assembly into position and install all bolts and nuts only finger-tight until the header pipe nuts and washers are installed and securely tightened. This will minimize the chance of an exhaust leak at the cylinder head.

10. Tighten all bolts and nuts to the torque specifications listed in **Table 2**.

11. After installation is complete, make sure there are no exhaust leaks.

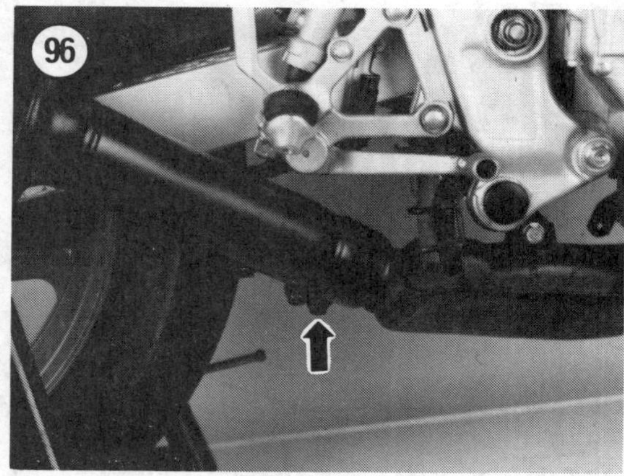

Table 1 CARBURETOR SPECIFICATIONS

	1987-on CBR600F (49-state)	1987-on CBR600F (California)
Identification No.	VG20A	VG21A
Throttle valve diameter	32 mm (1.3 in.)	32 mm (1.3 in.)
Main jet	105	105
Pilot jet	35	35
Float level	8 mm (5.8 in.)	8 mm (5.8 in.)
Pilot screw initial opening	2 1/4 turns out	2 1/2 turns out
Idle speed	1200 ±100 rpm	1300 ±100 rpm

Table 2 TIGHTENING TORQUES

	N·m	ft.-lb.
Fuel tank		
Front mounting bolt	10	7
Rear mounting bolt	27	20
Exhaust pipe		
Cylinder head joint bolts	12	9
Muffler bolts	27	20

7

CHAPTER EIGHT

ELECTRICAL SYSTEMS

The electrical system consists of the following:
a. Charging system.
b. Ignition system.
c. Starting system
d. Lighting system.
e. Directional signal system.
f. Switches.
g. Electrical components.

Tables 1-5 are located at the end of this chapter. Wiring diagrams are at the end of the book.

NOTE
Most motorcycle dealers and parts houses will not accept any returns on electrical parts. When testing electrical components, make sure that you perform the test procedures as described in this chapter and that your test equipment is working properly. If a test result shows that the component is defective, but the reading is close to the service limit, have the component tested by a Honda dealer to verify the test results.

ELECTRICAL CONNECTORS

The CBR600F Hurricane is equipped with a number of electrical components, connectors and wires. Corrosion-causing moisture can enter these electrical connectors and cause poor electrical connections leading to component failure. Troubleshooting an electrical circuit with one or more corroded electrical connectors can be time consuming and frustrating.

To prevent corrosion buildup in connectors, pack the connectors with a special Honda sealing compound that looks like a cream-colored grease similar to Lubriplate. This sealing compound is called Hondaline Dielectric Compound and is available at most Honda dealers. Dielectric grease is also available under other brand names and sold at most automotive supply stores.

Dielectric grease is formulated for sealing and waterproofing electrical connectors and will *not* interfere with the current flow through the electrical connectors. Use only this compound or an equivalent designed for this specific purpose. Do *not* use a substitute that may interfere with the current flow within the electrical connector.

To properly service electrical connectors, first clean male and female connectors with aerosol electrical contact cleaner and allow it to dry thoroughly. Using a dielectric grease, pack the interior of one of the connectors before connecting the 2 connector halves. On multi-pin connectors, pack the male side and on single-wire connectors, pack the female side. Use a good size glob so that it will squish out when the two halves are pushed together. For best results, the compound should fill the entire inner area of the connector. On multi-pin connectors, also pack the exposed backside of both male and female sides with the grease to preent moisture from entering the connector. After the connector is fully packed, wipe the exterior of all excessive grease.

Get into the practice of cleaning and sealing all electrical connectors every time they are unplugged. This may prevent a breakdown on the road and also save you time when troubleshooting a circuit.

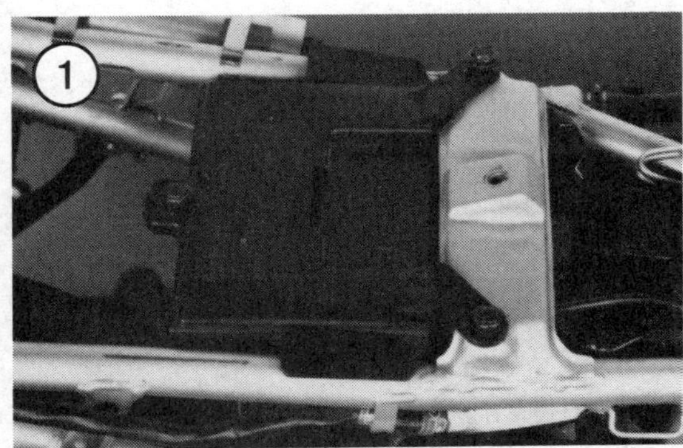

NOTE
If the bike was involved in a fire, the chemical compounds used in some fire extinguishers will severely corrode electrical connectors that they come in contact with.

BATTERY

The battery installed on all CBR600F models is a sealed type. The battery electrolyte level cannot be serviced. When replacing the battery, always use a sealed type; do not install a non-sealed battery.

Removal/Installation

The battery is installed in a battery box below the seat.

1. Remove both side covers and the seat. See Chapter Thirteen.
2. Remove the battery cover bolts and remove the cover (**Figure 1**).
3. Disconnect the battery negative cable (A, **Figure 2**) from the battery.
4. Disconnect the battery positive cable (B, **Figure 2**).
5. Lift the battery up slightly and disconnect the vent tube from the side of the battery.
6. Lift the battery (**Figure 3**) out of the battery box and remove it.

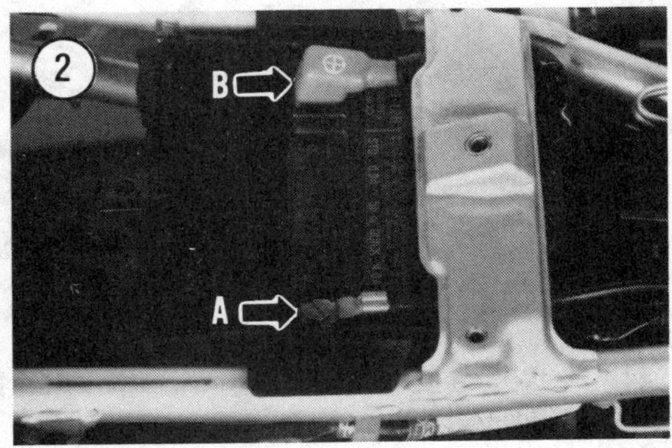

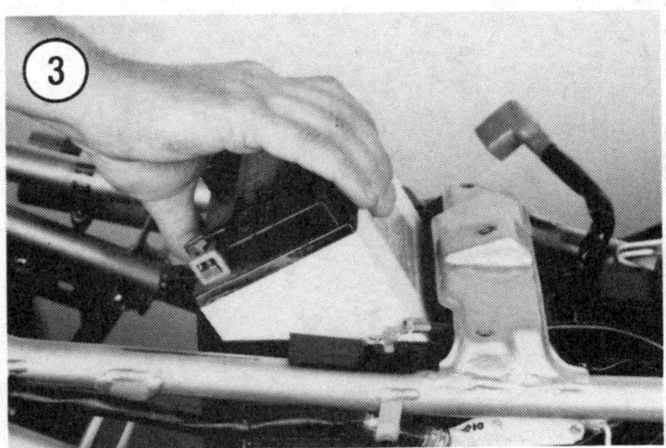

WARNING
Even though the battery is a sealed type, protect your eyes, skin and clothing. The battery case may be damaged and could be leaking. If electrolyte gets into your eyes, flush your eyes thoroughly with clean water and get immediate medical attention.

7. Wipe off the battery case (**Figure 4**) with a shop rag moistened with water. Clean the battery terminals and bolts with a brush and solution of water and baking soda. Rinse thoroughly with clean water.

NOTE
The battery terminal bolts are made of steel and lead coated. If the battery bolts are excessively corroded or damaged, replace with bolts that are designed for battery cable use.

8. Check the battery box and the frame tubes surrounding the battery box for corrosion or damage. Clean corrosion from all parts as required; replace parts damaged by excessive corrosion.

9. Check the battery cables for corrosion or fraying. Poor or corrosion damaged cables will cause the battery to be undercharged because current can't fully enter and charge the battery. Clean the cables with a solution of baking soda and water. If necessary, clean the cable ends with a piece of sandpaper. Rinse thoroughly. Replace battery cables that are excessively corroded. Remember, properly maintained battery cables ensures good electrical contact.

10. Install the battery as follows:
   a. Slip the battery into the battery box so that the battery terminals face to the rear of the bike (**Figure 3**).
   b. Apply a very thin coating of dielectric grease to the battery terminals before reattaching the cables. After connecting the cables, apply a light coating to the connections also—this will delay future corrosion.
   c. Reconnect the positive cable (B, **Figure 2**) to the battery positive terminal first.
   d. Reconnect the negative cable (A, **Figure 2**) to the battery negative terminal.
   e. Install the battery cover and secure it with its mounting bolts.

CAUTION
Make sure the battery box is not cracked and that the battery cover is properly installed. A damaged battery box and cover will allow the battery to vibrate. Vibration can damage the battery plates and short out the battery.

   f. Install the seat and side covers.

Testing

The battery can be tested while installed in the motorcycle. A voltmeter is required for this procedure.

1. Remove both side covers and the seat. See Chapter Thirteen.

2. Remove the battery cover bolts and remove the cover (**Figure 1**).

3. Connect a voltmeter between the battery negative and positive leads (**Figure 5**). Interpret results as follows:
   a. 13.0-13.2 volts: Fully charged.
   b. 12.3 volts or less: Undercharged.

4. If the battery charge is incorrect, perform the troubleshooting procedures described under *Charging System* in Chapter Two.

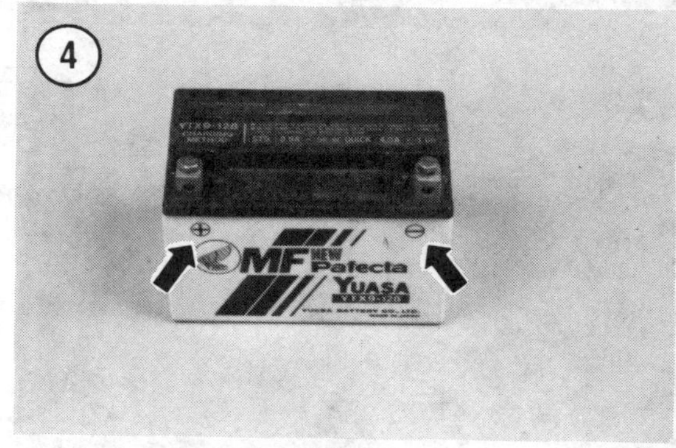

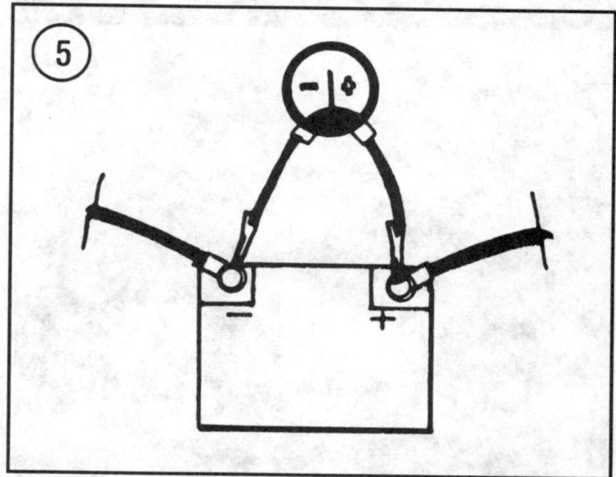

Charging

CAUTION
Always remove the battery from the motorcycle before connecting charging equipment.

WARNING
During charging, highly explosive hydrogen gas is released from the battery. The battery should be charged only in a well-ventilated area, and open flames and cigarettes should be kept away. Never check the charge of the battery by arcing across the terminals; the resulting spark can ignite the hydrogen gas.

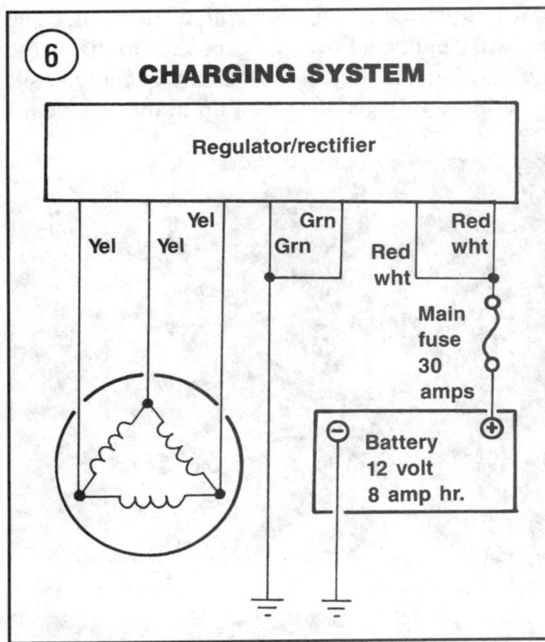

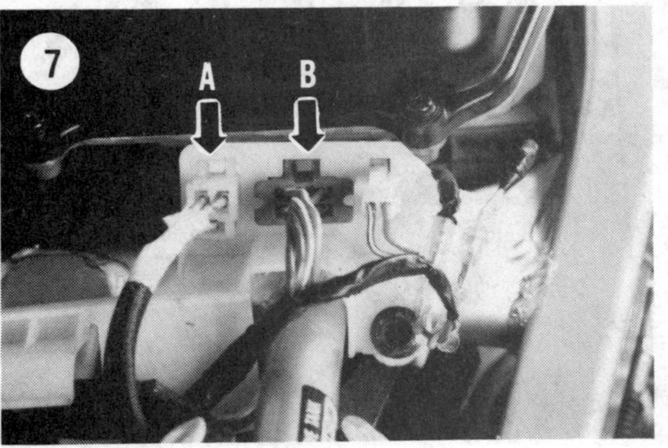

1. Remove the battery from the motorcycle as described in this chapter.
2. Connect the positive (+) charger lead to the battery positive terminal and the negative (−) charger lead to the battery negative terminal.
3. Set the charger at 12 volts, and switch it on. Normally, a battery should be charged at a slow charge rate of 1/10 its given capacity. The recommended charging rate for the CBR600 battery is listed in **Table 1**.
4. Check the battery as described under *Testing* in this section.

New Battery Installation

When replacing the old battery with a new one, be sure to charge it completely before installing it in the bike. Failure to do so will permanently damage the battery.

Be sure to install a sealed battery. Do not install a non-sealed type.

CHARGING SYSTEM

The charging system consists of the battery, alternator and a voltage regulator/rectifier. See **Figure 6**.

Alternating current generated by the alternator is rectified to direct current. The voltage regulator maintains the voltage to the battery and additional electrical loads (lights, ignition, etc.) at a constant voltage regardless of variations in engine speed and load.

Troubleshooting

Refer to *Charging System* in Chapter Two for complete troubleshooting procedures.

ALTERNATOR

Stator Coil
Removal/Installation

The stator coil assembly is mounted on the backside of the clutch cover.
1. Remove the fuel tank as described in Chapter Seven.
2. Disconnect the stator coil 3-pin connector (A, **Figure 7**) from the connector block behind the air filter housing. Pull the wires and connector out of the frame so that they hang free.

3. Remove the clutch cover. Refer to *Clutch Cover Removal/Installation* in Chapter Five.

4. Place the clutch cover on the workbench.

5. Remove the bolt (A, **Figure 8**) and the wire guide.

6. Pull the rubber wire grommet (B, **Figure 8**) out of the notch in the clutch cover.

7. Remove the 4 Allen screws (A, **Figure 9**) and remove the stator coil assembly (B, **Figure 9**).

8. Installation is the reverse of these steps. Note the following:

   a. Make sure to push the rubber wire grommet (B, **Figure 8**) all the way into the clutch cover notch.

   b. Apply Loctite 242 (blue) to the bolt (A, **Figure 8**); tighten the bolt securely.

Rotor
Removal/Installation

Refer to *Alternator Rotor Removal/Installation* in Chapter Four.

VOLTAGE
REGULATOR/RECTIFIER

Removal/Installation

1. Remove the fuel tank as described in Chapter Seven.

2. Remove the left-hand lower fairing as described in Chapter Thirteen.

3. Disconnect the regulator/rectifier 3-pin and 4-pin connectors from the connector block behind the air filter housing (A and B, **Figure 7**). Pull the wires and connectors out of the frame so they hang free.

NOTE
The regulator/rectifier assembly is mounted on the left-hand side of the frame behind the carburetor assembly.

4. Remove the bolts securing the regulator/rectifier assembly and remove it.

5. Install by reversing these steps. Make sure all electrical connections are tight and free of corrosion.

IGNITION SYSTEM

The ignition system consists of 2 ignition coils, 2 ignition pulse generators, 4 spark plugs and a spark unit. Refer to **Figure 10A** or **Figure 10B** for a diagram of the ignition circuit.

All models are equipped with a solid state capacitor discharge ignition (CDI) system that uses no breaker points. This system provides a longer component life than breaker-point ignitions and delivers a more efficient spark throughout the entire speed range of the engine. Ignition timing is fixed with no means of adjustment. If ignition timing is incorrect, it is due to a faulty unit within the ignition system. Direct current charges the capacitor. As the piston approaches the firing position, a pulse from the pulse generator coil triggers the silicone controlled rectifier. The rectifier in turn allows the capacitor to discharge quickly into the primary circuit of the ignition coil, where the voltage is stepped up in the secondary

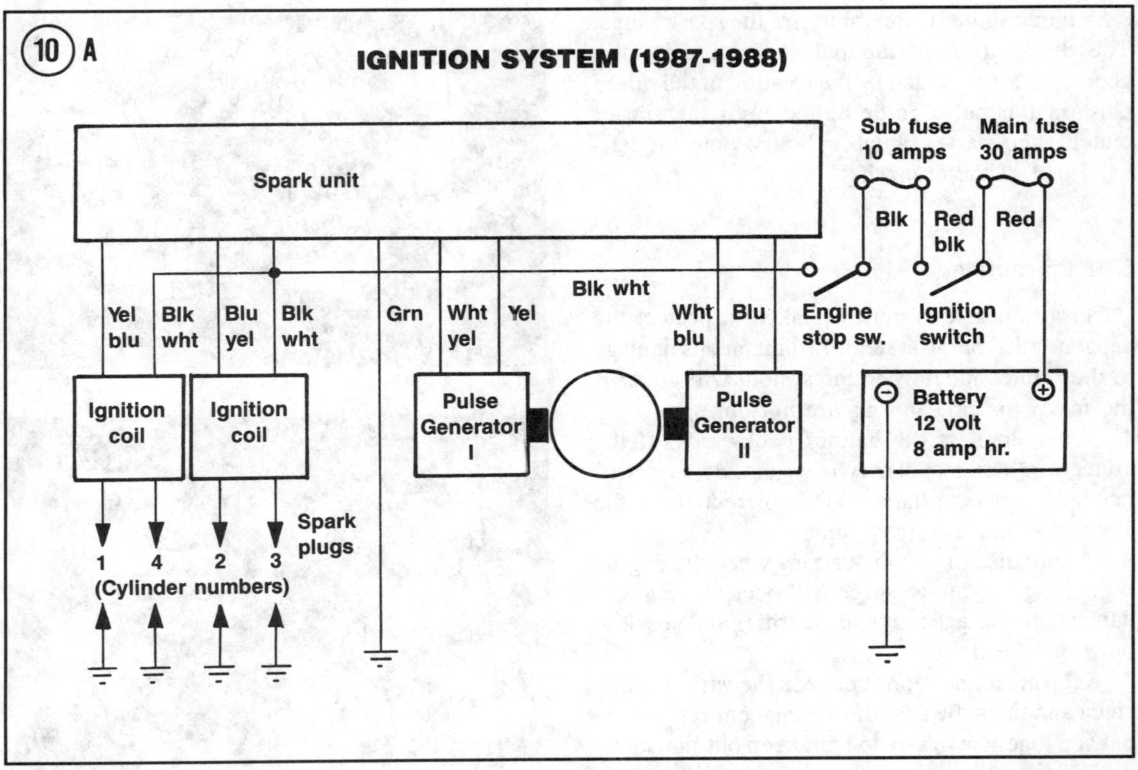
10 A
IGNITION SYSTEM (1987-1988)
Spark unit
Sub fuse
10 amps
Main fuse
30 amps
Blk
Red
blk
Red
Blk wht
Yel
blu
Blk
wht
Blu
yel
Blk
wht
Grn
Wht
yel
Yel
Wht
blu
Blu
Engine
stop sw.
Ignition
switch
Ignition
coil
Ignition
coil
Pulse
Generator
I
Pulse
Generator
II
Battery
12 volt
8 amp hr.
Spark
plugs
1 4 2 3
(Cylinder numbers)

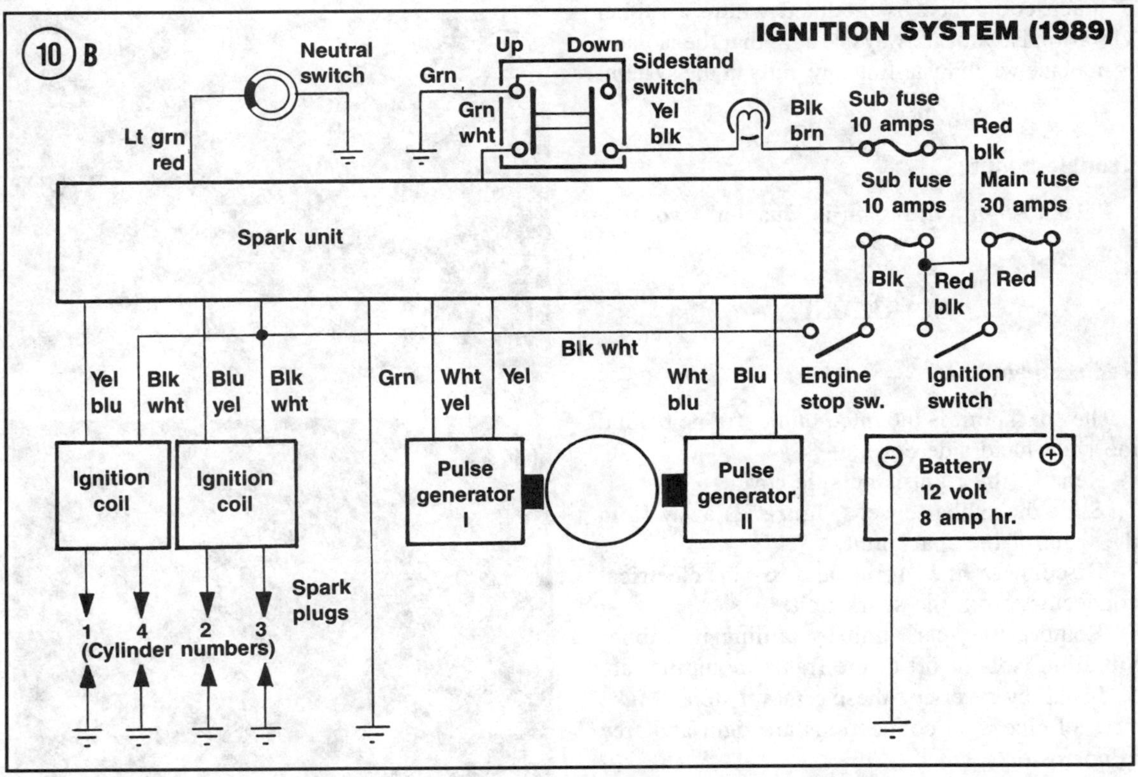
10 B
IGNITION SYSTEM (1989)
Neutral
switch
Up
Down
Sidestand
switch
Grn
Grn
wht
Yel
blk
Blk
brn
Lt grn
red
Sub fuse
10 amps
Red
blk
Sub fuse
10 amps
Main fuse
30 amps
Spark unit
Blk
Red
blk
Red
Blk wht
Yel
blu
Blk
wht
Blu
yel
Blk
wht
Grn
Wht
yel
Yel
Wht
blu
Blu
Engine
stop sw.
Ignition
switch
Ignition
coil
Ignition
coil
Pulse
generator
I
Pulse
generator
II
Battery
12 volt
8 amp hr.
Spark
plugs
1 4 2 3
(Cylinder numbers)

8

circuit to a value sufficient to fire the spark plugs. The distribution of the pulses from the pulse generator is controlled by the rotation of the raised tabs on the pulse rotor bolted onto the starter clutch. The starter clutch is bolted onto the left-hand end of the crankshaft.

CDI Precautions

Certain measures must be taken to protect the capacitor discharge system. Instantaneous damage to the semiconductors in the system will occur if the following precautions are not observed.

1. Never connect the battery backwards. If the connected battery polarity is wrong, damage will occur to the voltage regulator/rectifier, the alternator and the spark units.

2. Do not disconnect the battery when the engine is running. A voltage surge will occur which will damage the voltage regulator/rectifier and possibly burn out the lights.

3. Keep all connections between the various units clean and tight. Be sure the wiring connections are pushed together firmly to help keep out moisture.

4. Do not substitute another type of ignition coil.

5. Each component is mounted within a rubber vibration isolator. Always be sure that the isolator is in place when installing any units in the system.

Troubleshooting

Refer to *Ignition System* in Chapter Two.

SPARK UNIT

Replacement

The spark unit is mounted on the frame behind the right-hand side cover.

1. Remove the right-hand side cover.

2. Slide the rubber cover (**Figure 11**) away from the front of the spark unit.

3. Disconnect the 4-pin and 6-pin electrical connectors from the spark unit.

4. Remove the spark unit by pulling its rubber vibration isolator off of the frame mounting tab.

5. Install by reversing these removal steps. Make sure all electrical connections are tight and free of corrosion.

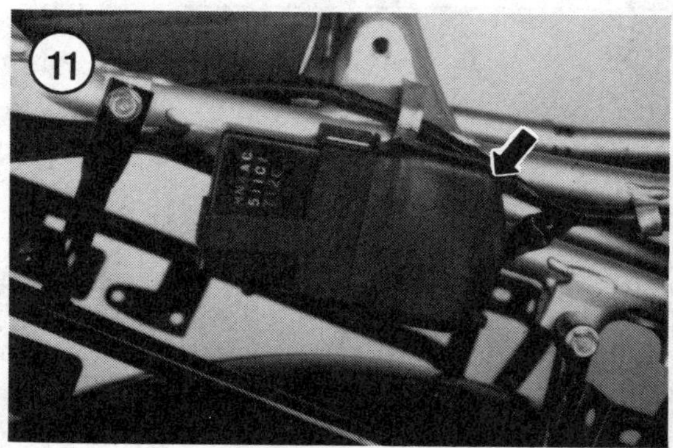

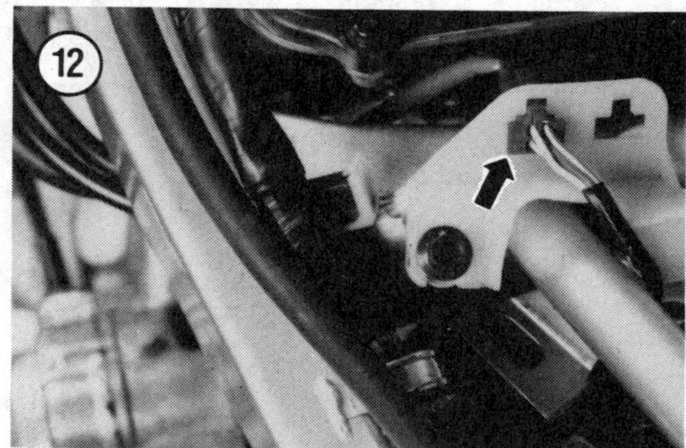

IGNITION COIL

There are 2 ignition coils; one fires the plugs for the No. 1 and No. 4 cylinders and the other fires the plugs for the No. 2 and No. 3 cylinders.

The ignition coil is a form of transformer which develops the high voltage required to jump the spark plug gap. The only maintenance required is that of keeping the electrical connections clean and tight and occasionally checking to see that the coils are mounted securely.

Removal/Installation

1. Remove the seat and fuel tank.

2. Label and disconnect the spark plug leads.

3. Disconnect the primary terminals from both coils. The No. 1 and No. 4 coil wires are yellow/blue and black/white. The No. 2 and No. 3 coil wires are blue/yellow and black/white.

4. Remove the bolts securing the ignition coils to the frame and remove both coils.

5. Install by reversing these removal steps; note the following.
6. Make sure all electrical connections are tight and free of corrosion.
7. Make sure to reconnect the wires to the primary terminals as described in Step 3.
8. Route the spark plug wires to the correct cylinders.

PULSE GENERATOR

Removal/Installation

1. Remove the side covers and seat as described in Chapter Thirteen.
2. Remove the battery cover and disconnect the negative battery lead.
3. Remove the fuel tank as described in Chapter Seven.
4. Remove the left-hand side lower fairing as described in Chapter Thirteen.
5. Drain the engine oil as described in Chapter Three.
6. Disconnect the pulse generator 4-pin connector (**Figure 12**). Pull the wires and connector out of the frame so that they hang free.
7. Remove the bolts securing the left-hand crankcase cover (**Figure 13**) and remove the cover and gasket. Remove the dowel pin (**Figure 14**) if it is loose. It is not necessary to remove the dowel pin if it is secure.
8. Remove the Allen bolts (A, **Figure 15**) securing the pulse generators and the wire harness guide.
9. Carefully pull the rubber grommet (**Figure 16**) and electrical wires from the left-hand crankcase cover and remove the pulse generators (B, **Figure 15**).
10. Install by reversing these removal steps, noting the following.
11. Insert the rubber grommet (**Figure 16**) into the left-hand crankcase so that it seats fully.
12. Apply Loctite 242 (blue) to the pulse generator Allen bolts prior to installation. Tighten the bolts securely.
13. Make sure the pulse generator wires are routed correctly. Reconnect the connector (**Figure 12**).
14. Make sure the dowel pin is installed (**Figure 14**), then install a new left-hand crankcase gasket.
15. Tighten the crankcase cover bolts securely.
16. Reconnect the 4-pin connector (**Figure 12**).

17. Refill the engine with the recommended viscosity and quantity of engine oil as described in Chapter Three.

STARTING SYSTEM

The starting system consists of the starter motor, starter gears, solenoid and the starter button.

The starting system is shown in **Figure 17A** or **Figure 17B**. When the starter button is pressed, it allows current flow through the solenoid coil. The coil contacts close, allowing electricity to flow from the battery to the starter motor.

CAUTION
Do not operate the starter for more than 5 seconds at a time. Let it rest approximately 10 seconds, then use it again.

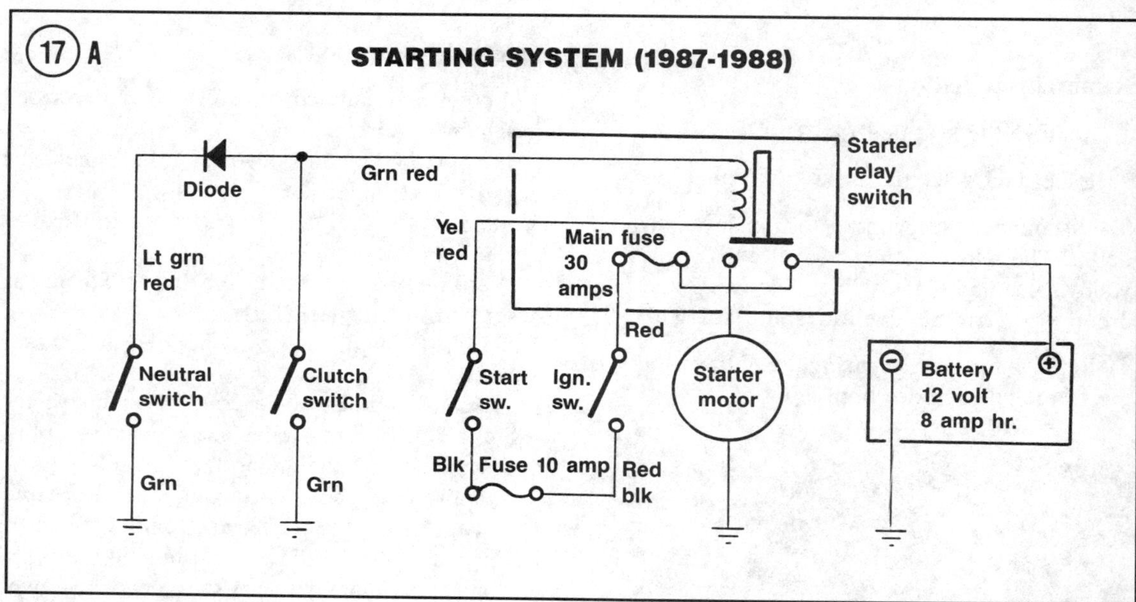

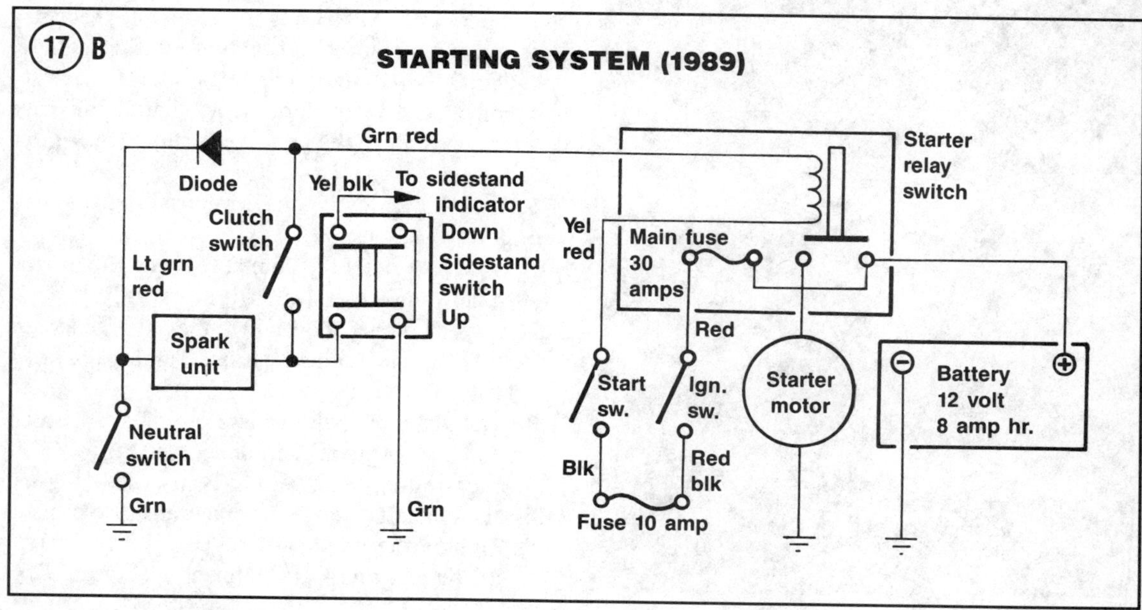

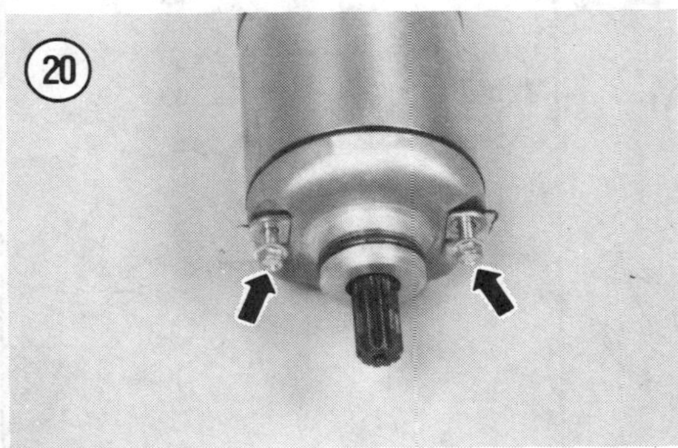

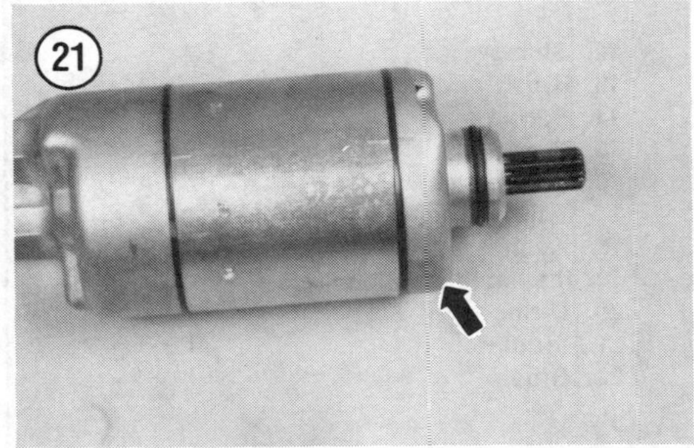

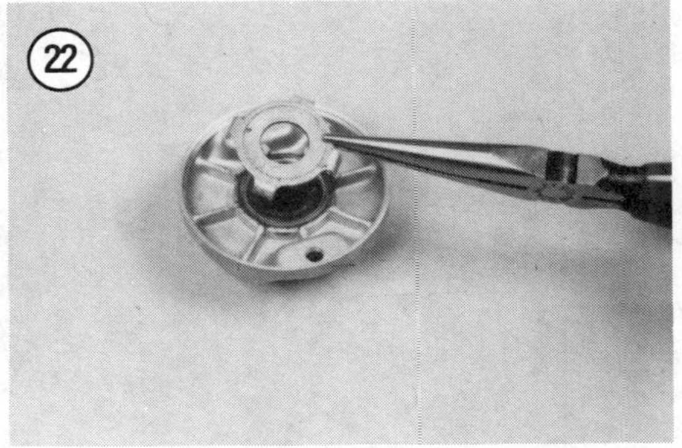

The starter gears and starter clutch assembly are covered in Chapter Four.

Troubleshooting

Refer to *Starting System* in Chapter Two.

Starter
Removal/Installation

1. Remove the side covers and seat.
2. Disconnect the negative battery lead.
3. Remove the left-hand lower fairing as described in Chapter Thirteen.
4. Disconnect the electric starter cable from the starter (**Figure 18**).
5. Remove the bolts securing the starter to the crankcase.
6. Slide the starter towards the right-hand side. Then lift the starter up and remove it.
7. Install by reversing these removal steps. Make sure the electrical wire connection is tight and free of corrosion.

Disassembly/Inspection

Refer to **Figure 19** for this procedure.
1. Loosen the 2 case screws (**Figure 20**). Then remove the screws, lockwashers and flat washers.

> *NOTE*
> *Write down the number of shims used on the shaft next to the commutator. Be sure to install the same number when reassembling the starter.*

2. Slide the front cover (**Figure 21**) off of the armature shaft.
3. Remove the lockwasher (**Figure 22**) from the front cover.
4. Slide the shims (**Figure 23**) off of the armature shaft. Record the number of shims and their location. Store the shims in a marked plastic bag.

> *NOTE*
> *Labeling and storing these shims removed in Step 4 is important because other shims are also used on the opposite side of the armature.*

(19)

STARTER MOTOR

1. Through-bolt
2. Lockwasher
3. Set plate
4. O-ring
5. O-ring
6. Front cover
7. O-ring
8. Case
9. Lockwasher
10. Shims
11. Armature
12. Shims
13. Brush and holder
14. Springs
15. O-ring
16. Rear cover
17. Nuts
18. Washer
19. Insulated washers
20. O-ring
21. Terminal
22. Brush

(23)

(24)

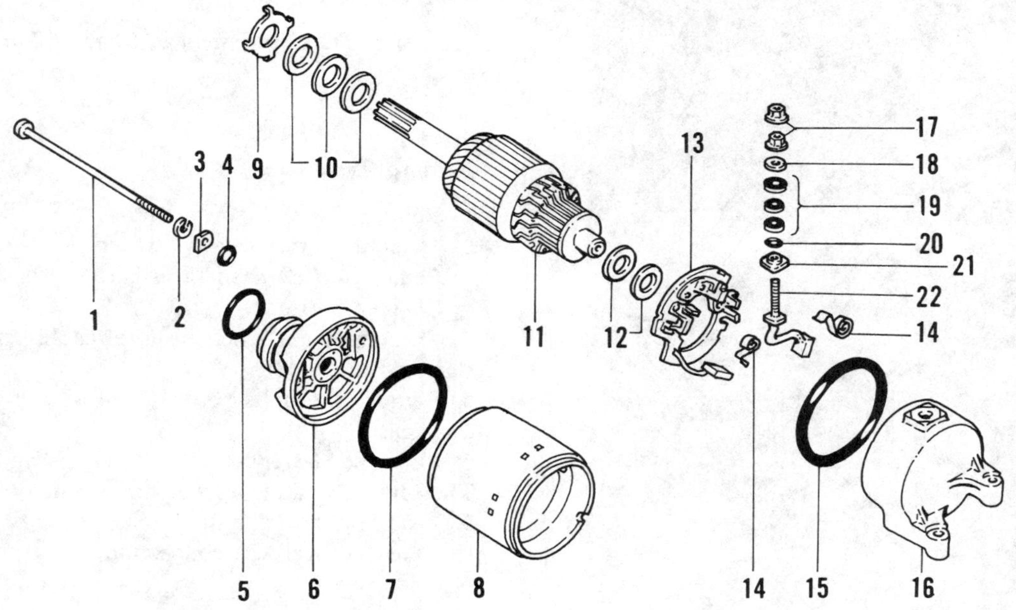

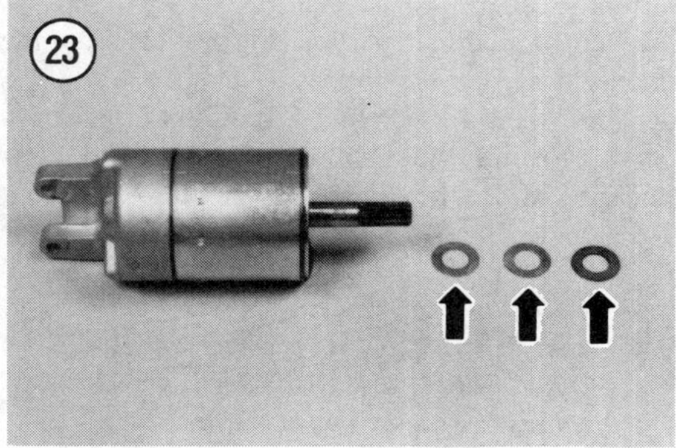

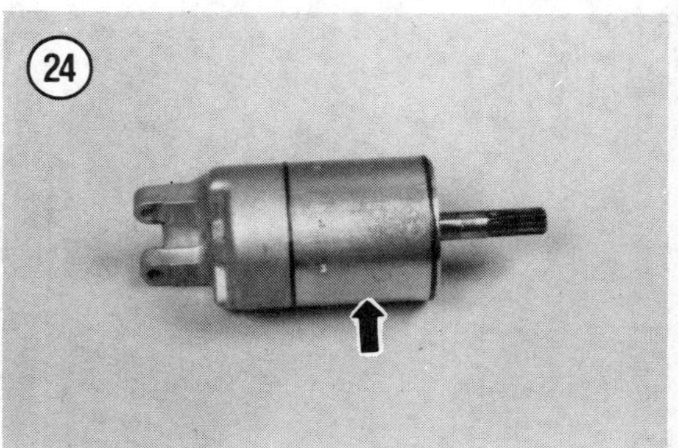

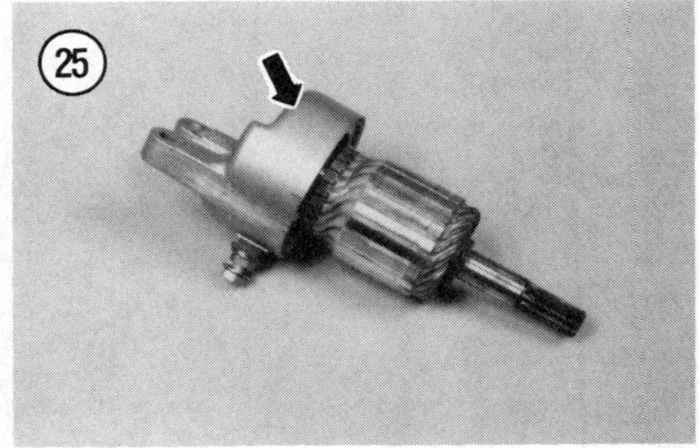

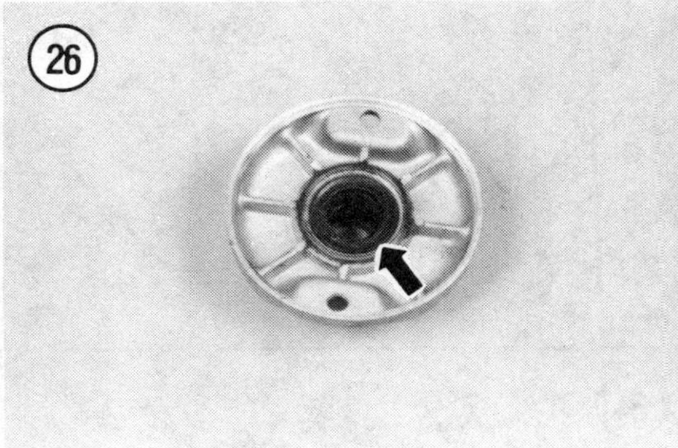

NOTE
The number of shims used in each starter varies. The starter shown in Figure 23 uses 3 shims. Your starter may use a different number of shims.

5. Slide the case (**Figure 24**) off of the armature.
6. Slide the end cover (**Figure 25**) off of the armature.
7. Slide the shims off of the armature shaft. Record the number of shims and their location. Store the shims in a marked plastic bag.
8. Clean all grease, dirt and carbon from the armature, case and end covers.

CAUTION
Do not immerse brushes or the wire windings in solvent as the insulation may be damaged. Wipe the windings with a cloth lightly moistened with solvent and dry thoroughly.

9. Check the dust seal (**Figure 26**) in the front cover for tearing or excessive wear. Replace the seal by prying it out of the front cover with a screwdriver. Work carefully when removing the seal so that you don't damage the front cover. Drive the new seal into the cover with a suitable size socket placed on the outer portion of the seal. Service old and new seals by applying a small amount of grease to the seal lips.
10. Check the 2 case O-rings (**Figure 27**) for wear or deterioration. Replace the O-rings if necessary.
11. Use an ohmmeter and check for continuity between the cable terminal and the end cover case (**Figure 28**); there should be no continuity. Check for continuity between the cable terminal and the brush black wire (**Figure 29**); there should be continuity. If the unit fails either of these tests the brush holder assembly is faulty and must be replaced as described later in this procedure.
12. Pull the brush holder (A, **Figure 30**) out of the end cover and carefully turn it over to expose the brushes (B, **Figure 30**).
13. Pull the spring away from each brush (B, **Figure 30**) and pull the brushes out of their guide.
14. Measure the length of each brush with a vernier caliper (**Figure 31**). If the length is worn to the wear limit specified in **Table 2**, the brush holder assembly must be replaced. The brushes cannot be replaced individually.

15. To replace the brush holder, perform the following:

> *NOTE*
> *The cable terminal assembly (C,*
> ***Figure 30***) *is composed of 3 insulated*
> *washers, a regular washer and nut.*
> *Label each component when removed,*
> *especially the insulated washers, as*

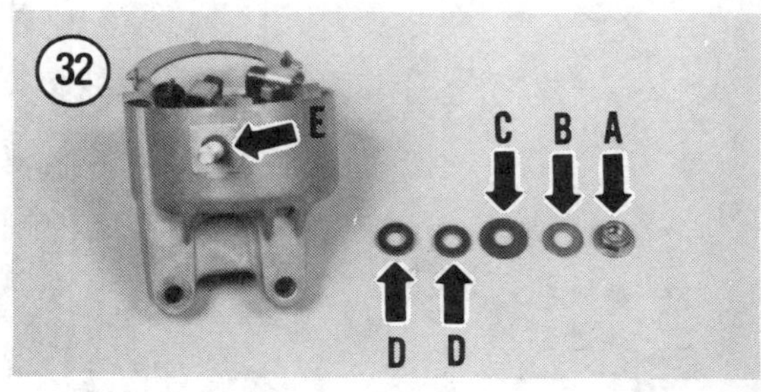

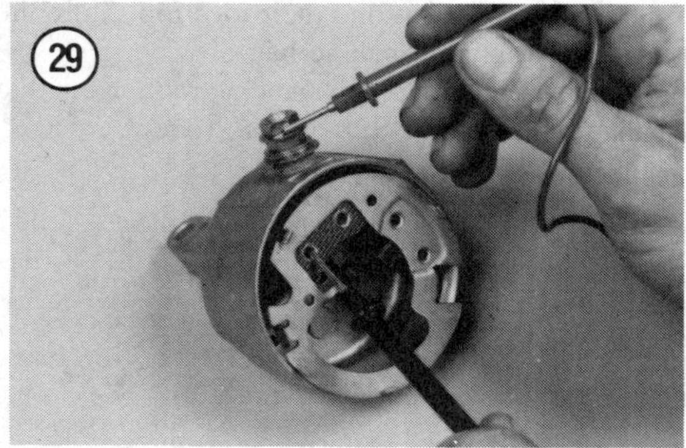

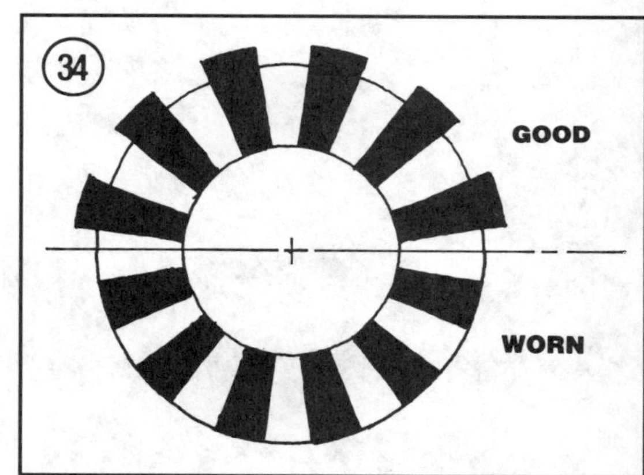

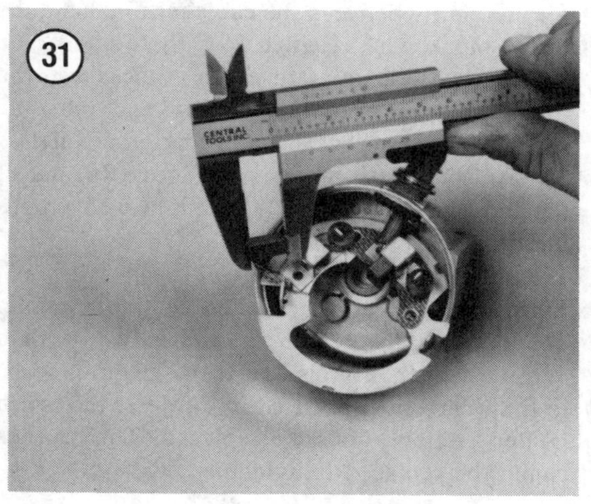

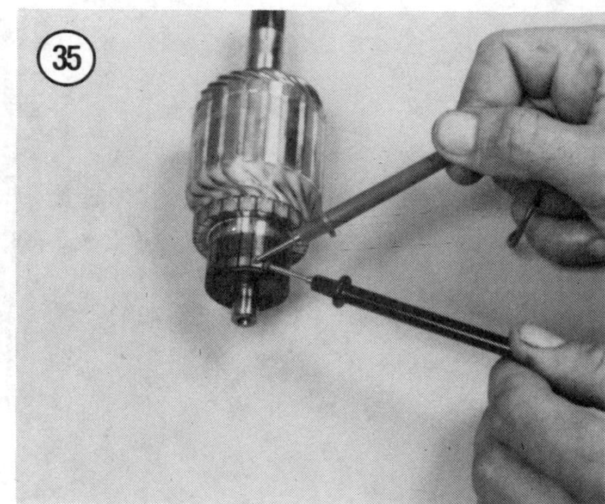

they must be reinstalled in the same order to insulate the brushes from the case.

a. Remove the nut (A, **Figure 32**) from the cable terminal and slide off the regular washer (B, **Figure 32**).

b. See **Figure 32**. Remove the large insulated washer (C) and the 2 small insulated washers (D).

c. Slide the O-ring (E, **Figure 32**) off of the cable terminal.

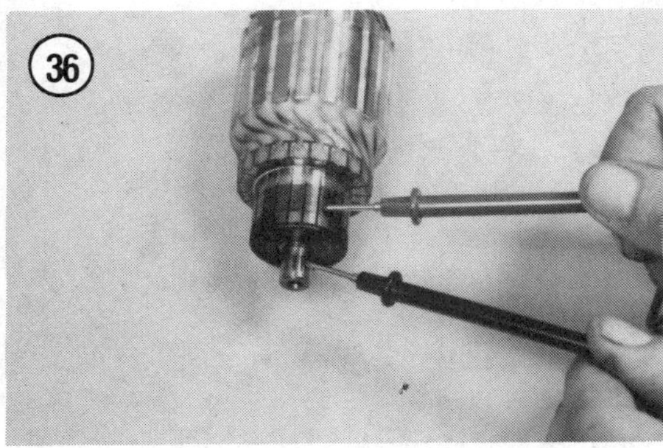

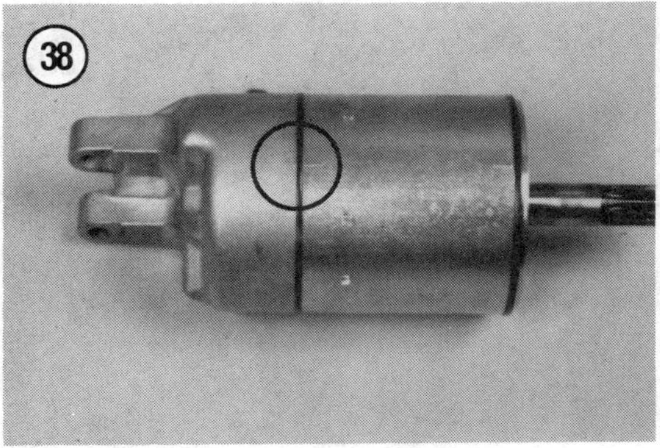

d. Push the cable terminal into the end cover and remove the brush holder assembly.

e. Install a new brush holder assembly by reversing these steps. Make sure to install the nut and washers in their original order.

16. Inspect the commutator (**Figure 33**). The mica in a good commutator is below the surface of the copper bars. On a worn commutator the mica and copper bars may be worn to the same level. See **Figure 34**. If necessary, have the commutator serviced by a dealer or electrical repair shop.

17. Inspect the commutator copper bars (**Figure 33**) for discoloration. If a pair of bars are discolored, grounded armature coils are indicated.

18. Use an ohmmeter and check for continuity between the commutator bars (**Figure 35**); there should be continuity between pairs of bars. Also check for continuity between the commutator bars and the shaft (**Figure 36**); there should be no continuity. If the unit fails either of these tests the armature is faulty and must be replaced.

19. Replace worn or damaged parts as determined by these tests.

Assembly

1. Insert the brushes (B, **Figure 30**) into their holders and secure the brushes with the springs.

2. When the brushes are installed, install the brush holder. Align the tab on the brush holder with the notch in the rear cover and install the brush holder. **Figure 37** shows the brush holder properly installed. The arrow in **Figure 37** shows the tab and notch alignment.

3. Install the correct number of shims on the armature shaft next to the commutator.

4. Insert the armature into the end cover (**Figure 25**). Turn the armature during installation so that the brushes engage the commutator properly. Make sure the armature is not turned upside down so that the shims could slide off the end of the shaft.

5. Make sure the 2 O-rings are installed on the case (**Figure 27**). Then slide the case over the armature (**Figure 24**). Align the mark on the case and end cover (**Figure 38**).

6. Install the correct number of shims on the armature shaft (**Figure 23**).

7. Install the lockwasher (**Figure 22**) onto the front cover so that the lockwasher tabs engage the cover slots as shown in **Figure 39**.

8. Slide the front cover (A, **Figure 40**) over the armature shaft. Align the marks on front cover with the case (B, **Figure 40**).

9. Install the through-bolts, flat washers and lockwashers (**Figure 20**). Tighten the bolts securely.

10. Replace the front cover O-ring (A, **Figure 41**) if deteriorated or damaged. Apply clean engine oil to the O-ring.

11. Clean the end cover mounting lugs (B, **Figure 41**) of all dirt and other contamination as they act as the ground for the starter motor.

STARTER RELAY SWITCH

Removal/Installation

The starter relay switch (**Figure 42**) is mounted behind the right-hand side cover.

1. Remove the seat and the right-hand side cover. See Chapter Thirteen.

2. Remove the battery cover and disconnect the negative battery lead.

NOTE
Label the switch wires before disconnecting them in Step 3.

3. Slide off the rubber protective boots and disconnect the electrical wires from the top relay switch terminals.

4. Remove the relay switch from the rubber mounting receptacle on the frame.

5. Install by reversing these removal steps, noting the following.

6. If installing a new relay switch, transfer the fuse holder to the new relay switch.

7. Make sure the electrical connections are tight and free of corrosion.

Testing

1. Check the starter relay switch (**Figure 42**). Turn the ignition switch on and depress the starter switch button on the right-hand handlebar switch. When the starter button is depressed, the starter relay switch should "click" once. If the starter relay switch did not click, perform Step 2.

2. *Voltage check:* Perform the following. A voltmeter is required for this test procedure.

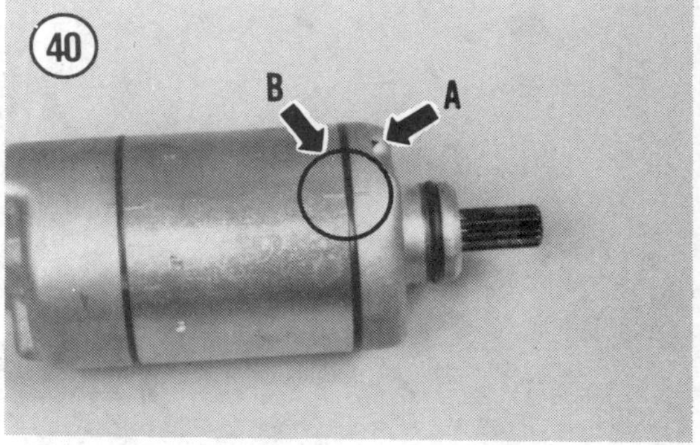

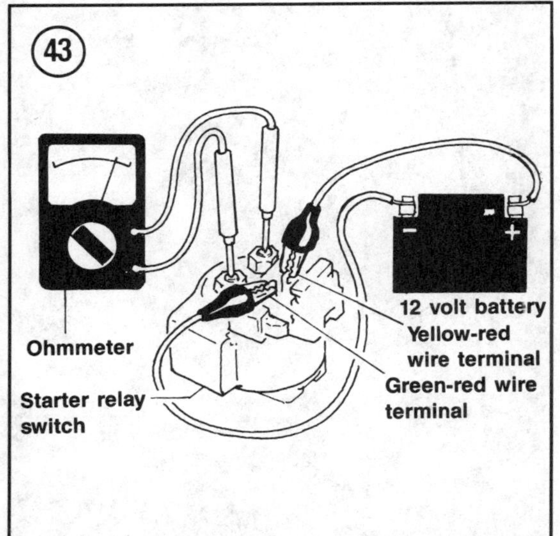

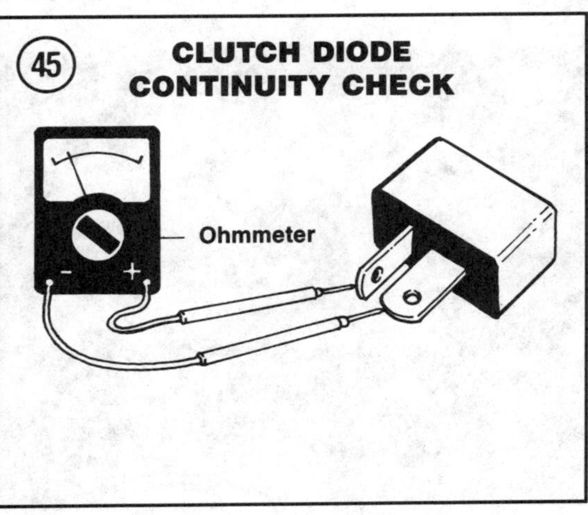

a. At the starter relay switch 4-pin connector, connect a positive voltmeter (+) lead to the yellow/red wire and the negative (−) lead to the green/red wire.

b. Shift the transmission into neutral. On 1989 models, also raise the sidestand to the UP position. Turn the ignition switch on and depress the starter button. The voltmeter should read battery voltage.

c. If the voltmeter reading is correct, perform Step 3. If the voltmeter did not read battery voltage, replace the starter relay switch.

3. *Continuity check:* Perform the following. An ohmmeter and a fully charged 12-volt battery is required for this test.

a. Remove the starter relay switch as described in this chapter.

b. Connect an ohmmeter to the starter relay switch as shown in **Figure 43**.

c. See **Figure 43**. Connect the positive cable from a 12-volt battery to the starter relay switch yellow/red wire terminal and the negative battery cable to the green/red wire terminal.

d. With the battery connected to the starter relay switch as described in sub-step c, the ohmmeter should show continuity (low resistance). Now disconnect the battery from the starter relay switch. The ohmmeter should show no continuity (infinite resistance).

e. Replace the starter relay switch if it failed the test procedures in sub-step d.

CLUTCH DIODE

Testing

1. Remove the fuel tank (see Chapter Seven).
2. Disconnect the clutch diode (**Figure 44**) from the wire harness.
3. See **Figure 45**. Use an ohmmeter and check for continuity between the 2 terminals on the clutch diode. There should be continuity (low resistance) in one direction and no continuity (infinite resistance) with the leads reversed. Replace the diode if it fails this test.

LIGHTING SYSTEM

The lighting system consists of a headlight, taillight/brake light combination, turn signals, indicator lights and meter illumination lights. **Table 4** lists replacement bulbs for these components.

Always use the correct wattage bulb as indicated in this section. The use of a larger wattage bulb will give a dim light and a smaller wattage bulb will burn out prematurely.

Headlight Bulb Replacement

The headlight bulb can be replaced without having to remove any of the fairing assembly. This procedure is shown with the fairing assembly removed for clarity. The headlight is equipped with a quartz halogen bulb. Special handling of the quartz halogen bulb is required as specified in this procedure.

1. Working inside the fairing, disconnect the headlight connector.
2. Pull the rubber cover away from the headlight bulb.

CAUTION
*Carefully read all instructions shipped with the replacement quartz halogen bulb (**Figure 46**). Do not touch the bulb glass with your fingers. Any traces of oil on the glass will drastically reduce the life of the bulb. Clean any traces of oil from the bulb with a cloth moistened in alcohol or lacquer thinner.*

3. Lift the tension spring up (**Figure 47**) and swing toward the left-hand side.
4. Pull the bulb (**Figure 48**) out of the holder.
5. Replace with a new bulb assembly—do not touch the bulb (**Figure 46**) with your fingers.
6. Install the rubber cover so that the TOP mark faces up.
7. Install by reversing these removal steps.
8. Adjust the headlight as described in this chapter.

Headlight Housing
Removal/Installation

1. Remove the upper fairing assembly as described in Chapter Thirteen.
2. Remove the 3 headlight mounting screws (A, **Figure 49**) and remove the headlight assembly.
3. Install by reversing these removal steps, noting the following:

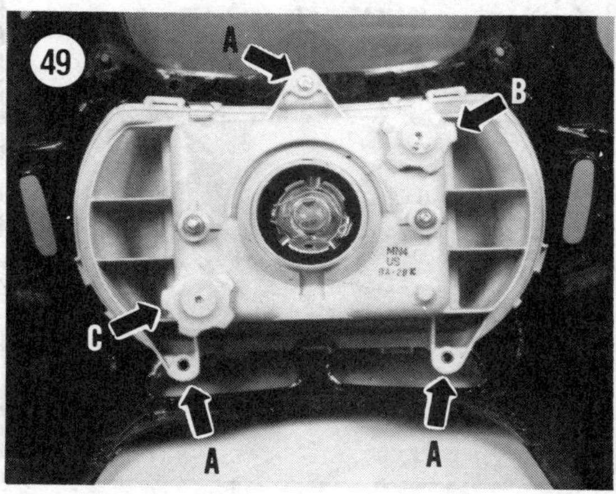

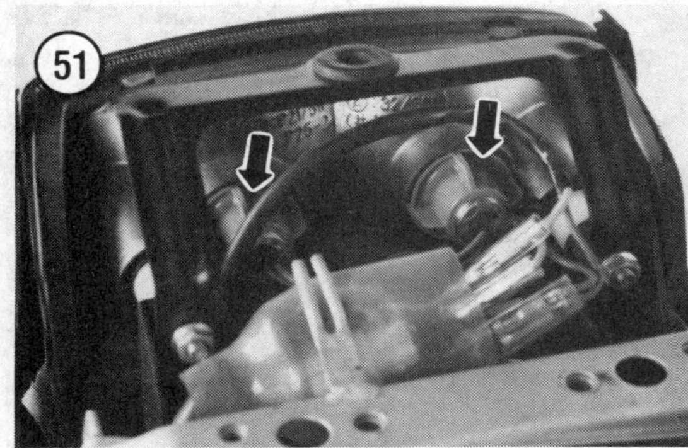

a. Install the rubber cover so that the TOP mark faces up.

b. Check and adjust the headlight as described in this chapter.

Headlight Adjustment

Adjust the headlight horizontally and vertically according to Department of Motor Vehicles regulations in your state.

1. *Vertical adjustment:* Turn the large knob on the right-hand side of the headlight housing (B, **Figure 49**) as required for adjustment. Turning the knob clockwise lowers the beam.

2. *Horizontal adjustment:* Turn the large knob on the left-hand side of the headlight housing (C, **Figure 49**) as required for adjustment. Turning the knob clockwise directs the headlight beam to the right-hand side.

Taillight/Brake Light Replacement

1. Remove the seat.

2. Remove the bolts securing the seat cowling (**Figure 50**) and remove it.

3. Twist the bulb socket and remove it from the housing. See **Figure 51**.

4. Remove the bulb from the socket (**Figure 52**) and replace it.

5. Wipe off all oil or dirt from the bulb before installing the bulb socket into the housing.

6. Repeat for the other bulb if necessary.

7. Install by reversing these steps.

Turn Signal Light Replacement

Front

1. Remove the bulb socket from the rear of the light assembly (**Figure 53**).

2. Remove the bulb from the socket.

3. Reverse to install.

Rear

1. Remove the screws securing the lens and remove the lens (**Figure 54**).

2. Wash the inside and outside of the lens with a mild detergent and wipe dry. Wipe off the reflective base surrounding the bulbs with a soft cloth.

3. Inspect the lens gasket and replace if it is damaged or deteriorated.

4. Replace the bulb (**Figure 55**) and install the lens; do not overtighten the screws as the lens may crack.

License Plate Bulb Replacement

1. Remove the license plate lens.
2. Wash the inside and outside of the lens with a mild detergent and wipe dry.
3. Replace the bulb and install the lens; don't overtighten the screws or the lens may crack.

Instrument Panel Light Replacement

1. Remove the instrument panel as described in this chapter.

> *CAUTION*
> *In the next step do not allow the instruments to remain upside-down any longer than necessary as the needle damping fluid will leak out onto the instrument face and lens.*

2. Turn the instrument cluster upside-down on the workbench on shop cloths to protect the finish.
3. Carefully pull the socket/bulb assembly out of the backside of the housing.
4. Replace the defective bulb(s).
5. Assemble and install by reversing these disassembly steps.

SWITCHES

Switches can be tested for continuity with an ohmmeter (see Chapter One) or a test light at the switch connector plug by operating the switch in each of its operating positions and comparing results with the switch operation. For example, **Figure 56** shows a continuity diagram for a typical horn button. It shows which terminals should show continuity when the horn button is in a given position.

When the horn button is pushed, there should be continuity between terminals light green and white/green. This is indicated by the line on the continuity diagram. An ohmmeter connected between these 2 terminals should indicate little or no resistance and a test lamp should light. When

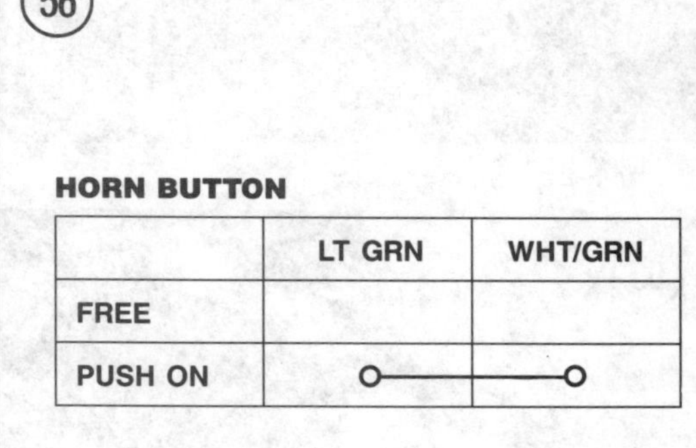

HORN BUTTON

	LT GRN	WHT/GRN
FREE		
PUSH ON	o———	———o

the horn button is free, there should be no continuity between the same terminals.

If the switch or button doesn't perform properly, replace it. Refer to **Figure 56** and **Figure 57** for switch continuity diagrams.

When testing switches, note the following:
a. First check the fuses as described under *Fuses* in this chapter.
b. Check the battery as described under *Battery* in this chapter; bring the battery to the correct state of charge, if required.
c. Disconnect the negative cable from the battery if the switch connectors are not disconnected in the circuit.

CAUTION
Do not attempt to start the engine with the battery negative cable disconnected or you will damage the wiring.

d. When separating 2 connectors, pull on the connector housings and not the wires.

e. After locating a defective circuit, check the connectors to make sure they are clean and properly connected. Check all wires going into a connector housing to make sure each wire is properly positioned and that the wire end is not loose.

---

(57) SWITCHES

TURN SIGNAL SWITCH

	GRN	LT BLU	ORG	BRN/WHT	LT BLU/WHT	ORG/WHT
R	o——	——o		o——	——o
N				o——	——o	——o
L	o——	——o	o——	——o	

IGNITION SWITCH

	RED	RED/BLK	BLU/ORG	BRN/WHT	BRN	YEL/BLK
ON	o——	——o	——o	o——	——o	
OFF						
P (PARK)	o——	——	——	——	——o

STARTER SWITCH

	YEL RED	BLK	BLU WHT	BLK RED
FREE			o——	——o
PUSH ON	o——	——o		

DIMMER SWITCH

	BLU WHT	WHT	BLU
LOW	o——	——o	
(N)	o——	——o	——o
HI	o——	——	——o
	HL	LO	HI

ENGINE STOP SWITCH

	BLK	BLK/WHT
OFF		
RUN	o——	——o

f. To properly connect connectors, push them together until they click into place.

g. When replacing handlebar switch assemblies, make sure the cables are routed correctly so that they are not crimped when the handlebar is turned from side to side.

Ignition Switch
Removal/Installation

NOTE
This procedure is shown with the front fairing assembly removed for clarity. It is not necessary to remove the front fairing assembly when removing the ignition switch.

1. Remove the inner fairing covers as described in Chapter Thirteen.
2. Disconnect the ignition switch 6-pin connector (black) (A, **Figure 58**).
3. Remove the ignition switch mounting bolts and remove the switch (**Figure 59**).
4. Install by reversing these steps. Tighten the ignition switch mounting bolts to the torque specification listed in **Table 3**.

Ignition Switch
Disassembly/Assembly

The ignition switch can be disassembled. Disassembly allows separation of the contact base from the cylinder.
1. Remove the ignition switch as described in this chapter.
2. Cut the wire clamp on the wire harness.
3. Remove the 3 screws at the bottom of the ignition switch assembly.
4. Separate the contact base from the cylinder.
5. Assemble the ignition switch by reversing these steps. Align the hole in the contact base with the cylinder shaft during assembly.

Engine Stop Switch and Starter Button
Removal/Installation

The engine stop switch and starter button are an integral part of the right-hand switch assembly (**Figure 60**). If either of these switches are faulty the entire switch assembly must be replaced.
1. Remove the right-hand inner cover as described in Chapter Thirteen.

2. Disconnect the engine stop switch connector from the right-hand side (**Figure 61**).

NOTE
Figure 61 shows the upper fairing removed for clarity. It is not necessary to remove the fairing when removing the engine stop switch assembly.

3. Remove the wire clamps that secure the engine stop switch connector harness to the frame and fairing.
4. Remove the screws securing the switch/throttle housing (**Figure 60**) to the right-hand handlebar.
5. Open the switch housing and disconnect the throttle cables.
6. Remove the engine stop switch assembly and its wire harness from the motorcycle.

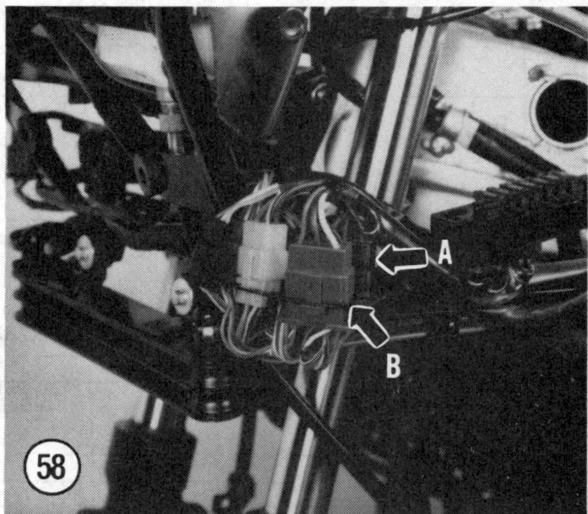

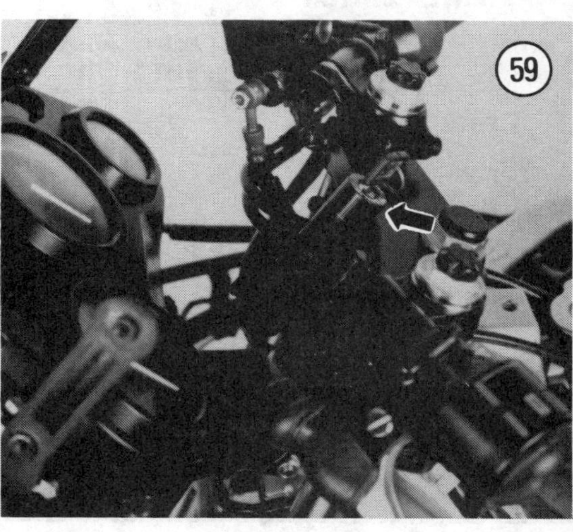

7. Install a new switch by reversing these removal steps. Make sure all electrical connections are tight and free of corrosion.

Sidestand Switch (1989 Models) Testing/Replacement

The sidestand switch allows the ignition circuit to be completed only with the sidestand in the UP position. If the sidestand is down you will be unable to start the engine.

Preliminary test

If the sidestand switch passes this test, the switch is operating correctly. If it does not pass, proceed to the next test.
1. Sit on the bike and raise the sidestand.
2. Start the engine with the transmission in NEUTRAL.
3. Shift the transmission into gear with the clutch lever applied.
4. Move the sidestand all the way down.
5. The engine should stop as the sidestand is lowered.

Testing

1. Remove the fuel tank as described in Chapter Seven.
2. Disconnect the 3-pin electrical connector (containing 3 wires—1 green, 1 green/white and 1 yellow/black).
3. Use an ohmmeter and check for continuity between the following terminals:
   a. Sidestand in the UP position: check between the green/white and green wire terminal. There should be no continuity (infinite resistance).
   b. Sidestand in the UP position: check between the yellow/black and green wire terminal. There should be continuity (low resistance).
   c. Sidestand in the DOWN position: check between the green/white and green wire terminal. There should be continuity (low resistance).
   d. Sidestand in the DOWN position: check between the yellow/black and green wire terminal. There should be no continuity (infinite resistance).
4. If the switch fails any of these tests the switch must be replaced.
5. Reconnect the 3-pin electrical connector.
6. Install the fuel tank as described in Chapter Seven.

Replacement

1. Remove the fuel tank as described in Chapter Seven.
2. Disconnect the 3-pin electrical connector (containing 3 wires—1 green, 1 green/white and 1 yellow/black).
3. Remove the screws securing the sidestand switch to the frame.
4. Carefully pull the switch wire harness out from the frame and remove the switch.
5. Install by reversing these removal steps, noting the following.
6. Make sure the electrical connector is tight and free of corrosion.

Headlight Dimmer Switch, Horn Button and Turn Signal Switch Removal/Installation

The headlight dimmer switch, horn button and turn signal switch are an integral part of the left-hand switch assembly (**Figure 62**). If any one switch is faulty the entire switch assembly must be replaced.

1. Remove the left-hand inner cover as described in Chapter Thirteen.
2. Disconnect the left-hand switch connector (B, **Figure 58**).

> *NOTE*
> ***Figure 58*** *shows the upper fairing removed for clarity. It is not necessary to remove the fairing to remove the switch assembly.*

3. Remove the wire clamps that secure the switch connector harness to the frame and fairing.
4. Remove the screws securing the switch housing (**Figure 62**) to the left-hand handlebar.
5. Remove the left-hand switch assembly and electrical wires from the frame.
6. Install a new switch by reversing these removal steps. Make sure all electrical connections are tight and free of corrosion.

Clutch Switch
Testing/Replacement

1. Disconnect the electrical wires (**Figure 63**) from the clutch switch.
2. Use an ohmmeter and check for continuity between the 2 terminals on the clutch switch. There should be no continuity (infinite resistance) with the clutch lever released. With the clutch lever applied there should be continuity (low resistance). If the switch fails either of these tests the switch must be replaced.
3. Remove the screw securing the clutch switch and remove the clutch switch.
4. Install a new switch by reversing these removal steps. Make sure all electrical connections are tight and free of corrosion.

Front Brake Light Switch
Testing/Replacement

1. Disconnect the electrical wires to the brake light switch (**Figure 64**).
2. Use an ohmmeter and check for continuity between the 2 terminals on the brake light switch. There should be no continuity (infinite resistance) with the brake lever released. With the brake lever

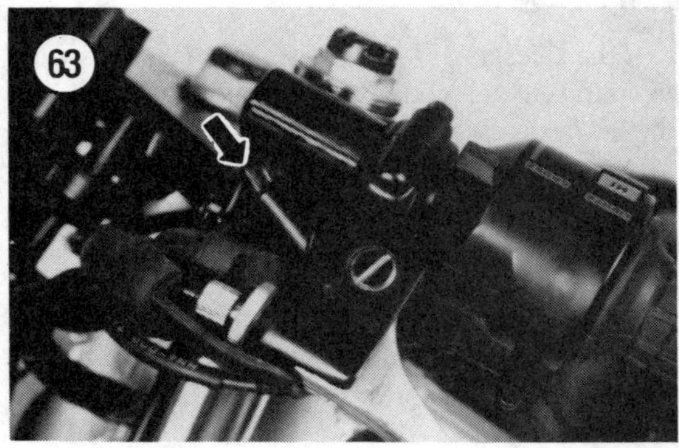

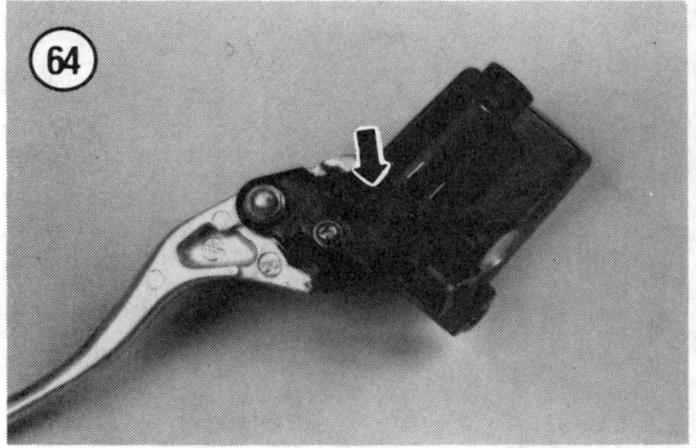

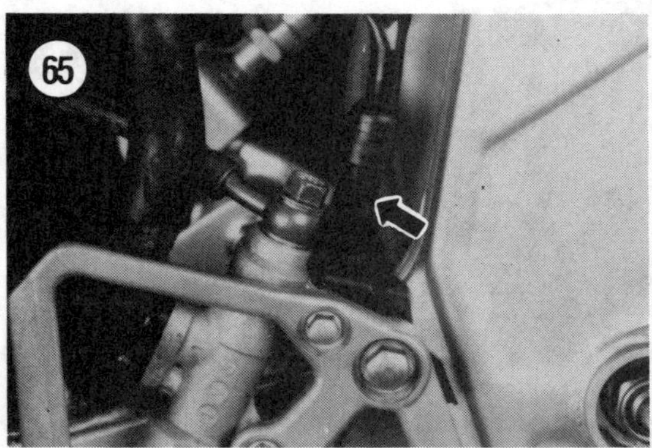

applied there should be continuity (low resistance). If the switch fails either of these tests the switch must be replaced.

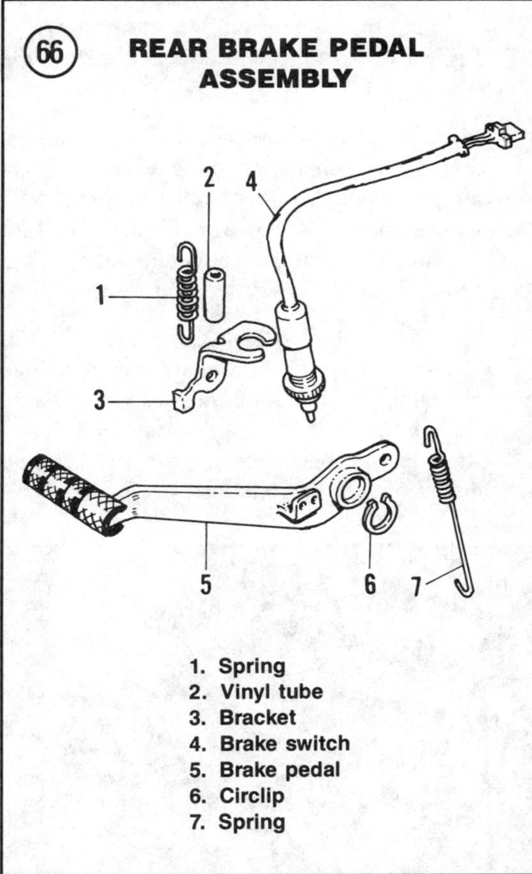

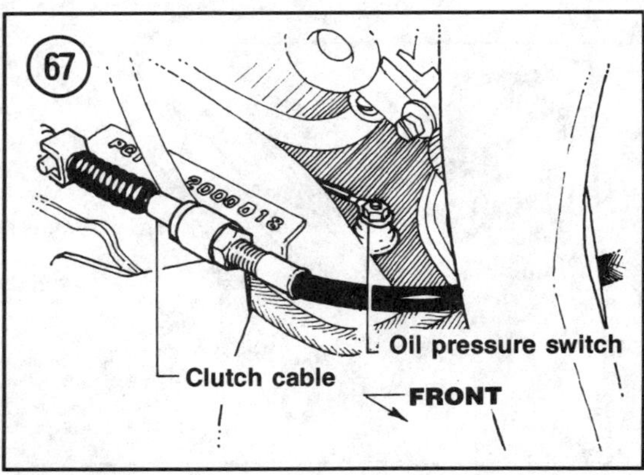

for clarity. It is not necessary to remove the master cylinder to remove the brake switch.

3. Remove the screw securing the brake switch and remove the brake switch (**Figure 64**) from the brake master cylinder.

4. Install a new switch by reversing these removal steps. Make sure all electrical connections are tight and free of corrosion.

**Rear Brake Light Switch
Testing/Replacement**

1. Disconnect the electrical wires to the rear brake light switch. **Figure 65** shows the rear brake light switch.

2. Use an ohmmeter and check for continuity between the 2 terminals on the brake light switch. There should be no continuity (infinite resistance) with the brake pedal released. With the brake pedal down or applied there should be continuity (low resistance). If the switch fails either of these tests the switch must be replaced.

3. Remove the rear brake pedal mounting bracket as described in Chapter Twelve.

4. Unhook the return spring and unscrew the locknut (**Figure 66**) securing the rear brake light switch to the mounting tab. Remove the switch from the frame.

5. Install a new switch by reversing these removal steps, noting the following.

6. Make sure all electrical connections are tight and free of corrosion.

7. Adjust the switch as described under *Rear Brake Light Switch Adjustment* in Chapter Three.

**Oil Pressure Switch
Testing/Replacement**

1. Remove the right-hand lower fairing as described in Chapter Thirteen.

2. Remove the terminal screws and disconnect the oil pressure switch wire at the switch (**Figure 67**).

3. Connect a jumper wire from the oil pressure switch wire to ground.

4. Turn the ignition switch to ON. The oil pressure switch light should come on. Interpret results as follows:

    a. *Light did not come on:* Check the fuse and the oil pressure light bulb. Then check the wires for a loose connection or an open circuit.

    b. *Light came on:* Start the engine and make sure the light goes off. If the light does not go out, check the oil pressure as described in Chapter Four under *Oil Pump*.

5. If necessary, replace the oil pressure switch as follows:

    a. Unscrew and remove the oil pressure switch (**Figure 67**).

    b. Apply a non-hardening gasket sealer to the switch threads.

    c. Install the switch and tighten to the torque specification in **Table 3**.

    d. Attach the electrical wire. Make sure the connection is tight and free from oil.

Thermostatic Switch Testing/Replacement

The thermostatic switch controls the radiator cooling fan according to engine coolant temperature.

> *NOTE*
> *If the cooling fan is not operating correctly, make sure that one of the fuses has not blown before starting this test. There is no specific fuse for the fan, so check all fuses. Also clean off any rust or corrosion from the electrical terminals on the thermostatic switch.*

If the fan does not run, perform the following.

1. Remove the left-hand maintenance cover (Chapter Thirteen).

2. Disconnect the electrical wire from the back of the thermostatic switch located on the lower left-hand side of the radiator. See **Figure 68**.

3. Place a jumper wire between the thermostatic switch wire and ground.

4. Turn the ignition switch on; the cooling fan should start running.

5. If the fan now runs, perform Step 6. If the fan does not run, check for battery voltage between the fan motor connector black/blue and green wires with the ignition switch turned on. If there is no voltage, check for a blown fuse, loose connectors or an open circuit.

6. Check the thermostatic switch as follows:

    a. Drain the cooling system as described in Chapter Three.

    b. Remove the thermostatic switch (**Figure 68**) from the radiator.

    c. Place the thermostatic switch in a pan filled with a 50:50 mixture of antifreeze and water. Suspend the switch with a rod as shown in **Figure 69** so that the coolant is below the switch threads.

    d. Place a thermometer in the pan (use a cooking thermometer that is rated higher than the test temperature). Check switch continuity with an ohmmeter as shown in **Figure 69**. With the coolant mixture at room temperature, the switch should have no continuity (infinity).

    e. Heat the coolant to 208-216° F (98-102° C). The switch should show continuity. Continue to heat the coolant for 3 minutes to make sure the continuity reading is maintained.

    f. Replace the thermostatic switch if it failed either of the previous test(s).

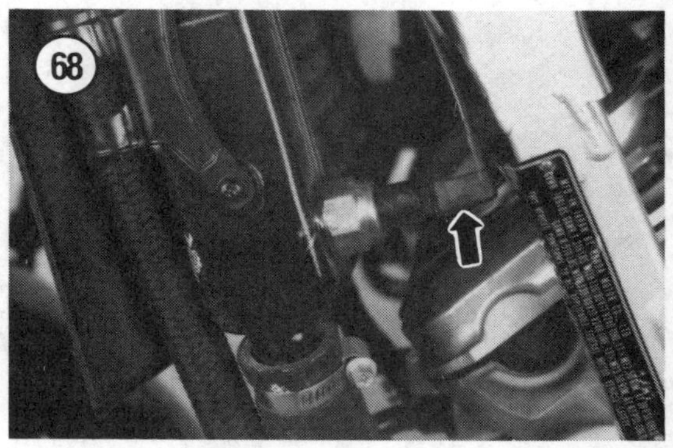

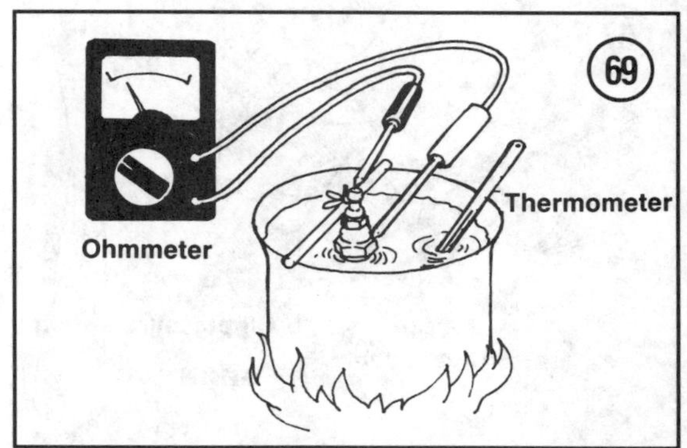

7. Install the thermostatic switch if removed. Apply a non-hardening sealer to the switch threads before installation. Tighten the switch securely.

8. Install all items removed.

9. Refill the cooling system with the recommended type and quantity of coolant. Refer to Chapter Three.

Neutral Switch Testing

1. Remove the fuel tank as described in Chapter Seven.

2. Disconnect the neutral switch light green connector. The connector is located beside the electrical connector junction block on the right-hand side behind the air filter housing. See **Figure 70**.

3. Use an ohmmeter and check for continuity between the light green connector and ground. There should be no continuity (infinite resistance) with the transmission in any gear. With the transmission in NEUTRAL, there should be continuity (low resistance). If the switch fails either of these tests the switch must be replaced. Refer to *Neutral Switch Removal/Installation* in Chapter Six.

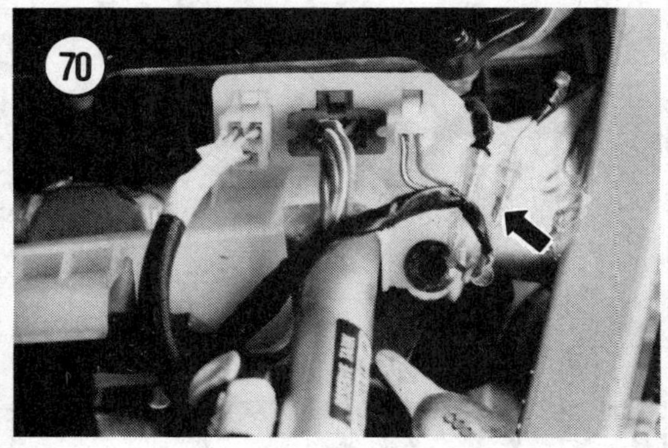

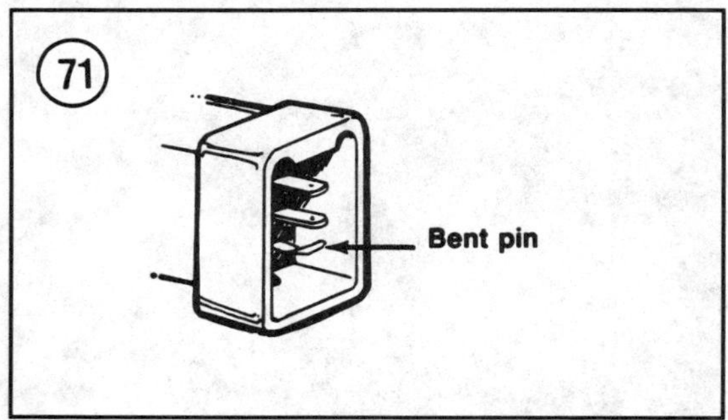

ELECTRICAL COMPONENTS

This section contains information on electrical components other than switches.

Some of the test procedures covered in this section specify taking a meter reading with the electrical connector attached to a specific part. Under these conditions, make sure that the meter test lead has penetrated into the connector and is touching the bare metal wire, *not* the insulation on the wire. If the test lead does not touch the bare metal wire, the readings will be false and may lead to the unnecessary purchase of an expensive electrical part that cannot be returned for a refund. Most dealers and parts houses will not accept any returns on electrical parts.

If you are having trouble with electrical components, these quick preliminary checks may save a lot of time.

    a. Disconnect each electrical connector and check that there are no bent metal pins on the male side of the electrical connector (**Figure 71**). A bent pin will not connect to its mating receptacle in the female end of the connector, causing an open circuit.

    b. Check each female end of the connector. Make sure that the metal connector on the end of each wire (**Figure 72**) is pushed all the way into the plastic connector. If not, carefully push them in with a narrow-blade screwdriver.

    c. Check all electrical wires where they enter the individual metal connector in both the male and female plastic connector.

    d. After all is checked out, push the connectors together and make sure they are fully engaged and locked together (**Figure 73**).

Thermosensor Testing/Replacement

The engine must be cold for this test, preferably not operated for 12 hours.

1. Remove the air filter housing as described under *Carburetor Assembly Removal/Installation* in Chapter Seven.

2. Remove the bolts securing the guard plate (**Figure 74**) to the frame and remove the plate.

3. Loosen the left-hand water hose clamp (**Figure 75**) at the thermostat housing. Then twist the hose slightly and slide it off the thermostat.

NOTE
Figure 76 shows the thermostat housing removed for clarity. The thermostat housing must be installed on the motorcycle and the thermosensor must be installed in the thermostat housing when performing Step 5.

4. Disconnect the electrical connector at the thermosensor (**Figure 76**).

5. Using an ohmmeter, check for continuity between the thermosensor body and ground. There should be continuity. If not, check the thermostat housing for looseness. Tighten the housing and recheck.

WARNING
*To accurately test the thermosensor, the thermosensor is placed in a container of oil that is heated to very high temperatures. Because heated oil is very flammable, make sure to keep the oil away from all open flames. Ideally, the oil could be heated in a container placed on a hot plate. Place the hot plate on a cement floor that is cleared of all newspapers or any other flammable materials. Do not leave the area while performing this test and make sure to turn the hot plate **off** when the test is completed. If you do not feel you can safely perform this test, have it performed by a Honda dealer.*

6. Performance testing of the thermosensor is listed as follows. Make sure to read the previous *WARNING* and read this entire procedure before starting.
   a. Unscrew the thermosensor from the thermostat housing.
   b. Place the thermosensor in a pan filled with new engine oil. Suspend the switch with a rod.
   c. Place a thermometer in the pan (use a cooking thermometer that is rated higher than the test temperature).
   d. Heat the oil and check resistance between the terminal on the thermosensor and ground. As the oil temperature increases, compare to the temperature and resistance values listed in **Table 5**.
   e. If the resistance values do not match those listed in **Table 5**, the thermosensor must be replaced.
   f. Apply a non-hardening sealer to the threads and install the thermosensor. Tighten the thermosensor securely.
   g. Connect the electrical wires to the temperature sensor.
   h. Install all items removed.

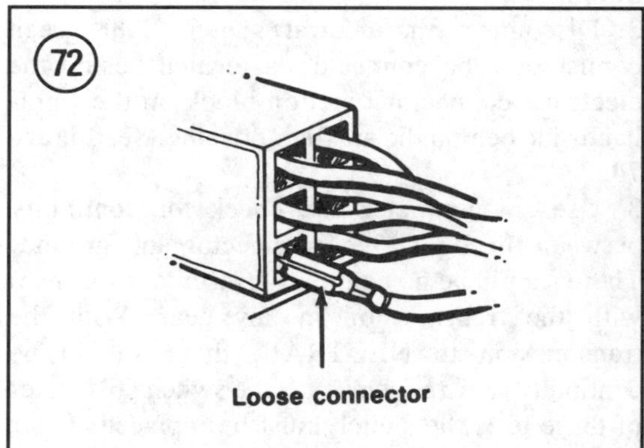

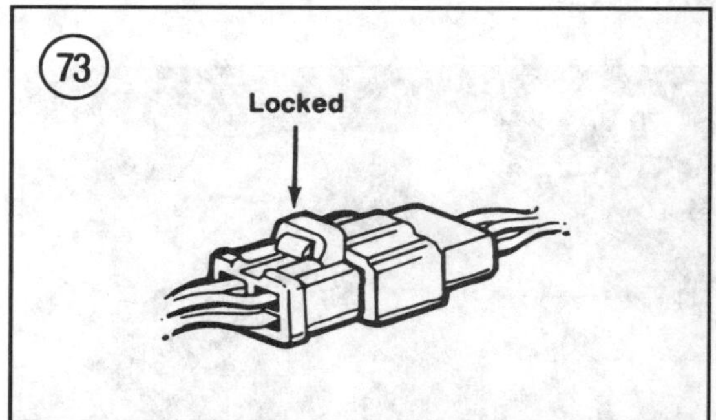

Temperature Gauge Testing

1. Remove the air filter housing as described under *Carburetor Assembly Removal/Installation* in Chapter Seven.
2. Remove the bolts securing the guard plate (**Figure 74**) to the frame and remove the plate.
3. Loosen the left-hand water hose clamp (**Figure 75**) at the thermostat housing. Twist the hose slightly and slide it off the thermostat.

NOTE
Figure 76 shows the thermostat housing removed for clarity. The thermostat housing must be installed on the motorcycle and the thermosensor must be installed in the thermostat housing when performing the following test procedure.

4. Disconnect the electrical wire going to the thermosensor on the thermostat housing.

CAUTION
Do not short the temperature sensor wire to ground for longer than a few seconds or the temperature gauge will be damaged.

5. Run a jumper wire from the electrical connector and short the other end to ground.
6. Turn the ignition switch to ON.
7. When the wire is grounded the gauge needle should move all the way to the right to the "H" position on the gauge face.
8. If the gauge fails the test the gauge must be replaced.
9. Remove the jumper wire and reconnect the thermosensor electrical connector.

Turn Signal Relay Replacement

1. Remove the right-hand side cover.
2. Pull the turn signal relay (**Figure 77**) out of the rubber mount.
3. Transfer the electrical wires to the new relay and install the relay in the rubber mount. Install all parts removed.

Instrument Cluster Removal/Installation

NOTE
The photographs in this procedure show the front fairing removed. The fairing has been removed for clarity; it is not necessary to remove it when removing the instrument cluster.

1. Remove the seat and the side covers.

2. Remove the battery cover and disconnect the negative battery lead.

3. Remove the left- and right-hand inner covers.

4. Remove the instrument panel mounting bolts. **Figure 78** shows 2 of the mounting bolts. There is another mounting bolt between the instrument cluster and the ignition switch.

5. Loosen the speedometer cable knurled nut (**Figure 79**) and pull the cable out of the speedometer housing.

6. Disconnect the instrument cluster 6-pin and 4-pin connectors (**Figure 80**).

> *WARNING*
> *After the instrument cluster has been removed, set the cluster down with the meter face and needles facing upward. If the cluster is set face-down the needle damping fluid will leak out onto the instrument face and lens.*

7. Carefully lift the instrument cluster (**Figure 78**) away from its mounting position on the fairing mount.

8. Install by reversing these removal steps.

Tachometer Testing

If the tachometer is not operating at all or operating erratically, perform this test.

1. Check the fuses as described under *Fuses* in this chapter. If the fuses are okay, perform the following.

2. Remove the front fairing as described in Chapter Thirteen.

> *NOTE*
> *The tachometer terminals described in Step 3 are located directly underneath the tachometer.*

3. Turn the ignition switch to ON. Check the voltage between the black/brown (+) and green (−) tachometer terminals. If there is voltage (12 volts), perform Step 4. If there is no voltage, check the tachometer wires for damaged or loose connections and an open circuit.

4. Test for an open circuit as follows.

  a. Disconnect the negative battery lead.

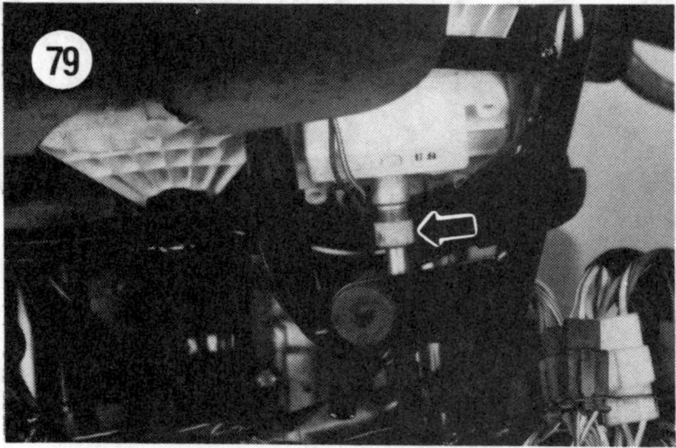

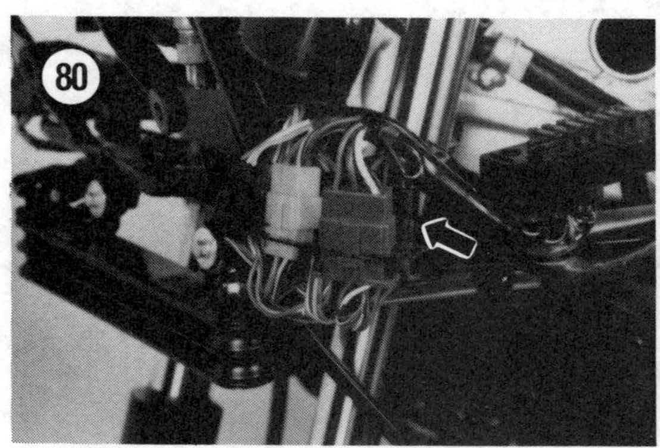

b. Attach one ohmmeter test lead to the tachometer and the other to the 6-pin connector (**Figure 80**). Refer to the wiring diagram at the end of this book for wire colors. The ohmmeter should read low resistance.

c. Remove the right-hand side cover. Attach one ohmmeter test lead to the 6-pin connector (**Figure 80**) and the other test lead to the spark unit 6-pin connector (**Figure 81**). The ohmmeter should read low resistance.

5. Replace the tachometer if the resistance readings in Step 4 are excessive.

Horn Removal/Installation

The horn is mounted underneath the steering stem.

1. Disconnect the electrical connections from the horn.

2. Remove the bolt and remove the horn and its mounting bracket.

3. Install by reversing these removal steps. Make sure the electrical connections are tight and free of corrosion.

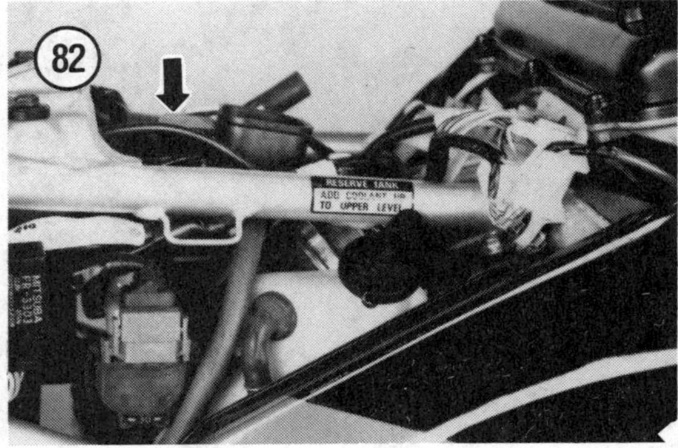

Horn Testing

Remove the horn as described in this chapter. Connect a 12-volt battery to the horn. If the horn is good, it will sound. If not, replace it.

Fuel Pump Testing

Fuel pump flow test

Fuel pump removal and installation is covered in Chapter Seven.

1. Remove the fuel tank as described in Chapter Seven.

2. Turn the ignition switch off.

3. Disconnect the fuel pump relay wire 3-pin connector (**Figure 82**).

4. Connect a jumper wire between the black/blue and black terminals at the fuel pump relay 3-pin connector on the wire harness side.

5. Temporarily install the fuel tank and reconnect the fuel hose. Support the fuel tank with a block of wood so that it doesn't cause the jumper wire to disconnect.

6. Disconnect the outlet fuel line at the fuel pump (**Figure 83**).

NOTE
The outlet fuel line connects the fuel
pump to the carburetors.

7. Connect an auxiliary fuel hose to the fuel pump (same inside diameter as that of the stock hose) that is long enough to reach from the fuel pump to a graduated beaker placed on the ground beside the motorcycle.

8. Place the loose end of the auxiliary fuel hose into a graduated beaker.

9. Turn the ignition switch on and allow the fuel to run out of the fuel hose (into the graduated beaker) for 5 seconds.

10. Turn the ignition off.

11. Multiply the amount of fuel in the beaker by 12 (12 × 5 = 60 seconds). This will give the fuel pump flow capacity for one minute.

12. The fuel pump flow capacity for one minute should be 650 cc (21.9 oz.) per minute.

13. Reconnect the fuel line to the carburetors.

14. Disconnect the jumper wire from the fuel pump relay and reconnect the 3-pin connector (**Figure 82**).

Fuel pump relay check

1. If the fuel pump does not flow to the specified capacity, check the fuel pump circuit as follows.
2. Connect a voltmeter positive lead to the fuel pump relay connector black pin and the negative voltmeter lead to a good engine ground. Turn the ignition switch on. The voltmeter should read battery voltage.
3. Turn the ignition switch off and disconnect the voltmeter leads.
4. Using an ohmmeter, check for continuity at the yellow/blue wire between the fuel pump relay connector and the spark unit.
5. Using an ohmmeter, check for continuity at the black/blue wire between the fuel pump relay connector and the fuel pump.
6. If any test in Steps 2-6 was incorrect, replace or repair damaged wiring.
7. Reconnect the fuel pump relay connector.

FUSES

The fuse box is located on the left-hand fairing underneath the inner fairing cover (**Figure 84**).

The main fuse is located on the starter solenoid (A, **Figure 85**). A spare main fuse is located underneath the starter solenoid (B, **Figure 85**).

Whenever a fuse blows, find out why before replacing the fuse. Usually the trouble is a short circuit in the wiring. This may be caused by worn-through insulation or a disconnected wire shorted to ground.

CAUTION
Never substitute aluminum foil or wire for a fuse. Never use a higher amperage fuse than specified. An overload could cause a fire and complete loss of the motorcycle.

CAUTION
When replacing a fuse, make sure the ignition switch is in the OFF position. This will lessen the chance of a short circuit.

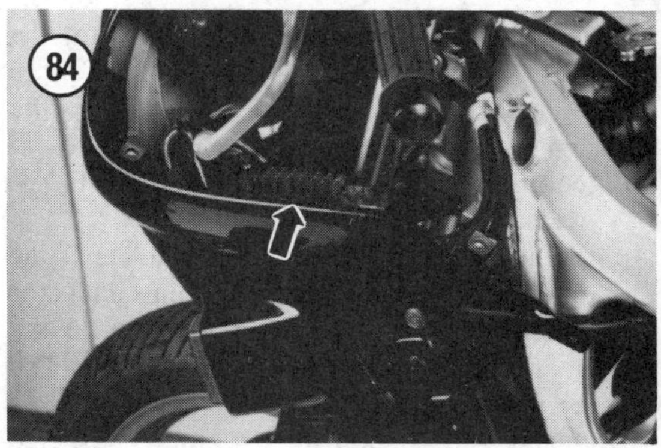

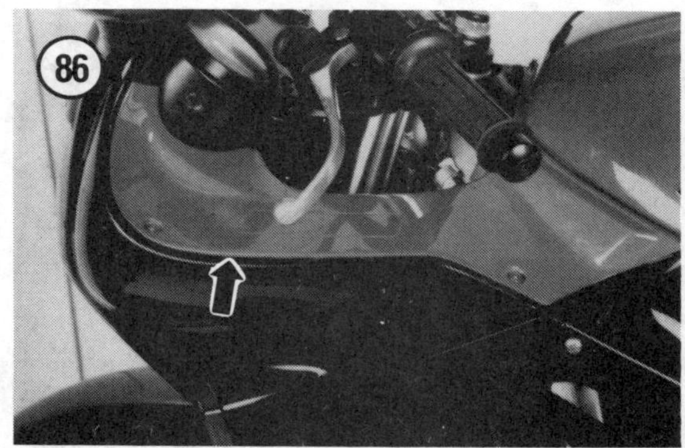

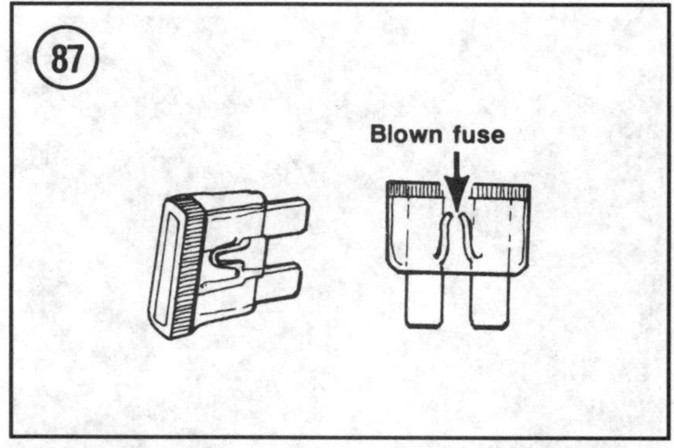

Fuse Replacement

If a fuse in the fuse box blows, perform the following.

1. Remove the screws securing the inner fairing cover (**Figure 86**) and remove the cover.
2. Remove the fuse box cover.
3. Remove the fuse remover from the fuse box.
4. Remove the old fuse by pulling it out of the fuse box (**Figure 84**) with the fuse remover.

NOTE
*These fuses (**Figure 87**) are not the typical glass tube with metal ends. Extra fuses are installed in the fuse box. When replacing a blown fuse, make sure to purchase additional spare fuses as necessary and store them in the fuse box or your bike's tool kit.*

5. Install a new fuse of the correct amperage.
6. Install the fuse box cover and the inner fairing cover.

Main Fuse Replacement

If the main fuse blows, perform the following.

1. Remove the right-hand side cover.
2. Disconnect the connector on top of the starter solenoid (A, **Figure 85**).
3. Remove the old fuse and install a new one.
4. Install the right-hand side cover.

Tables are on the following pages.

8

Table 1 CHARGING SYSTEM SPECIFICATIONS

Battery	
Capacity	12V-8 amp hours
Voltage @ 68° F (20° C)	
Fully charged	13.0-13.2 volts
Requires charging	12.3 volts or less
Charging current	0.9 amps
Charging time	5 hours
Alternator	
Charging coil resistance*	0.1-1.0 ohms
Charging test rpm	1,000 ±100 rpm

* Tests made at 68° F (20° C).

Table 2 STARTER SPECIFICATIONS

	Specification mm (in.)	Wear limit mm (in.)
Starter brush length	12.5 (0.49)	8.5 (0.33)

Table 3 ELECTRICAL SYSTEM TIGHTENING TORQUES

	N•m	ft.-lb.
Ignition switch bolts	25	18
Flywheel bolt	85	61
Starter clutch bolt	85	61
Starter clutch setting socket bolt*	16	12
Pulse generator socket bolt*	5.3	3.8
Oil pressure switch	12	9

* Apply Loctite 242 (blue) to threads before installation.

Table 4 REPLACEMENT BULBS

	Voltage/wattage
Headlight	12V 60/55W
Stop/taillight	12V 32/3cp
Front turn signal/position light	12V 32/3cp
Rear turn signal light	12V 32cp
License light	12V 3cp
Instrument lights	
1987-1988	12V 3W
1989	12V 1.7W
Indicator lights	
1987-1988	12V 3W
1989	12V 3.4W

Table 5 THERMOSENSOR TEST SPECIFICATIONS

Temperature	Test specifications
140° F (60° C)	104 ohms
185° F (85° C)	43.9 ohms
230° F (110° C)	20.3 ohms
248° F (120° C)	16.1 ohms

CHAPTER NINE

LIQUID COOLING SYSTEM

The pressurized cooling system consists of the radiator, water pump, radiator cap, thermostat, electric cooling fan and a coolant reservoir tank. **Figure 1** shows the major components of the liquid cooling system.

The water pump requires no routine maintenance and is replaced as a complete unit if defective. Replacement parts are not available for the unit.

It is important to keep the coolant level to the UP mark on the coolant reservoir tank (**Figure 2**). Check the level with the engine at normal operating temperature and the bike held upright. If the level is low, remove the right-hand side cover and add coolant to the reservoir tank (**Figure 3**), not to the radiator.

CAUTION
*Drain and flush the cooling system at least every 2 years. Refill with a mixture of ethylene glycol antifreeze (formulated for aluminum engines) and distilled water. Do not reuse the old coolant as it deteriorates with use. Do **not** operate the cooling system with only distilled water (even in climates where antifreeze protection is not*

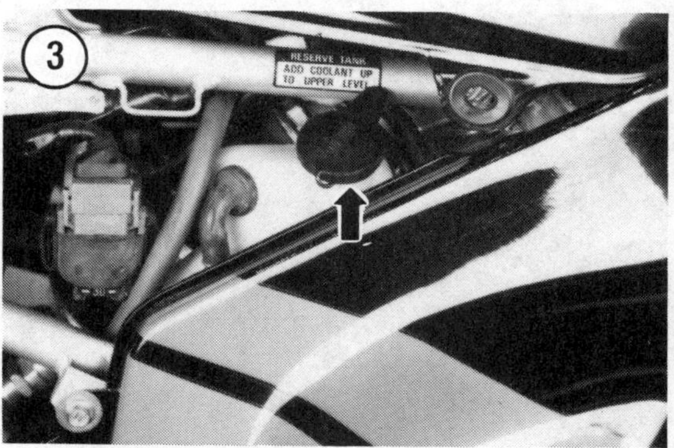

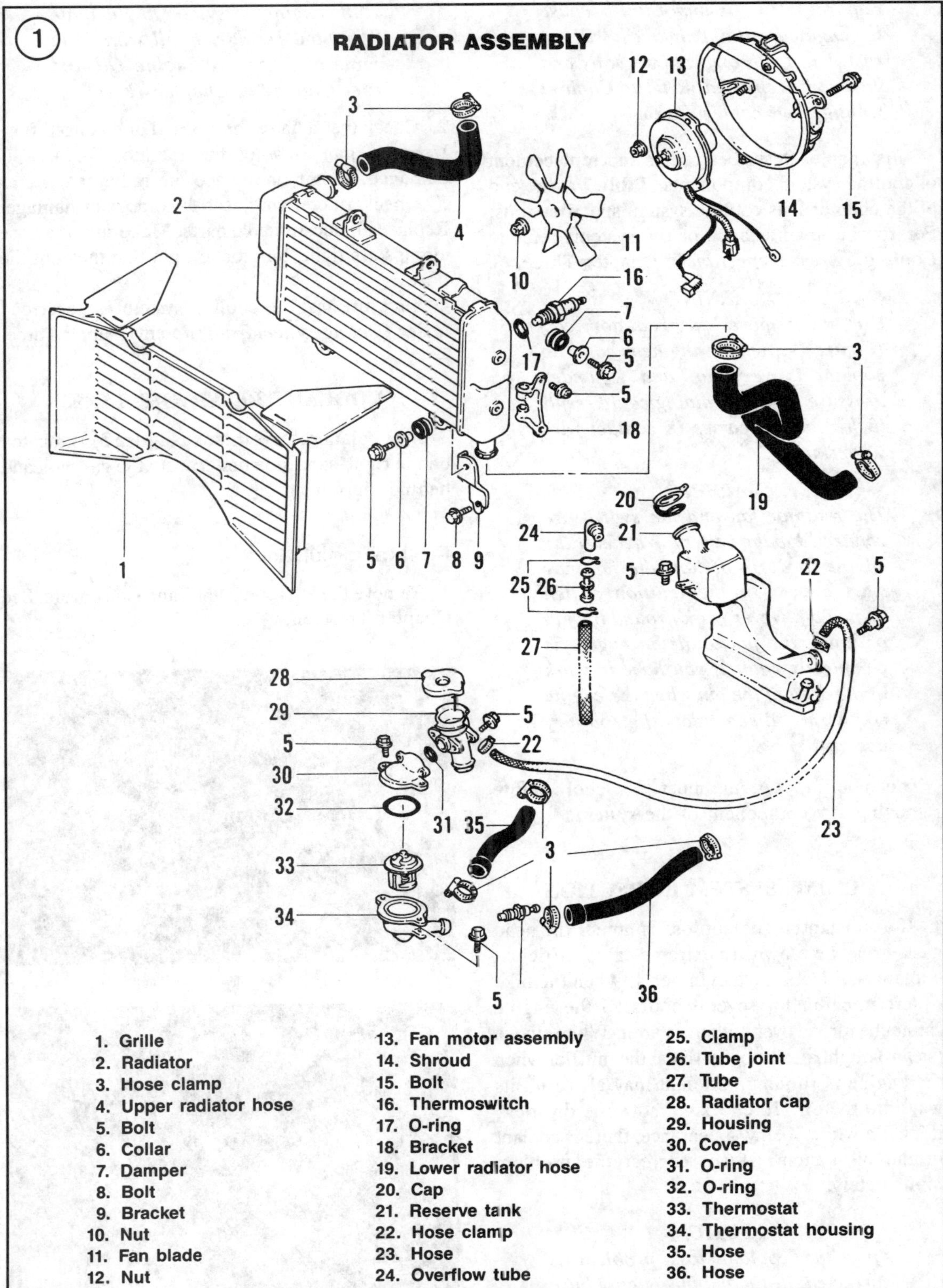

1. Grille	13. Fan motor assembly	25. Clamp
2. Radiator	14. Shroud	26. Tube joint
3. Hose clamp	15. Bolt	27. Tube
4. Upper radiator hose	16. Thermoswitch	28. Radiator cap
5. Bolt	17. O-ring	29. Housing
6. Collar	18. Bracket	30. Cover
7. Damper	19. Lower radiator hose	31. O-ring
8. Bolt	20. Cap	32. O-ring
9. Bracket	21. Reserve tank	33. Thermostat
10. Nut	22. Hose clamp	34. Thermostat housing
11. Fan blade	23. Hose	35. Hose
12. Nut	24. Overflow tube	36. Hose

required). This is important because the engine is all aluminum; it will not rust, but it will oxidize internally and have to be replaced. Refer to **Coolant Change** *in Chapter Three.*

This chapter describes repair and replacement of cooling system components. **Table 1** at the end of the chapter lists cooling system specifications. For routine maintenance of the system, refer to *Cooling System Inspection* in Chapter Three.

WARNING
*Do not remove the radiator cap (**Figure 4**) when the engine is hot. The coolant is very hot and is under pressure. Severe scalding could result if the coolant comes in contact with your skin.*

WARNING
The radiator fan and fan switch are connected to the battery. Whenever the engine is warm or hot, the fan may start even with the ignition switch turned off. Never work around the fan or touch the fan until the engine is completely cool. If you have to work in the area of the fan when the engine is warm, disconnect the battery negative cable.

The cooling system must be cool before removing any component of the system.

COOLING SYSTEM INSPECTION

1. If a substantial coolant loss is noted, the head gasket may be blown. In extreme cases sufficient coolant will leak into a cylinder(s) when the bike is left standing for several hours so the engine cannot be turned over with the starter. White smoke (steam) might also be observed at the muffler when the engine is running. Coolant may also find its way into the oil. To check, remove the dipstick; if it has a white, foamy appearance, there is coolant in the oil system. If so, correct the problem immediately.

CAUTION
After the coolant loss problem is corrected, drain and thoroughly flush

out the engine oil system to eliminate all coolant residue. Refill with fresh engine oil; refer to **Engine Oil and Filter Change** *in Chapter Three.*

2. Check the radiator for clogged or damaged fins. If more than 20% of the radiator fin area is damaged, repair or replace the radiator.
3. Check all coolant hoses for cracks or damage. Replace all questionable parts. Make sure the hose clamps are tight, but not so tight that they cut the hoses.
4. Pressure test the cooling system as described under *Cooling System Inspection* in Chapter Three.

COOLANT RESERVOIR TANK

The coolant reservoir tank (**Figure 5**) is located on the right-hand side underneath the gas tank and behind the fairing.

Removal/Installation

1. Remove the left- and right-hand side covers. See Chapter Thirteen.

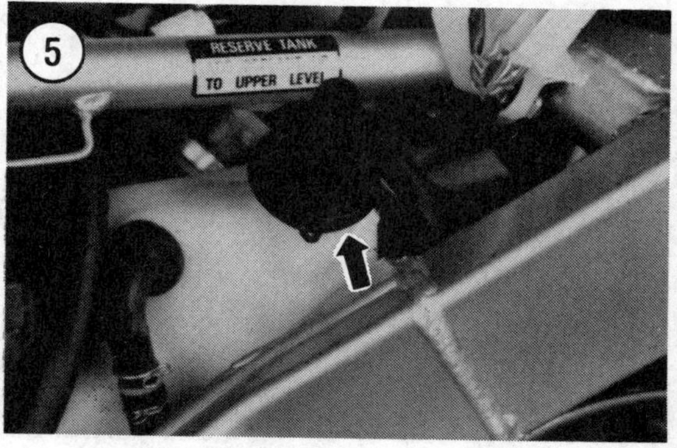

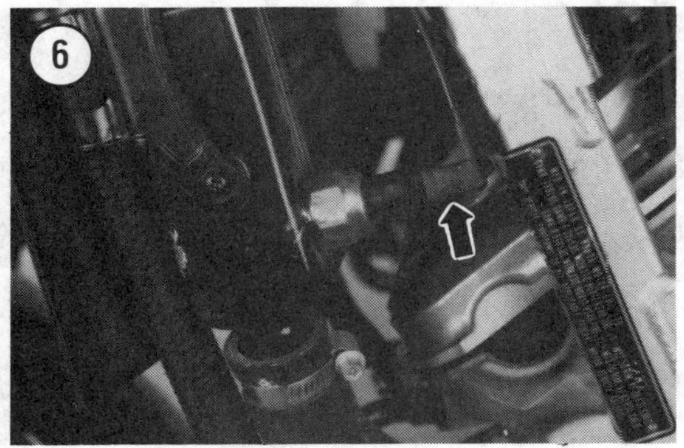
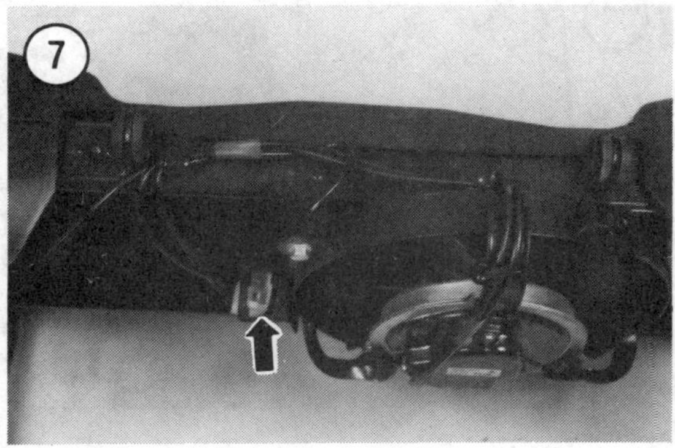
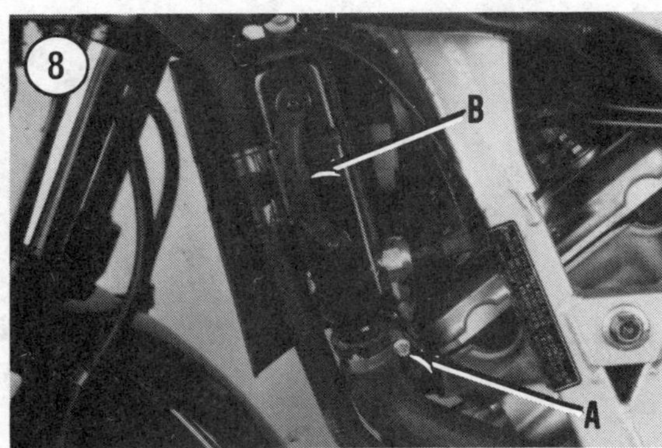

2. Remove the shock absorber as described in Chapter Eleven.

3. Remove the upper and lower reservoir tank mounting bolts.

4. Disconnect the hoses at the reservoir.

5. Remove the reservoir tank from the left-hand side.

6. Install by reversing these steps.

RADIATOR

WARNING
The radiator fan and fan switch are connected to the battery. Whenever the engine is warm or hot, the fan may start with the ignition switch turned off. Never work around the fan or touch the fan until the engine is completely cool. If you have to work in the area of the fan when the engine is hot, disconnect the battery negative cable.

Removal/Installation

The radiator and fan are removed as an assembly.

1. Support the bike on a bike stand.

2. Remove the upper and lower fairings as described in Chapter Thirteen.

3. Drain the cooling system as described under *Coolant Change* in Chapter Three.

4. Remove the fuel tank as described in Chapter Seven.

5. Disconnect the thermostatic switch connector (**Figure 6**).

6. Disconnect the fan motor switch connector (**Figure 7**).

NOTE
Figure 7 shows the switch connector with the radiator removed for clarity.

7. Refer to **Figure 8**. Perform the following:
   a. Disconnect the radiator lower hose (A).
   b. Remove the left-hand oil hose clamp (B).

8. Refer to **Figure 9**. Perform the following:
   a. Disconnect the radiator upper hose (A).
   b. Remove the right-hand oil hose clamp (B).

9. Remove the radiator upper mounting bolt from the left-hand side.

10. Remove the lower radiator mounting bolts.

11. Lower the radiator from the frame and remove

12. Install by reversing these removal steps, noting the following.

13. Make sure the electrical connections are free of corrosion and are tight.

14. Refill the cooling system with the recommended type and quantity of coolant as described in Chapter Three.

Inspection

CAUTION
When flushing the radiator fins with a garden hose on low pressure, always point the hose perpendicular to the radiator and at a distance of 20 in. Never point a water hose or air hose at an angle to the radiator fins.

1. Flush off the exterior of the radiator with a garden hose on low pressure. Spray both the front and the back to remove all road dirt and bugs. Carefully use a whisk broom or stiff paint brush to remove any stubborn dirt.

CAUTION
Do not press too hard or the cooling fins and tubes may be damaged, causing a leak.

2. Release the grille tabs and lift the grille (**Figure 10**) off of the radiator.

3. Carefully straighten out any bent cooling fins with a broad-tipped screwdriver.

4. Check for cracks or leakage (usually a moss-green colored residue) at the filler neck, the inlet and outlet hose fittings and the upper and lower tank seams. See **Figure 11**.

5. Refer to **Figure 12**. Inspect the radiator cap top (A) and bottom (B) seals for deterioration or damage. Check the spring for damage. Pressure test the radiator cap as described under *Cooling System Inspection* in Chapter Three. Replace the radiator cap if necessary.

6. If the condition of the radiator is doubtful, have it checked as described under *Pressure Check* in Chapter Three.

7. To prevent oxidation to the radiator, touch up any area where the black paint is worn off. Use a good quality spray paint and apply several *light* coats of paint. Do not apply heavy coats as this will cut down on the cooling efficiency of the radiator.

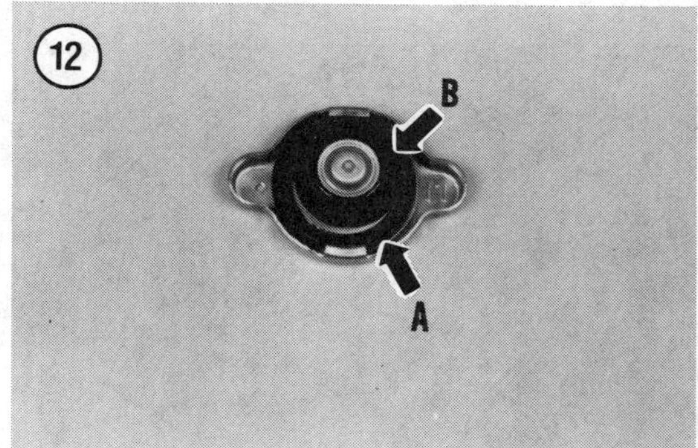

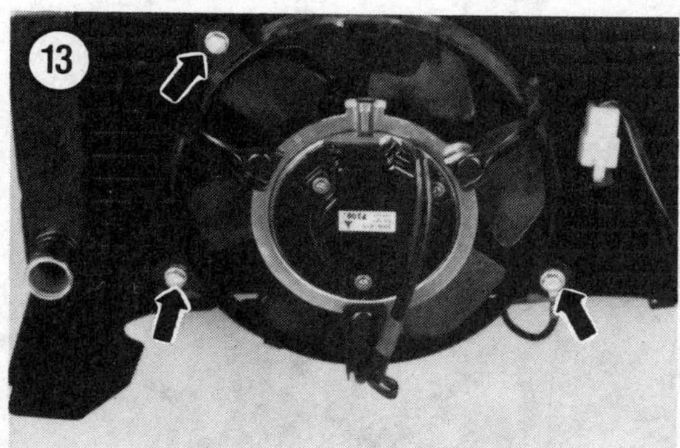

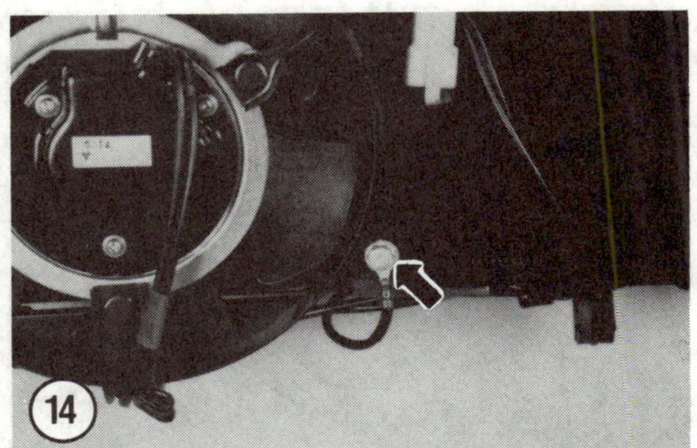

COOLING FAN

Removal/Installation

1. Remove the radiator as described in this chapter.
2. Remove the bolts (**Figure 13**) securing the fan shroud and fan assembly and remove the assembly.
3. To remove the fan blade from the motor, remove the nut securing the fan blade. Remove the fan blade from the motor.
4. If necessary remove the screws securing the fan motor to the fan shroud and remove the motor assembly.
5. Install by reversing these removal steps, noting the following.
6. If the fan was removed, align the motor shaft with the fan groove.
7. Apply Loctite 242 (blue) to the threads on the fan motor shaft before installing the fan blade nut. Install the nut and tighten securely.
8. Make sure to install the fan ground wire (**Figure 14**).
9. Install the radiator as described in this chapter.

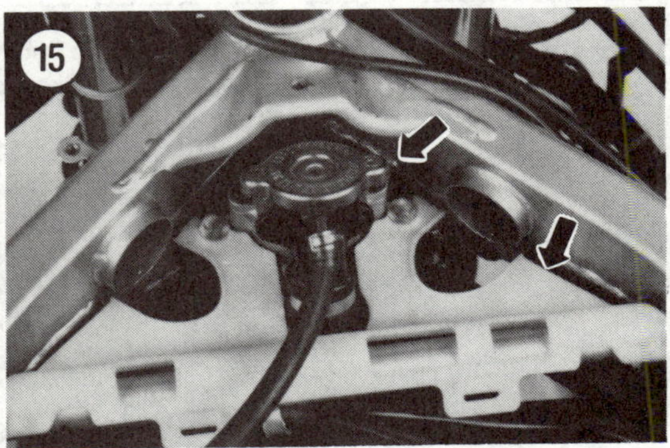

THERMOSTAT

Removal/Installation

1. Remove the fuel tank as described in Chapter Seven.
2. Drain the cooling system as described under *Coolant Change* in Chapter Three.

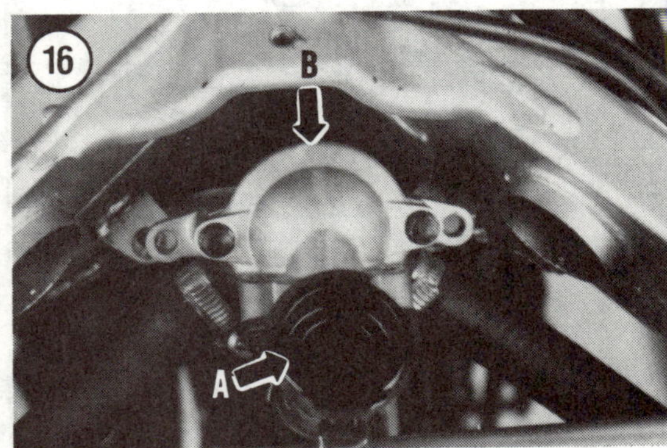

> *NOTE*
> *The following procedure is shown with the air filter housing removed for clarity. It is not necessary to remove the air filter housing when servicing the thermostat.*

3. Remove the radiator cap and guard plate (**Figure 15**).
4. Remove the radiator cap housing bolts and remove the cap housing (A, **Figure 16**).
5. Remove the thermostat cover bolts and lift the cover (B, **Figure 16**) off of the housing.
6. Lift the thermostat (**Figure 17**) out of the housing.
7. Test the thermostat as described in this chapter.
8. Install by reversing these steps. Note the following.

9. Replace the radiator and thermostat housing O-ring if deteriorated or damaged. See **Figure 18**.

10. Refill the cooling system with the recommended type and quantity of coolant as described under *Coolant Change* in Chapter Three.

Inspection

Test the thermostat to ensure proper operation. The thermostat should be replaced if it remains open at normal room temperature or stays closed after the specified temperature has been reached during the test procedure.

Place the thermostat on a small piece of wood in a pan of water (**Figure 19**). Place a thermometer in the pan of water (use a cooking or candy thermometer that is rated higher than the test temperature). Gradually heat the water and continue to gently stir the water until it reaches 80-84° C (176-183° F). At this temperature the thermostat should open.

> *NOTE*
> *Valve operation is sometimes sluggish; it usually takes 3-5 minutes for the valve to operate properly.*

If the valve fails to open, the thermostat should be replaced (it cannot be serviced). Be sure to replace it with one of the same temperature rating.

WATER PUMP

Refer to **Figure 20** when servicing the water pump.

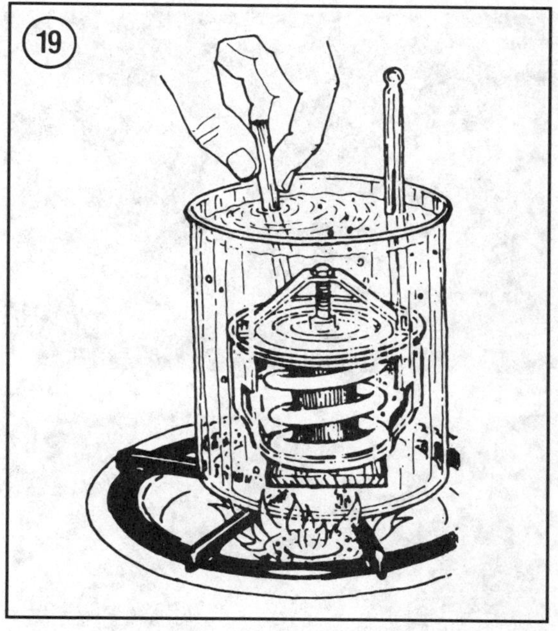

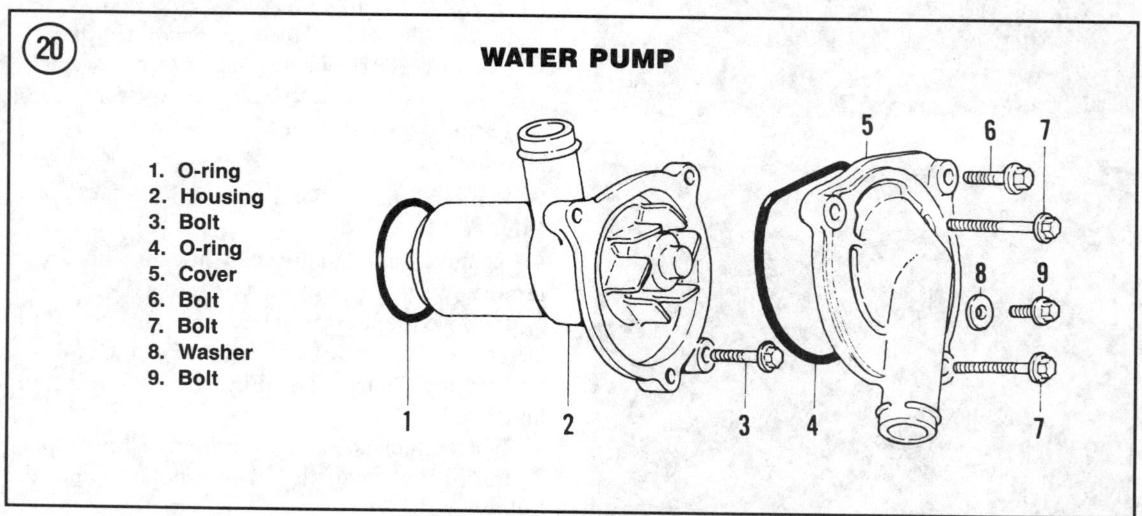

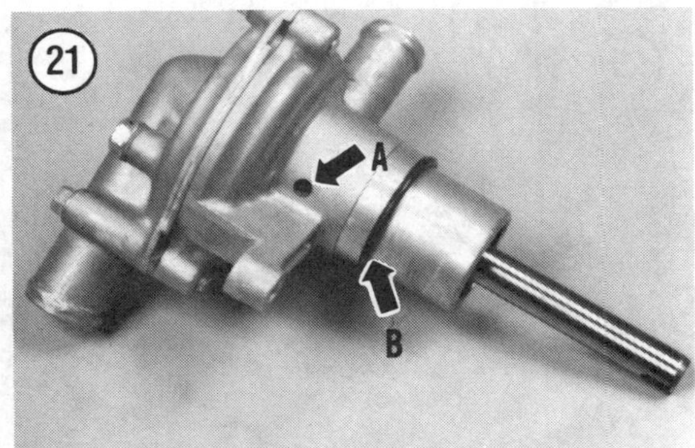

Inspection

NOTE
Figure 21 shows the water pump removed for clarity. The hole can be observed with the water pump installed on the bike.

Check the water pump body drainage outlet passage (A, **Figure 21**) for leakage. If coolant leaks from the outlet passage, an internal seal is damaged; replace the water pump unit. If there is no indication of coolant leakage from the outlet passage, pressure test the cooling system as described under *Cooling System Inspection* in Chapter Three.

Removal/Installation

1. Remove the left-hand lower fairing as described in Chapter Thirteen.
2. Drain the engine oil as described under *Engine Oil and Filter Change* in Chapter Three.
3. Drain the cooling system as described under *Coolant Change* in Chapter Three.
4. Loosen the hose clamps at the water pump. Twist the hoses and slide them off (**Figure 22**) of the water pump fittings.
5. Remove the 2 water pump mounting bolts and remove the water pump (**Figure 23**).
6. Installation is the reverse of these steps. Note the following:
7. Replace the O-ring (B, **Figure 21**) if worn or damaged.
8. Align the groove in the water pump shaft (**Figure 24**) with the tab on the oil pump shaft and install the water pump.
9. Tighten the water pump mounting bolts securely.
10. Refill the cooling system with the recommended type and quantity of coolant as described under *Coolant Change* in Chapter Three.

Disassembly/Inspection/Reassembly

NOTE
The water pump is sold as a complete unit only. If any component is damaged, the entire water pump must be replaced. The 2 O-rings, however, can be replaced separately.

1. Check the O-ring (B, **Figure 21**) for flat spots or damage; replace if necessary.
2. Remove the water pump cover bolts (**Figure 25**) and separate the pump assembly.
3. Check the impeller blades (**Figure 26**) for corrosion or damage. If corrosion is minor, clean the blades. If corrosion is severe or if the blades are cracked or broken, replace the water pump unit.
4. Turn the impeller shaft (**Figure 27**) and check the bearing for excessive noise or roughness. If the bearing operation is rough, replace the water pump unit.
5. Replace the water pump O-ring (**Figure 28**) if deformed or cracked or if there are indications of coolant leakage.
6. Reverse Step 2 to assemble the water pump assembly. Tighten the bolts securely.

HOSES

Hoses deteriorate with age and should be replaced periodically or whenever they show signs of cracking or leakage. To be safe, replace the hoses every 2 years. The spray of hot coolant from a cracked hose can injure the rider and passenger. Loss of coolant can also cause the engine to overheat causing damage.

Whenever any component of the cooling system is removed, inspect the hoses(s) and determine if replacement is necessary.

Inspection

1. With the engine cool, check the cooling hoses for brittleness or hardness. A hose in this condition will usually show cracks and must be replaced.
2. With the engine hot, examine the hoses for swelling along the entire hose length. Eventually a hose will rupture at this point.
3. Check area around hose clamps. Signs of rust around clamps indicate possible hose leakage.

Replacement

Hose replacement should be performed when the engine is cool.
1. Drain the cooling system as described under *Coolant Change* in Chapter Three.

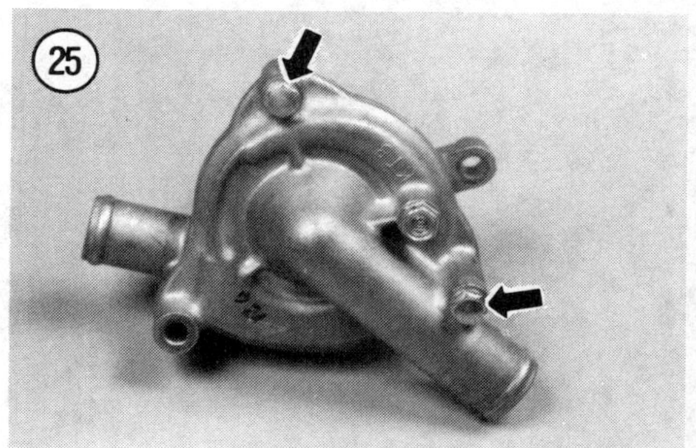

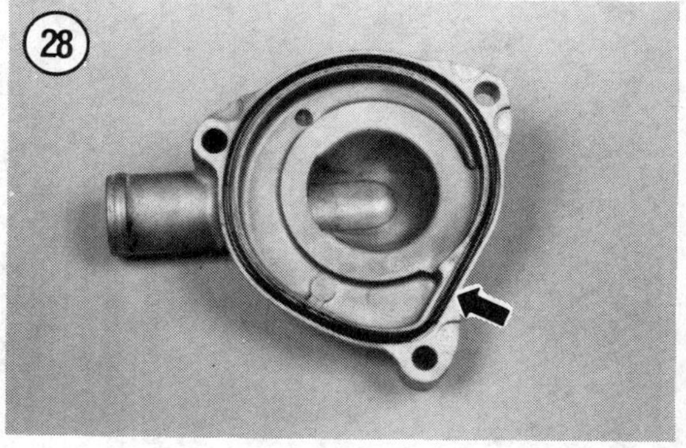

2. Loosen the hose clamps from the hose to be replaced. Slide the clamps along the hose and out of the way.

CAUTION
Excessive force applied to the hose during removal could damage the connecting joint.

3. Twist the hose end to break the seal and remove from the connecting joint. If the hose has been on for some time, it may have become fused to the joint. If so, cut the hose parallel to the joint connections with a knife or razor. The hose can then be carefully pried loose with a screwdriver.
4. Examine the connecting joint for cracks or other damage. Repair or replace parts as required. If the joint is okay, clean it of any rust with sandpaper.
5. Inspect hose clamps and replace as necessary.

NOTE
If it is difficult to install a hose on a joint, soak the end of the hose in hot water for approximately 2 minutes. This will soften the hose and ease installation.

6. Slide hose clamps over outside of hose and install hose to inlet and outlet connecting joint. Make sure hose clears all obstructions and is routed properly.
7. With the hose positioned correctly on joint, position clamps back away from end of hose slightly. Tighten clamps securely, but not so much that hose is damaged.
8. Refill cooling system as described under *Coolant Change* in Chapter Three. Start the engine and check for leaks. Retighten hose clamps as necessary.

Table 1 COOLING SYSTEM SPECIFICATIONS

Coolant capacity	
Total system	2.0 liters (2.11 qt.)
Radiator cap relief pressure	0.95-1.25 kg/cm^2 (14-18 psi)
Thermostat	
Begins to open	80-84° C
	(176-183° F)
Valve lift	Minimum of 8 mm @ 95° C
	(0.32 in. at 203° F)
Boiling point (50:50 mixture)	
Unpressurized	107.7° C (226° F)
Pressurized (cap on)	125.6° C (258° F)
Freezing point (hydrometer test)	
45:55 Water:antifreeze ratio	-32° C (-25° F)
50:50 Water:antifreeze ratio	-37° C (-34° F)
45:55 Water:antifreeze ratio	-44.5° C (-48° F)

9

CHAPTER TEN

FRONT SUSPENSION AND STEERING

This chapter discusses service operations on suspension components, steering, wheels and related items. **Table 1** lists service specifications. **Tables 1-5** are at the end of the chapter.

FRONT WHEEL

Removal

> *NOTE*
> *Honda CBR600 models are not equipped with a centerstand. An accessory centerstand, for non-California models only, is available from Honda dealers. To raise the front wheel off of the ground, a special front wheel stand can be used (available from accessory manufacturers) or the lower fairing assembly must be removed so that a jack can be used underneath the engine. Make sure the bike is securely supported before removing and servicing the front wheel.*

> *NOTE*
> *This procedure is shown with the front fender (Figure 1) removed for clarity. It is not necessary to remove the front fender when servicing the front wheel.*

1. Support the motorcycle so that the front wheel is clear of the ground.

2. Remove the speedometer cable set screw (**Figure 2**) and pull the cable out of the speedometer drive unit. Reinstall the set screw.

3. Remove the right-hand brake caliper bracket bolts (**Figure 3**) and lift the caliper (**Figure 4**) off of the brake disc. Support the caliper with a Bunjee cord to prevent stress buildup on the brake hose.

4. Remove the right-hand axle pinch bolts (A, **Figure 5**).

5. Loosen and remove the axle bolt (B, **Figure 5**) from the right-hand side.

6. Remove the left-hand axle pinch bolts (**Figure 6**).

7. Remove the axle (**Figure 7**) from the left-hand side.

8. Pull the wheel forward to disengage the attached caliper from the brake disc. See **Figure 8**.

9. Remove the speedometer drive gear (**Figure 9**) from the left-hand side.

10. Remove the spacer (**Figure 10**) from the right-hand side.

> *CAUTION*
> *Do not set the wheel down on the disc surface as it may be scratched or warped. Either lean the wheel against a wall or place it on a couple of wood blocks.*

> *NOTE*
> *Insert a piece of wood in the calipers to hold the brake pads in place (**Figure 11**). That way, if the brake lever is inadvertently squeezed, the pistons will not be forced out of the cylinder. If this does happen, the calipers might have to be disassembled to reseat the pistons and the system will have to be bled.*

11. When servicing the wheel assembly, install the spacer, speedometer drive gear and axle bolt on the axle to prevent misplacing them. See **Figure 12**.

Installation

1. Align the 2 tabs in the speedometer gear housing (A, **Figure 13**) with the 2 speedometer drive slots (B, **Figure 13**) in the front wheel and install the gear housing. See **Figure 9**.

2. Insert the spacer into the right-hand side of the wheel (**Figure 10**). Install the spacer so that the large diameter end faces out.

3. To prevent axle seizure, coat the axle lightly with wheel bearing grease.

4. Remove the wood block between the left-hand brake caliper brake pads.

5. Position the front wheel between the fork tubes so that the speedometer drive gear is on the left-hand side (**Figure 8**).

6. Raise the wheel assembly to align the front fork slider and wheel axle holes and insert the axle (**Figure 7**) from the left-hand side. Also make sure to carefully align the left-hand brake disc with the brake caliper brake pads.

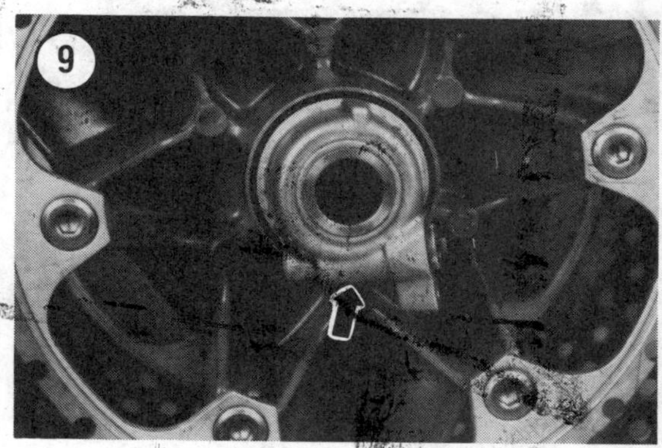

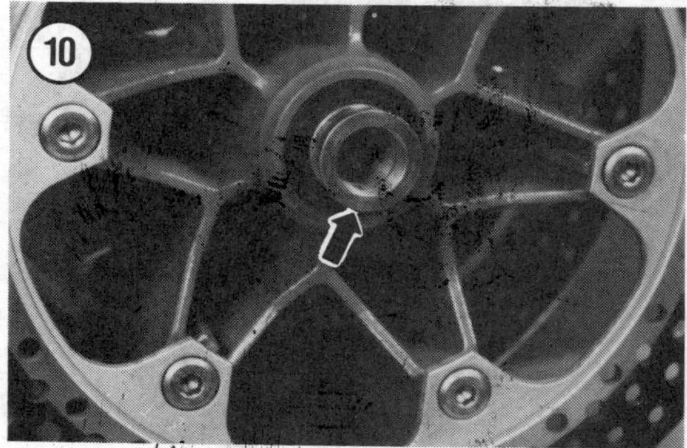

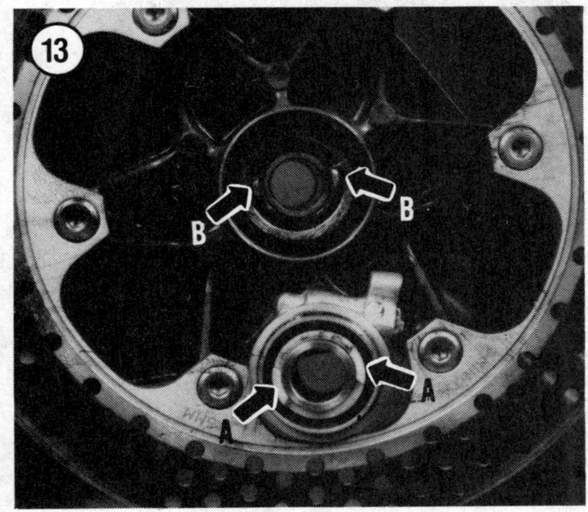

7. Align the slot on the speedometer gear housing with the tab on the back of the left-hand fork tube (**Figure 14**). This procedure locates the speedometer drive gear and prevents it from rotating when the wheel turns.

8. Install the axle bolt (B, **Figure 5**) and tighten to the torque specifications in **Table 2**.

9. Check the O-ring on the end of the speedometercable; replace if necessary. Then insert the speedometer cable into the speedometer drive housing and secure the cable with the screw.

10. Remove the right-hand brake caliper from the Bunjee cord and remove the wood block from between the brake pads.

11. Carefully align the right-hand brake disc with the brake pads and install the right-hand brake caliper (**Figure 4**). Install the brake caliper bolts and tighten to the torque specifications in **Table 2**.

> *WARNING*
> *Step 12 checks for adequate brake disc-to-caliper clearance. Failure to maintain adequate clearance may cause brake disc damage and reduced braking efficiency.*

12. See **Figure 15**. Check left-hand brake caliper holder-to-disc clearance as follows:

a. Using a 0.7 mm (0.028 in.) feeler gauge, measure the clearance between brake disc and the caliper bracket as shown in **Figure 15**. Check the clearance on both sides of the brake disc.

> *NOTE*
> *A 0.7 mm (0.028 in.) feeler gauge is included in your bike's tool kit (**Figure 16**).*

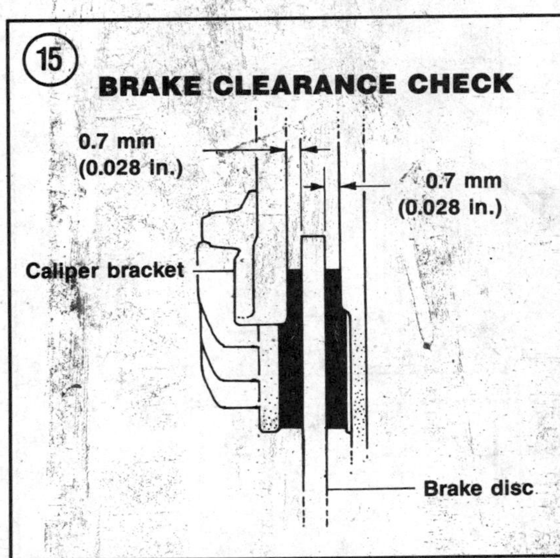

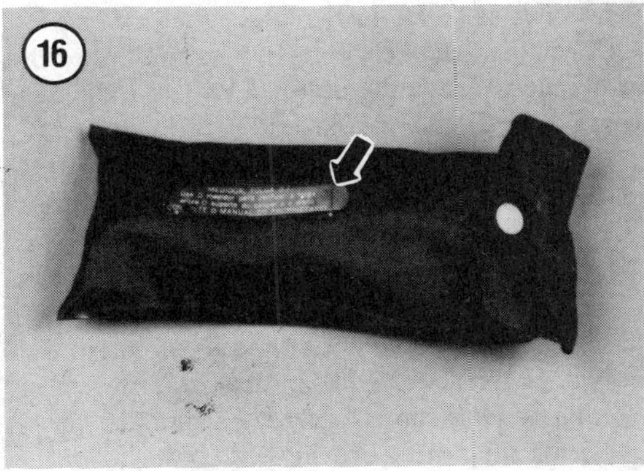

b. If the feeler gauge can be inserted and withdrawn easily (but not loose), the clearance is correct. Proceed to Step 13. If the feeler gauge cannot be inserted or if it is too tight, perform the following.

c. If the brake caliper holder-to-disc clearance is too tight, pull the left-hand fork slider in or out by hand. Then reinsert the feeler gauge and recheck the clearance. Continue to adjust slider positioning by hand until the clearance is correct.

d. Leave the feeler gauge in place while performing Step 13.

13. Tighten the left- and right-hand axle pinch bolts to the torque specifications listed in **Table 2**. Remove the feeler gauge, if necessary.

> *WARNING*
> *Failure to remove the feeler gauge will cause brake damage or brake lockup.*

14. Spin the wheel and apply the front brake a few times. Then recheck brake disc-to-caliper bracket clearance with the 0.7 mm (0.028 in.) feeler gauge.

15. Apply the front brake as many times as necessary to make sure the brake pads are against both brake discs correctly.

Inspection

1. Remove any corrosion on the front axle (A, **Figure 17**) with a piece of fine emery cloth.

2. Check axle runout. Place the axle on V-blocks (**Figure 18**). Place the tip of a dial indicator in the middle of the axle. Rotate the axle and check runout. If the runout exceeds the wear limit specifications in **Table 1**, replace the front axle.

3. Check the front axle bolt (B, **Figure 17**) threads for damage. Check the bolt head for rounding or other damage. Replace the axle bolt if necessary.

4. Check rim runout as follows:

a. Measure the radial (up and down) runout of the wheel rim with a dial indicator as shown in **Figure 19**. If runout exceeds 2.0 mm (0.08 in.), check the wheel bearings.

b. Measure the axial (side to side) runout of the wheel rim with a dial indicator as shown in **Figure 19**. If runout exceeds 2.0 mm (0.08 in.), check the wheel bearings.

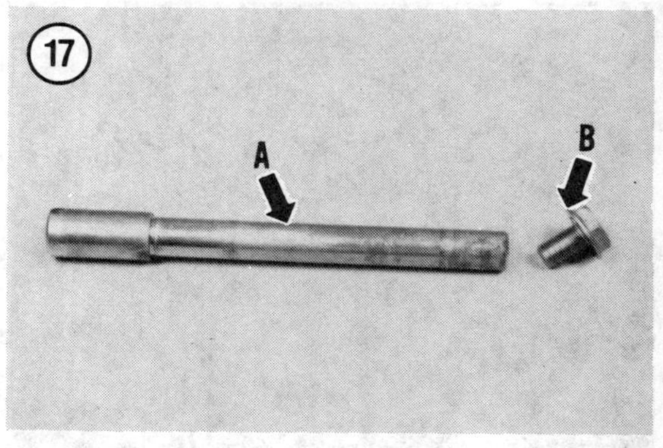

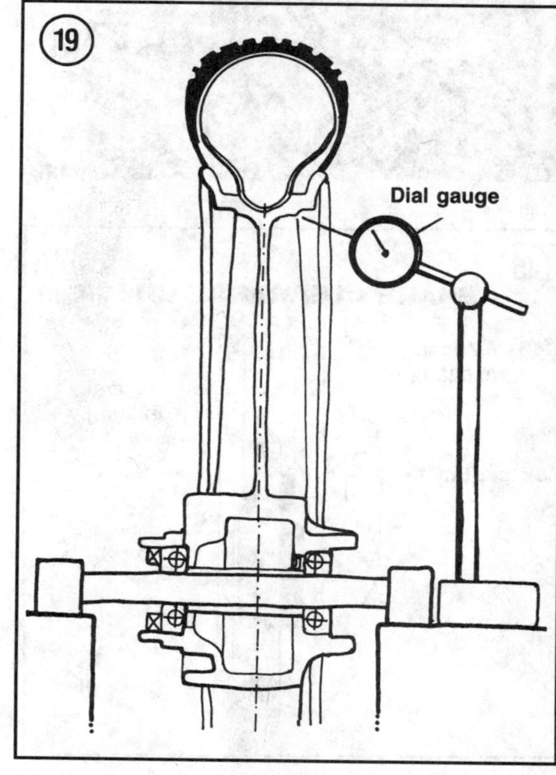

c. Check the wheel bearings as described under *Front Hub* in this chapter. If the wheel bearings are okay, the wheel cannot be serviced, but must be replaced.

d. If necessary, replace the front wheel bearings as described under *Front Hub* in this chapter.

5. Inspect the wheel rim for dents, bending or cracks. Check the rim and rim sealing surface for scratches that are deeper than 0.5 mm (0.02 in.). If any of these conditions are present, replace the wheel.

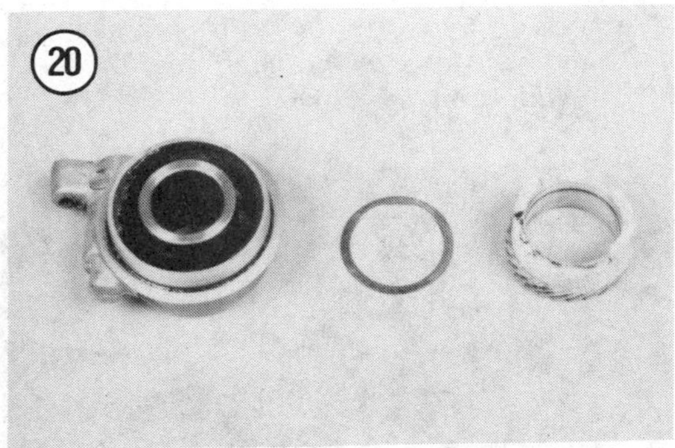

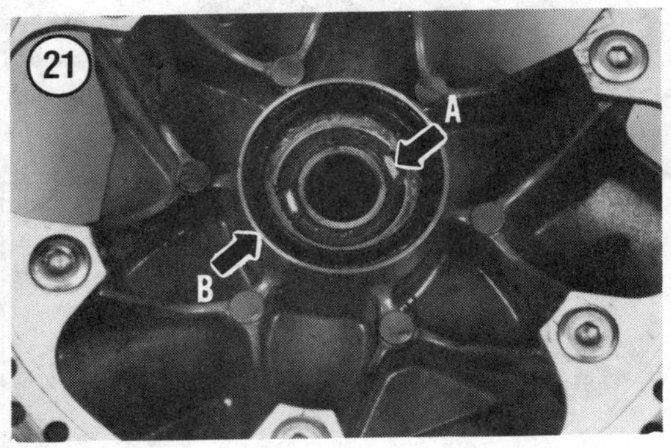

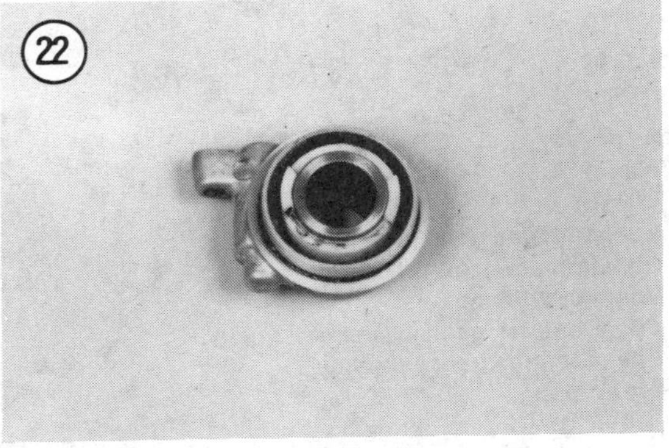

Speedometer Gear Inspection
Inspection and Lubrication

Periodically, the speedometer drive gear should be removed from the speedometer housing for inspection.

1. Remove the front wheel from the motorcycle as described in this chapter.

2. Remove the drive gear and washers from the speedometer gear housing (**Figure 20**).

3. Inspect the drive gear teeth for breakage or other damage. Check the slots on the top of the gear for cracks or other damage that would cause inaccurate speedometer readings. Replace the drive gear if necessary.

4. Inspect the metal ring (A, **Figure 21**) in the left-hand side of the front wheel that engages with the drive gear. Check the metal ring tabs for cracks or breakage. If necessary, replace the metal ring (A, **Figure 21**) by first prying the oil seal (B, **Figure 21**) out of the hub with a screwdriver. Disengage the metal ring from the hub and replace it. Make sure to align the tangs on the metal ring with the slots in the hub. Install a new oil seal by driving it into the hub with a suitable size socket placed on the seal. Drive the seal in until it seats against the metal ring.

5. Clean all old grease from the speedometer gear housing and gear. Lightly pack the housing with high-temperature grease.

6. Assemble the speedometer gear assembly (**Figure 20**) by installing the spacers and drive gear. Install the gear so that the gear teeth are at the bottom of the housing. See **Figure 22**.

7. Install the front wheel as described in this chapter.

FRONT HUB

Disassembly/Inspection/Reassembly

Refer to **Figure 23** for this procedure.

1. Check the wheel bearings by rotating the inner race. Check for bearing roughness, excessive noise or damage. If necessary, replace the bearings as follows. Always replace bearings as a set.

> *CAUTION*
> *Never reinstall bearings removed from the hub as removal usually damages the bearings. Always install new bearings.*

2. Remove the left-hand oil seal and metal ring as follows:

  a. Pry the oil seal (B, **Figure 21**) out of the hub with a screwdriver.

  b. Disengage the metal ring from the hub and remove it from the hub.

3. Remove the right-hand oil seal by prying it out of the hub with a large screwdriver. See **Figure 24**.

NOTE

Before removing the wheel bearings, check the tightness of the bearings in the hub by trying to pull the bearing up and then from side to side. The outer bearing race should be tight against the hub with no movement. If the outer bearing race is loose and wobbles, the bearing area in the hub may be cracked or damaged. Remove the bearings as described in this procedure and check the hub bearing area carefully. If any cracks or damage are found, the hub must be replaced. It cannot be repaired.

4. Using a long drift and hammer, tilt the center spacer away from one side of the left-hand bearing (**Figure 25**). Drive the left-hand bearing out of the hub. See **Figure 25**.

5. Lift the center spacer out of the hub.

6. Using a large socket with an extension or a piece of pipe, drive the right-hand bearing out of the hub.

7. Clean the center spacer and hub thoroughly in solvent.

8. Pack the wheel bearings with grease before installation.

CAUTION

Use care when installing the new wheel bearings. Drive the bearings into the hub by hitting on the outer bearing race only. Never drive the bearings in by applying force on the inner race. This will destroy the bearing.

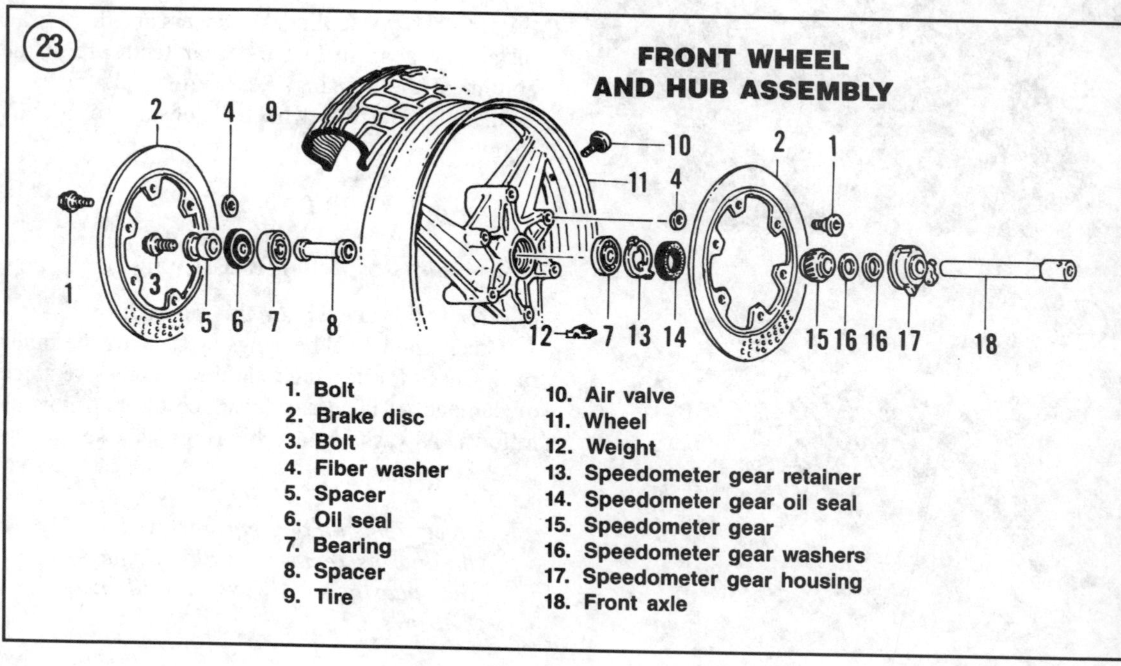

FRONT WHEEL AND HUB ASSEMBLY

1. Bolt
2. Brake disc
3. Bolt
4. Fiber washer
5. Spacer
6. Oil seal
7. Bearing
8. Spacer
9. Tire
10. Air valve
11. Wheel
12. Weight
13. Speedometer gear retainer
14. Speedometer gear oil seal
15. Speedometer gear
16. Speedometer gear washers
17. Speedometer gear housing
18. Front axle

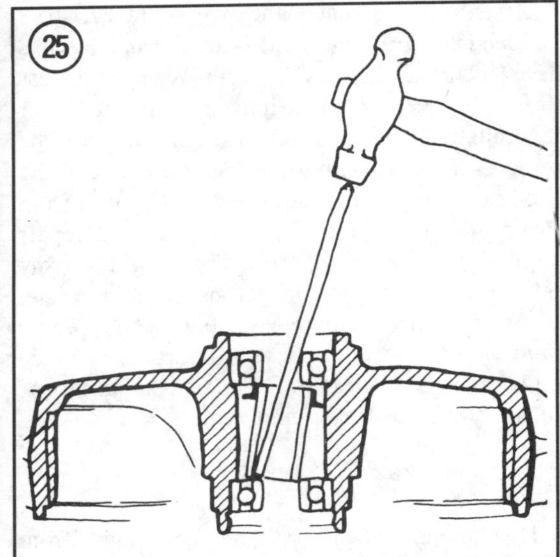

NOTE
Drive the bearings into the hub until
they seat against the hub shoulder.

9. Tap the right-hand bearing into place carefully using a suitable size socket placed on the outer bearing race (**Figure 26**).

10. Install the center spacer.

11. Use the procedure outlined for the right-hand bearing in Step 9 and install the left-hand bearing into the hub.

12. Install the left-hand oil seal and metal ring as follows:

   a. Align the tangs on the metal ring with the slots in the hub and install the metal ring (A, **Figure 21**).

   b. Install the oil seal (B, **Figure 21**) by driving it into the hub with a suitable size socket placed on the seal. Drive the seal in until it seats against the metal ring.

13. Install the right-hand oil seal (**Figure 27**). Drive the oil seal in with a suitable size socket placed on the seal. Drive the seal in until it is flush with the side of the hub as shown in **Figure 27**.

14. Spin the left- and right-hand bearing inner races by hand. Make sure they spin smoothly without any roughness or excessive noise.

15. Check that the bearings are tight in the hub.

WHEEL BALANCE

An unbalanced wheel results in unsafe riding conditions. Depending on the degree of unbalance and the speed of the motorcycle, the rider may experience anything from a mild vibration to a violent shimmy and loss of control.

Weights are attached to the rim (**Figure 28**). Adhesive weight kits are available from motorcycle

10

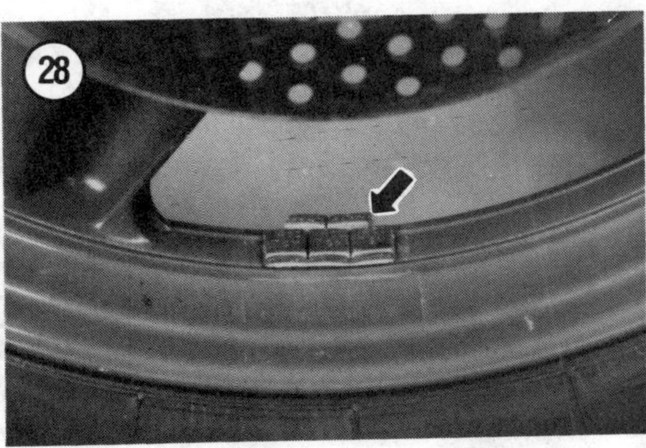

dealers. These kits contain test weights and strips of adhesive-backed weights that can be cut to the desired length and attached directly to the rim.

> *NOTE*
> *Be sure to balance the wheel with the brake discs attached as they are part of the rotating mass and they affect balance.*

Before attempting to balance the wheels, check to be sure that the wheel bearings are in good condition and properly lubricated. The wheel must rotate freely. See *Front Hub* in this chapter. Also check that the tire balance mark (paint dot on tire) is aligned with the valve stem (**Figure 29**). If not, break the tire loose from the rim and realign. See *Tire Changing* in this chapter.

1. Remove the wheel as described in this chapter or in Chapter Eleven (rear wheel).
2. Mount the wheel on a fixture such as the one in **Figure 30** so it can rotate freely.
3. Give the wheel a spin and let it coast to a stop. Mark the tire at the lowest point.
4. Spin the wheel several more times. If the wheel keeps coming to rest at the same point, it is out of balance.
5. Tape a test weight to the upper (or light) side of the wheel.
6. Experiment with different weights until the wheel, when spun, comes to rest at a different position each time.
7. Remove the test weight and install the correct size weight.

> *CAUTION*
> *When adding balance weight, do not add more than 60 grams to the front or rear wheel.*

> *NOTE*
> *When installing crimp-type weights to aluminum rims, it may be necessary to let some air out of the tire. After installing the weight, refill the tire to the correct air pressure. See **Table 3**.*

TUBELESS TIRES

> *WARNING*
> *Do not install an inner tube inside a tubeless tire. The tube will cause an abnormal heat buildup in the tire.*

Tubeless tires have the word TUBELESS molded in the tire sidewall (**Figure 31**) and the rims have "TUBELESS" cast on them. When a tubeless tire is flat, it's best to take it to a motorcycle dealer for repair. Punctured tubeless tires should be removed from the rim to inspect the inside of the tire and to apply a combination plug/patch from the inside. Don't rely on a plug or cord repair applied from outside the tire. They might be okay on a car, but they're too dangerous on a motorcycle.

After repairing a tubeless tire, don't exceed 50 mph (80 kph) form the first 24 hours. Never race on a repaired tubeless tire. The patch could work loose from tire flexing and heat.

Repair

Do not relay on a plug or cord patch applied from outside the tire. Use a combination plug/patch applied from inside the tire (**Figure 32**).

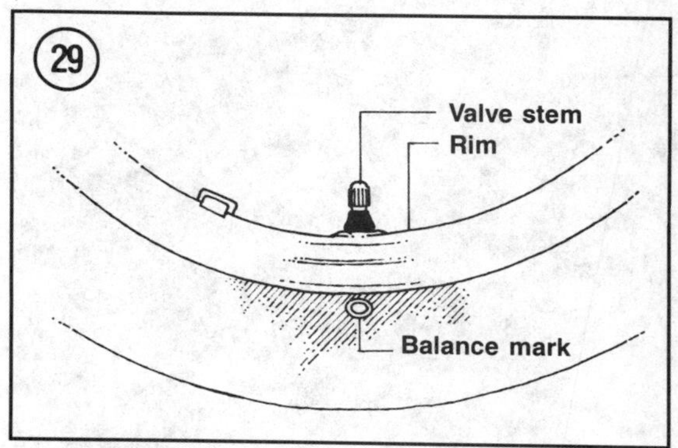

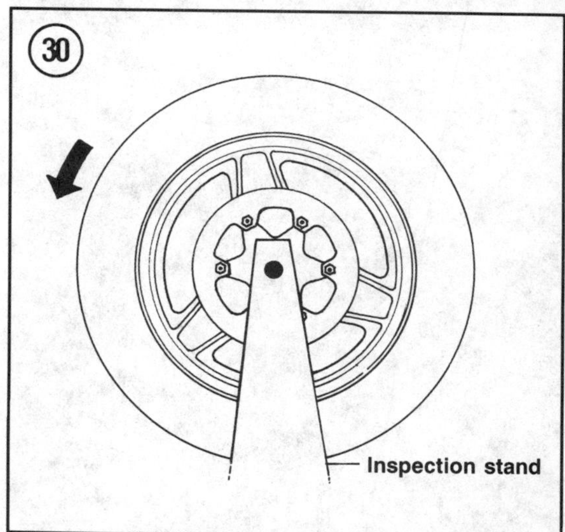

1. Remove the tire from the rim as described in this chapter.

2. Inspect the rim inner flange. Smooth any scratches on the sealing surface with emery cloth. If a scratch is deeper than 0.5 mm (0.020 in.), the wheel should be replaced.

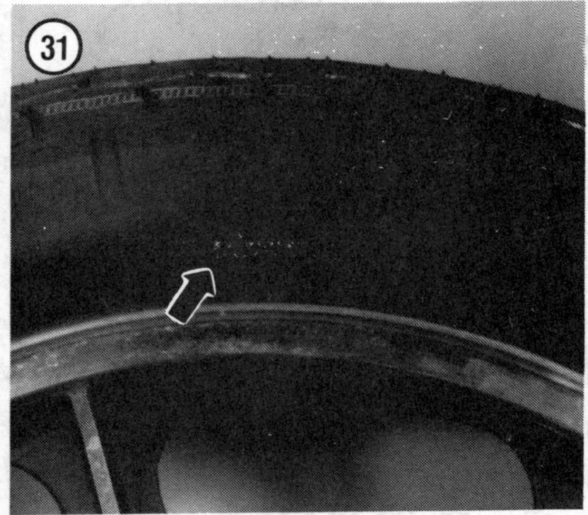

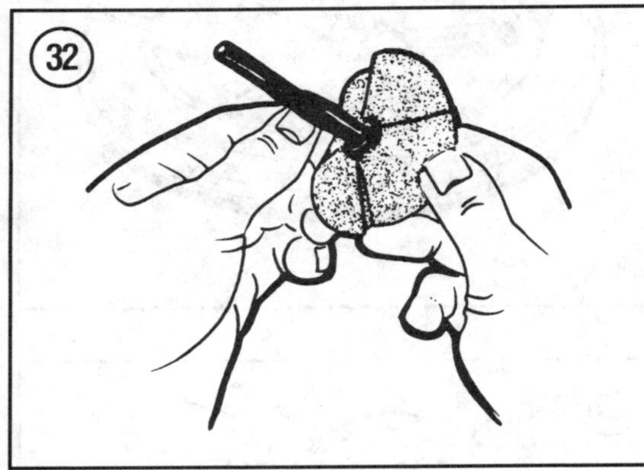

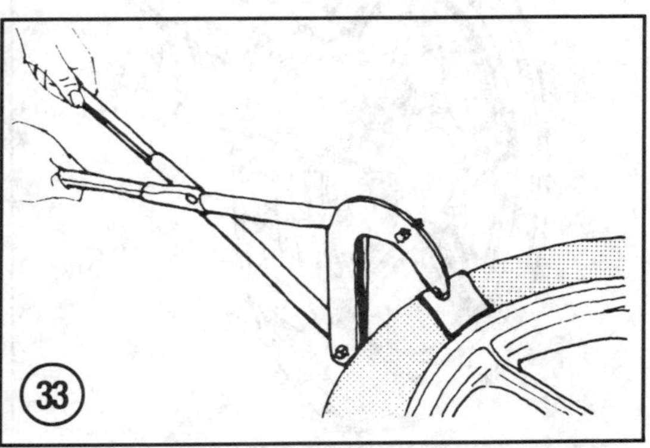

3. Inspect the tire inside and out. Replace a tire if any of the following is found:
  a. A puncture larger than 3 mm (1/8 in.) diameter.
  b. A punctured or damaged sidewall.
  c. More than 2 punctures in the tire.
4. Apply the plug/patch, following the instructions supplied with the patch kit.

TUBELESS TIRE CHANGING

The wheels can easily be damaged during tire removal. Special care must be taken with tire irons when changing a tire to avoid scratches and gouges to the outer rim surface. Insert scraps of leather between the tire iron and the rim to protect the rim from damage.

The stock cast wheels are designed for use with tubeless tires.

When removing a tubeless tire, take care not to damage the tire beads, inner liner of the tire or the wheel rim flange. Use tire levers or flat handled tire irons with rounded ends.

Tire Removal

CAUTION
While removing a tire, support the wheel on 2 blocks of wood, so the brake disc doesn't contact the floor or bench top.

1. Mark the valve stem location on the tire, so the tire can be installed in the same position for easier balancing. See **Figure 29**.
2. Remove the valve core to deflate the tire.

NOTE
*Removal of tubeless tires from their rims can be very difficult because of the exceptionally tight bead/rim seal. Breaking the bead seal may require the use of a special tool (**Figure 33**). If you have trouble breaking the seal, take the tire to a motorcycle dealer.*

CAUTION
The inner rim and tire bead area are sealing surfaces on a tubeless tire. Do not scratch the inside of the rim or damage the tire bead.

3. Press the entire bead on both sides of the tire into the center of the rim.

4. Lubricate the beads with soapy water.

NOTE
*Use rim protectors (**Figure 34**) or insert scraps of leather between the tire irons and the rim to protect the rim from damage.*

5. Insert the tire iron under the bead next to the valve (**Figure 35**). Force the bead on the opposite side of the tire into the center of the rim and pry the bead over the rim with the tire iron.

6. Insert a second tire iron next to the first to hold the bead over the rim. Work around the tire with the first tool, prying the bead over the rim (**Figure 36**).

NOTE
Step 7 is required only if it is necessary to completely remove the tire from the rim.

7. Turn the wheel over or stand it upright. Insert a tire tool between the second bead and the same side of the rim that the first bead was pried over (**Figure 37**). Force the bead on the opposite side from the tool into the center of the rim. Pry the second bead off the rim, working around the wheel with 2 tire irons as with the first.

8. Inspect the valve stem seal. Because rubber deteriorates with age, it is advisable to replace the valve stem when replacing a tire.

Tire Installation

1. Carefully inspect the tire for any damage, especially inside.

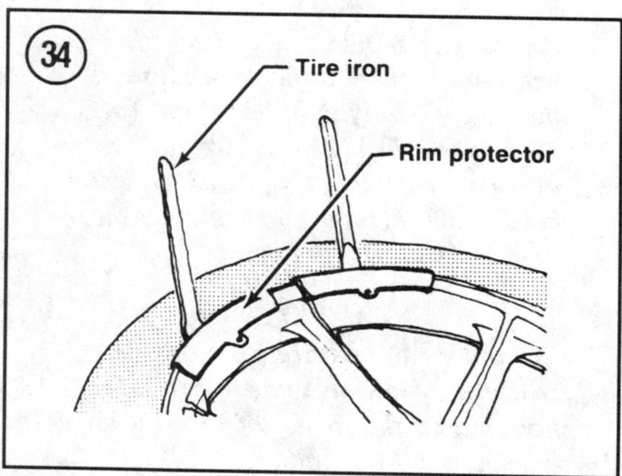

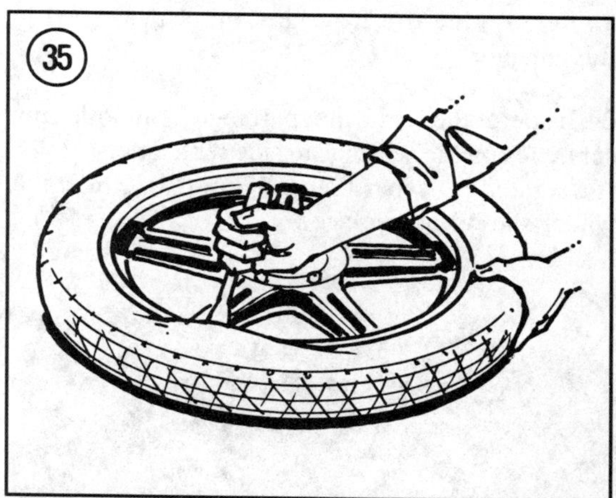

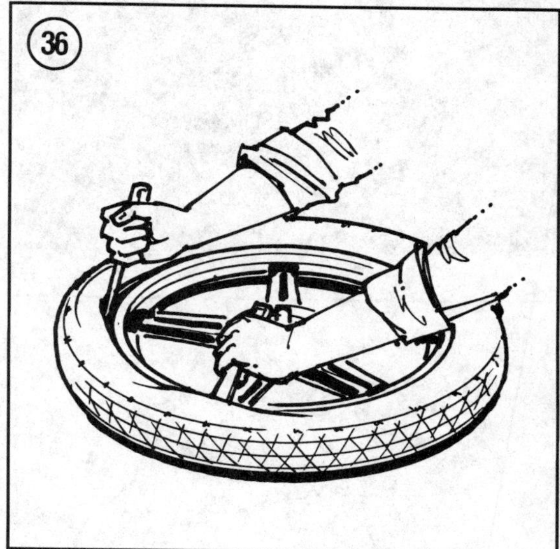

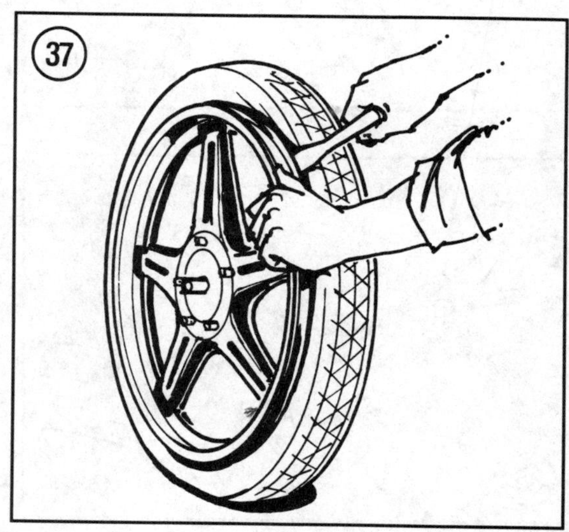

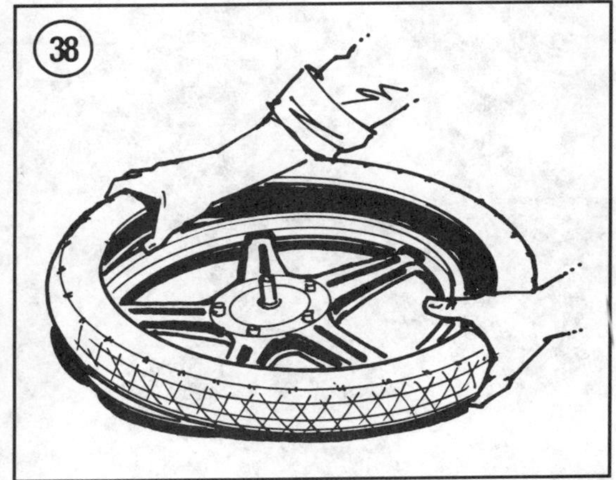

2. A new tire may have balancing rubbers inside. These are not patches and should not be disturbed. A colored spot near the bead indicates a lighter point on the tire. This spot should be placed next to the valve stem (**Figure 29**). In addition, most tires have directional arrows labeled on the side of the tire that indicates in which direction the tire should rotate. Be sure to install the tire accordingly.

3. Lubricate both beads of the tire with soapy water.

4. Place the backside of the tire into the center of the rim. The lower bead should go into the center of the rim and the upper bead outside. Work around the tire in both directions (**Figure 38**). Use a tire iron for the last few inches of bead (**Figure 39**).

5. Press the upper bead into the rim opposite the valve. Pry the bead into the rim on both sides of the initial point with a tire tool, working around the rim to the valve (**Figure 40**).

6. Check the bead on both sides of the tire for an even fit around the rim.

7. Place an inflatable band around the circumference of the tire. Slowly inflate the band until the tire beads are pressed against the rim. Inflate the tire enough to seat it, deflate the band and remove it.

> *WARNING*
> *Never exceed 56 psi (4.0 kg/cm²) inflation pressure as the tire could burst causing severe injury. Never stand directly over the tire while inflating it.*

8. After inflating the tire, check to see that the beads are fully seated and that the tire rim lines (**Figure 41**) are the same distance from the rim all

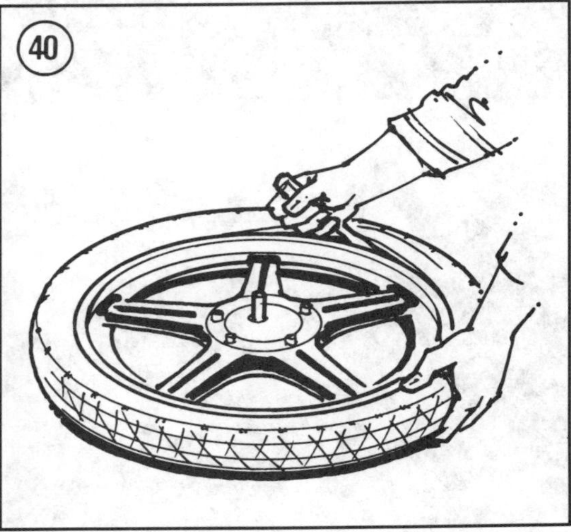

the way around the tire. If the beads won't seat, deflate the tire, relubricate the rim and beads an with soapy water and reinflate the tire.

9. Inflate the tire to the required pressure listed in **Table 3**. Screw on the valve stem cap.

10. Balance the wheel assembly as described in this chapter.

HANDLEBARS

Removal/Installation

The CBR600 uses separate handlebar (**Figure 42**) assemblies that slip over the top of the fork tubes and are bolted directly to the upper fork bridge.

1. Remove the left-hand handlebar as follows:
   a. Remove the screws securing the left-hand handlebar switch (**Figure 43**) to the handlebar.
   b. Separate the switch halves and disconnect the choke cable at the choke lever.
   c. Allow the switch assembly to hang down from the handlebar assembly.
   d. Remove the clutch lever clamp screws. Separate the clamp from the lever housing and remove the lever housing assembly (**Figure 44**).
   e. Pry the upper fork tube retainer ring (A, **Figure 44**) out of the fork tube groove. Then loosen the handlebar pinch bolt (B, **Figure 44**) and slide the handlebar assembly (**Figure 45**) off of the fork tube.

2. Remove the right-hand handlebar as follows:

> *NOTE*
> *It is not necessary to disconnect the brake hydraulic line when removing the master cylinder in sub-step a.*

   a. Disconnect the electrical connector at the master cylinder. Remove the master cylinder clamp bolts and lift the master cylinder (A, **Figure 46**) away from the handlebar. Secure the master cylinder with a piece of wire so that it is level and as high as its mounting position to prevent air from entering into the brake fluid.
   b. Remove the throttle grip/switch housing screws (B, **Figure 46**) and separate the housing slightly. Then disconnect the throttle cables at the throttle grip and remove the

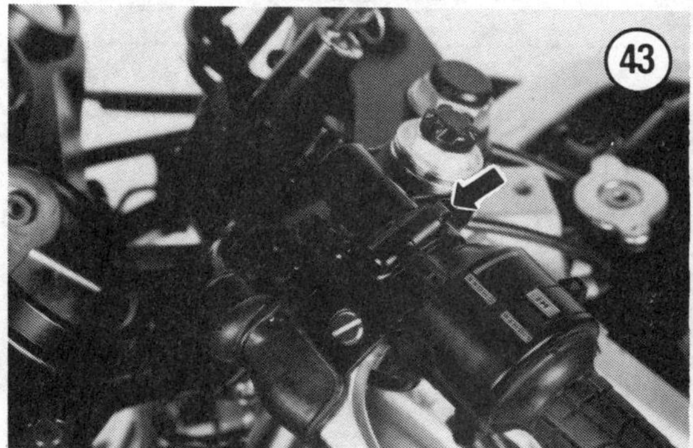

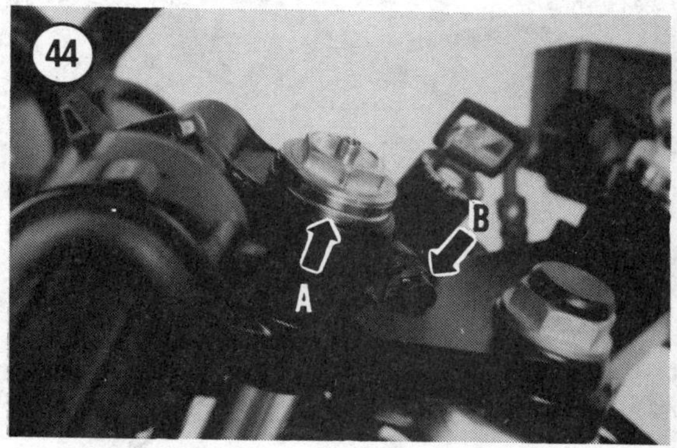

throttle grip assembly. Allow the switch housing assembly to hang down and away from the handlebar. It is not necessary to disconnect the throttle cable from the lower housing assembly.

c. Pry the upper fork tube retainer ring (C, **Figure 46**) out of the fork tube groove. Loosen the handlebar pinch bolt (D, **Figure 46**) and slide the handlebar assembly off of the fork tube.

3. Inspect the handlebar assemblies as described in this chapter.

4. Installation of the handlebar assemblies is the reverse of these steps, noting the following.

5. Note the following when installing the left-hand handlebar:

a. After sliding the handlebar over the fork tube, align the pin on the bottom of the handlebar holder with the slot in the top of the upper steering stem. Seat the handlebar against the upper steering stem.

b. Slide the retainer ring over the fork tube and seat it in the fork tube groove (A, **Figure 44**).

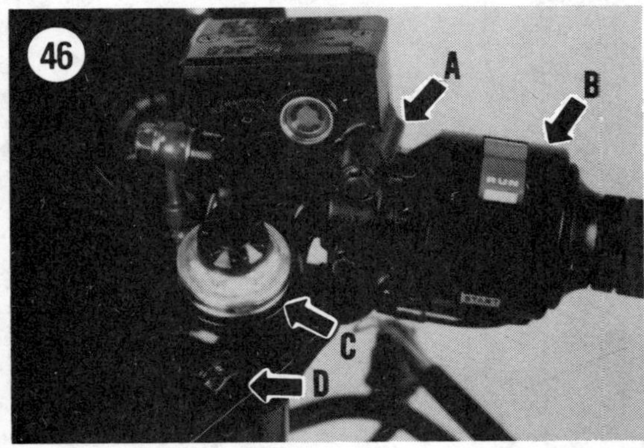

Make sure the retainer ring seats in the groove completely.

c. Tighten the handlebar pinch bolt to the torque specifications in **Table 2**.

d. Slide the choke lever on the handlebar away from the grip and position the switch assembly around the handlebar. Then connect the choke cable to the choke lever.

e. When installing the switch assembly, align the locating pin in the lower switch housing with the hole in the handlebar. Install the 2 switch housing screws. Tighten the front screw and then the rear screw securely.

f. Install the clutch lever bracket so that the front clamp with the UP mark faces up. Install the bracket holder bolts to the torque specifications in **Table 2**.

6. Note the following when installing the right-hand handlebar:

a. After sliding the handlebar over the fork tube, align the pin on the bottom of the handlebar holder with the slot in the top of the upper steering stem. Seat the handlebar against the upper steering stem.

b. Slide the retainer ring over the fork tube and seat it in the fork tube groove (C, **Figure 46**). Make sure the retainer ring seats in the groove completely.

c. Tighten the handlebar pinch bolt to the torque specifications in **Table 2**.

d. Apply a light weight machine oil onto the right-hand handlebar.

e. Slide the throttle grip onto the handlebar.

f. Align the switch housing with the throttle grip assembly. Then connect the end of the throttle cables with the throttle grip.

g. When installing the switch assembly, align the locating pin in the lower switch housing with the hole in the handlebar. Install the 2 switch housing screws. Tighten the front screw and then the rear screw securely.

h. Remove the master cylinder from the piece of wire. Place the master cylinder next to the handlebar. Install the master cylinder clamp so that the UP mark faces up. Install the 2 master cylinder clamp bolts snugly. Then align the upper end of the clamp with the punch mark on the handlebar (**Figure 47**). Tighten the clamp bolts securely.

Inspection

1. Check the handlebars at their bolt holes and along the entire mounting area for cracks or damage. Replace a bent or damaged handlebar immediately. If the bike is involved in a crash, examine the handlebars, steering stem and front forks carefully.

2. To replace a hand grip (A, **Figure 48**), perform the following:

   a. Remove the screw from the end of the handlebar and remove the weight (B, **Figure 48**).

   b. Insert a thin-blade screwdriver part way underneath the hand grip. Then insert a plastic nozzle attached to a can of aerosol electrical contact cleaner and spray a blast of cleaner underneath the grip. Quickly turn the grip to break the adhesive seal. Spray contact cleaner as required until the grip slides off the handlebar.

   c. Clean the handlebar (left side) or throttle grip (right side) thoroughly of all old adhesive.

> *NOTE*
> *The 3-5 minute waiting period in sub-step d applies to the use of Honda Bond A. If you are using another manufacturer's adhesive, follow the direction on the container for application, installation and cure time.*

   d. Apply Honda Bond A (or equivalent) to the inside of the grip and onto the mating handlebar or throttle grip surface. Wait approximately 3-5 minutes and install the grip. Turn the grip slowly to position it and to provide even application of the applied adhesive.

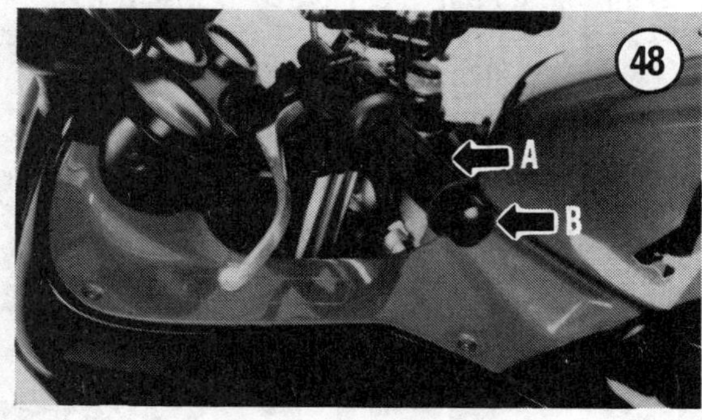

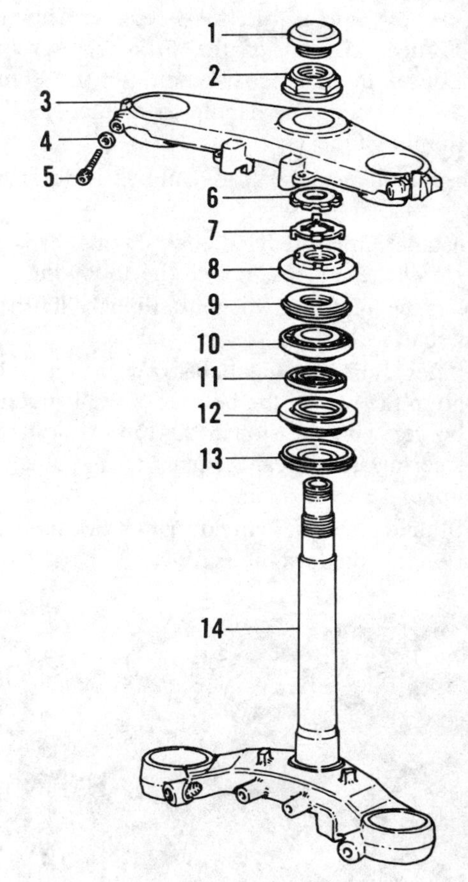

1. Cap
2. Steering stem nut/washer
3. Top fork bridge
4. Washer
5. Bolt
6. Locknut
7. Lockwasher
8. Bearing adjust nut and dust cap
9. Upper inner race
10. Upper bearing outer race
11. Grease holder (1987)
12. Lower bearing
13. Grease seal
14. Steering stem

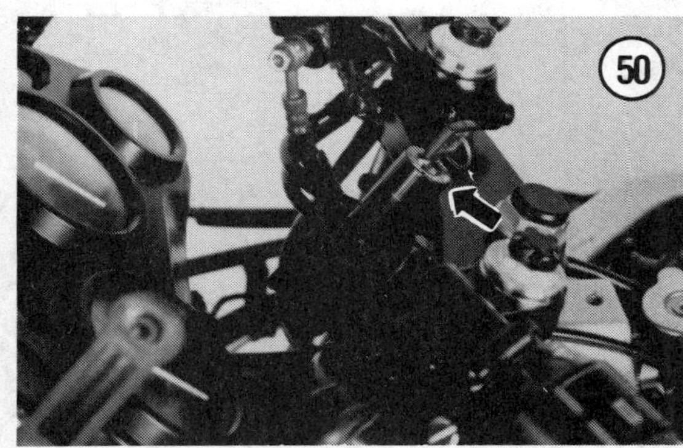

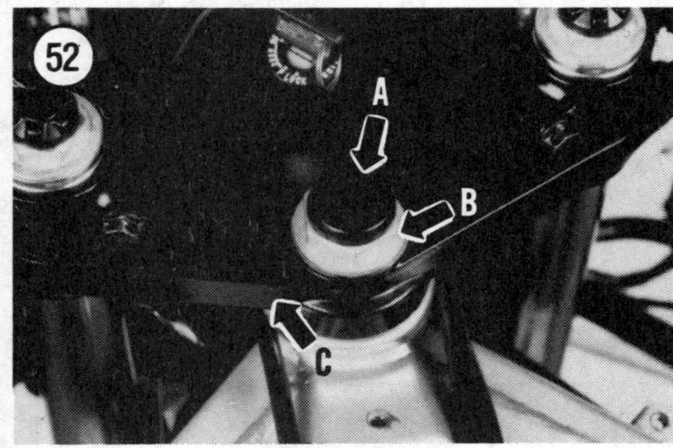

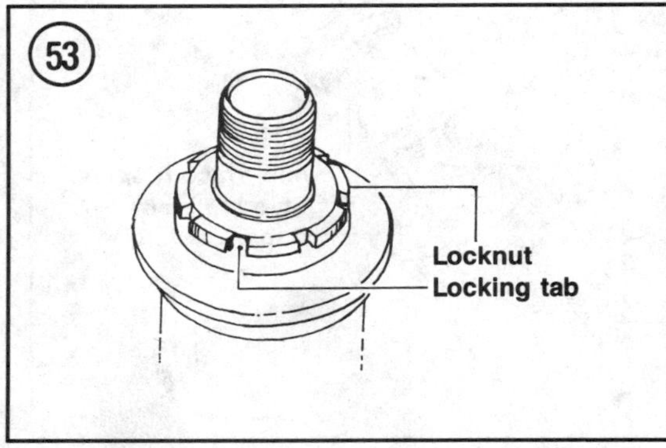

> *WARNING*
> *Allow the adhesive to dry at least one hour (cure time) before riding the bike. If the bike is ridden sooner the hand grip may work loose.*

STEERING HEAD AND STEM

Removal

Refer to **Figure 49** for this procedure.

1. Remove the front wheel as described in this chapter.
2. Remove the upper and lower fairings as described in Chapter Thirteen.
3. Remove the fuel tank as described in Chapter Seven.
4. Disconnect the ignition switch electrical connector. Remove the ignition switch bolts and separate the switch (**Figure 50**) from the upper steering stem.
5. Remove the horn from underneath the steering stem.
6. Remove the bolts securing the brake hose 2-way joint (**Figure 51**) and allow it to hang down. It is not necessary to disconnect the brake hoses.
7. Remove the rubber cap (A, **Figure 52**) from the top of the steering nut.
8. Loosen the steering nut (B, **Figure 52**).
9. Remove the fork tubes as described in this chapter.
10. Remove the steering nut and washer.
11. Remove the upper fork bridge (C, **Figure 52**).
12. Pry the lockwasher tab away from the locknut groove. Then remove the locknut (**Figure 53**) and lockwasher.
13. Secure the steering stem so it will not fall out or the steeing head portion of the frame. Remove the steering stem adjust nut, dust cap and grease holder (1987) (**Figure 54**). Pull the steering stem out of the frame with the lower bearing attached (**Figure 55**).
14. Remove the upper bearing inner race and the upper bearing assembly from the frame tube.

Inspection

1. Clean the bearings and the bearing races in the steering head with solvent.

10

2. Check the welds around the steering head in the frame for cracks and fractures. If any are found, have them repaired by a competent frame shop or welding service.

3. Check the bearings for pitting, scratches or discoloration indicating wear or corrosion. Replace the bearings if they show these conditions. Lower bearing removal and installation are described in this chapter.

4. Check the races for pitting, galling and corrosion. If any of these conditions exist, replace the races as described in this chapter.

5. Check the steering stem for cracks and check its races for damage or wear. Replace if necessary.

6. Thread the steering nut onto the steering stem. Make sure it screws on easily with no roughness. The threads cut onto the steering stem are fine and will damage easily.

Installation

Refer to **Figure 49** for this procedure.

1. Make sure both steering head bearing outer races are properly seated in the steering head tube.

2. Pack the bearing cavities of both ball bearings with bearing grease. Coat the outer bearing races in the steering head with bearing grease also.

3. Install the steering stem, with the lower bearing in place (**Figure 55**), into the steering head tube and hold it firmly in place.

4. Install a new grease holder (1987 only) and the upper bearing assembly.

5. Apply grease to the bottom of the dust seal and install it.

6. Install the steering stem adjust nut and tighten to the torque specification in **Table 2**.

7. Turn the steering stem from side-to-side 5 to 6 times to help seat the bearings.

8. Loosen the steering stem adjust nut and repeat Step 6 and Step 7 twice more to make sure the bearings are properly seated.

9. Install a new lockwasher. Position 2 opposite tabs of the lockwasher into the notches in the steering stem adjust nut as shown in **Figure 57**. Always install a new lockwasher; never reinstall a used one as the tabs may break off, making the lockwasher ineffective.

10. Install the locknut and hand-tighten it. Further tighten the locknut just until the grooves align with 2 of the lockwasher tabs. Bend the 2 tabs up into the grooves in the locknut as shown in **Figure 57**.

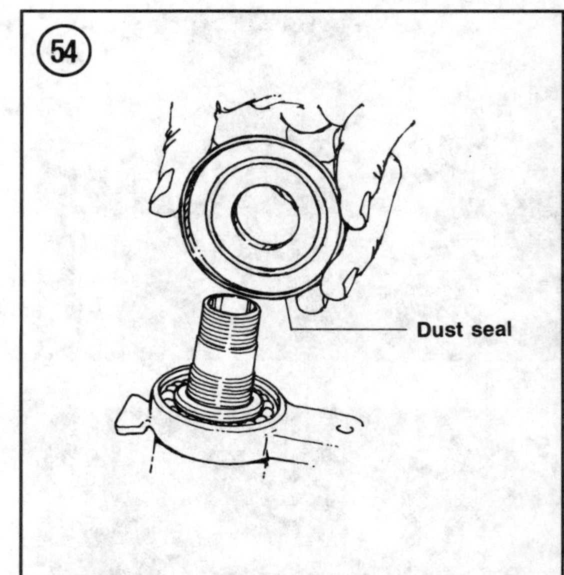

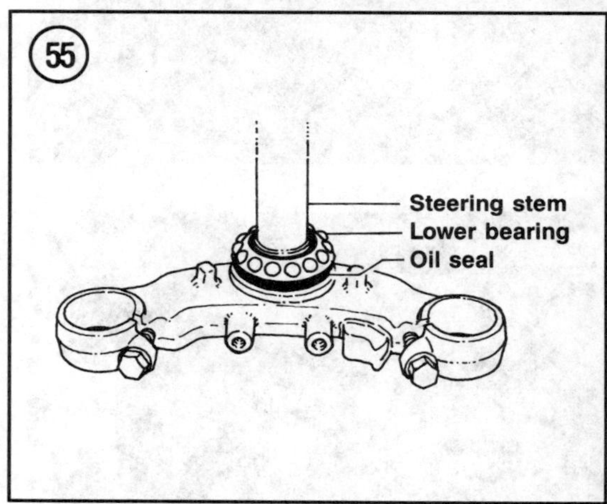

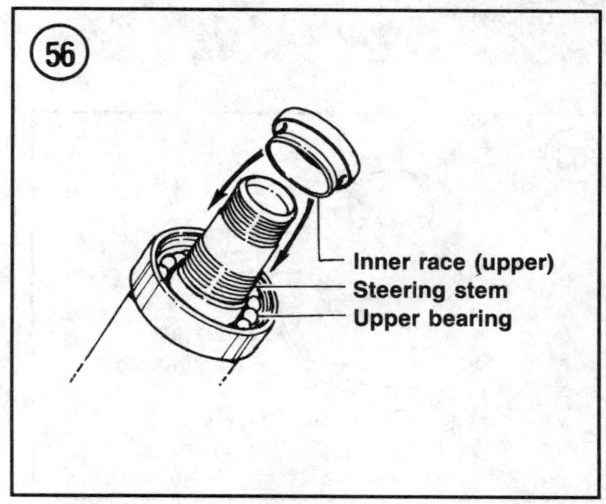

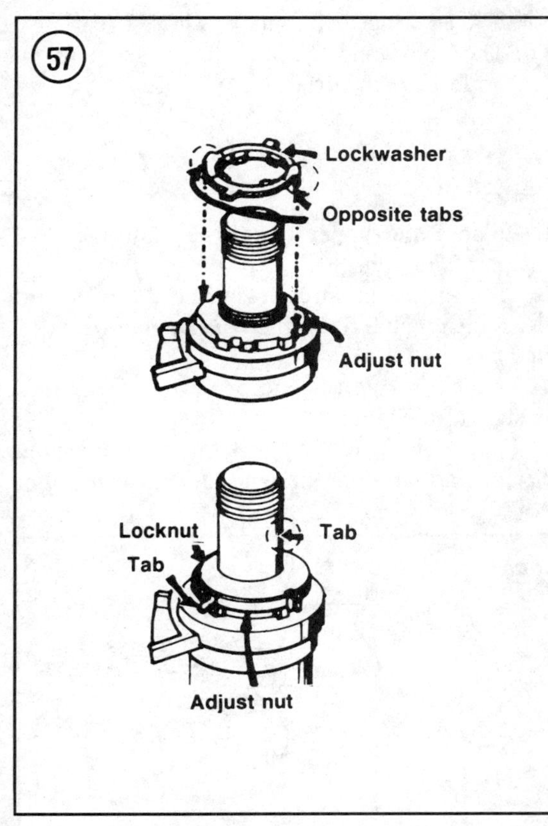

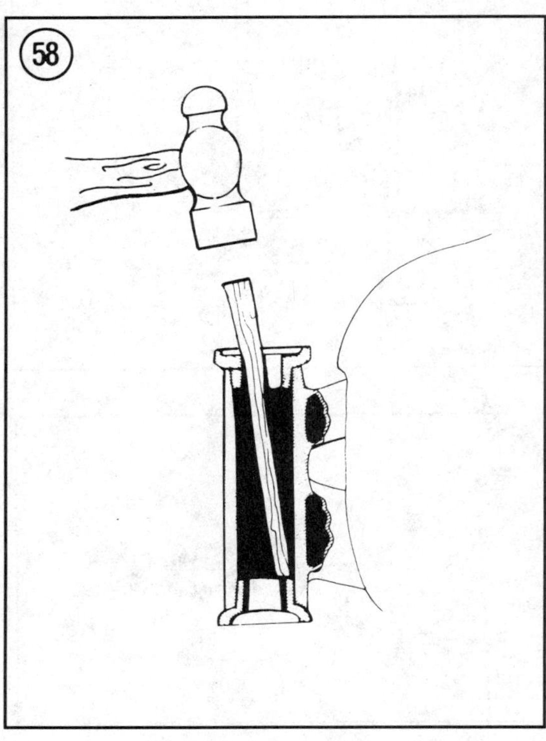

11. Install the upper fork bridge, washer and the steering stem nut. Tighten the nut only finger-tight at this time.

12. Temporarily install the fork tubes at this time.

13. Tighten the steerng stem nut to the torque specification listed in **Table 2**.

14. Remove the fork tubes.

15. Turn the steering stem by hand to make sure it turns freely and does not bind. If the steering stem is too tight, the bearings can be damaged; if the steering stem is too loose, the steering will become unstable. Repeat if necessary.

16. Install the rubber cap (A, **Figure 52**) onto the steering stem nut.

17. Install the 2-way brake hose joint (**Figure 51**). Tighten the mounting bolts securely.

18. Mount the horn underneath the steering stem. Reconnect the horn connector.

19. Install the ignition switch (**Figure 50**) and its attaching bolts. Tighten the bolts securely and reconnect the switch electrical connector.

20. Install the fork tubes as described in this chapter.

21. Reinstall the fuel tank as described in Chapter Seven.

22. Install the front wheel as described in this chapter.

23. Check the steering stem adjustment as described in this chapter.

24. Install the upper and lower fairings as described in Chapter Thirteen.

Steering Head Bearing Races

The headset and steering stem bearing races are pressed into place. Because they are easily bent, do not remove them unless they are worn and require replacement.

The top and bottom bearing races are not the same size. Be sure that you install them in the proper ends of the frame steering head tube.

Steering Head Bearing Outer Race Replacement

To remove the headset race, insert a hardwood stick or soft punch into the head tube (**Figure 58**) and carefully tap the race out from the inside. After it is started, tap around the race so that neither the race nor the steering head tube is damaged. The inside diameters of the inner races are different.

The lower bearing race has a *larger* inside diameter than the upper.

To install the steering head bearing race, tap it in slowly with a block of wood, a suitable size socket or piece of pipe (**Figure 59**). Make sure that the race is squarely seated in the steering head tube bore before tapping it into place. Tap the race in until is flush with the steering head surface.

Steering Stem Lower Bearing Assembly and Dust Seal Removal/Installation

NOTE
Do not remove the steering stem lower bearing race unless it is going to be replaced with a new bearing race. Do not reinstall a bearing race that has been removed as it is no longer true to alignment.

1. Install the steering stem adjust nut onto the steering stem to protect the threads during this procedure.
2. To remove the steering stem lower bearing assembly (**Figure 55**), carefully pry it up from the base of the steering stem with a screwdriver; work around in a circle, prying a little at a time. Remove the bearing assembly and the dust seal.
3. Remove the steering stem adjust nut.
4. Clean the steering stem bearing area of all old grease.
5. Slide a new dust seal over the steering stem and seat it at the bottom of the steering stem.
6. Slide the new bearing onto the steering stem until it stops.
7. Align the bearing with the machined portion of the shaft and slide a long hollow pipe over the steering stem (**Figure 60**). The end of the pipe should fit the bearing's inner race diameter.
8. Drive the bearing on until it rests against the seal. Make sure the bearing is seated squarely and is all the way down.

STEERING PLAY

The steering head should be checked for looseness at the intervals specified in Chapter Three or whenever the following symptoms or conditions exist:

  a. The handlebars vibrate more than normal.
  b. The front forks make a clicking or clunking noise when the front brake is applied.
  c. The steering feels tight or slow.
  d. The motorcycle does not want to steer straight on level road surfaces.

Inspection

1. Remove the upper and lower fairings. See Chapter Thirteen.
2. Prop up the motorcycle so that the front tire clears the ground. See *Front Wheel Removal* in this chapter.
3. Attach a spring scale to one of the fork tubes as shown in **Figure 61**.
4. Center the wheel. Pull the spring scale and note the reading on the scale when the steering stem

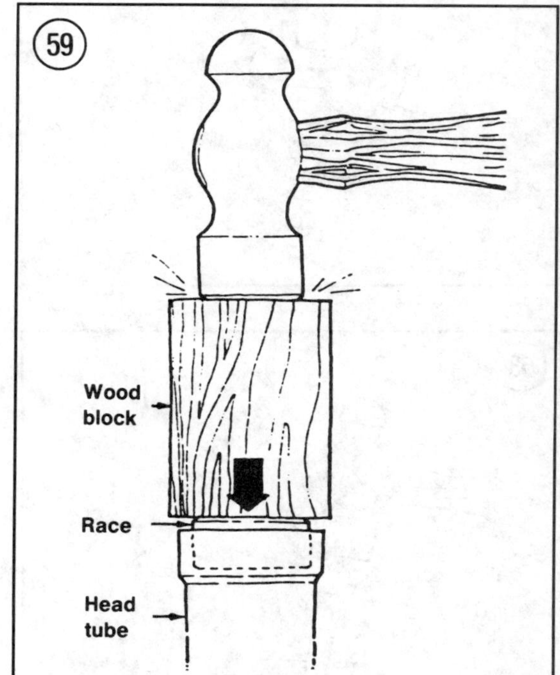

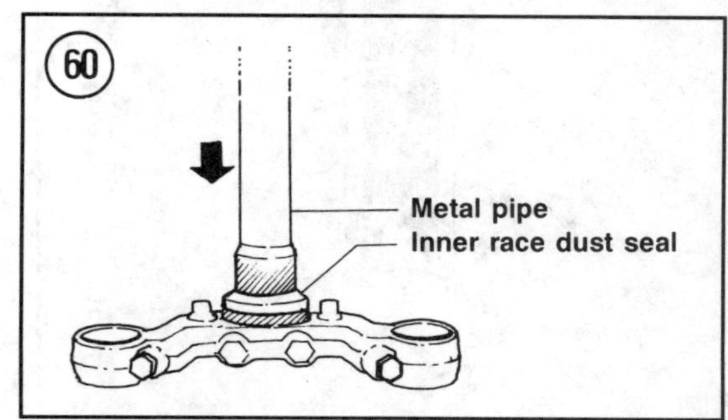

begins to turn. The correct preload adjustment is 1.1-1.6 kg (2.43-3.53 lb.) for right and left turns. If any other reading is obtained, perform the *Adjustment* procedure in this section.

5. If you do not have a spring scale, check steering adjustment as follows:

  a. Center the front wheel. Push lightly against the left handlebar grip to start the wheel turning to the right, then let go. The wheel should continue turning under its own momentum until the forks hit their stop.

  b. Center the wheel, and push lightly against the right handlebar grip. Again, the wheel should turn until the forks hit their stop.

  c. If, with a light push in either direction, the front wheel will turn all the way to the stop, the steering adjustment is not too tight.

  d. If the front wheel would not turn all the way to the stop, the steering is too tight. Adjust the steering as described in this chapter.

  e. Center the front wheel and kneel in front of it. Grasp the bottoms of the 2 front fork slider

legs. Try to pull the forks toward you, and then try to push them toward the engine. If no play is felt, the steering adjustment is not too loose.

  f. If the steering adjustment is too tight or too loose, adjust it as described in this chapter.

5. Reinstall the upper and lower fairings as described in Chapter Thirteen.

Adjustment

1. Prop up the motorcycle so that the front tire clears the ground. See *Front Wheel Removal* in this chapter.

2. Remove the upper and lower fairings. See Chapter Thirteen.

3. Remove the fuel tank.

4. Recheck the steering play as described under *Inspection* in this chapter.

5. If bearing preload is incorrect, lower the front wheel to the ground. Adjust the bearing adjustment nut (**Figure 49**) as described under *Steering Head and Stem Installation* in this chapter. Be sure to install a new lockwasher after making the adjustment.

6. Install the fuel tank and the upper and lower fairings.

FRONT FORKS

If the front forks are going to be removed without disassembly, perform the following *Removal/ Installation* procedure. If the front forks require disassembly, refer to *For Leg Disassembly* and the *Fork Leg Assembly* procedures in this chapter.

Removal/Installation

1. Remove the brake caliper(s) as described under *Front Caliper Removal/Installation* in Chapter Twelve.

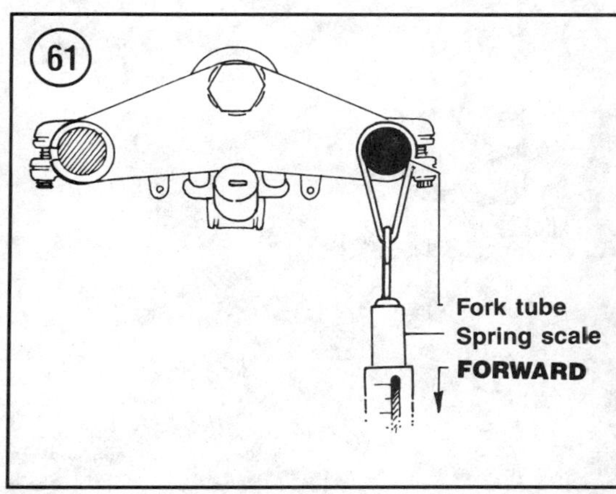

NOTE
*Insert a piece of wood between the brake pads (**Figure 62**) place of the disc. That way, if the brake lever is inadvertently squeezed, the piston will not be forced out of the calipers. If it does happen, the calipers might have to be disassembled to reseat the pistons.*

2. Remove the front fender mounting bolts and remove the fender (**Figure 63**).

3. Remove the front wheel as described in this chapter.

4. Remove the pivot spacer (**Figure 64**) after removing the left-hand brake caliper.

5. Remove the handlebars as described under *Handlebars* in this chapter.

6. Remove the air valve cap (**Figure 65**) from both fork tubes.

> *WARNING*
> *Protect your eyes and clothing when releasing the front fork air pressure as described in Step 7 as fork oil may come out if the air is release too fast.*

7. Depress the air valve (**Figure 66**) to release all fork air pressure.

8. Loosen the upper (**Figure 67**) and lower fork tube pinch bolts.

9. Twist the upper fork tube and slide the fork tube assembly (**Figure 68**) out of the steering stem.

10. Repeat for the opposite side.

11. Install by reversing these removal steps. Note the following:

12. Slide each fork tube into the steering stem assembly until the lower groove in the fork tube aligns with the top of the fork bridge (**Figure 69**).

13. Tighten the upper and lower fork tube pinch bolts to the torque specifications in **Table 2**.

14. Install the front wheel as described in this chapter.

15. Apply a moly base grease onto the pivot spacer (**Figure 64**) and insert it all the way in the fork tube bearing (**Figure 70**)

16. Install the front brake calipers as described in Chapter Twelve.

> *WARNING*
> *After installing the front brake calipers, squeeze the front brake lever. If the brake lever feels spongy, bleed the brake(s) as described under* **Bleeding the System** *in Chapter Twelve.*

> *WARNING*
> *During the next step, never use any type of compressed gas as an explosion may be lethal. Never heat the fork assembly with a torch or place it near an open*

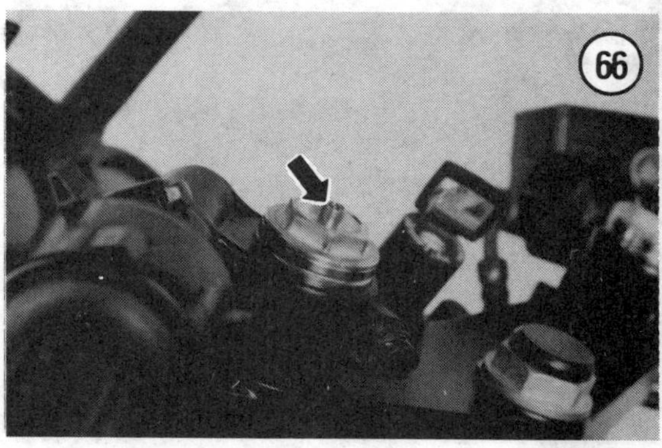

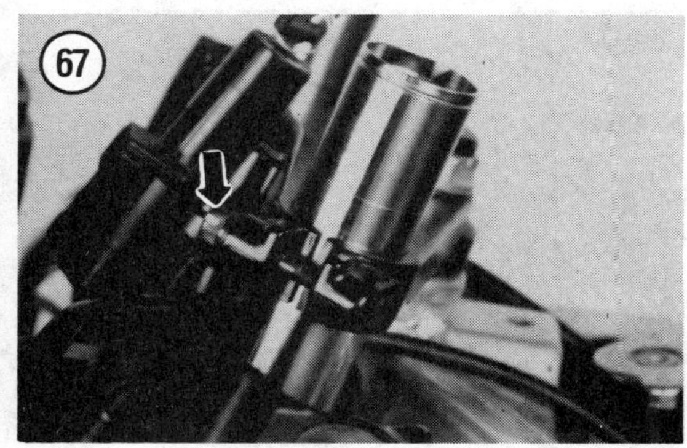

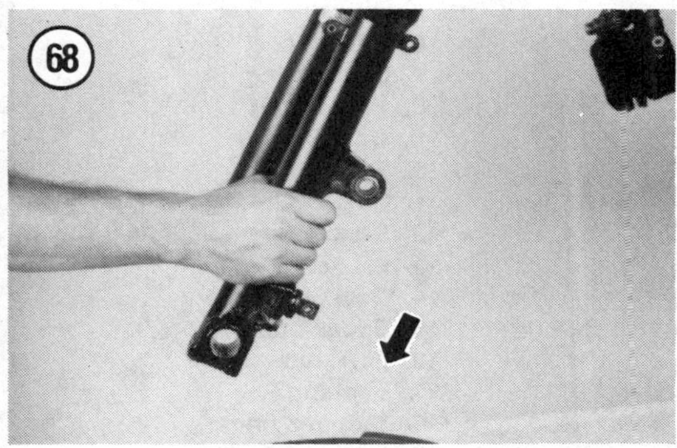

flame or extreme heat, as this will also result in an explosion.

17. Make sure the front wheel is off the ground and inflate the forks to within the specifications listed in **Table 4**. Do not use compressed air; use only a small hand-operated air pump.

18. Apply Loctite 242 (blue) to the front fender bolts prior to installation. Tighten the bolts securely.

Fork Leg Disassembly

Refer to **Figure 71** (left-hand side) and **Figure 72** (right-hand side) when performing this procedure.

Fork tube disassembly is easier if some of the procedures are performed while the fork tubes are mounted on the bike.

1. Perform Steps 1-5 described under *Front Fork Removal/Installation*.

2. Remove the air valve cap (**Figure 65**) from both fork tubes.

> *WARNING*
> *Protect your eyes and clothing when releasing the front fork air pressure as described in Step 3 as for oil may come out if the air is released too fast.*

3. Depress the air valve (**Figure 66**) to release all fork air pressure.

> *NOTE*
> *The lower fork tube Allen bolt is normally secured with Loctite and can be very difficult to remove because the damper rod will turn inside the slider. The Allen bolt can be removed easily with an air impact driver. If you do not have access to an air impact driver, it is best to loosen the Allen bolt before removing the fork tube cap and spring. This method allows the fork spring to apply pressure to the damper rod to keep it from turning when the Allen bolt is loosened. If you are unable to loosen the Allen bolt, take the fork tubes to a dealer and have them remove the bolts.*

4. Place a drain pan underneath one of the fork tubes.

LEFT FORK LEG

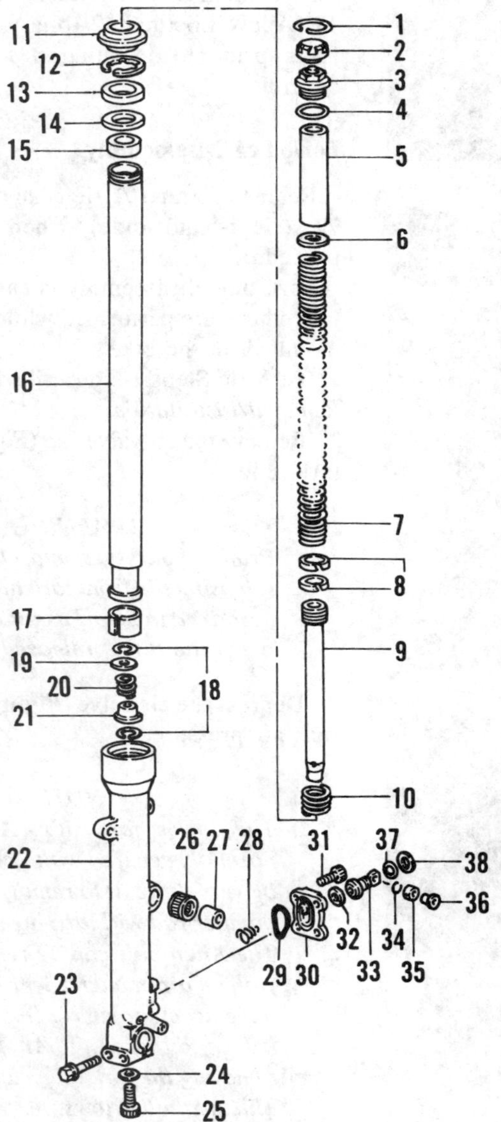

1. Clip
2. Air valve cap
3. Fork tube cap
4. O-ring
5. Spacer
6. Spring seat
7. Fork spring
8. Piston ring
9. Damper rod
10. Spring
11. Dust seal
12. Snap ring
13. Oil seal
14. Backup ring
15. Slider bushing
16. Fork tube
17. Bushing
18. Stopper rings
19. Seat
20. Spring
21. Oil lock valve
22. Slider
23. Bolt
24. Special washer
25. Allen bolt
26. Needle bearing
27. Bushing
28. Spring
29. O-ring
30. Anti-dive cover
31. Bolt
32. Rubber stopper
33. Piston
34. Stopper ring
35. Rubber bushing
36. Cover
37. O-ring
38. Piston case boot

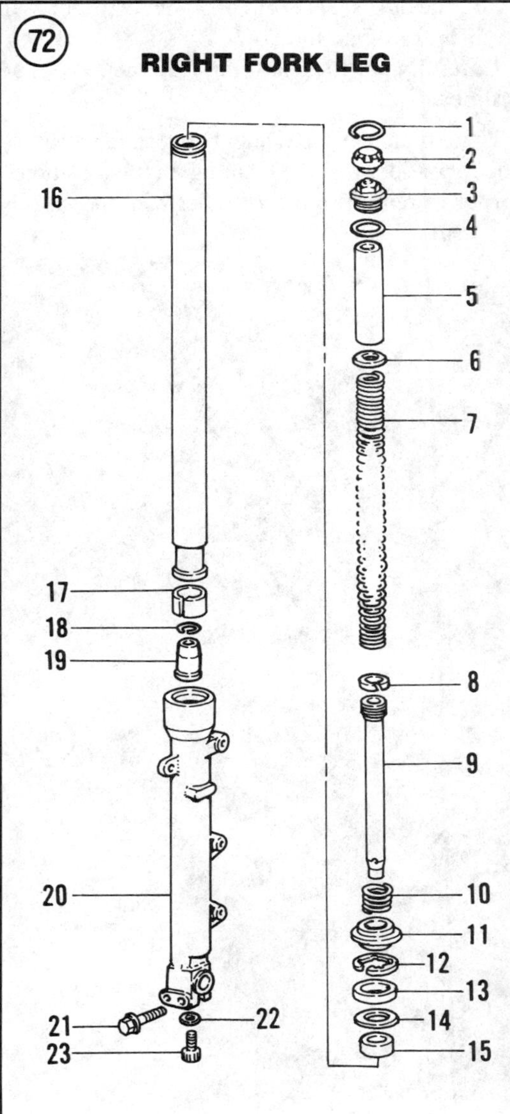

1. Clip
2. Air valve cap
3. Fork tube cap
4. O-ring
5. Spacer
6. Spring seat
7. Fork spring
8. Piston ring
9. Damper rod
10. Spring
11. Dust seal
12. Snap ring
13. Oil seal
14. Backup ring
15. Slider bushing
16. Fork tube
17. Bushing
18. Stopper ring
19. Oil lock piece
20. Slider
21. Bolt
22. Special washer
23. Allen bolt

5. Using an allen bit fixed to a socket, loosen and remove the fork tube Allen bolt (**Figure 73**). Allow the oil to drain out of the fork tube when the bolt is removed.

NOTE
*With the front fender removed, the slider will turn when the Allen bolt is turned. Hold the slider with a large adjustable wrench as shown in **Figure 73**.*

WARNING
The fork caps are held under spring pressure. Take precautions to prevent the caps from flying into your face during removal. Furthermore, if the fork tubes are bent, the fork caps will be under considerable pressure; have them removed by a Honda dealer.

6. Using a socket, loosen and remove the fork cap (**Figure 74**).

7. Remove the following parts from the top of the fork tube:

   a. Spacer (**Figure 75**).
   b. Spring seat (**Figure 76**).
   c. Fork spring (**Figure 77**).

8. Remove the Allen bolt (**Figure 73**) loosened in Step 5.

9 Work the dust seal (**Figure 78**) out of slider and slide it up the fork tube.

10. Carefully pry the snap ring (**Figure 79**) out of the slider.

11. There is an interference fit between the bushing in the fork slider and the bushing on the fork tube. In order to remove the fork tube from the slider,

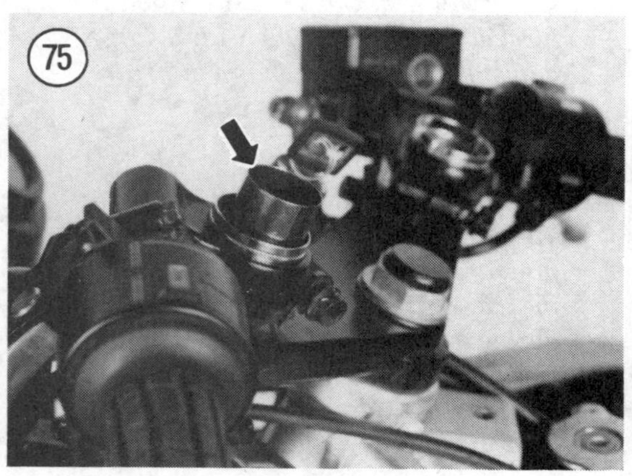

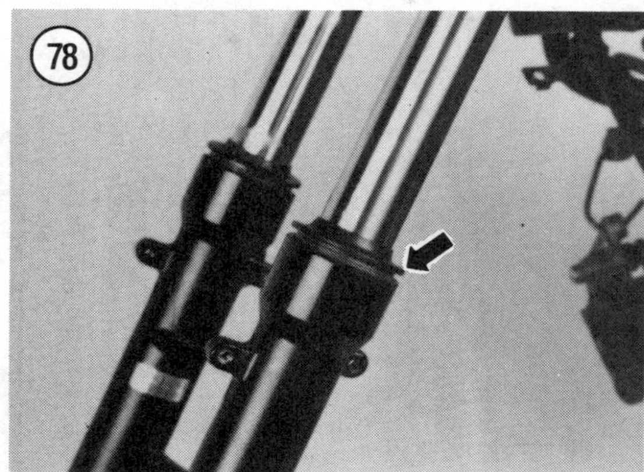

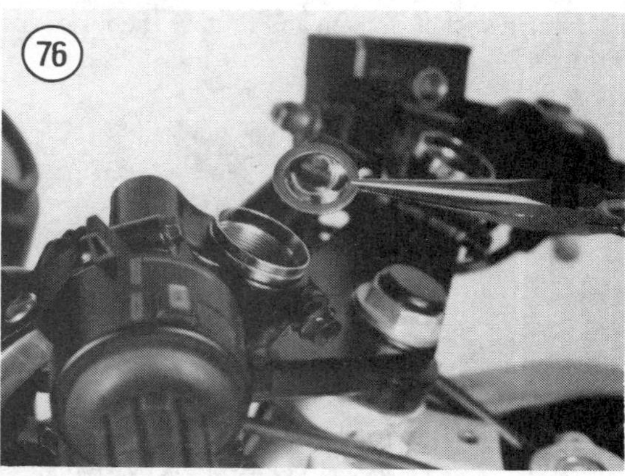

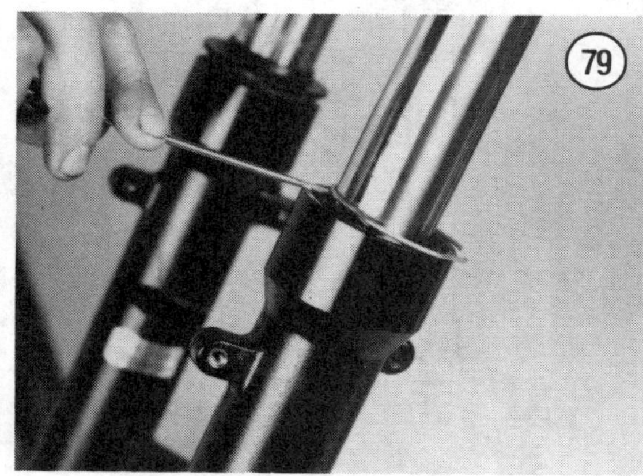

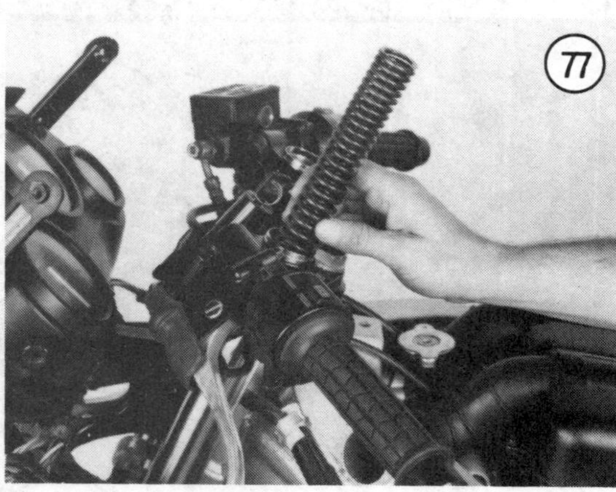

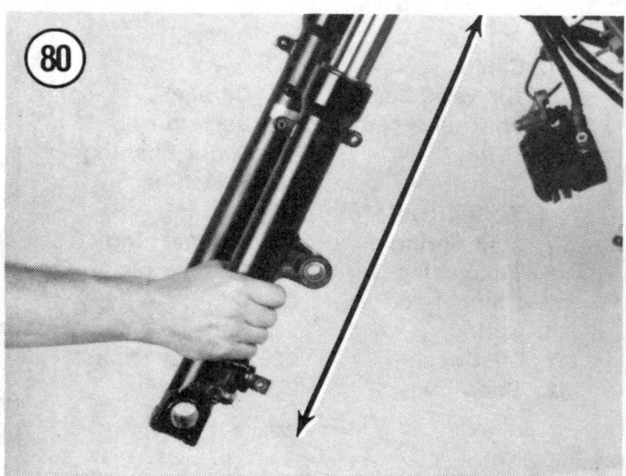

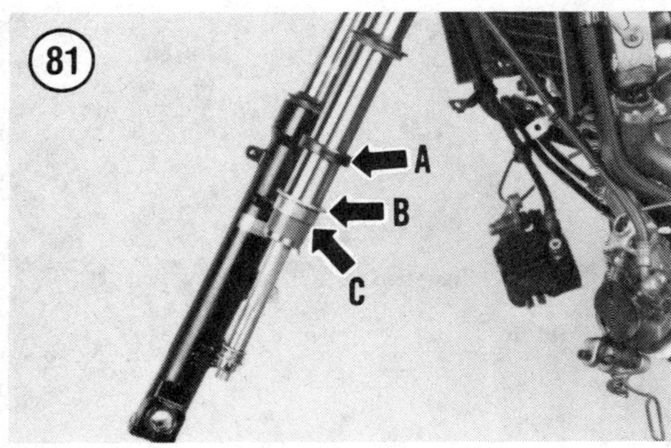

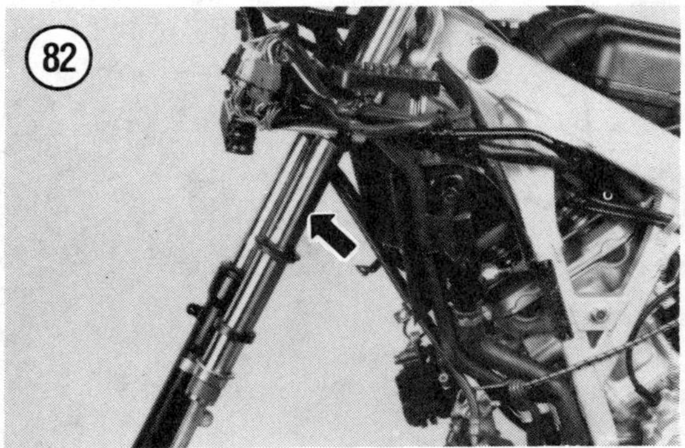

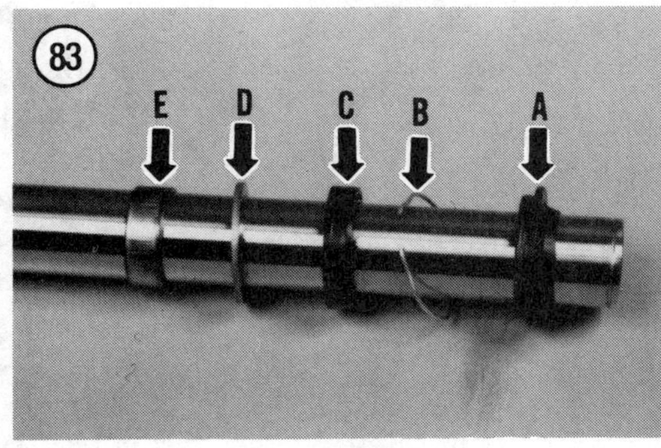

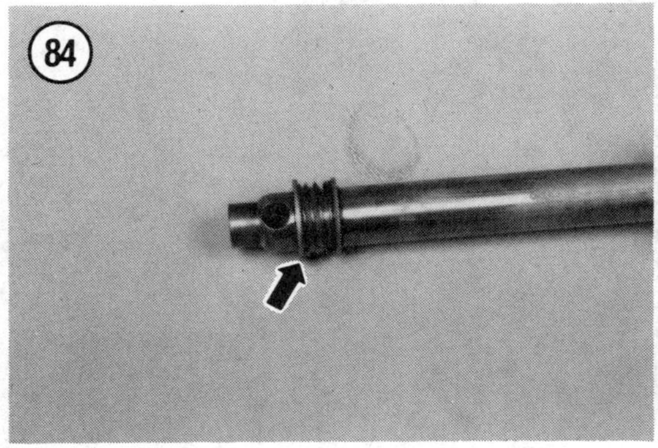

pull hard on the fork tube using quick in-and-out strokes (**Figure 80**). Doing this will withdraw the oil seal (A), backup ring (B) and slider bushing (C). See **Figure 81**.

12. Loosen the upper and lower fork tube pinch bolts and remove the fork tube assembly (**Figure 82**).

13. See **Figure 83**. Slide the following parts off of the fork tube:
   a. Dust seal (A).
   b. Snap ring (B).
   c. Oil seal (C).
   d. Backup ring (D).
   e. Slider bushing (E).

14A. *Left-hand fork tube*: Complete fork tube disassembly by performing the following:
   a. Remove the circlip from the damper rod (**Figure 84**).
   b. Slide off the oil lock valve (**Figure 85**).
   c. Remove the spring (**Figure 86**).

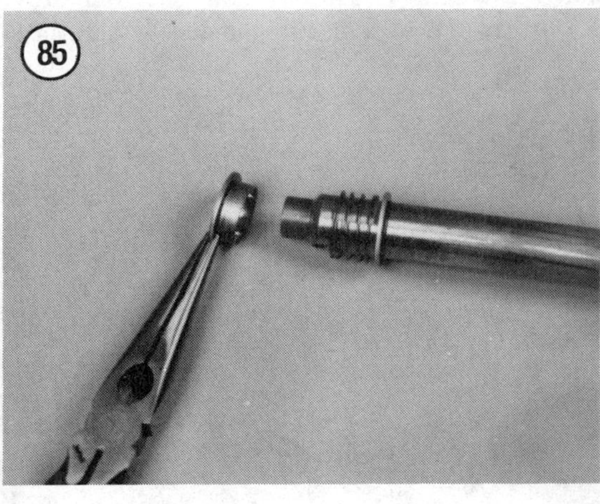

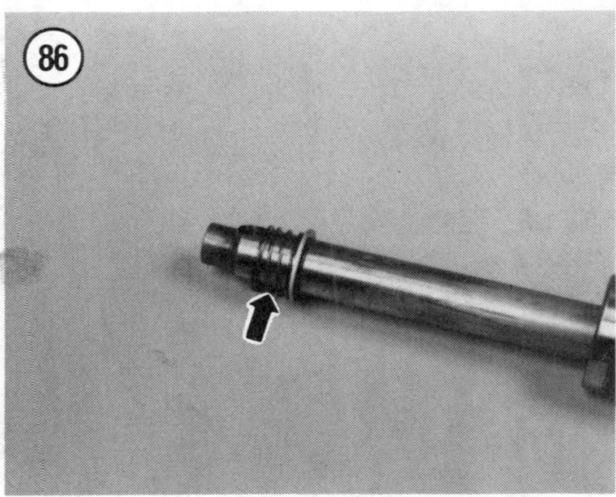

d. Remove the circlip from the damper rod (**Figure 87**).

e. Slide the damper rod and spring out through the top of the fork tube (**Figure 88**).

14B. *Right-hand fork tube*: Complete fork tube disassembly by performing the following:

a. Slide the oil lock valve (A, **Figure 89**) off of the damper rod.

b. Remove the circlip (B, **Figure 89**) from the damper rod.

c. Slide the damper rod and spring out through the top of the fork tube (**Figure 90**).

Inspection

1. Thoroughly clean all parts in solvent and dry them.

2. Check both fork tubes for wear or scratches.

3. Check the fork tube for straightness. Place the fork tube on V-blocks and check runout with a dial indicator (**Figure 91**). If the runout is 0.2 mm (0.01 in.) or greater, have it straightened by a Honda

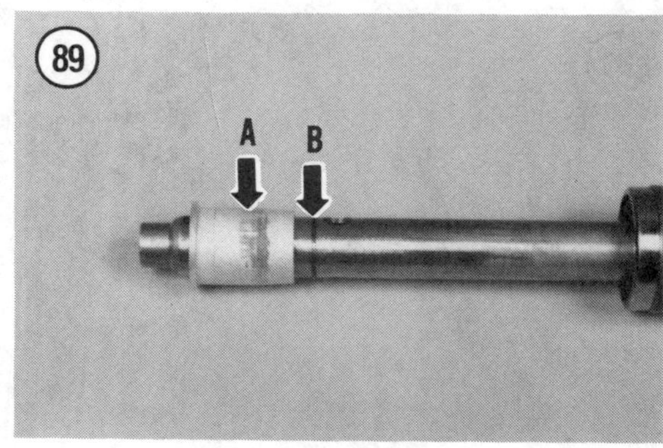

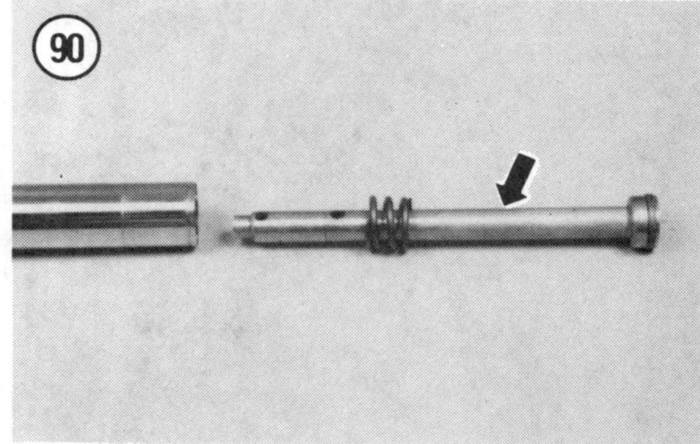

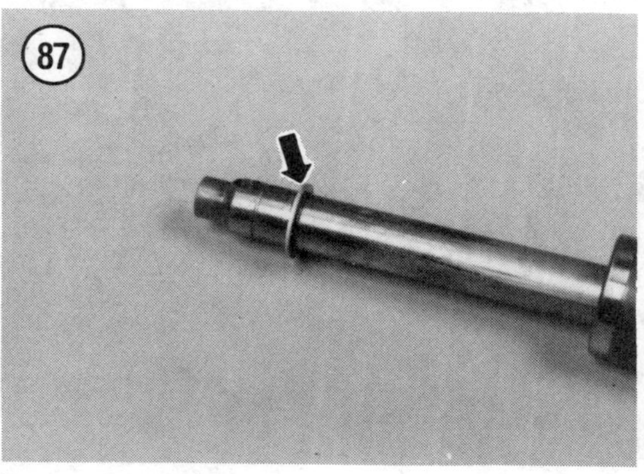

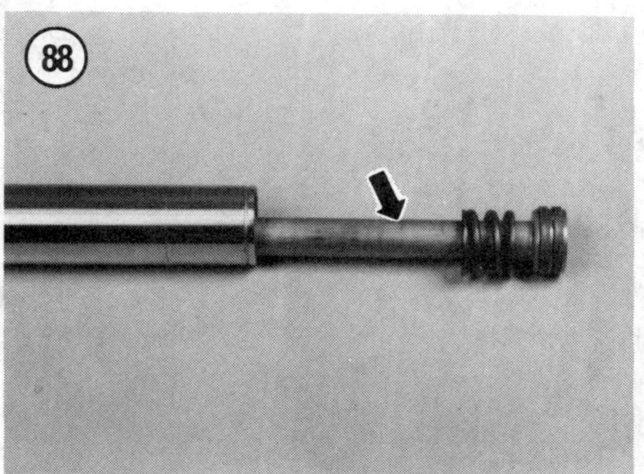

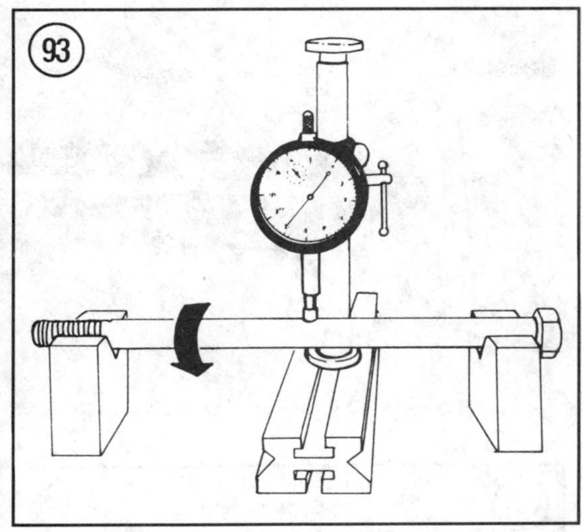

dealer. If the fork tube is bent to the point that it has creased or the chrome has flaked, the fork tube must be replaced.

4. Check the oil seal area in the slider (**Figure 92**) for dents or other damage that would allow oil leakage. Replace the slider if necessary.

5. Check the damper rod for straightness. Place the damper rod on V-blocks and check runout with a dial indicator (**Figure 93**). The rod should be replaced if the runout is 0.2 mm (0.008 in.) or greater.

6. Carefully check the damper rod and piston ring(s) for wear or damage. Refer to **Figure 94** for the left-hand fork leg and **Figure 95** for the right-hand fork leg.

7. Check the damper rod circlip grooves (**Figure 96**) for damage that would allow the circlips to loosen; replace the damper rod if necessary.

8. Measure the uncompressed length of the stock Honda fork springs (**Figure 97**) with a tape measure and compare to specifications in **Table 1**. Replace the fork spring(s) if too short.

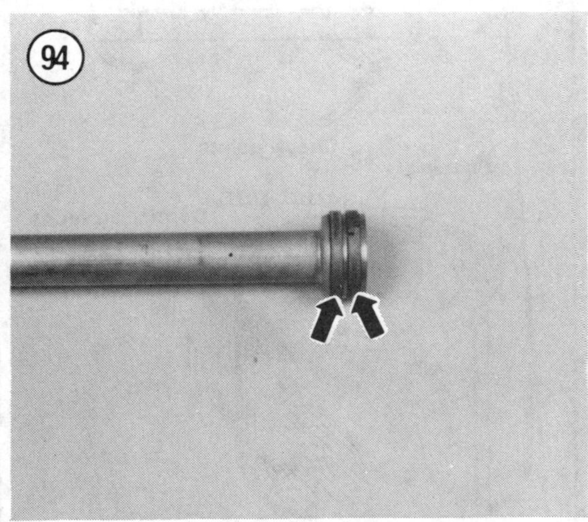

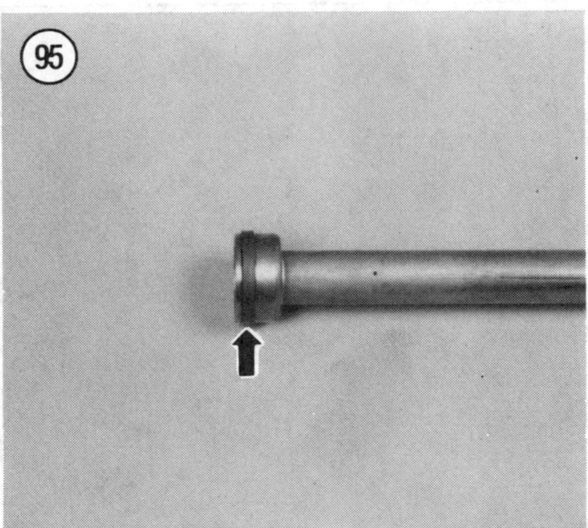

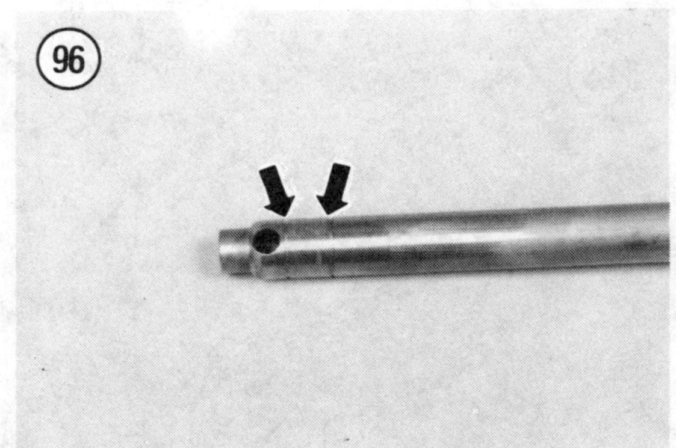

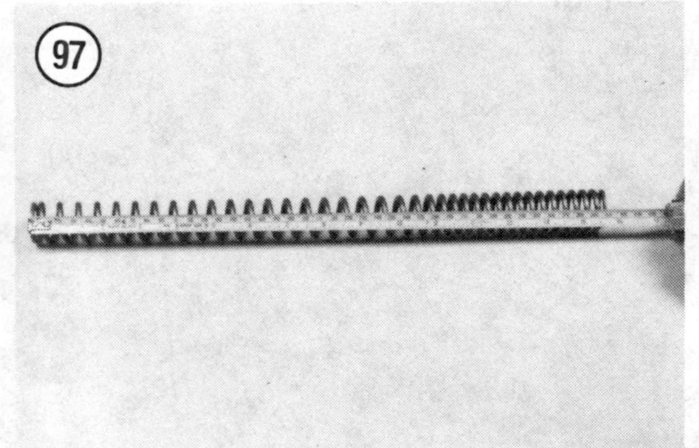

NOTE
If one fork spring is replaced, compare the measurement of the new and the remaining old spring. If the length difference is great between a new and the old usable spring, it is best to replace both springs to keep the forks balanced for steering stability.

9. Replace the fork cap O-ring (**Figure 98**) if deformed or damaged.

10. Check the fork tube Allen bolt washer (**Figure 99**) for damage that would allow oil leakage; replace if necessary.

11. Inspect the slider and fork tube bushing. Refer to **Figure 100**. If the Teflon coating is worn off so that the copper base material is showing on approximately 3/4 of the total surface, the bushing must be replaced. Also check for distortion on the check points of the backup ring; replace as necessary. Refer to **Figure 101**.

12. Check the oil seal (**Figure 102**) for tears, deterioration or other damage that would allow oil leakage. Replace both seals if necessary.

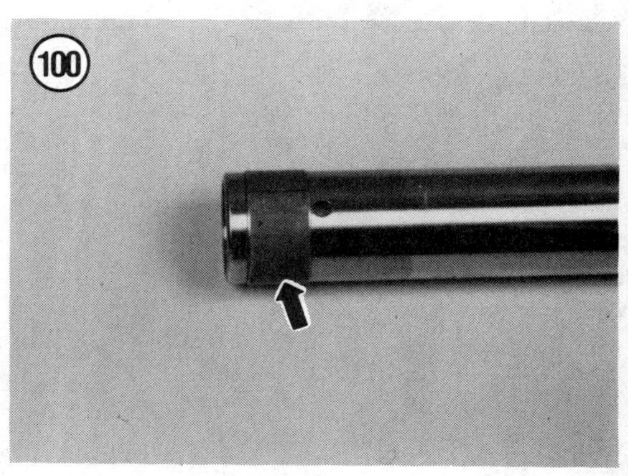

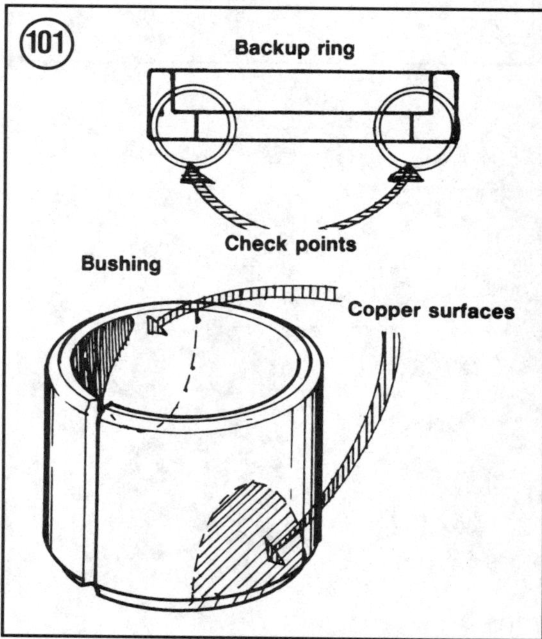

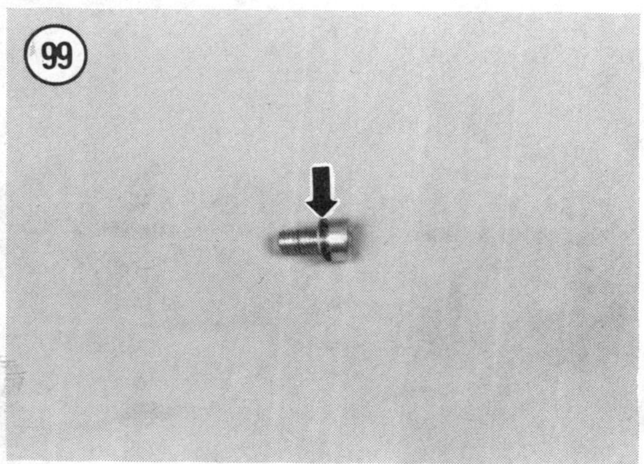

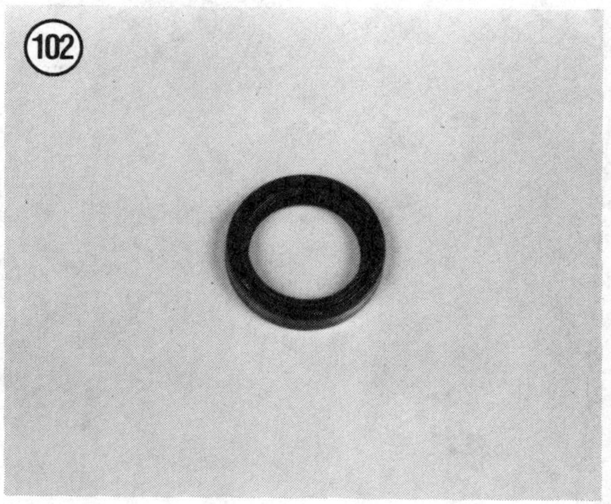

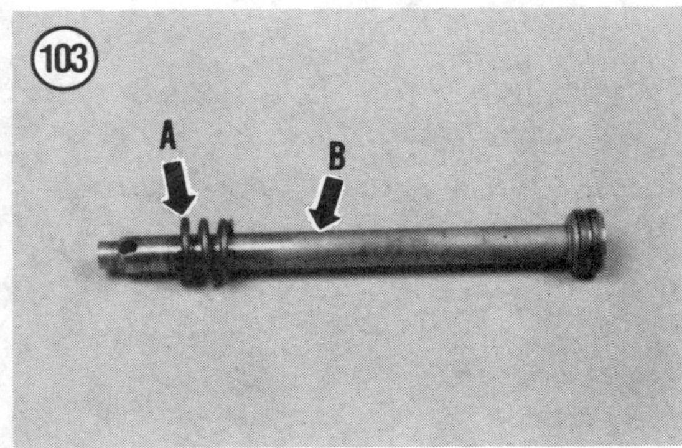

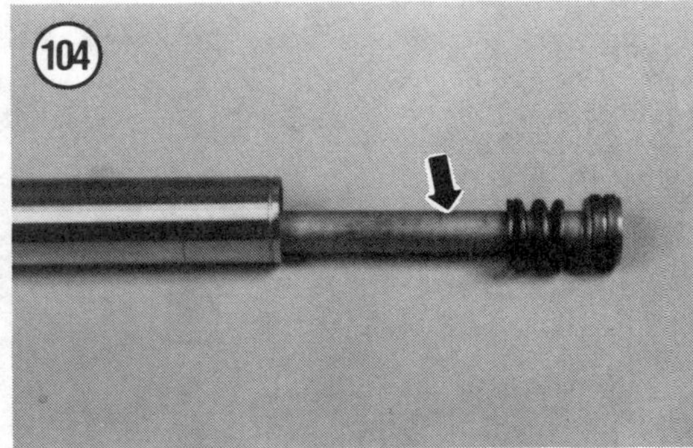

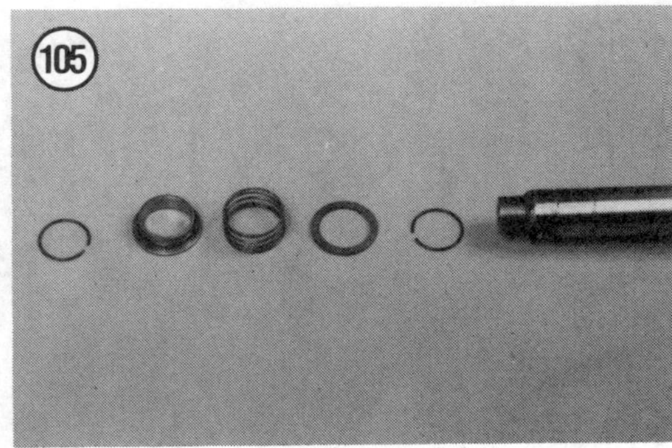

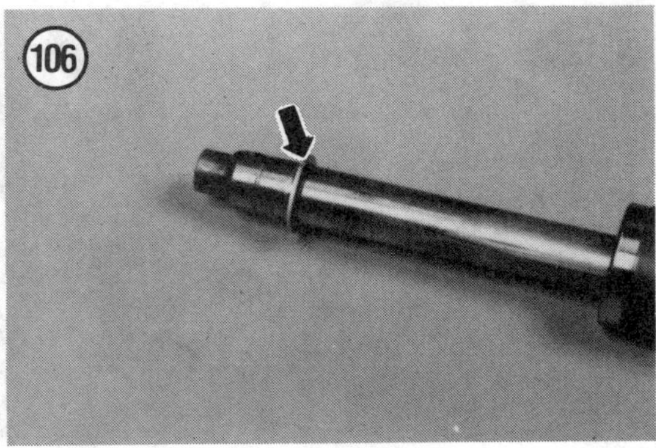

Fork Leg Assembly
(Left-Hand Fork Leg)

Refer to **Figure 71** when performing this procedure.

1. Coat all parts with fresh DEXRON automatic transmission fluid before installation.

2. If removed, install a new fork tube bushing (**Figure 100**).

3. Install the rebound spring (A) onto the damper rod (B). See **Figure 103**.

4. Insert the damper rod assembly into the fork tube as shown in **Figure 104**.

5. Assemble the damper rod oil lock valve assembly (**Figure 105**) in the following order:

  a. Install the circlip and spring seat (**Figure 106**).

  b. Install the spring (**Figure 107**).

  c. Install the oil lock valve as shown in **Figure 108**.

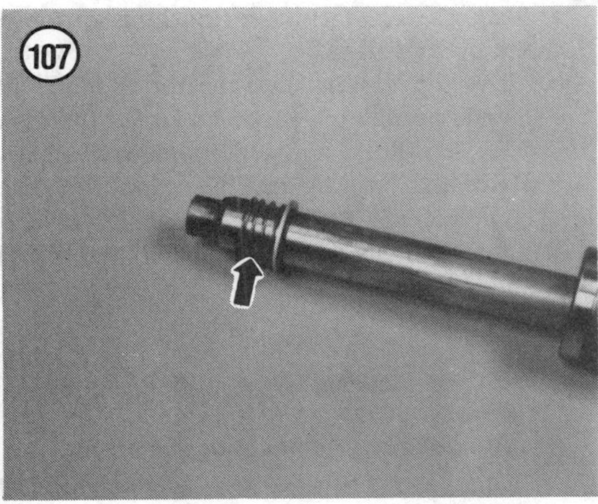

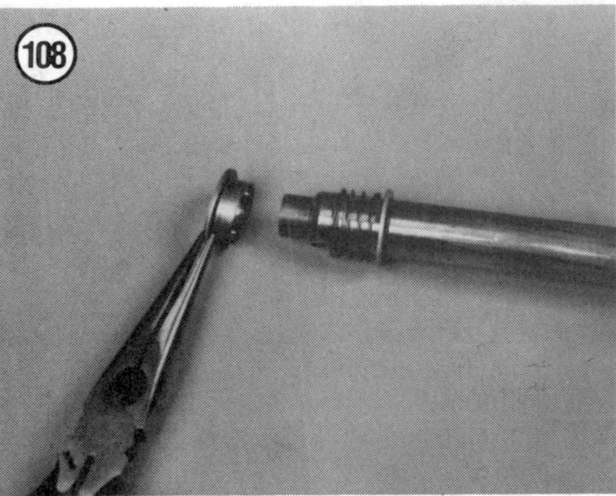

10

d. Secure the oil lock valve assembly with the circlip (**Figure 109**).

6. Temporarily install the fork spring, spring seat, spacer and fork cap to hold the damper rod in place. Install the fork cap while pushing down on the spacer and spring. Start the cap slowly; don't cross thread it.

7. Install the fork tube assembly into the slider.

8. Make sure the gasket (**Figure 99**) is on the Allen head screw.

9. Apply Loctite 242 (blue) to the threads of the Allen head screw before installation. Install it in the fork slider (**Figure 110**) and tighten to the torque specification listed in **Table 2**.

10. Install the fork slider bushing (A, **Figure 111**) down the fork tube and rest it on the slider.

11. Slide the fork slider backup ring (D, **Figure 111**) down the fork tube and rest it on top of the fork slider bushing.

12. To install the fork slider bushing, perform the following:

a. Place the old fork slider bushing on top of the backup ring.

b. Drive the bushing into the fork slider with Honda special tool Fork Seal Driver (part No. 07947-3710101) or a suitable piece of pipe.

c. Drive the bushing into place until it seats completely in the recess in the slider.

d. Remove the installation tool and the old fork slider bushing.

> *NOTE*
> *The slider bushing can be driven in with a homemade tool (**Figure 112**). This tool can be made at a machine shop from a piece of aluminum.*

> *NOTE*
> *A piece of galvanized pipe can also work as a tool. If both ends are threaded (a close nipple pipe fitting), wrap one end with duct tape to prevent the threads from damaging the interior of the slider.*

13. To install the fork seal (C, **Figure 111**), perform the following:

a. Coat the new seal with DEXRON automatic transmission fluid or fork oil.

b. Position the seal with the marking (**Figure 102**) facing upward and slide it down onto the fork tube.

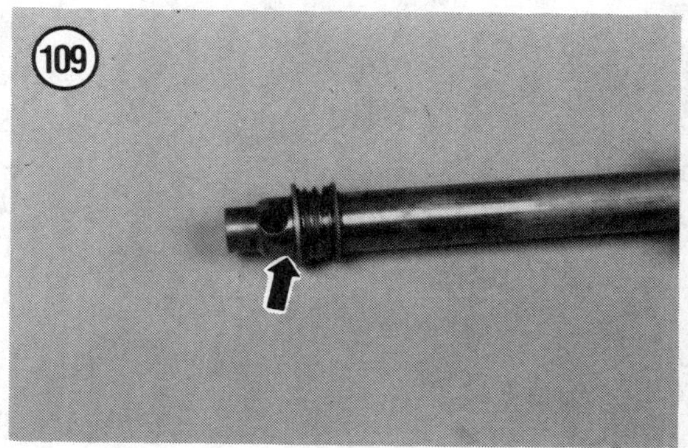

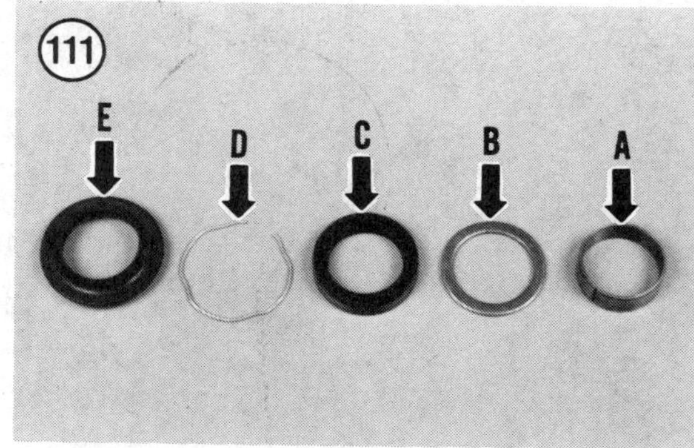

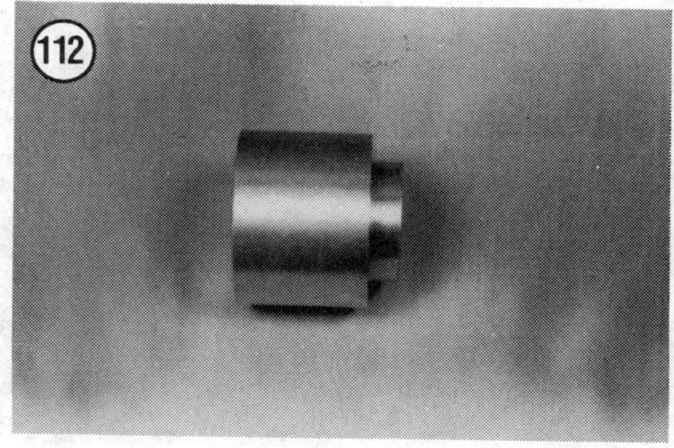

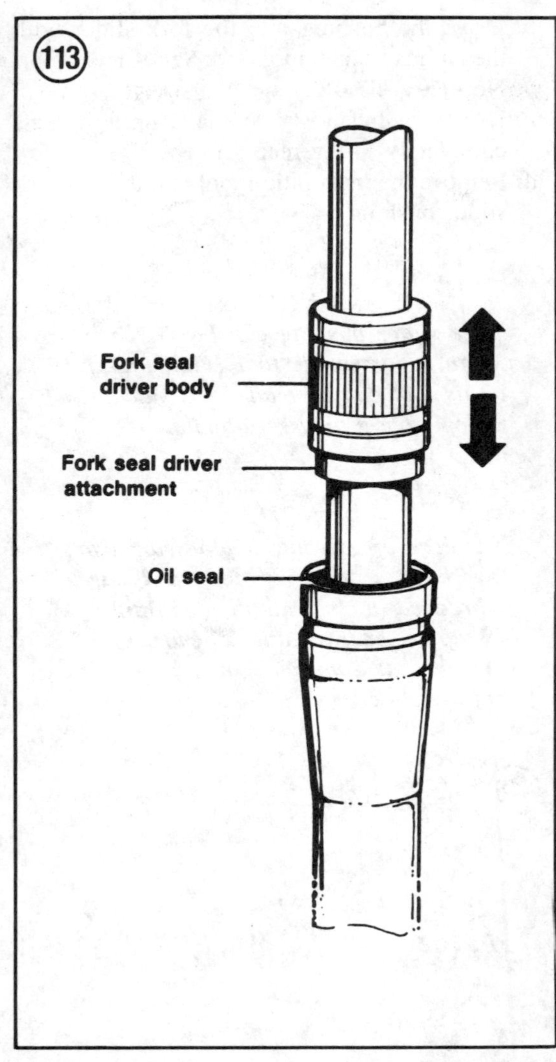

c. Drive the seal into the slider with Honda special tool Fork Seal Driver (part No. 07947-3710101) and Attachment (part No. 07747-0010600). See **Figure 113**.

d. Drive the oil seal in until the groove in the slider can be seen above the top surface of the oil seal.

NOTE
The seal can be driven in with a homemade tool described in the NOTES following Step 11.

14. Install the snap ring (**Figure 114**). Make sure the snap ring is completely seated in the groove in the fork slider.

15. Install the dust seal (**Figure 115**) into the slider.

16. Install the fork tube as described in this chapter.

WARNING
The fork caps are held under spring pressure. Take precautions to prevent the caps from flying into your face during removal.

17. Using a socket, loosen and remove the fork cap.

18. Remove the following parts from the top of the fork tube:
   a. Spacer.
   b. Spring seat.
   c. Fork spring.

19. Fill the fork tube with the correct quantity of DEXRON automatic transmission fluid or fork oil. See **Table 5**.

NOTE
Note that in Table 5 the fork quantity is different for both fork tubes.

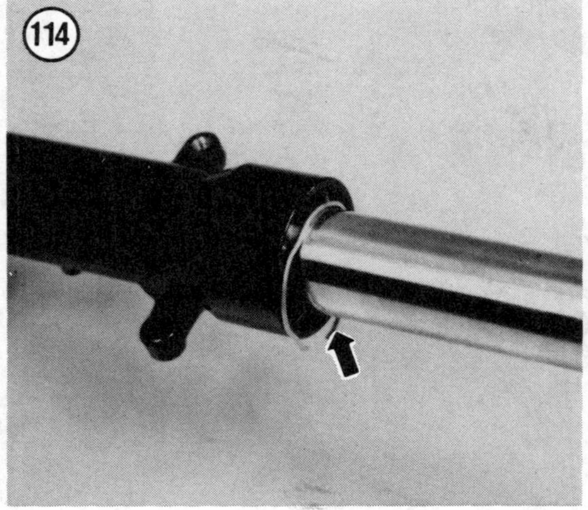

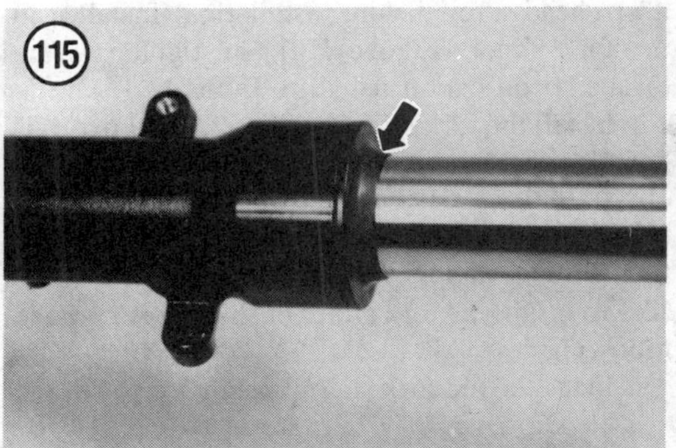

20. Position the fork spring with the closer wound coils at one end facing *down* (**Figure 116**) toward the slider and install the fork spring.

21. Install the spring seat and spacer.

22. Install the fork tube cap while pushing down on the spacer and spring. Start the cap slowly; don't cross thread it. Tighten the fork tube cap to the tightening torque in **Table 2**.

23. Complete fork tube installation as described in this chapter.

Fork Leg Assembly (Right-Hand Fork Leg)

Refer to **Figure 117** when performing this procedure.

1. Coat all parts with fresh **DEXRON** automatic transmission fluid or fork oil before installation.

2. If removed, install a new fork tube bushing (**Figure 100**).

3. Install the rebound spring (A) onto the damper rod (B). See **Figure 118**.

4. Insert the damper rod assembly into the fork tube as shown in **Figure 119**.

5. See **Figure 120**. Install the circlip (A) and oil lock piece (B) onto the damper rod. Make sure the circlip seats in the groove completely. See **Figure 121**.

6. Temporarily install the fork spring, spring seat, spacer and fork cap to hold the damper rod in place. Install the fork cap while pushing down on the spacer and spring. Start the cap slowly; don't cross thread it.

7. Install the fork tube assembly into the slider (**Figure 122**).

8. Make sure the gasket (**Figure 99**) is on the Allen head screw.

9. Apply Loctite 242 (blue) to the threads of the Allen head screw before installation. Install it in the fork slider (**Figure 110**) and tighten to the torque specification listed in **Table 2**.

10. Install the fork slider bushing (A, **Figure 111**) down the fork tube and rest it on the slider.

11. Slide the fork slider backup ring (B, **Figure 111**) down the fork tube and rest it on top of the fork slider bushing.

12. To install the fork slider bushing, perform the following:

  a. Place the old fork slider bushing on top of the backup ring.

  b. Drive the bushing into the fork slider with the Honda special tool Fork Seal Driver (part No. 07947-3710101).

  c. Drive the bushing into place until it seats completely in the recess in the slider.

  d. Remove the installation tool and the old fork slider bushing.

NOTE
*The slider bushing can be driven in with a homemade tool (**Figure 112**). This tool can be made at a machine shop from a piece of aluminum.*

NOTE
A piece of galvanized pipe can also work as a tool. If both ends are threaded (a close nipple pipe fitting), wrap one end with duct tape to prevent the threads from damaging the interior of the slider.

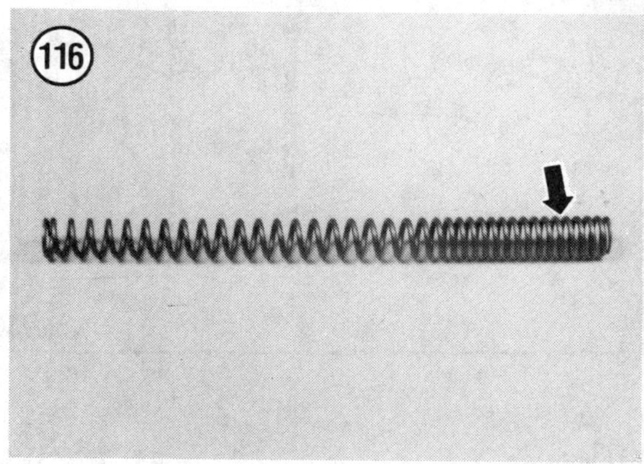

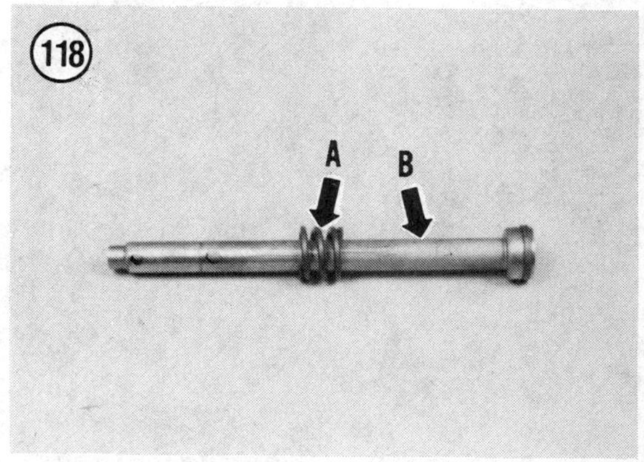

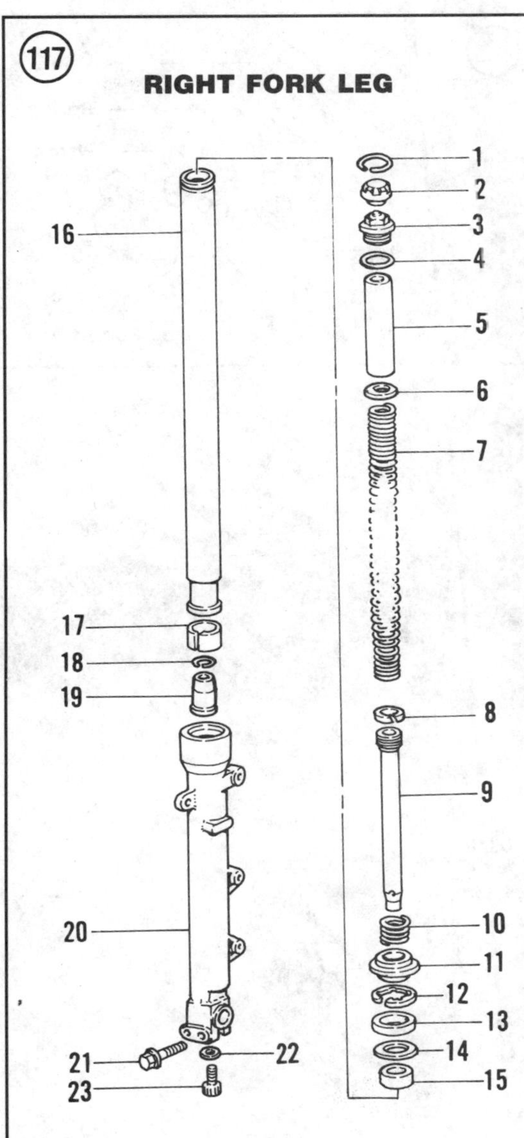

1. Clip
2. Air valve cap
3. Fork tube cap
4. O-ring
5. Spacer
6. Spring seat
7. Fork spring
8. Piston ring
9. Damper rod
10. Spring
11. Dust seal
12. Snap ring
13. Oil seal
14. Backup ring
15. Slider bushing
16. Fork tube
17. Bushing
18. Stopper ring
19. Oil lock piece
20. Slider
21. Bolt
22. Special washer
23. Allen bolt

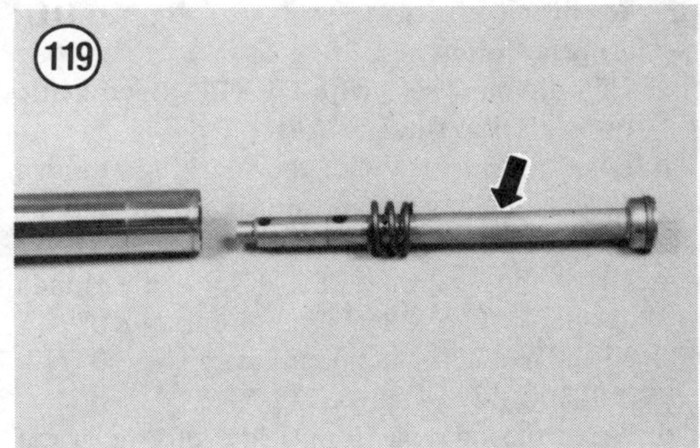

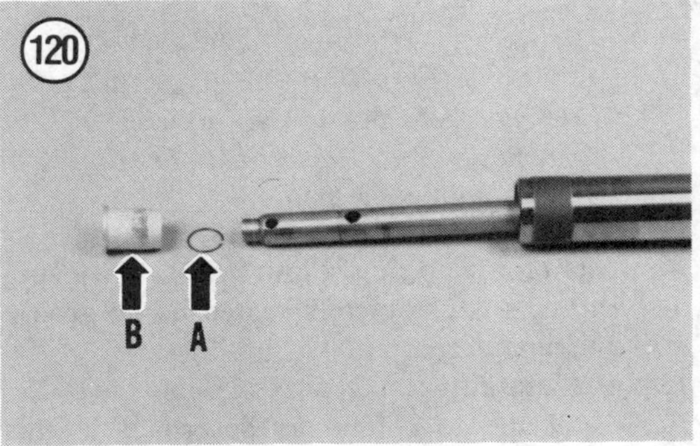

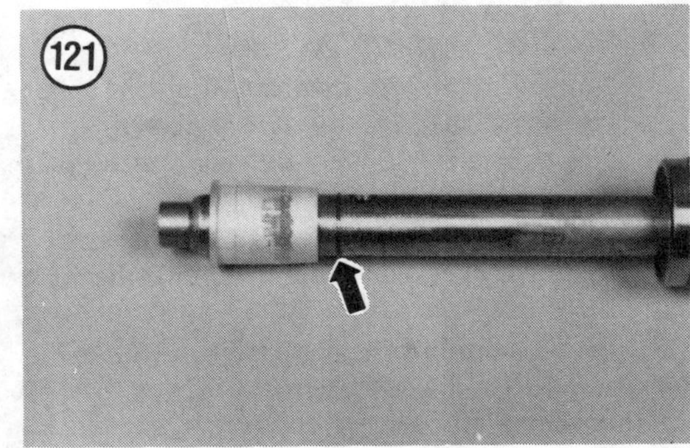

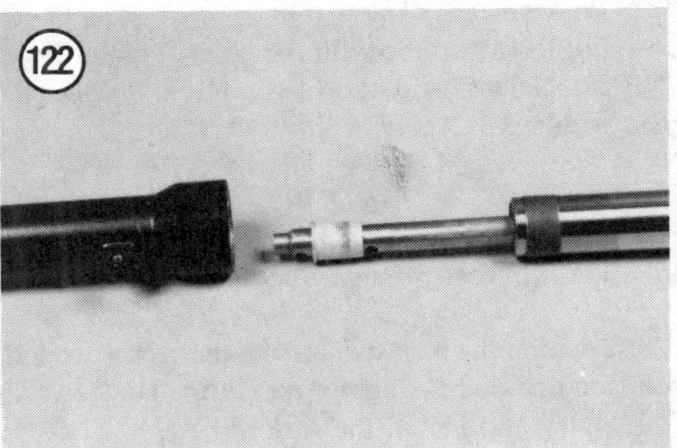

13. To install the fork seal (C, **Figure 111**), perform the following:

   a. Coat the new seal with DEXRON automatic transmission fluid or fork oil.

   b. Position the seal with the marking (**Figure 102**) facing upward and slide it down onto the fork tube.

   c. Drive the seal into the slider with Honda special tool Fork Seal Driver (part No. 07947-3710101) and Attachment (part No. 07747-0010600). See **Figure 113**.

   d. Drive the oil seal in until the groove in the slider can be seen above the top surface of the oil seal.

> *NOTE*
> *The seal can be driven in with a homemade tool described in the NOTES following Step 12.*

14. Install the snap ring (**Figure 114**). Make sure the snap ring is completely seated in the groove in the fork slider.

15. Install the dust seal (**Figure 115**) into the slider.

16. Install the fork tube as described in this chapter.

> *WARNING*
> *The fork caps are held under spring pressure. Take precautions to prevent the caps from flying into your face during removal.*

17. Using a socket, loosen and remove the fork cap.

18. Remove the following parts from the top of the fork tube:

   a. Spacer.

   b. Spring seat.

   c. Fork spring.

19. Fill the fork tube with the correct quantity of DEXRON automatic transmission fluid or fork oil. See **Table 5**.

> *NOTE*
> *Note that in **Table 5** the fork quantity is different for both fork tubes.*

20. Position the fork spring with the closer wound coils at one end facing *down* (**Figure 116**) toward the slider and install the fork spring.

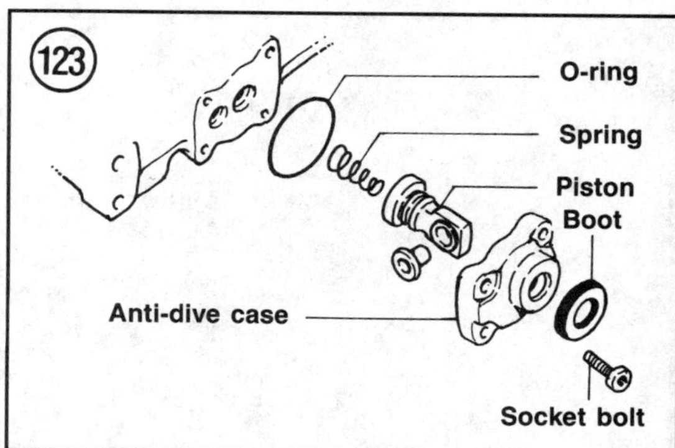

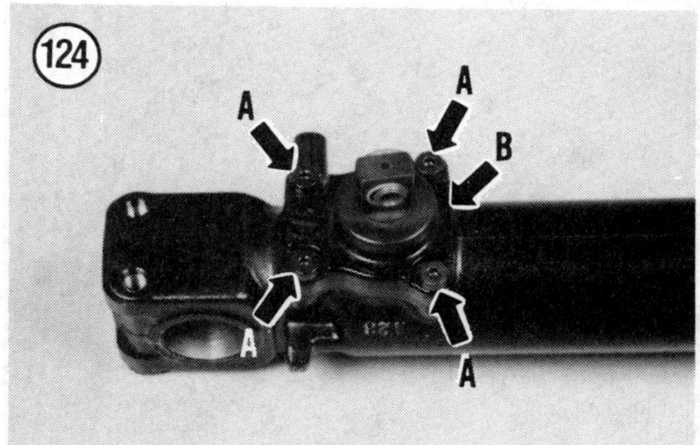

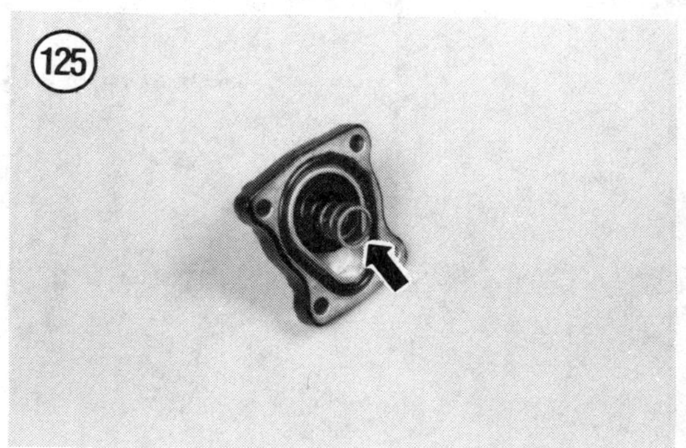

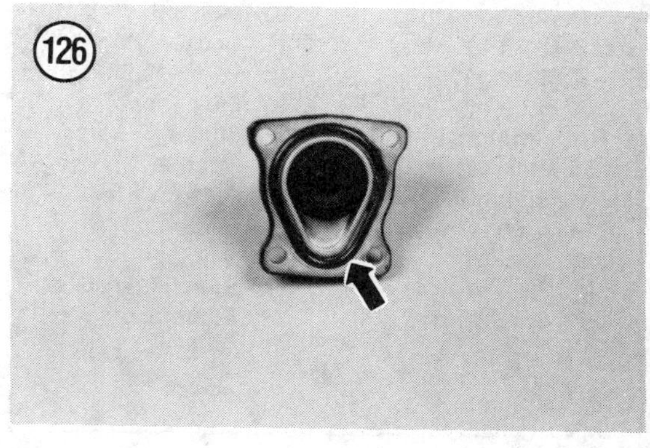

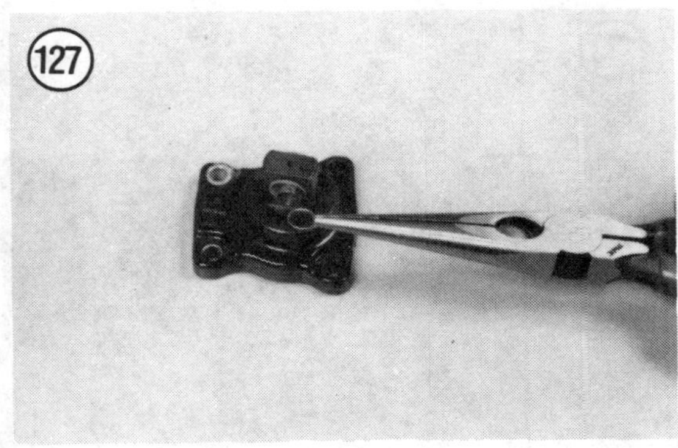

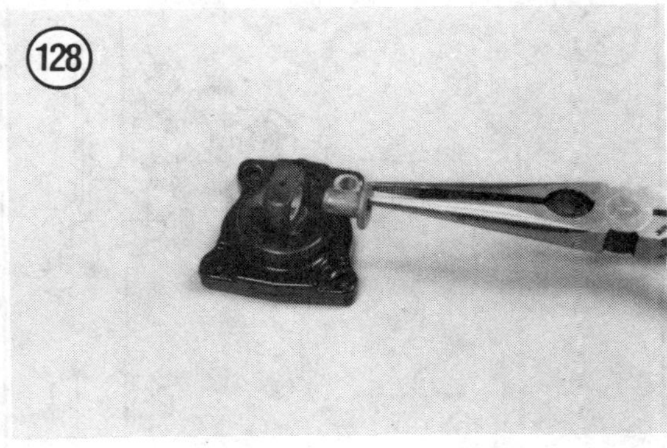

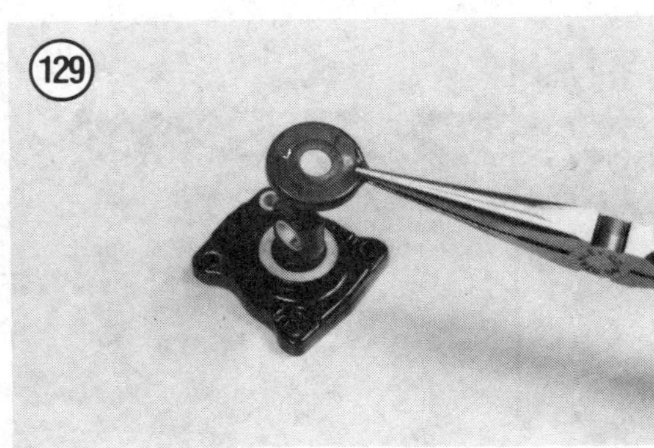

21. Install the spring seat and spacer.

22. Install the fork tube cap (**Figure 117**) while pushing down on the spacer and spring. Start the cap slowly; don't cross thread it. Tighten the fork tube cap to the tightening torque in **Table 2**.

23. Complete fork tube installation as described in this chapter.

ANTI-DIVE FRONT SUSPENSION

All models are equipped with an anti-dive system that is integrated into the left-hand fork leg. The system reacts to the forward weight transfer of the bike and rider(s) during braking. This system is strictly mechanical; some other systems rely on brake fluid pressure.

Disassembly/Assembly

Refer to **Figure 123** for this procedure.

1. Remove the left-hand brake caliper assembly as described in Chapter Twelve.

2. Drain the fork oil from the left-hand fork tube as described in Chapter Three.

3. Remove the left-hand fork assembly from the bike as described in this chapter.

4. Remove the Allen bolts (A, **Figure 124**) securing the anti-dive case to the fork slider and remove the anti-dive case (B, **Figure 124**).

5. Remove the spring (**Figure 125**) and O-ring (**Figure 126**) from the anti-dive case.

6. Remove the stopper ring (**Figure 127**) from the piston collar. Remove the piston collar (**Figure 128**) from the piston.

7. Remove the seal (**Figure 129**) from around the piston.

8. Pull the piston (**Figure 130**) out of the anti-dive case.

9. Remove the seal (**Figure 131**) off of the piston.

10. Assemble by reversing these removal steps. Note the following:

11. See **Figure 132**. Apply DEXRON automatic transmission fluid or fork oil to the piston (A), piston O-ring (B) and seal (C) before installation.

12. Make sure the stopper rings seats in the piston collar completely (**Figure 127**).

13. Apply Loctite 242 (blue) to all Allen bolt threads before installation.

14. Tighten the case mounting bolts (A, **Figure 124**) securely in a crisscross pattern.

10

15. After assembly is complete, push on the piston (**Figure 133**) and measure its stroke. The stroke should be 1.5 mm (1/16 in.). See **Figure 134**. If the stroke is incorrect, the anti-dive unit is assembled incorrectly or the piston is damaged.

Inspection

1. Clean all parts (**Figure 135**) in solvent and dry thoroughly.
2. Inspect the piston return spring for wear or damage.
3. Inspect all piston seals and O-rings for wear or deterioration. Replace if necessary.
4. Inspect the piston and piston collar for scratches and wear. Replace as necessary.
5. Inspect the anti-dive machined surface (**Figure 136**) on the slider for scratches, nicks or other damage.

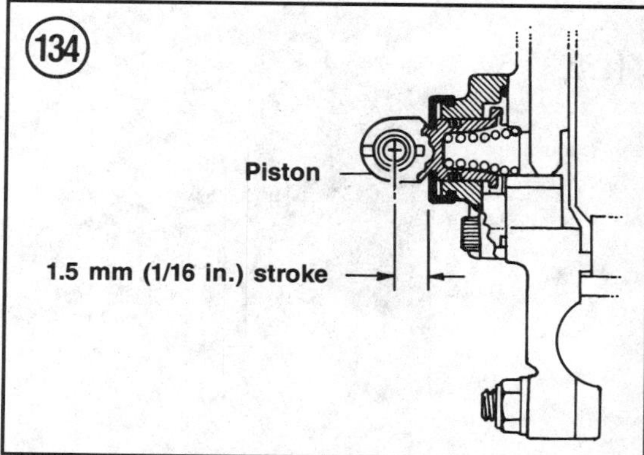

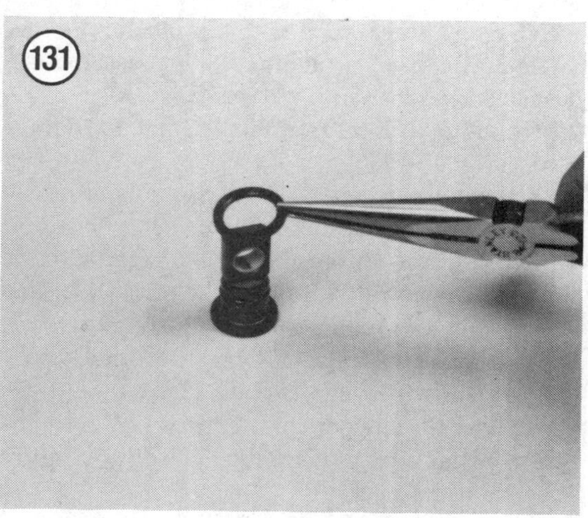

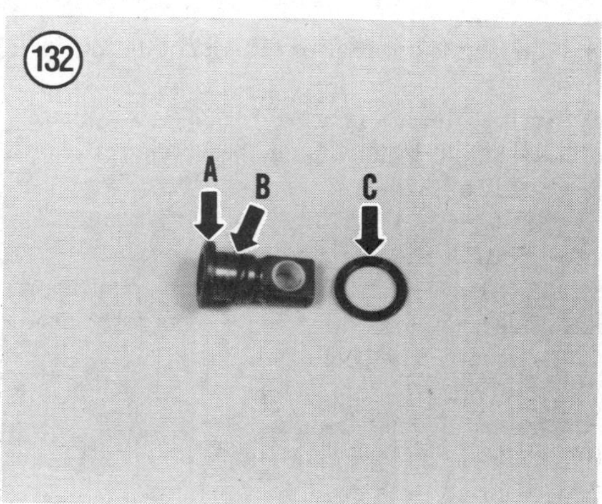

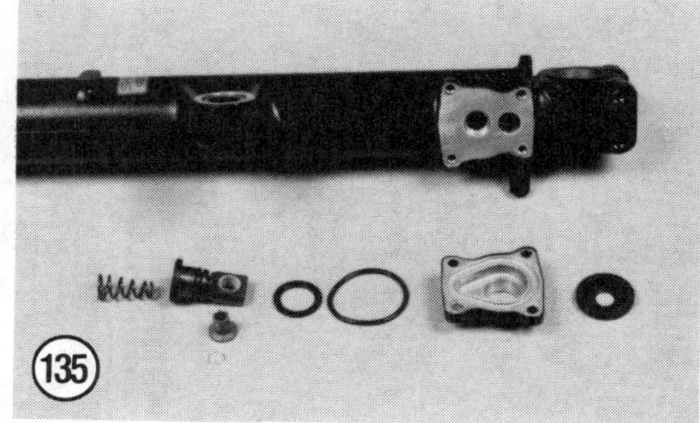

Table 1 FRONT SUSPENSION WEAR LIMITS

	mm	in.
Fork spring free length	389.0	15.31
Front axle runout	0.2	0.008
Front wheel rim runout		
Radial	2.0	0.08
Axial	2.0	0.08
Fork tube runout	0.2	0.008

Table 2 FRONT SUSPENSION TORQUE SPECIFICATIONS

	N•m	ft.-lb.
Front axle		
Axle bolt	60	43
Pinch bolt	22	16
Handlebar pinch bolt	27	20
Left handlebar bracket holder bolt	9	7
Fork tube cap	22	16
Fork tube pinch bolts		
Upper	11	8
Lower	35	25
Fork damper rod Allen screw*	20	14
Steering stem nut	105	76
Steering stem adjust nut	22	16
Brake caliper bracket bolts	27	20

* Apply Loctite 242 (blue) to threads before installation.

Table 3 TIRE SPECIFICATIONS

Tire size	Air pressure (cold)*	Minimum tread depth
Front		
110/80-17	36 psi (2.50 kg/cm²)	1.5 mm (1/16 in.)
Rear		
130/80-17	42 psi (2.90 kg/cm²)	2.0 mm (3/32 in.)

* Up to maximum load limit of 200 lb. (89 kg) including total weight of motorcycle with accessories, rider(s) and luggage.

Table 4 FRONT FORK AIR PRESSURE

Normal	0-6 psi (0-0.4 kg/cm²)

* Do not exceed the maximum air pressure or internal parts of the fork will be damaged.

Table 5 FRONT FORK OIL CAPACITY

Left-hand side	371 cc (12.5 oz.)
Right-hand side	361 cc (12.2 oz.)

CHAPTER ELEVEN

REAR SUSPENSION

This chapter includes repair and replacement procedures for the rear wheel, drive chain and rear suspension components.

Tire changing and balancing are covered in Chapter Ten.

Table 1 lists rear suspension service specifications. **Table 1** and **Table 2** are listed at the end of this chapter.

REAR WHEEL

Removal/Installation

NOTE
Honda CBR600 models are not equipped with a centerstand. To raise the rear wheel off of the ground, a special rear wheel stand can be used (available from accessory manufacturers) or the lower fairing assembly must be removed so that a jack can be used underneath the engine. Make sure the bike is securely supported before removing and servicing the rear wheel. An accessory centerstand can be purchased from Honda dealers for use on non-California models.

1. Support the bike so that the rear wheel clears the ground.
2. Loosen the drive chain locknut and adjusting nut (A, **Figure 1**).
3. Remove the rear axle nut (B, **Figure 1**) and washer (**Figure 2**).

4. Push the rear wheel forward and remove the rear axle from the left-hand side. Allow the wheel to drop to the ground.

5. Lift the drive chain off the sprocket and pull the wheel away from the swing arm (**Figure 3**).

6. Remove the left- (**Figure 4**) and right-hand (**Figure 5**) axle spacers.

CAUTION
Do not set the wheel down on the disc surface as it may be scratched or warped. Either lean the wheel against a wall or place it on a couple of wood blocks.

NOTE
Insert a piece of wood in the caliper in place of the disc. That way, if the brake pedal is inadvertently depressed, the pistons will not be forced out of the cylinders. If this does happen, the caliper might have to be disassembled to reseat the pistons and the system will have to be bled. By using the wood, bleeding the brake is not necessary when installing the wheel.

7. Leave the drive chain adjusters in the swing arm (**Figure 6**).

8. If the wheel is going to be off for any length of time, or if it is to be taken to a shop for repair, install the chain adjusters and axle spacers on the axle along with the axle nut to prevent misplacing any parts.

9. If necessary, service the rear sprocket as described under *Rear Sprocket and Coupling* in this chapter.

10. Installation is the reverse of these steps. Note the following:

   a. To prevent axle seizure, lightly coat the axle with wheel bearing grease.

   b. If removed, insert the rear sprocket/coupling assembly into the rear hub as described in this chapter.

   c. Adjust the drive chain as described in Chapter Three.

   d. Tighten the axle nut to the torque specification in **Table 2**.

   e. Adjust the rear brake as described under *Rear Brake Pedal Height Adjustment* and *Rear Brake Light Switch Adjustment* in Chapter Three.

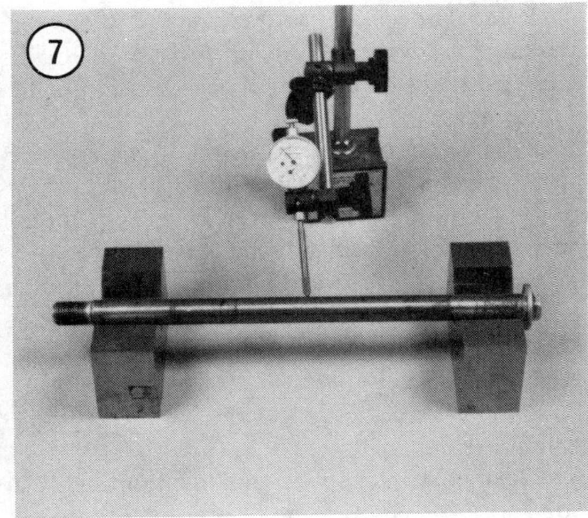

f. Spin the wheel several times to make sure it rotates freely. Apply the rear brake as many times as necessary to make sure the brake pads are against the brake disc correctly.

Inspection

1. Remove any corrosion on the rear axle with a piece of fine emery cloth.

2. Check axle runout. Place the axle on V-blocks and place the tip of a dial indicator in the middle of the axle (**Figure 7**). Rotate the axle and check runout. If the runout exceeds the service limit in **Table 1**, replace it.

3. Check rim runout as follows:

   a. Measure the radial (up and down) runout of the wheel rim with a dial indicator as shown in **Figure 8**. If runout exceeds the wear limit in **Table 1**, check the wheel bearings as described under *Rear Hub* in this chapter.

   b. Measure the axial (side to side) runout of the wheel rim with a dial indicator as shown in **Figure 8**. If runout exceeds the wear limit in **Table 1**, check the wheel bearings as described under *Rear Hub* in this chapter.

   c. If the wheel bearings are okay, the wheel cannot be serviced, but must be replaced.

   d. Replace the rear wheel bearings as described under *Rear Hub* in this chapter.

4. Inspect the wheel rim for dents, bending or cracks. Check the rim and rim sealing surface for scratches that are deeper than 0.5 mm (0.01 in.). If any of these conditions are present, replace the wheel.

REAR HUB

Inspection

Inspect each wheel bearing before removing it. Refer to **Figure 9** for this procedure.

CAUTION
Do not remove the wheel bearings for inspection as they will be damaged during removal. Remove wheel bearings only if they require replacement.

1. Perform Step 1 and Step 2 of *Rear Hub Disassembly* in this section.

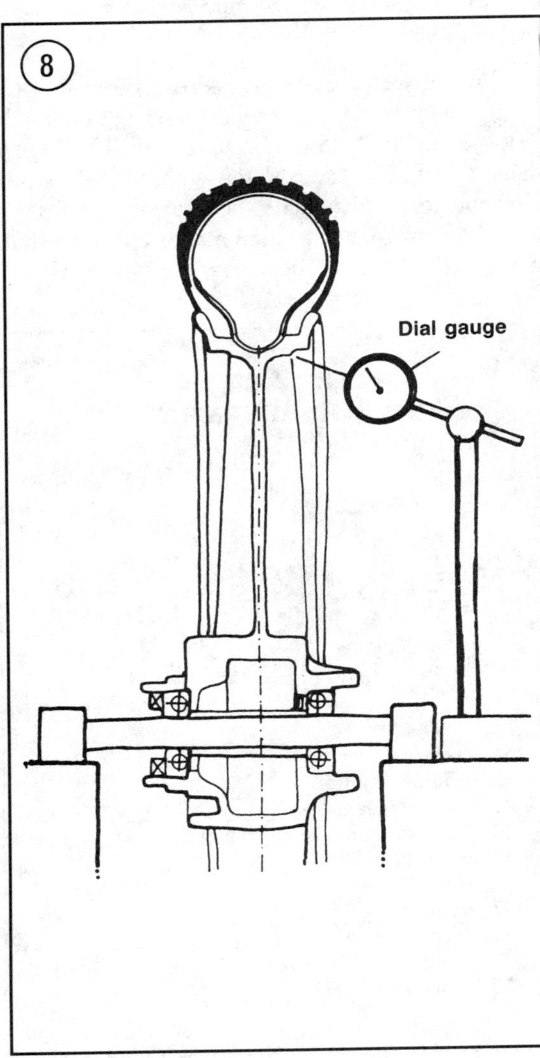

2. Check the wheel bearings (A, **Figure 10**) by rotating the inner race. Check for bearing roughness, excessive noise or damage. If necessary, replace the bearings as described in the following section. Always replace bearings as a set.

Disassembly

Refer to **Figure 9** for this procedure.

1. Remove the rear wheel as described in this chapter.
2. Lift the rear sprocket/coupling assembly (**Figure 11**) out of the rear hub. Don't lose the spacer on the backside of the rear sprocket/coupling housing (**Figure 12**).
3. Remove the rubber dampers from the hub (**Figure 13**).

> *NOTE*
> *If the driven flange assembly is difficult to remove, tap on the backside of the sprocket (from the opposite side of the wheel through the wheel spokes) with a wooden hammer handle. Tap evenly around the perimeter of the sprocket until the assembly is free.*

4. Before proceeding further, inspect the wheel bearings as described under *Inspection* in this chapter. If they must be replaced, perform the following steps.
5. Remove the bolts securing the brake disc and remove the brake disc (B, **Figure 10**).
6. Using a long drift or screwdriver, pry the oil seal from the right-hand side. See **Figure 14**.
7. Using a long drift and hammer, tilt the center spacer away from one side of the left-hand bearing (**Figure 15**). Then drive the left-hand bearing out of the hub. See **Figure 16**.
8. Remove the center spacer and remove the right-hand bearing.
9. Clean the center spacer and hub thoroughly in solvent.

Assembly

1. On non-sealed bearings, pack the bearings with a good quality bearing grease. Work the grease in between the balls thoroughly; turn the bearing by hand a couple of times to make sure the grease is distributed evenly inside the bearing.
2. Blow any dirt or foreign matter out of the hub before installing the bearings.

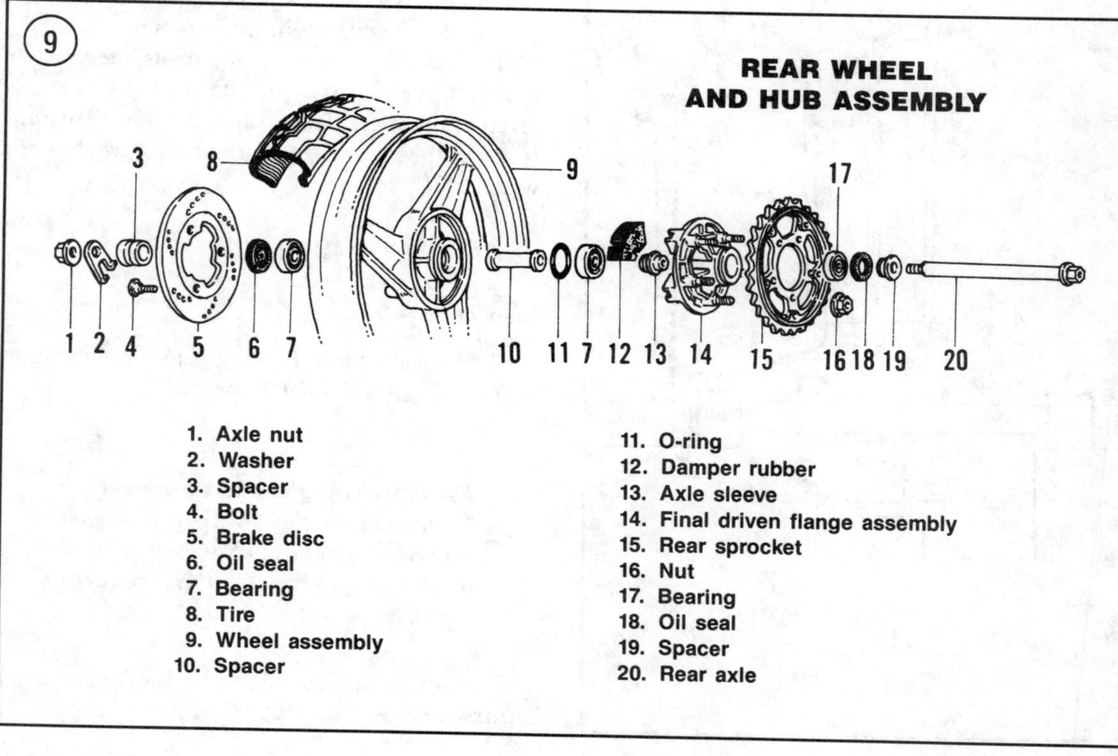

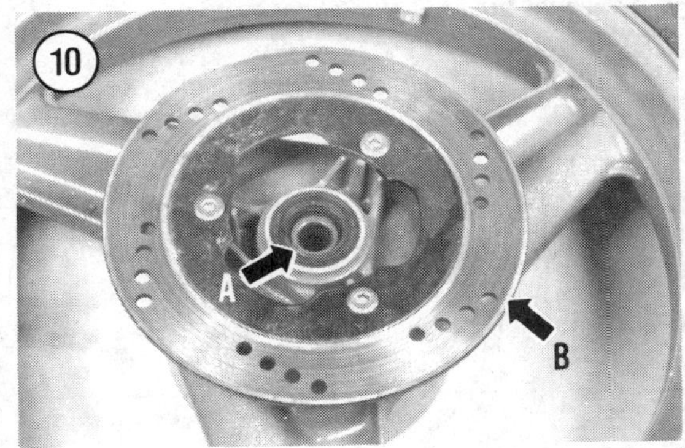

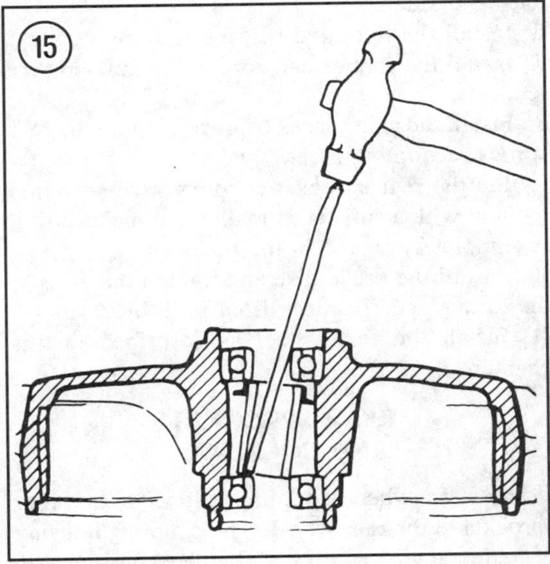

3. Pack the hub with multipurpose grease.

NOTE
Install the standard bearings (they are sealed on one side only) with the sealed side facing out.

CAUTION
*Tap the bearings squarely into place and tap on the outer race only. Use a socket (**Figure 17**) that matches the outer bearing race diameter. Do not tap on the inner race or the bearing might be damaged. Be sure that the bearings are completely seated.*

4. Install the right-hand bearing into the hub.
5. Install the center spacer into the hub from the left-hand side.
6. Install the left-hand bearing into the hub.
7. Install the rubber dampers in the hub (**Figure 13**).
8. Install the axle spacer (**Figure 12**) into the rear sprocket/coupling assembly.
9. Tap the rear sprocket/coupling assembly into the hub with a soft-faced mallet and make sure it is completely seated in the hub.
10. Install the brake disc and tighten the bolts to the torque specification listed in **Table 2**.
11. Install the rear wheel as described in this chapter.

REAR SPROCKET AND COUPLING

The rear wheel coupling connects the rear sprocket to the rear wheel. The coupling housing is equipped with an oil seal, ball bearing and axle sleeve. Rubber shock dampers installed in the coupling absorb some of the shock that results from torque changes during acceleration and braking.

Removal/Installation

1. Remove the rear wheel as described in this chapter.
2. Pull the rear wheel coupling assembly (**Figure 11**) up and out of the wheel hub.

NOTE
If the driven flange assembly is difficult to remove, tap on the backside of the sprocket (from the opposite side of the wheel through the wheel spokes) with a wooden hammer handle. Tap evenly around the perimeter of the sprocket until the assembly is free.

3. Pull the dampers (**Figure 13**) out of the housing.
4. Remove the axle spacer (**Figure 12**).
5. Perform *Inspection/Disassembly/Reassembly* as described in this chapter.
6. Install by reversing these steps.

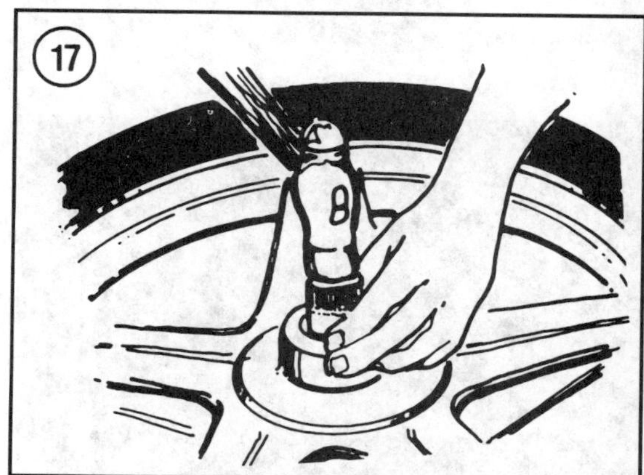

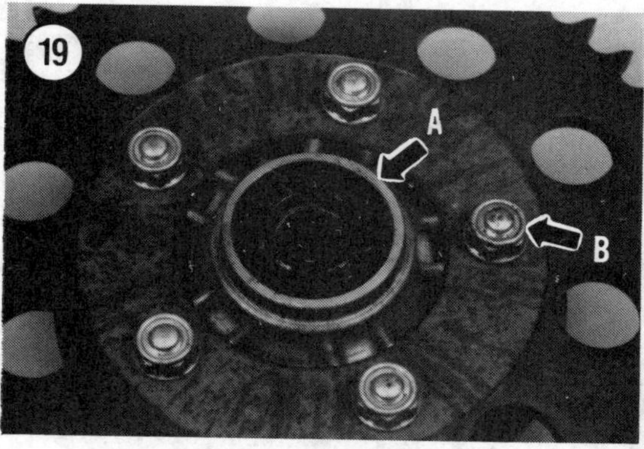

Inspection/Disassembly/Reassembly

1. Visually inspect the rubber dampers (**Figure 13**) for damage or deterioration. Replace, if necessary, as a complete set.

2. Inspect the flange assembly housing and damper separators (**Figure 18**) for cracks or damage. Replace the coupling housing if necessary.

3. If necessary, replace the coupling housing bearing as follows:

   a. Pry the seal from the housing (A, **Figure 19**).

   b. Using a large diameter socket or drift on the bearing (**Figure 20**), drive it out from the inner surface of the housing.

   c. Discard the bearing.

   d. Clean the housing thoroughly in solvent and check for cracks or damage in the bearing area.

   e. Blow any dirt or foreign matter out of the housing prior to installing the bearing.

> *NOTE*
> *The standard bearing is sealed on both sides.*

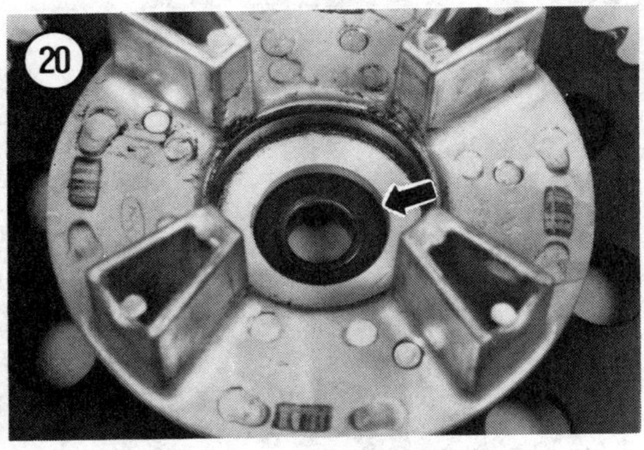

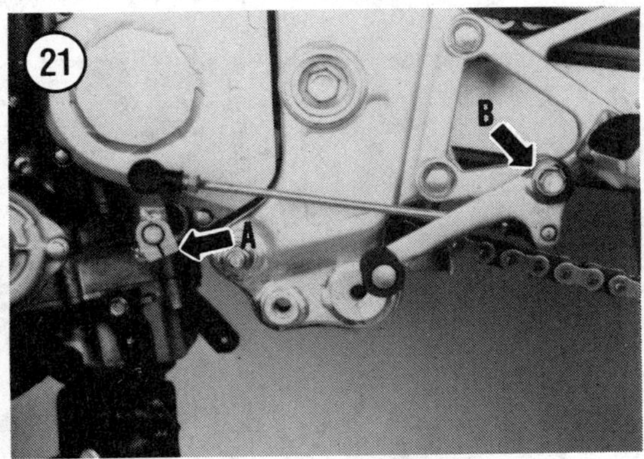

f. Tap the bearing into position with a socket placed on the outer bearing race.

g. Install a new seal (A, **Figure 19**) by driving it in squarely with a suitable size socket and hammer.

Sprocket Inspection

Inspect the teeth of the sprocket. If the teeth are visibly worn, replace both sprockets and the drive chain. Never replace any one sprocket or chain as a separate item; worn parts will cause rapid wear of the new component.

1. If the driven sprocket requires replacement, remove the nuts (B, **Figure 19**) securing the sprocket and remove the sprocket.

2. If necessary, replace the front sprocket as described under *Engine Sprocket* in Chapter Six.

DRIVE SPROCKET AND DRIVE CHAIN

This procedure describes removal and installation of the drive sprocket and drive chain. Because the drive chain is endless (has no master link), the swing arm must be removed to remove the drive chain. Drive chain lubrication is covered in Chapter Three.

> *WARNING*
> *Honda uses an endless chain on this model for strength and reliability. Do not cut the chain with a chain cutter or install a chain with a master link. The chain may fail and rear wheel lockup and loss of control may result under riding conditions.*

Removal/Installation

1. Support the bike and raise the rear wheel off the ground as described under *Rear Wheel Removal/Installation* in this chapter.

2. Remove the lower fairing assembly. See Chapter Thirteen.

3. Remove the shift linkage (**Figure 21**); remove the pinch screw (A) and the pivot screw (B) securing the shift linkage and pull the shift linkage off. If the pivot boss is tight on the shaft, spread the slot open with a screwdriver.

4. Remove the screws securing the engine sprocket cover and remove the cover (**Figure 22**). Remove the washer gasket (A, **Figure 23**), and the spacer from behind the cover (B, **Figure 23**).

5. Have an assistant apply the rear brake to keep the drive chain taut and keep the drive sprocket from turning. Loosen and remove the drive sprocket bolt (**Figure 24**).

6. Remove the rear wheel as described in this chapter.

7. With slack in the drive chain, pull the drive sprocket and chain off of the transmission countershaft. See **Figure 25**. Remove the drive sprocket from the drive chain.

8. Remove the swing arm as described in this chapter.

9. Slip the drive chain off of the swing arm (**Figure 26**).

10. Install by reversing the removal steps. Note the following:

a. Be sure to slip the drive chain over the swing arm (**Figure 26**) before installing the swing arm.

b. Install the swing arm as described in this chapter.

c. Tighten the drive sprocket bolts to the torque specification in **Table 2**.

d. Make sure to install the washer gasket (A, **Figure 23**) and the spacer (B, **Figure 23**) behind the sprocket cover.

e. Adjust the drive chain as described under *Drive Chain Adjustment* in Chapter Three.

f. Rotate the wheel several times to make sure it rotates smoothly. Apply the brake several times to make sure it operates correctly.

g. Adjust the rear brake as described under *Rear Brake Pedal Height Adjustment* and *Rear Brake Light Switch Adjustment* in Chapter Three.

Drive Chain Cleaning

> *CAUTION*
> *The factory drive chain is equipped with O-rings between the side plates that seal lubricant between the pins and bushings. To prevent damaging these O-rings, use only kerosene or*

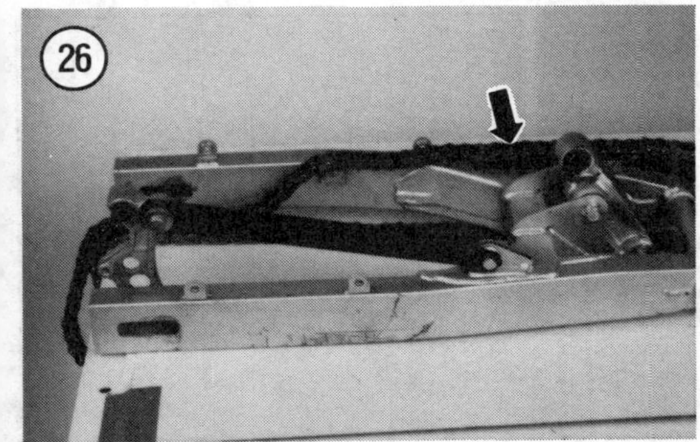

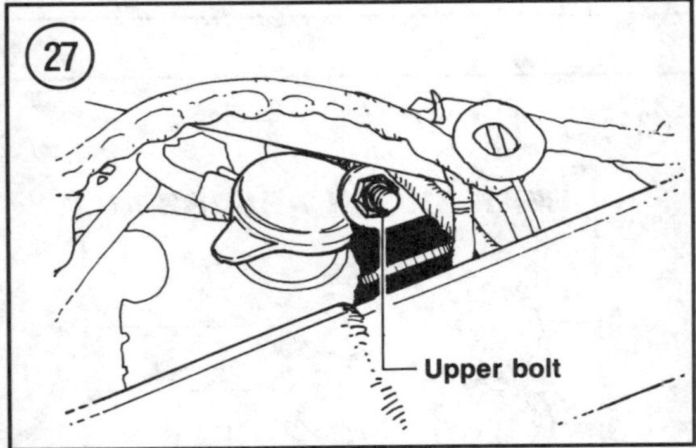

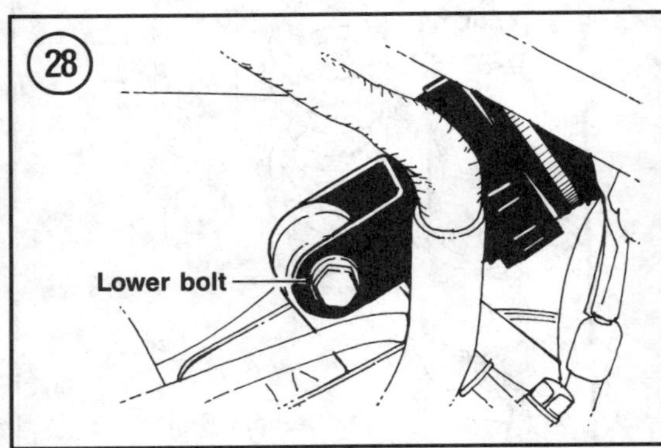

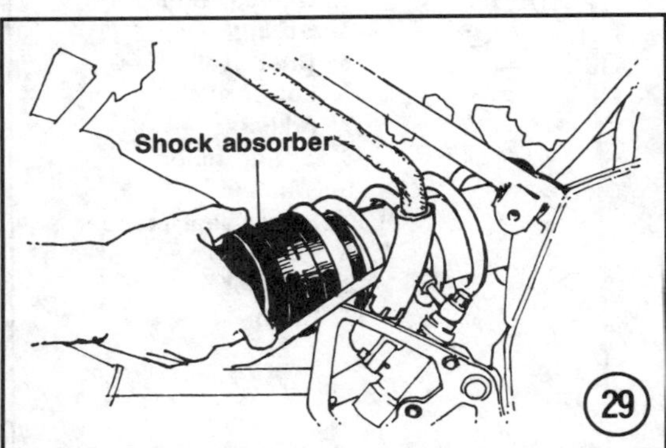

diesel oil for cleaning. Do not use gasoline or other solvents that will cause the O-rings to swell or deteriorate.

Occasionally, the drive chain should be removed from the bike for a thorough cleaning and soak lubrication. Perform the following:

a. Brush off excess dirt and grit.

b. Remove the drive chain as described in this chapter.

c. Soak the chain in kerosene or diesel oil for about half an hour and clean it thoroughly. Hang the chain from a piece of wire and allow it to dry.

d. Lubricate the drive chain, referring to *Drive Chain Lubrication* in Chapter Three.

e. Install the chain on the motorcycle as described in this chapter.

REAR SHOCK ABSORBER

Removal/Installation

1. Support the bike and raise the rear wheel off the ground as described under *Rear Wheel Removal/Installation* in this chapter.

2. Remove the right-hand side cover. See Chapter Thirteen.

3. Remove the upper shock absorber mounting bolt (**Figure 27**).

4. Remove the lower shock absorber mounting bolt (**Figure 28**).

5. Remove the shock absorber out through the right-hand side as shown in **Figure 29**.

WARNING
The shock absorber contains highly compressed nitrogen gas. Do not tamper with or attempt to open the housing. Do not place it near an open flame or other extreme heat. Do not weld on the frame near it. Do not dispose of the shock absorber yourself. Take it to a Honda dealer where it can be deactivated and disposed of properly.

6. Install by reversing these steps. Note the following:
   a. Install the shock absorber so that the point where the spring guide and spring seat align is facing *up*. See **Figure 30**.
   b. Install the shock absorber bolts from the left-hand side.
   c. Tighten the shock absorber bolts to the torque specification in **Table 2**.

Disassembly

Refer to **Figure 31** for this procedure.

> *NOTE*
> *A shock absorber spring compressor is required for this procedure. Use the Honda shock absorber compressor attachment (part No. 07959-MB1000) and shock absorber compressor screw assembly (part No. 07GME-0010100) or equivalent. The Honda tools are shown in* **Figure 32**.

1. Assemble the shock absorber into a spring compressor (**Figure 32**). Compress the shock spring until the stopper ring (**Figure 33**) can be removed. Remove the stopper ring and release tension on the shock spring.
2. Remove the shock absorber from the spring compressor.
3. Referring to **Figure 31**, remove the following parts in order:
   a. Upper spring seat.
   b. Spring.
   c. Dust seal.
   d. Lower spring seat.
   e. Adjuster.
   f. Spring guide.
4. Referring to **Figure 34**, remove the lower joint as follows:
   a. Remove the adjuster screw. Then pull the adjuster knob off of the shock absorber.
   b. Slide the rubber stopper and the seat stopper towards the shock housing. Loosen the locknut.
   c. Remove the lower joint, locknut and seat stopper.

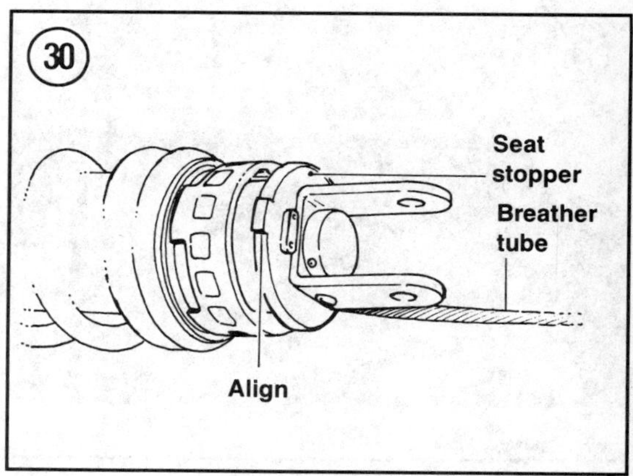

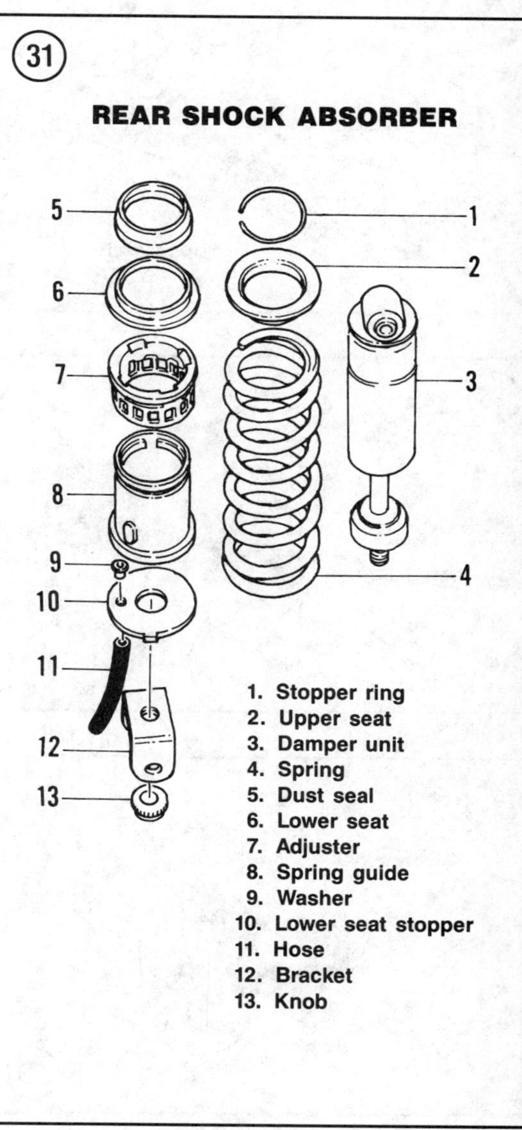

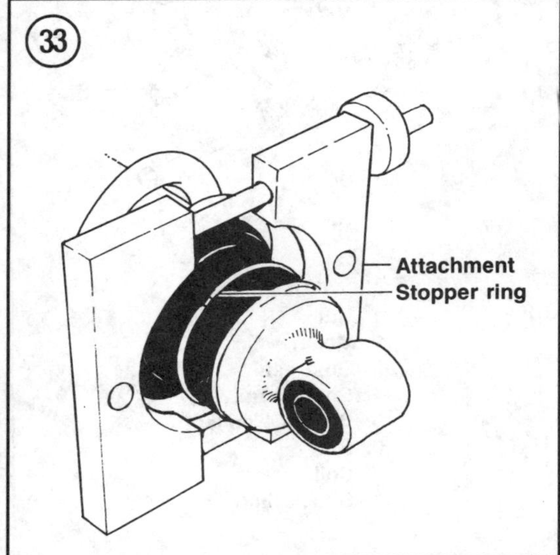

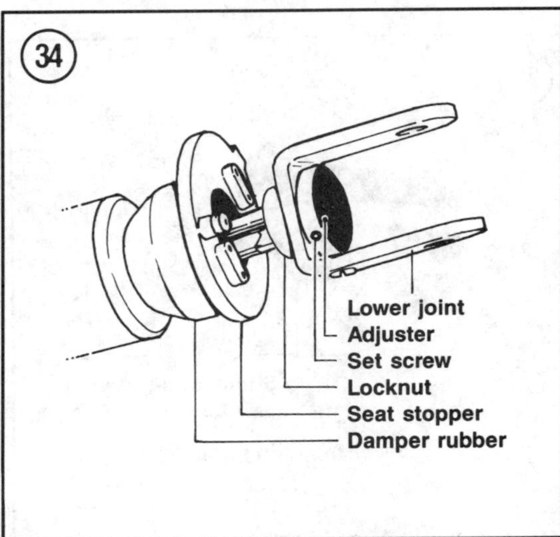

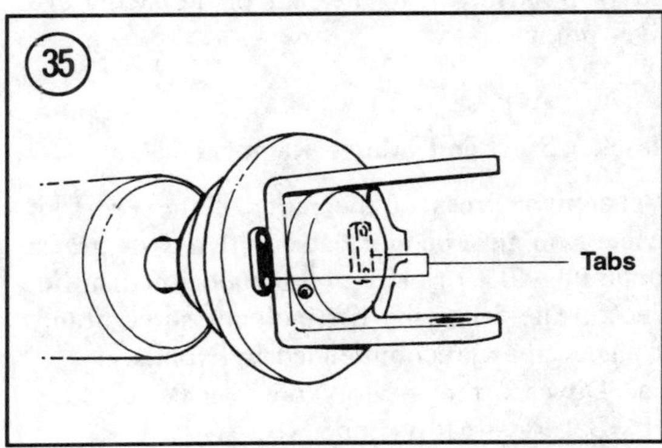

Inspection

1. Measure the length of the stock Honda shock spring and compare it to the specification in **Table 1**. Replace the spring if it is too short.

2. Check the shock absorber housing for dents, damage or oil leakage. Replace the housing if necessary.

> *WARNING*
> *The shock absorber contains highly compressed nitrogen gas. Do not tamper with or attempt to open the housing. Do not place it near an open flame or other extreme heat. Do not weld on the frame near it. Do not dispose of the shock absorber yourself. Take it to a Honda dealer where it can be deactivated and disposed of properly.*

3. Check all of the components for wear and damage; replace worn and damaged parts as required.

Assembly

Refer to **Figure 31** for this procedure.

1. Apply Loctite 242 (blue) onto the shock absorber shaft. Install the locknut and screw it on all the way.

2. See **Figure 34**. Install the seat stopper.

3. Screw the lower joint onto the shock absorber shaft all the way. Then hold the lower joint and tighten the locknut to the torque specification listed in **Table 2**.

4. After tightening the lower joint locknut in Step 3, turn the seat stopper and align the tabs on the stopper with the lower joint as shown in **Figure 35**.

5. Install the adjuster knob and secure it with its set screw (**Figure 34**).

6. Install the following parts in order onto the shock absorber:

> *NOTE*
> *Install the spring guide so that the notch in the guide aligns with the tab on the seat stopper (**Figure 30**).*

  a. Spring guide.
  b. Adjuster.
  c. Lower seat.
  d. Dust seal.
  e. Spring.
  f. Upper spring seat.

7. Install the shock absorber assembly into the shock spring compressor used during disassembly and compress the spring enough to allow installation of the stopper ring. Install the stopper ring and slowly release the spring compressor. Check the stopper ring to make sure it is completely seated in the shock absorber groove. If the stopper ring is not completely seated it could work free when riding the bike.

8. Remove the shock assembly from the spring compressor.

9. Apply paste grease containing 40% or more of molybdenum disulfide grease to the upper shock bushing and joint collar.

10. Install the shock absorber as described in this chapter.

PRO-LINK
SUSPENSION SYSTEM

The single shock absorber and linkage of the Pro-Link rear suspension system are attached to the swing arm just to the rear of the swing arm pivot point.

Shock Absorber Linkage Removal

The pivot areas of the parts of the Pro-Link suspension must be lubricated with a paste grease containing 40% or more of molybdenum disulfide grease. The following list includes some brands of paste grease recommended by Honda:
  a. Dow Corning—Molykote G-n Paste.
  b. Bel-Ray—Moly-Lube NIC-8.

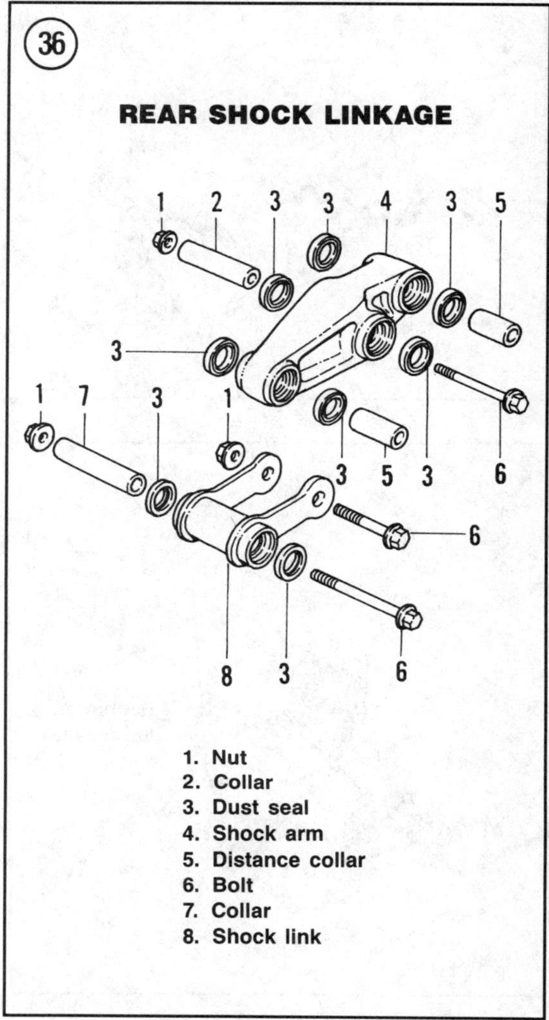

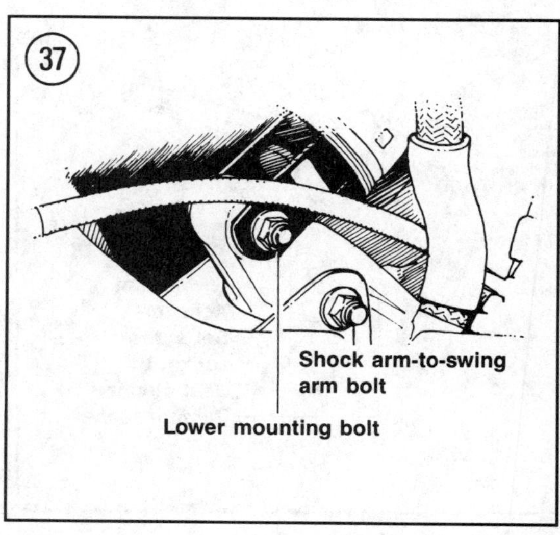

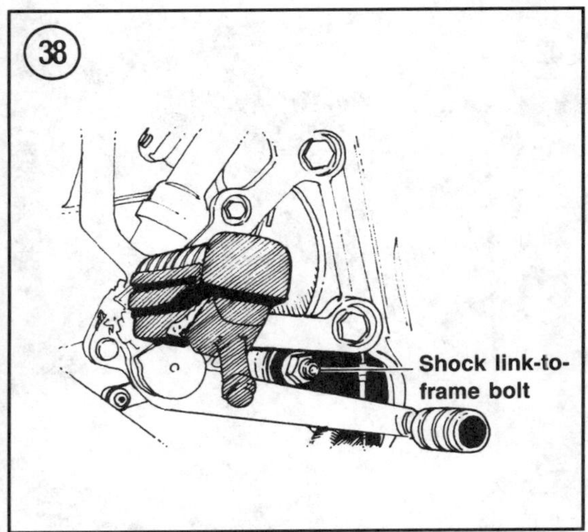

c. Sumico Lubricant—Locol Paste (Japan).

d. Any other brand that meets these requirements.

Refer to **Figure 36** for this procedure.

1. Support the bike and raise the rear wheel off the ground as described under *Rear Wheel Removal/Installation* in this chapter.

2. Remove the side covers as described in Chapter Thirteen.

3. Remove the shock absorber lower mounting bolt and nut (**Figure 28**).

4. Remove the shock arm-to-swing arm bolt and nut (**Figure 37**).

5. Remove the shock link-to-frame bolt and nut (**Figure 38**). Remove the shock arm and shock link as an assembly (**Figure 39**).

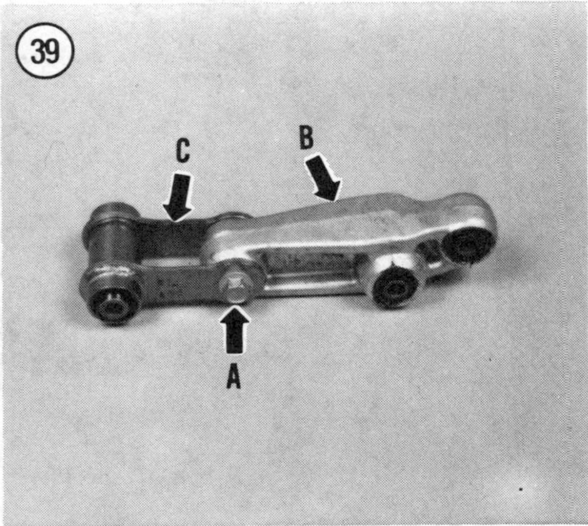

Inspection

1. Remove the shock arm-to-shock link bolt and nut (A, **Figure 39**). Separate the shock arm (B) from the shock link (C).

2. Withdraw the shock arm pivot collars (**Figure 40**).

3. Withdraw the shock link pivot collar (**Figure 41**).

4. Pry the dust seals out of all pivot points. See **Figure 42** (shock arm) and **Figure 43** (shock link).

5. Clean all parts in solvent and dry thoroughly with compressed air.

6. Inspect the pivot collars for scratches, abrasion or abnormal wear; replace as necessary.

11

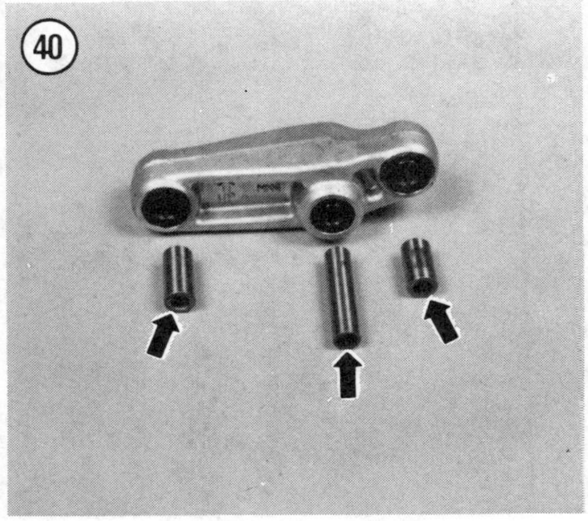

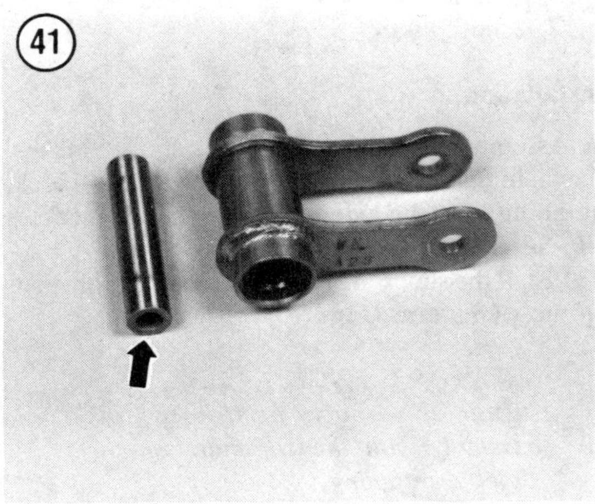

7. Inspect the needle bearings for abnormal wear. If any of the bearings are damaged, they must be replaced. Refer to *Bearing Replacement* in this section.

8. Inspect the dust seals. Replace all of them as a set if any are worn or starting to deteriorate. If the dust seals are in poor condition they will allow dirt to enter into the pivot areas and cause the pivot collars to wear.

9. Coat the inside of the dust seals with molybdenum disulfide paste grease.

10. Install the dust seals by driving them into place with a suitable size socket. See **Figure 44** (shock arm) and **Figure 45** (shock link). Install the seals so that they are flush with the shock arm and shock link. See **Figure 46**.

> *NOTE*
> *Make sure the dust seal lips seat correctly. If not they will allow dirt and moisture into the pivot collar areas and cause premature wear.*

11. Coat all surfaces of the pivot receptacles and pivot collars with molybdenum disulfide paste grease.

12. Insert the shock link pivot collar (**Figure 47**).

> *NOTE*
> *The shock link pivot collar is 80 mm long.*

13. Install the shock arm pivot collars. Match the length of the collars listed below to the letters in **Figure 48**.

   a. 37 mm.
   b. 67 mm.
   c. 32 mm.

Installation

1. Assemble the shock arm and shock link as shown in **Figure 49**. Insert the shock arm-to-shock link bolt from the side of the shock arm marked UP. See **Figure 49**.

2. Install the shock arm onto the mounting bracket on the swing arm (**Figure 37**).

> *NOTE*
> *Install the shock arm/shock link assembly with the UP mark on the shock arm facing up.*

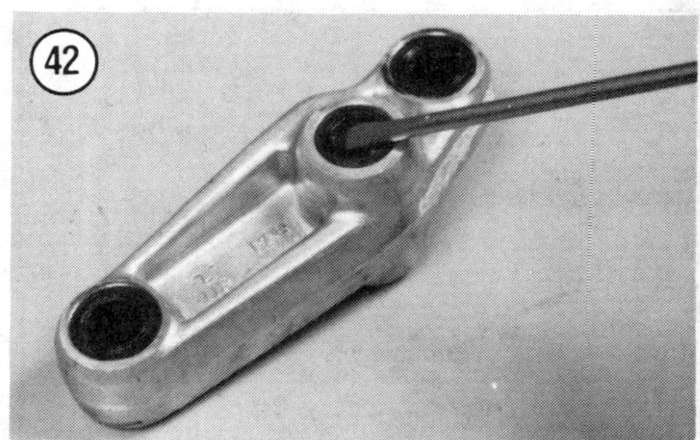

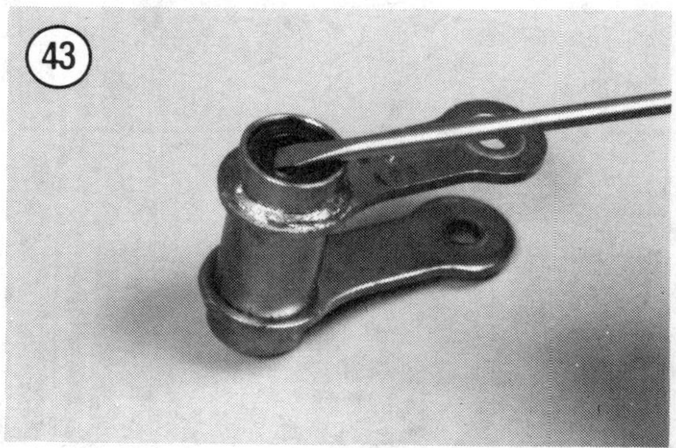

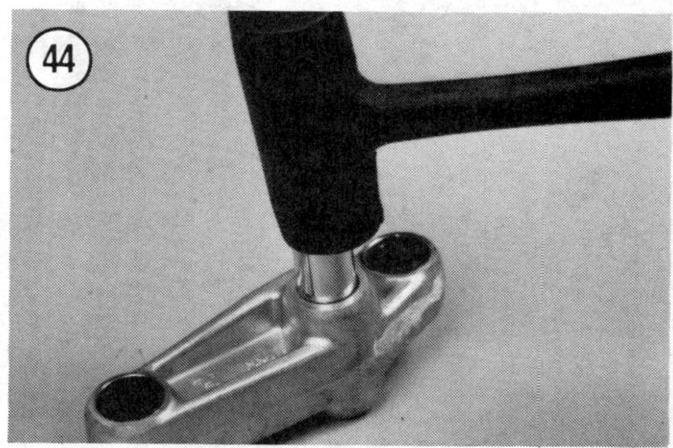

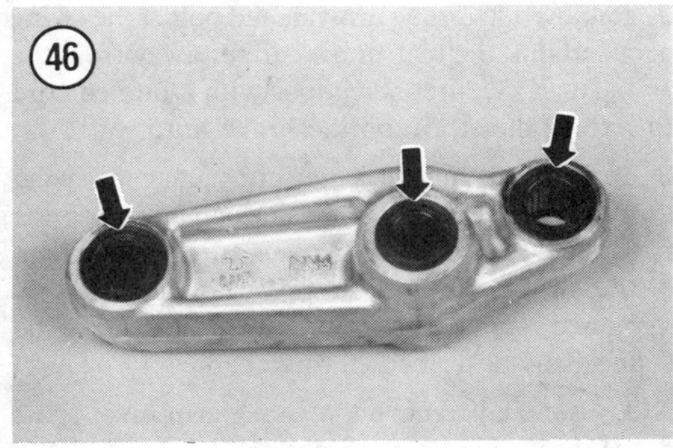

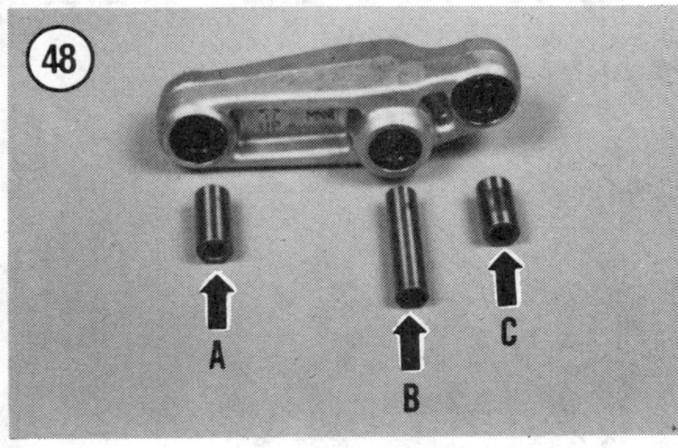

3. Install the shock arm-to-shock link bolt from the left-hand side and tighten it to the torque specification in **Table 2**.

4. Install the shock arm-to-swing arm pivot bolt from the left-hand side. Tighten to the torque specification in **Table 2**.

5. Install the shock absorber lower mounting bolt from the left-hand side. Tighten to the torque specification in **Table 2**.

6. Install the side covers. See Chapter Thirteen.

Bearing Replacement

A hydraulic press is required for this procedure.

1. Remove the shock arm as described in this chapter.

2. Perform Steps 1-4 under *Inspection*.

3. Replace the shock arm bearing as follows:
   a. Support the shock arm in a press.
   b. Press the bearings out of the shock arm housing.
   c. Apply grease onto the needle bearings.
   d. Press the needle bearings into the shock arm assembly.

4. Replace shock link bearings as follows:
   a. Remove the needle bearings with a universal bearing remover as shown in **Figure 50**.
   b. Apply grease to the needle bearings.
   c. Press the needle bearings into the shock link assembly.

SWING ARM

In time, the needle bearings will wear and will have to be replaced. The condition of the bearings

11

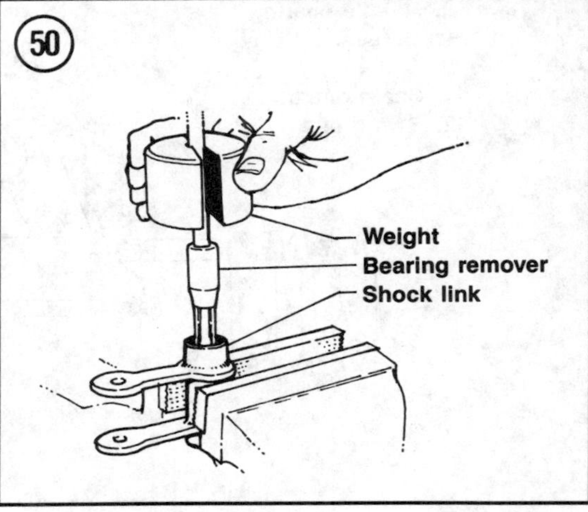

can greatly affect handling performance and if worn parts are not replaced they can produce erratic and dangerous handling. Common symptoms are wheel hop, pulling to one side during acceleration and pulling to the other side during braking.

Refer to **Figure 51** when servicing the swing arm.

Removal/Installation

1. Remove the muffler as described in Chapter Seven.

2. Remove the rear fender (**Figure 52**) mounting bolts. Tilt the fender to the left-hand side and remove it.

3. Remove the rear wheel as described in this chapter.

4. Remove the shock arm-to-swing arm bolt (**Figure 37**).

5. Remove the lower shock absorber mounting bolt (**Figure 37**).

6. Remove the drive sprocket as described under *Drive Sprocket and Drive Chain* in this chapter.

7. Remove the torque arm nut and bolt at the swing arm and pull the rear brake caliper away from the swing arm. Secure the caliper with a Bunjee cord to relieve the strain on the brake hose.

8. Before removing the swing arm, grasp the swing arm and move it from side to side and up and down. If you feel any more than a very slight movement of the swing arm and the pivot bolt is correctly tightened, remove the swing arm and check the bearings as described in this chapter.

9. Loosen and remove the swing arm pivot shaft nut (**Figure 53**) on the right-hand side.

10. Remove the swing arm pivot shaft (**Figure 54**) out from the left-hand side. Pull the swing arm (**Figure 55**) and drive chain toward the rear and remove it from the frame.

11. Inspect the swing arm as described in this chapter.

12. With the swing arm removed, check the frame pivot areas (**Figure 56**) for cracks or other damage. Check on both sides of the frame.

13. Install the swing arm assembly by reversing these steps. Note the following.

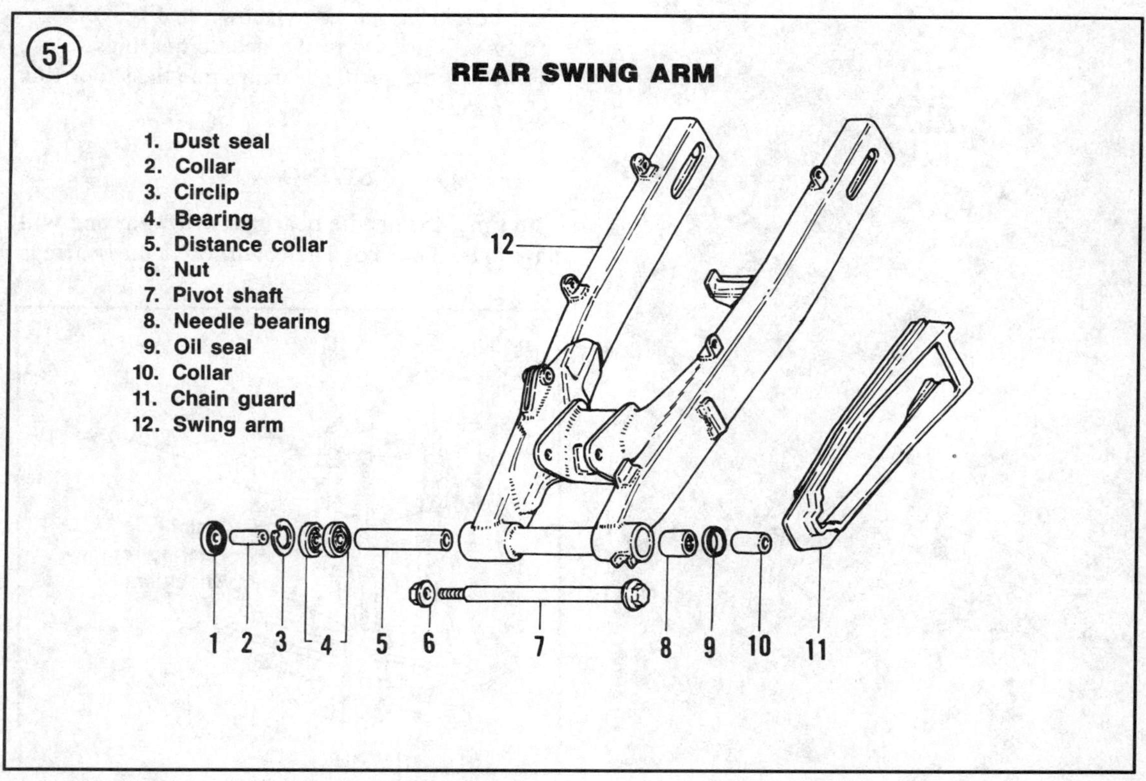

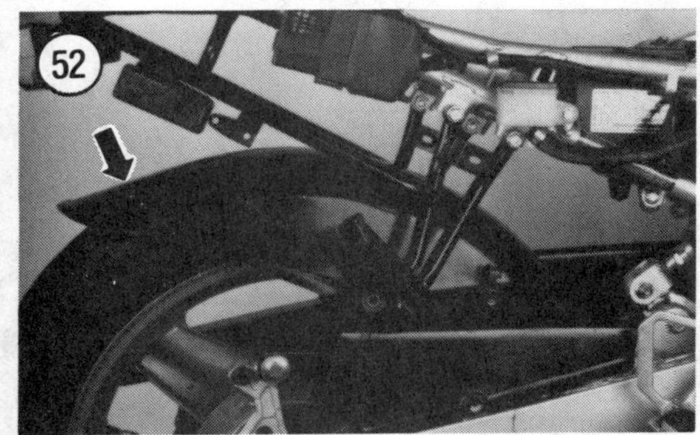

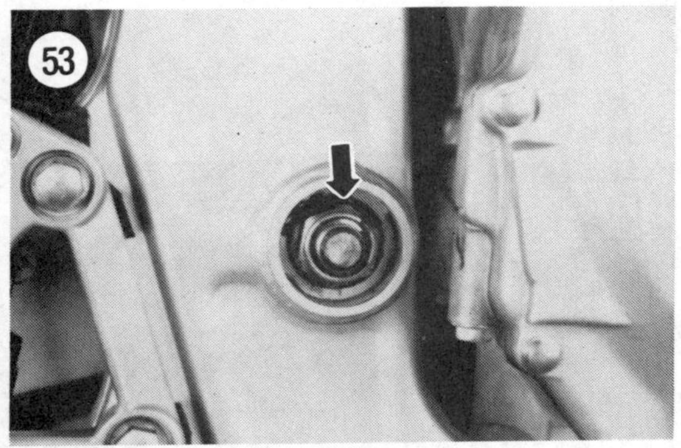

14. Make sure the drive chain is installed over the swing arm before installing the swing arm and the pivot shaft.

15. Coat the swing arm pivot shaft with a light coat of waterproof bearing grease.

16. Install the pivot shaft in from the left-hand side (**Figure 54**).

17. Tighten the swing arm pivot shaft nut to the tightening torque in **Table 2**.

18. Tighten the shock arm-to-swing arm bolt (**Figure 37**) to the torque specification in **Table 2**.

19. Tighten the shock absorber lower mounting bolt (**Figure 28**) to the torque specification in **Table 2**.

20. Tighten the brake torque rod nut to the torque specification in **Table 2**. Secure the nut with a new cotter pin and bend the ends over completely.

Inspection

Refer to **Figure 51**.

1. Slip the drive chain off of the swing arm.

2. Pull the chain guard (A, **Figure 57**) off of the swing arm. Replace the chain guard if worn severely or damaged.

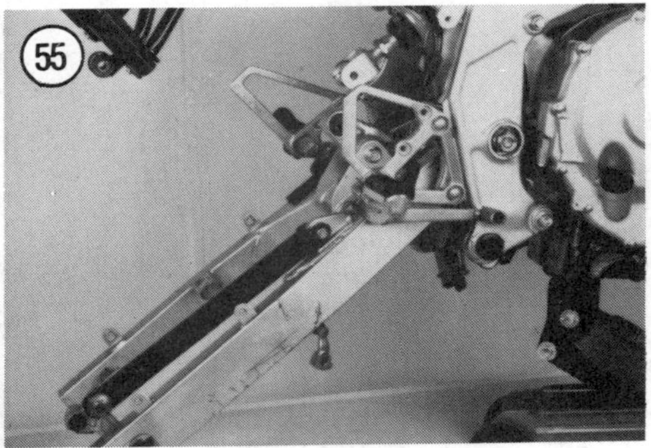

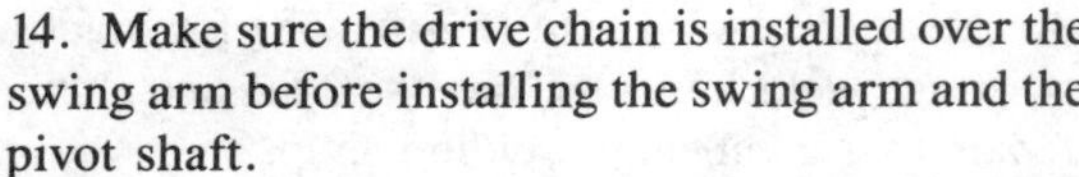

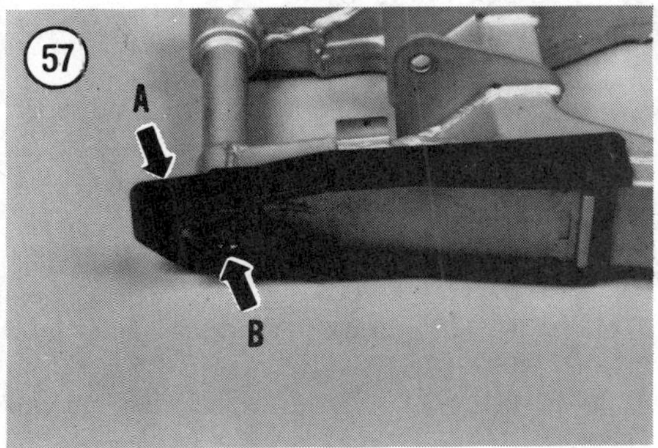

3. Check the swing arm (**Figure 58**) for cracks, twisting, weld breakage or other damage. Refer repair to a competent welding shop.

4. Pry the bearing seals (B, **Figure 57**) out of the swing arm.

5. Referring to **Figure 59**, remove the following from the swing arm:

   a. Right-hand pivot collar (A).

   b. Distance collar (B).

   c. Left-hand pivot collar (C).

6. Needle bearing wear is difficult to measure. Turn the bearings by hand. Make sure they rotate smoothly. Check the rollers for evidence of wear, pitting or color change indicating heat from lack of lubrication. If the bearing is damaged or severely worn, the needles may fall out of the bearing cage. If necessary, replace the bearings as described under *Bearing Replacement* in this chapter.

7. Assemble the swing arm by reversing Steps 1-5. Apply a light coat of waterproof grease to the collars, bearings and seals (inside lip) before installation.

Bearing Replacement

The swing arm is equipped with a needle bearing on the left-hand side and a ball bearing on the right-hand side.

Bearing removal requires a hydraulic press and the following Honda special tools (or equivalent bearing tools and drivers):

   a. Driver handle, Honda part No. 07949-3710001.

   b. Driver attachment (24 × 26 mm), Honda part No. 07746-0010700.

   c. Needle bearing remover, Honda part No. 07GMD-KT70200.

   d. Driver handle, Honda part No. 07749-0010000.

   e. Driver attachment (28 × 30 mm), Honda part No. 07946-1870100.

   f. Pilot (22 mm), Honda part No. 07746-0041000.

   g. Driver attachment (32 × 35 mm), Honda part No. 07746-0010100.

   h. Pilot (15 mm), Honda part No. 07746-0040300.

1. Remove the swing arm as described in this chapter.

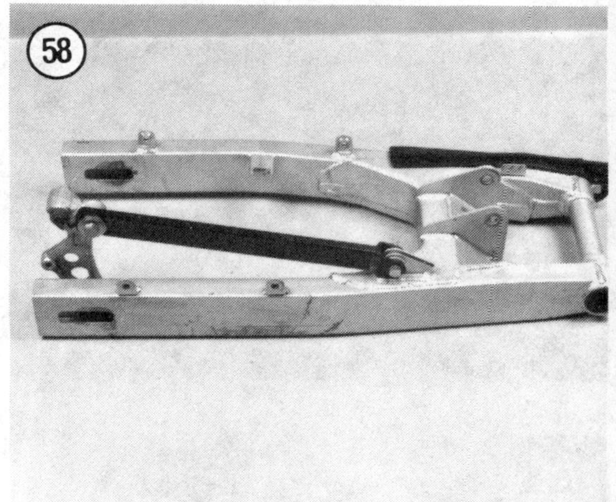

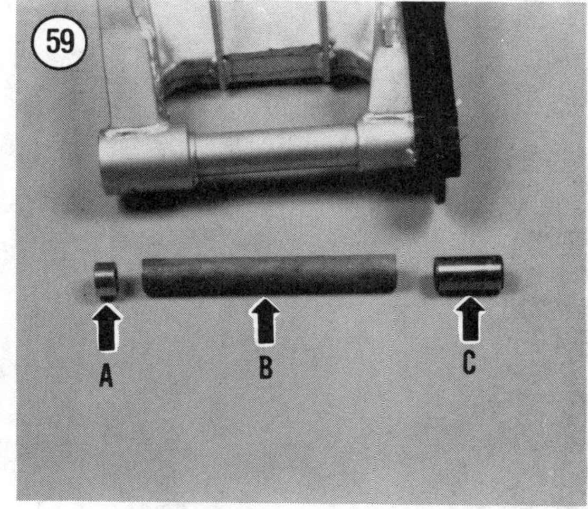

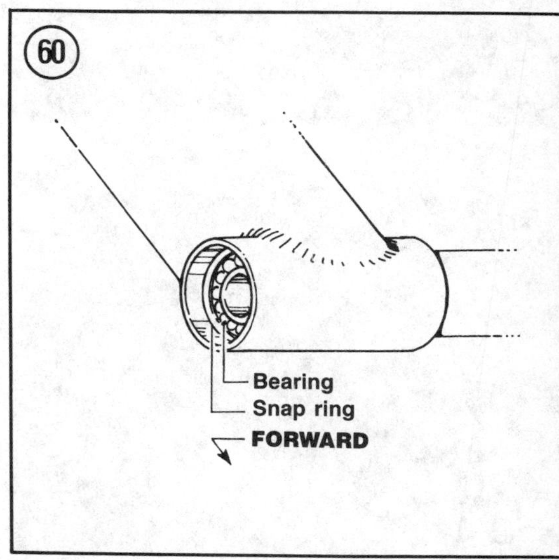

2. Perform Steps 1-5 under *Swing Arm Inspection*.

3. To remove the right-hand ball bearing, perform the following:

  a. Remove the snap ring (**Figure 60**).

  b. Support the swing arm in a press so that the right-hand side faces down (**Figure 61**).

  c. Install driver attachment (part No. 07746-0010700) onto driver handle (part No. 07949-3710001). Insert the driver handle through the swing arm and engage it with the right-hand ball bearing.

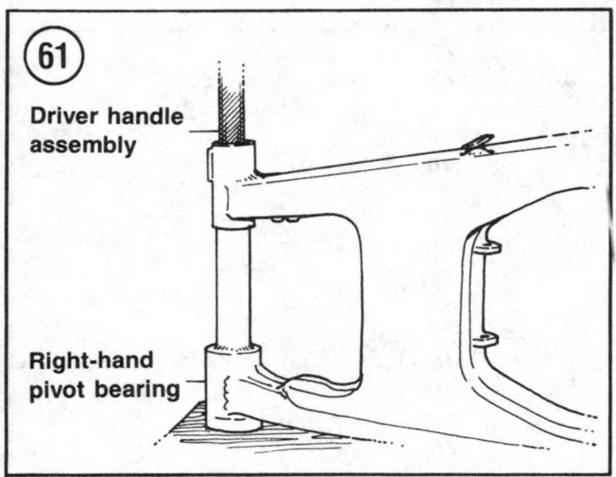

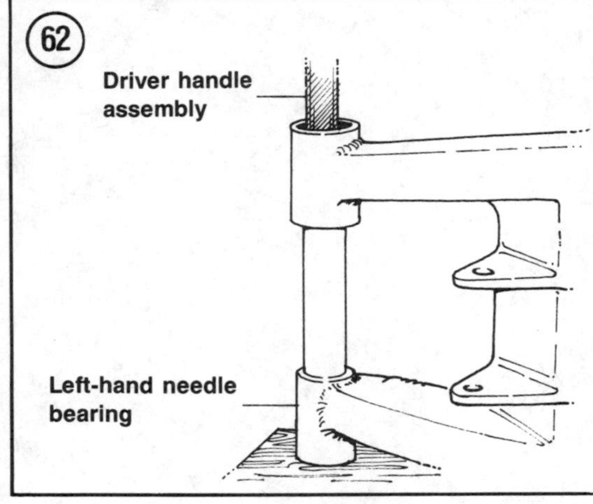

  d. Press the right-hand ball bearing out of the swing arm.

4. Remove the left-hand needle bearing as follows:

  a. Install the needle bearing remover (part No. 07GMD-KT70200) through the left-hand bearing as shown in **Figure 62**.

  b. Support the swing arm in a press so that the left-hand side faces down.

  c. Install driver attachment (part No. 07746-0010700) onto driver handle (part No. 07949-3710001). Insert the driver handle through the swing arm so that the attachment fits into the needle bearing remover.

  d. Press the left-hand needle bearing out of the swing arm.

5. Thoroughly clean out the inside of the swing arm with solvent and dry with compressed air.

6. Apply a light coat of waterproof grease to all parts before installation.

7. Install the left-hand needle bearing as follows:

  a. Support the swing arm in a press so that the left-hand side faces up.

  b. Install attachment (part No. 07946-1870100) onto driver handle (part No. 07749-0010000). Install pilot (part No. 07746-0041000) onto the attachment.

  c. Align the new needle bearing with the top of the swing arm and then press it into the swing arm with the driver handle assembly.

8. Install the right-hand ball bearing as follows:

  a. Support the swing arm in a press so that the right-hand side faces up.

  b. Install attachment (part No. 07746-0010100) onto driver handle (part No. 07749-0010000). Install pilot (part No. 07746-0040300) onto the attachment.

  c. Align the new ball bearing with the top of the swing arm and then press it into the swing arm with the driver handle assembly.

  d. Install the snap ring (**Figure 60**).

9. Assemble the pivot collars and dust seals as described under *Inspection*.

Tables are on the following page.

Table 1 REAR SUSPENSION SPECIFICATIONS

	Specification mm (in.)	Wear limit mm (in.)
Rear axle runout	—	0.2 (0.008)
Rear wheel rim runout		
Radial	—	2.0 (0.08)
Axial	—	2.0 (0.08)
Shock absorber spring free length	150.0 (5.91)	145.9 (5.74)

Table 2 REAR SUSPENSION TIGHTENING TORQUES

	N·m	ft.-lb.
Rear axle nut	90	65
Sprocket bolts	65	47
Shock absorber		
Upper mounting bolt	55	40
Lower mounting bolt	55	40
Lower joint locknut	65	47
Shock arm-to-shock link bolt	55	40
Shock link-to-frame bolt	55	40
Shock arm-to-swing arm bolt	55	40
Swing arm pivot shaft nut	65	47
Brake torque rod		
Nut (front)	22	16
Bolt (rear)	35	25
Brake disc bolts	40	29
Drive sprocket bolt	55	40

CHAPTER TWELVE

BRAKES

The brake system consists of dual discs on the front wheel and a single disc on the rear.

Refer to **Table 1** for brake specifications. **Table 1** and **Table 2** are found at the end of the chapter.

DISC BRAKES

The disc brake units are actuated by hydraulic fluid controlled by the hand lever (front brake) or brake pedal (rear brake). As the front brake pads wear, the brake fluid level drops in the master cylinder reservoir and automatically adjusts for pad wear. Rear disc brake pad wear must be compensated for by periodic rear brake pedal adjustment; see *Rear Brake Pedal Height Adjustment* and *Rear Brake Light Switch Adjustment* in Chapter Three.

When working on a hydraulic brake system, it is necessary that the work area and all tools be absolutely clean. Any tiny particles of foreign matter or grit on the caliper assembly or the master cylinder can damage the components. Also, sharp tools must not be used inside a caliper or on a caliper piston. If there is any doubt about your ability to correctly and safely carry out major service on the brake components, take the job to a Honda dealer or brake specialist.

When adding brake fluid use only a type clearly marked DOT 4 and use it from a sealed container. Brake fluid will draw moisture which greatly reduces its ability to perform correctly, so it is a good idea to purchase brake fluid in small containers.

Whenever *any* component has been removed from the brake system the system is considered "opened" and must be bled to remove air bubbles. Also, if the brake feels "spongy," this usually means there are air bubbles in the system and it must be bled. For safe brake operation, refer to *Bleeding the System* in this chapter for complete details.

CAUTION
Disc brake components rarely require disassembly, so do not disassemble unless necessary. Do not use solvents of any kind on the brake system's internal components. Solvents will cause the seals to swell and distort. When disassembling and cleaning brake components (except brake pads) use new DOT 4 brake fluid.

WARNING
*When working on the brake system, do **not** inhale brake dust. It may contain asbestos, which can cause lung injury and cancer. Wear a disposable face mask and wash your hands thoroughly after completing the work.*

FRONT BRAKE PAD REPLACEMENT

There is no recommended mileage interval for changing the friction pads on the disc brakes. Pad wear depends greatly on riding habits and conditions. The pads should be checked for wear every 4,000 miles (6,400 km) by observing the pads through the slot in the caliper housing (**Figure 1**) and replaced when the wear line (**Figure 2**) reaches the edge of the brake disc. To maintain an even brake pressure on the disc, always replace both pads in each caliper at the same time.

Service Notes

Observe the following service notes before replacing brake pads.
1. Brake pads should be replaced only as a set.
2. Disconnecting the hydraulic brake hose is not required for brake pad replacement. Disconnect the hose only if caliper removal is required.

WARNING
Use brake fluid clearly marked DOT 4 from a sealed container. Other types may vaporize and cause brake failure. Always use the same brand name; do not intermix brake fluids, many brands are not compatible.

WARNING
*Do not ride the motorcycle until you are sure the brake is operating correctly. If necessary, bleed the brake as described under **Bleeding the System** in this chapter.*

Front Pad Replacement

Refer to **Figure 3** for this procedure.

1. To prevent the accidental application of the front brake lever, place a spacer between the front brake lever and the hand grip. Hold the spacer in place with tape or a large rubber band.

2. *Left-hand caliper:* Perform the following:
   a. Remove the speedometer cable set screw (**Figure 4**) and pull the cable out of the speedometer drive housing. Pull the cable out of the cable guide (**Figure 5**).

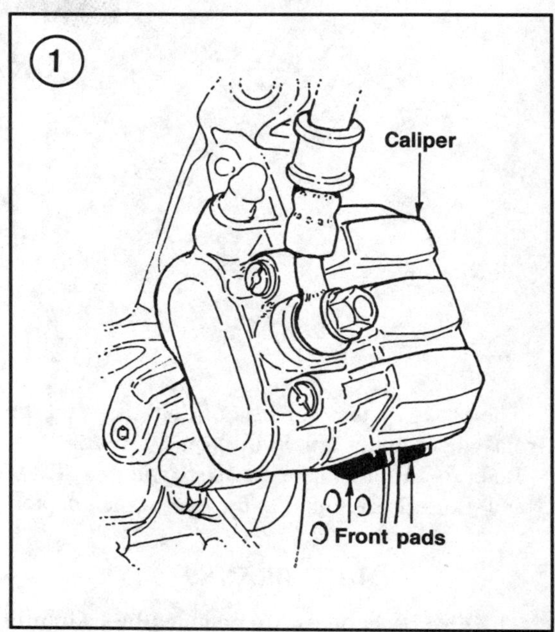

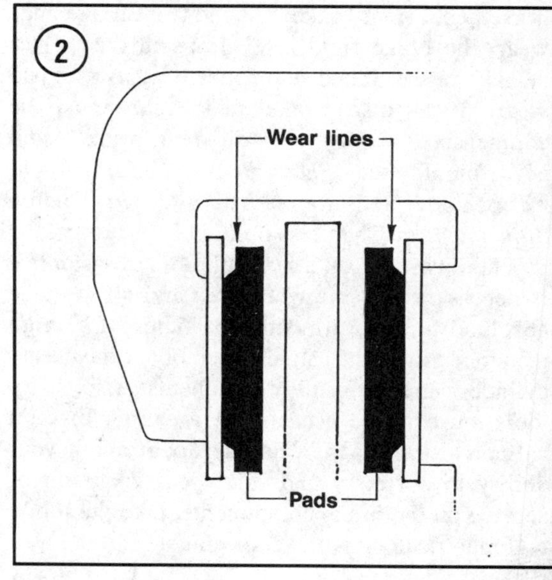

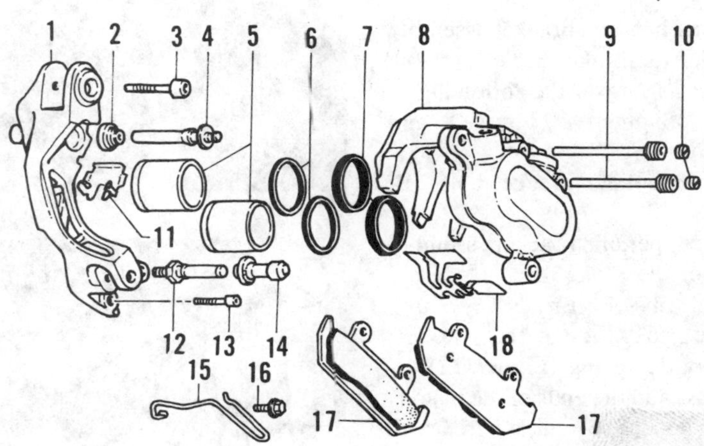

1. Caliper support
2. Boot
3. Bolt
4. Bolt
5. Pistons
6. Dust seals
7. Piston seals
8. Caliper housing
9. Pad pins
10. Pad pin plugs
11. Anti-rattle spring
12. Bolt
13. Bolt
14. Pin bushing
15. Cable guide
16. Bolt
17. Brake pads

b. Remove the pad pin plugs (A, **Figure 6**). Loosen the pad pins.

c. Remove the caliper bracket bolt (B, **Figure 6**).

d. Remove the anti-dive piston bolt (C, **Figure 6**).

e. Slide the brake caliper and bracket assembly (**Figure 7**) off of the brake disc.

3. *Right-hand caliper:* Perform the following:

a. Remove the pad pin plugs (A, **Figure 8**) and loosen the pad pins.

b. Remove the brake caliper bracket bolts (B, **Figure 8**).

c. Slide the brake caliper and bracket assembly (**Figure 9**) off of the brake disc.

4. Remove the 2 pad pins (**Figure 10**).

5. Remove the brake pads (**Figure 11**).

6. Remove the anti-rattle spring (**Figure 12**).

7. Clean the pad recess and the ends of the pistons with a shop cloth. Do not use solvent, a wire brush or any hard tool which would damage the cylinders or pistons.

8. When new pads are installed in the caliper, the master cylinder brake fluid will rise as the caliper pistons are repositioned. Perform the following:

a. Clean the top of the master cylinder of all dirt and foreign matter. Remove the screws securing the cap (**Figure 13**) and remove the cap and the diaphragm from the front master cylinder.

b. Slowly push both pistons into the caliper.

c. Constantly check the reservoir to make sure brake fluid does not overflow. Siphon brake fluid, if necessary, before it overflows.

d. The pistons should move freely. If they don't, and there is evidence of them sticking in the cylinder, the caliper should be removed and serviced as described under *Front Caliper Rebuilding* in this chapter.

9. Push the caliper pistons in all the way to allow room for the new pads.

10. Install the anti-rattle spring as shown in **Figure 12**.

11. Insert the brake pads into the caliper housing so that the friction surfaces face each other. See **Figure 11**.

12. Install one brake pad pin, then the other (**Figure 10**). Screw the pad pins in all the way.

13. *Left-hand caliper:* Perform the following:

a. Align the brake pads with the brake disc and install the brake caliper assembly.

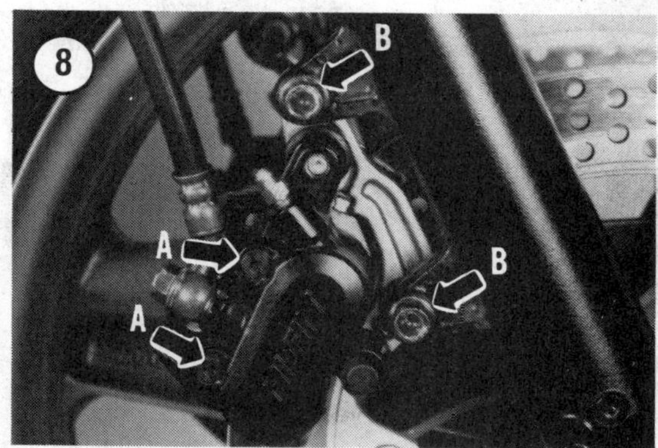

b. Tighten the caliper bracket bolt (B, **Figure 6**) to the torque specification in **Table 2**.

c. Tighten the anti-dive piston bolt (C, **Figure 6**) to the torque specification in **Table 2**.

d. Tighten the pad pins (A, **Figure 6**) to the torque specification in **Table 2**.

e. Insert the speedometer cable into the speedometer housing. Install the attaching screw (**Figure 4**) securely. Make sure to route the speedometer cable into the cable guide as shown in **Figure 5**.

14. *Right-hand caliper:* Perform the following:

a. Align the brake pads with the brake disc and install the brake caliper assembly.

b. Tighten the caliper bracket bolts (B, **Figure 6**) to the torque specification in **Table 2**.

c. Tighten the pad pins (**Figure 8**) to the torque specification in **Table 2**.

15. Support the motorcycle with the front wheel off the ground. Spin the wheel and pump the brake until the pads are seated against the disc.

16. Refill the master cylinder reservoir, if necessary, to maintain the correct fluid level. Install the diaphragm and top cap. Tighten the screws securely.

> *WARNING*
> *Use brake fluid clearly marked DOT 4 from a sealed container. Other types may vaporize and cause brake failure. Always use the same brand name; do not intermix brake fluids, many brands are not compatible.*

> *WARNING*
> *Do not ride the motorcycle until you are sure the brakes are working correctly.*

FRONT BRAKE CALIPER

Removal

Refer to **Figure 3**.

1. Drain the master cylinder as follows:

a. Attach a hose to the brake caliper bleed screw (A, **Figure 14**).

b. Place the end of the hose in a clean container (**Figure 15**).

c. Open the bleed screw (A, **Figure 14**) and operate the brake lever to drain all brake fluid from the master cylinder reservoir.

d. Close the bleed screw and disconnect the
   hose.
e. Discard the brake fluid.

2. Remove the banjo bolt (B, **Figure 14**) and
sealing washers attaching the brake hose to the
caliper. To prevent the loss of brake fluid, cap the
end of the brake hose and tie it up to the fender.
Be sure to cap or tape the ends to prevent the entry
of moisture and dirt.

3. Remove the brake pads as described under *Front
Brake Pad Replacement* in this chapter.

4. Installation is the reverse of these steps. Note
the following:

a. Tighten the caliper bracket bolts to the torque
   specification in **Table 2**.
b. Install the brake hose using new sealing
   washers (**Figure 16**) on each side of the hose
   fitting.
c. Tighten the brake banjo bolt to the torque
   specification in **Table 2**.
d. Bleed the brakes as described under *Bleeding
   the System* in this chapter.

Disassembly

Refer to **Figure 3** for this procedure.

1. Remove the brake caliper as described in this
chapter.

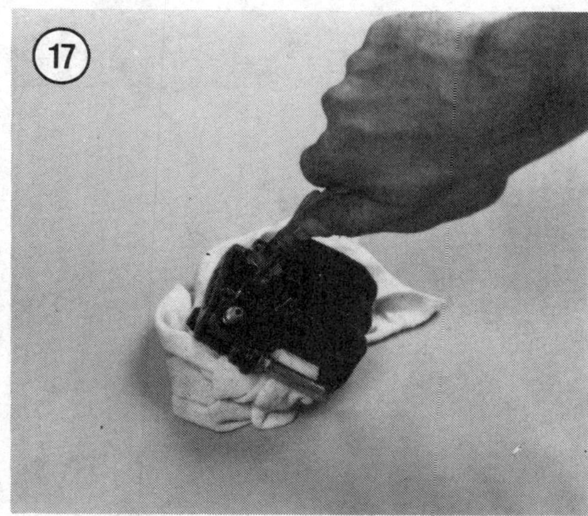

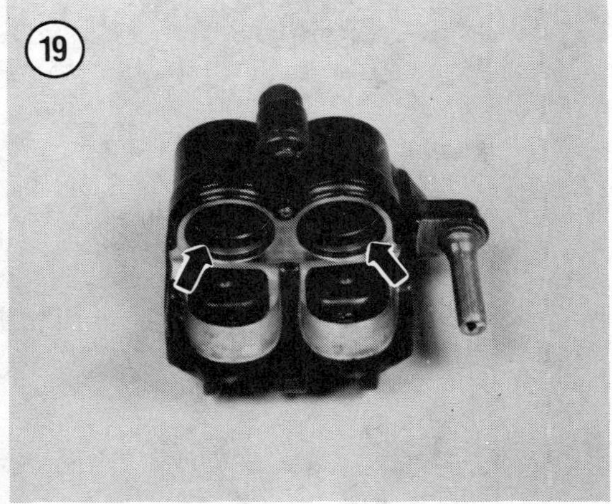

2. Pull the caliper bracket out of the housing.

> *NOTE*
> *Compressed air will be required to remove the pistons.*

> *WARNING*
> *Keep your fingers and hand out of the caliper bore area when removing the pistons in Step 3. The pistons will fly out of the bore with considerable force and could crush your fingers or hand.*

3. Pad the pistons with shop rags or wood blocks as shown in **Figure 17**. Then apply compressed air through one of the caliper ports and blow the pistons out of the caliper (**Figure 18**).

4. Carefully pry the dust and piston seals (**Figure 19**) out of the caliper. Be sure not to damage the piston bore when removing the seals.

Inspection

1. Clean all caliper parts (except brake pads) in new DOT 4 brake fluid. Place the clean parts on a lint-free cloth while performing the following inspection procedures.

2. Check the caliper bore (**Figure 19**) for cracks, deep scoring or excessive wear. Measure the cylinder bore (**Figure 20**). Replace the caliper housing if the bore exceeds the specifications given in **Table 1**.

3. Check the caliper pistons (**Figure 21**) for deep scoring, excessive wear or rust. Then measure the

piston outside diameter with a micrometer (**Figure 22**). Replace the pistons if the outside diameter is less than the specifications given in **Table 1**.

4. The piston seal (A, **Figure 23**) maintains correct brake pad to disc clearance. If the seal is worn or damaged, the brake pads will drag and cause excessive pad wear and brake fluid temperatures. Replace the piston (A, **Figure 23**) and dust seals (B, **Figure 23**) if the following conditions exist:

a. Brake fluid leaks around the inner brake pad.
b. The piston seal(s) is stuck in the caliper groove.
c. There is a large difference in inner and outer brake pad wear thickness (**Figure 24**).

5. Check the caliper bracket (A, **Figure 25**) for cracks or other damage; replace the support if necessary. Replace the dust boot (B, **Figure 25**) on the caliper bracket if torn or damaged.

6. Replace the retainer (A, **Figure 26**) on the caliper bracket if cracked or damaged. Be sure the retainer is positioned as shown in **Figure 26**.

7. Check the pad pins for cracks, deep scoring or excessive wear. Replace the pins if necessary.

8. Check the anti-rattle spring (**Figure 27**) for cracks or other damage; replace if necessary.

Assembly

1. Coat the seals, pistons and piston bores in clean DOT 4 brake fluid.

2. Refer to **Figure 23**. Install the piston (A) and dust (B) seals as follows:

a. Install the piston seals (**Figure 28**) in the rear piston bore grooves.
b. Install the dust seals (B, **Figure 23**) in the front piston bore grooves.

3. Install the pistons so that the insulated ends will face toward the brake pads. See **Figure 29**.

4. Coat the caliper bracket pins (B, **Figure 26**) with silicone grease.

5. Install the caliper bracket onto the caliper housing.

6. Install the brake pads and the caliper housing as described under *Front Brake Pad Replacement* in this chapter.

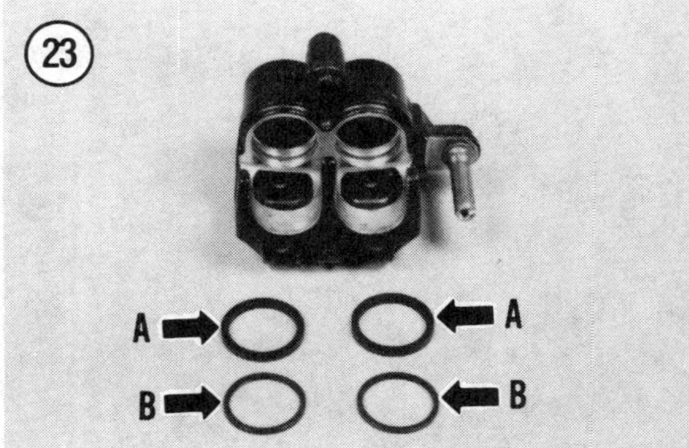

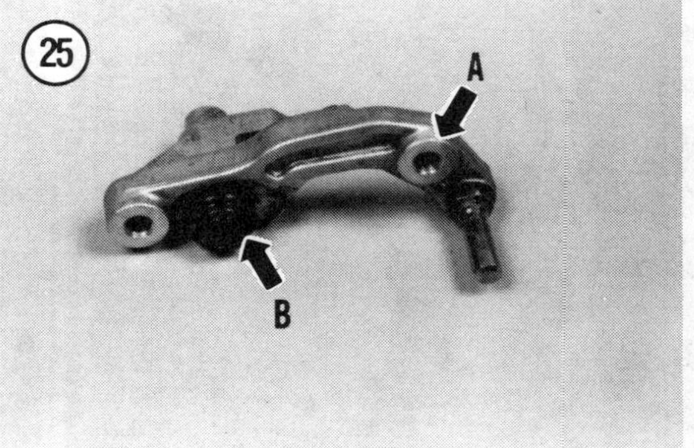

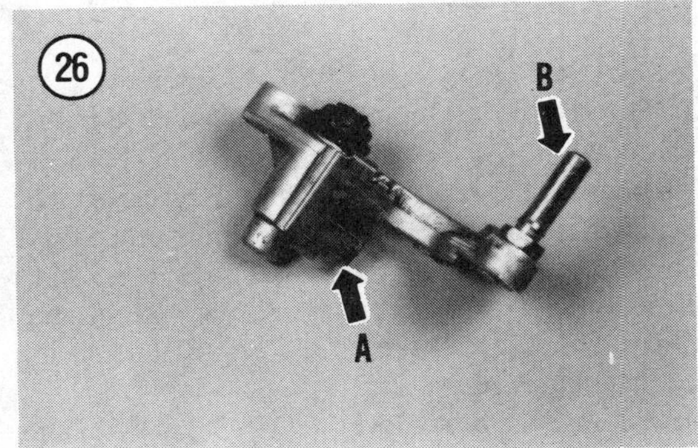

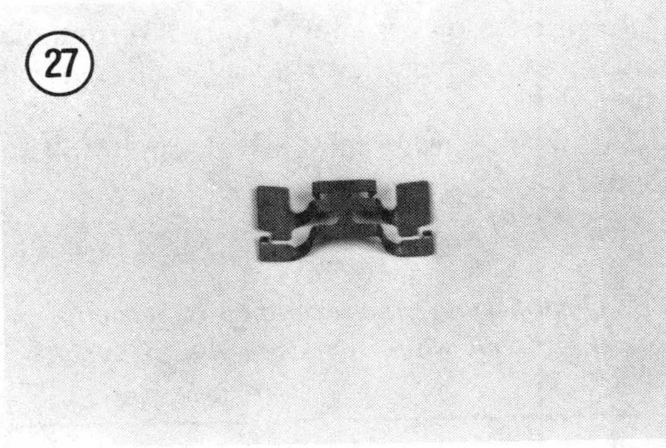

FRONT MASTER CYLINDER

Removal/Installation

CAUTION
Cover the fuel tank, front fender and instrument cluster with a heavy cloth or plastic tarp to protect them from accidental spilling of brake fluid. Wash any spilled brake fluid off any plastic, painted or plated surfaces immediately, as it will destroy the finish. Use soapy water and rinse completely.

1. Drain the master cylinder as follows:
   a. Attach a hose to the brake caliper bleed screw (A, **Figure 14**).
   b. Place the end of the hose in a clean container (**Figure 15**).
   c. Open the bleed screw (A, **Figure 14**) and operate the brake lever to drain all brake fluid from the master cylinder reservoir.
   d. Close the bleed screw and disconnect the hose (B, **Figure 14**).
   e. Discard the brake fluid.
2. Disconnect the brake switch wires at the master cylinder.
3. Remove the banjo bolt securing the brake hose to the master cylinder (A, **Figure 30**). Remove the brake hose and both sealing washers. Cover the end of the hose to prevent the entry of foreign matter and moisture. Tie the hose end up to the handlebar to prevent the loss of brake fluid.
4. Remove the 2 clamp bolts (B, **Figure 30**) and clamp securing the master cylinder to the handlebar and remove the master cylinder.

12

5. Install by reversing these removal steps. Note the following:

   a. Install the master cylinder clamp with the arrow facing upward.

   b. Align the top end of the handlebar clamp with the punch mark on the handlebar.

   c. Tighten the upper clamp bolt first, then the lower clamp bolt securely. There should be a gap at the lower part of the clamp after tightening is complete.

   d. Install the brake hose onto the master cylinder. Be sure to place a sealing washer on each side of the hose fitting and install the banjo bolt. Tighten the banjo bolt to the torque specification in **Table 2**.

   e. Bleed the brake system as described under *Bleeding the System* in this chapter.

WARNING
Do not ride the motorcycle until the front brake is operating correctly.

Disassembly

Refer to **Figure 31** for this procedure.

1. Remove the master cylinder as described in this chapter.

2. Remove the screws securing the reservoir cap and diaphragm. Pour out the remaining brake fluid and discard it. *Never* reuse brake fluid.

3. Remove the brake switch screw and lift the brake switch (A, **Figure 32**) off of the master cylinder housing.

4. Remove the brake lever nut (B, **Figure 32**) and pivot bolt and remove the brake lever (C, **Figure 32**).

5. Remove the rubber boot (**Figure 33**) from the area where the hand lever actuates the internal piston.

6. Remove the piston circlip with circlip pliers (**Figure 34**).

CAUTION
Do not remove the secondary cup from the piston when removing the piston

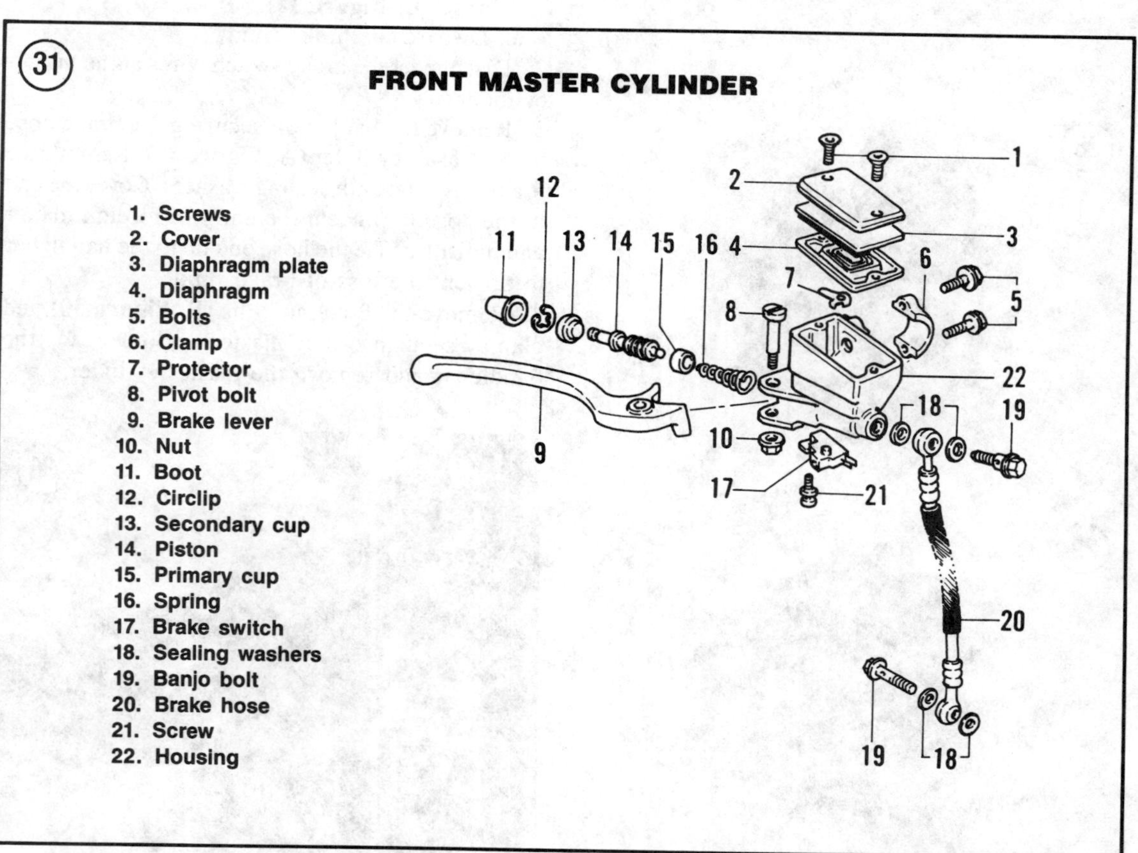

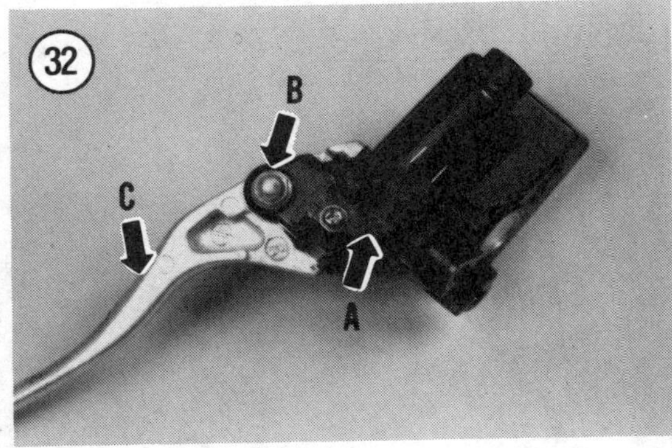

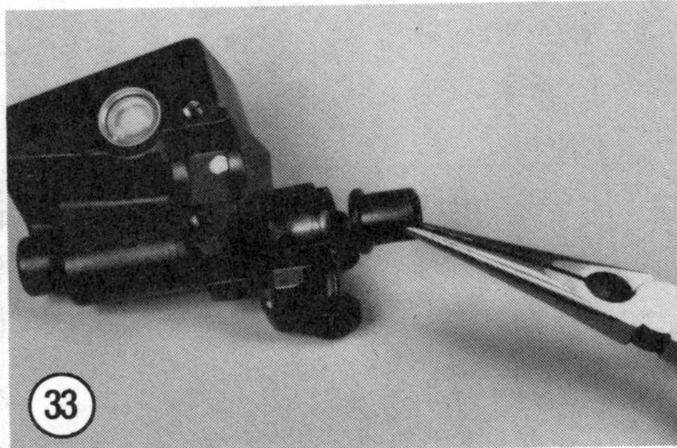

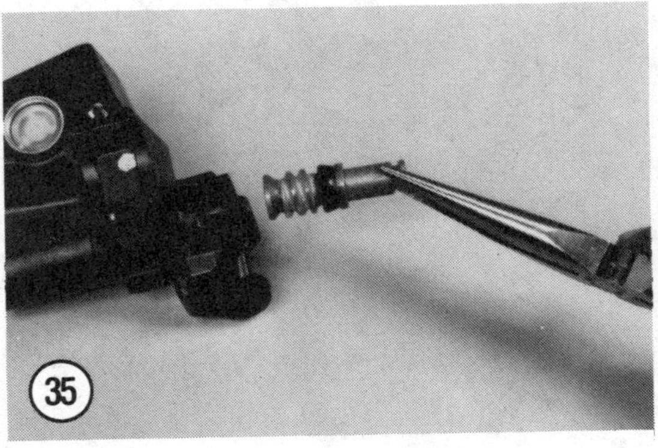

assembly in Step 7. Removing the secondary cup from the piston will damage the cup.

7. Remove the piston/secondary cup assembly (**Figure 35**).
8. Remove the primary cup/spring assembly (**Figure 36**).
9. Remove the protector from inside the master cylinder (**Figure 37**).

Inspection

1. Clean all parts (**Figure 38**) in fresh DOT 4 brake fluid. Place the master cylinder components on a clean lint-free cloth when performing the following inspection procedures.

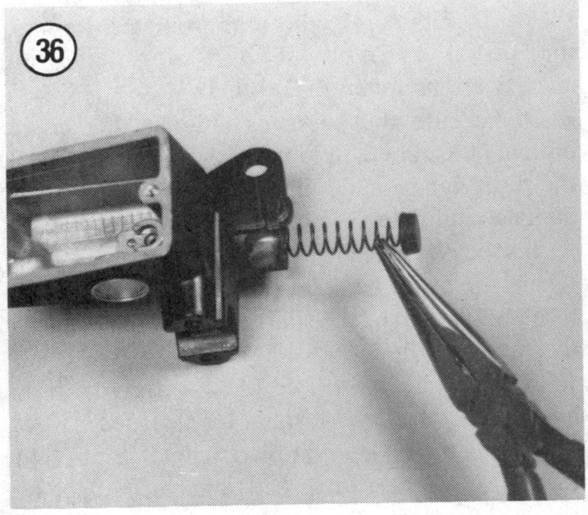

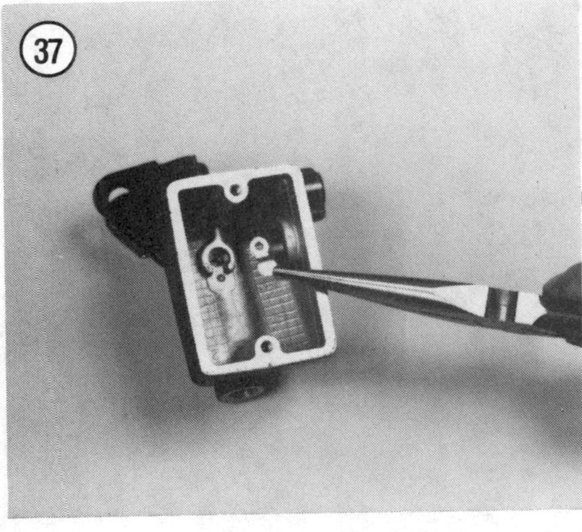

2. Check the end of the piston (A, **Figure 39**) for wear caused by the hand lever. Replace the entire piston assembly if any portion of it requires replacement. If the piston assembly is replaced, also replace the primary cup (B, **Figure 39**).

3. Check the secondary cup (on the piston) for damage, softness or for swollen conditions. See C, **Figure 39**. Replace the piston assembly if the secondary cup is damaged.

4. Check the primary cup (B, **Figure 39**) for the same conditions in Step 3. Replace the primary cup if necessary.

5. Check the spring (D, **Figure 39**) for cracks or other damage; replace if necessary.

6. Measure the cylinder bore (**Figure 40**). Replace the master cylinder if the bore exceeds the specifications given in **Table 1**.

7. Measure the outside diameter of the piston as shown in **Figure 41** with a micrometer. Replace the piston assembly if it is less than the specifications given in **Table 1**.

8. Make sure the passages (**Figure 42**) in the bottom of the brake fluid reservoir are clear. Check the reservoir cap and diaphragm (**Figure 43**) for damage and deterioration; replace if necessary.

9. Inspect the threads in the master cylinder body where the brake hose banjo bolt screws in. If the threads are damaged or partially stripped, replace the master cylinder.

10. Inspect the pivot hole (A, **Figure 44**) in the hand lever. If worn, it must be replaced.

11. Check the brake lever pivot bolt (B, **Figure 44**) for excessive wear or thread damage; replace the bolt if necessary.

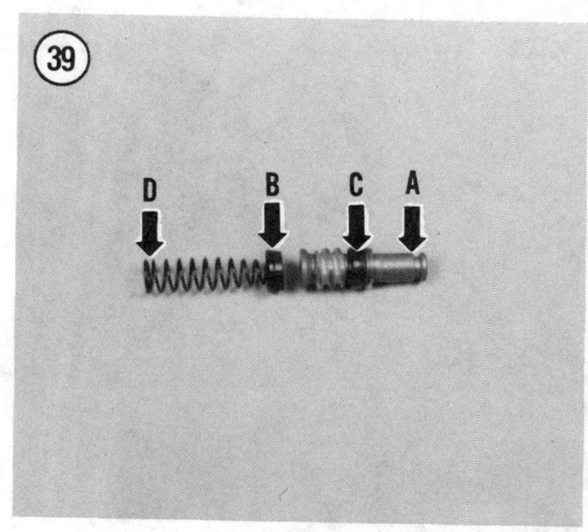

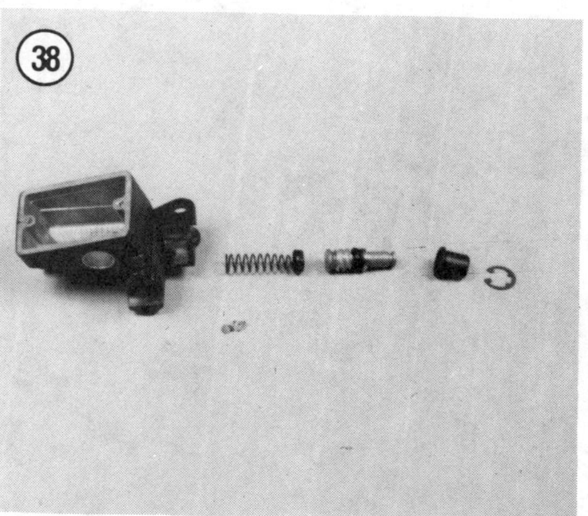

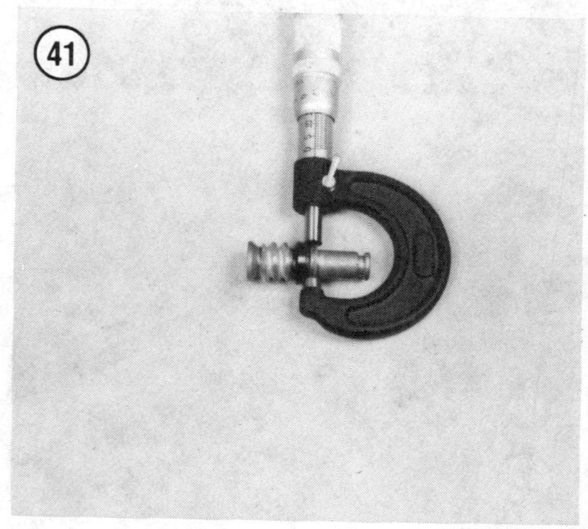

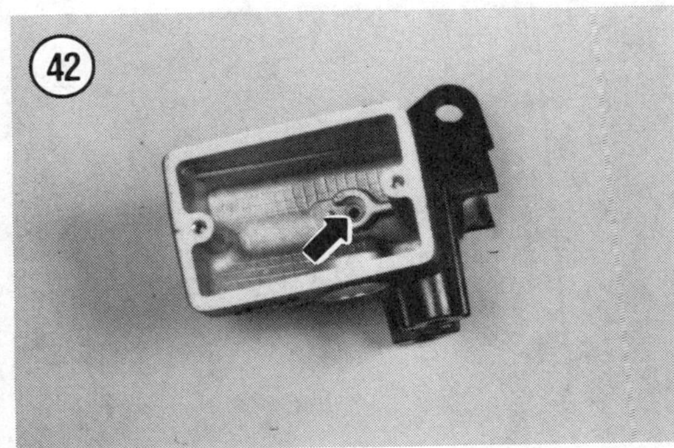

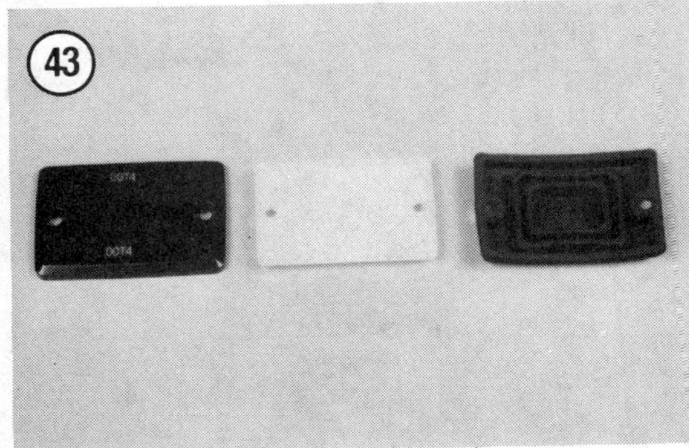

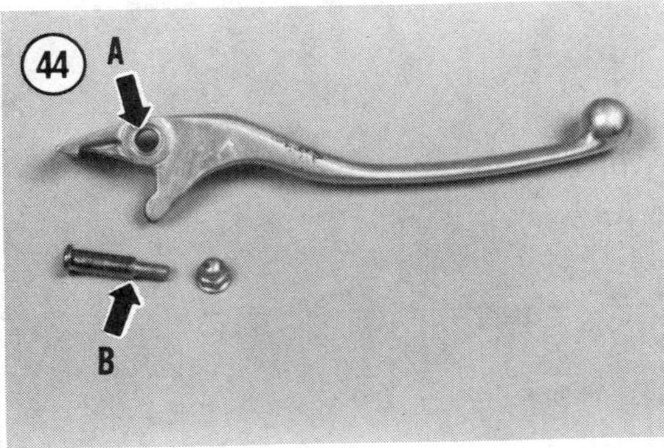

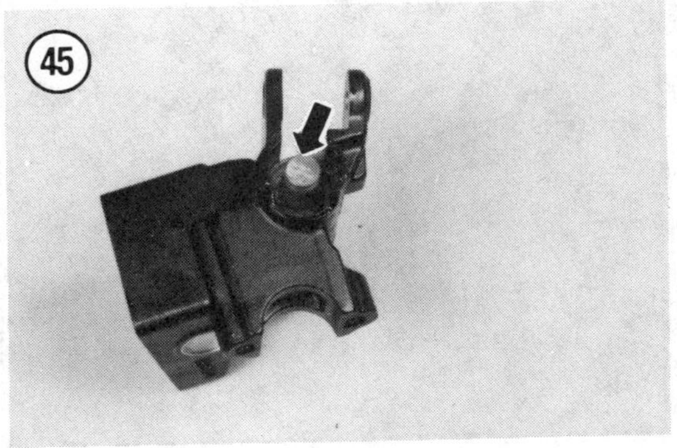

Assembly

1. Soak the new cups in fresh DOT 4 brake fluid for at least 15 minutes to make them pliable. Coat the inside of the cylinder with fresh brake fluid before assembling the parts.

> *CAUTION*
> *When installing the piston assembly, do not allow the cups to turn inside out as they will be damaged and allow brake fluid to leak within the cylinder bore.*

2. Install the primary cup onto the spring (B, **Figure 39**) and insert the assembly into the master cylinder as shown in **Figure 36**.

> *NOTE*
> *Be sure to install the primary cup (B, **Figure 39**) with the open end in first, toward the spring.*

3. Install the piston/secondary cup assembly into the master cylinder as shown in **Figure 35**.

4. Push the piston (**Figure 45**) into the master cylinder and install the circlip (**Figure 34**) into the master cylinder groove. Make sure the circlip is seated completely in the groove.

5. Install the rubber boot (**Figure 33**). Make sure the boot seats completely in the master cylinder (**Figure 46**).

6. Install the brake lever (A, **Figure 47**) onto the master cylinder. Then install the pivot bolt (B, **Figure 47**) through the brake lever and secure it with the nut (B, **Figure 32**). Tighten the nut securely.

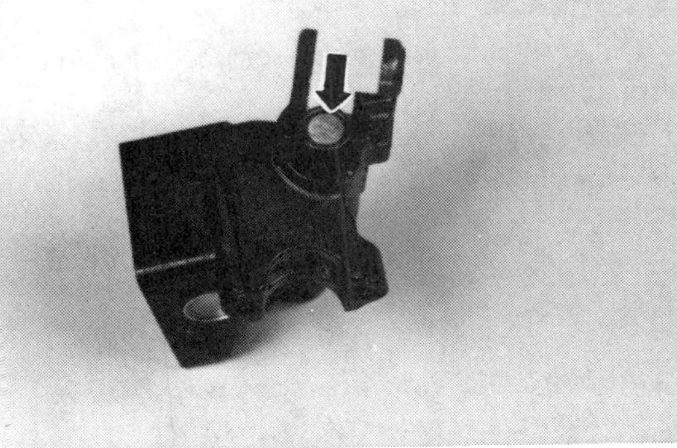

7. Install the front brake switch onto the master cylinder (A, **Figure 32**). Secure the switch with the screw.

8. Install the protector into the master cylinder (**Figure 37**). Seat the protector into the brake fluid passage as shown in **Figure 48**.

9. Install the diaphragm and cover. Do not tighten the cover screws at this time as fluid will have to be added later.

REAR DISC BRAKE

The rear disc brake is actuated by hydraulic fluid and is controlled by the right-hand foot pedal. The brake pedal is connected to the master cylinder. As the brake pads wear, the caliper pistons move out automatically to keep pedal freeplay constant. Over a period of time, this gradual repositioning of the pistons in response to brake pad wear will drop the level of the hydraulic fluid in the master cylinder reservoir.

REAR BRAKE PAD REPLACEMENT

There is no recommended mileage interval for changing the friction pads on the disc brake. Pad wear depends greatly on riding habits and conditions. The pads should be checked for wear every 4,000 miles (6,400 km) by observing the pads through the slot in the caliper housing (**Figure 49**) and replaced when the wear lines (**Figure 50**) reach the edge of the brake disc. To maintain an even brake pressure on the disc, always replace both pads in each caliper at the same time.

Service Notes

Observe the following service notes before replacing brake pads.

1. Brake pads should be replaced only as a set.

2. Disconnecting the hydraulic brake hose is not required for brake pad replacement. Disconnect the hose only if caliper removal is required.

WARNING
Use brake fluid clearly marked DOT 4 from a sealed container. Other types

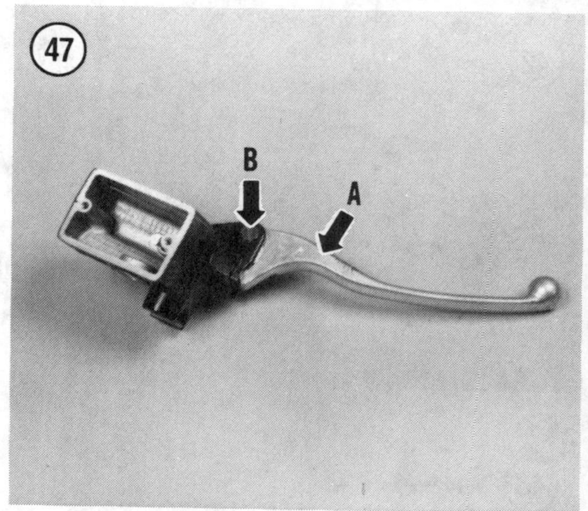

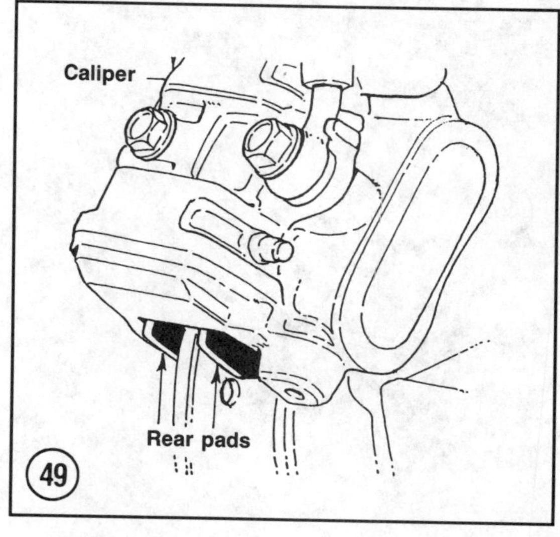

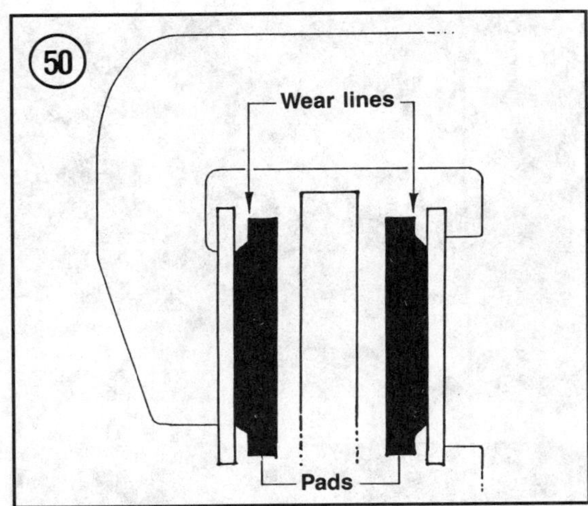

may vaporize and cause brake failure. Always use the same brand name; do not intermix brake fluids as many brands are not compatible.

WARNING
Do not ride the motorcycle until you are sure the brake is operating correctly. If necessary, bleed the brake as described under **Bleeding the System** in this chapter.

NOTE
Refer to **Figure 51** for Steps 3-22.

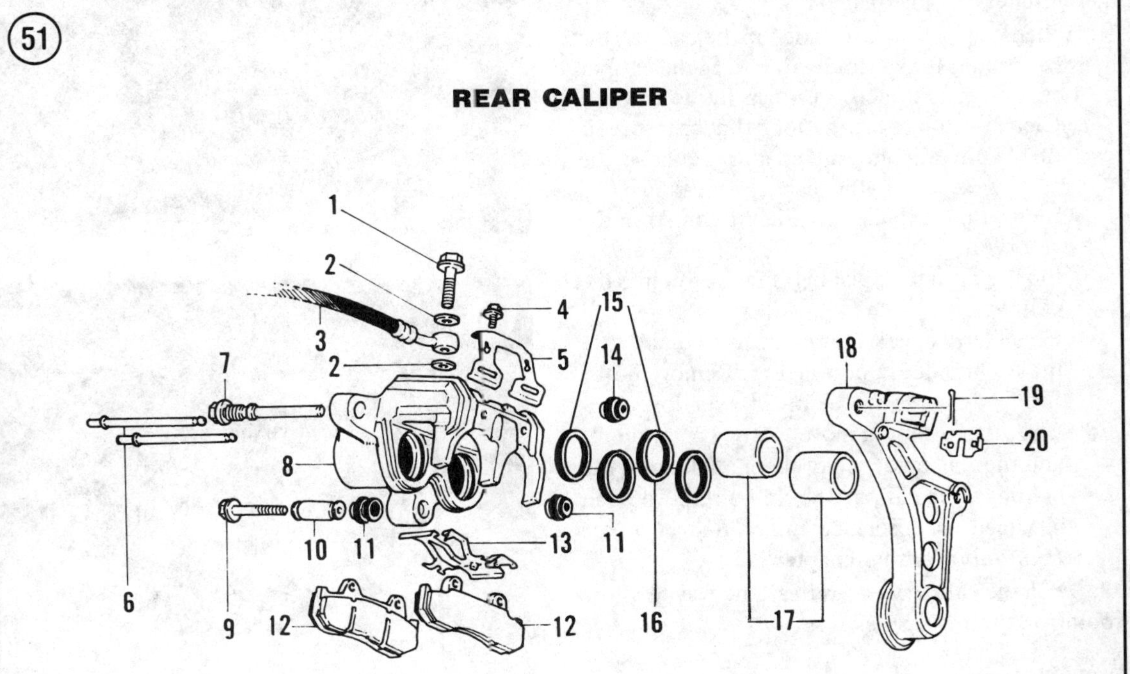

1. Union bolt
2. Sealing washers
3. Brake hose
4. Screw
5. Pad pin retainer
6. Pad pins
7. Bolt
8. Caliper housing
9. Bolt
10. Sleeve
11. Boot
12. Brake pads
13. Pad spring
14. Boot
15. Piston seals
16. Dust seals
17. Pistons
18. Caliper support
19. Cotter pin
20. Retainer

12

3. Remove the brake caliper mounting bolt (A, **Figure 52**) and the caliper pivot bolt (B, **Figure 52**).

4. Pivot the caliper upwards (**Figure 53**) and away from the brake disc. Then slide the caliper outward and remove it.

5. Remove the pad pin retainer bolt (**Figure 54**).

6. Lift the pad pin retainer (**Figure 55**) off of the master cylinder.

7. Slide the 2 pad pins out of the master cylinder and remove them (**Figure 56**).

8. Remove both brake pads (**Figure 57**).

9. Remove the anti-rattle spring (**Figure 58**).

10. Clean the pad recess and the ends of the pistons (**Figure 59**) with a shop cloth. Do not use solvent, a wire brush or any hard tool which would damage the cylinders or pistons.

11. When new pads are installed in the caliper, the master cylinder brake fluid will rise as the caliper pistons are repositioned. Perform the following:

   a. Clean the top of the master cylinder reservoir of all dirt and foreign matter. Remove the screws securing the cap (**Figure 60**) and remove the cap and the diaphragm from the reservoir.

   b. Slowly push both pistons (**Figure 59**) into the caliper.

   c. Constantly check the reservoir to make sure brake fluid does not overflow. Remove brake fluid, if necessary, before it overflows.

   d. The pistons should move freely. If they don't, and there is evidence of them sticking in the cylinder, the caliper should be removed and serviced as described under *Rear Caliper Rebuilding* in this chapter.

12. Push the caliper pistons in all the way to allow room for the new pads.

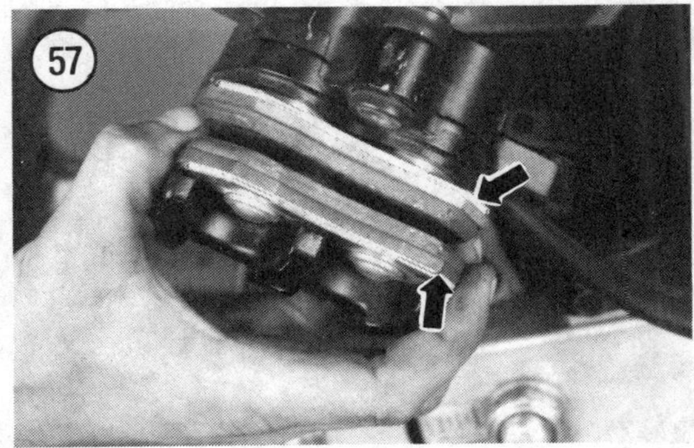

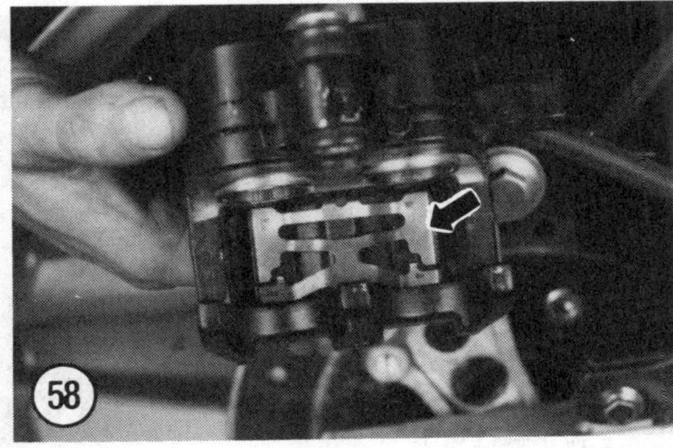

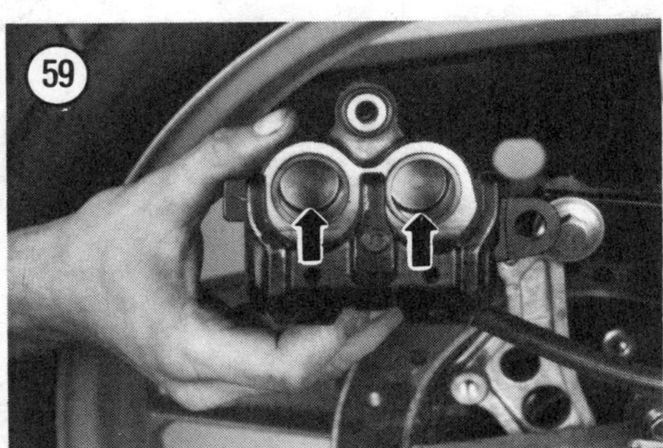

13. Install the anti-rattle spring as shown in **Figure 58**.

14. Insert the brake pads into the caliper housing so that the friction surfaces face each other. See **Figure 57**.

15. Install one brake pad pin, then the other (**Figure 56**).

16. Install silicone grease onto the caliper bracket pin and the caliper mounting bolt.

17. Install the pad pin retainer so that the retainer locks the pad pins as shown in **Figure 55**.

18. Install the pad pin retainer bolt (**Figure 54**) and tighten to the torque specification in **Table 2**.

19. Slide the caliper assembly onto the brake disc (**Figure 53**) so that the brake disc is between the brake pads.

20. Install the pivot bolt (**Figure 61**) and the caliper mounting bolt (A, **Figure 52**). Tighten the pivot pin securely. Tighten the rear caliper mounting bolt to the torque specification in **Table 2**.

21. Support the motorcycle with the rear wheel off the ground. Spin the wheel and pump the brake until the pads are seated against the disc.

22. Refill the master cylinder reservoir, if necessary, to maintain the correct fluid level. Install the diaphragm and top cap (**Figure 60**). Tighten the screws securely.

> *WARNING*
> *Use brake fluid clearly marked DOT 4 from a sealed container. Other types may vaporize and cause brake failure. Always use the same brand name; do not intermix brake fluids, as many brands are not compatible.*

REAR BRAKE CALIPER

Removal

Refer to **Figure 51** for this procedure.

1. Drain the master cylinder as follows:
   a. Attach a hose to the brake caliper bleed screw (A, **Figure 62**).
   b. Place the end of the hose in a clean container.
   c. Open the bleed screw (A, **Figure 62**) and operate the brake pedal to drain all brake fluid from the master cylinder reservoir.
   d. Close the bleed screw and disconnect the hose.
   e. Discard the brake fluid.

2. Remove the banjo bolt and sealing washers attaching the brake hose to the caliper (B, **Figure 62**). To prevent the loss of brake fluid, cap the end of the brake hose and tie it up to the fender. Be sure to cap or tape the ends to prevent the entry of moisture and dirt.

3. Remove the brake pads as described under *Rear Brake Pad Replacement* in this chapter.

4. Installation is the reverse of these steps. Note the following:
   a. Install the rear brake pads (and brake caliper) as described in this chapter.
   b. Install the brake hose using new sealing washers (B, **Figure 62**) on each side of the hose fitting.
   c. Tighten the brake banjo bolt to the torque specification in **Table 2**.
   d. Bleed the brakes as described under *Bleeding the System* in this chapter.

WARNING
Do not ride the motorcycle until you are sure that the brakes are operating properly.

Disassembly

Refer to **Figure 51** for this procedure.

1. Remove the brake caliper as described in this chapter.

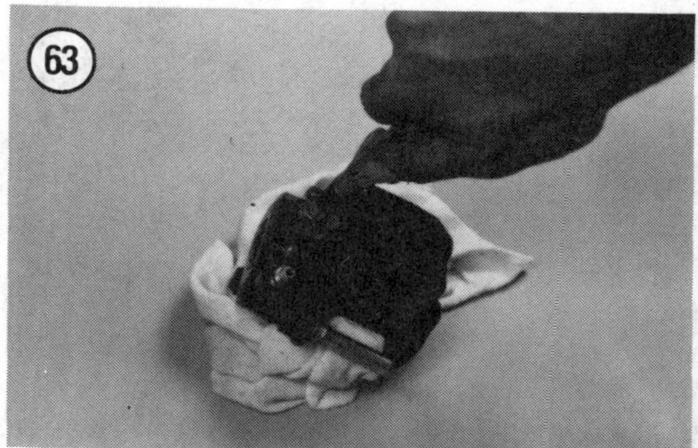

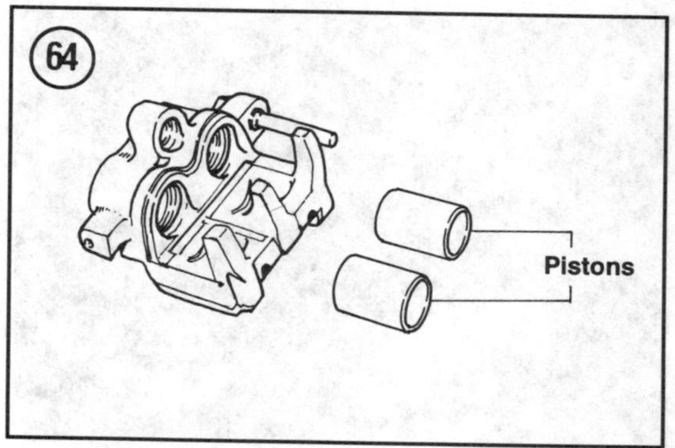

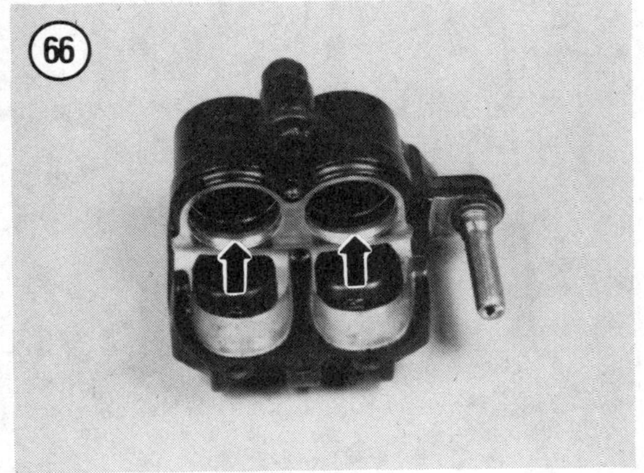

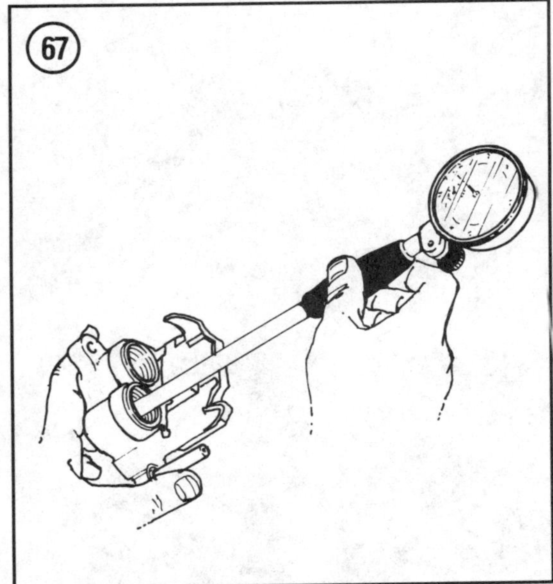

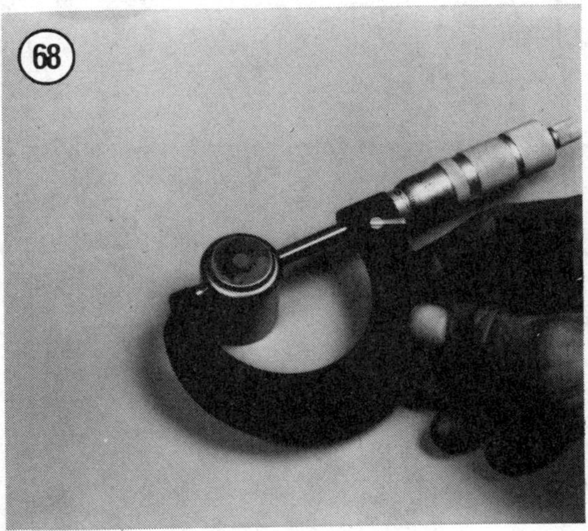

2. Remove the pivot collar and rubber boots from the caliper housing.

> *NOTE*
> *Compressed air will be required to remove the pistons.*

> *WARNING*
> *Keep your fingers and hand out of the caliper bore area when removing the pistons in Step 3. The pistons will fly out of the bore with considerable force and could crush your fingers or hand.*

3. Pad the piston with shop rags or wood blocks as shown in **Figure 63**. Apply compressed air through one of the caliper ports and blow the pistons out of the caliper (**Figure 64**).

4. Carefully pry the dust (**Figure 65**) and piston seals (**Figure 66**) out of the caliper. Be sure not to damage the piston bore when removing the seals.

Inspection

1. Clean all caliper parts (except brake pads) in new DOT 4 brake fluid. Place the cleaned parts on a lint-free cloth while performing the following inspection procedures.

2. Check the caliper bore for cracks, deep scoring or excessive wear. Measure the cylinder bore (**Figure 67**). Replace the caliper housing if the bore exceeds the specification given in **Table 1**.

3. Check the caliper piston for deep scoring, excessive wear or rust. Measure the piston outside diameter with a micrometer (**Figure 68**). Replace the pistons if the outside diameter is less than the specification given in **Table 1**.

4. Replace the piston seals (A, **Figure 69**) and dust seals (B, **Figure 69**) whenever the caliper is disassembled.

12

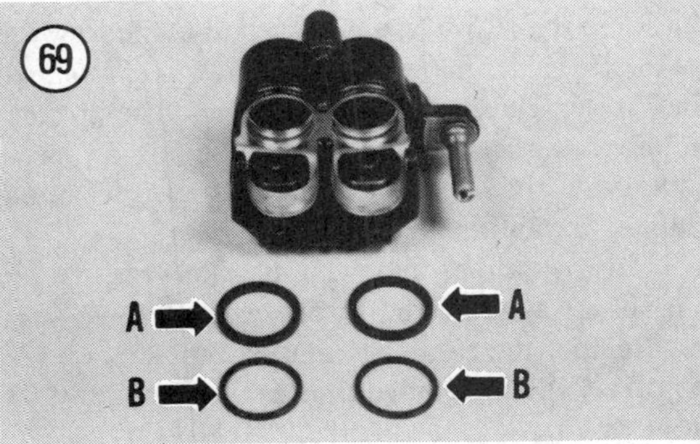

5. Check the pad pins (A, **Figure 70**) for cracks, deep scoring or excessive wear. Replace the pins if necessary.

6. Check the pad pin retainer (B, **Figure 70**) for cracks or damage where the retainer engages the pad pins. Replace the retainer if necessary.

7. Check the pivot bolt (**Figure 71**) for cracks, scoring or other damage; replace if necessary.

8. Check the anti-rattle spring for cracks or other damage; replace if necessary.

9. Check the brake pad friction material for severe wear or oil contamination. If the friction material is okay, check the back of the pads for cracks or other damage (**Figure 72**).

Assembly

1. Coat the seals, pistons and piston bores in clean DOT 4 brake fluid.

2. Refer to **Figure 69**. Install the piston (A) and dust (B) seals as follows:
   a. Install the piston seals (**Figure 66**) in the rear piston bore grooves.
   b. Install the dust seals (**Figure 65**) in the front piston bore grooves.

3. Install the pistons so that the open end faces to the outside as shown in **Figure 64**.

4. Coat the pivot collar and the inside of the rubber boots with silicone grease.

5. Install the pivot collar and boots.

6. Install the brake pads and the caliper housing as described under *Rear Brake Pad Replacement* in this chapter.

Caliper Mounting Bracket Removal/Installation

1. Remove the rear caliper assembly as described in this chapter.

2. Raise the rear wheel and partially withdraw the rear axle as described under *Rear Wheel Removal* in Chapter Eleven. It is not necessary to completely remove the rear axle from the swing arm. Withdraw the rear axle only until it clears the caliper mounting bracket.

3. Lift the caliper mounting bracket (**Figure 73**) up and away from the rear wheel.

4. Remove the caliper mounting bracket bolt (A, **Figure 74**) and remove the bracket assembly (B, **Figure 74**).

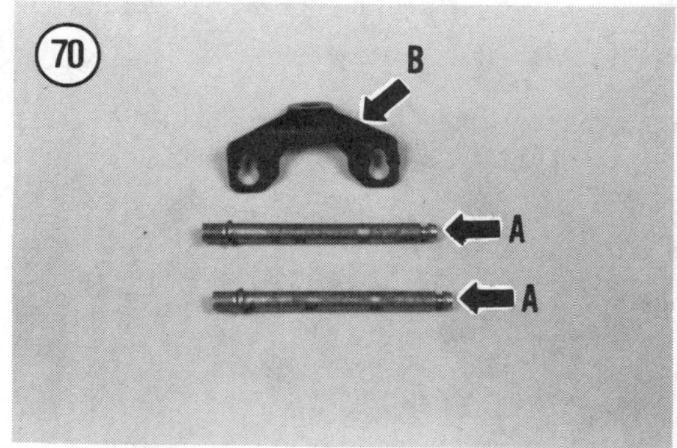

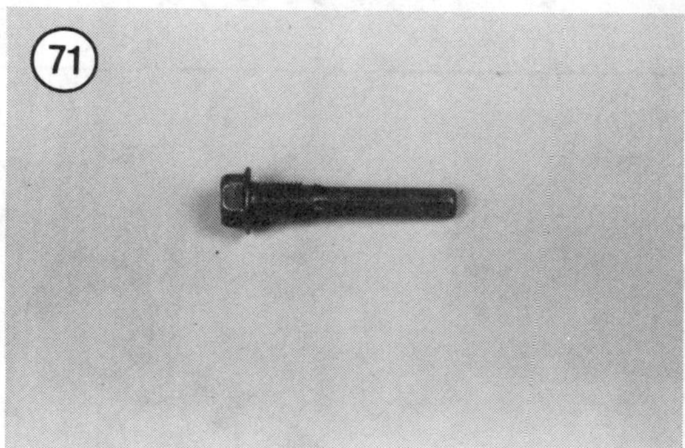

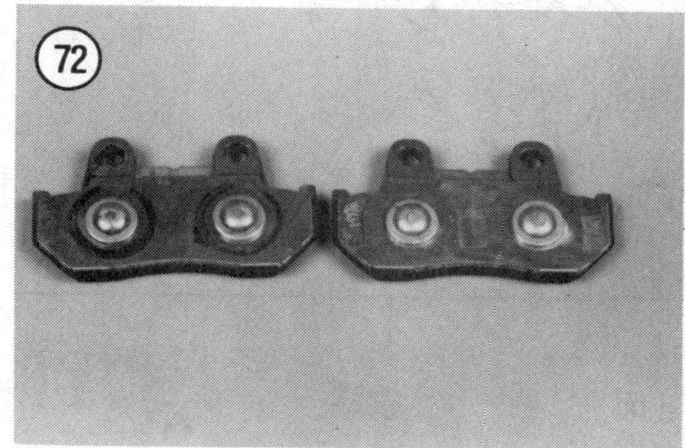

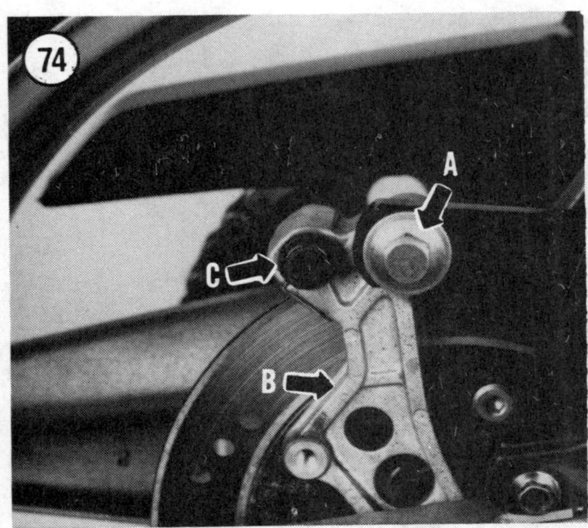

5. Install by reversing these removal steps. Note the following:
   a. Make sure the retainer (C, **Figure 74**) is installed on the caliper bracket.
   b. Tighten the caliper mounting bracket bolt securely.
   c. When installing the rear wheel, make sure the axle spacer on the left-hand side is still installed on the rear wheel. See *Rear Wheel Installation* in Chapter Eleven.

REAR MASTER CYLINDER

Removal/Installation

Refer to **Figure 75** for this procedure.

(75)

REAR MASTER CYLINDER

1. Banjo bolt
2. Sealing washers
3. Brake hose
4. Bolt
5. Housing
6. O-ring
7. Joint
8. Bolt
9. Clamp
10. Brake hose
11. Bolt
12. Clamp
13. Spacer
14. Reservoir
15. Screws
16. Cover
17. Diaphragm plate
18. Diaphragm
19. Spring
20. Piston cup
21. Spring
22. Piston cup
23. Pushrod
24. Circlip
25. Dust boot
26. Cotter pin
27. Washer
28. Nut
29. Nut
30. Joint
31. Pivot pin

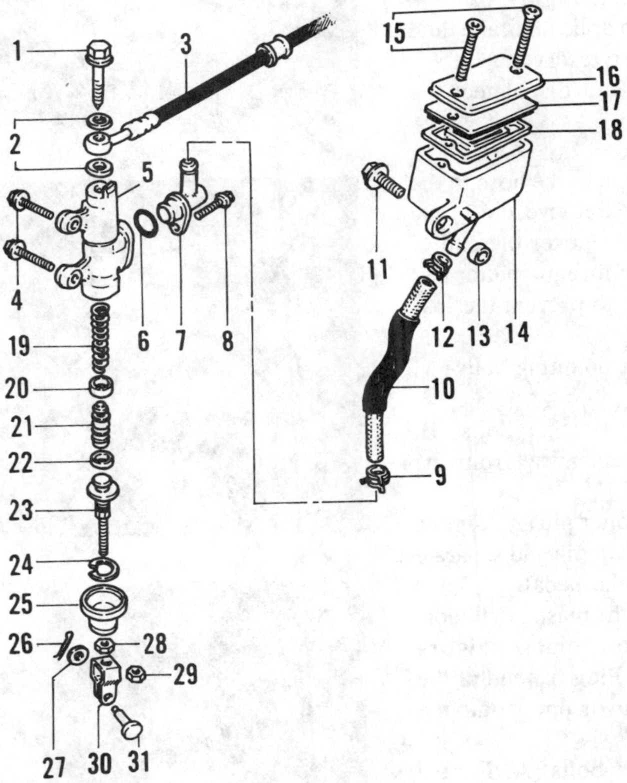

1. Remove the muffler as described under *Exhaust System* in Chapter Seven. It is not necessary to remove the muffler but this will prevent any accidental damage to it during this procedure.

CAUTION
Cover the swing arm with a heavy cloth or plastic tarp to protect it from accidental spilling of brake fluid. Wash any spilled brake fluid off any plastic, painted or plated surfaces immediately, as it will destroy the finish. Use soapy water and rinse completely.

2. Remove the right-hand side cover. See Chapter Thirteen.

3. Drain the master cylinder as follows:
   a. Attach a hose to the brake caliper bleed screw (A, **Figure 62**).
   b. Place the end of the hose in a clean container.
   c. Open the bleed screw (A, **Figure 62**) and operate the brake pedal to drain all brake fluid from the master cylinder reservoir.
   d. Close the bleed screw and disconnect the hose.
   e. Discard the brake fluid.

4. Remove the bolt securing the brake hose to the master cylinder (**Figure 76**). Remove the brake hose and both sealing washers. Cover the end of the hose to prevent the entry of foreign matter and moisture. Tie the hose end up to prevent the loss of brake fluid.

5. Loosen the master cylinder mounting bolts (A, **Figure 77**).

6. Remove the right footpeg bracket bolts (B, **Figure 77**) and pull the bracket away from the frame.

7. Remove the pushrod joint cotter pin (A, **Figure 78**). Remove the washer and pivot pin and separate the pushrod from the rear brake pedal.

8. Remove the screw securing the master cylinder-to-reservoir hose and lift the hose joint (B, **Figure 78**) off of the master cylinder. Plug the end of the hose to prevent brake fluid from dripping onto the bike.

9. Remove the master cylinder bolts (A, **Figure 77**) and remove the master cylinder assembly.

10. Install by reversing these removal steps. Note the following.

11. Replace the reservoir hose O-ring (**Figure 79**) if deteriorated or otherwise damaged.

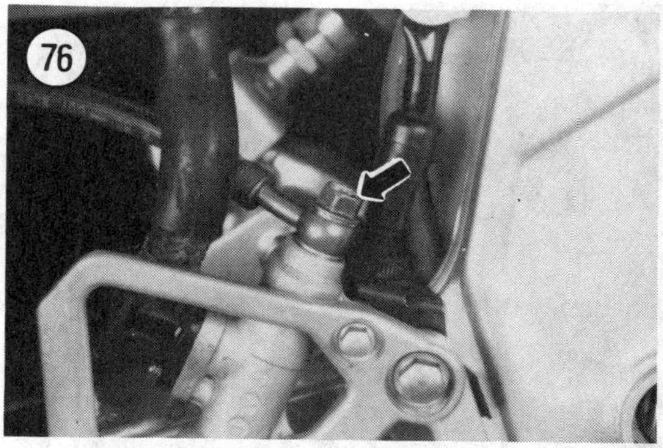

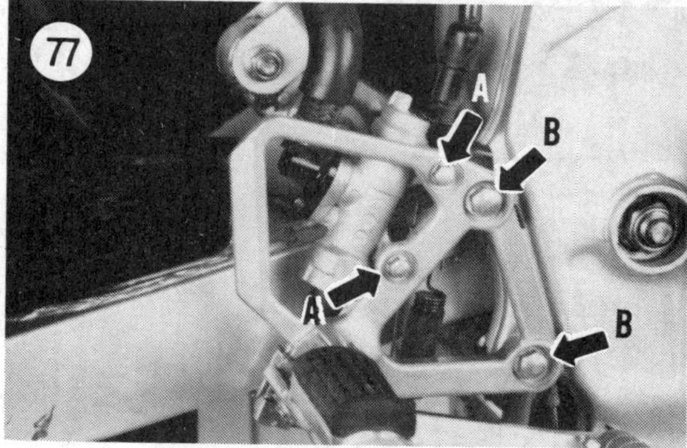

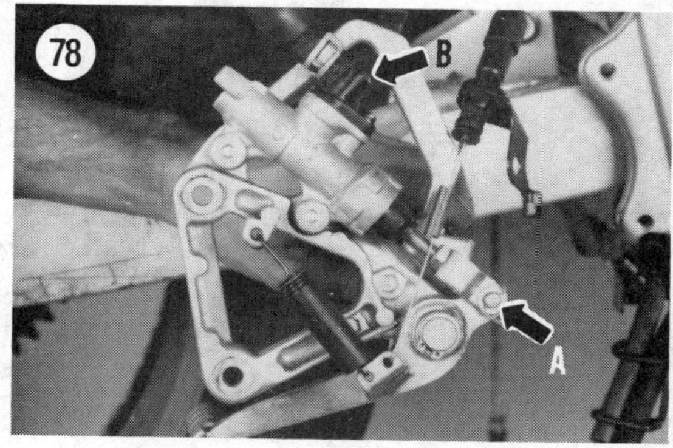

12. Connect the pushrod joint to the brake pedal with the pivot pin and washer. Secure with a *new* cotter pin (A, **Figure 78**).

13. Temporarily install the master cylinder onto the right-hand footpeg bracket before installing the footpeg bracket.

14. Tighten the right-hand footpeg bracket bolts to the torque specification in **Table 2**.

15. Tighten the master cylinder bolts to the torque specification in **Table 2**.

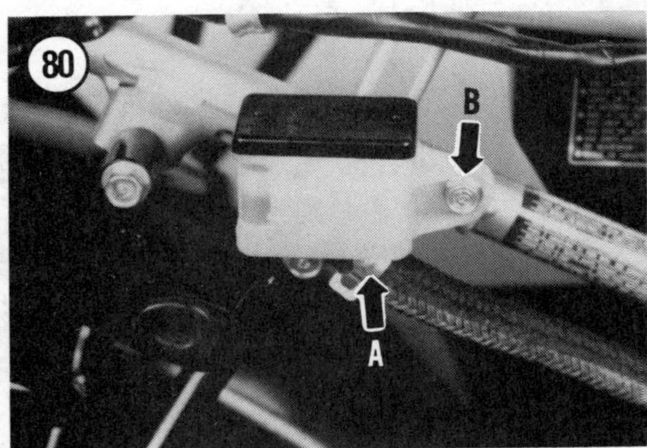

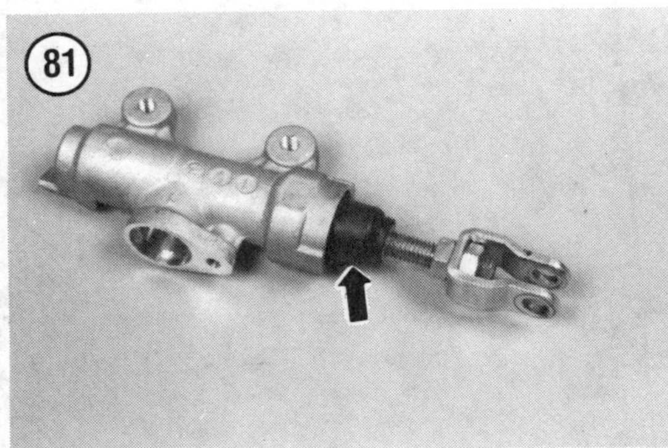

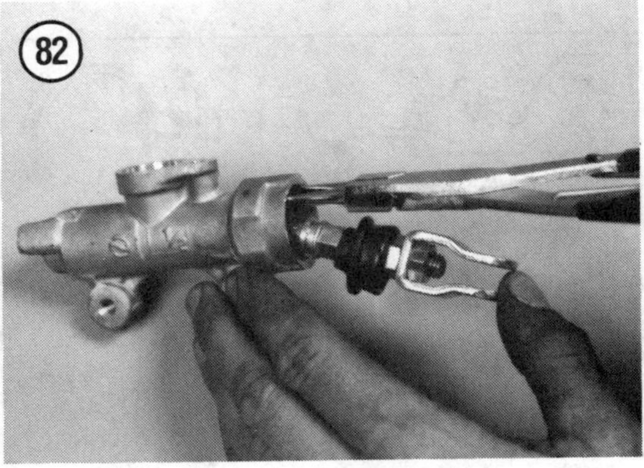

16. Install the brake hose onto the master cylinder. Be sure to place a sealing washer on each side of the hose fitting and install the banjo bolt. Tighten the banjo bolt to the torque specification in **Table 2**.

17. Bleed the brake system as described under *Bleeding the System* in this chapter.

18. Adjust the rear brake pedal as described in Chapter Three; refer to *Rear Brake Pedal Height Adjustment* and *Rear Brake Light Switch Adjustment*.

19. Install the right-hand side cover.

20. Install the muffler, if removed.

> *WARNING*
> *Do not ride the motorcycle until the rear brake is operating correctly.*

Reservoir
Removal/Installation

The master cylinder reservoir can be removed by first draining the master cylinder as described under *Master Cylinder Removal/Installation*. Disconnect the hose at the reservoir (A, **Figure 80**) and remove the reservoir bolt (B, **Figure 80**). Remove the reservoir. Reverse to install. Bleed the brake as described under *Bleeding the System* in this chapter.

Disassembly

Refer to **Figure 75**.

1. Remove the master cylinder as described in this chapter.

2. Pull the rubber boot (**Figure 81**) away from the master cylinder housing.

> *CAUTION*
> *When the circlip is removed in Step 3, the pushrod will fly out of the housing under spring pressure. Protect yourself accordingly.*

3. Remove the circlip (**Figure 82**).

4. Remove the pushrod assembly (**Figure 83**).

5. Remove the piston, cups and spring (**Figure 84**).

Inspection

1. Clean all parts (**Figure 85**) in fresh DOT 4 brake fluid. Place the master cylinder components on a clean lint-free cloth when performing the following inspection procedures.

2. Check the end of the piston (A, **Figure 86**) for wear caused by the pushrod. Replace the entire piston assembly if any portion of it requires replacement. If the piston assembly is replaced, the cups (B, **Figure 86**) must be replaced also.

3. Check the cups for damage, softness or for swollen conditions. See B, **Figure 86**. Replace the piston assembly if necessary.

4. Check the spring for cracks or other damage; replace if necessary.

5. Measure the cylinder bore (**Figure 87**). Replace the master cylinder if the bore exceeds the specifications given in **Table 1**.

6. Measure the outside diameter of the piston as shown in **Figure 88** with a micrometer. Replace the piston assembly if it is less than the specifications given in **Table 1**.

7. Make sure the passages (**Figure 89**) in the bottom of the master cylinder are clear.

8. Inspect the threads in the master cylinder body where the brake hose banjo bolt screws in. If the threads are damaged or partially stripped, replace the master cylinder.

9. Inspect the pushrod assembly (**Figure 90**). Inspect the threads for strippage. Inspect the rubber boot for tears and replace if necessary.

10. Check the snap ring groove in the master cylinder (**Figure 91**) for damage; replace the master cylinder if necessary.

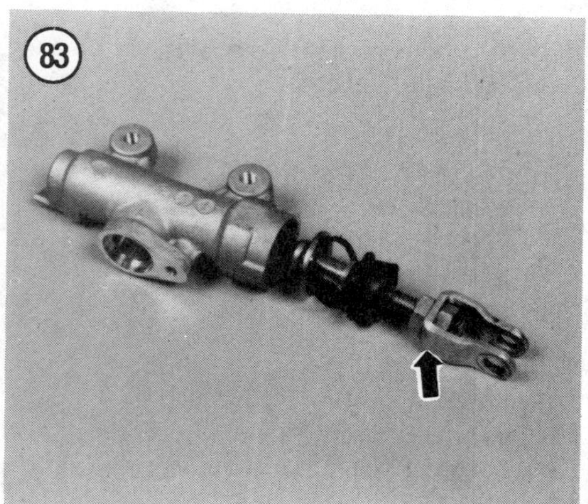

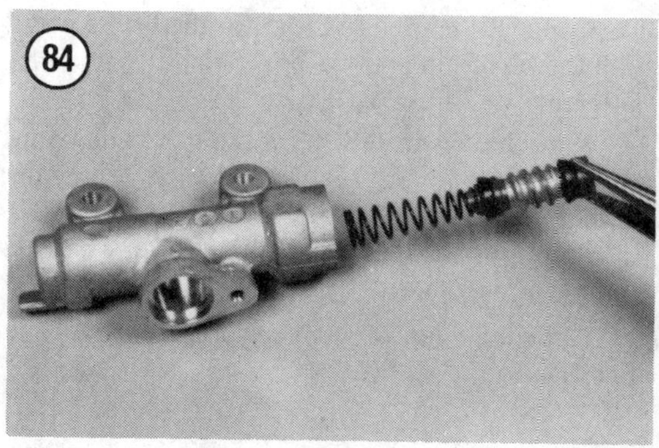

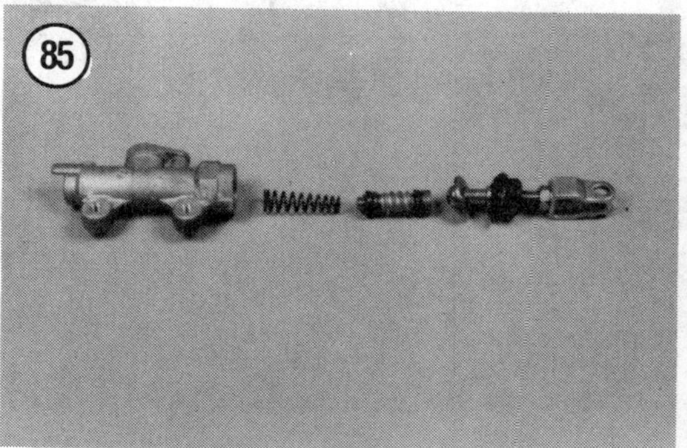

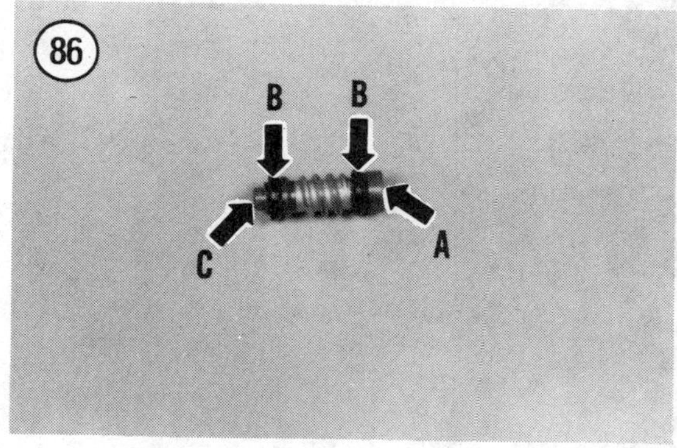

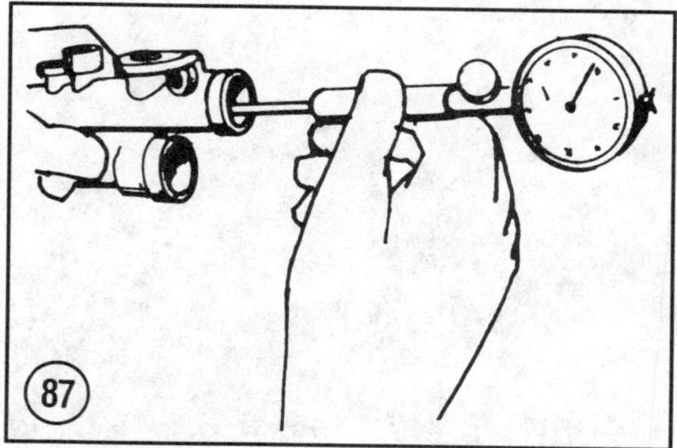

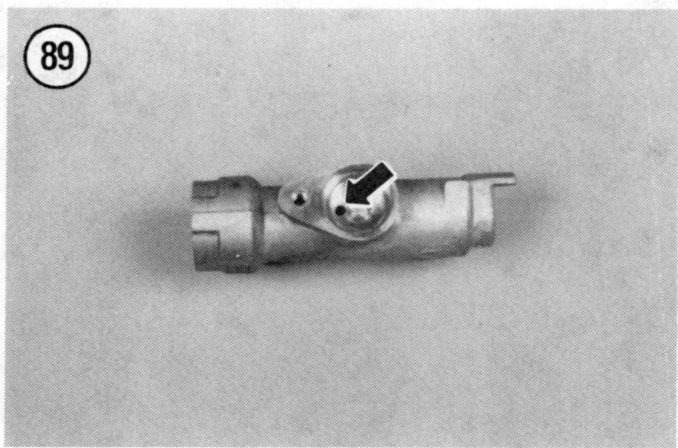

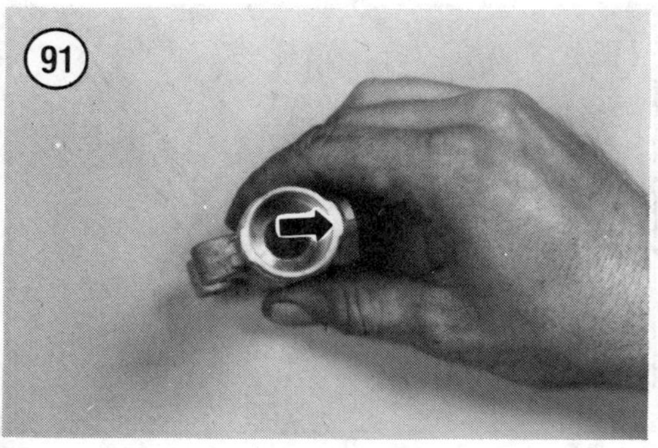

Assembly

1. Soak the new cups in fresh brake fluid for at least 15 minutes to make them pliable. Coat the inside of the cylinder with fresh brake fluid before assembling the parts.

CAUTION
When installing the piston assembly, do not allow the cups to turn inside out as they will be damaged and allow brake fluid to leak within the cylinder bore.

2. Place the master cylinder in a vise with soft jaws. Do not tighten the jaws too tight or the master cylinder may be distorted or damaged.

NOTE
Be sure to install the primary cup with the open end in first, toward the spring (C, Figure 86).

3. Install the primary and secondary cups onto the piston as shown in B, **Figure 86**.
4. Insert the small end of the spring onto the end of the piston and install the spring/piston assembly as shown in **Figure 84**.
5. Install the circlip and washer onto the pushrod as shown in **Figure 90**.
6. Align the pushrod assembly with the master cylinder as shown in **Figure 83**. Compress the pushrod and install the washer below the circlip groove. Install the circlip (**Figure 82**). Make sure the circlip seats in the groove completely.
7. Slide on the rubber boot so that it seals the master cylinder. See **Figure 81**.
8. Install the master cylinder as described in this chapter.

BRAKE HOSE REPLACEMENT

A brake hose should replaced whenever it shows cracks, bulges or other damage. The deterioration of rubber by ozone and other atmospheric elements may require hose replacement every 4 years.

CAUTION
Cover components with a heavy cloth or plastic tarp to protect them from the accidental spilling of brake fluid. Wash any spilled brake fluid off of plastic, painted or plated surfaces immediately, as it will destroy the finish. Use soapy water and rinse completely.

1. Before replacing a brake hose, inspect the routing of the old hose carefully, noting any guides and grommets the hose may go through.

2. Drain the master cylinder as described under *Front Master Cylinder Removal/Installation* or *Rear Master Cylinder Removal/Installation* in this chapter.

3. Disconnect the banjo bolts securing the hose at either end and remove the hose with its banjo bolts and 2 washers at both ends (**Figure 92**).

4. To remove the front brake banjo joint, disconnect the hoses at the joint (**Figure 93**). Remove the attaching bolts and the joint.

5. Install new brake hoses, sealing washers and banjo bolts in the reverse order of removal. Be sure to install the new sealing washers in their correct positions (**Figure 92**). Tighten all banjo bolts to the torque specification in **Table 2**.

6. Refill the master cylinder(s) with fresh brake fluid clearly marked DOT 4. Bleed the brake as described under *Bleeding the System* in this chapter.

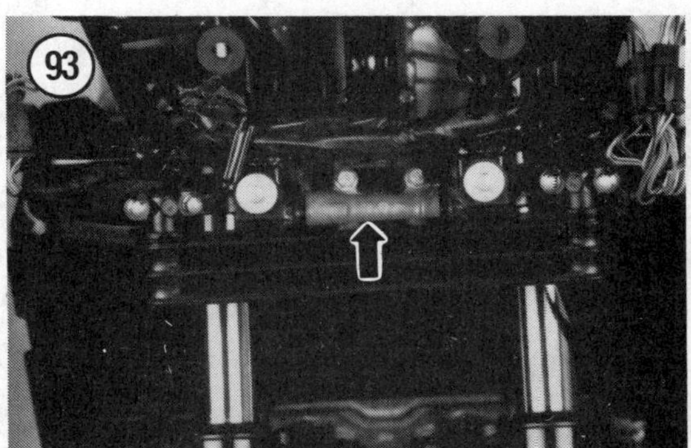

WARNING
Do not ride the motorcycle until you are sure that the brakes are operating properly.

BRAKE DISC

Inspection

It is not necessary to remove the disc from the wheel to inspect it. Small marks on the disc are not important, but deep radial scratches, deep enough to snag a fingernail, reduce braking effectiveness and increase brake pad wear. If these grooves are found, the disc should be resurfaced or replaced.

1. Measure the thickness around the disc at several locations with vernier calipers or a micrometer (**Figure 94**). The disc must be replaced if the thickness at any point is worn to the wear limit or less as specified in **Table 1**.

2. Make sure the disc bolts are tight before performing this check. Check the disc runout with a dial indicator as shown in **Figure 95**. Slowly

rotate the wheel and watch the dial indicator. If the runout is 0.3 mm (0.012 in.) or greater, the disc must be replaced.

3. Clean the disc of any rust or corrosion and wipe clean with lacquer thinner. Never use an oil based solvent that may leave an oil residue on the disc.

Removal/Installation

1. Remove the front or rear wheel as described in Chapter Ten or Chapter Eleven.

NOTE
Place a piece of wood in the calipers in place of the disc. This way, if the brake lever is inadvertently squeezed, the piston will not be forced out of the cylinder. If this does happen, the caliper might have to be disassembled to reseat the piston and the system will have to be bled.

2. *Front wheel:* Remove the bolts (**Figure 96**) securing the disc to the wheel and remove the disc. Remove the paper washers (**Figure 97**) from the mounting bosses on the wheel.

3. *Rear wheel:* Remove the bolts (**Figure 98**) securing the disc to the wheel and remove the disc.

4. Install by reversing these removal steps. Note the following:

   a. Apply Loctite 242 (blue) to the bolts before installation.
   b. Tighten the disc bolts to the torque specifications in **Table 2**.

REAR BRAKE PEDAL

Removal/Installation

Refer to **Figure 99** for this procedure.

1. Remove the right-hand side cover. See Chapter Thirteen.

2. Remove the bolt securing the rear master cylinder reservoir to the frame (B, **Figure 80**) and remove the reservoir. Secure the reservoir so that it is next to the frame and parallel to the ground.

3. Remove the right-hand footpeg bracket bolts (**Figure 100**).

4. Referring to **Figure 101**, perform the following:

   a. Using a pair of Vise Grips or a spring tool, disconnect the return spring (A) at the brake pedal.

b. Disconnect the stop light switch spring (B) at the brake pedal.

c. Remove the cotter pin (C) and disconnect the pivot pin and washer at the brake pedal.

d. Remove the circlip (D) and remove the brake pedal assembly.

5. Install by reversing these removal steps. Note the following.

6. Apply a light coat of multipurpose grease to all pivot areas before assembly and installation.

7. When installing the circlip (D, **Figure 101**) make sure it seats in the brake pedal groove completely.

8. Install a *new* pivot pin cotter pin (C, **Figure 101**). Bend the ends of the cotter pin over completely to lock it in place.

9. Tighten the right-hand footpeg bracket bolts to the torque specification in **Table 2**.

10. Tighten the reservoir mounting bolt to the torque specification in **Table 2**.

BLEEDING THE SYSTEM

This procedure is necessary only when the brakes feel spongy, there is a leak in the hydraulic system, a component has been replaced or the brake fluid has been replaced.

1. Flip off the rubber cap on the bleed valve.

2. Connect a length of clear tubing to the bleeder valve on the caliper. See **Figure 102** (front) or **Figure 103** (rear). Place the other end of the tube in a clean container. Fill the container with enough fresh DOT 4 brake fluid to keep the end submerged. The tube should be long enough so that a loop can be made higher than the bleeder valve to prevent air from being drawn into the caliper during bleeding. See **Figure 104**.

> *CAUTION*
> *Cover parts with a heavy cloth or plastic tarp to protect them from the accidental spilling of brake fluid. Wash any spilled brake fluid off of plastic, painted or plated surfaces immediately, as it will destroy the finish. Use soapy water and rinse completely.*

3. Clean the top of the master cylinder of all dirt and foreign matter. Remove the cap and diaphragm. Fill the reservoir to about 10 mm (3/8 in.) from the top. Install the diaphragm to prevent the entry of dirt and moisture.

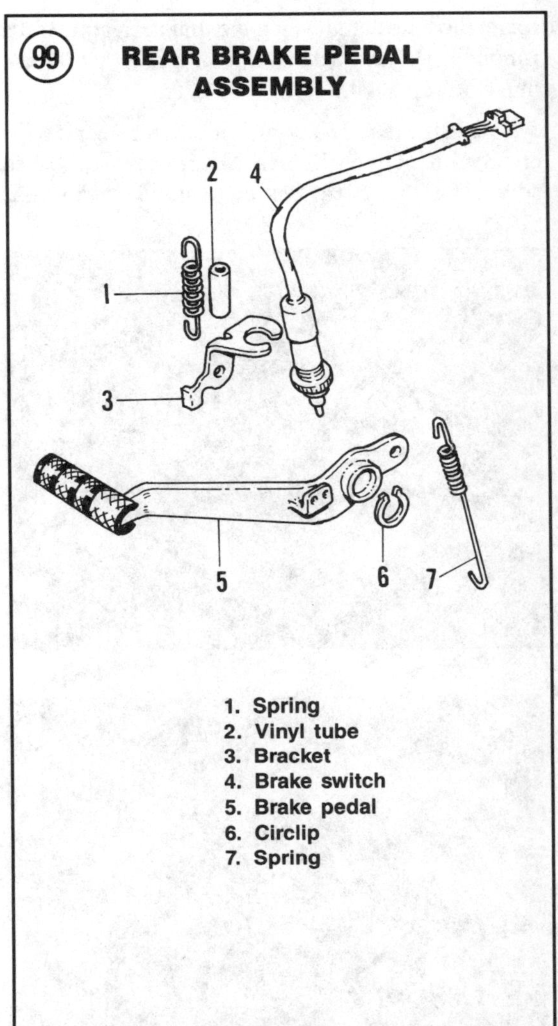

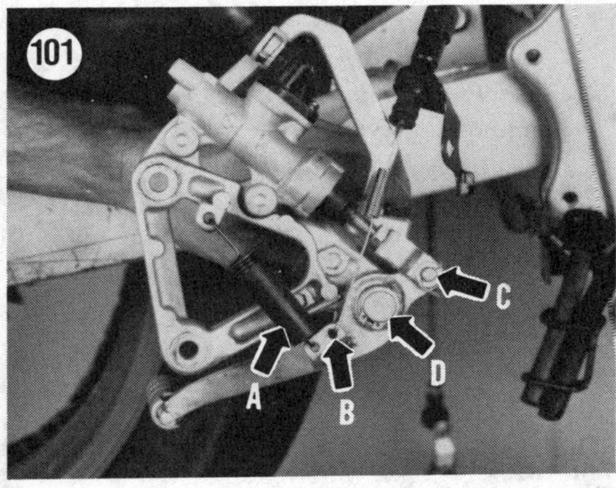

4. Slowly apply the brake lever (front) or pedal (rear) several times. Hold the lever in the applied position and open the bleeder valve about 1/2 turn. Allow the lever to travel to its limit. When this limit is reached, tighten the bleeder screw. As the brake fluid enters the system, the level will drop in the master cylinder reservoir. Maintain the level at about 10 mm (3/8 in.) from the top of the reservoir to prevent air from being drawn into the system.

5. Continue to pump the lever or pedal and fill the reservoir until the fluid emerging from the hose is completely free of air bubbles.

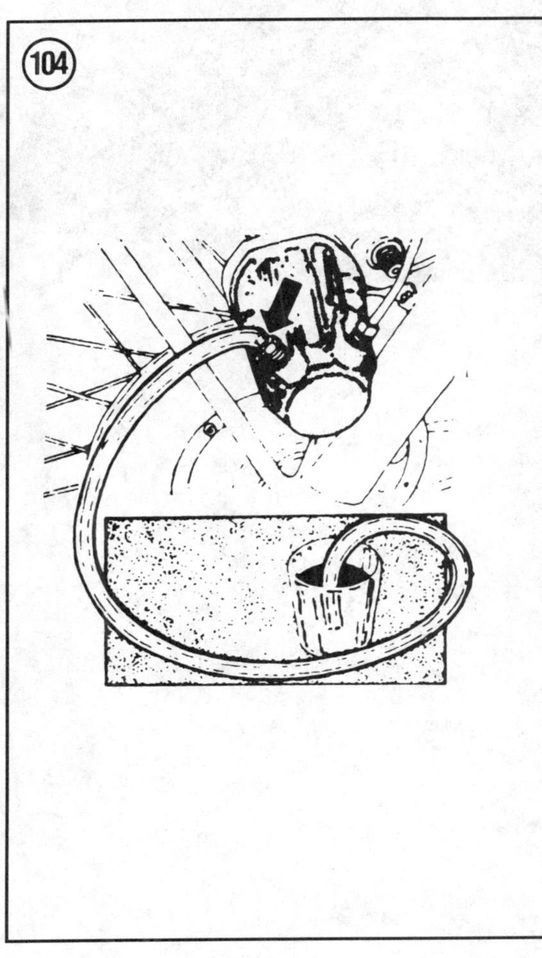

12

6. Hold the lever or pedal in the applied position and tighten the bleeder valve. Remove the bleeder tube and install the bleeder valve dust cap.

7. If necessary, add fluid to correct the level in the master cylinder reservoir. It must be above the LOWER level line. See A, **Figure 105** (front) or A, **Figure 106** (rear).

8. Install the cap and tighten the screws. See B, **Figure 105** (front) or B, **Figure 106** (rear).

9. Test the feel of the brake lever or pedal. It should feel firm and should offer the same resistance each time it's operated. If it feels spongy, it is likely that air is still in the system and it must be bled again. When all air has been bled from the system, and the brake fluid level is correct in the reservoir, double-check for leaks and tighten all fittings and connections.

> *WARNING*
> *Before riding the motorcycle, make certain that the brakes are operating correctly by operating the lever or pedal several times. Then make the test ride a slow one at first to make sure the brake is operating correctly.*

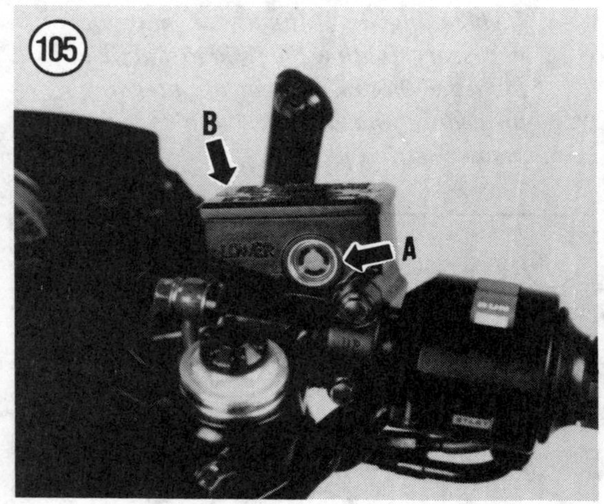

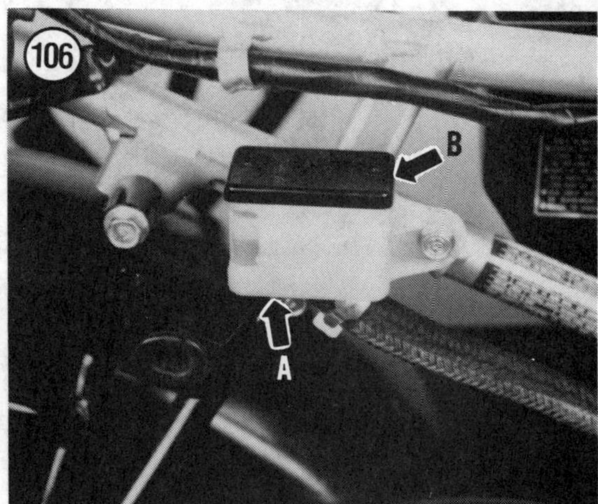

Table 1 BRAKE SPECIFICATIONS

	Specification mm (in.)	Wear limit mm (in.)
Brake disc		
Thickness		
Front	4.0-4.7 (2.89-3.40)	3.5 (0.14)
Rear	4.8-5.2 (3.47-3.76)	4.0 (0.16)
Warpage	0.3	(0.01)
Master cylinder ID		
Front	14.000-14.043 (0.5512-0.5529)	14.055 (0.5022)
Rear	12.700-12.743 (0.5000-0.5017)	12.755 (0.5022)
Master cylinder piston OD		
Front	13.957-13.984 (0.5495-0.5506)	13.984 (0.5506)
Rear	12.657-12.684 (0.4983-0.4994)	12.645 (0.4978)
Brake caliper		
Cylinder ID	27.000-27.050 (1.0630-1.0650)	27.06 (1.065)
Piston OD	26.918-26.968 (1.0598-1.0617)	26.91 (1.059)

Table 2 BRAKE TIGHTENING TORQUES

	N·m	ft.-lb.
Brake caliper bracket bolt	27	20
Brake caliper bleed valve	5.5	4
Brake caliper pad pins (front)	18	13
Anti-dive piston bolt	12	9
Pad pin retainer bolt (rear)	11	8
Rear brake caliper mounting bolt	23	17
Brake hose banjo bolt		
1987-1988	30	22
1989	35	25
Brake hose 2-way joint bolt	35	25
Rear master cylinder mounting bolts	12	9
Reservoir mounting bolts	9	7
Footpeg bracket bolts	27	20
Brake disc bolts	40	29

12

CHAPTER THIRTEEN

BODY

This chapter contains removal and installation procedures for the fairing assembly (**Figure 1**).

When removing a fairing component, it is best to reinstall all mounting hardware onto the removed part or store it in plastic bags taped to the inside of the fairing. After removal, fairing components should be placed away from the service area to prevent accidental damage.

SIDE COVERS

Removal/Installation

Turn the clip (A, **Figure 2**) at the lower front edge of the side cover 90° counterclockwise. Pull the side cover out slightly to disconnect the attaching prongs. Pull the side cover down to disconnect the rear tab (B, **Figure 2**) and remove the side cover (C, **Figure 2**). Installation is the reverse of these steps.

SEAT

Removal/Installation

1. Remove each side cover as described in this chapter.

2. Remove the left- and right-hand bolts at the rear of the seat.

3. Pull the seat back and remove it.

4. Install by reversing these steps. Be sure to engage the front seat bracket with the recess under the frame during installation. Tighten the seat bolts securely.

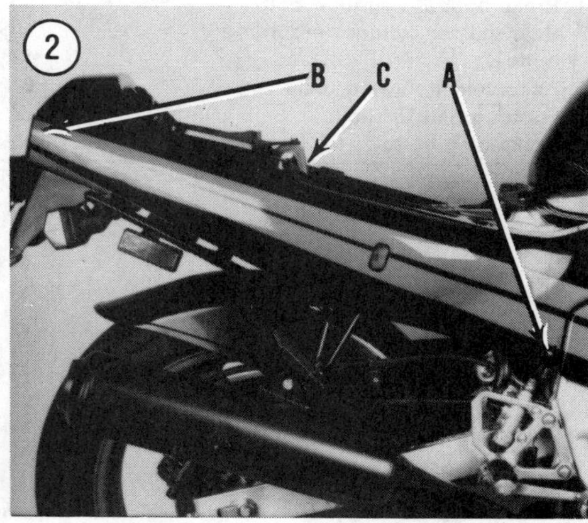

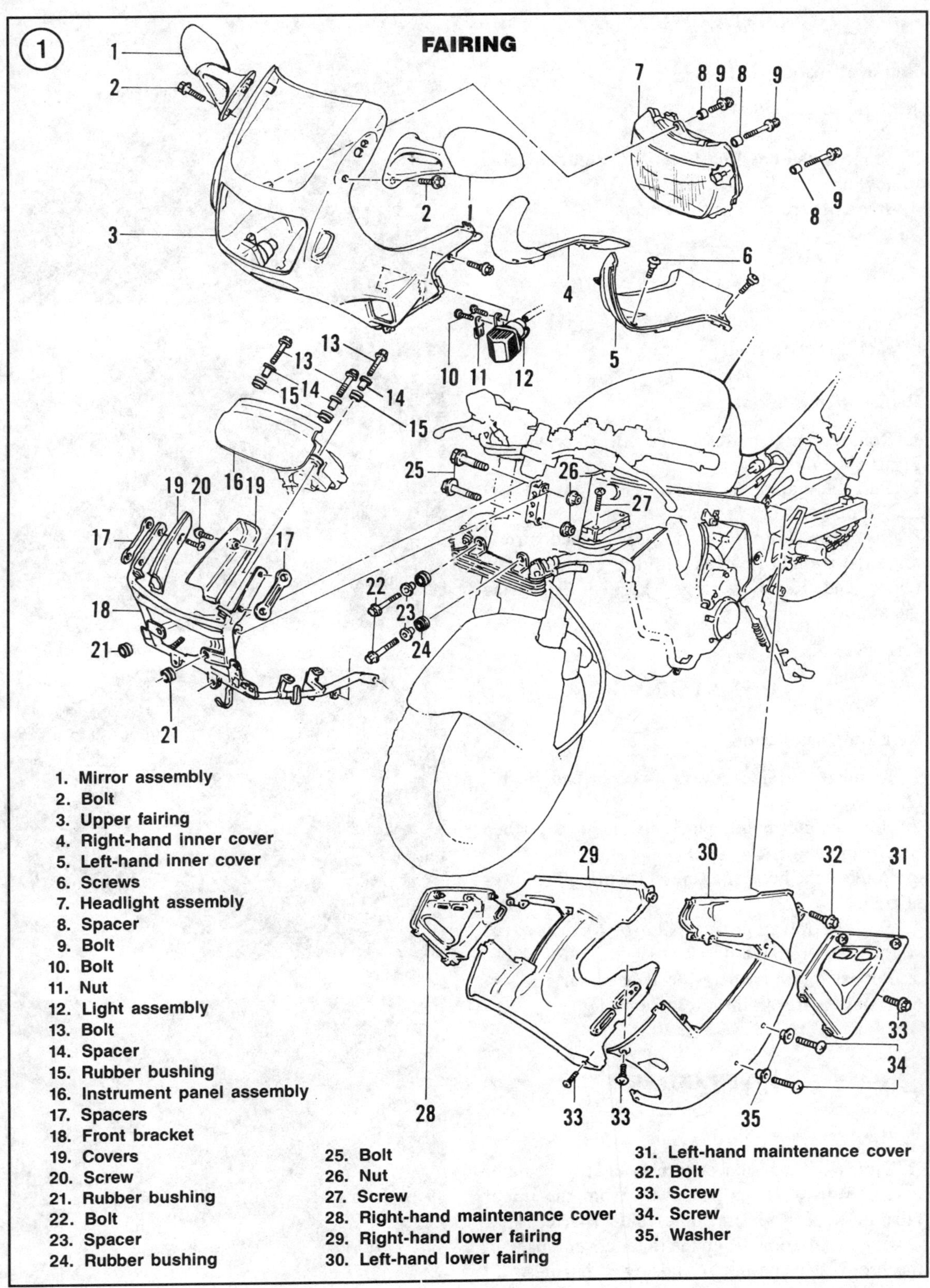

1. Mirror assembly
2. Bolt
3. Upper fairing
4. Right-hand inner cover
5. Left-hand inner cover
6. Screws
7. Headlight assembly
8. Spacer
9. Bolt
10. Bolt
11. Nut
12. Light assembly
13. Bolt
14. Spacer
15. Rubber bushing
16. Instrument panel assembly
17. Spacers
18. Front bracket
19. Covers
20. Screw
21. Rubber bushing
22. Bolt
23. Spacer
24. Rubber bushing
25. Bolt
26. Nut
27. Screw
28. Right-hand maintenance cover
29. Right-hand lower fairing
30. Left-hand lower fairing
31. Left-hand maintenance cover
32. Bolt
33. Screw
34. Screw
35. Washer

SEAT COWLING

Removal/Installation

1. Remove the side covers.
2. Remove the seat.
3. Remove the cowling bolts (A, **Figure 3**) and remove the cowling (B, **Figure 3**).
4. Install by reversing these steps.

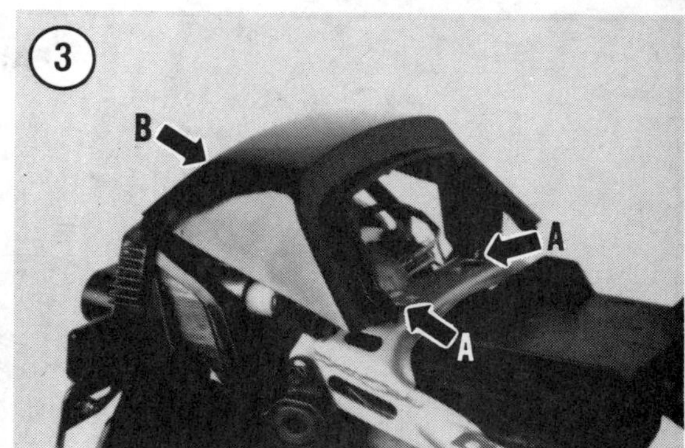

MAINTENANCE COVERS

A maintenance cover is installed in the center of each lower fairing.

Removal/Installation

1. Remove the 2 maintenance cover screws (A, **Figure 4**).
2. Pull the maintenance cover (B, **Figure 4**) out and remove it.
3. Install by reversing these steps. Make sure to align the front cover tabs with the grooves in the upper and lower fairings (**Figure 5**) during installation.

LOWER FAIRING

Removal/Installation

1. Remove the side covers as described in this chapter.
2. Remove the maintenance covers as described in this chapter.
3. Remove the bolts and screws securing the lower fairing.
4. Slip the lower fairing (**Figure 6**) backwards slightly and remove it.
5. Repeat for the other side if necessary.
6. Install by reversing these steps.

INNER COVER

Removal/Installation

Remove the inner cover screws and lift the inner cover (**Figure 7**) up and away from the upper fairing. Repeat for the other side if necessary. During installation, align the inner cover tabs with the grooves in the upper and lower fairings.

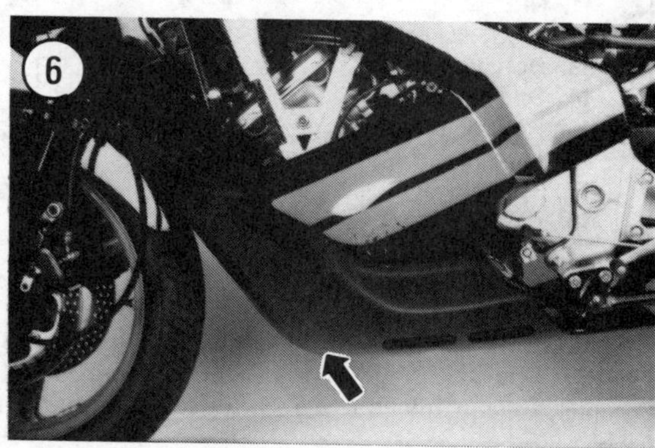

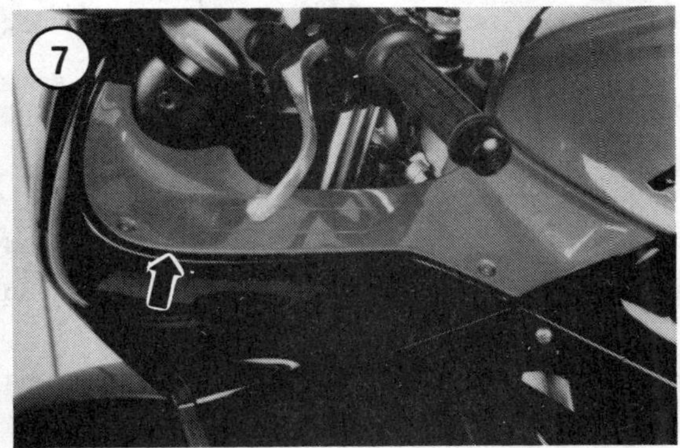

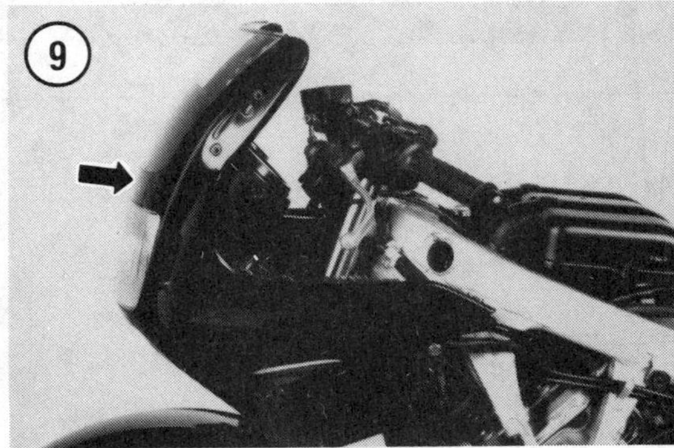

UPPER FAIRING

Removal/Installation

1. Remove the left- and right-hand lower fairings as described in this chapter.
2. Remove the left- and right-hand inner covers as described in this chapter.
3. Remove the screws securing the rear view mirrors to the upper fairing and remove both mirrors (**Figure 8**).
4. Disconnect the electrical connectors connected to the upper fairing components.
5. Remove the upper fairing bolts and remove the upper fairing (**Figure 9**).
6. Install by reversing these steps.

WINDSHIELD

Removal/Installation

The windshield can be removed without removing the upper fairing.
1. From inside the windshield, remove the 2 screws and the windshield holders (**Figure 10**).
2. From outside the windshield, remove the 2 screws. From the inside, remove the washers and collars. See **Figure 11**.
3. Lift the windshield off of the upper fairing.
4. Install by reversing these steps. Tighten the screws (**Figure 11**) to 1.5 N·m (1.1 ft.-lb.).

> *CAUTION*
> *Do not overtighten the screws as the windshield may crack.*

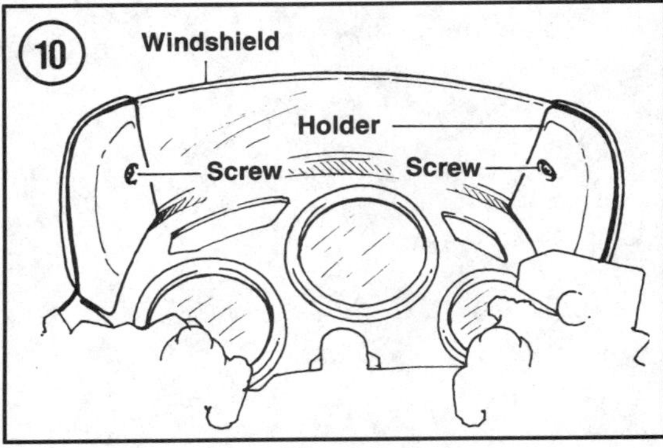

Windshield Cleaning

Be very careful when cleaning the windshield (**Figure 10**) as it can be scratched or damaged. Do not use a cleaner with an abrasive, a combination cleaner and wax or any solvent that contains ethyl or methyl alcohol. Never use gasoline or cleaning solvent. These products will either scratch or destroy the surface of the windshield.

To remove oil, grease or road tar use isopropyl alcohol. Then, wash the windshield with a solution

of mild soap and water. Dry gently with a soft cloth or chamois—do not press hard.

> *NOTE*
> *When removing road tar, make sure there are no small stones or sand embedded in it. Carefully remove any abrasive particles before performing any rubbing action with a cleaner. This will help minimize scratching.*

Many commercial windshield cleaners are available. If using a cleaner, make sure it is safe for use on plastic and test it on a small area first.

FRONT FENDER

Removal/Installation

Remove the front fender mounting screws and remove the front fender (**Figure 12**). Reverse to install.

REAR FENDERS

Rear Fender A
Removal/Installation

Remove the rear fender A (**Figure 13**) as follows:

1. Remove the seat cowling screws and remove the cowling.

2. Disconnect the electrical connector at the taillight and remove the taillight assembly.

3. Remove the spark unit as described in Chapter Eight.

4. Remove the seat cowling stay screws and remove the stay.

5. Remove the rear fender A mounting bolts and remove the fender.

6. Install by reversing these steps.

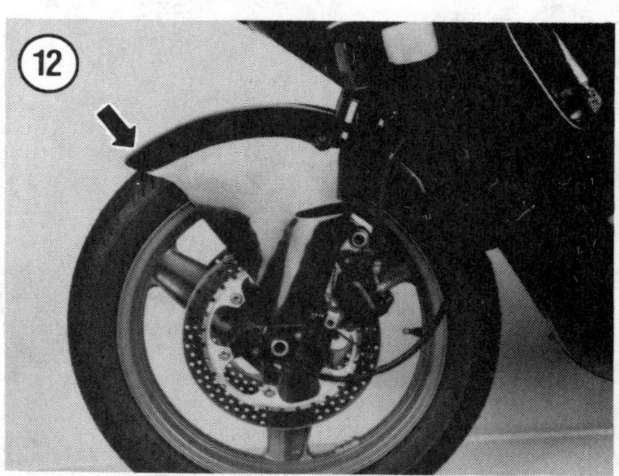

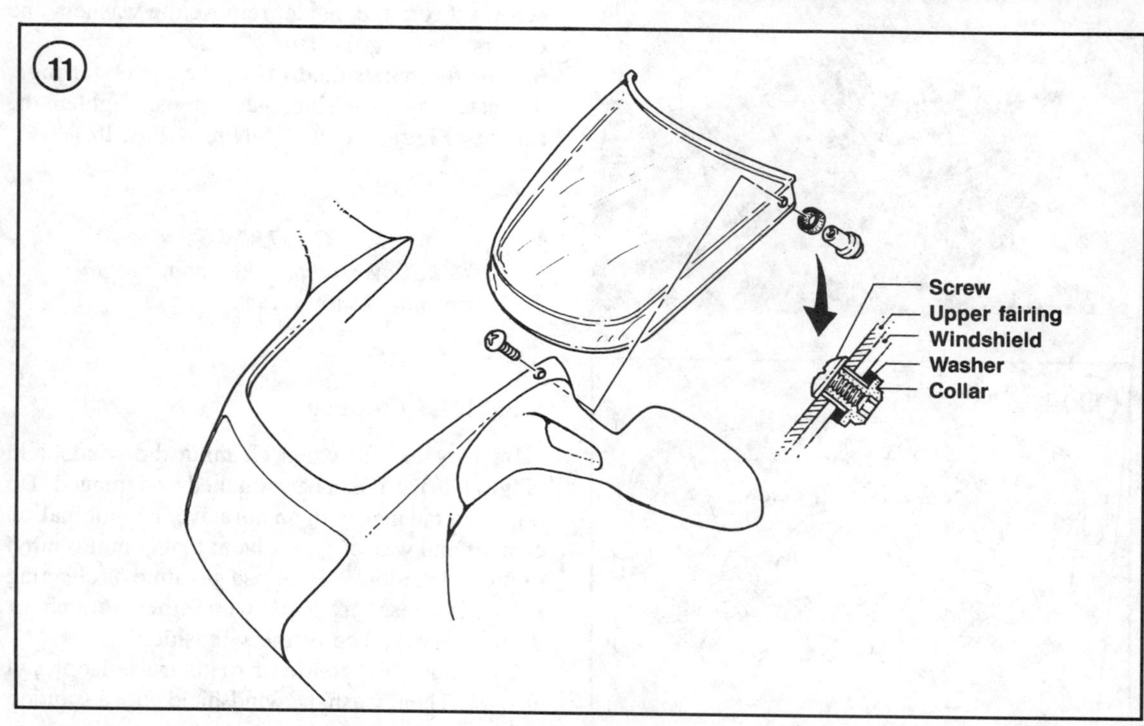

13

REAR FENDER A
ASSEMBLY
1
2
3
4
5
6
5
7
1. Bolts
2. Seat cowling
3. Bracket
4. Nuts
5. Bolts
6. Spacers
7. Rear fender A

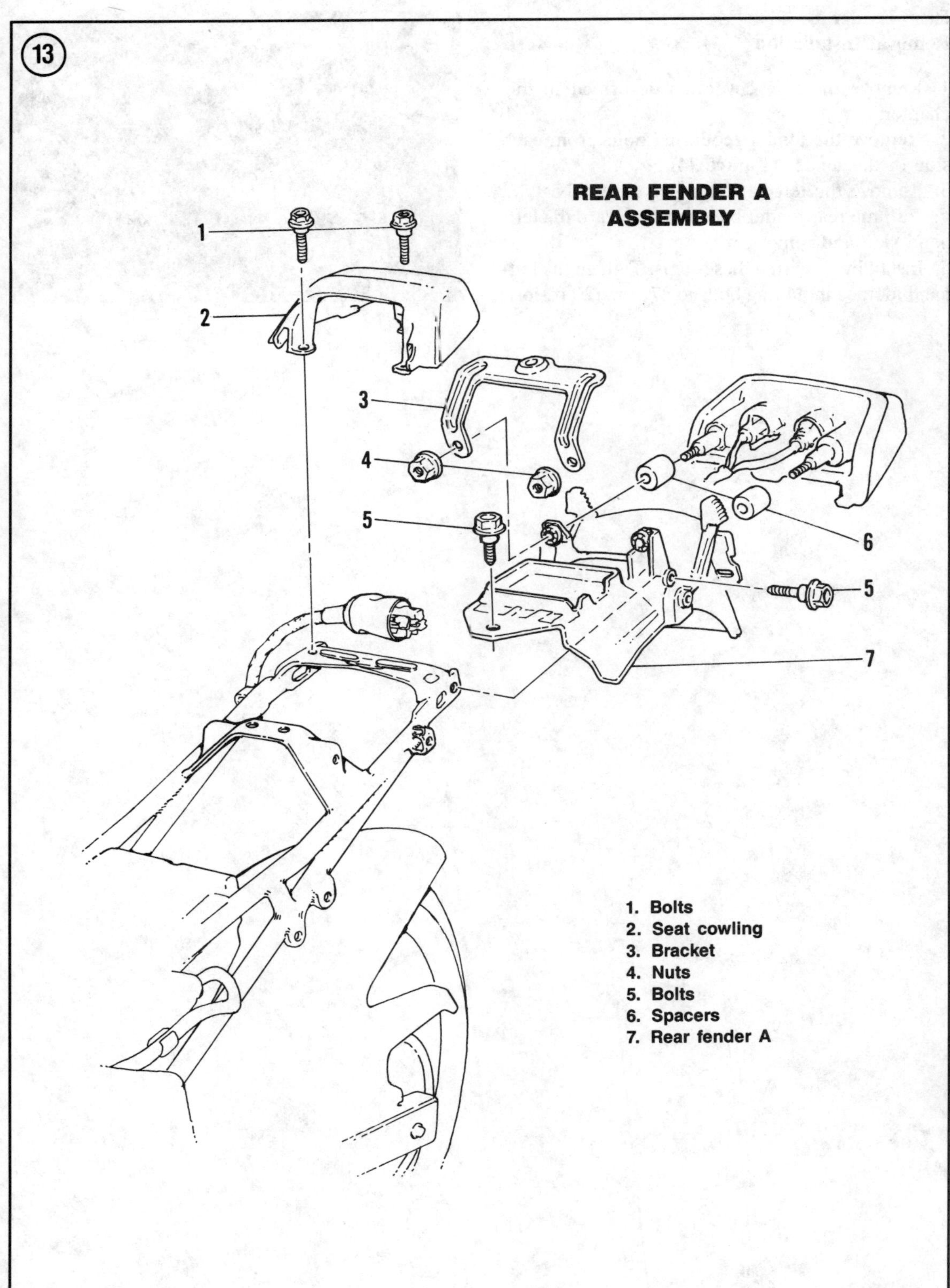

13

Rear Fender B
Removal/Installation

1. Remove the side covers as described in this chapter.

2. Remove the fender mounting bolts from each side of the fender (**Figure 14**).

3. Remove the left-hand footpeg assembly.

4. Pull the rear fender backwards toward the left-hand side and remove it.

5. Install by reversing these steps. Tighten the left-hand footpeg mounting bolts to 27 N·m (20 ft.-lb.).

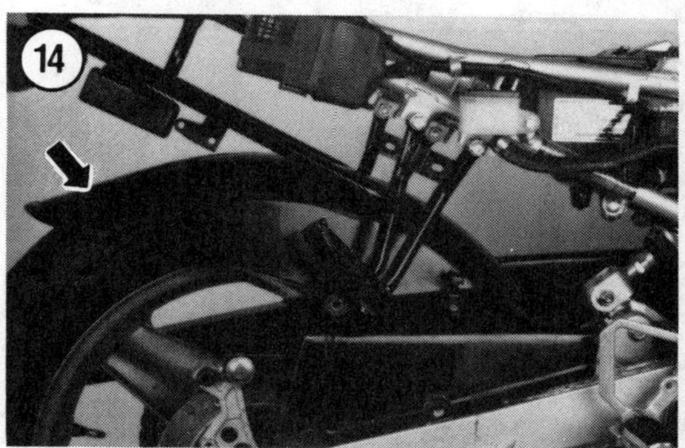

INDEX

WIRING DIAGRAMS

1987-1988 CBR600F

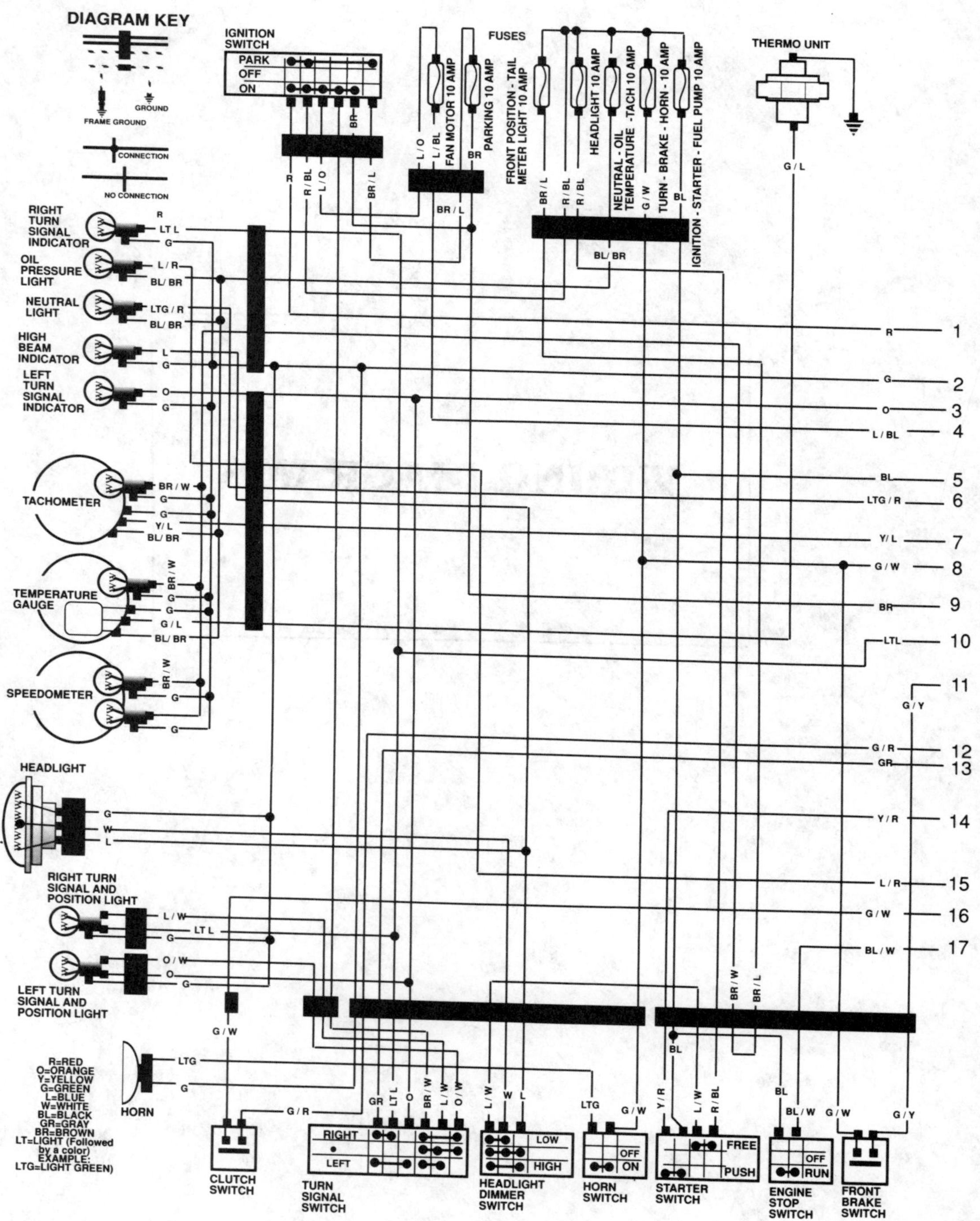

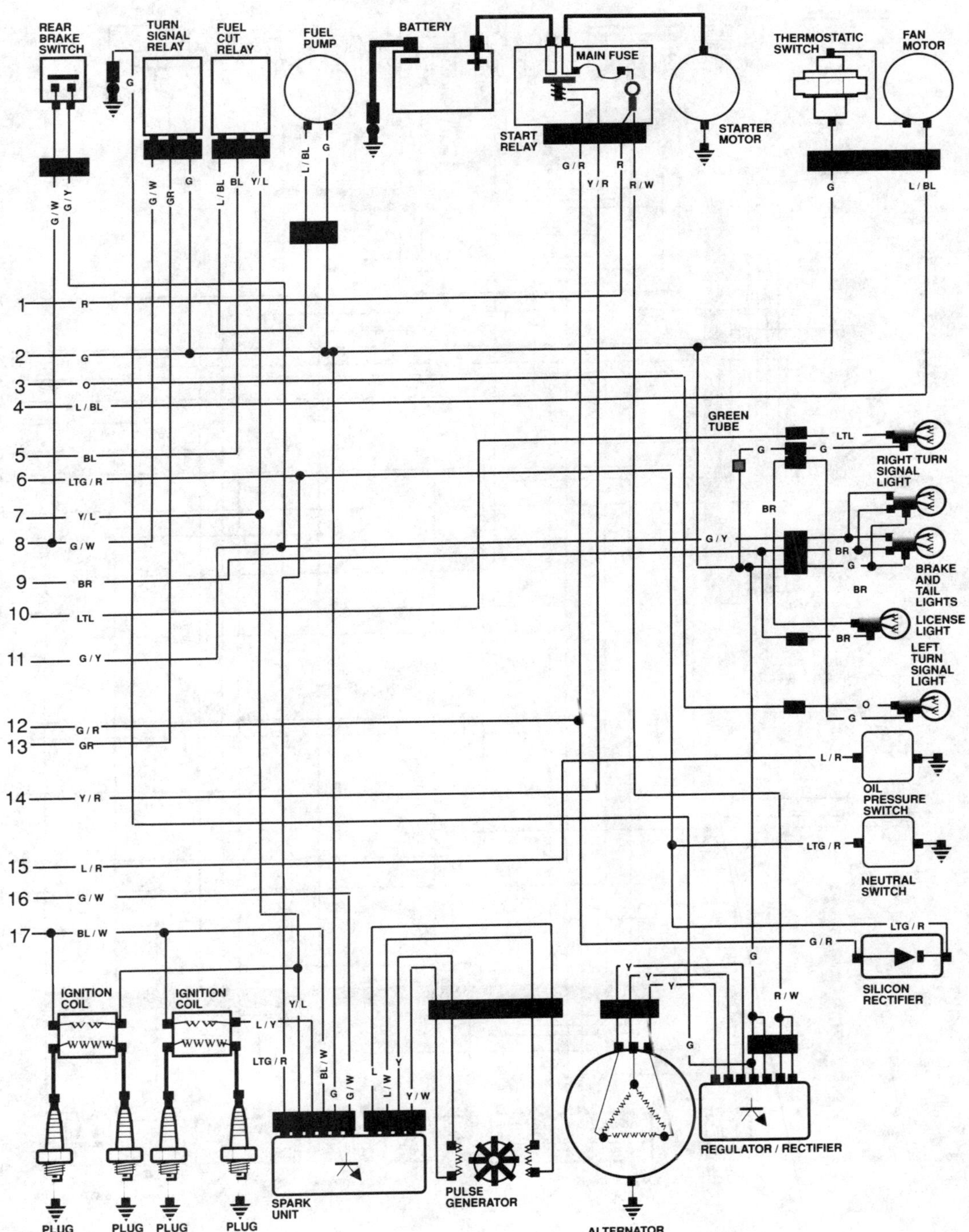
REAR BRAKE SWITCH
TURN SIGNAL RELAY
FUEL CUT RELAY
FUEL PUMP
BATTERY
MAIN FUSE
START RELAY
STARTER MOTOR
THERMOSTATIC SWITCH
FAN MOTOR
G
G / W
G / Y
G / W
GR
G
L / BL
BL
Y / L
L / BL
G
G / R
Y / R
R / W
R
G
L / BL
1 R
2 G
3 O
4 L / BL
5 BL
6 LTG / R
7 Y / L
8 G / W
9 BR
10 LTL
11 G / Y
12 G / R
13 GR
14 Y / R
15 L / R
16 G / W
17 BL / W
GREEN TUBE
LTL
G
G
BR
G / Y
BR
G
BR
BR
RIGHT TURN SIGNAL LIGHT
BRAKE AND TAIL LIGHTS
LICENSE LIGHT
LEFT TURN SIGNAL LIGHT
O
G
L / R
OIL PRESSURE SWITCH
LTG / R
NEUTRAL SWITCH
LTG / R
G / R
G
R / W
SILICON RECTIFIER
IGNITION COIL
IGNITION COIL
Y / L
L / Y
LTG / R
BL / W
G / W
L
L / Y
Y / W
Y
Y
Y
G
SPARK UNIT
PULSE GENERATOR
ALTERNATOR
REGULATOR / RECTIFIER
PLUG #1
PLUG #4
PLUG #2
PLUG #3
15

1989 CBR600F

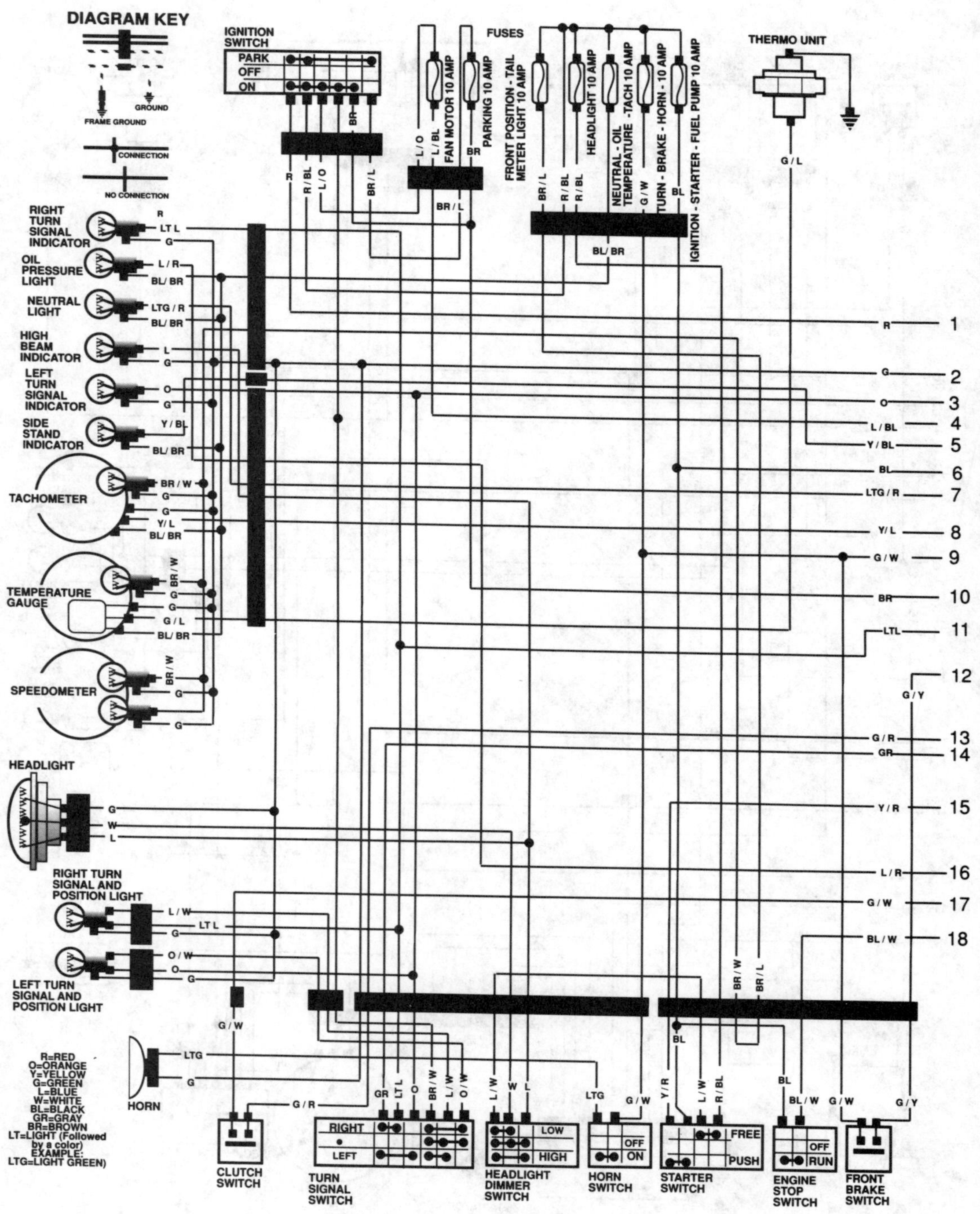

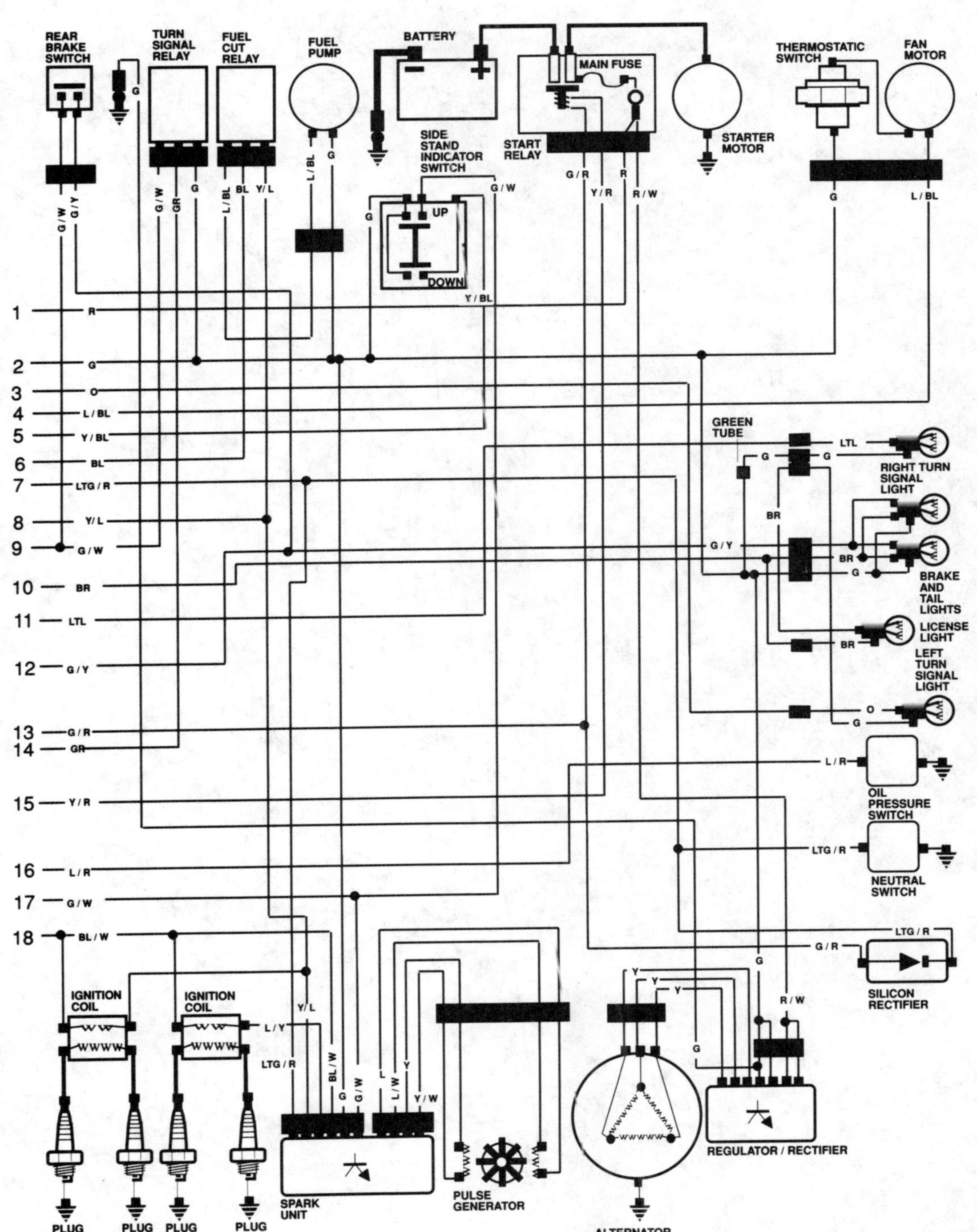
REAR BRAKE SWITCH
TURN SIGNAL RELAY
FUEL CUT RELAY
FUEL PUMP
BATTERY
MAIN FUSE
SIDE STAND INDICATOR SWITCH
START RELAY
STARTER MOTOR
THERMOSTATIC SWITCH
FAN MOTOR
UP
DOWN
G
G/W
G/Y
G/W
GR
G
L/BL
BL
Y/L
L/BL
G
G/W
G/R
R
Y/R
R/W
G
L/BL
Y/BL
GREEN TUBE
LTL
G
G
RIGHT TURN SIGNAL LIGHT
BR
G/Y
BR
G
BRAKE AND TAIL LIGHTS
BR
LICENSE LIGHT
LEFT TURN SIGNAL LIGHT
O
G
L/R
OIL PRESSURE SWITCH
LTG/R
NEUTRAL SWITCH
LTG/R
G/R
SILICON RECTIFIER
1 R
2 G
3 O
4 L/BL
5 Y/BL
6 BL
7 LTG/R
8 Y/L
9 G/W
10 BR
11 LTL
12 G/Y
13 G/R
14 GR
15 Y/R
16 L/R
17 G/W
18 BL/W
IGNITION COIL
IGNITION COIL
Y/L
L/Y
LTG/R
BL/W
G/W
L/W
Y/W
L
SPARK UNIT
PULSE GENERATOR
Y
Y
Y
G
R/W
ALTERNATOR
REGULATOR / RECTIFIER
PLUG #1
PLUG #4
PLUG #2
PLUG #3
15

NOTES

NOTES

NOTES

NOTES

NOTES